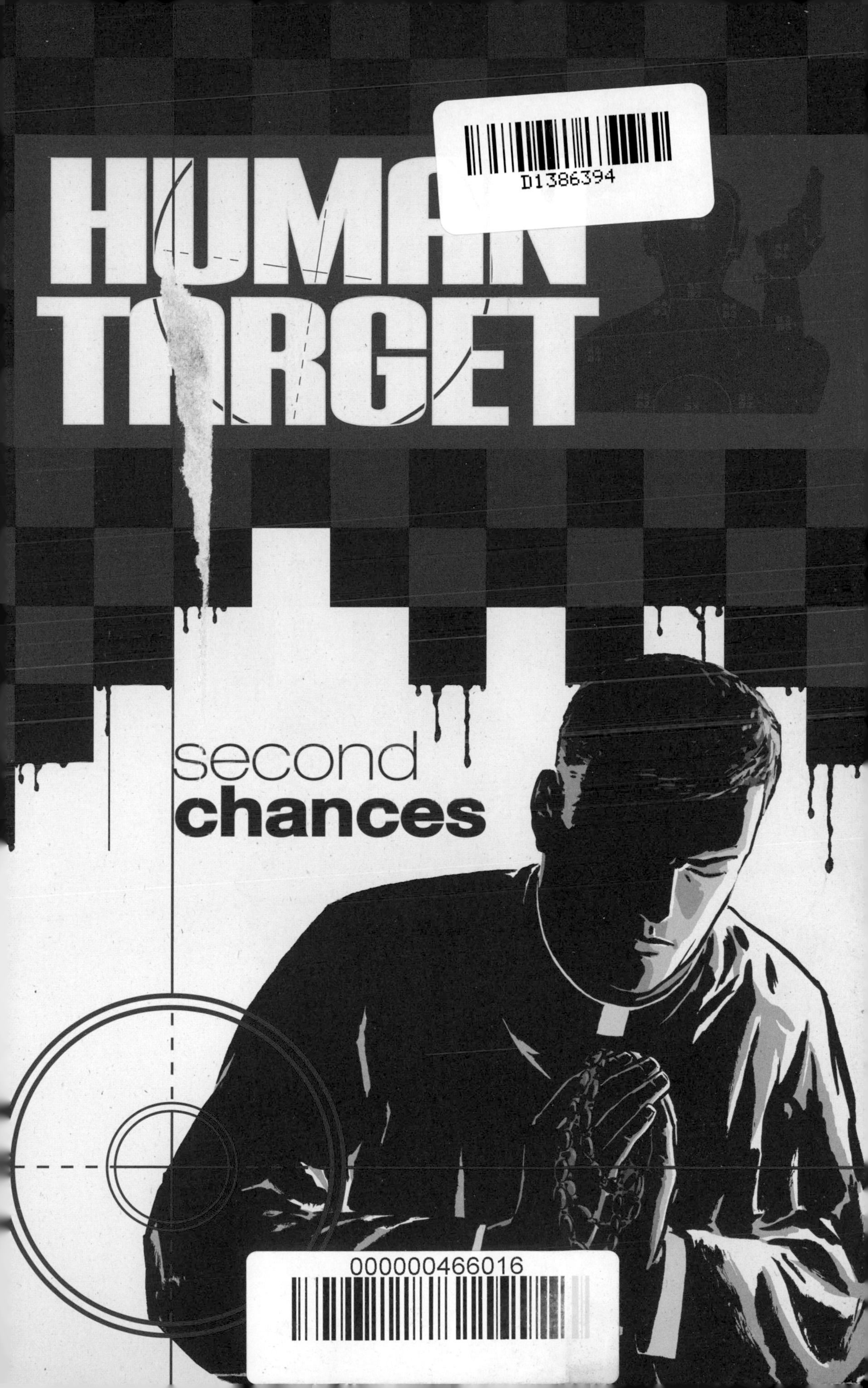
HUMAN TARGET
second
chances

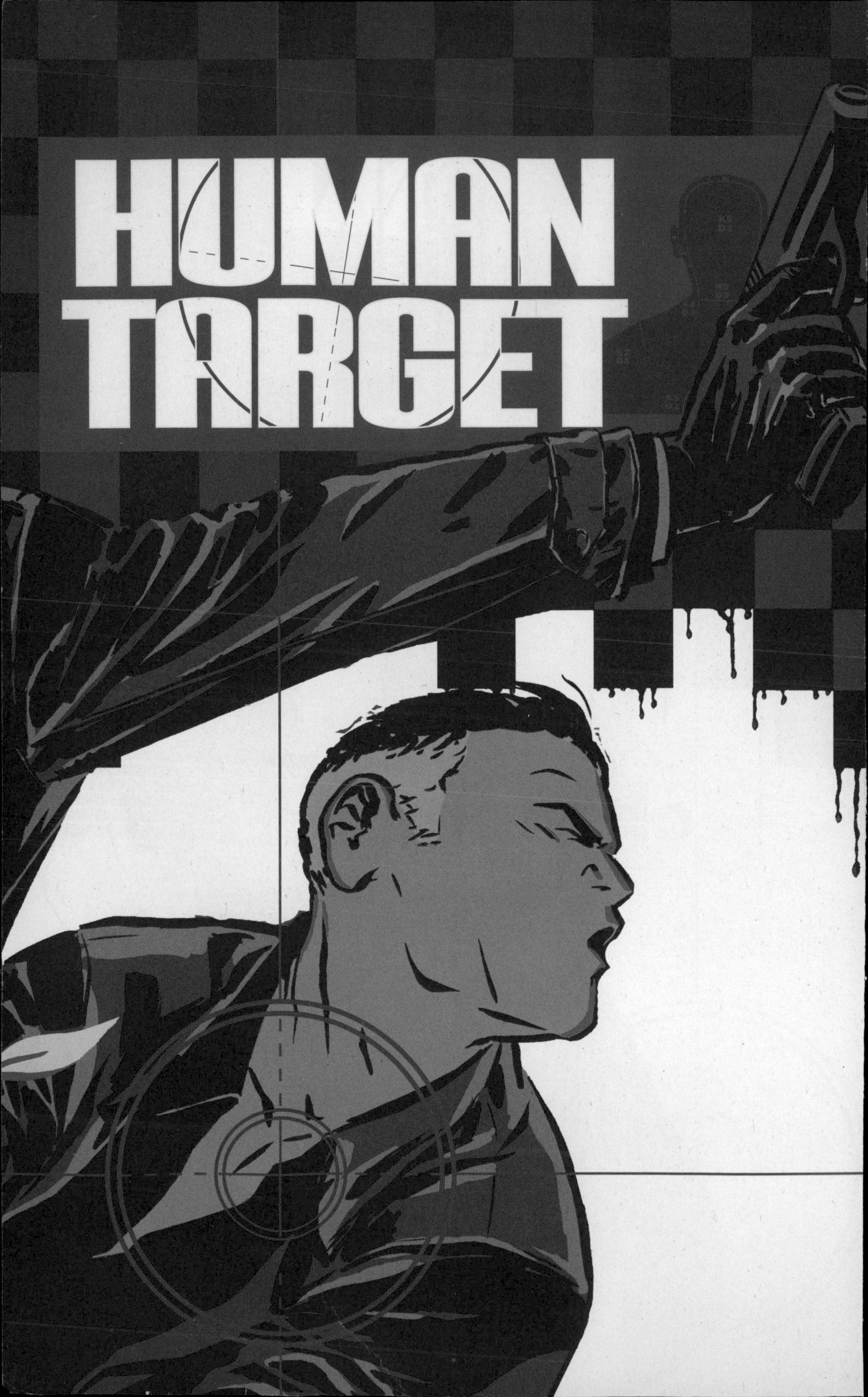
HUMAN
TARGET

second
chances

PETER MILLIGAN
Writer

JAVIER PULIDO
CLIFF CHIANG
Artists

LEE LOUGHRIDGE
JAVIER RODRIGUEZ
Colorists

CLEM ROBINS
Letterer

JAVIER PULIDO
Cover Artist

JAVIER PULIDO
CLIFF CHIANG
JOHN WATKISS
Original series covers

**THE HUMAN TARGET created by
LEN WEIN and CARMINE INFANTINO**

Karen Berger   SVP – Executive Editor and Editor – Original Series
Pornsak Pichetshote
Zachary Rau   Associate Editors – Original Series
Bob Harras   Group Editor – Collected Editions
Scott Nybakken   Editor
Robbin Brosterman   Design Director – Books

DC COMICS
Diane Nelson   President
Dan DiDio and **Jim Lee**   Co-Publishers
Geoff Johns   Chief Creative Officer
Patrick Caldon   EVP – Finance and Administration
John Rood   EVP – Sales, Marketing and Business Development
Amy Genkins   SVP – Business and Legal Affairs
Steve Rotterdam   SVP – Sales and Marketing
John Cunningham   VP – Marketing
Terri Cunningham   VP – Managing Editor
Alison Gill   VP – Manufacturing
David Hyde   VP – Publicity
Sue Pohja   VP – Book Trade Sales
Alysse Soll   VP – Advertising and Custom Publishing
Bob Wayne   VP – Sales
Mark Chiarello   Art Director

HUMAN TARGET: SECOND CHANCES

DC COMICS
1700 Broadway, New York, NY 10019
A Warner Bros. Entertainment Company.

Printed in the USA.
First Printing
ISBN: 978-1-4012-3061-6

SUSTAINABLE
FORESTRY
INITIATIVE
Certified Fiber Sourcing
www.sfiprogram.org
Fiber used in this product line meets the
sourcing requirements of the SFI program.
www.sfiprogram.org SGS-SFICOC-0130

Table of Contents

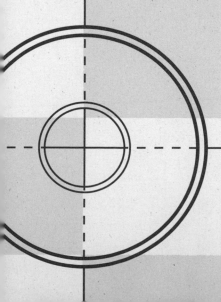

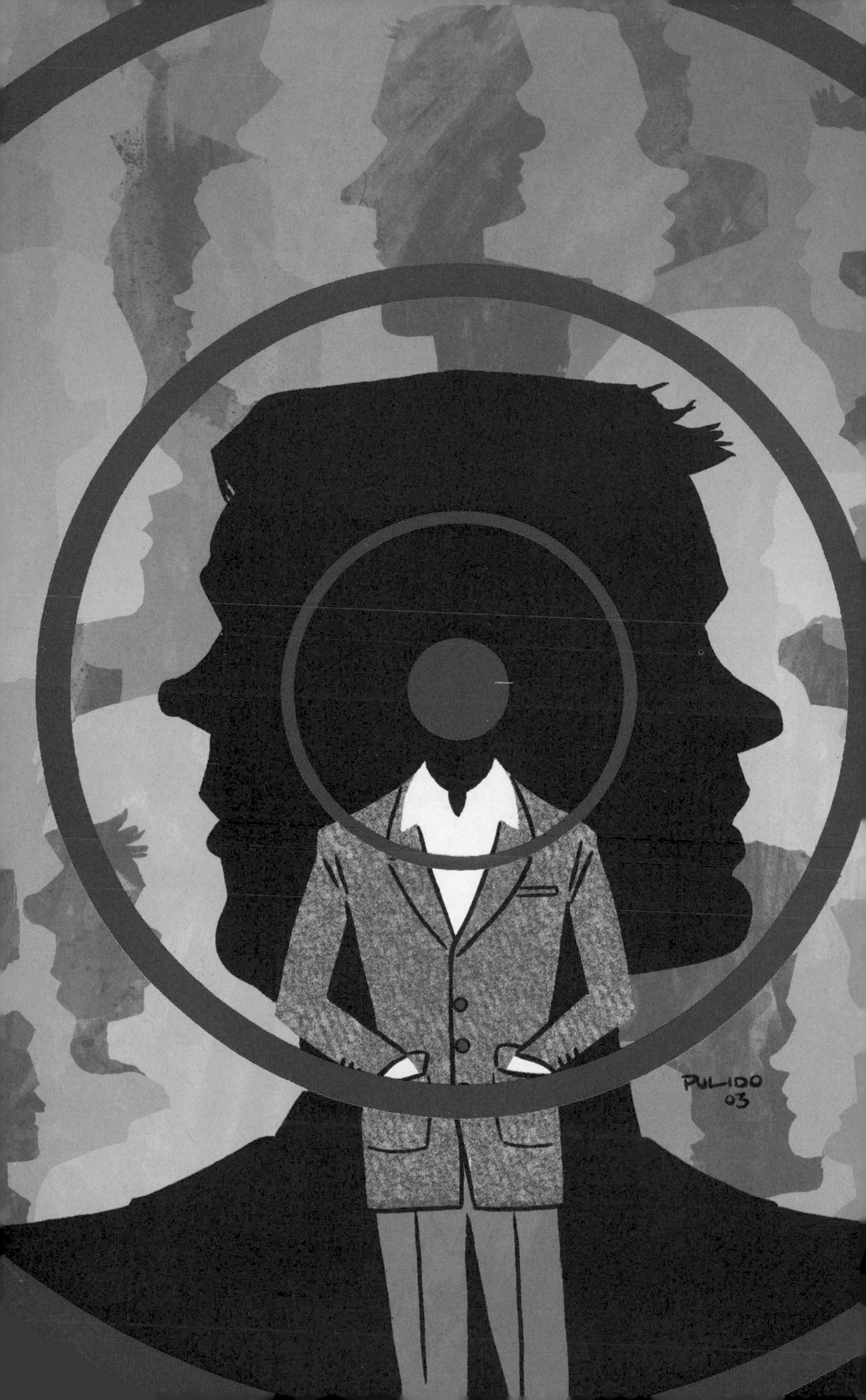
PULIDO
03

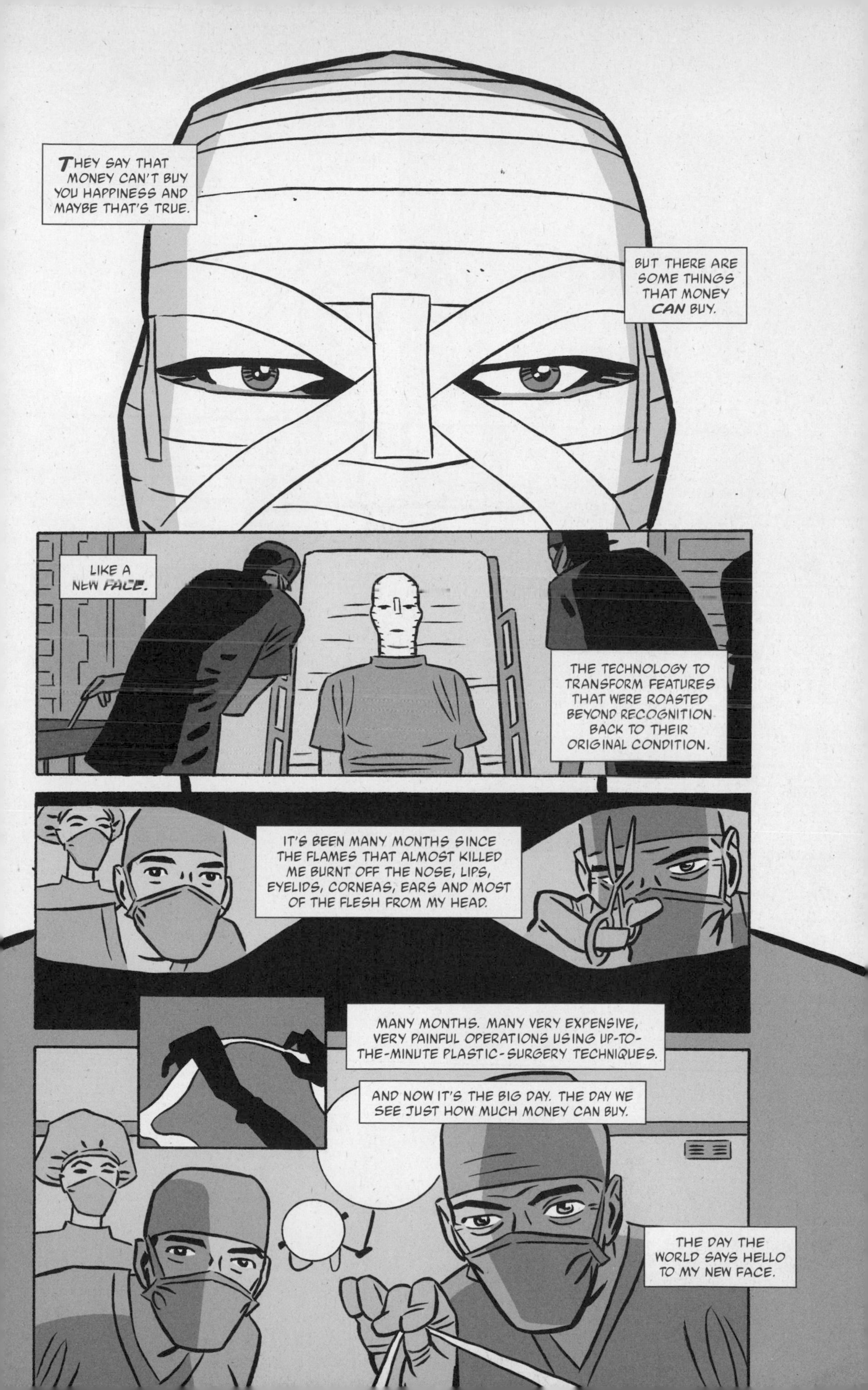
THEY SAY THAT MONEY CAN'T BUY YOU HAPPINESS AND MAYBE THAT'S TRUE.
BUT THERE ARE SOME THINGS THAT MONEY CAN BUY.
LIKE A NEW FACE.
THE TECHNOLOGY TO TRANSFORM FEATURES THAT WERE ROASTED BEYOND RECOGNITION BACK TO THEIR ORIGINAL CONDITION.
IT'S BEEN MANY MONTHS SINCE THE FLAMES THAT ALMOST KILLED ME BURNT OFF THE NOSE, LIPS, EYELIDS, CORNEAS, EARS AND MOST OF THE FLESH FROM MY HEAD.
MANY MONTHS. MANY VERY EXPENSIVE, VERY PAINFUL OPERATIONS USING UP-TO-THE-MINUTE PLASTIC-SURGERY TECHNIQUES.
AND NOW IT'S THE BIG DAY. THE DAY WE SEE JUST HOW MUCH MONEY CAN BUY.
THE DAY THE WORLD SAYS HELLO TO MY NEW FACE.

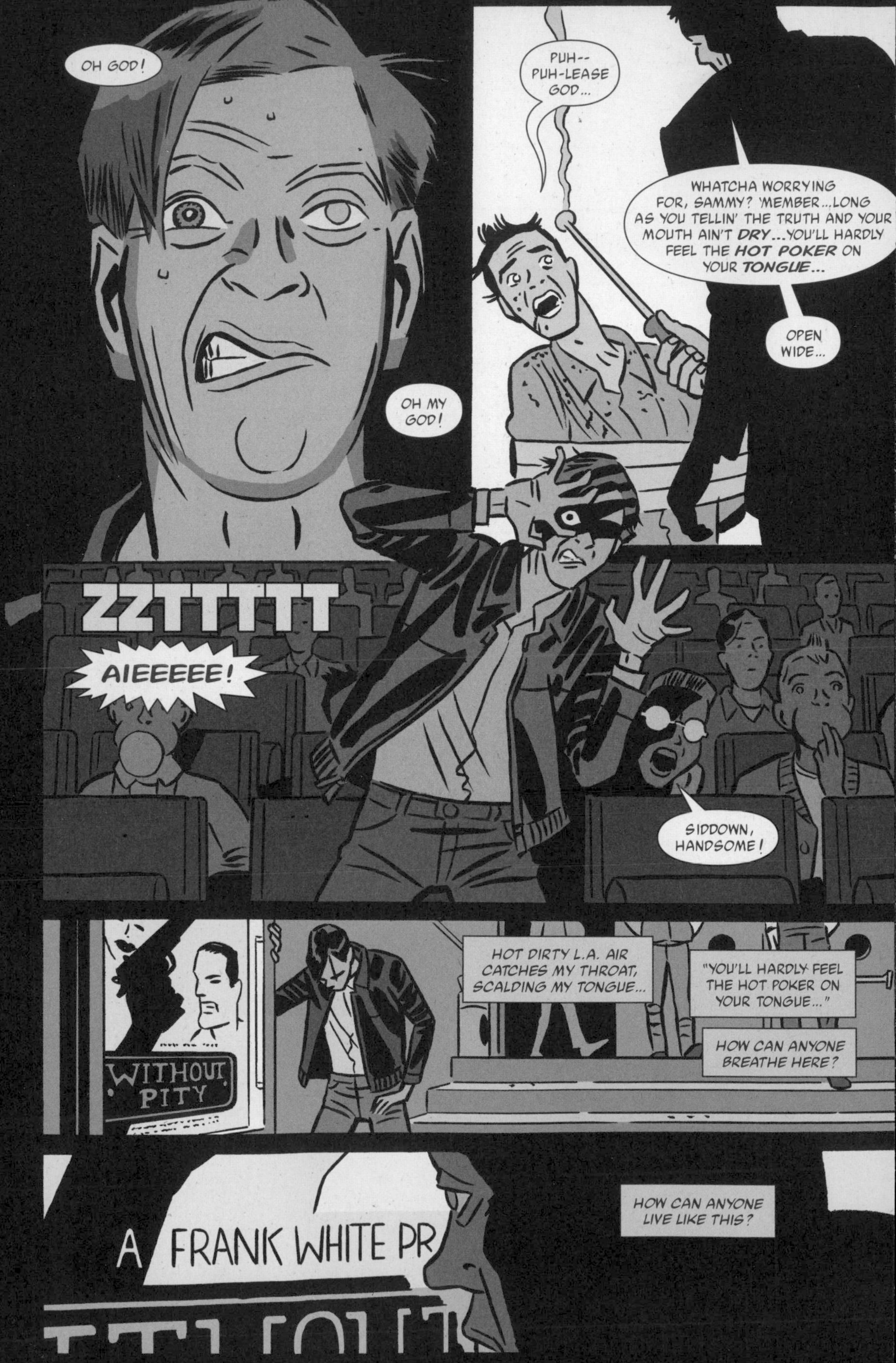
OH GOD!
PUH-- PUH-LEASE GOD...
WHATCHA WORRYING FOR, SAMMY? 'MEMBER...LONG AS YOU TELLIN' THE TRUTH AND YOUR MOUTH AIN'T DRY...YOU'LL HARDLY FEEL THE HOT POKER ON YOUR TONGUE...
OPEN WIDE...
OH MY GOD!
ZZTTTTT
AIEEEEE!
SIDDOWN, HANDSOME!
WITHOUT PITY
HOT DIRTY L.A. AIR CATCHES MY THROAT, SCALDING MY TONGUE...
"YOU'LL HARDLY FEEL THE HOT POKER ON YOUR TONGUE..."
HOW CAN ANYONE BREATHE HERE?
A FRANK WHITE PR
HOW CAN ANYONE LIVE LIKE THIS?

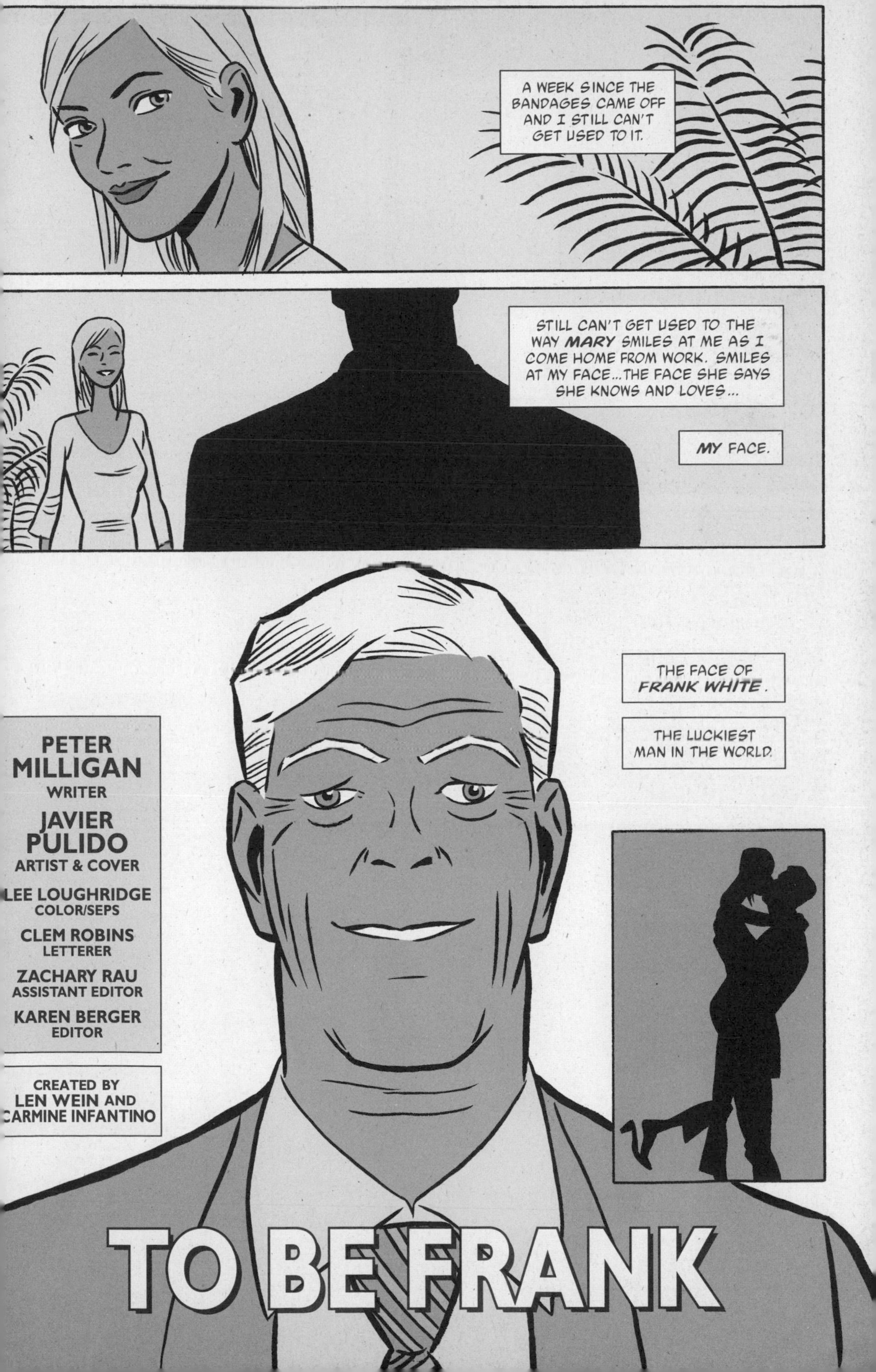
A WEEK SINCE THE BANDAGES CAME OFF AND I STILL CAN'T GET USED TO IT.
STILL CAN'T GET USED TO THE WAY MARY SMILES AT ME AS I COME HOME FROM WORK. SMILES AT MY FACE...THE FACE SHE SAYS SHE KNOWS AND LOVES...
MY FACE.
THE FACE OF FRANK WHITE.
THE LUCKIEST MAN IN THE WORLD.
PETER MILLIGAN
WRITER
JAVIER PULIDO
ARTIST & COVER
LEE LOUGHRIDGE
COLOR/SEPS
CLEM ROBINS
LETTERER
ZACHARY RAU
ASSISTANT EDITOR
KAREN BERGER
EDITOR
CREATED BY
LEN WEIN AND
CARMINE INFANTINO
TO BE FRANK

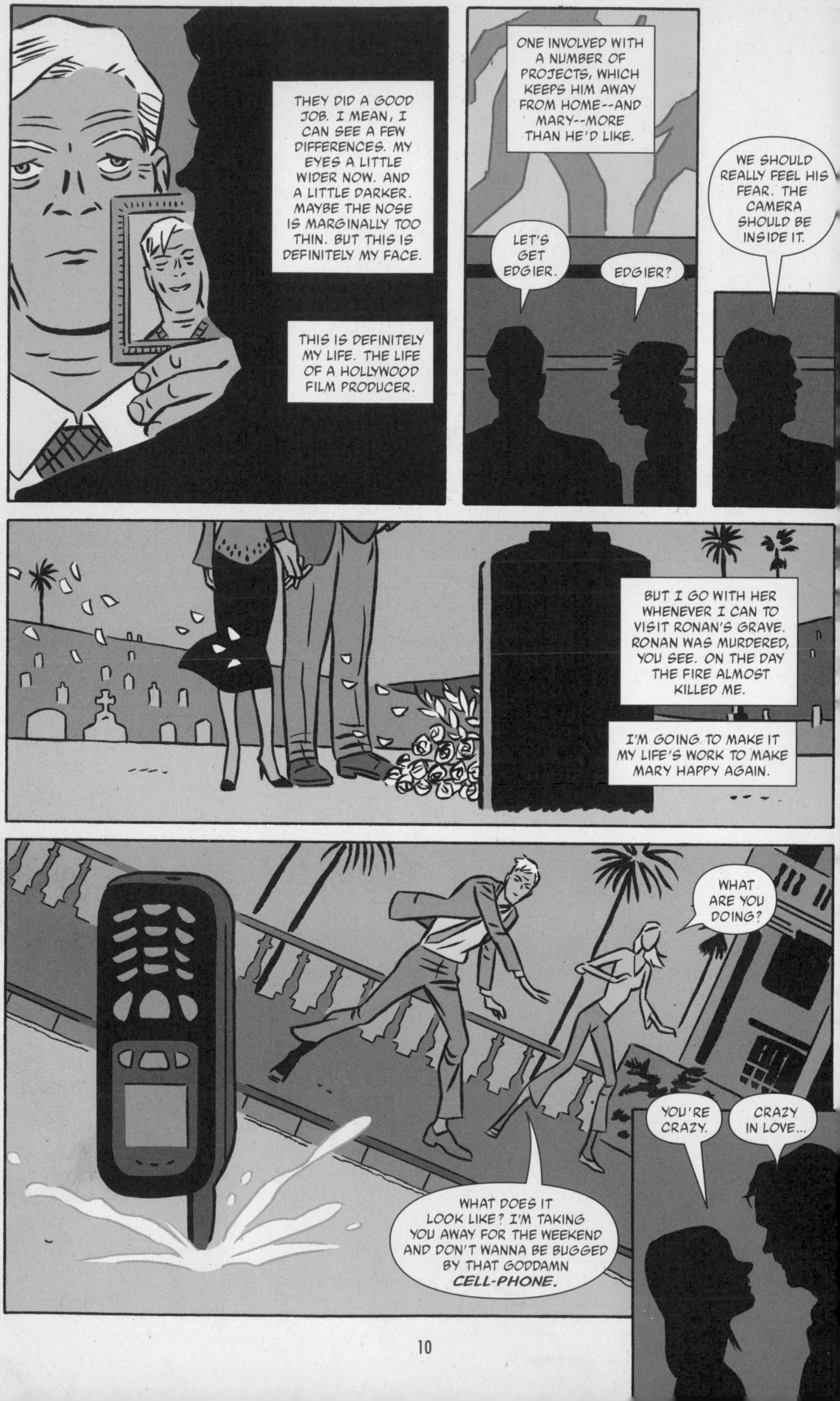
THEY DID A GOOD JOB. I MEAN, I CAN SEE A FEW DIFFERENCES. MY EYES A LITTLE WIDER NOW. AND A LITTLE DARKER. MAYBE THE NOSE IS MARGINALLY TOO THIN. BUT THIS IS DEFINITELY MY FACE.
THIS IS DEFINITELY MY LIFE. THE LIFE OF A HOLLYWOOD FILM PRODUCER.
ONE INVOLVED WITH A NUMBER OF PROJECTS, WHICH KEEPS HIM AWAY FROM HOME--AND MARY--MORE THAN HE'D LIKE.
LET'S GET EDGIER.
EDGIER?
WE SHOULD REALLY FEEL HIS FEAR. THE CAMERA SHOULD BE INSIDE IT.
BUT I GO WITH HER WHENEVER I CAN TO VISIT RONAN'S GRAVE. RONAN WAS MURDERED, YOU SEE. ON THE DAY THE FIRE ALMOST KILLED ME.
I'M GOING TO MAKE IT MY LIFE'S WORK TO MAKE MARY HAPPY AGAIN.
WHAT ARE YOU DOING?
WHAT DOES IT LOOK LIKE? I'M TAKING YOU AWAY FOR THE WEEKEND AND DON'T WANNA BE BUGGED BY THAT GODDAMN ***CELL-PHONE.***
YOU'RE CRAZY.
CRAZY IN LOVE...

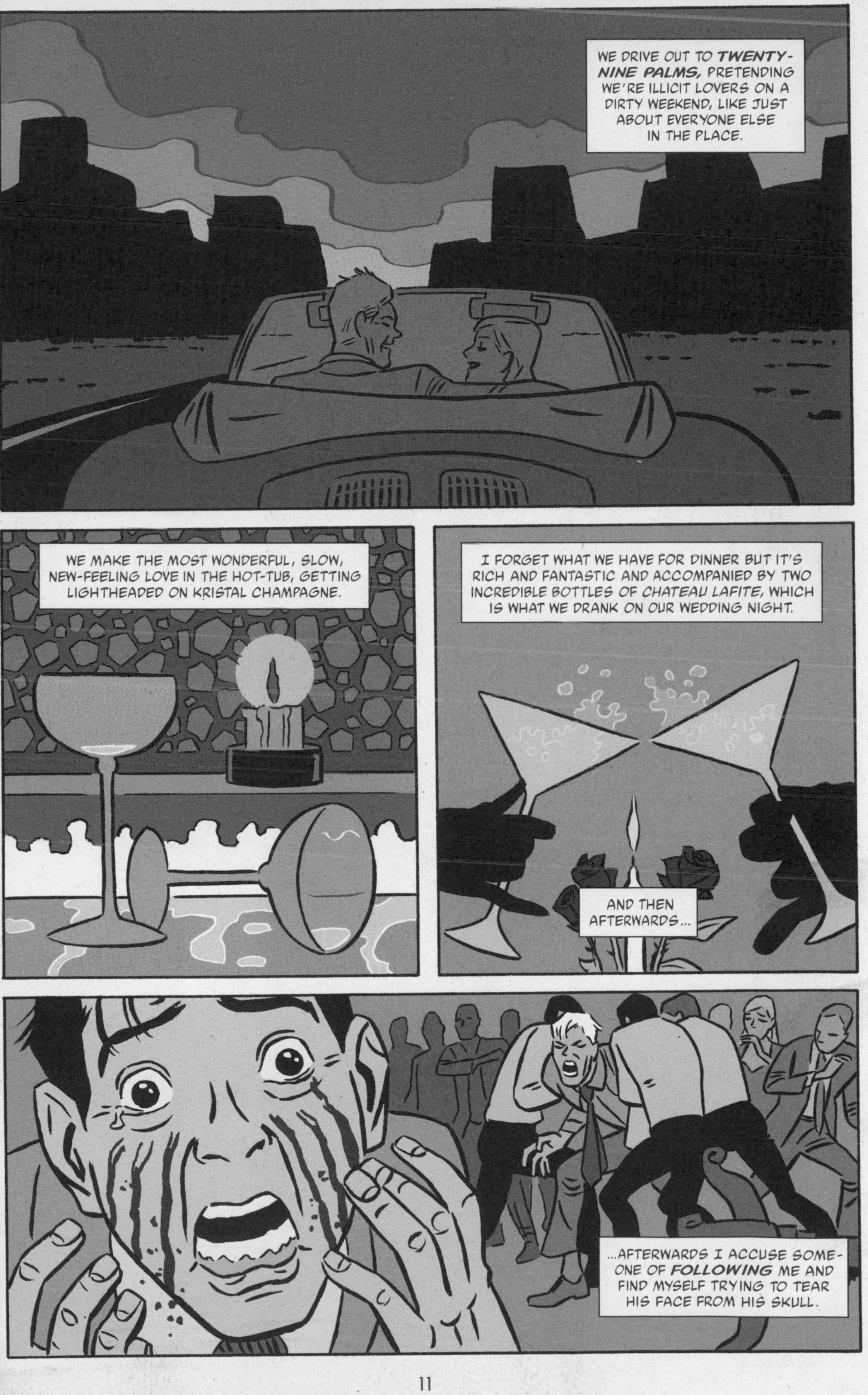
WE DRIVE OUT TO **TWENTY-NINE PALMS,** PRETENDING WE'RE ILLICIT LOVERS ON A DIRTY WEEKEND, LIKE JUST ABOUT EVERYONE ELSE IN THE PLACE.
WE MAKE THE MOST WONDERFUL, SLOW, NEW-FEELING LOVE IN THE HOT-TUB, GETTING LIGHTHEADED ON KRISTAL CHAMPAGNE.
I FORGET WHAT WE HAVE FOR DINNER BUT IT'S RICH AND FANTASTIC AND ACCOMPANIED BY TWO INCREDIBLE BOTTLES OF *CHATEAU LAFITE,* WHICH IS WHAT WE DRANK ON OUR WEDDING NIGHT.
AND THEN AFTERWARDS...
...AFTERWARDS I ACCUSE SOME-ONE OF **FOLLOWING** ME AND FIND MYSELF TRYING TO TEAR HIS FACE FROM HIS SKULL.

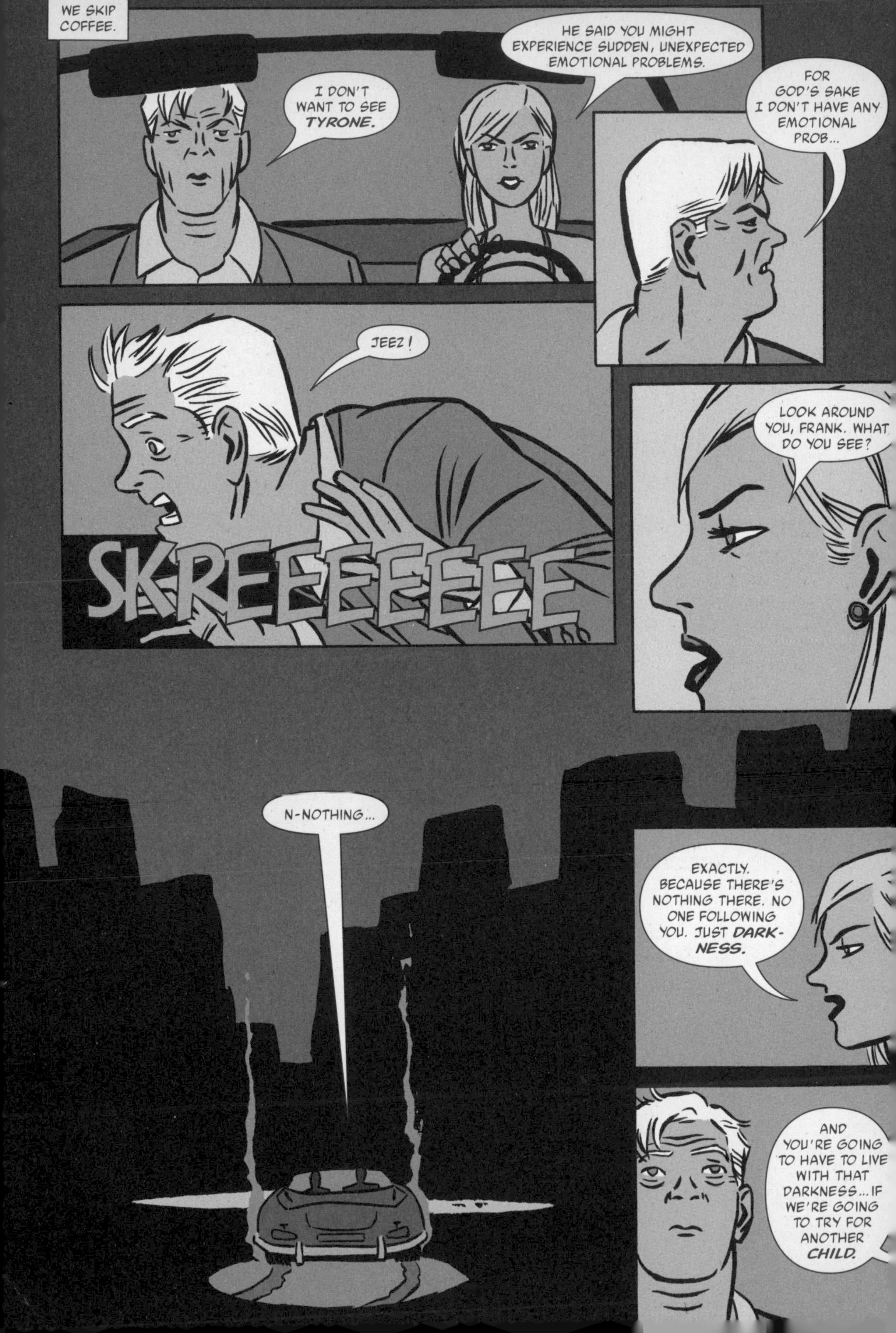
WE SKIP COFFEE.
I DON'T WANT TO SEE TYRONE.
HE SAID YOU MIGHT EXPERIENCE SUDDEN, UNEXPECTED EMOTIONAL PROBLEMS.
FOR GOD'S SAKE I DON'T HAVE ANY EMOTIONAL PROB...
JEEZ!
SKREEEEEEEE
LOOK AROUND YOU, FRANK. WHAT DO YOU SEE?
N-NOTHING...
EXACTLY. BECAUSE THERE'S NOTHING THERE. NO ONE FOLLOWING YOU. JUST DARKNESS.
AND YOU'RE GOING TO HAVE TO LIVE WITH THAT DARKNESS... IF WE'RE GOING TO TRY FOR ANOTHER CHILD.

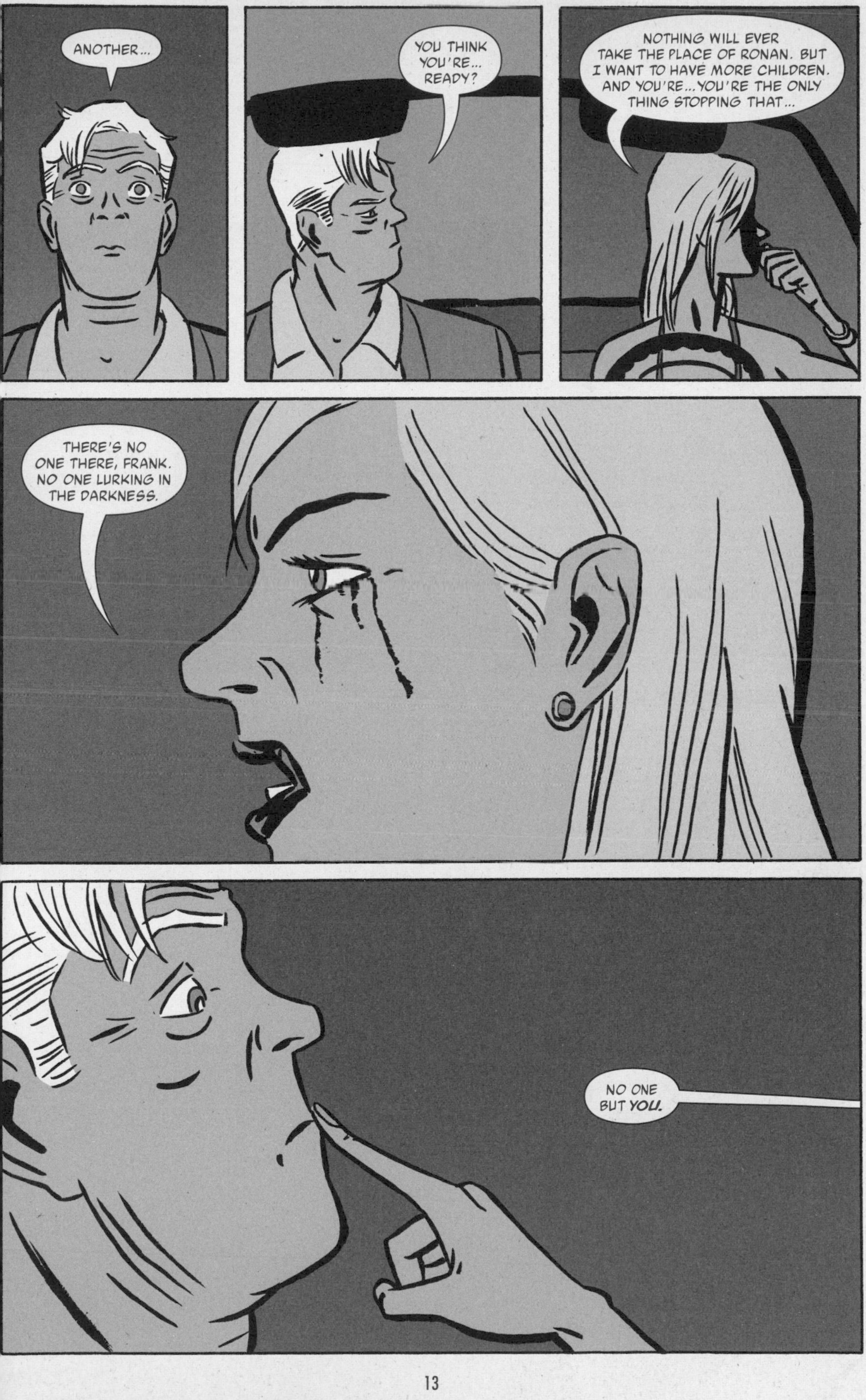
ANOTHER...
YOU THINK YOU'RE... READY?
NOTHING WILL EVER TAKE THE PLACE OF RONAN. BUT I WANT TO HAVE MORE CHILDREN. AND YOU'RE... YOU'RE THE ONLY THING STOPPING THAT...
THERE'S NO ONE THERE, FRANK. NO ONE LURKING IN THE DARKNESS.
NO ONE BUT *YOU.*

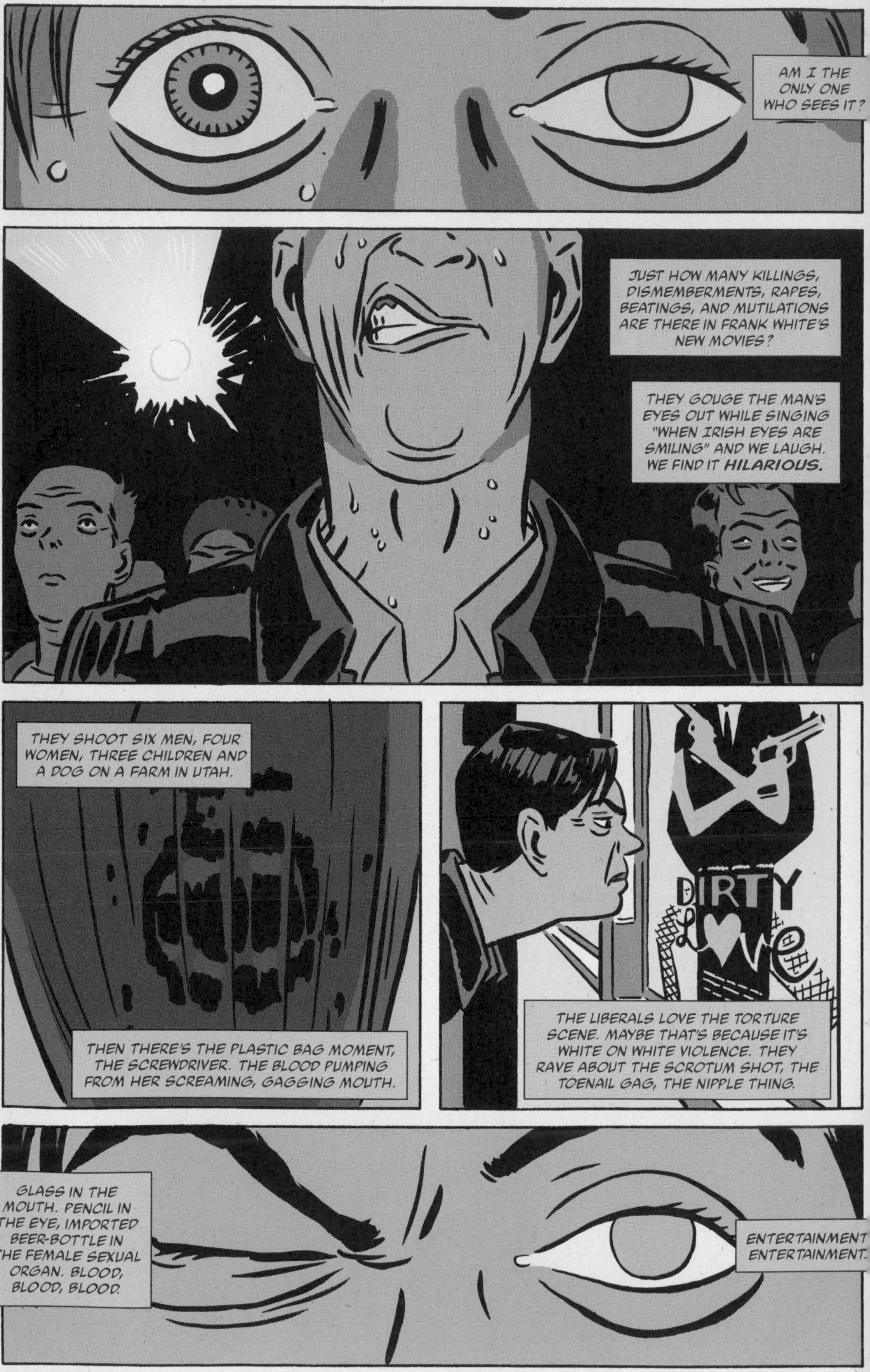
AM I THE ONLY ONE WHO SEES IT?
JUST HOW MANY KILLINGS, DISMEMBERMENTS, RAPES, BEATINGS, AND MUTILATIONS ARE THERE IN FRANK WHITE'S NEW MOVIES?
THEY GOUGE THE MAN'S EYES OUT WHILE SINGING "WHEN IRISH EYES ARE SMILING" AND WE LAUGH. WE FIND IT HILARIOUS.
THEY SHOOT SIX MEN, FOUR WOMEN, THREE CHILDREN AND A DOG ON A FARM IN UTAH.
THEN THERE'S THE PLASTIC BAG MOMENT, THE SCREWDRIVER. THE BLOOD PUMPING FROM HER SCREAMING, GAGGING MOUTH.
DIRTY LOVE
THE LIBERALS LOVE THE TORTURE SCENE. MAYBE THAT'S BECAUSE IT'S WHITE ON WHITE VIOLENCE. THEY RAVE ABOUT THE SCROTUM SHOT, THE TOENAIL GAG, THE NIPPLE THING.
GLASS IN THE MOUTH. PENCIL IN THE EYE, IMPORTED BEER-BOTTLE IN THE FEMALE SEXUAL ORGAN. BLOOD, BLOOD, BLOOD.
ENTERTAINMENT ENTERTAINMENT.

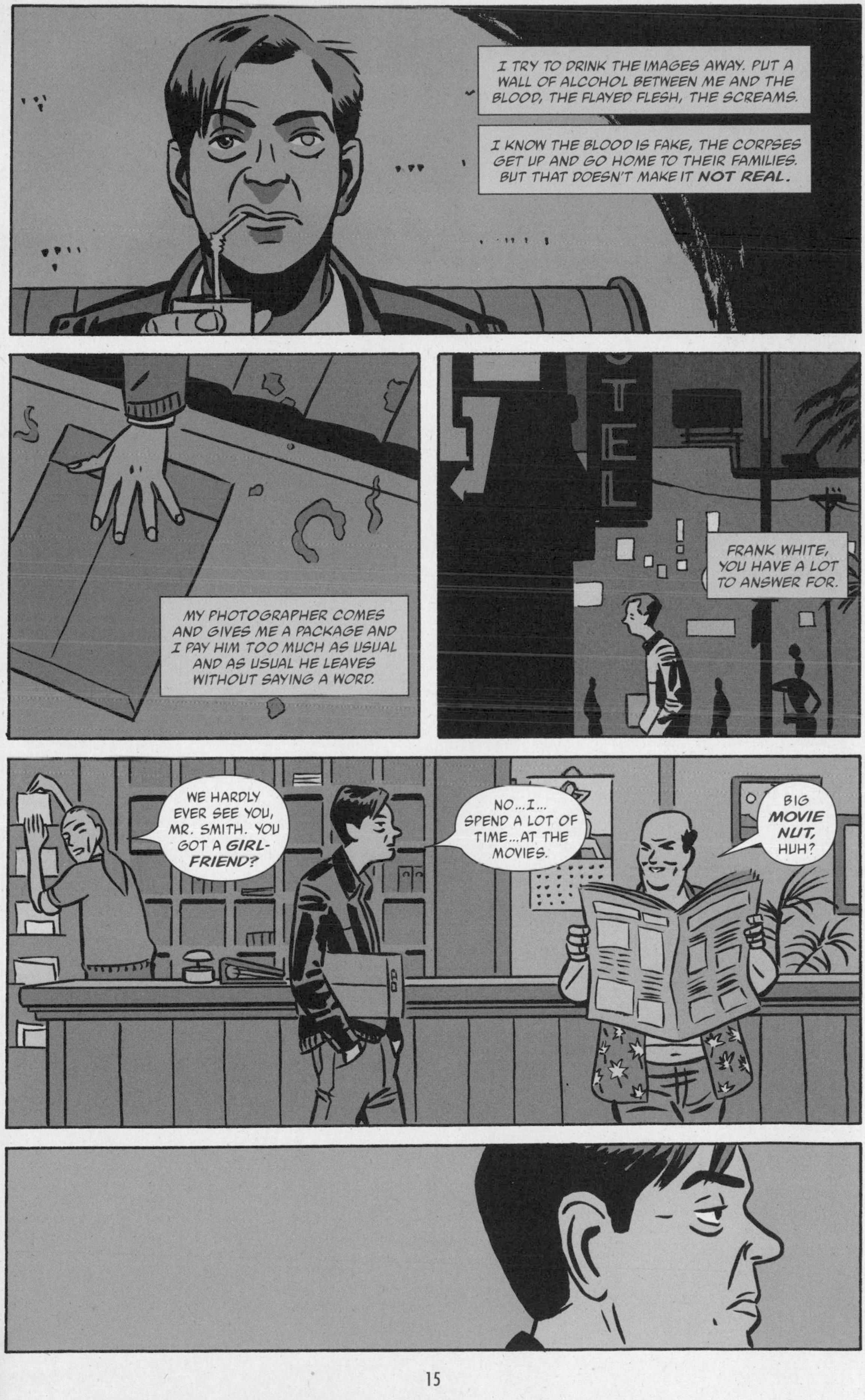
I TRY TO DRINK THE IMAGES AWAY. PUT A WALL OF ALCOHOL BETWEEN ME AND THE BLOOD, THE FLAYED FLESH, THE SCREAMS.
I KNOW THE BLOOD IS FAKE, THE CORPSES GET UP AND GO HOME TO THEIR FAMILIES. BUT THAT DOESN'T MAKE IT **NOT REAL.**
MY PHOTOGRAPHER COMES AND GIVES ME A PACKAGE AND I PAY HIM TOO MUCH AS USUAL AND AS USUAL HE LEAVES WITHOUT SAYING A WORD.
FRANK WHITE, YOU HAVE A LOT TO ANSWER FOR.
WE HARDLY EVER SEE YOU, MR. SMITH. YOU GOT A ***GIRL-FRIEND?***
NO...I... SPEND A LOT OF TIME...AT THE MOVIES.
BIG ***MOVIE NUT,*** HUH?

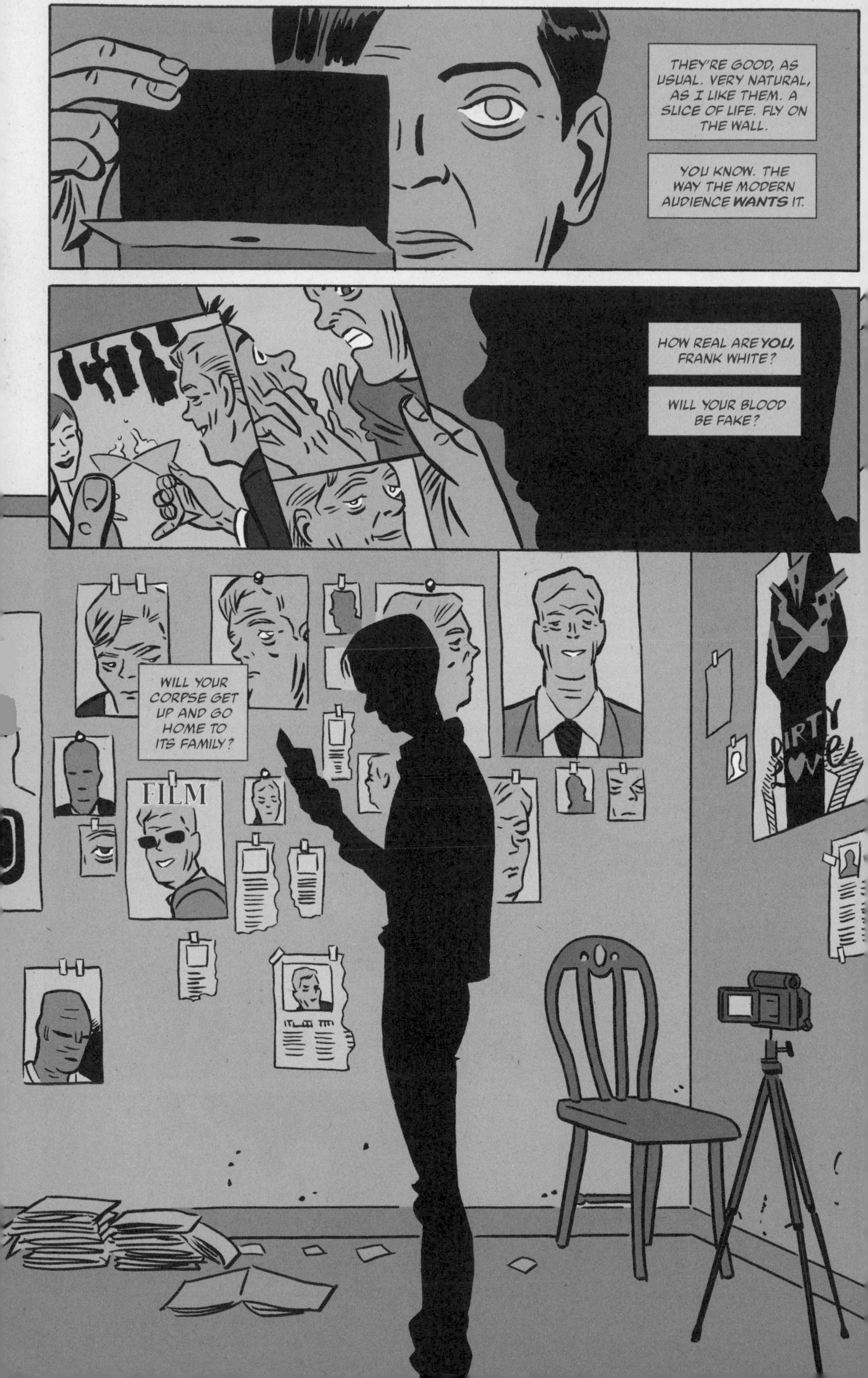
THEY'RE GOOD, AS USUAL. VERY NATURAL, AS I LIKE THEM. A SLICE OF LIFE. FLY ON THE WALL.
YOU KNOW. THE WAY THE MODERN AUDIENCE WANTS IT.
HOW REAL ARE YOU, FRANK WHITE?
WILL YOUR BLOOD BE FAKE?
WILL YOUR CORPSE GET UP AND GO HOME TO ITS FAMILY?
FILM
DIRTY LOVE

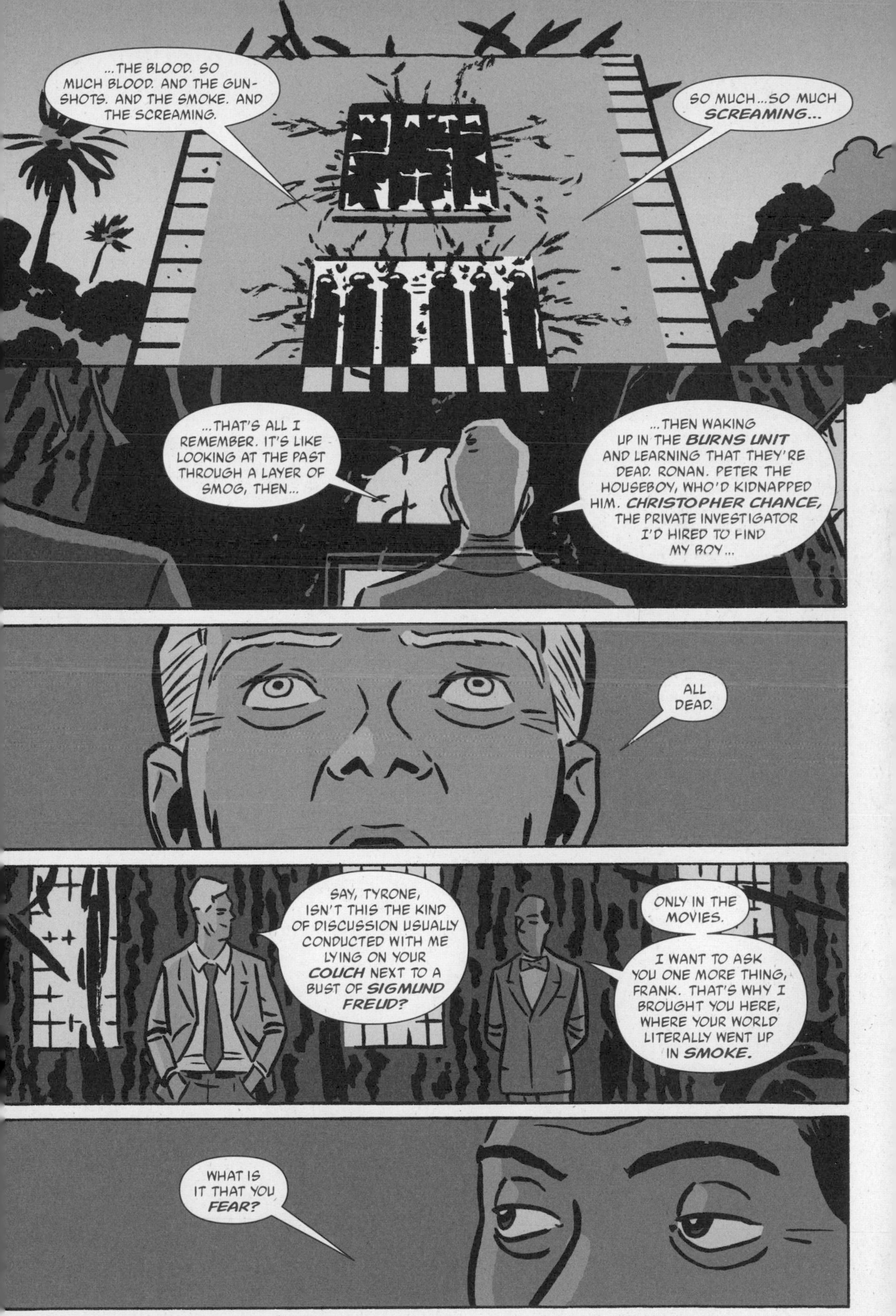
...THE BLOOD. SO MUCH BLOOD. AND THE GUN-SHOTS. AND THE SMOKE. AND THE SCREAMING.
SO MUCH...SO MUCH SCREAMING...
...THAT'S ALL I REMEMBER. IT'S LIKE LOOKING AT THE PAST THROUGH A LAYER OF SMOG, THEN...
...THEN WAKING UP IN THE BURNS UNIT AND LEARNING THAT THEY'RE DEAD. RONAN. PETER THE HOUSEBOY, WHO'D KIDNAPPED HIM. CHRISTOPHER CHANCE, THE PRIVATE INVESTIGATOR I'D HIRED TO FIND MY BOY...
ALL DEAD.
SAY, TYRONE, ISN'T THIS THE KIND OF DISCUSSION USUALLY CONDUCTED WITH ME LYING ON YOUR COUCH NEXT TO A BUST OF SIGMUND FREUD?
ONLY IN THE MOVIES.
I WANT TO ASK YOU ONE MORE THING, FRANK. THAT'S WHY I BROUGHT YOU HERE, WHERE YOUR WORLD LITERALLY WENT UP IN SMOKE.
WHAT IS IT THAT YOU FEAR?

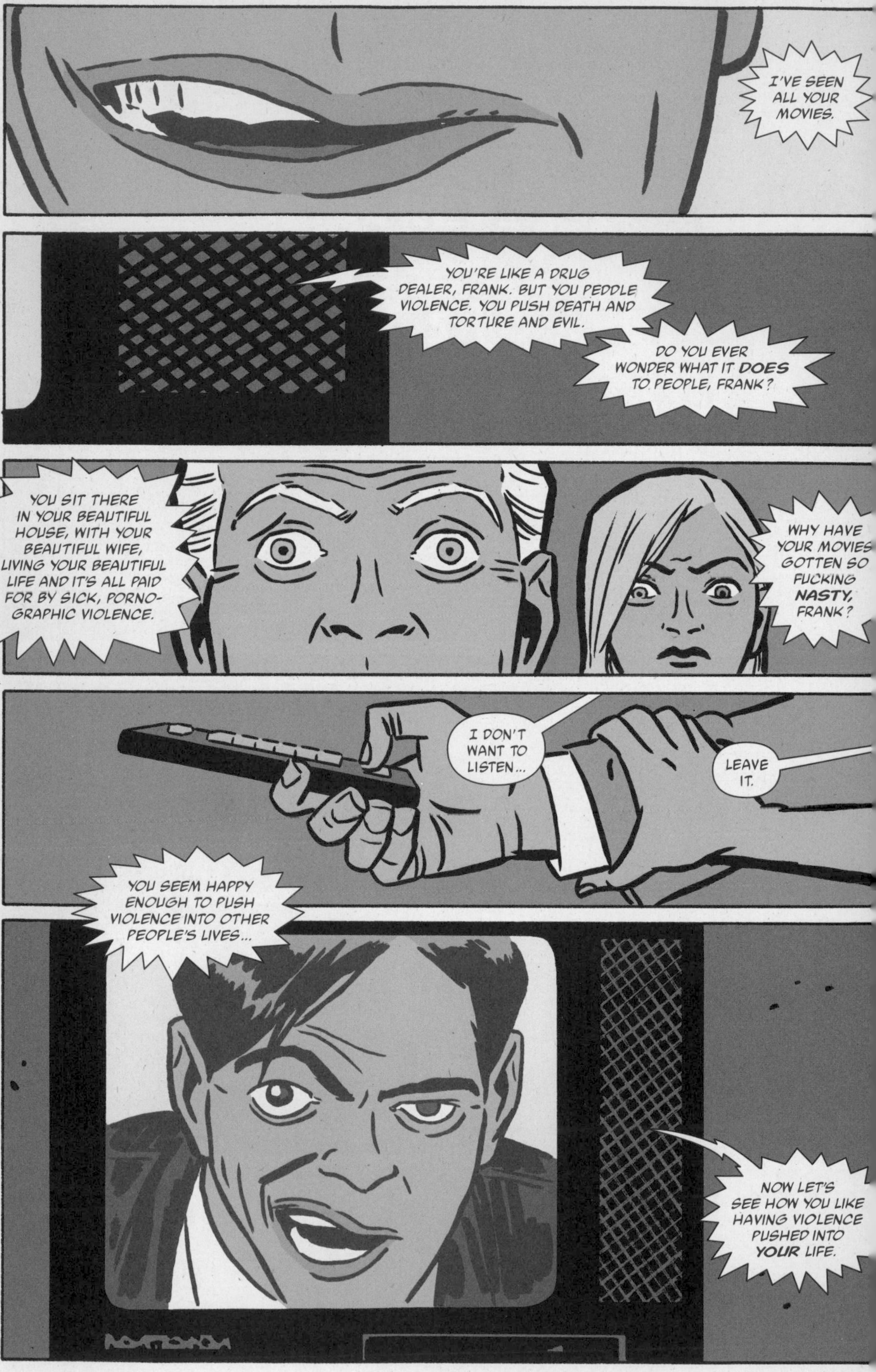
I'VE SEEN ALL YOUR MOVIES.
YOU'RE LIKE A DRUG DEALER, FRANK. BUT YOU PEDDLE VIOLENCE. YOU PUSH DEATH AND TORTURE AND EVIL.
DO YOU EVER WONDER WHAT IT **DOES** TO PEOPLE, FRANK?
YOU SIT THERE IN YOUR BEAUTIFUL HOUSE, WITH YOUR BEAUTIFUL WIFE, LIVING YOUR BEAUTIFUL LIFE AND IT'S ALL PAID FOR BY SICK, PORNO-GRAPHIC VIOLENCE.
WHY HAVE YOUR MOVIES GOTTEN SO FUCKING **NASTY,** FRANK?
I DON'T WANT TO LISTEN...
LEAVE IT.
YOU SEEM HAPPY ENOUGH TO PUSH VIOLENCE INTO OTHER PEOPLE'S LIVES...
NOW LET'S SEE HOW YOU LIKE HAVING VIOLENCE PUSHED INTO **YOUR** LIFE.

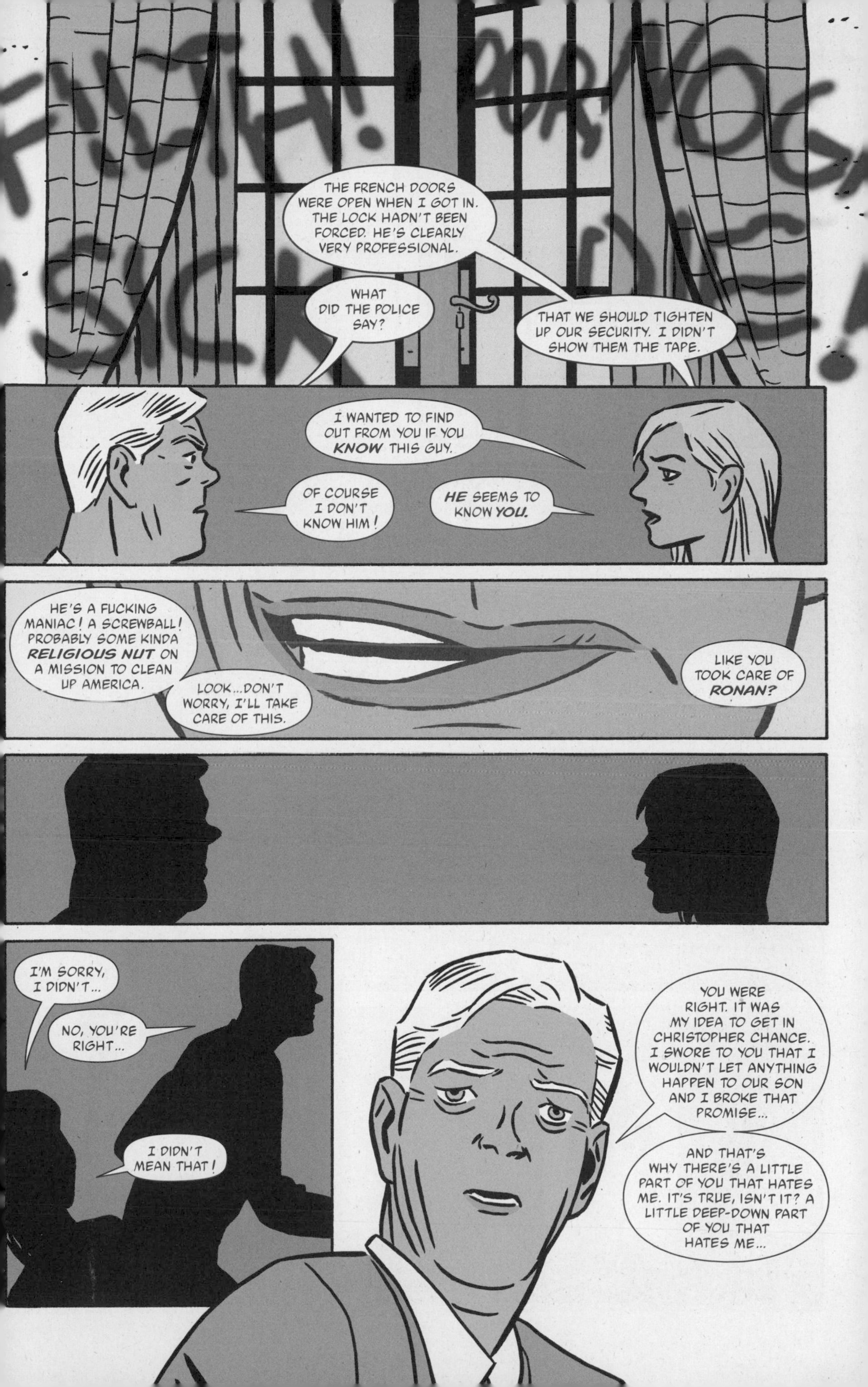
THE FRENCH DOORS WERE OPEN WHEN I GOT IN. THE LOCK HADN'T BEEN FORCED. HE'S CLEARLY VERY PROFESSIONAL.
WHAT DID THE POLICE SAY?
THAT WE SHOULD TIGHTEN UP OUR SECURITY. I DIDN'T SHOW THEM THE TAPE.
I WANTED TO FIND OUT FROM YOU IF YOU KNOW THIS GUY.
OF COURSE I DON'T KNOW HIM!
HE SEEMS TO KNOW YOU.
HE'S A FUCKING MANIAC! A SCREWBALL! PROBABLY SOME KINDA RELIGIOUS NUT ON A MISSION TO CLEAN UP AMERICA.
LOOK...DON'T WORRY, I'LL TAKE CARE OF THIS.
LIKE YOU TOOK CARE OF RONAN?
I'M SORRY, I DIDN'T...
NO, YOU'RE RIGHT...
I DIDN'T MEAN THAT!
YOU WERE RIGHT. IT WAS MY IDEA TO GET IN CHRISTOPHER CHANCE. I SWORE TO YOU THAT I WOULDN'T LET ANYTHING HAPPEN TO OUR SON AND I BROKE THAT PROMISE...
AND THAT'S WHY THERE'S A LITTLE PART OF YOU THAT HATES ME. IT'S TRUE, ISN'T IT? A LITTLE DEEP-DOWN PART OF YOU THAT HATES ME...

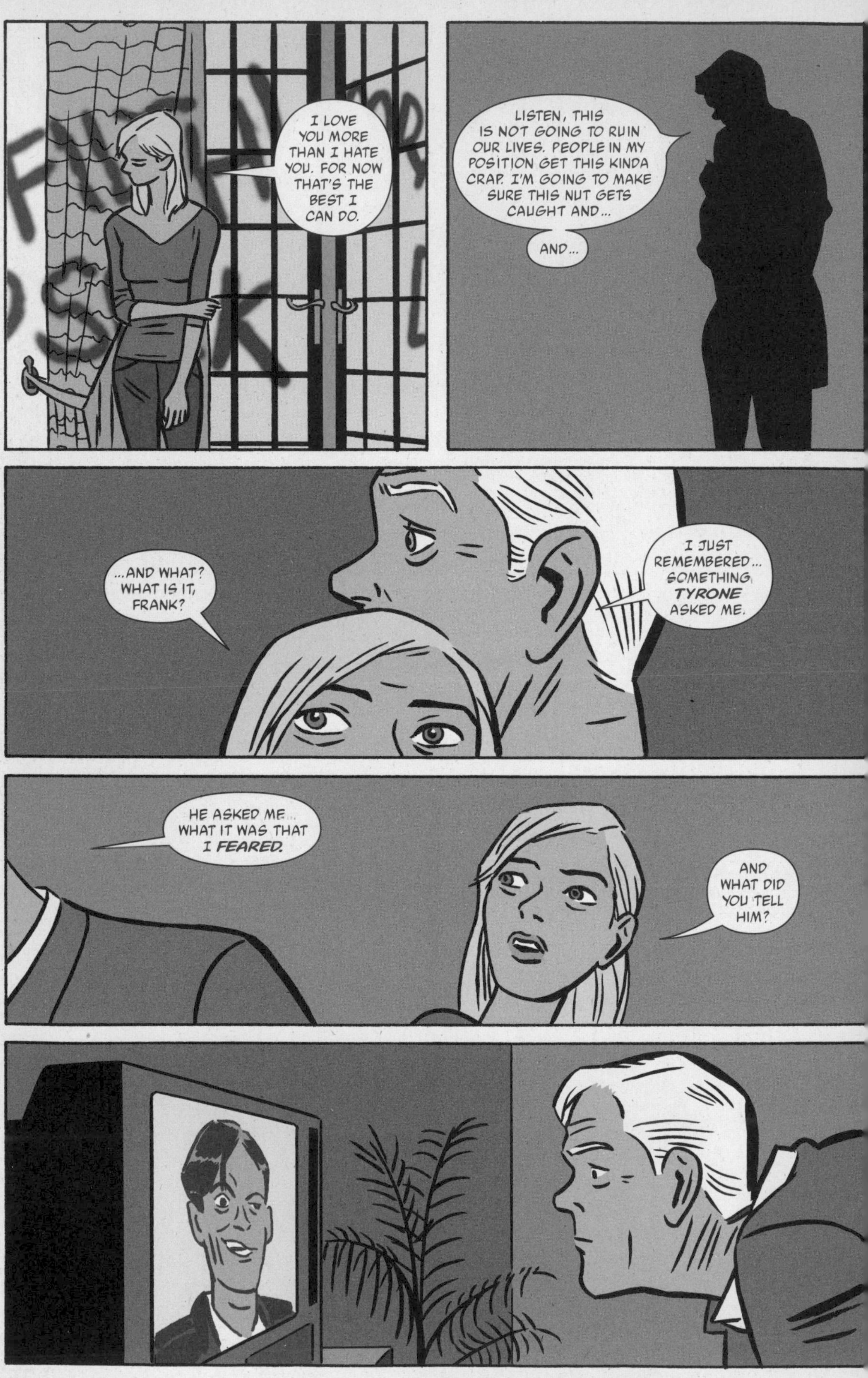
I LOVE YOU MORE THAN I HATE YOU. FOR NOW THAT'S THE BEST I CAN DO.
LISTEN, THIS IS NOT GOING TO RUIN OUR LIVES. PEOPLE IN MY POSITION GET THIS KINDA CRAP. I'M GOING TO MAKE SURE THIS NUT GETS CAUGHT AND...
AND...
...AND WHAT? WHAT IS IT, FRANK?
I JUST REMEMBERED... SOMETHING TYRONE ASKED ME.
HE ASKED ME... WHAT IT WAS THAT I FEARED.
AND WHAT DID YOU TELL HIM?

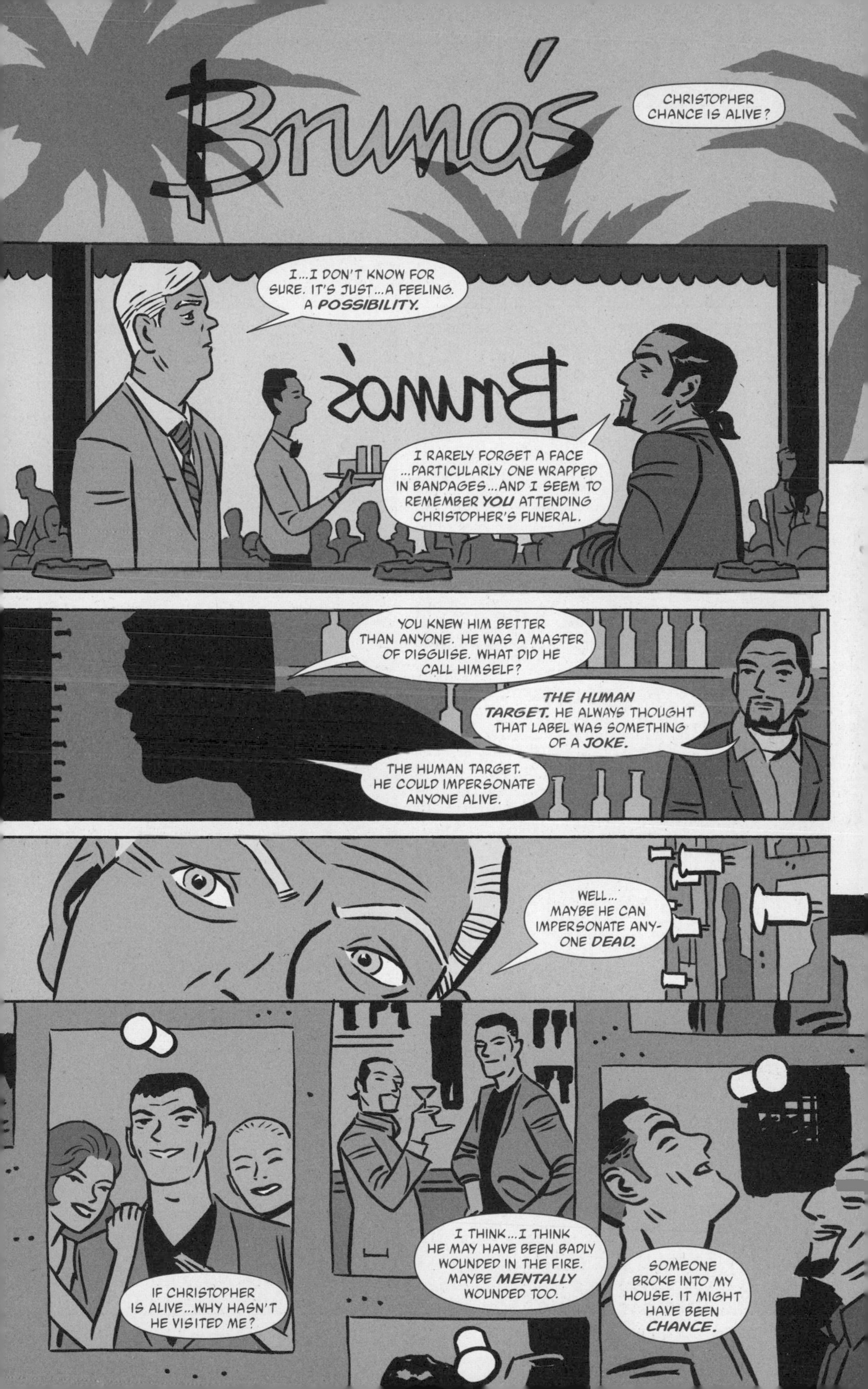
Bruno's
CHRISTOPHER CHANCE IS ALIVE?
I...I DON'T KNOW FOR SURE. IT'S JUST...A FEELING. A POSSIBILITY.
Bruno's
I RARELY FORGET A FACE ...PARTICULARLY ONE WRAPPED IN BANDAGES...AND I SEEM TO REMEMBER YOU ATTENDING CHRISTOPHER'S FUNERAL.
YOU KNEW HIM BETTER THAN ANYONE. HE WAS A MASTER OF DISGUISE. WHAT DID HE CALL HIMSELF?
THE HUMAN TARGET. HE ALWAYS THOUGHT THAT LABEL WAS SOMETHING OF A JOKE.
THE HUMAN TARGET. HE COULD IMPERSONATE ANYONE ALIVE.
WELL... MAYBE HE CAN IMPERSONATE ANY-ONE DEAD.
IF CHRISTOPHER IS ALIVE...WHY HASN'T HE VISITED ME?
I THINK...I THINK HE MAY HAVE BEEN BADLY WOUNDED IN THE FIRE. MAYBE MENTALLY WOUNDED TOO.
SOMEONE BROKE INTO MY HOUSE. IT MIGHT HAVE BEEN CHANCE.

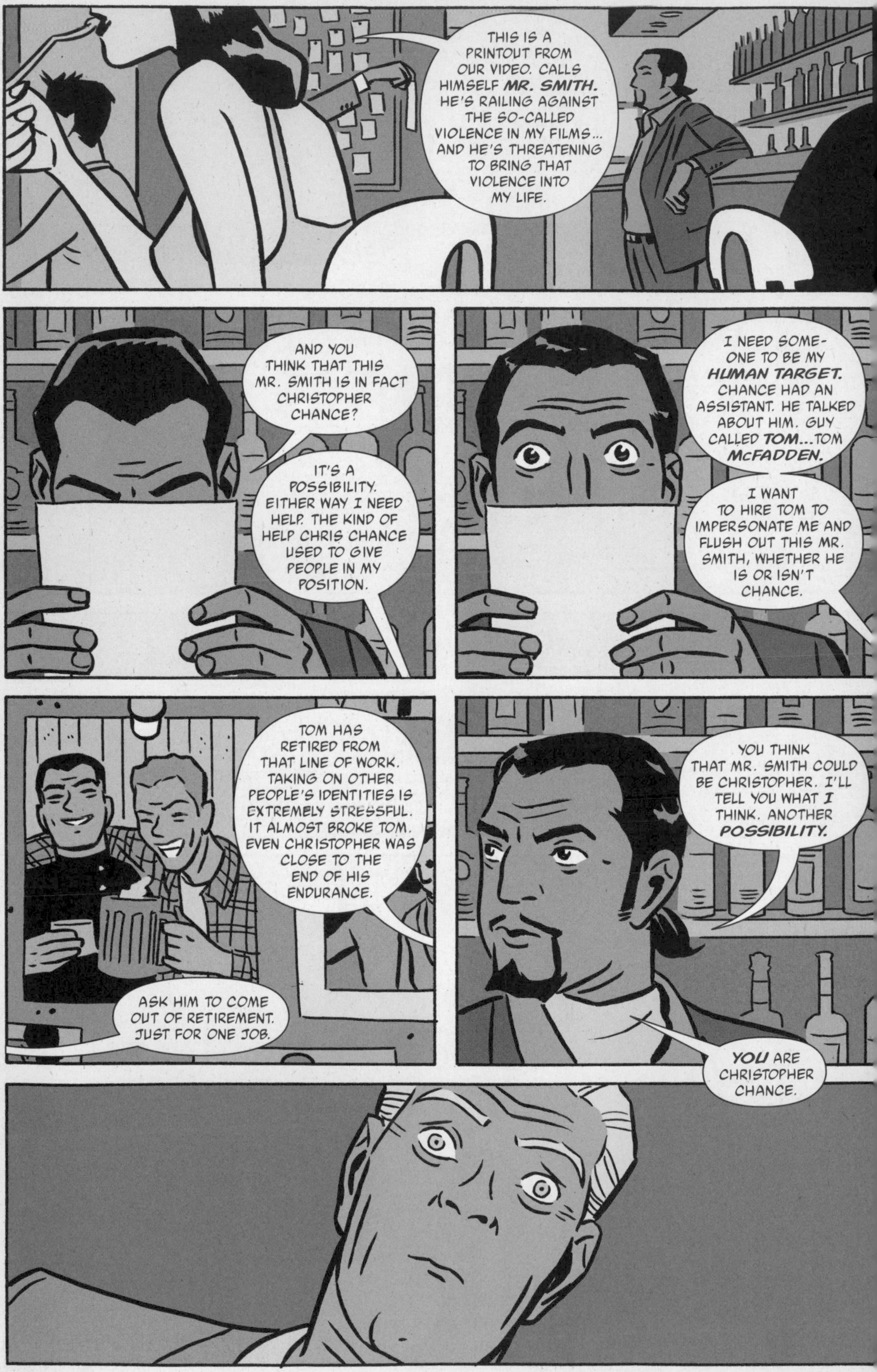

THIS IS A PRINTOUT FROM OUR VIDEO. CALLS HIMSELF **MR. SMITH.** HE'S RAILING AGAINST THE SO-CALLED VIOLENCE IN MY FILMS... AND HE'S THREATENING TO BRING THAT VIOLENCE INTO MY LIFE.
AND YOU THINK THAT THIS MR. SMITH IS IN FACT CHRISTOPHER CHANCE?
IT'S A POSSIBILITY. EITHER WAY I NEED HELP. THE KIND OF HELP CHRIS CHANCE USED TO GIVE PEOPLE IN MY POSITION.
I NEED SOME-ONE TO BE MY **HUMAN TARGET.** CHANCE HAD AN ASSISTANT. HE TALKED ABOUT HIM. GUY CALLED **TOM...**TOM **McFADDEN.**
I WANT TO HIRE TOM TO IMPERSONATE ME AND FLUSH OUT THIS MR. SMITH, WHETHER HE IS OR ISN'T CHANCE.
TOM HAS RETIRED FROM THAT LINE OF WORK. TAKING ON OTHER PEOPLE'S IDENTITIES IS EXTREMELY STRESSFUL. IT ALMOST BROKE TOM. EVEN CHRISTOPHER WAS CLOSE TO THE END OF HIS ENDURANCE.
ASK HIM TO COME OUT OF RETIREMENT. JUST FOR ONE JOB.
YOU THINK THAT MR. SMITH COULD BE CHRISTOPHER. I'LL TELL YOU WHAT **I** THINK. ANOTHER **POSSIBILITY.**
YOU ARE CHRISTOPHER CHANCE.

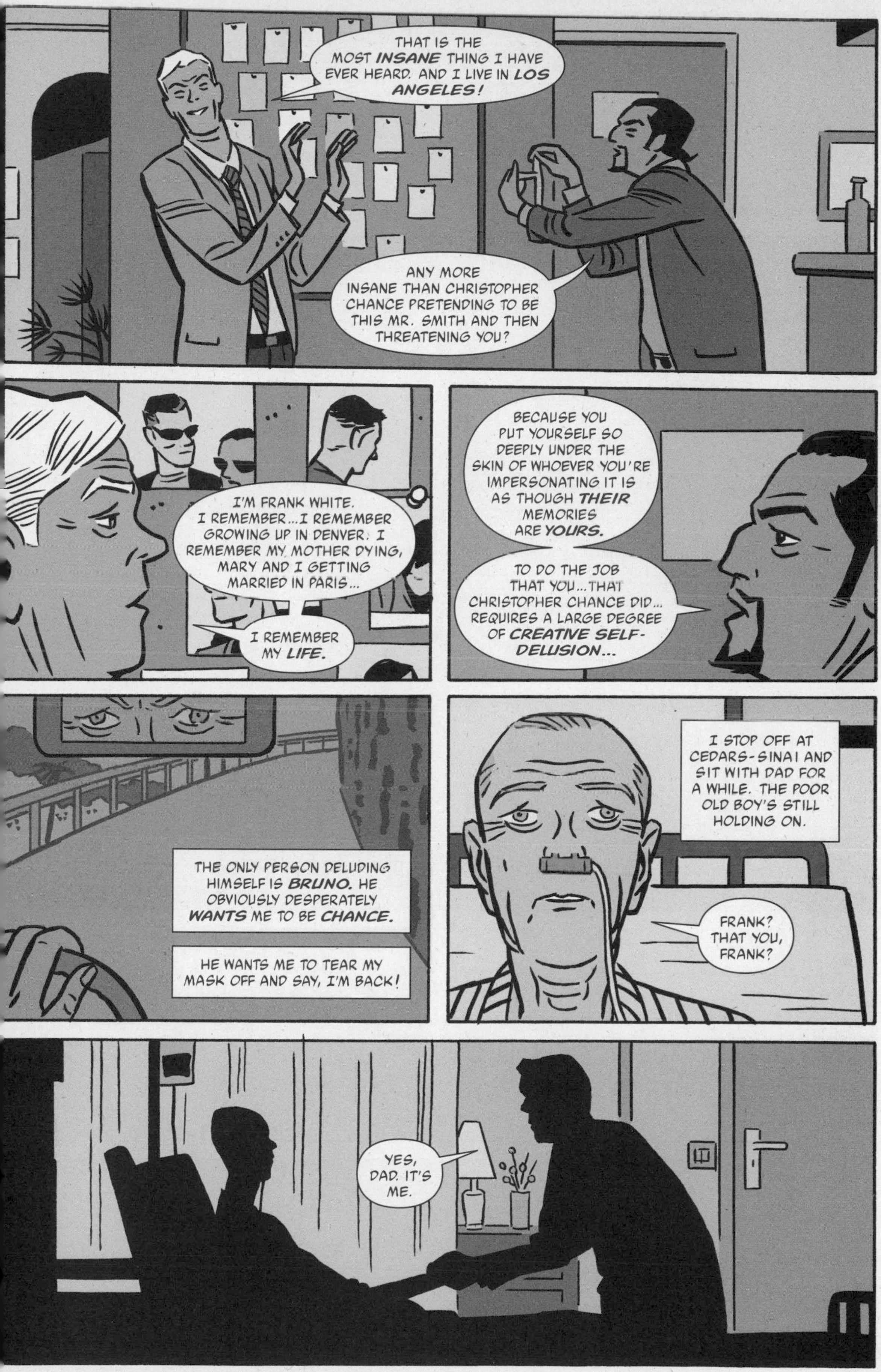
THAT IS THE MOST INSANE THING I HAVE EVER HEARD. AND I LIVE IN LOS ANGELES!
ANY MORE INSANE THAN CHRISTOPHER CHANCE PRETENDING TO BE THIS MR. SMITH AND THEN THREATENING YOU?
I'M FRANK WHITE. I REMEMBER...I REMEMBER GROWING UP IN DENVER. I REMEMBER MY MOTHER DYING, MARY AND I GETTING MARRIED IN PARIS...
I REMEMBER MY LIFE.
BECAUSE YOU PUT YOURSELF SO DEEPLY UNDER THE SKIN OF WHOEVER YOU'RE IMPERSONATING IT IS AS THOUGH THEIR MEMORIES ARE YOURS.
TO DO THE JOB THAT YOU...THAT CHRISTOPHER CHANCE DID... REQUIRES A LARGE DEGREE OF CREATIVE SELF-DELUSION...
THE ONLY PERSON DELUDING HIMSELF IS BRUNO. HE OBVIOUSLY DESPERATELY WANTS ME TO BE CHANCE.
HE WANTS ME TO TEAR MY MASK OFF AND SAY, I'M BACK!
I STOP OFF AT CEDARS-SINAI AND SIT WITH DAD FOR A WHILE. THE POOR OLD BOY'S STILL HOLDING ON.
FRANK? THAT YOU, FRANK?
YES, DAD. IT'S ME.

WE'VE SEEN THIS MOVIE BEFORE. BUT IT STILL WORKS FOR US. IT STILL ZINGS ON OUR JADED MORAL PALATE.

IT'S PROBABLY ALL THAT DOES NOW.

AH, YES. THE INTRUDERS INSIDE YOUR HOME. THE VIOLATION OF YOUR SPACE. HOW VERY **PRIMAL**!

SEE HOW SCARED THE POOR WOMAN IS: WHAT DELIGHTFUL NERVE-ENDINGS ARE TICKLED BY THE SIGHT OF HER DREAD?

ARE THEY GOING TO RAPE HER? KILL HER? DOES SHE HAVE LITTLE KIDDIES UPSTAIRS? JUST HOW HORRIFIC IS THIS GOING TO GET?

JUST HOW HORRIFIC DO WE **WANT** IT TO GET?

LET'S CONSIDER THE INTRUDERS FOR A MOMENT. THEY'RE WHITE. MIDDLE-CLASS. THEY COULD EASILY HAVE BEEN BLACK OR LATINO BUT THAT WOULD HAVE RAISED OTHER ISSUES.

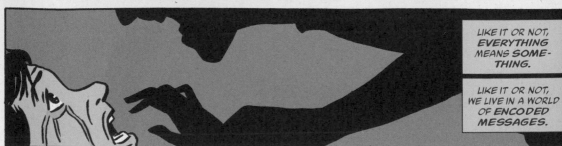

LIKE IT OR NOT, **EVERYTHING** MEANS **SOMETHING**.

LIKE IT OR NOT, WE LIVE IN A WORLD OF **ENCODED MESSAGES**.

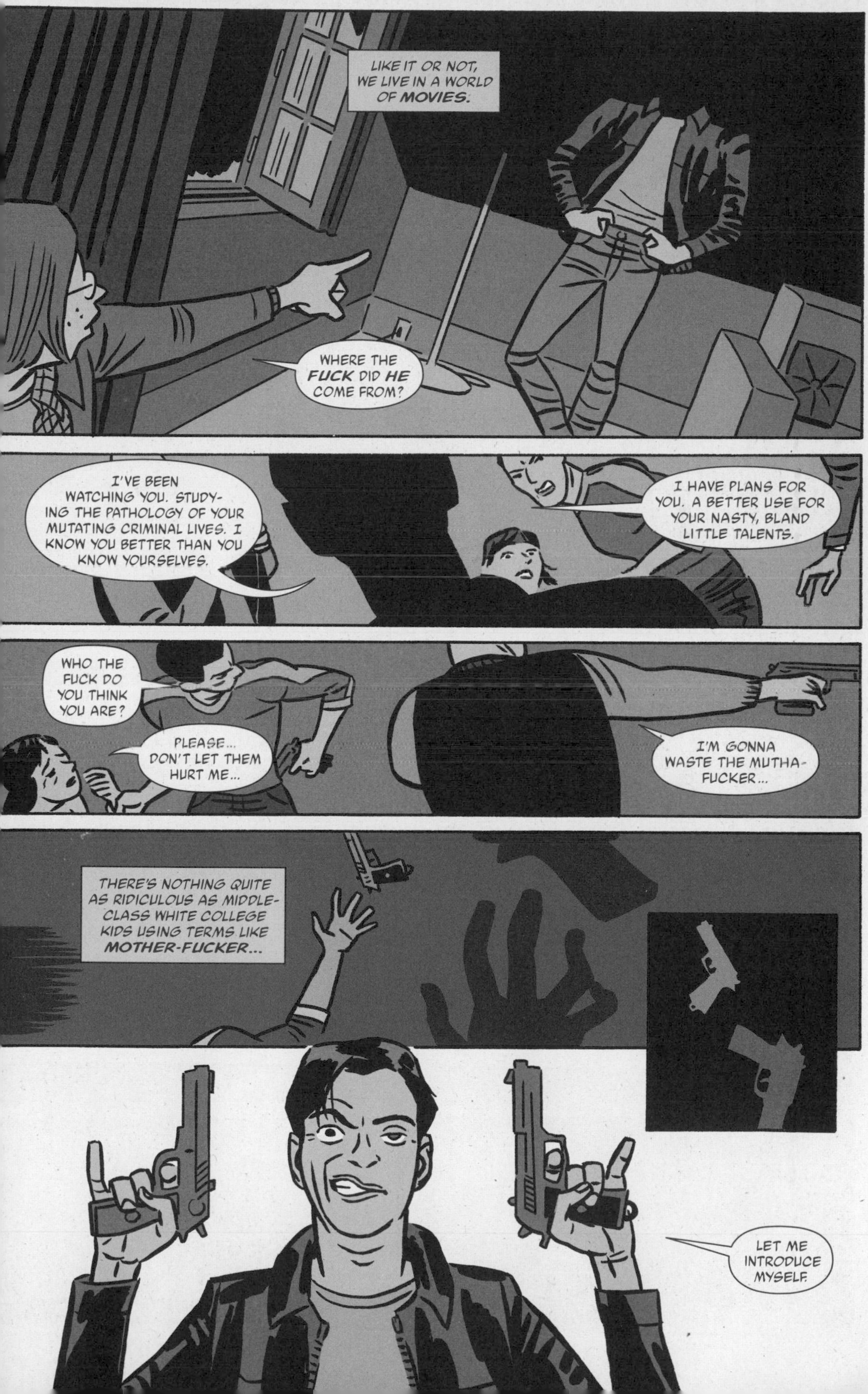

LIKE IT OR NOT, WE LIVE IN A WORLD OF MOVIES:
WHERE THE FUCK DID HE COME FROM?
I'VE BEEN WATCHING YOU. STUDYING THE PATHOLOGY OF YOUR MUTATING CRIMINAL LIVES. I KNOW YOU BETTER THAN YOU KNOW YOURSELVES.
I HAVE PLANS FOR YOU. A BETTER USE FOR YOUR NASTY, BLAND LITTLE TALENTS.
WHO THE FUCK DO YOU THINK YOU ARE?
PLEASE... DON'T LET THEM HURT ME...
I'M GONNA WASTE THE MUTHA-FUCKER...
THERE'S NOTHING QUITE AS RIDICULOUS AS MIDDLE-CLASS WHITE COLLEGE KIDS USING TERMS LIKE MOTHER-FUCKER...
LET ME INTRODUCE MYSELF.

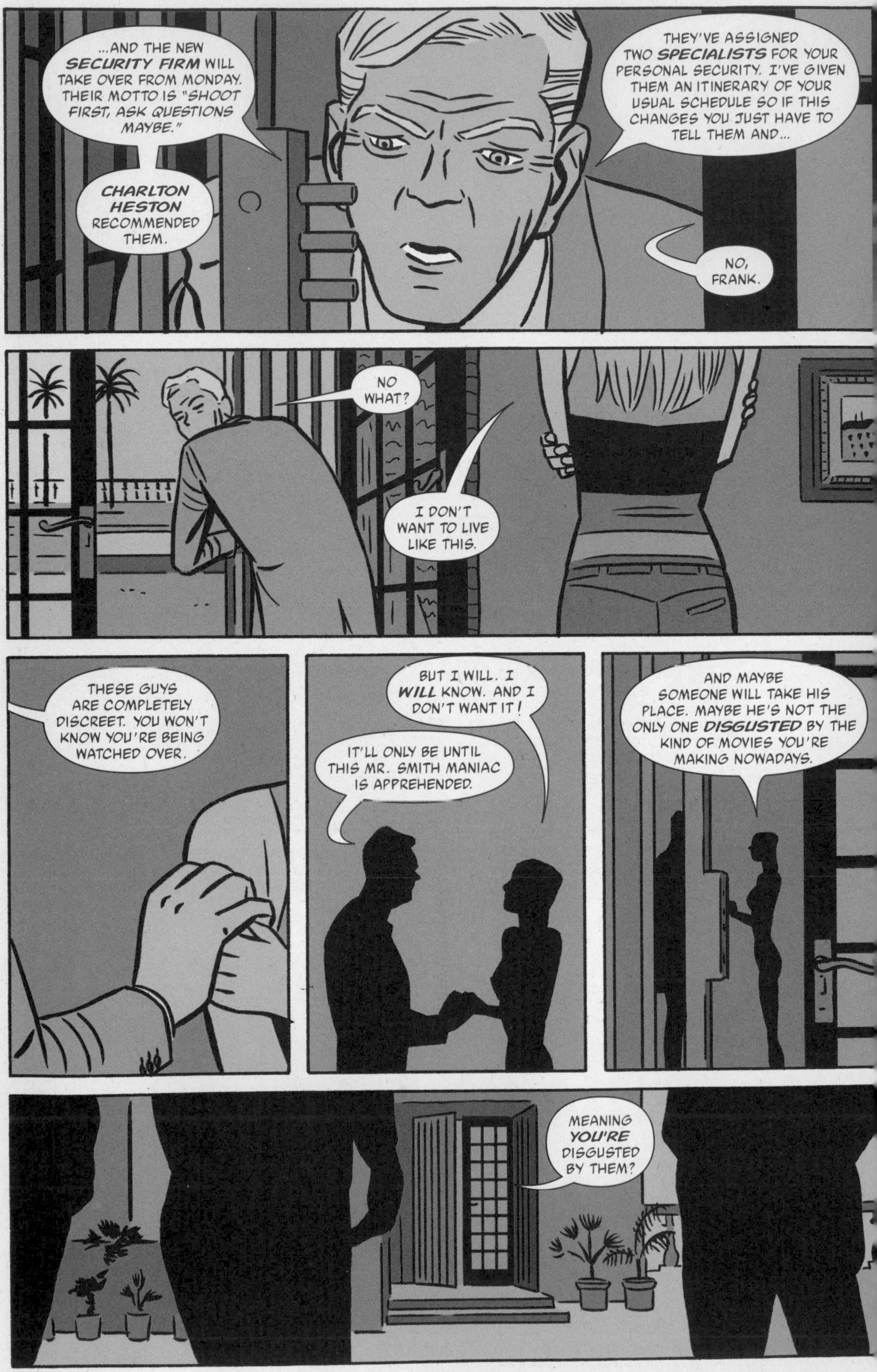
...AND THE NEW SECURITY FIRM WILL TAKE OVER FROM MONDAY. THEIR MOTTO IS "SHOOT FIRST, ASK QUESTIONS MAYBE."
CHARLTON HESTON RECOMMENDED THEM.
THEY'VE ASSIGNED TWO SPECIALISTS FOR YOUR PERSONAL SECURITY. I'VE GIVEN THEM AN ITINERARY OF YOUR USUAL SCHEDULE SO IF THIS CHANGES YOU JUST HAVE TO TELL THEM AND...
NO, FRANK.
NO WHAT?
I DON'T WANT TO LIVE LIKE THIS.
THESE GUYS ARE COMPLETELY DISCREET. YOU WON'T KNOW YOU'RE BEING WATCHED OVER.
BUT I WILL. I WILL KNOW. AND I DON'T WANT IT!
IT'LL ONLY BE UNTIL THIS MR. SMITH MANIAC IS APPREHENDED.
AND MAYBE SOMEONE WILL TAKE HIS PLACE. MAYBE HE'S NOT THE ONLY ONE DISGUSTED BY THE KIND OF MOVIES YOU'RE MAKING NOWADAYS.
MEANING YOU'RE DISGUSTED BY THEM?

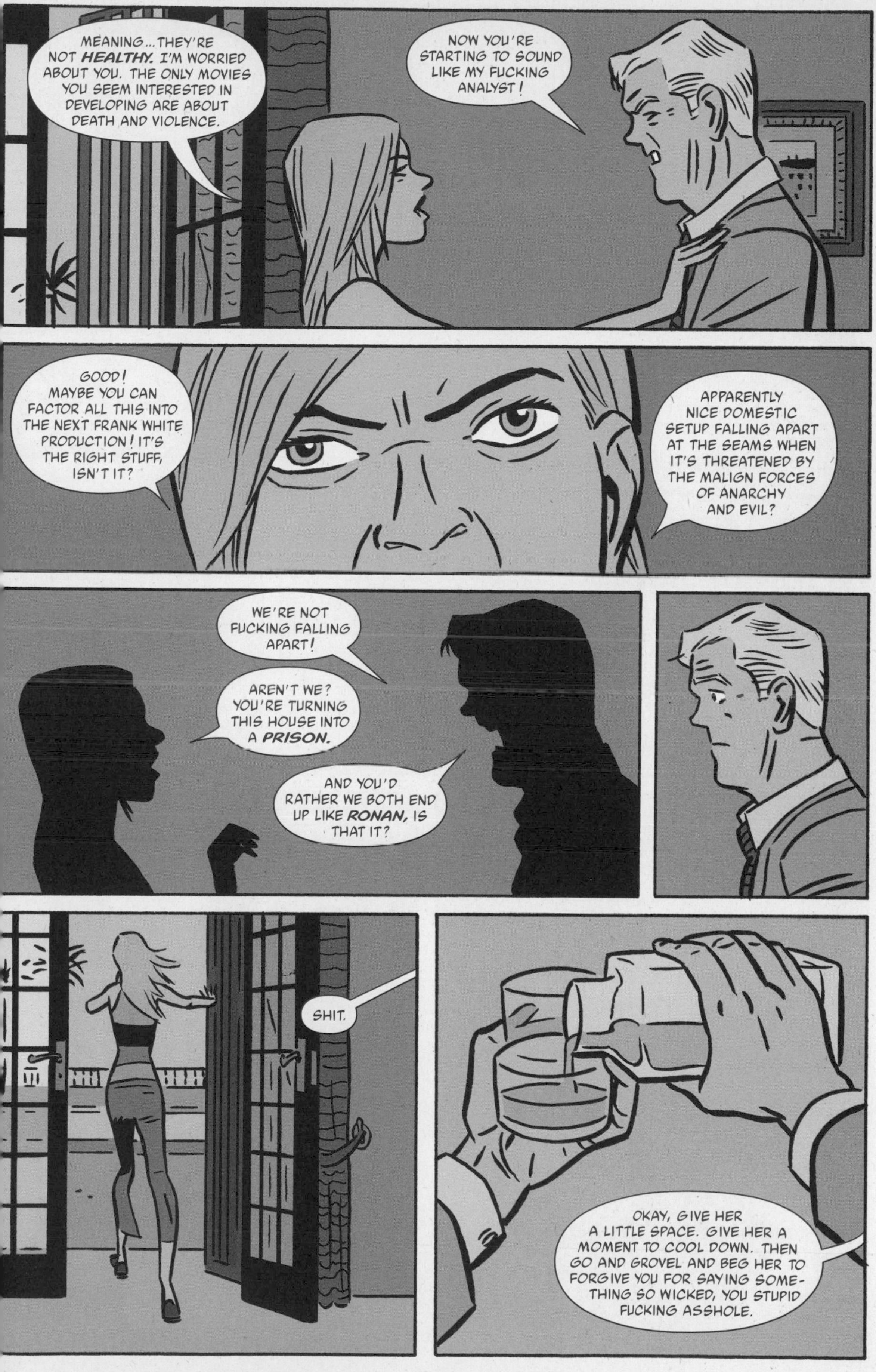
MEANING... THEY'RE NOT **HEALTHY.** I'M WORRIED ABOUT YOU. THE ONLY MOVIES YOU SEEM INTERESTED IN DEVELOPING ARE ABOUT DEATH AND VIOLENCE.
NOW YOU'RE STARTING TO SOUND LIKE MY FUCKING ANALYST!
GOOD! MAYBE YOU CAN FACTOR ALL THIS INTO THE NEXT FRANK WHITE PRODUCTION! IT'S THE RIGHT STUFF, ISN'T IT?
APPARENTLY NICE DOMESTIC SETUP FALLING APART AT THE SEAMS WHEN IT'S THREATENED BY THE MALIGN FORCES OF ANARCHY AND EVIL?
WE'RE NOT FUCKING FALLING APART!
AREN'T WE? YOU'RE TURNING THIS HOUSE INTO A **PRISON.**
AND YOU'D RATHER WE BOTH END UP LIKE **RONAN,** IS THAT IT?
SHIT.
OKAY, GIVE HER A LITTLE SPACE. GIVE HER A MOMENT TO COOL DOWN. THEN GO AND GROVEL AND BEG HER TO FORGIVE YOU FOR SAYING SOMETHING SO WICKED, YOU STUPID FUCKING ASSHOLE.

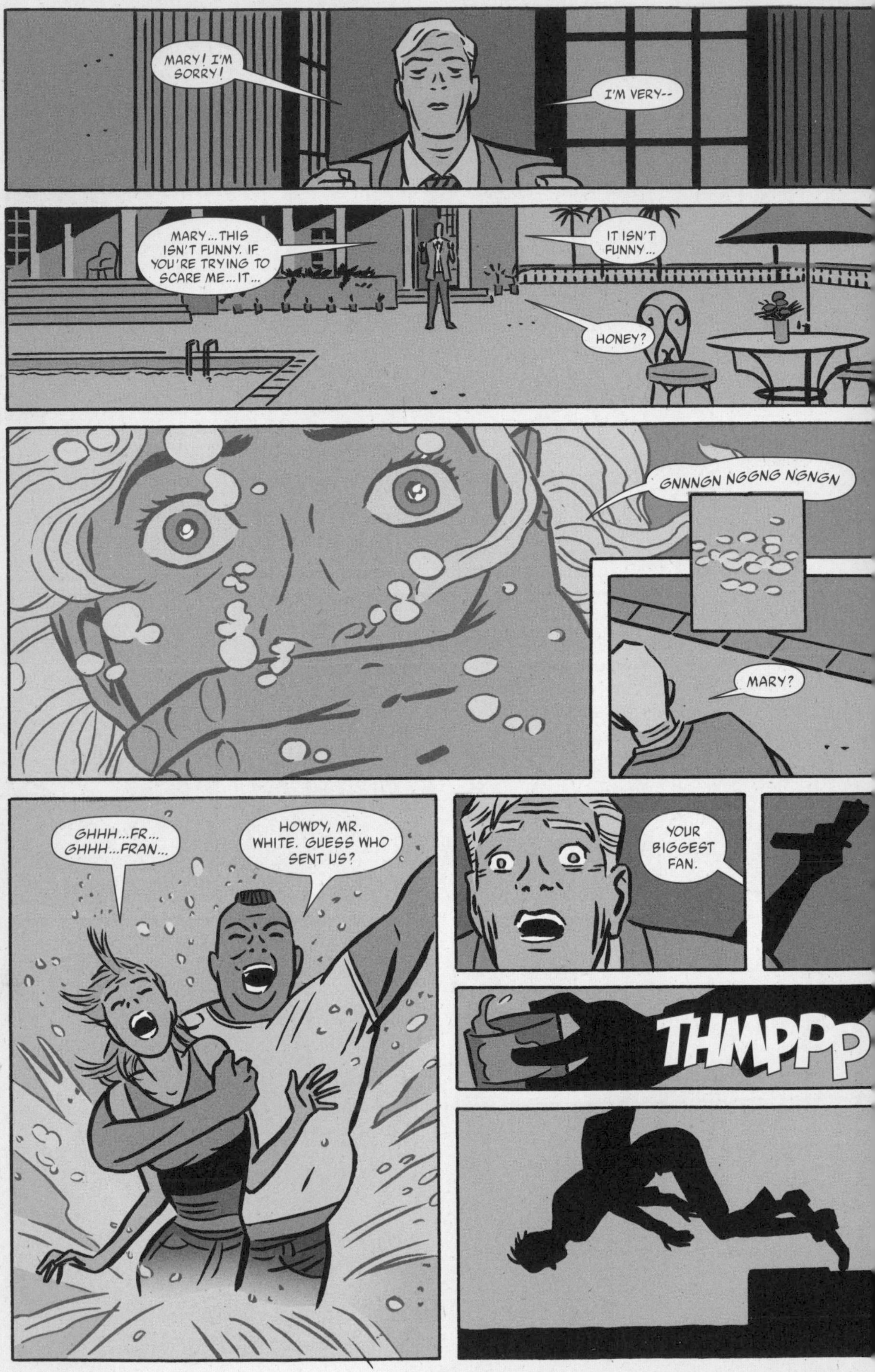
MARY! I'M SORRY!
I'M VERY--
MARY... THIS ISN'T FUNNY. IF YOU'RE TRYING TO SCARE ME... IT...
IT ISN'T FUNNY...
HONEY?
GNNNGN NGGNG NGNGN
MARY?
GHHH...FR... GHHH...FRAN...
HOWDY, MR. WHITE. GUESS WHO SENT US?
YOUR BIGGEST FAN.
THMPPP

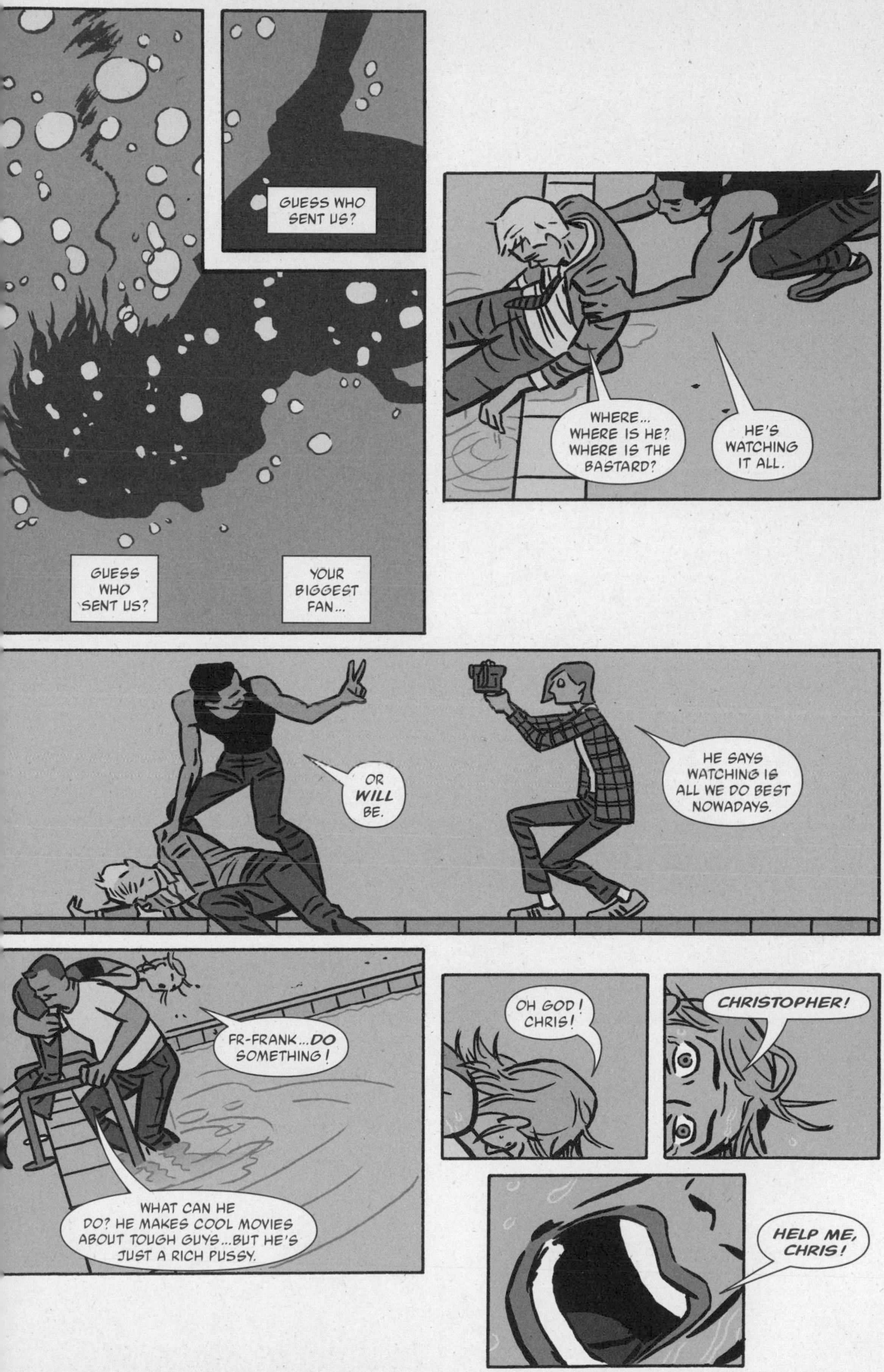
GUESS WHO SENT US?
GUESS WHO SENT US?
YOUR BIGGEST FAN...
WHERE... WHERE IS HE? WHERE IS THE BASTARD?
HE'S WATCHING IT ALL.
OR WILL BE.
HE SAYS WATCHING IS ALL WE DO BEST NOWADAYS.
FR-FRANK...DO SOMETHING!
WHAT CAN HE DO? HE MAKES COOL MOVIES ABOUT TOUGH GUYS...BUT HE'S JUST A RICH PUSSY.
OH GOD! CHRIS!
CHRISTOPHER!
HELP ME, CHRIS!

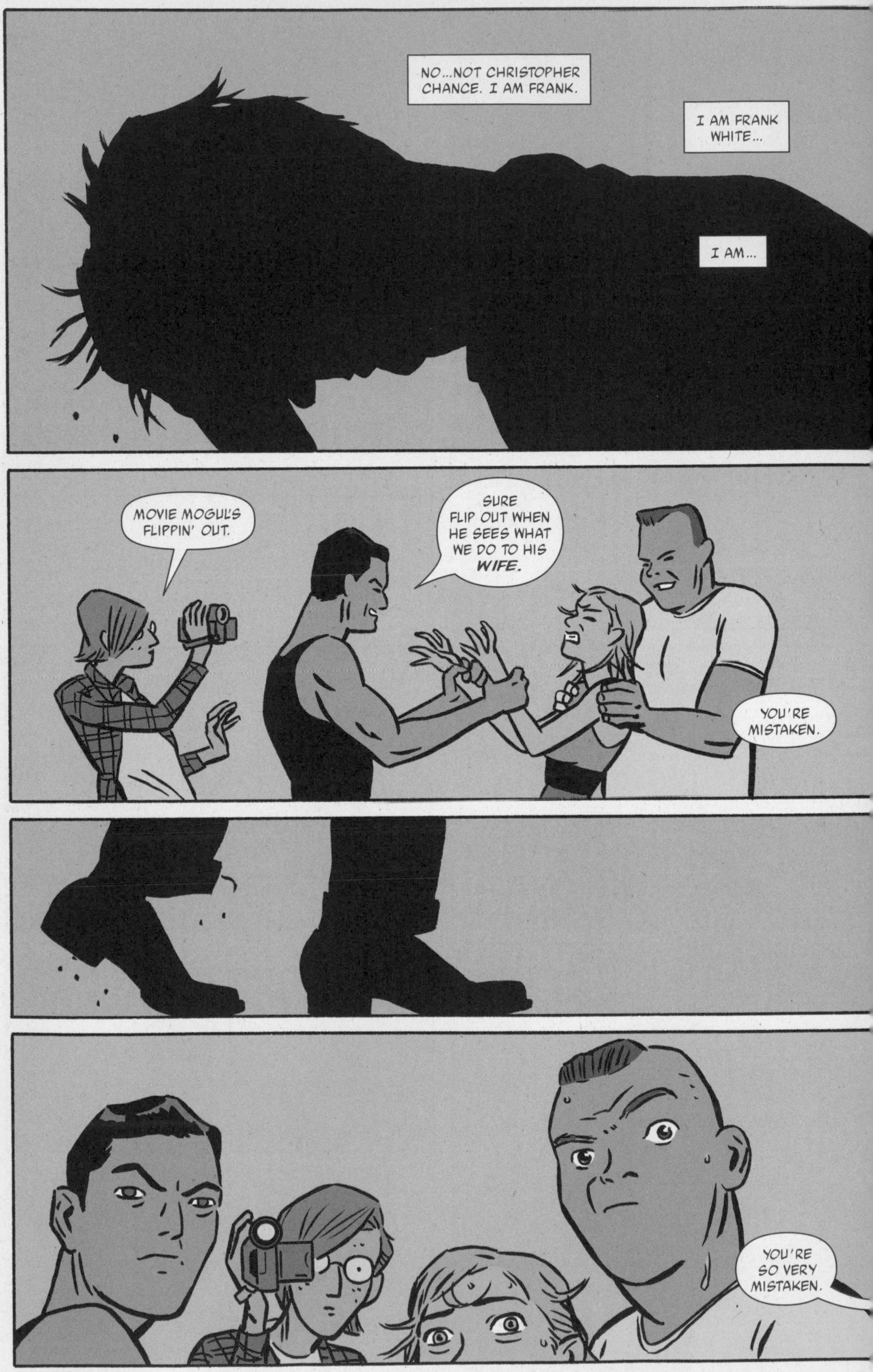
NO...NOT CHRISTOPHER CHANCE. I AM FRANK.
I AM FRANK WHITE...
I AM...
MOVIE MOGUL'S FLIPPIN' OUT.
SURE FLIP OUT WHEN HE SEES WHAT WE DO TO HIS WIFE.
YOU'RE MISTAKEN.
YOU'RE SO VERY MISTAKEN.

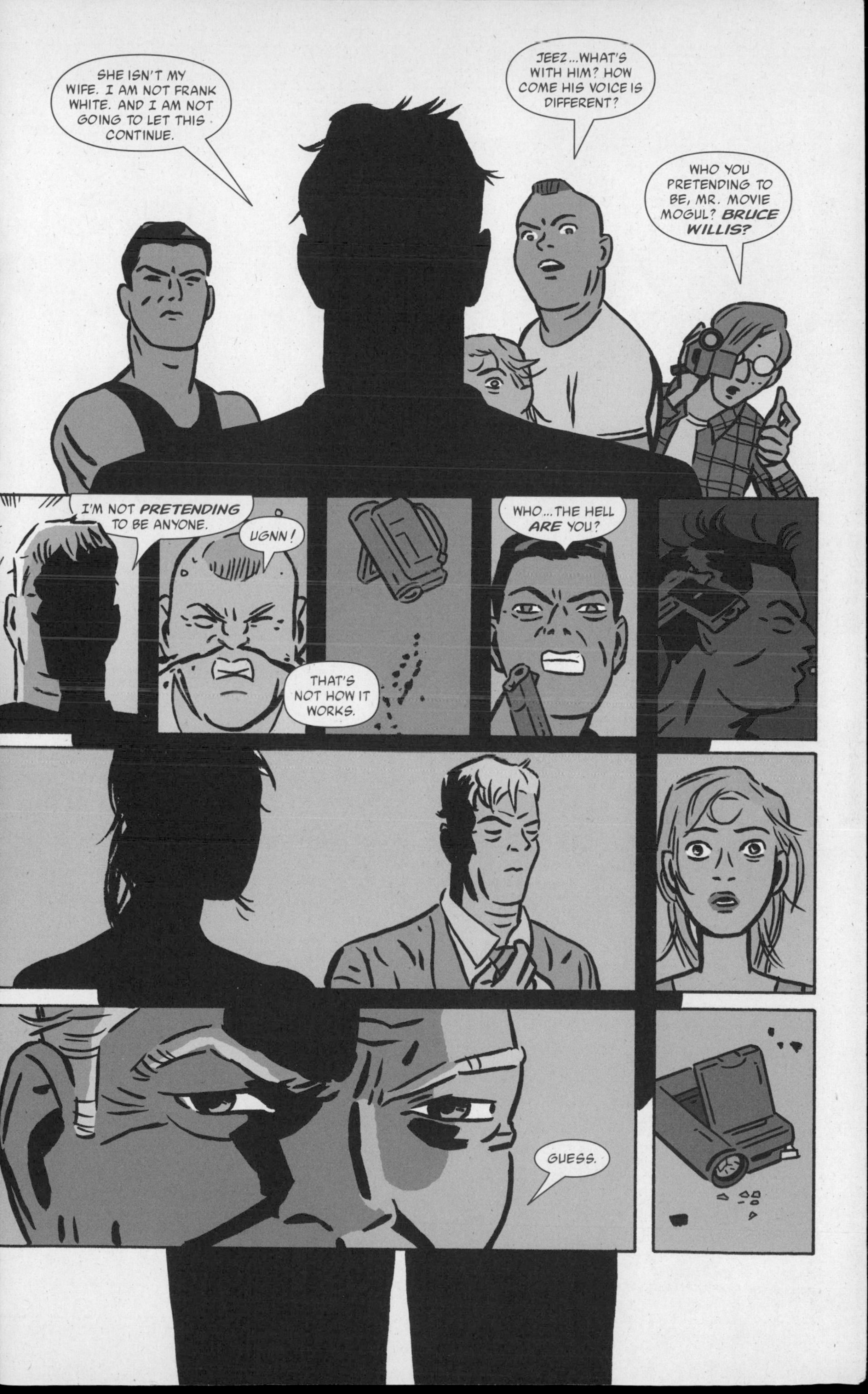
SHE ISN'T MY WIFE. I AM NOT FRANK WHITE. AND I AM NOT GOING TO LET THIS CONTINUE.
JEEZ...WHAT'S WITH HIM? HOW COME HIS VOICE IS DIFFERENT?
WHO YOU PRETENDING TO BE, MR. MOVIE MOGUL? BRUCE WILLIS?
I'M NOT PRETENDING TO BE ANYONE.
UGNN!
THAT'S NOT HOW IT WORKS.
WHO...THE HELL ARE YOU?
GUESS.

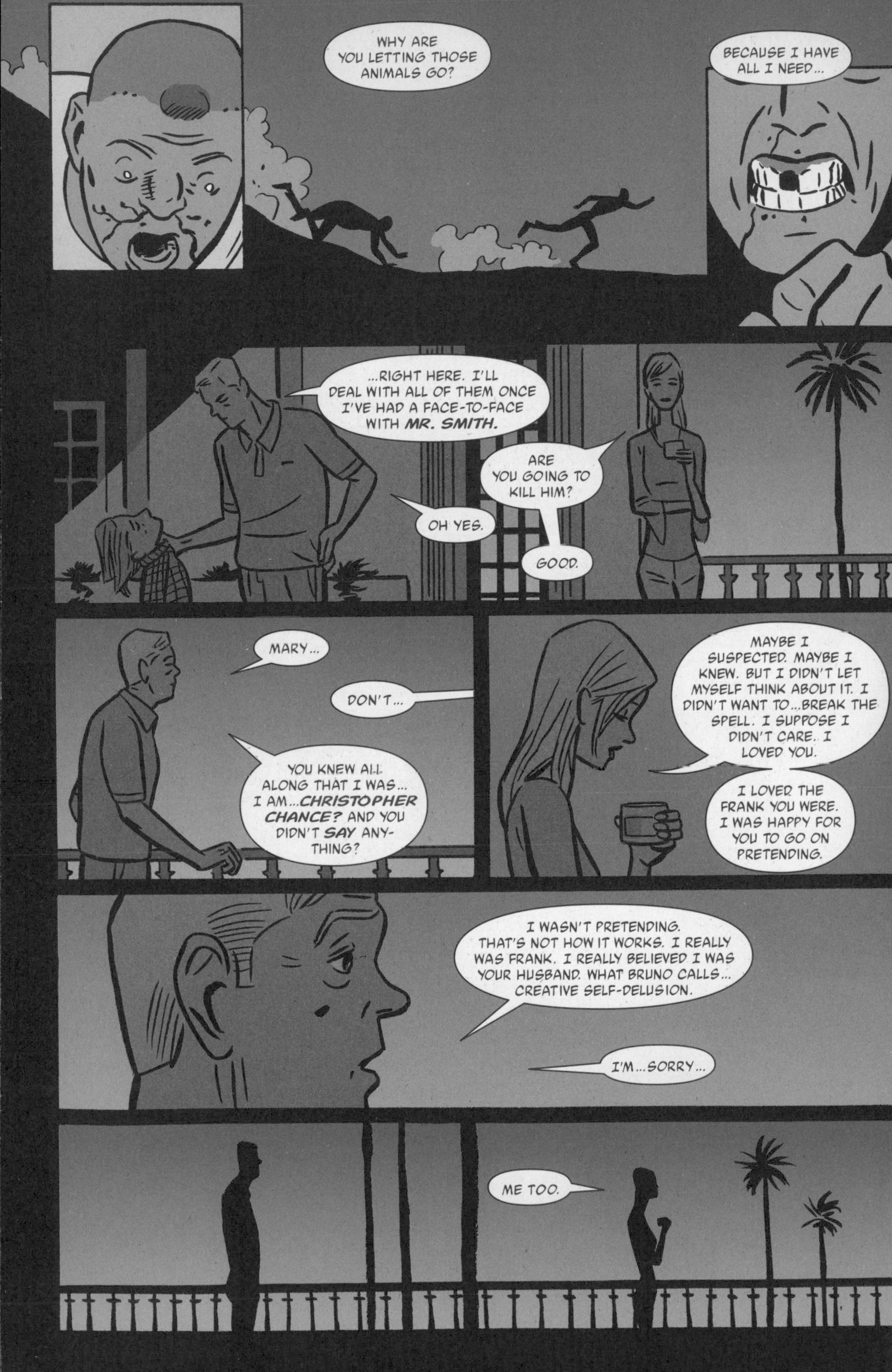
WHY ARE YOU LETTING THOSE ANIMALS GO?
BECAUSE I HAVE ALL I NEED...
...RIGHT HERE. I'LL DEAL WITH ALL OF THEM ONCE I'VE HAD A FACE-TO-FACE WITH MR. SMITH.
ARE YOU GOING TO KILL HIM?
OH YES.
GOOD.
MARY...
DON'T...
YOU KNEW ALL ALONG THAT I WAS... I AM...CHRISTOPHER CHANCE? AND YOU DIDN'T SAY ANYTHING?
MAYBE I SUSPECTED. MAYBE I KNEW. BUT I DIDN'T LET MYSELF THINK ABOUT IT. I DIDN'T WANT TO...BREAK THE SPELL. I SUPPOSE I DIDN'T CARE. I LOVED YOU.
I LOVED THE FRANK YOU WERE. I WAS HAPPY FOR YOU TO GO ON PRETENDING.
I WASN'T PRETENDING. THAT'S NOT HOW IT WORKS. I REALLY WAS FRANK. I REALLY BELIEVED I WAS YOUR HUSBAND. WHAT BRUNO CALLS... CREATIVE SELF-DELUSION.
I'M...SORRY...
ME TOO.

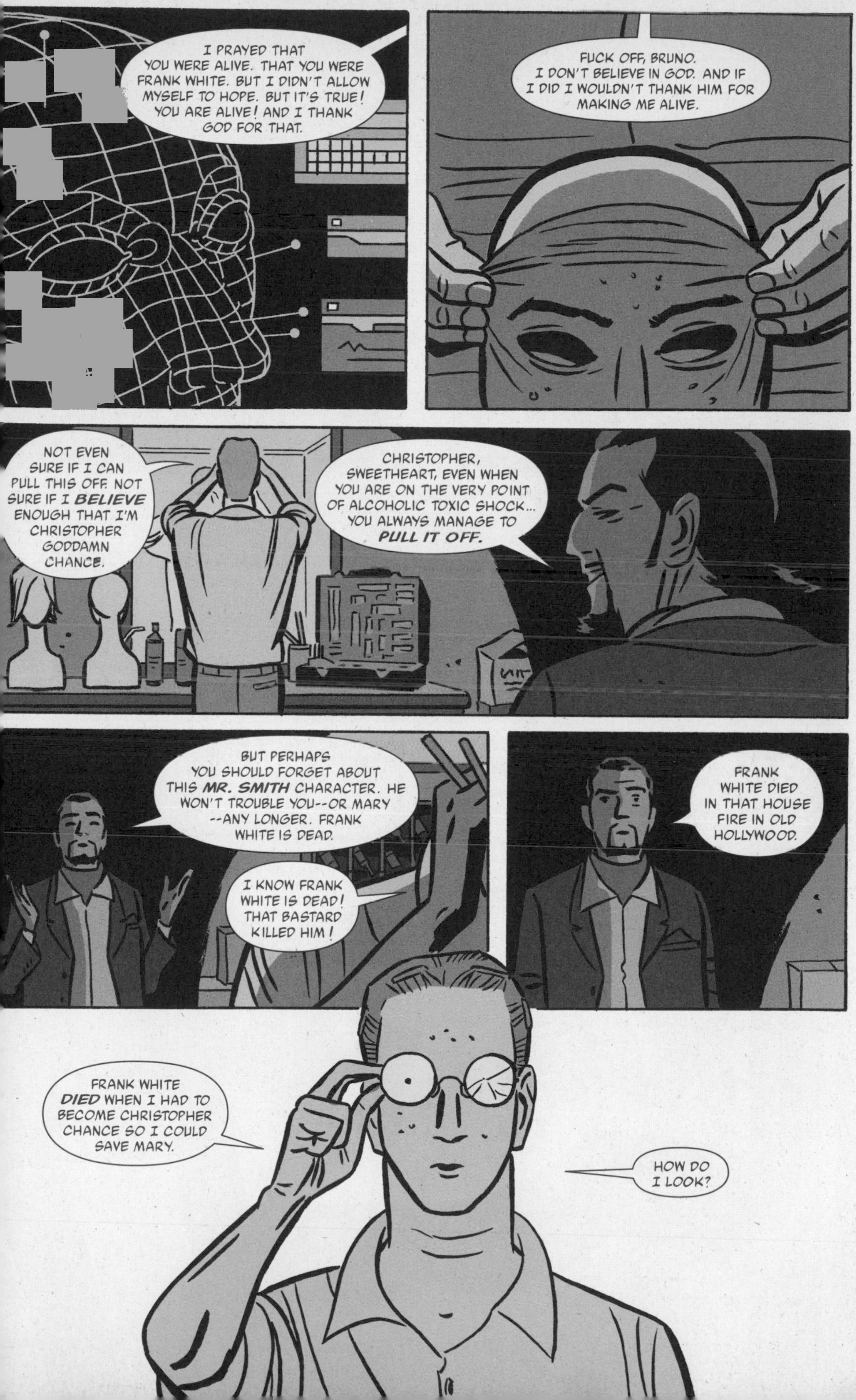
I PRAYED THAT YOU WERE ALIVE. THAT YOU WERE FRANK WHITE. BUT I DIDN'T ALLOW MYSELF TO HOPE. BUT IT'S TRUE! YOU ARE ALIVE! AND I THANK GOD FOR THAT.
FUCK OFF, BRUNO. I DON'T BELIEVE IN GOD. AND IF I DID I WOULDN'T THANK HIM FOR MAKING ME ALIVE.
NOT EVEN SURE IF I CAN PULL THIS OFF. NOT SURE IF I BELIEVE ENOUGH THAT I'M CHRISTOPHER GODDAMN CHANCE.
CHRISTOPHER, SWEETHEART, EVEN WHEN YOU ARE ON THE VERY POINT OF ALCOHOLIC TOXIC SHOCK... YOU ALWAYS MANAGE TO PULL IT OFF.
BUT PERHAPS YOU SHOULD FORGET ABOUT THIS MR. SMITH CHARACTER. HE WON'T TROUBLE YOU--OR MARY --ANY LONGER. FRANK WHITE IS DEAD.
I KNOW FRANK WHITE IS DEAD! THAT BASTARD KILLED HIM!
FRANK WHITE DIED IN THAT HOUSE FIRE IN OLD HOLLYWOOD.
FRANK WHITE DIED WHEN I HAD TO BECOME CHRISTOPHER CHANCE SO I COULD SAVE MARY.
HOW DO I LOOK?

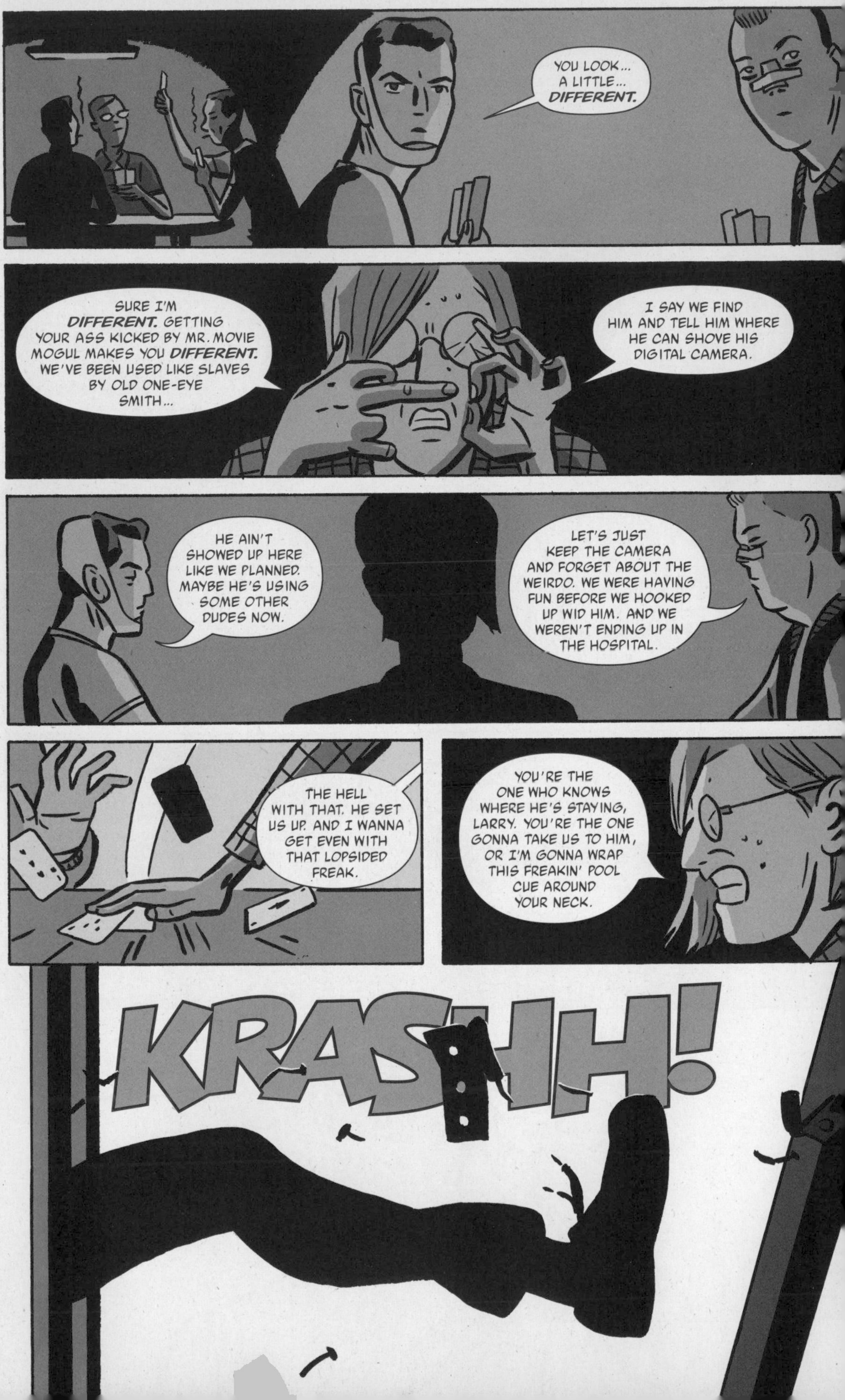
YOU LOOK... A LITTLE... DIFFERENT.
SURE I'M DIFFERENT. GETTING YOUR ASS KICKED BY MR. MOVIE MOGUL MAKES YOU DIFFERENT. WE'VE BEEN USED LIKE SLAVES BY OLD ONE-EYE SMITH...
I SAY WE FIND HIM AND TELL HIM WHERE HE CAN SHOVE HIS DIGITAL CAMERA.
HE AIN'T SHOWED UP HERE LIKE WE PLANNED. MAYBE HE'S USING SOME OTHER DUDES NOW.
LET'S JUST KEEP THE CAMERA AND FORGET ABOUT THE WEIRDO. WE WERE HAVING FUN BEFORE WE HOOKED UP WID HIM. AND WE WEREN'T ENDING UP IN THE HOSPITAL.
THE HELL WITH THAT. HE SET US UP. AND I WANNA GET EVEN WITH THAT LOPSIDED FREAK.
YOU'RE THE ONE WHO KNOWS WHERE HE'S STAYING, LARRY. YOU'RE THE ONE GONNA TAKE US TO HIM, OR I'M GONNA WRAP THIS FREAKIN' POOL CUE AROUND YOUR NECK.
KRASHH!

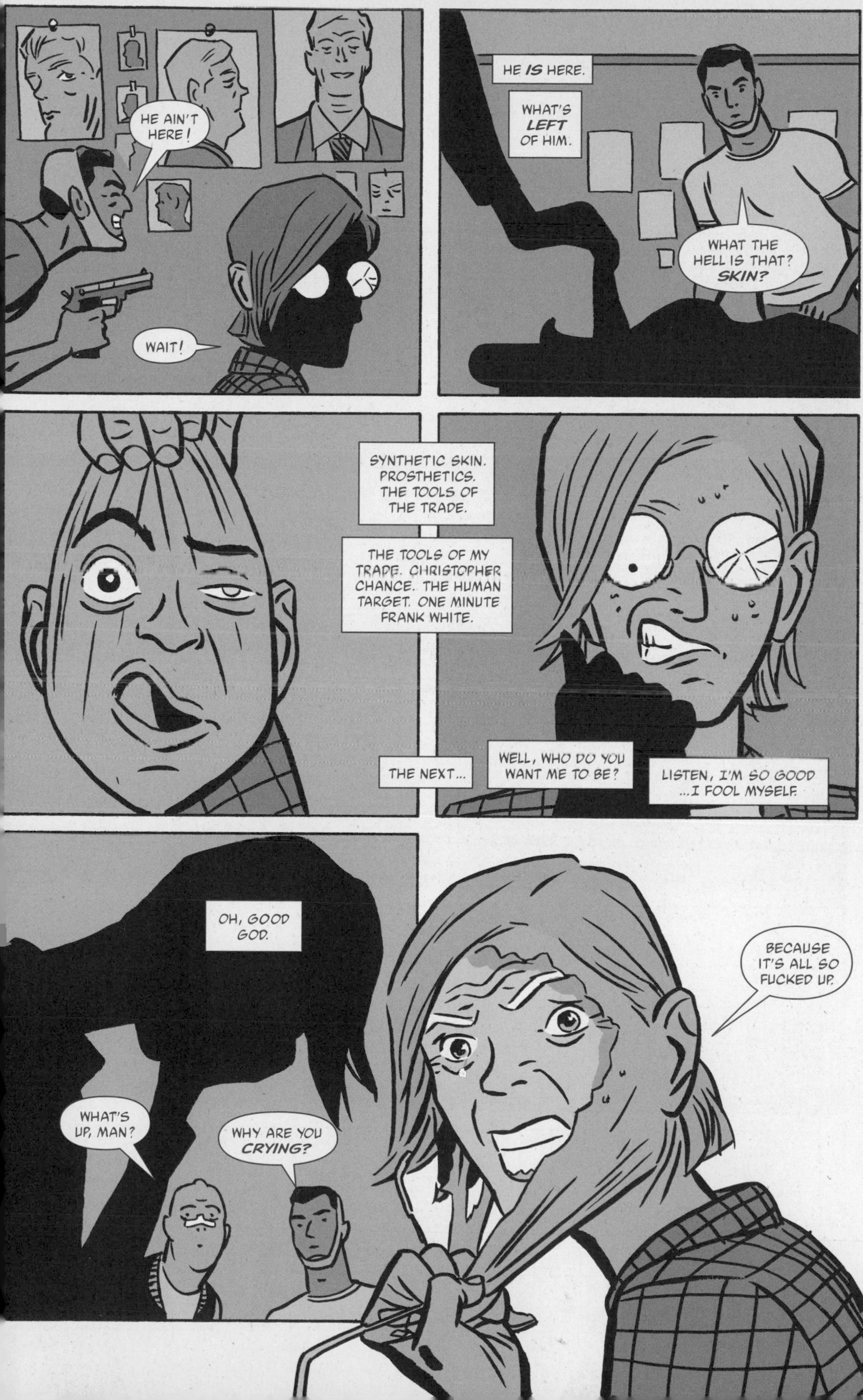
HE AIN'T HERE!
WAIT!
HE *IS* HERE.
WHAT'S *LEFT* OF HIM.
WHAT THE HELL IS THAT? *SKIN?*
SYNTHETIC SKIN. PROSTHETICS. THE TOOLS OF THE TRADE.
THE TOOLS OF MY TRADE. CHRISTOPHER CHANCE. THE HUMAN TARGET. ONE MINUTE FRANK WHITE.
THE NEXT...
WELL, WHO DO YOU WANT ME TO BE?
LISTEN, I'M SO GOOD ...I FOOL MYSELF.
OH, GOOD GOD.
BECAUSE IT'S ALL SO FUCKED UP.
WHAT'S UP, MAN?
WHY ARE YOU *CRYING?*

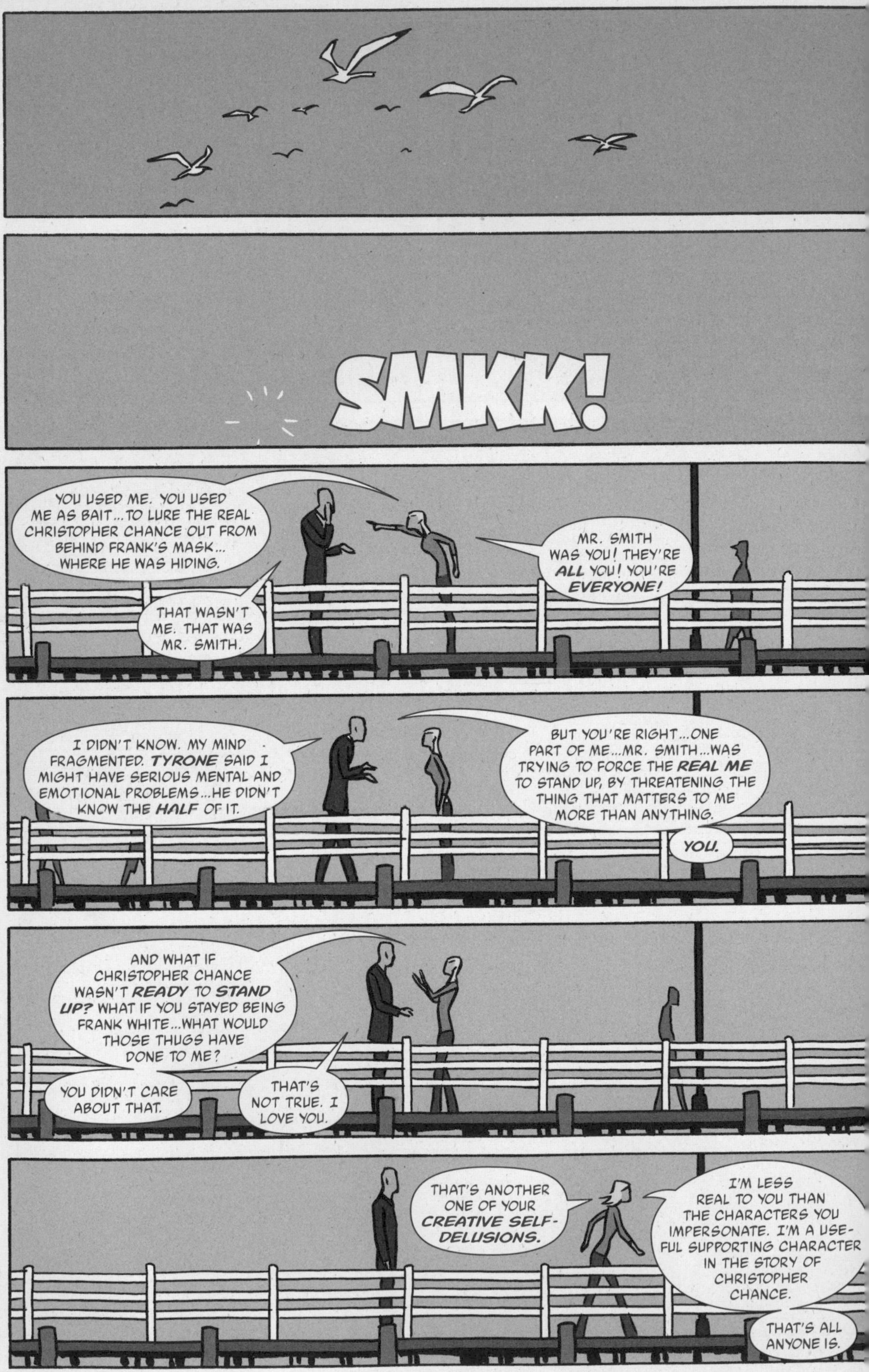
SMKK!
YOU USED ME. YOU USED ME AS BAIT... TO LURE THE REAL CHRISTOPHER CHANCE OUT FROM BEHIND FRANK'S MASK... WHERE HE WAS HIDING.
MR. SMITH WAS YOU! THEY'RE ALL YOU! YOU'RE EVERYONE!
THAT WASN'T ME. THAT WAS MR. SMITH.
I DIDN'T KNOW. MY MIND FRAGMENTED. TYRONE SAID I MIGHT HAVE SERIOUS MENTAL AND EMOTIONAL PROBLEMS... HE DIDN'T KNOW THE HALF OF IT.
BUT YOU'RE RIGHT... ONE PART OF ME... MR. SMITH... WAS TRYING TO FORCE THE REAL ME TO STAND UP, BY THREATENING THE THING THAT MATTERS TO ME MORE THAN ANYTHING.
YOU.
AND WHAT IF CHRISTOPHER CHANCE WASN'T READY TO STAND UP? WHAT IF YOU STAYED BEING FRANK WHITE... WHAT WOULD THOSE THUGS HAVE DONE TO ME?
YOU DIDN'T CARE ABOUT THAT.
THAT'S NOT TRUE. I LOVE YOU.
THAT'S ANOTHER ONE OF YOUR CREATIVE SELF-DELUSIONS.
I'M LESS REAL TO YOU THAN THE CHARACTERS YOU IMPERSONATE. I'M A USEFUL SUPPORTING CHARACTER IN THE STORY OF CHRISTOPHER CHANCE.
THAT'S ALL ANYONE IS.

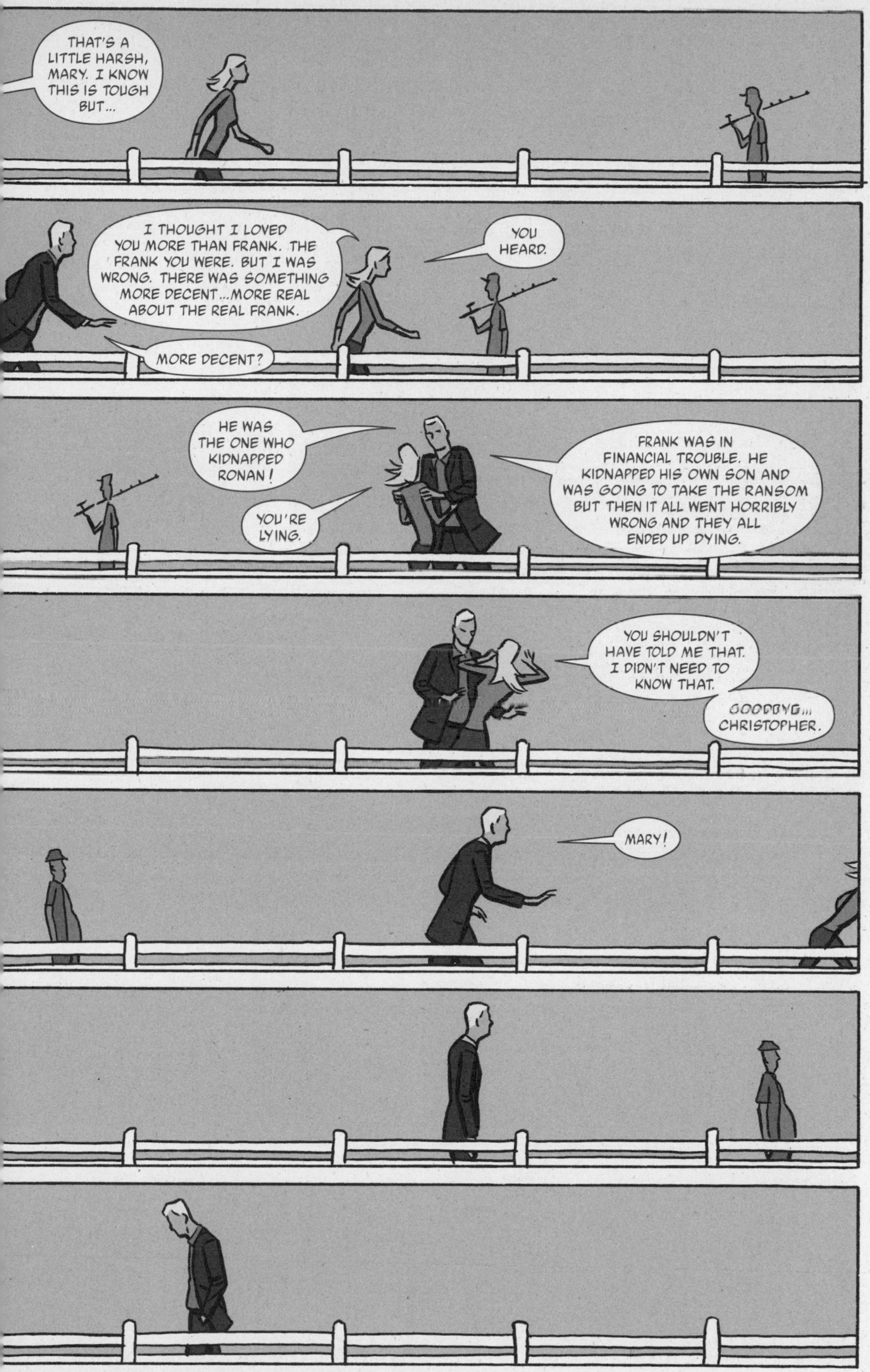
THAT'S A LITTLE HARSH, MARY. I KNOW THIS IS TOUGH BUT...
I THOUGHT I LOVED YOU MORE THAN FRANK. THE FRANK YOU WERE. BUT I WAS WRONG. THERE WAS SOMETHING MORE DECENT...MORE REAL ABOUT THE REAL FRANK.
YOU HEARD.
MORE DECENT?
HE WAS THE ONE WHO KIDNAPPED RONAN!
YOU'RE LYING.
FRANK WAS IN FINANCIAL TROUBLE. HE KIDNAPPED HIS OWN SON AND WAS GOING TO TAKE THE RANSOM BUT THEN IT ALL WENT HORRIBLY WRONG AND THEY ALL ENDED UP DYING.
YOU SHOULDN'T HAVE TOLD ME THAT. I DIDN'T NEED TO KNOW THAT.
GOODBYE... CHRISTOPHER.
MARY!

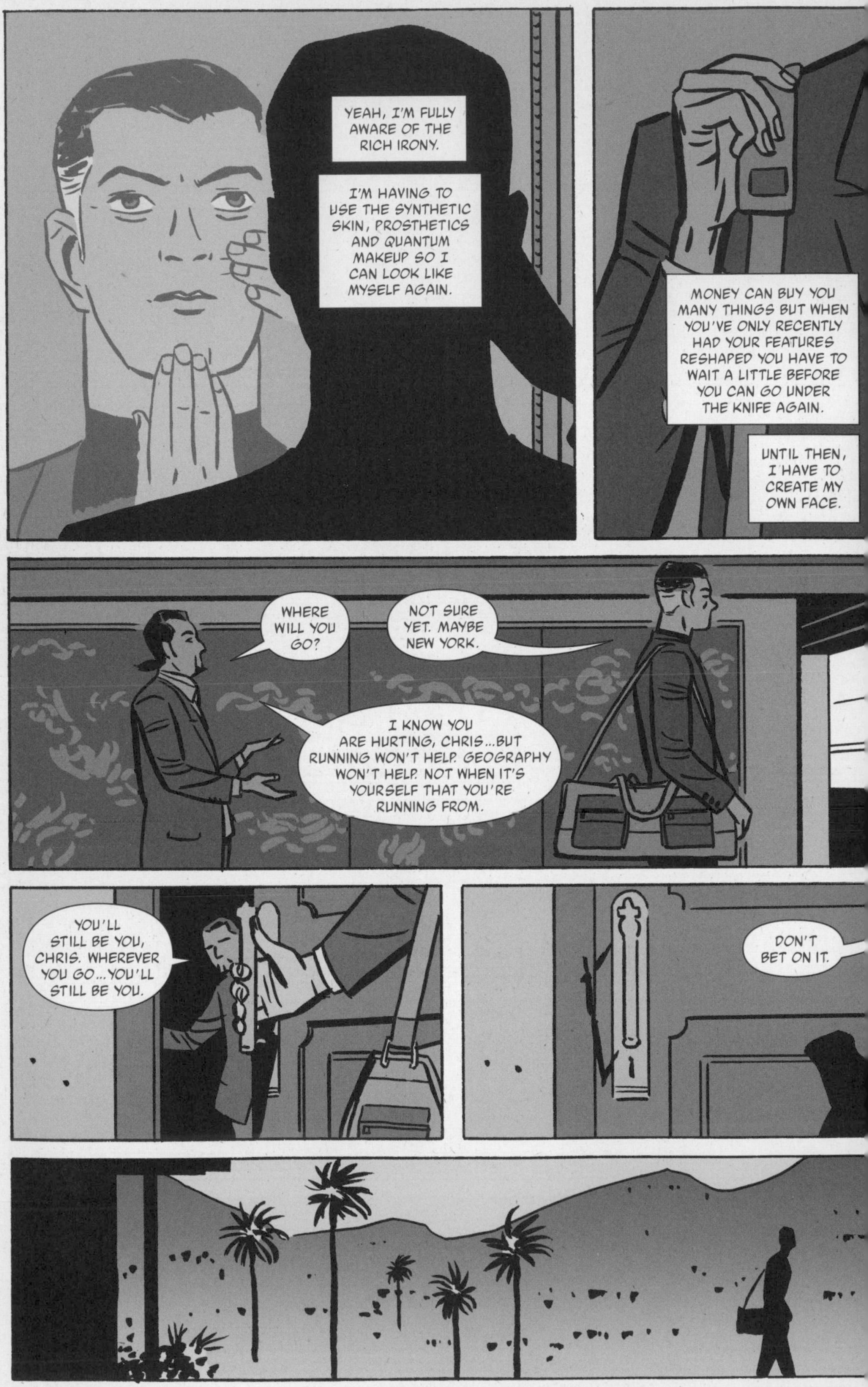
YEAH, I'M FULLY AWARE OF THE RICH IRONY.
I'M HAVING TO USE THE SYNTHETIC SKIN, PROSTHETICS AND QUANTUM MAKEUP SO I CAN LOOK LIKE MYSELF AGAIN.
MONEY CAN BUY YOU MANY THINGS BUT WHEN YOU'VE ONLY RECENTLY HAD YOUR FEATURES RESHAPED YOU HAVE TO WAIT A LITTLE BEFORE YOU CAN GO UNDER THE KNIFE AGAIN.
UNTIL THEN, I HAVE TO CREATE MY OWN FACE.
WHERE WILL YOU GO?
NOT SURE YET. MAYBE NEW YORK.
I KNOW YOU ARE HURTING, CHRIS...BUT RUNNING WON'T HELP. GEOGRAPHY WON'T HELP. NOT WHEN IT'S YOURSELF THAT YOU'RE RUNNING FROM.
YOU'LL STILL BE YOU, CHRIS. WHEREVER YOU GO...YOU'LL STILL BE YOU.
DON'T BET ON IT.

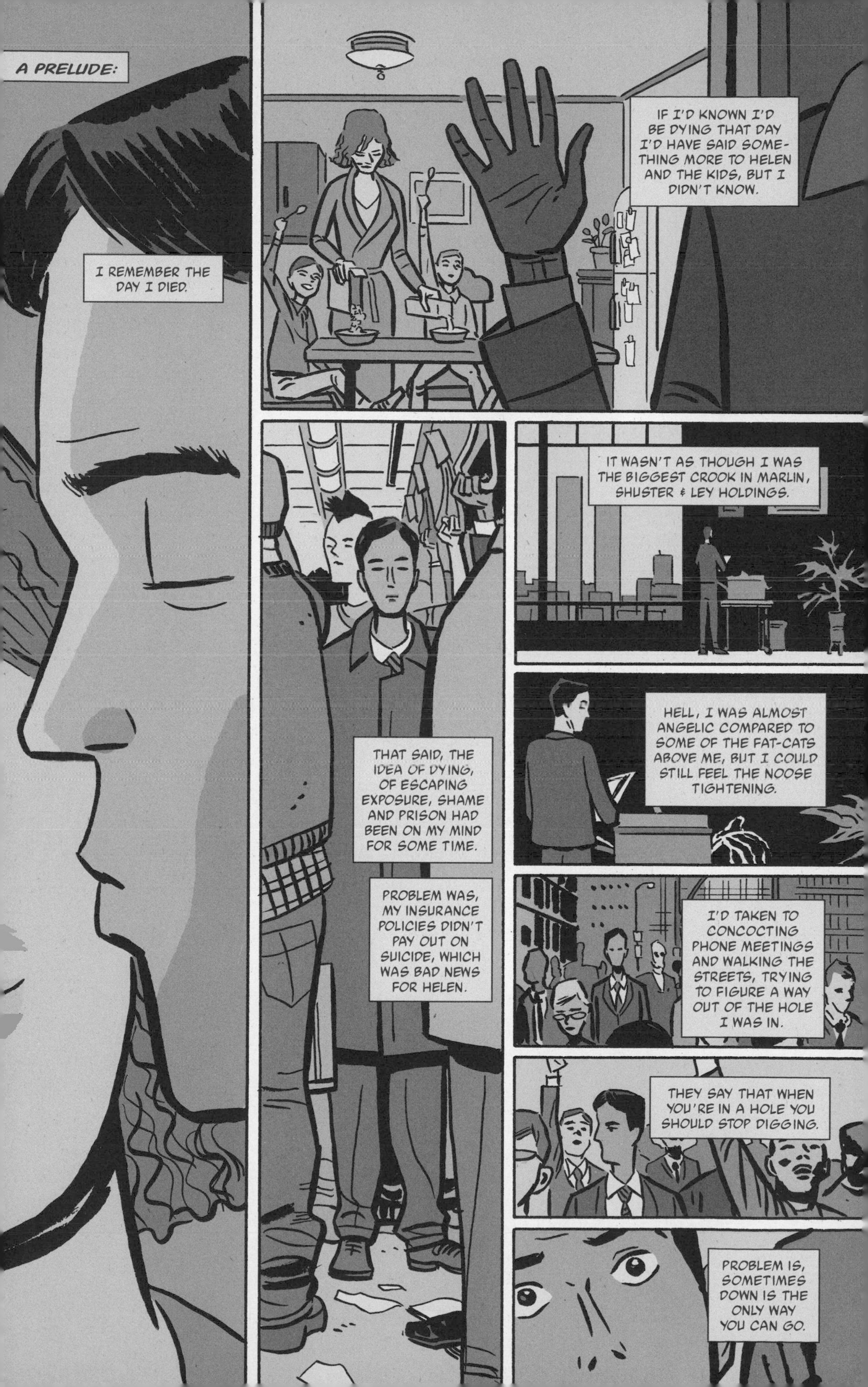
A PRELUDE:
I REMEMBER THE DAY I DIED.
IF I'D KNOWN I'D BE DYING THAT DAY I'D HAVE SAID SOMETHING MORE TO HELEN AND THE KIDS, BUT I DIDN'T KNOW.
THAT SAID, THE IDEA OF DYING, OF ESCAPING EXPOSURE, SHAME AND PRISON HAD BEEN ON MY MIND FOR SOME TIME.
PROBLEM WAS, MY INSURANCE POLICIES DIDN'T PAY OUT ON SUICIDE, WHICH WAS BAD NEWS FOR HELEN.
IT WASN'T AS THOUGH I WAS THE BIGGEST CROOK IN MARLIN, SHUSTER & LEY HOLDINGS.
HELL, I WAS ALMOST ANGELIC COMPARED TO SOME OF THE FAT-CATS ABOVE ME, BUT I COULD STILL FEEL THE NOOSE TIGHTENING.
I'D TAKEN TO CONCOCTING PHONE MEETINGS AND WALKING THE STREETS, TRYING TO FIGURE A WAY OUT OF THE HOLE I WAS IN.
THEY SAY THAT WHEN YOU'RE IN A HOLE YOU SHOULD STOP DIGGING.
PROBLEM IS, SOMETIMES DOWN IS THE ONLY WAY YOU CAN GO.

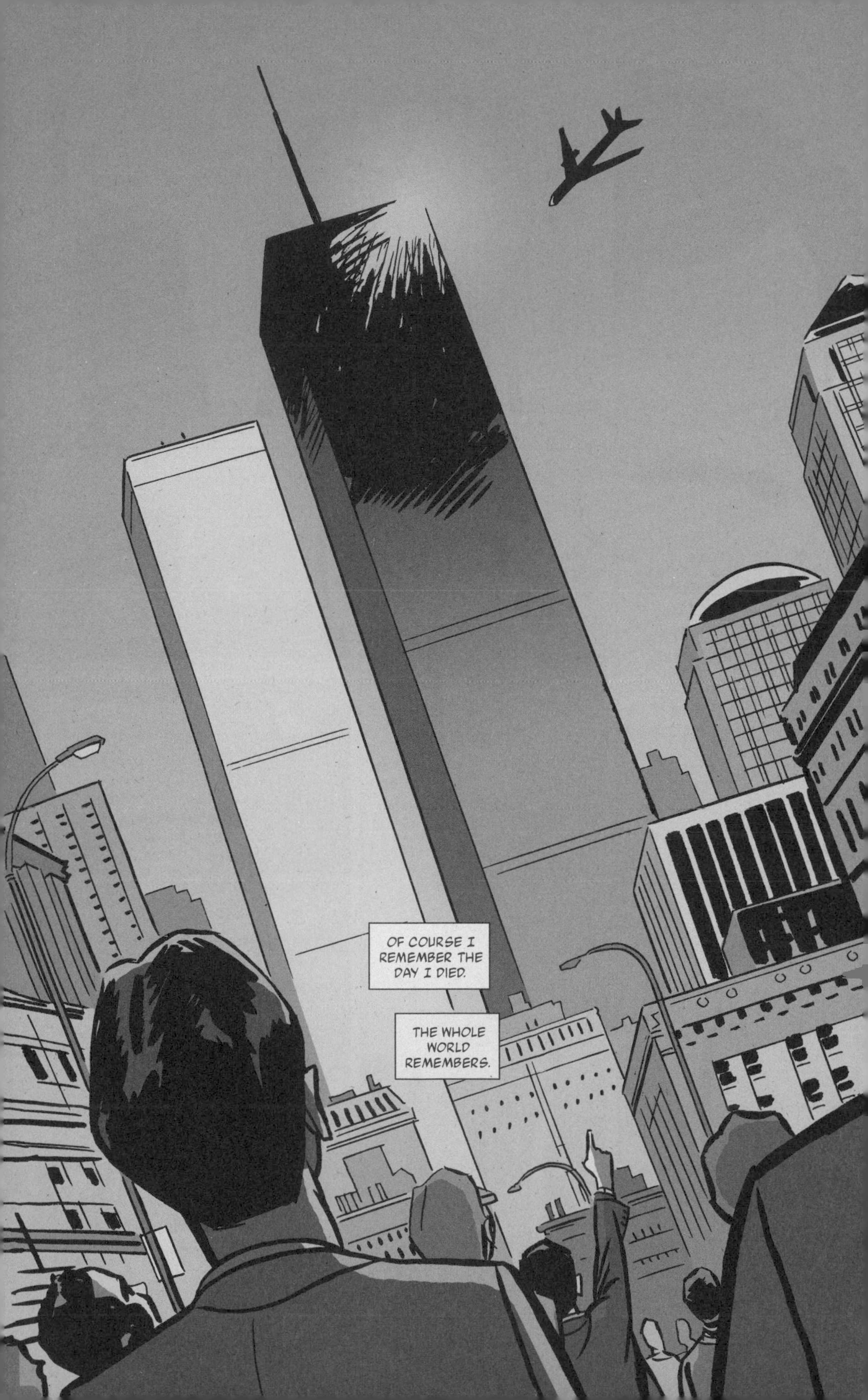
OF COURSE I REMEMBER THE DAY I DIED.
THE WHOLE WORLD REMEMBERS.

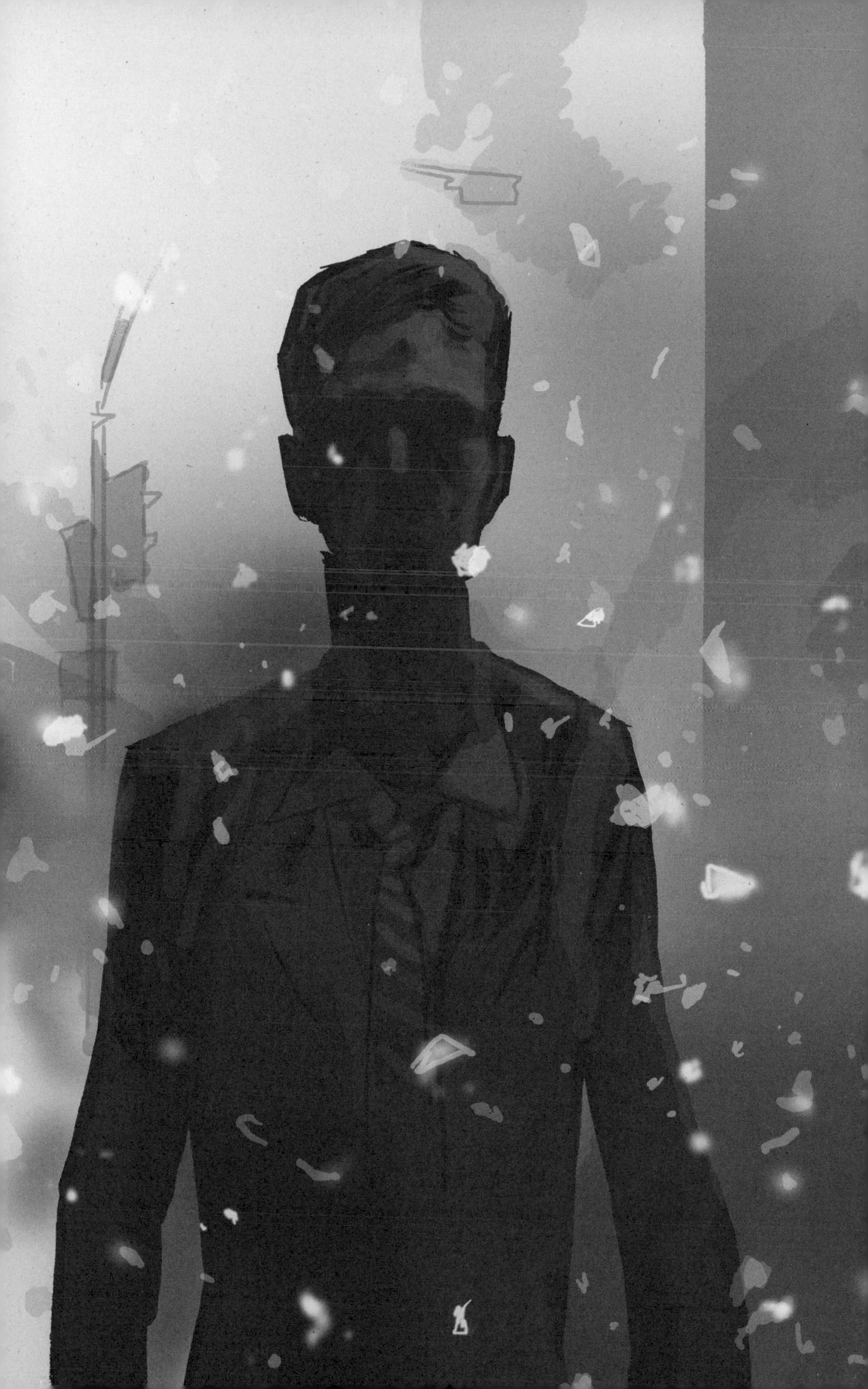

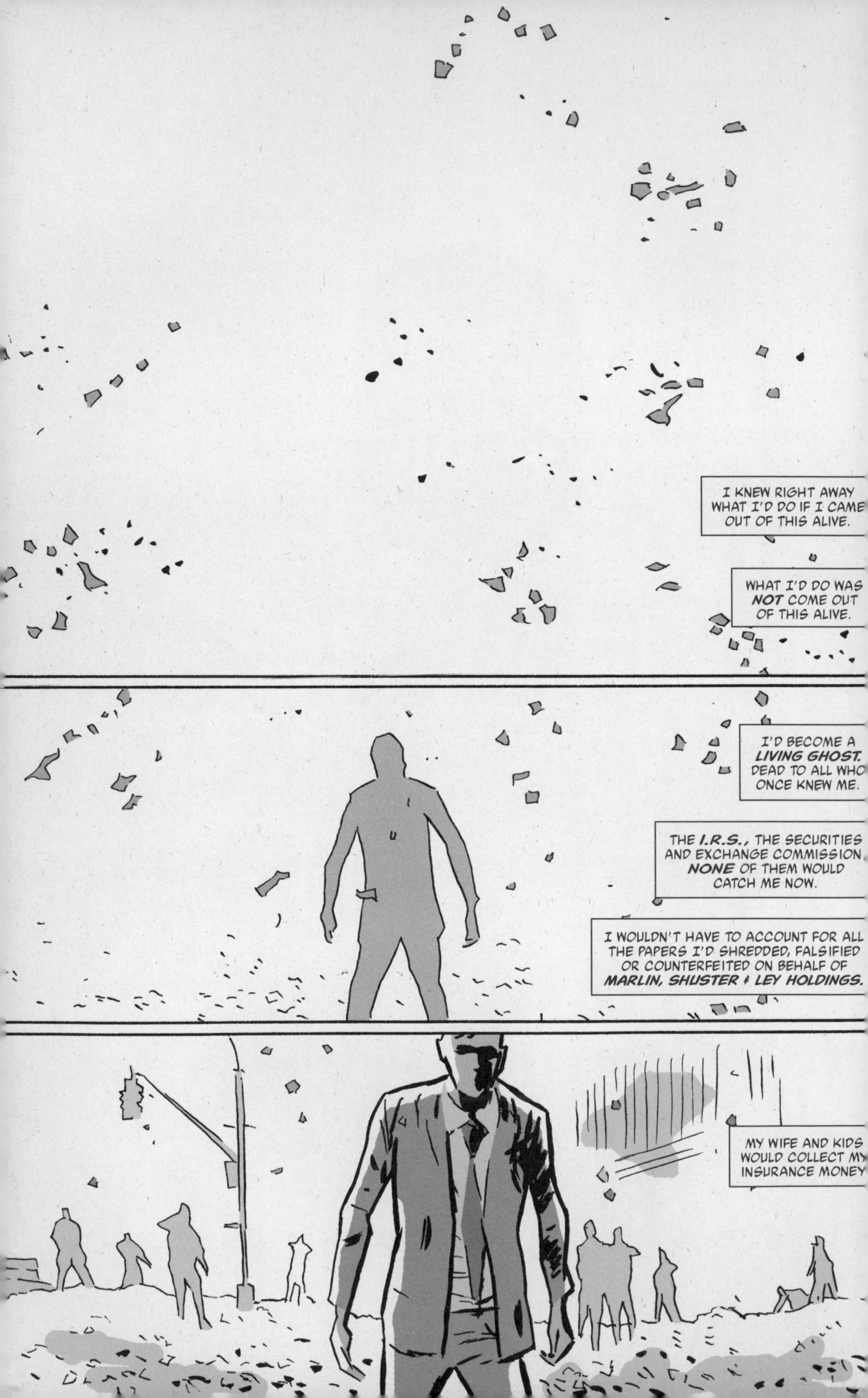
I KNEW RIGHT AWAY WHAT I'D DO IF I CAME OUT OF THIS ALIVE.
WHAT I'D DO WAS *NOT* COME OUT OF THIS ALIVE.
I'D BECOME A *LIVING GHOST.* DEAD TO ALL WHO ONCE KNEW ME.
THE *I.R.S.,* THE SECURITIES AND EXCHANGE COMMISSION, *NONE* OF THEM WOULD CATCH ME NOW.
I WOULDN'T HAVE TO ACCOUNT FOR ALL THE PAPERS I'D SHREDDED, FALSIFIED OR COUNTERFEITED ON BEHALF OF *MARLIN, SHUSTER & LEY HOLDINGS.*
MY WIFE AND KIDS WOULD COLLECT MY INSURANCE MONEY

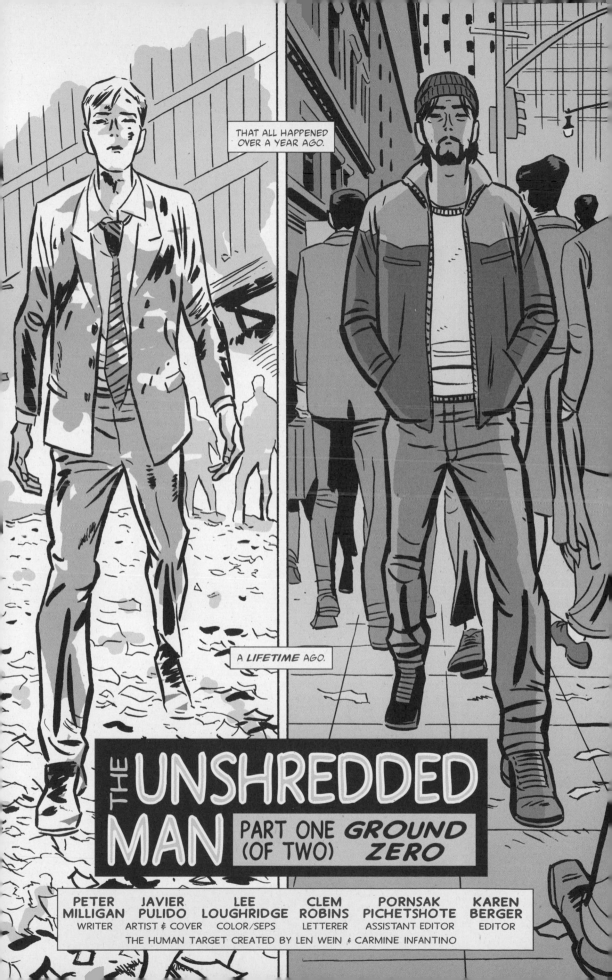

THAT ALL HAPPENED OVER A YEAR AGO.

A *LIFETIME* AGO.

THE UNSHREDDED MAN
PART ONE *GROUND* (OF TWO) *ZERO*

PETER MILLIGAN — WRITER
JAVIER PULIDO — ARTIST & COVER
LEE LOUGHRIDGE — COLOR/SEPS
CLEM ROBINS — LETTERER
PORNSAK PICHETSHOTE — ASSISTANT EDITOR
KAREN BERGER — EDITOR
THE HUMAN TARGET CREATED BY LEN WEIN & CARMINE INFANTINO

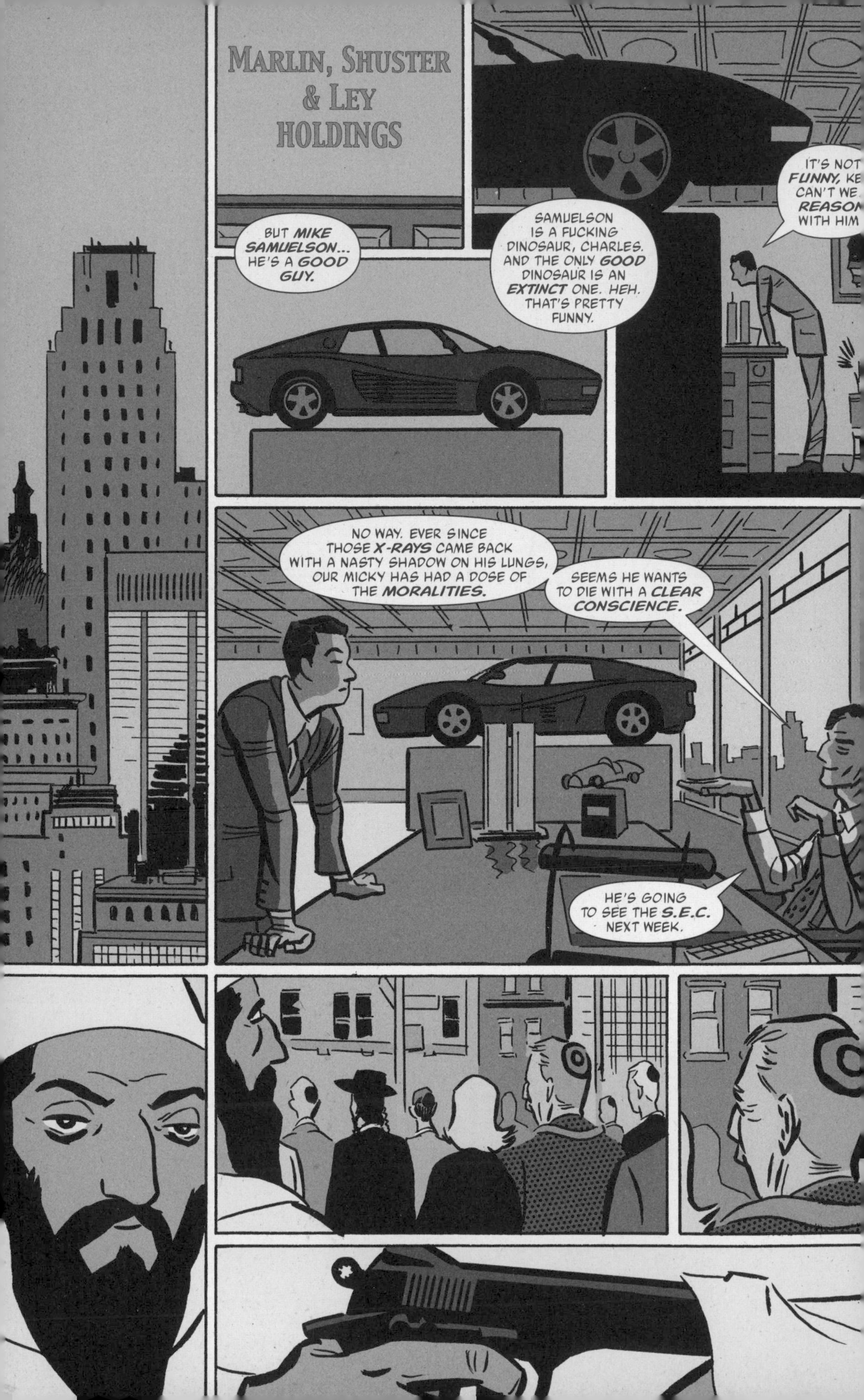
MARLIN, SHUSTER & LEY HOLDINGS
BUT MIKE SAMUELSON... HE'S A GOOD GUY.
SAMUELSON IS A FUCKING DINOSAUR, CHARLES. AND THE ONLY GOOD DINOSAUR IS AN EXTINCT ONE. HEH. THAT'S PRETTY FUNNY.
IT'S NOT FUNNY, KE CAN'T WE REASON WITH HIM
NO WAY. EVER SINCE THOSE X-RAYS CAME BACK WITH A NASTY SHADOW ON HIS LUNGS, OUR MICKY HAS HAD A DOSE OF THE MORALITIES.
SEEMS HE WANTS TO DIE WITH A CLEAR CONSCIENCE.
HE'S GOING TO SEE THE S.E.C. NEXT WEEK.

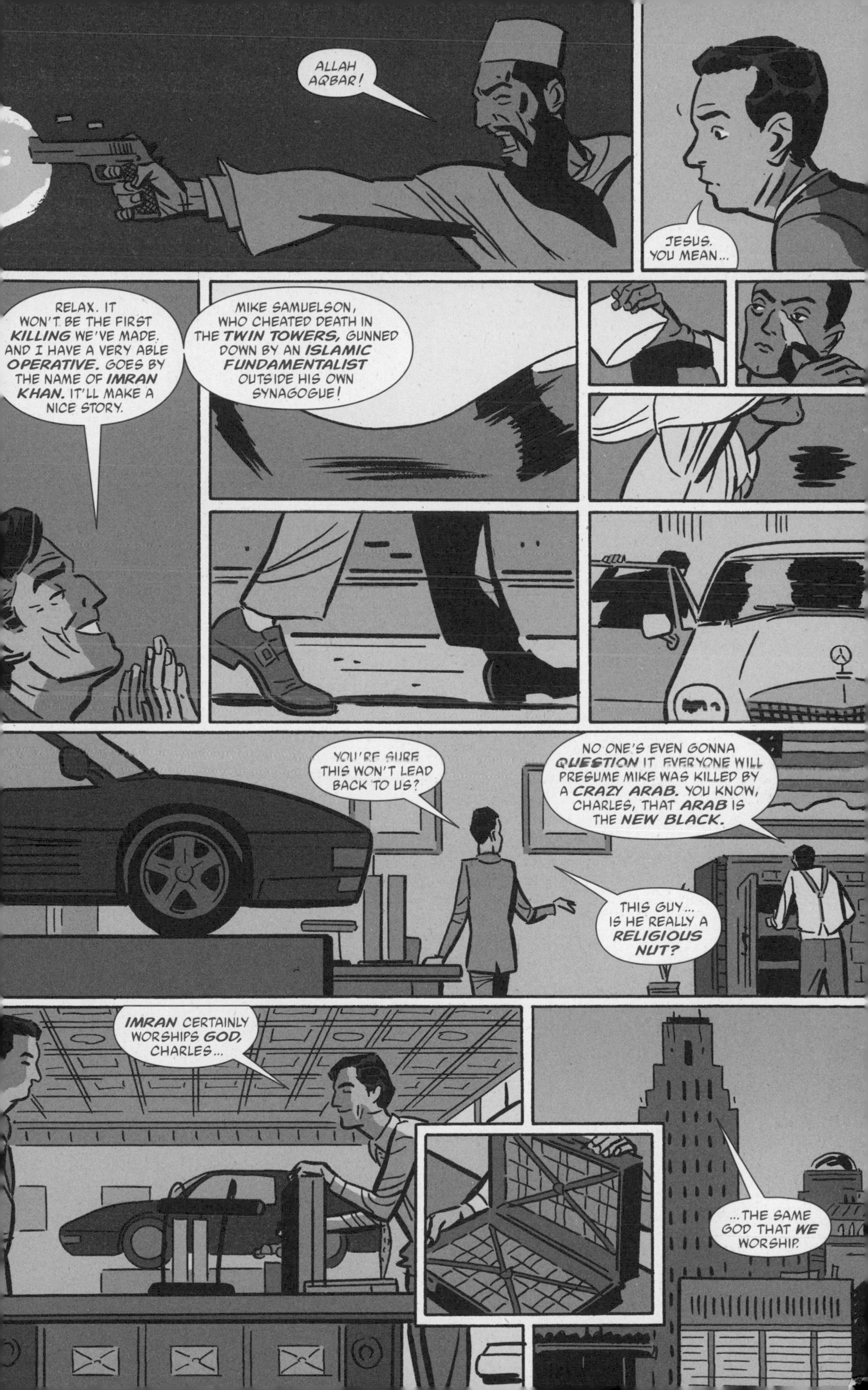
ALLAH AQBAR!
JESUS. YOU MEAN...
RELAX. IT WON'T BE THE FIRST KILLING WE'VE MADE. AND I HAVE A VERY ABLE OPERATIVE. GOES BY THE NAME OF IMRAN KHAN. IT'LL MAKE A NICE STORY.
MIKE SAMUELSON, WHO CHEATED DEATH IN THE TWIN TOWERS, GUNNED DOWN BY AN ISLAMIC FUNDAMENTALIST OUTSIDE HIS OWN SYNAGOGUE!
YOU'RE SURE THIS WON'T LEAD BACK TO US?
NO ONE'S EVEN GONNA QUESTION IT. EVERYONE WILL PRESUME MIKE WAS KILLED BY A CRAZY ARAB. YOU KNOW, CHARLES, THAT ARAB IS THE NEW BLACK.
THIS GUY... IS HE REALLY A RELIGIOUS NUT?
IMRAN CERTAINLY WORSHIPS GOD, CHARLES...
...THE SAME GOD THAT WE WORSHIP.

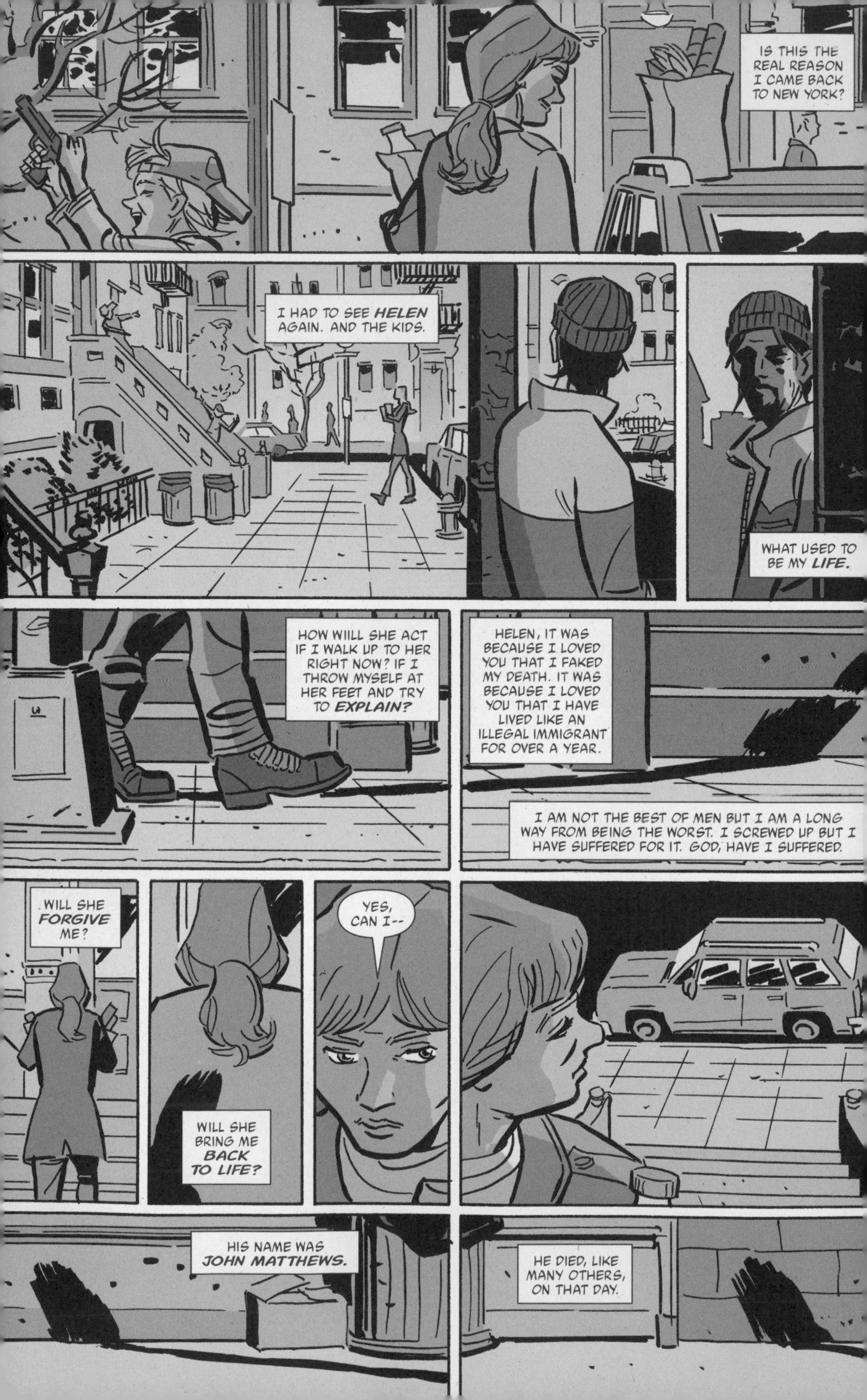
IS THIS THE REAL REASON I CAME BACK TO NEW YORK?
I HAD TO SEE HELEN AGAIN. AND THE KIDS.
WHAT USED TO BE MY LIFE.
HOW WIILL SHE ACT IF I WALK UP TO HER RIGHT NOW? IF I THROW MYSELF AT HER FEET AND TRY TO EXPLAIN?
HELEN, IT WAS BECAUSE I LOVED YOU THAT I FAKED MY DEATH. IT WAS BECAUSE I LOVED YOU THAT I HAVE LIVED LIKE AN ILLEGAL IMMIGRANT FOR OVER A YEAR.
I AM NOT THE BEST OF MEN BUT I AM A LONG WAY FROM BEING THE WORST. I SCREWED UP BUT I HAVE SUFFERED FOR IT. GOD, HAVE I SUFFERED.
WILL SHE FORGIVE ME?
WILL SHE BRING ME BACK TO LIFE?
YES, CAN I--
HIS NAME WAS JOHN MATTHEWS.
HE DIED, LIKE MANY OTHERS, ON THAT DAY.

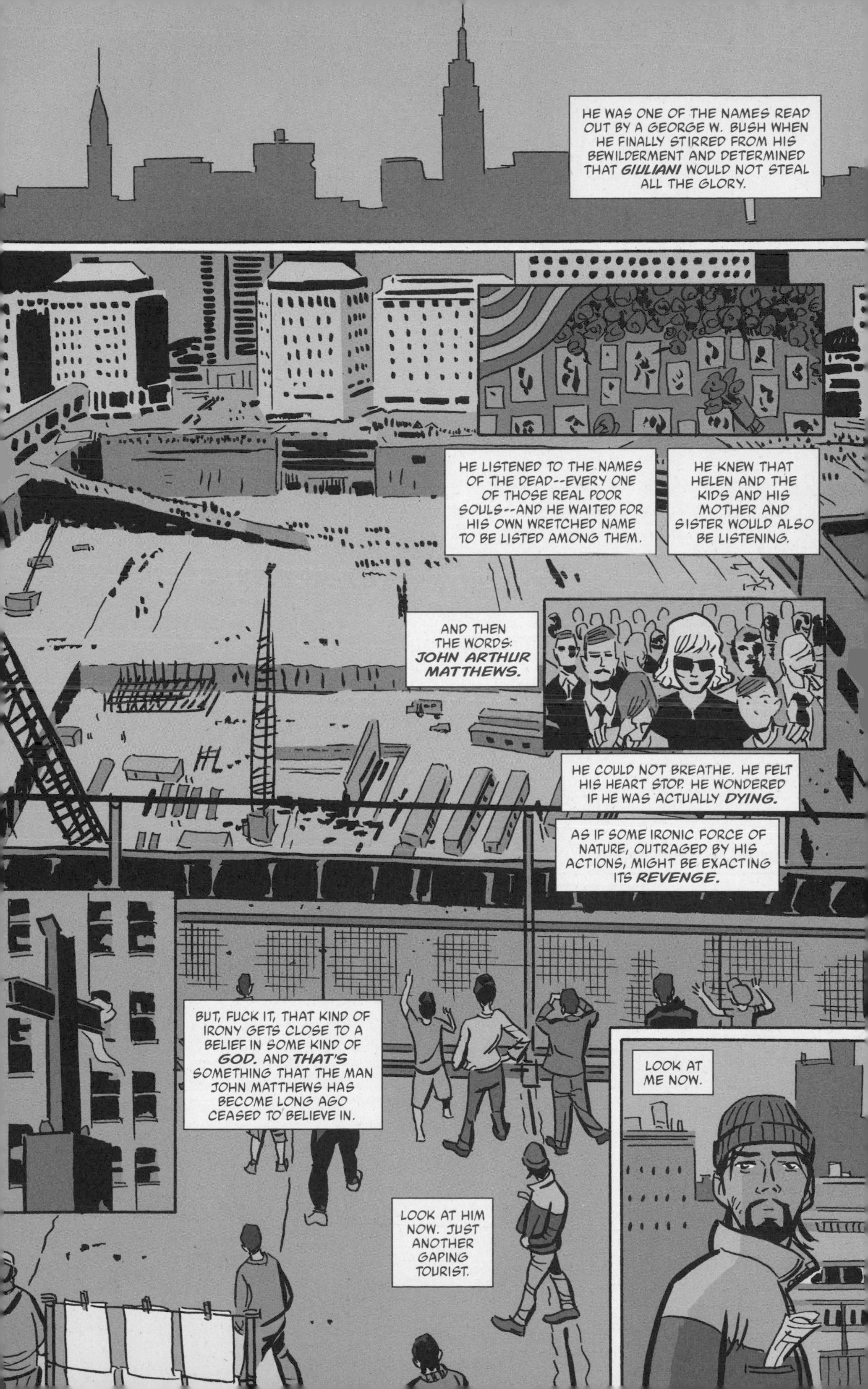
HE WAS ONE OF THE NAMES READ OUT BY A GEORGE W. BUSH WHEN HE FINALLY STIRRED FROM HIS BEWILDERMENT AND DETERMINED THAT GIULIANI WOULD NOT STEAL ALL THE GLORY.
HE LISTENED TO THE NAMES OF THE DEAD--EVERY ONE OF THOSE REAL POOR SOULS--AND HE WAITED FOR HIS OWN WRETCHED NAME TO BE LISTED AMONG THEM.
HE KNEW THAT HELEN AND THE KIDS AND HIS MOTHER AND SISTER WOULD ALSO BE LISTENING.
AND THEN THE WORDS: JOHN ARTHUR MATTHEWS.
HE COULD NOT BREATHE. HE FELT HIS HEART STOP. HE WONDERED IF HE WAS ACTUALLY DYING.
AS IF SOME IRONIC FORCE OF NATURE, OUTRAGED BY HIS ACTIONS, MIGHT BE EXACTING ITS REVENGE.
BUT, FUCK IT, THAT KIND OF IRONY GETS CLOSE TO A BELIEF IN SOME KIND OF GOD. AND THAT'S SOMETHING THAT THE MAN JOHN MATTHEWS HAS BECOME LONG AGO CEASED TO BELIEVE IN.
LOOK AT HIM NOW. JUST ANOTHER GAPING TOURIST.
LOOK AT ME NOW.

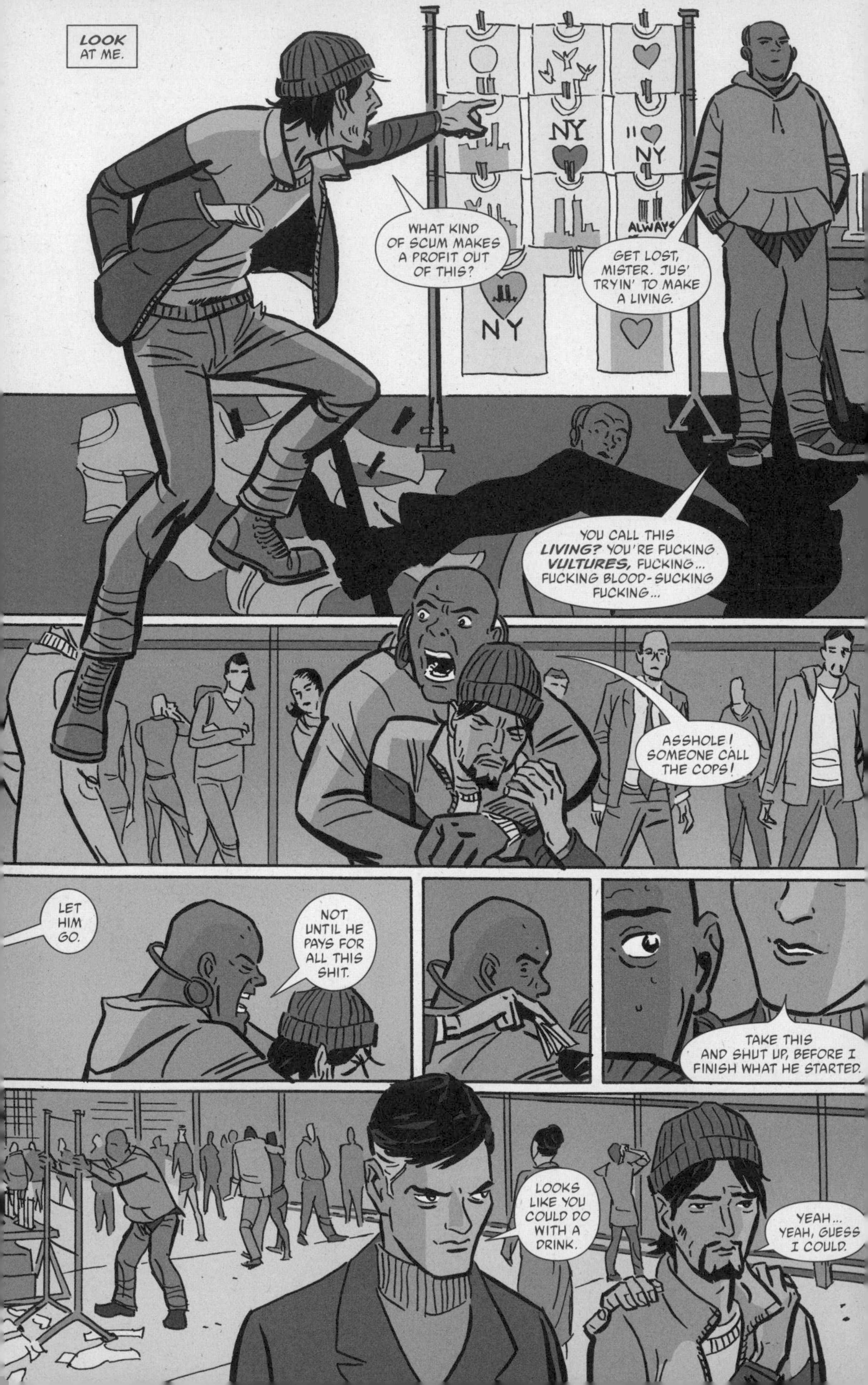
LOOK AT ME.
WHAT KIND OF SCUM MAKES A PROFIT OUT OF THIS?
GET LOST, MISTER. JUS' TRYIN' TO MAKE A LIVING.
NY
NY
ALWAYS
NY
YOU CALL THIS LIVING? YOU'RE FUCKING VULTURES, FUCKING... FUCKING BLOOD-SUCKING FUCKING...
ASSHOLE! SOMEONE CALL THE COPS!
LET HIM GO.
NOT UNTIL HE PAYS FOR ALL THIS SHIT.
TAKE THIS AND SHUT UP, BEFORE I FINISH WHAT HE STARTED.
LOOKS LIKE YOU COULD DO WITH A DRINK.
YEAH... YEAH, GUESS I COULD.

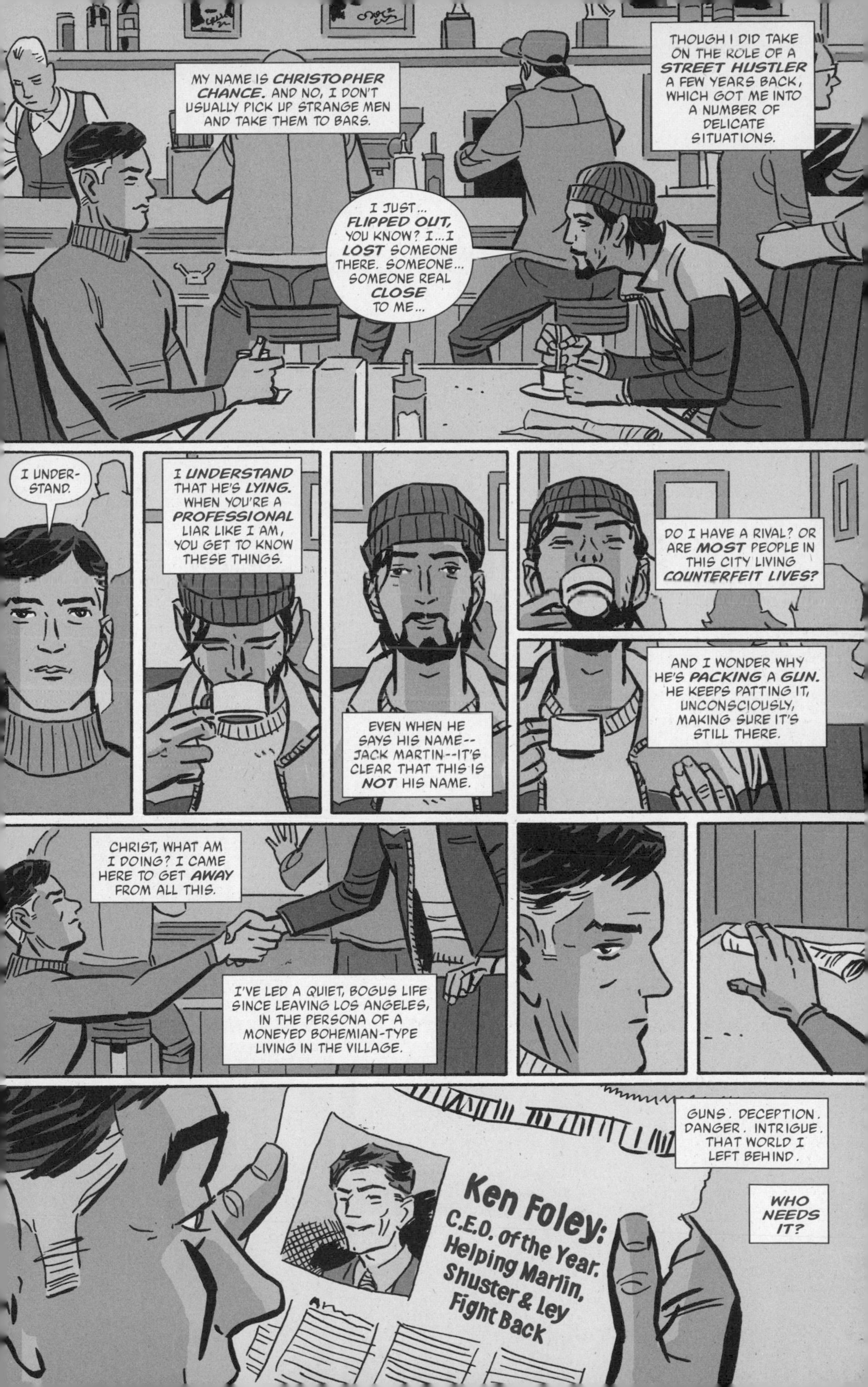
MY NAME IS CHRISTOPHER CHANCE. AND NO, I DON'T USUALLY PICK UP STRANGE MEN AND TAKE THEM TO BARS.
THOUGH I DID TAKE ON THE ROLE OF A STREET HUSTLER A FEW YEARS BACK, WHICH GOT ME INTO A NUMBER OF DELICATE SITUATIONS.
I JUST... FLIPPED OUT, YOU KNOW? I...I LOST SOMEONE THERE. SOMEONE... SOMEONE REAL CLOSE TO ME...
I UNDER-STAND.
I UNDERSTAND THAT HE'S LYING. WHEN YOU'RE A PROFESSIONAL LIAR LIKE I AM, YOU GET TO KNOW THESE THINGS.
EVEN WHEN HE SAYS HIS NAME--JACK MARTIN--IT'S CLEAR THAT THIS IS NOT HIS NAME.
DO I HAVE A RIVAL? OR ARE MOST PEOPLE IN THIS CITY LIVING COUNTERFEIT LIVES?
AND I WONDER WHY HE'S PACKING A GUN. HE KEEPS PATTING IT, UNCONSCIOUSLY, MAKING SURE IT'S STILL THERE.
CHRIST, WHAT AM I DOING? I CAME HERE TO GET AWAY FROM ALL THIS.
I'VE LED A QUIET, BOGUS LIFE SINCE LEAVING LOS ANGELES, IN THE PERSONA OF A MONEYED BOHEMIAN-TYPE LIVING IN THE VILLAGE.
GUNS. DECEPTION. DANGER. INTRIGUE. THAT WORLD I LEFT BEHIND.
Ken Foley: C.E.O. of the Year. Helping Marlin, Shuster & Ley Fight Back
WHO NEEDS IT?

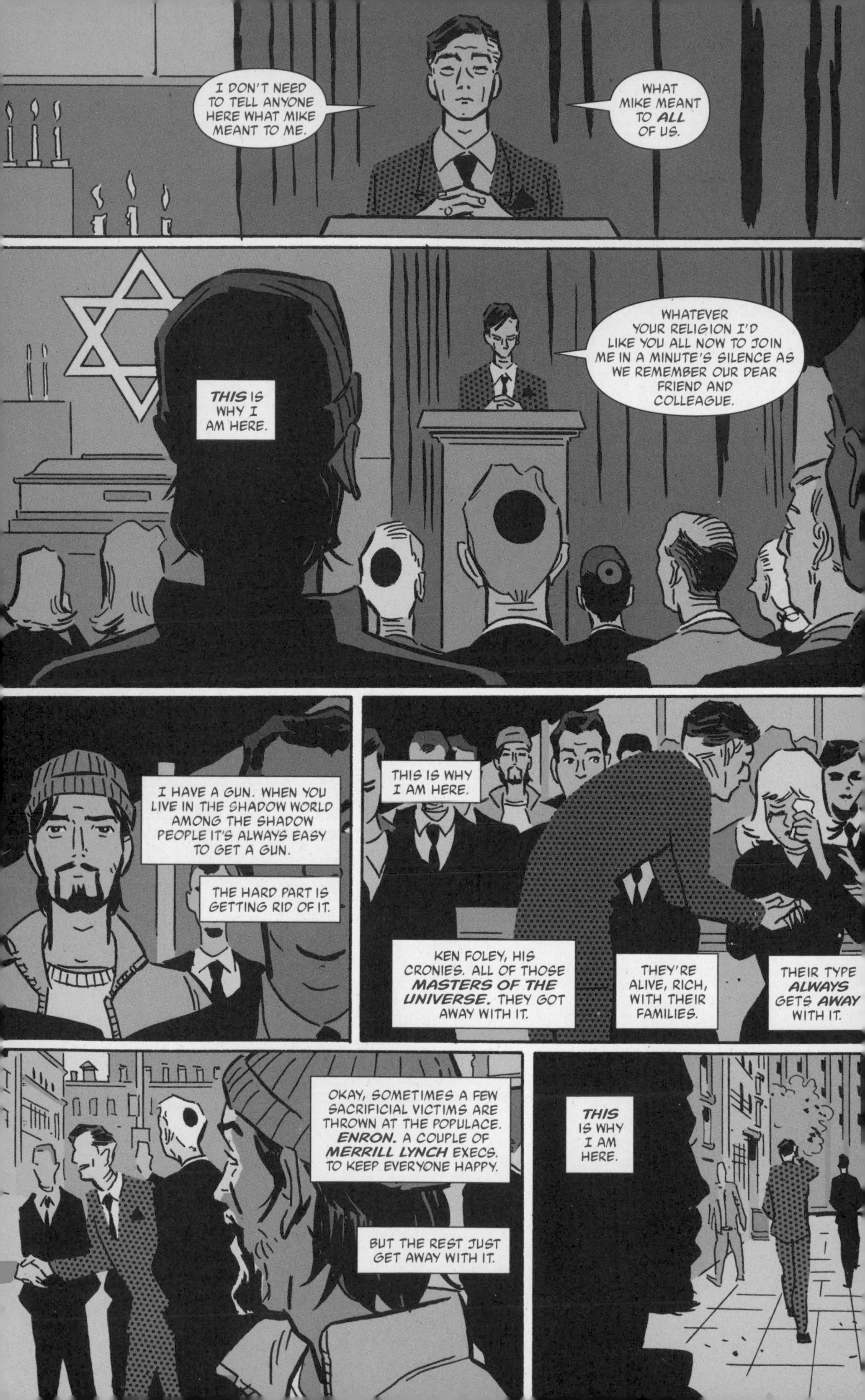
I DON'T NEED TO TELL ANYONE HERE WHAT MIKE MEANT TO ME.
WHAT MIKE MEANT TO ALL OF US.
THIS IS WHY I AM HERE.
WHATEVER YOUR RELIGION I'D LIKE YOU ALL NOW TO JOIN ME IN A MINUTE'S SILENCE AS WE REMEMBER OUR DEAR FRIEND AND COLLEAGUE.
I HAVE A GUN. WHEN YOU LIVE IN THE SHADOW WORLD AMONG THE SHADOW PEOPLE IT'S ALWAYS EASY TO GET A GUN.
THE HARD PART IS GETTING RID OF IT.
THIS IS WHY I AM HERE.
KEN FOLEY, HIS CRONIES. ALL OF THOSE MASTERS OF THE UNIVERSE. THEY GOT AWAY WITH IT.
THEY'RE ALIVE, RICH, WITH THEIR FAMILIES.
THEIR TYPE ALWAYS GETS AWAY WITH IT.
OKAY, SOMETIMES A FEW SACRIFICIAL VICTIMS ARE THROWN AT THE POPULACE. ENRON. A COUPLE OF MERRILL LYNCH EXECS. TO KEEP EVERYONE HAPPY.
BUT THE REST JUST GET AWAY WITH IT.
THIS IS WHY I AM HERE.

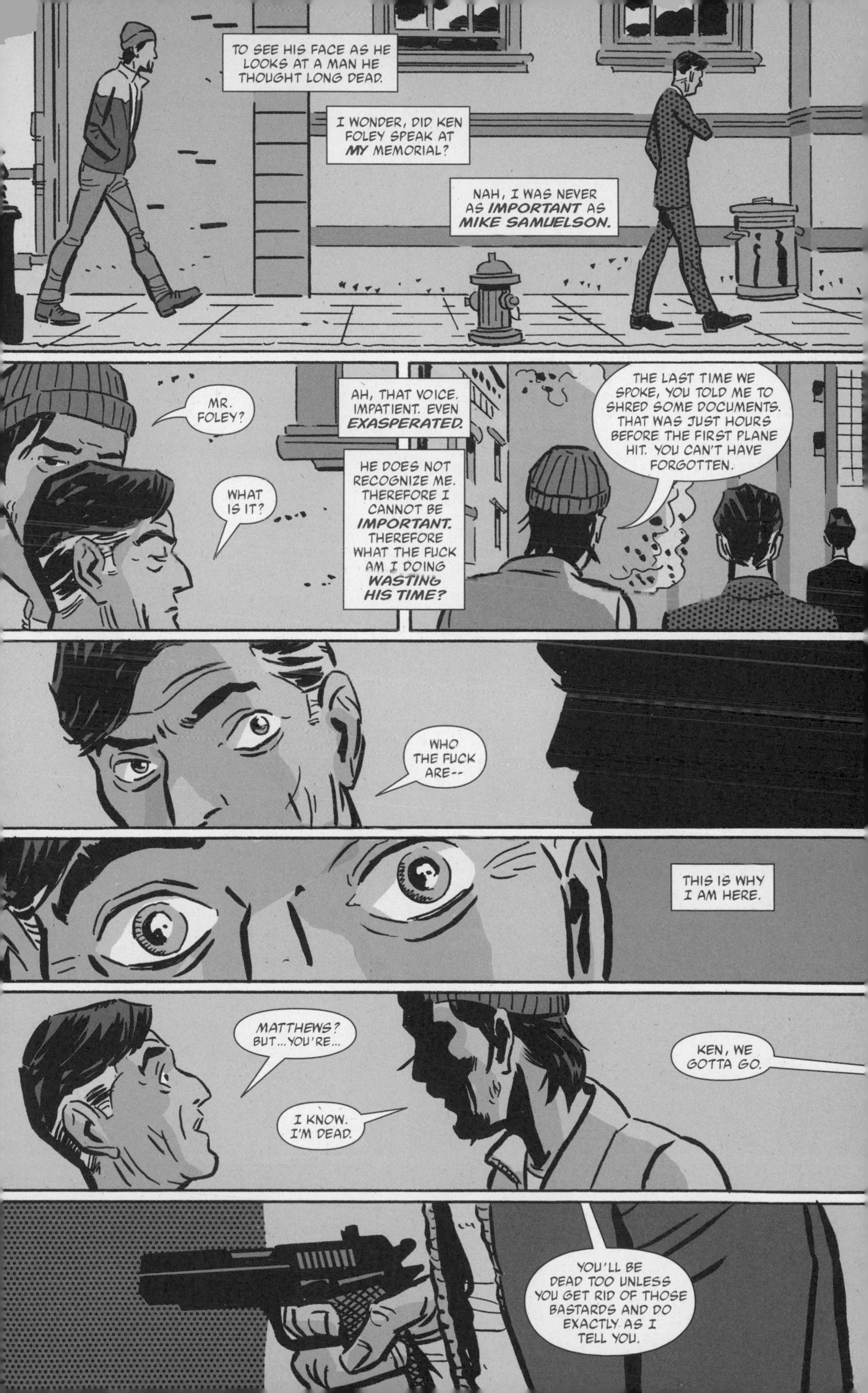
TO SEE HIS FACE AS HE LOOKS AT A MAN HE THOUGHT LONG DEAD.
I WONDER, DID KEN FOLEY SPEAK AT MY MEMORIAL?
NAH, I WAS NEVER AS IMPORTANT AS MIKE SAMUELSON.
MR. FOLEY?
WHAT IS IT?
AH, THAT VOICE. IMPATIENT. EVEN EXASPERATED.
HE DOES NOT RECOGNIZE ME. THEREFORE I CANNOT BE IMPORTANT. THEREFORE WHAT THE FUCK AM I DOING WASTING HIS TIME?
THE LAST TIME WE SPOKE, YOU TOLD ME TO SHRED SOME DOCUMENTS. THAT WAS JUST HOURS BEFORE THE FIRST PLANE HIT. YOU CAN'T HAVE FORGOTTEN.
WHO THE FUCK ARE--
THIS IS WHY I AM HERE.
MATTHEWS? BUT... YOU'RE...
I KNOW. I'M DEAD.
KEN, WE GOTTA GO.
YOU'LL BE DEAD TOO UNLESS YOU GET RID OF THOSE BASTARDS AND DO EXACTLY AS I TELL YOU.

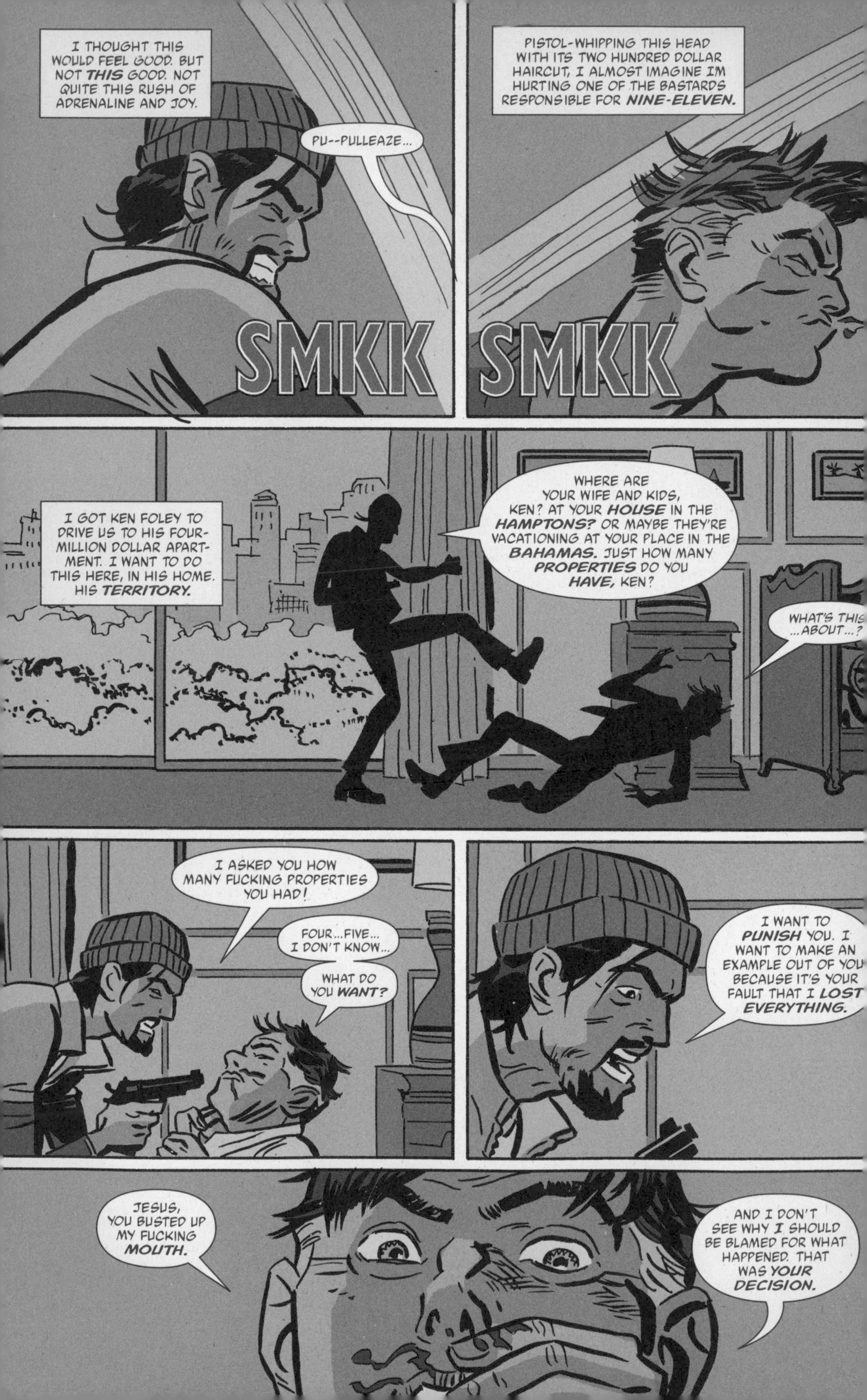
I THOUGHT THIS WOULD FEEL GOOD. BUT NOT THIS GOOD. NOT QUITE THIS RUSH OF ADRENALINE AND JOY.
PU--PULLEAZE...
SMKK
PISTOL-WHIPPING THIS HEAD WITH ITS TWO HUNDRED DOLLAR HAIRCUT, I ALMOST IMAGINE I'M HURTING ONE OF THE BASTARDS RESPONSIBLE FOR NINE-ELEVEN.
SMKK
I GOT KEN FOLEY TO DRIVE US TO HIS FOUR-MILLION DOLLAR APARTMENT. I WANT TO DO THIS HERE, IN HIS HOME. HIS TERRITORY.
WHERE ARE YOUR WIFE AND KIDS, KEN? AT YOUR HOUSE IN THE HAMPTONS? OR MAYBE THEY'RE VACATIONING AT YOUR PLACE IN THE BAHAMAS. JUST HOW MANY PROPERTIES DO YOU HAVE, KEN?
WHAT'S THIS ...ABOUT...?
I ASKED YOU HOW MANY FUCKING PROPERTIES YOU HAD!
FOUR...FIVE... I DON'T KNOW...
WHAT DO YOU WANT?
I WANT TO PUNISH YOU. I WANT TO MAKE AN EXAMPLE OUT OF YOU BECAUSE IT'S YOUR FAULT THAT I LOST EVERYTHING.
JESUS, YOU BUSTED UP MY FUCKING MOUTH.
AND I DON'T SEE WHY I SHOULD BE BLAMED FOR WHAT HAPPENED. THAT WAS YOUR DECISION.

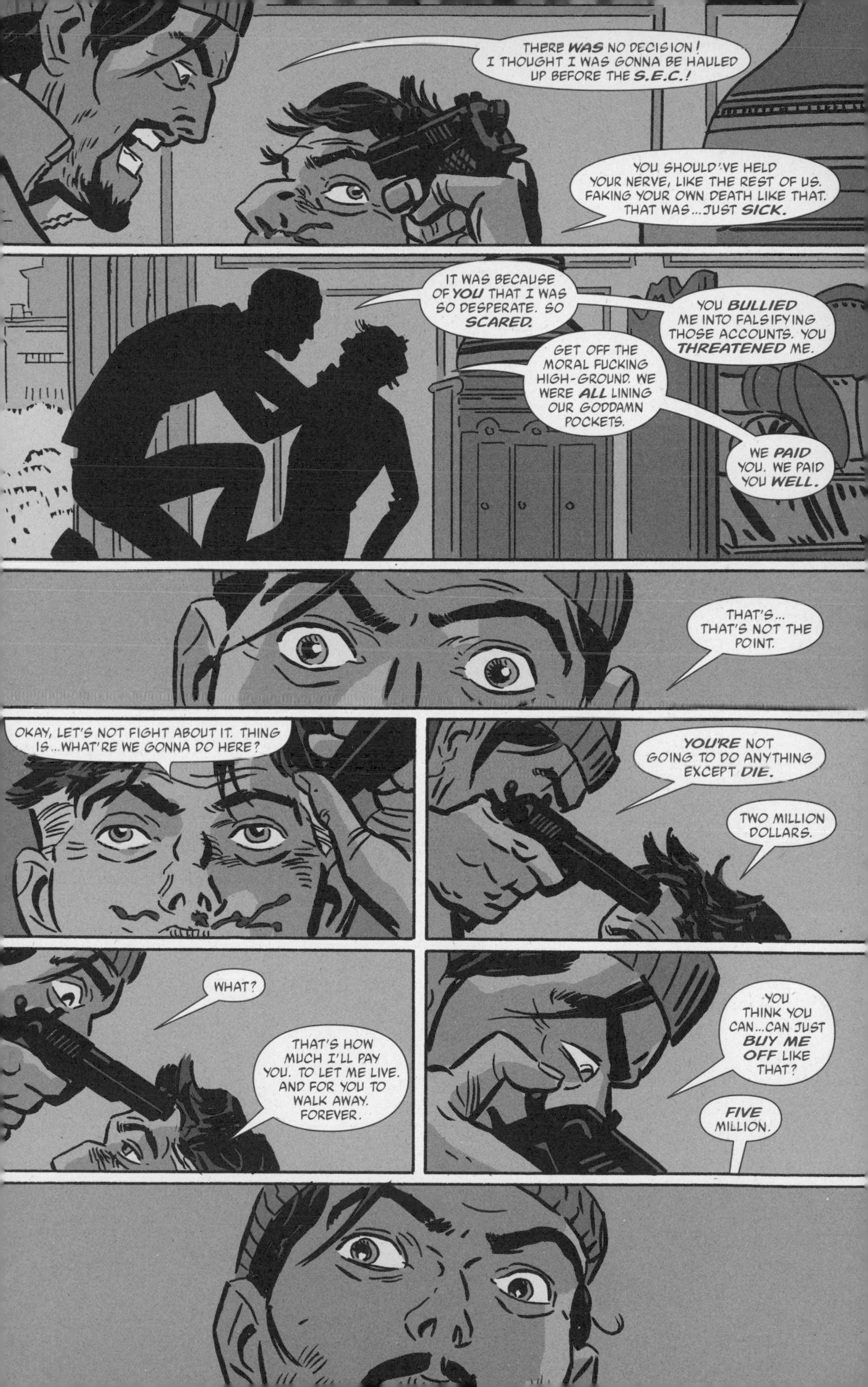
THERE WAS NO DECISION! I THOUGHT I WAS GONNA BE HAULED UP BEFORE THE S.E.C.!
YOU SHOULD'VE HELD YOUR NERVE, LIKE THE REST OF US. FAKING YOUR OWN DEATH LIKE THAT. THAT WAS... JUST SICK.
IT WAS BECAUSE OF YOU THAT I WAS SO DESPERATE. SO SCARED.
YOU BULLIED ME INTO FALSIFYING THOSE ACCOUNTS. YOU THREATENED ME.
GET OFF THE MORAL FUCKING HIGH-GROUND. WE WERE ALL LINING OUR GODDAMN POCKETS.
WE PAID YOU. WE PAID YOU WELL.
THAT'S... THAT'S NOT THE POINT.
OKAY, LET'S NOT FIGHT ABOUT IT. THING IS... WHAT'RE WE GONNA DO HERE?
YOU'RE NOT GOING TO DO ANYTHING EXCEPT DIE.
TWO MILLION DOLLARS.
WHAT?
THAT'S HOW MUCH I'LL PAY YOU. TO LET ME LIVE. AND FOR YOU TO WALK AWAY. FOREVER.
YOU THINK YOU CAN... CAN JUST BUY ME OFF LIKE THAT?
FIVE MILLION.

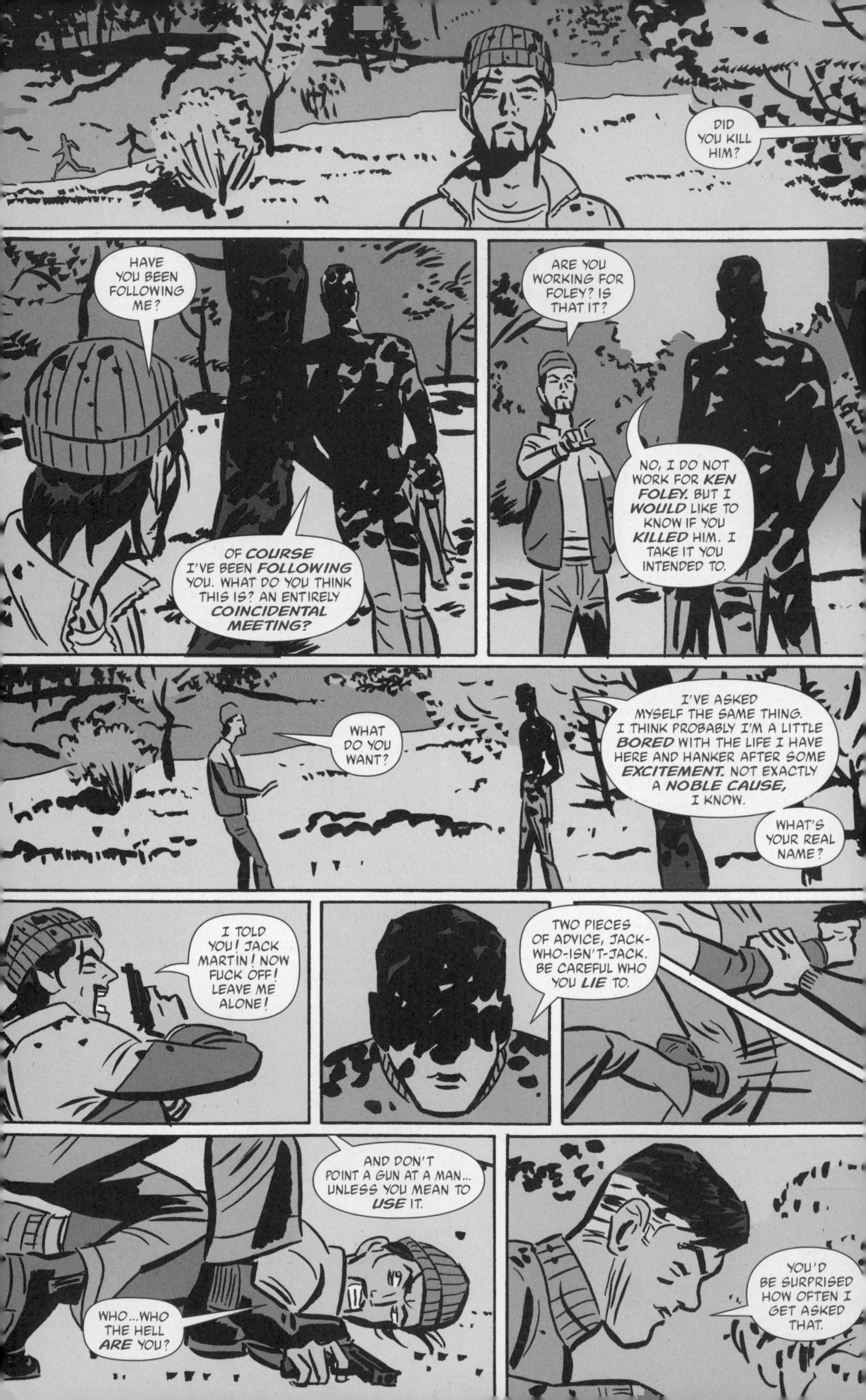
DID YOU KILL HIM?
HAVE YOU BEEN FOLLOWING ME?
OF COURSE I'VE BEEN FOLLOWING YOU. WHAT DO YOU THINK THIS IS? AN ENTIRELY COINCIDENTAL MEETING?
ARE YOU WORKING FOR FOLEY? IS THAT IT?
NO, I DO NOT WORK FOR KEN FOLEY. BUT I WOULD LIKE TO KNOW IF YOU KILLED HIM. I TAKE IT YOU INTENDED TO.
WHAT DO YOU WANT?
I'VE ASKED MYSELF THE SAME THING. I THINK PROBABLY I'M A LITTLE BORED WITH THE LIFE I HAVE HERE AND HANKER AFTER SOME EXCITEMENT. NOT EXACTLY A NOBLE CAUSE, I KNOW.
WHAT'S YOUR REAL NAME?
I TOLD YOU! JACK MARTIN! NOW FUCK OFF! LEAVE ME ALONE!
TWO PIECES OF ADVICE, JACK-WHO-ISN'T-JACK. BE CAREFUL WHO YOU LIE TO.
AND DON'T POINT A GUN AT A MAN... UNLESS YOU MEAN TO USE IT.
WHO...WHO THE HELL ARE YOU?
YOU'D BE SURPRISED HOW OFTEN I GET ASKED THAT.

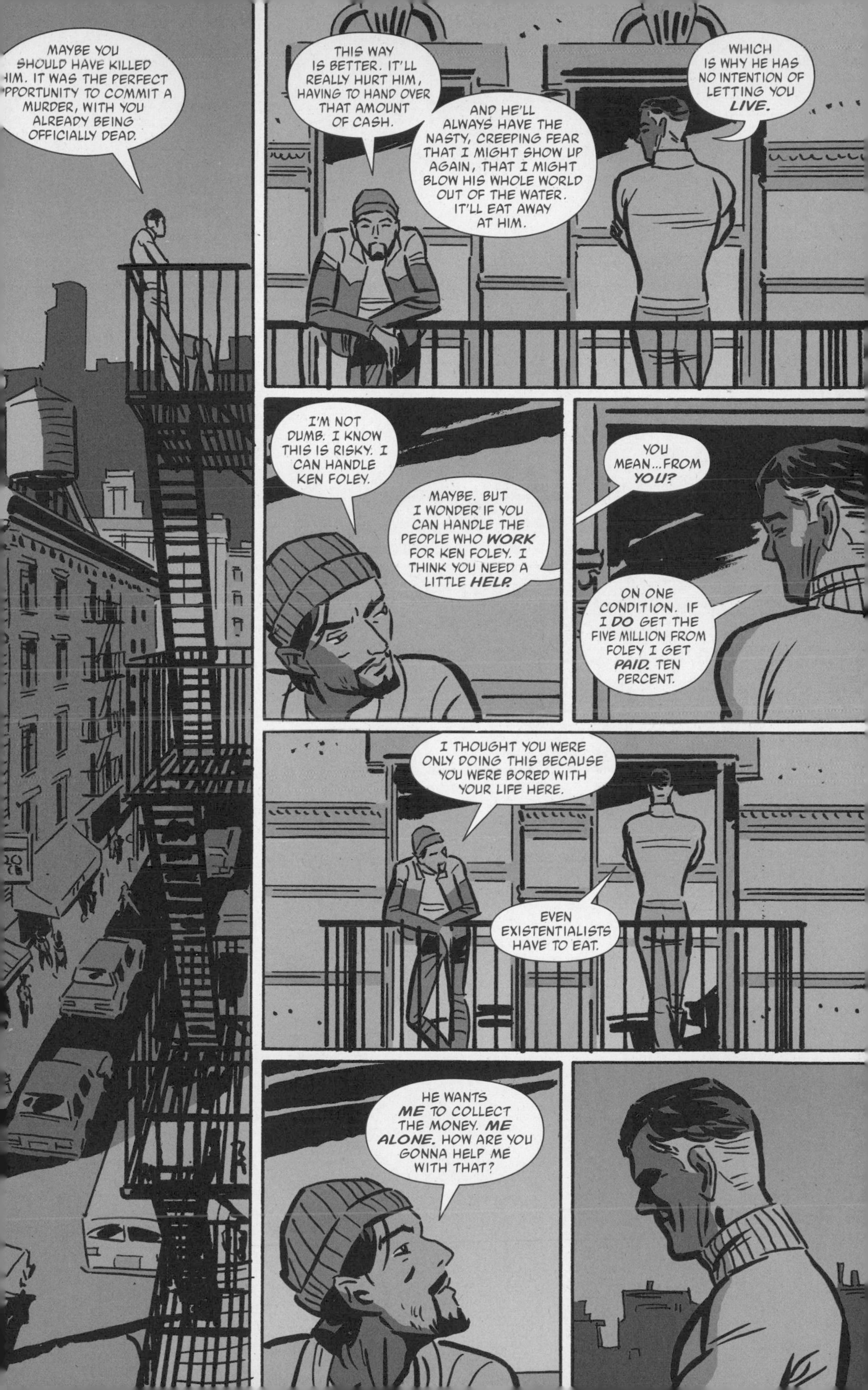
MAYBE YOU SHOULD HAVE KILLED HIM. IT WAS THE PERFECT OPPORTUNITY TO COMMIT A MURDER, WITH YOU ALREADY BEING OFFICIALLY DEAD.
THIS WAY IS BETTER. IT'LL REALLY HURT HIM, HAVING TO HAND OVER THAT AMOUNT OF CASH.
AND HE'LL ALWAYS HAVE THE NASTY, CREEPING FEAR THAT I MIGHT SHOW UP AGAIN, THAT I MIGHT BLOW HIS WHOLE WORLD OUT OF THE WATER. IT'LL EAT AWAY AT HIM.
WHICH IS WHY HE HAS NO INTENTION OF LETTING YOU LIVE.
I'M NOT DUMB. I KNOW THIS IS RISKY. I CAN HANDLE KEN FOLEY.
MAYBE. BUT I WONDER IF YOU CAN HANDLE THE PEOPLE WHO WORK FOR KEN FOLEY. I THINK YOU NEED A LITTLE HELP.
YOU MEAN...FROM YOU?
ON ONE CONDITION. IF I DO GET THE FIVE MILLION FROM FOLEY I GET PAID. TEN PERCENT.
I THOUGHT YOU WERE ONLY DOING THIS BECAUSE YOU WERE BORED WITH YOUR LIFE HERE.
EVEN EXISTENTIALISTS HAVE TO EAT.
HE WANTS ME TO COLLECT THE MONEY. ME ALONE. HOW ARE YOU GONNA HELP ME WITH THAT?

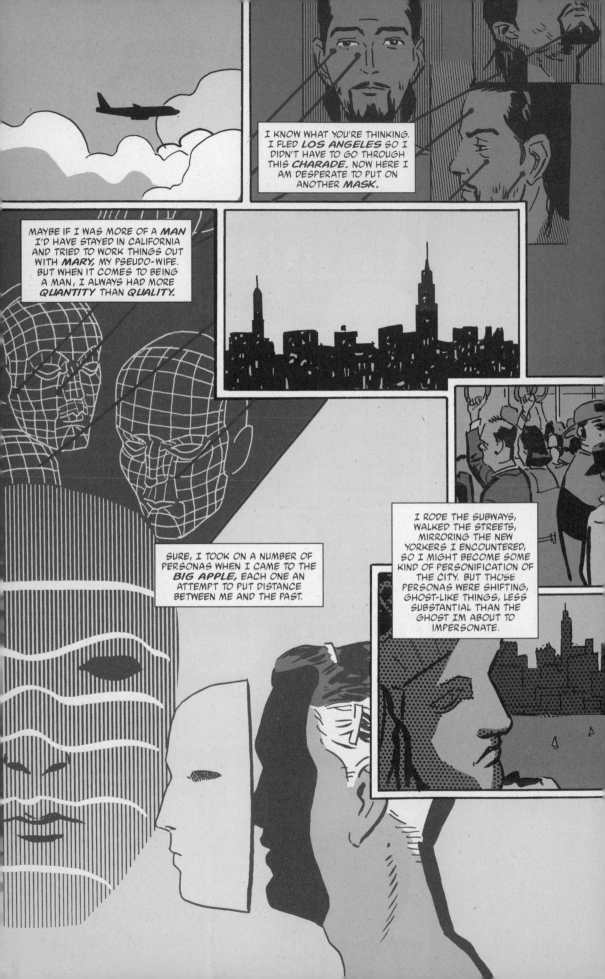

I KNOW WHAT YOU'RE THINKING. I FLED *LOS ANGELES* SO I DIDN'T HAVE TO GO THROUGH THIS *CHARADE*. NOW HERE I AM DESPERATE TO PUT ON ANOTHER *MASK*.

MAYBE IF I WAS MORE OF A *MAN* I'D HAVE STAYED IN CALIFORNIA AND TRIED TO WORK THINGS OUT WITH *MARY*, MY PSEUDO-WIFE. BUT WHEN IT COMES TO BEING A MAN, I ALWAYS HAD MORE *QUANTITY* THAN *QUALITY*.

SURE, I TOOK ON A NUMBER OF PERSONAS WHEN I CAME TO THE *BIG APPLE*, EACH ONE AN ATTEMPT TO PUT DISTANCE BETWEEN ME AND THE PAST.

I RODE THE SUBWAYS, WALKED THE STREETS, MIRRORING THE NEW YORKERS I ENCOUNTERED, SO I MIGHT BECOME SOME KIND OF PERSONIFICATION OF THE CITY. BUT THOSE PERSONAS WERE SHIFTING, GHOST-LIKE THINGS, LESS SUBSTANTIAL THAN THE GHOST I'M ABOUT TO IMPERSONATE.

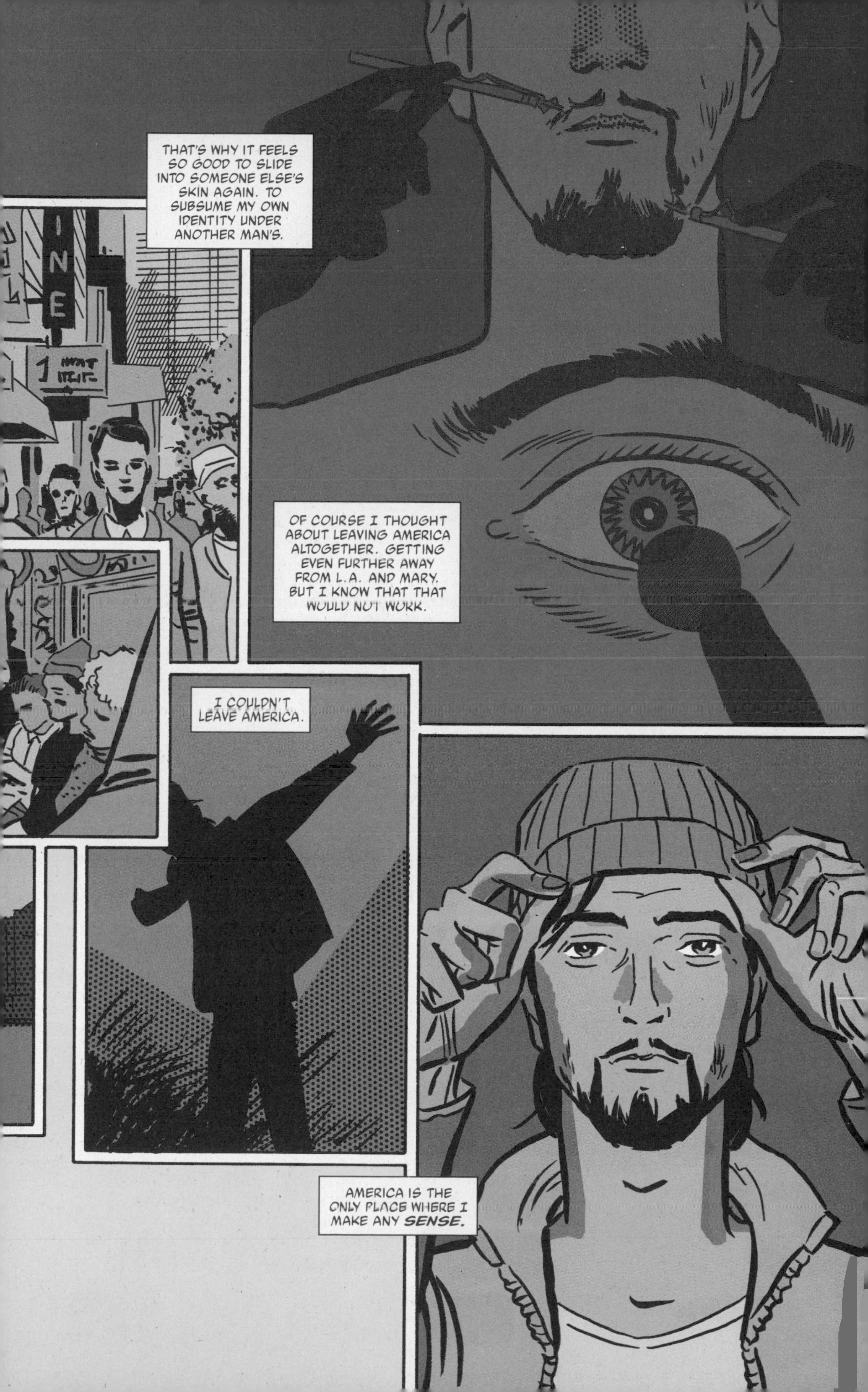
THAT'S WHY IT FEELS SO GOOD TO SLIDE INTO SOMEONE ELSE'S SKIN AGAIN. TO SUBSUME MY OWN IDENTITY UNDER ANOTHER MAN'S.
OF COURSE I THOUGHT ABOUT LEAVING AMERICA ALTOGETHER. GETTING EVEN FURTHER AWAY FROM L.A. AND MARY. BUT I KNOW THAT THAT WOULD NOT WORK.
I COULDN'T LEAVE AMERICA.
AMERICA IS THE ONLY PLACE WHERE I MAKE ANY *SENSE.*

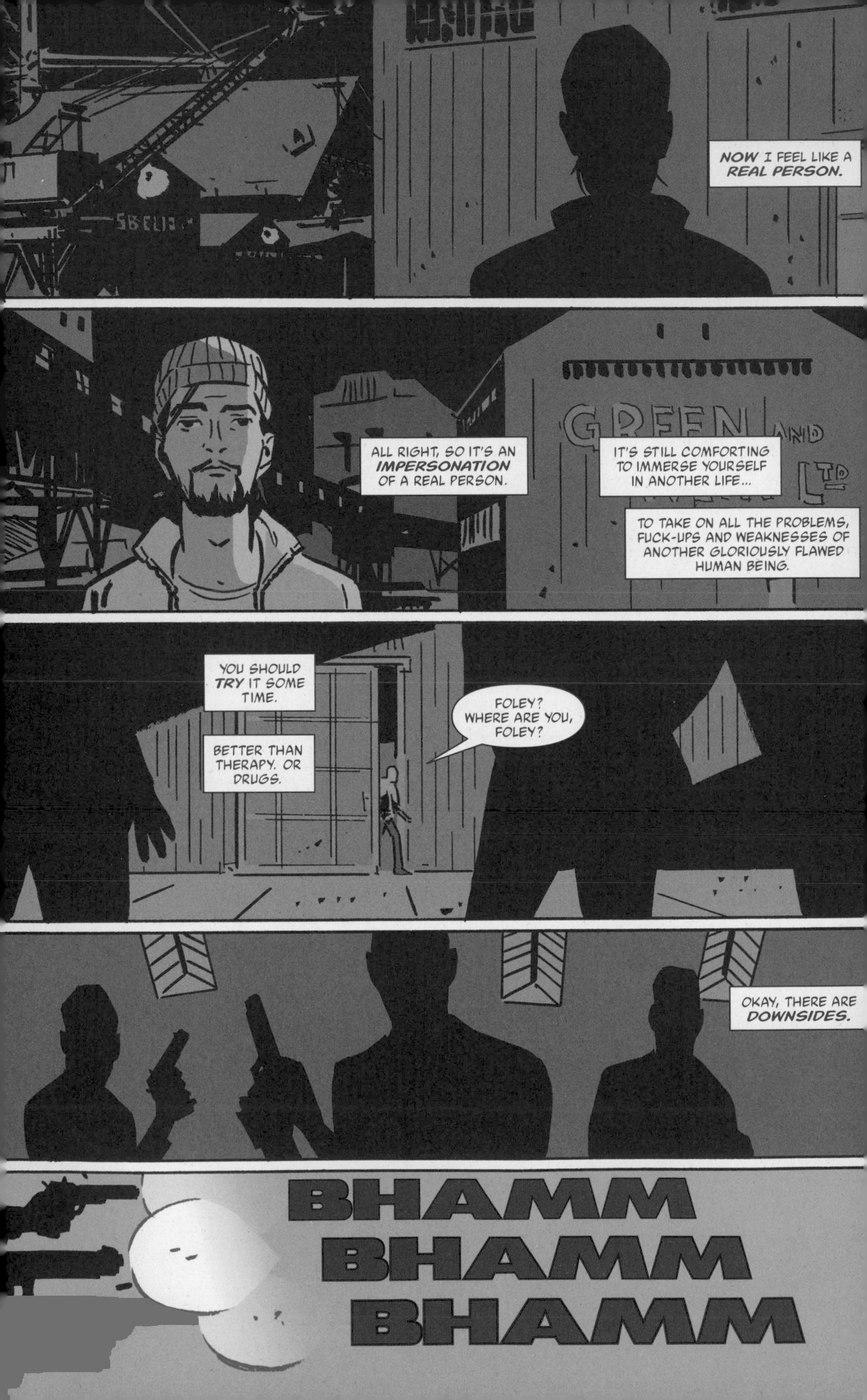
NOW I FEEL LIKE A REAL PERSON.
ALL RIGHT, SO IT'S AN IMPERSONATION OF A REAL PERSON.
IT'S STILL COMFORTING TO IMMERSE YOURSELF IN ANOTHER LIFE...
TO TAKE ON ALL THE PROBLEMS, FUCK-UPS AND WEAKNESSES OF ANOTHER GLORIOUSLY FLAWED HUMAN BEING.
YOU SHOULD TRY IT SOME TIME.
BETTER THAN THERAPY. OR DRUGS.
FOLEY? WHERE ARE YOU, FOLEY?
OKAY, THERE ARE DOWNSIDES.
BHAMM
BHAMM
BHAMM

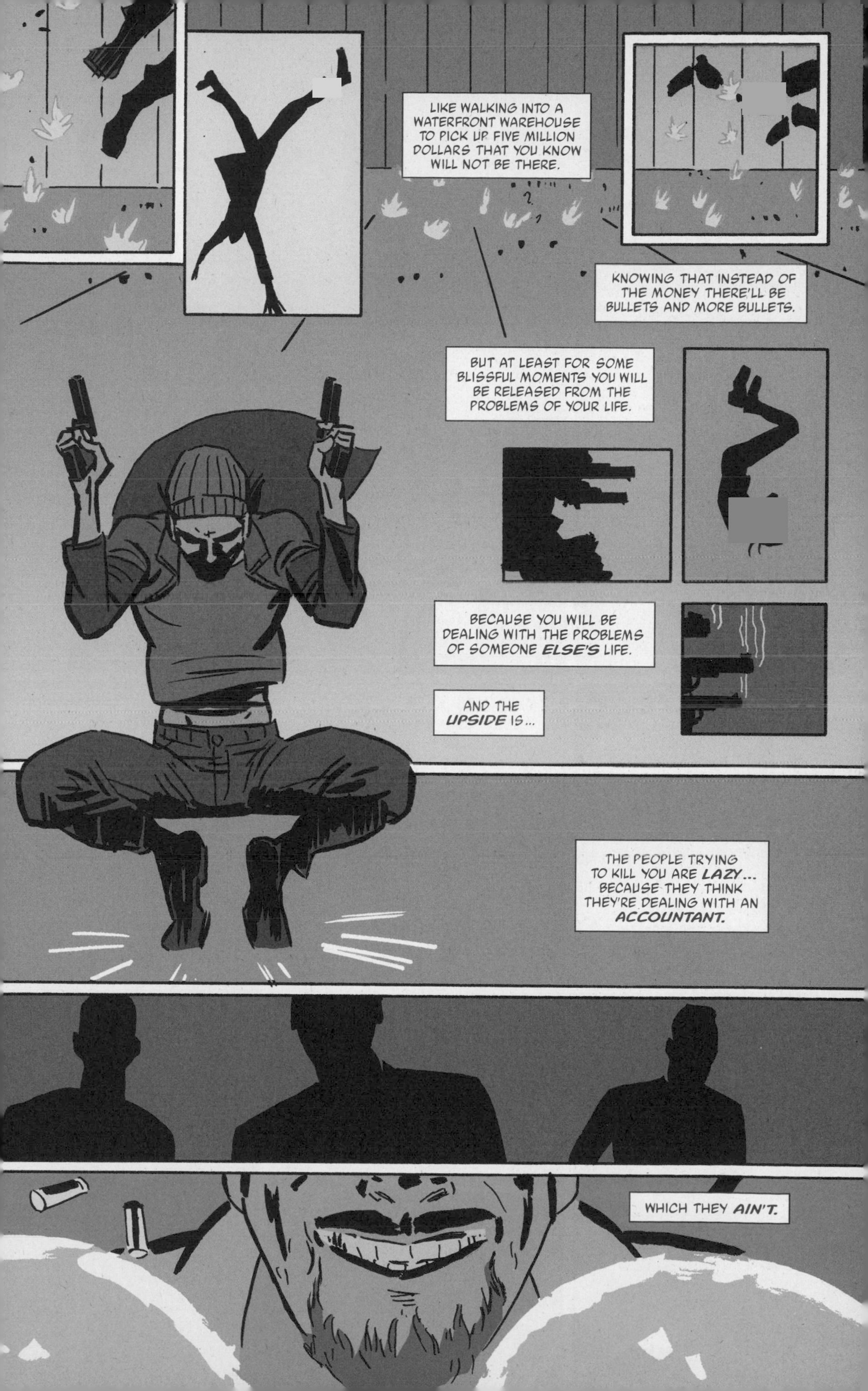
LIKE WALKING INTO A WATERFRONT WAREHOUSE TO PICK UP FIVE MILLION DOLLARS THAT YOU KNOW WILL NOT BE THERE.
KNOWING THAT INSTEAD OF THE MONEY THERE'LL BE BULLETS AND MORE BULLETS.
BUT AT LEAST FOR SOME BLISSFUL MOMENTS YOU WILL BE RELEASED FROM THE PROBLEMS OF YOUR LIFE.
BECAUSE YOU WILL BE DEALING WITH THE PROBLEMS OF SOMEONE ELSE'S LIFE.
AND THE UPSIDE IS...
THE PEOPLE TRYING TO KILL YOU ARE LAZY... BECAUSE THEY THINK THEY'RE DEALING WITH AN ACCOUNTANT.
WHICH THEY AIN'T.

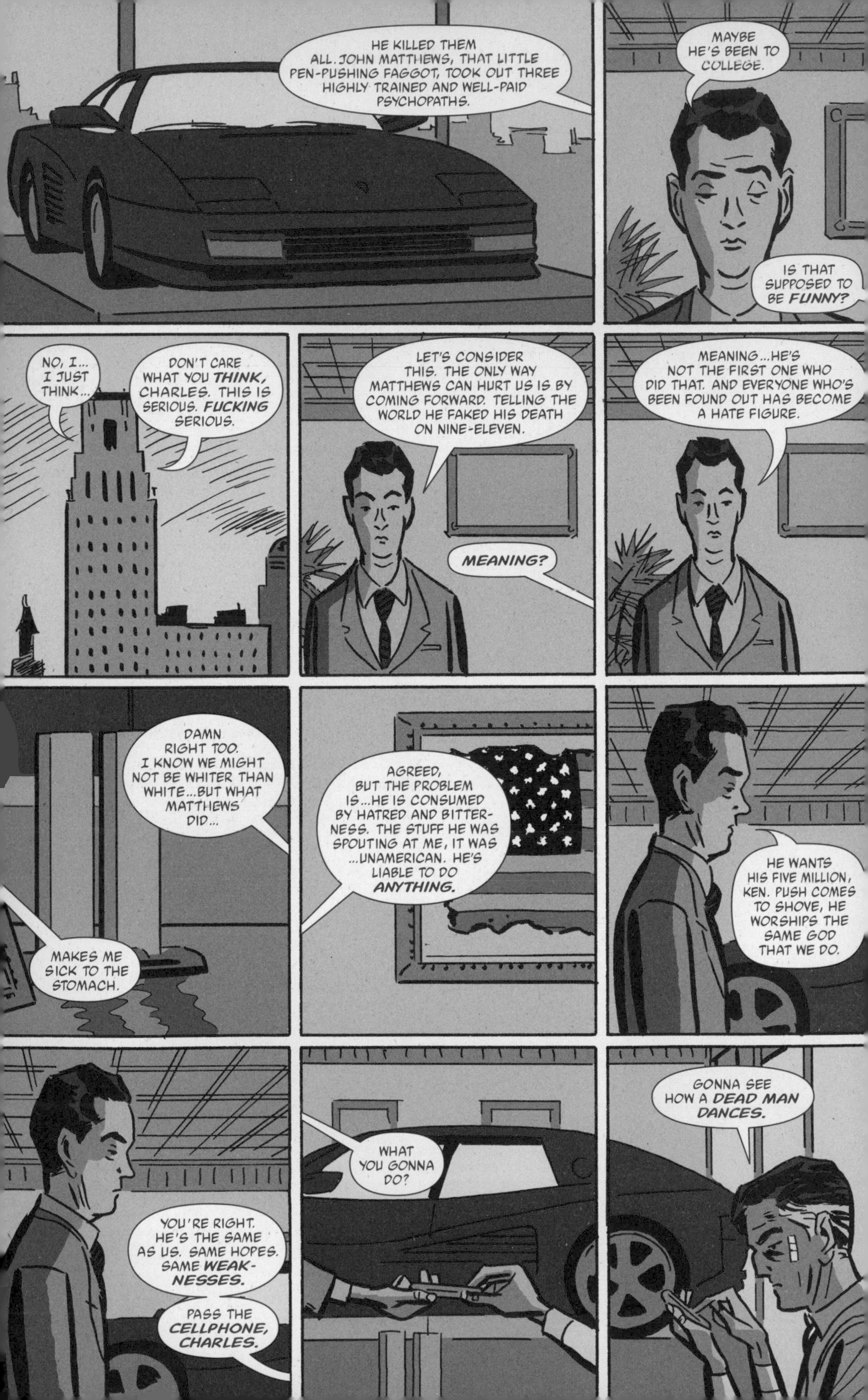
HE KILLED THEM ALL. JOHN MATTHEWS, THAT LITTLE PEN-PUSHING FAGGOT, TOOK OUT THREE HIGHLY TRAINED AND WELL-PAID PSYCHOPATHS.
MAYBE HE'S BEEN TO COLLEGE.
IS THAT SUPPOSED TO BE FUNNY?
NO, I... I JUST THINK...
DON'T CARE WHAT YOU THINK, CHARLES. THIS IS SERIOUS. FUCKING SERIOUS.
LET'S CONSIDER THIS. THE ONLY WAY MATTHEWS CAN HURT US IS BY COMING FORWARD. TELLING THE WORLD HE FAKED HIS DEATH ON NINE-ELEVEN.
MEANING?
MEANING...HE'S NOT THE FIRST ONE WHO DID THAT. AND EVERYONE WHO'S BEEN FOUND OUT HAS BECOME A HATE FIGURE.
DAMN RIGHT TOO. I KNOW WE MIGHT NOT BE WHITER THAN WHITE...BUT WHAT MATTHEWS DID...
MAKES ME SICK TO THE STOMACH.
AGREED, BUT THE PROBLEM IS...HE IS CONSUMED BY HATRED AND BITTERNESS. THE STUFF HE WAS SPOUTING AT ME, IT WAS ...UNAMERICAN. HE'S LIABLE TO DO ANYTHING.
HE WANTS HIS FIVE MILLION, KEN. PUSH COMES TO SHOVE, HE WORSHIPS THE SAME GOD THAT WE DO.
YOU'RE RIGHT. HE'S THE SAME AS US. SAME HOPES. SAME WEAKNESSES.
PASS THE CELLPHONE, CHARLES.
WHAT YOU GONNA DO?
GONNA SEE HOW A DEAD MAN DANCES.

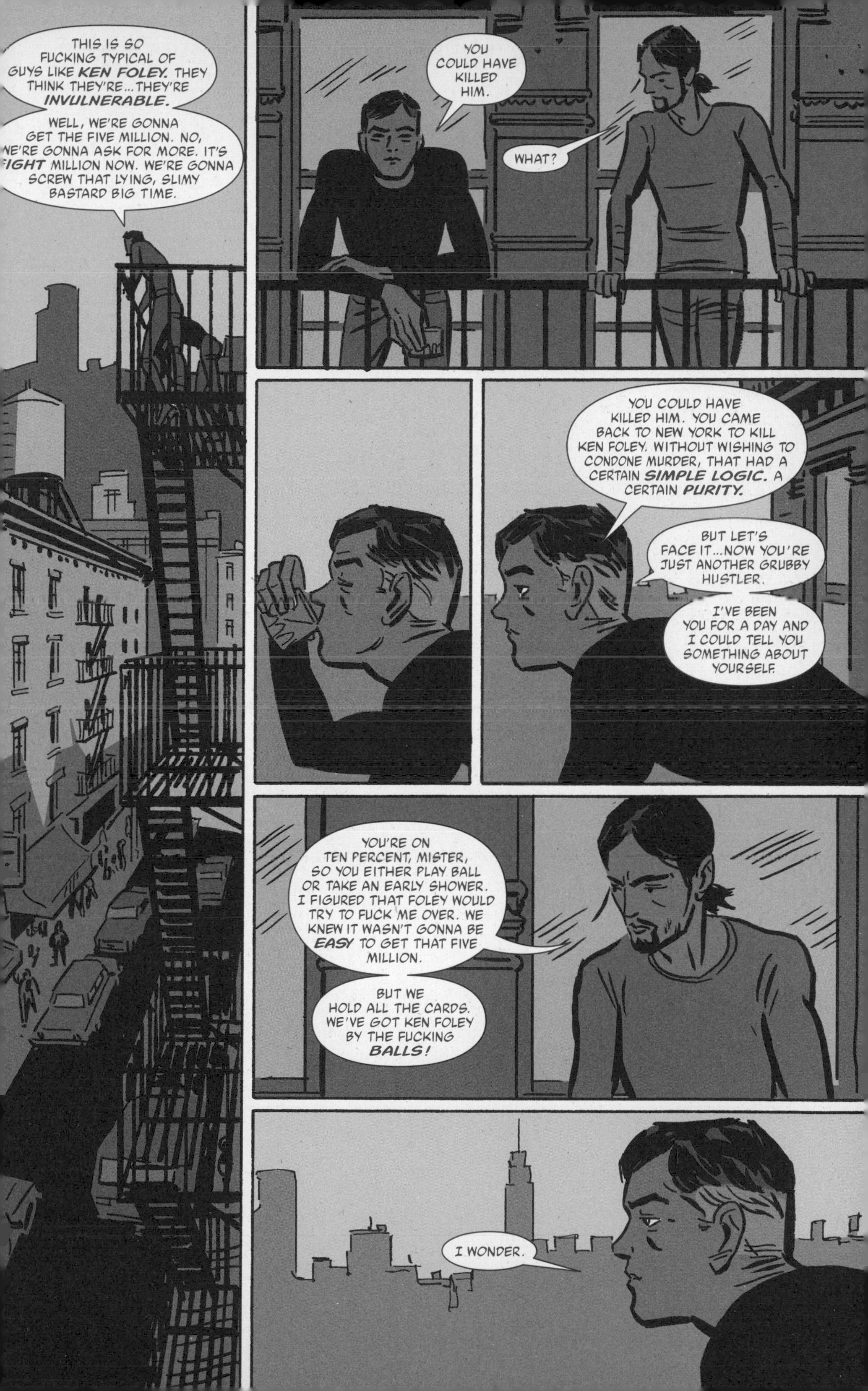
THIS IS SO FUCKING TYPICAL OF GUYS LIKE KEN FOLEY. THEY THINK THEY'RE... THEY'RE INVULNERABLE.
WELL, WE'RE GONNA GET THE FIVE MILLION. NO, WE'RE GONNA ASK FOR MORE. IT'S EIGHT MILLION NOW. WE'RE GONNA SCREW THAT LYING, SLIMY BASTARD BIG TIME.
YOU COULD HAVE KILLED HIM.
WHAT?
YOU COULD HAVE KILLED HIM. YOU CAME BACK TO NEW YORK TO KILL KEN FOLEY. WITHOUT WISHING TO CONDONE MURDER, THAT HAD A CERTAIN SIMPLE LOGIC. A CERTAIN PURITY.
BUT LET'S FACE IT... NOW YOU'RE JUST ANOTHER GRUBBY HUSTLER.
I'VE BEEN YOU FOR A DAY AND I COULD TELL YOU SOMETHING ABOUT YOURSELF.
YOU'RE ON TEN PERCENT, MISTER, SO YOU EITHER PLAY BALL OR TAKE AN EARLY SHOWER. I FIGURED THAT FOLEY WOULD TRY TO FUCK ME OVER. WE KNEW IT WASN'T GONNA BE EASY TO GET THAT FIVE MILLION.
BUT WE HOLD ALL THE CARDS. WE'VE GOT KEN FOLEY BY THE FUCKING BALLS!
I WONDER.

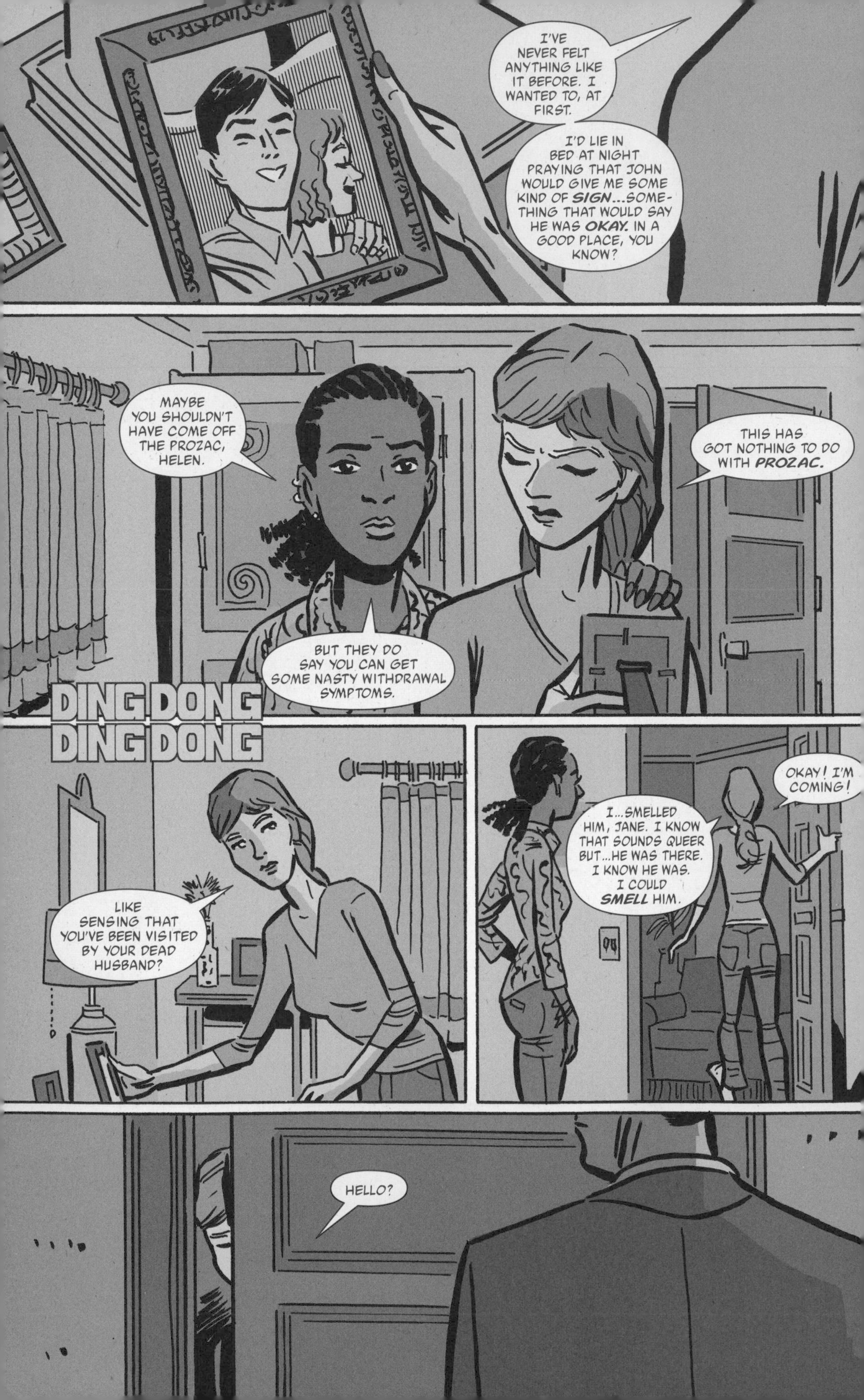
I'VE NEVER FELT ANYTHING LIKE IT BEFORE. I WANTED TO, AT FIRST.
I'D LIE IN BED AT NIGHT PRAYING THAT JOHN WOULD GIVE ME SOME KIND OF SIGN...SOMETHING THAT WOULD SAY HE WAS OKAY. IN A GOOD PLACE, YOU KNOW?
MAYBE YOU SHOULDN'T HAVE COME OFF THE PROZAC, HELEN.
THIS HAS GOT NOTHING TO DO WITH PROZAC.
BUT THEY DO SAY YOU CAN GET SOME NASTY WITHDRAWAL SYMPTOMS.
DING DONG
DING DONG
LIKE SENSING THAT YOU'VE BEEN VISITED BY YOUR DEAD HUSBAND?
I...SMELLED HIM, JANE. I KNOW THAT SOUNDS QUEER BUT...HE WAS THERE. I KNOW HE WAS. I COULD SMELL HIM.
OKAY! I'M COMING!
HELLO?

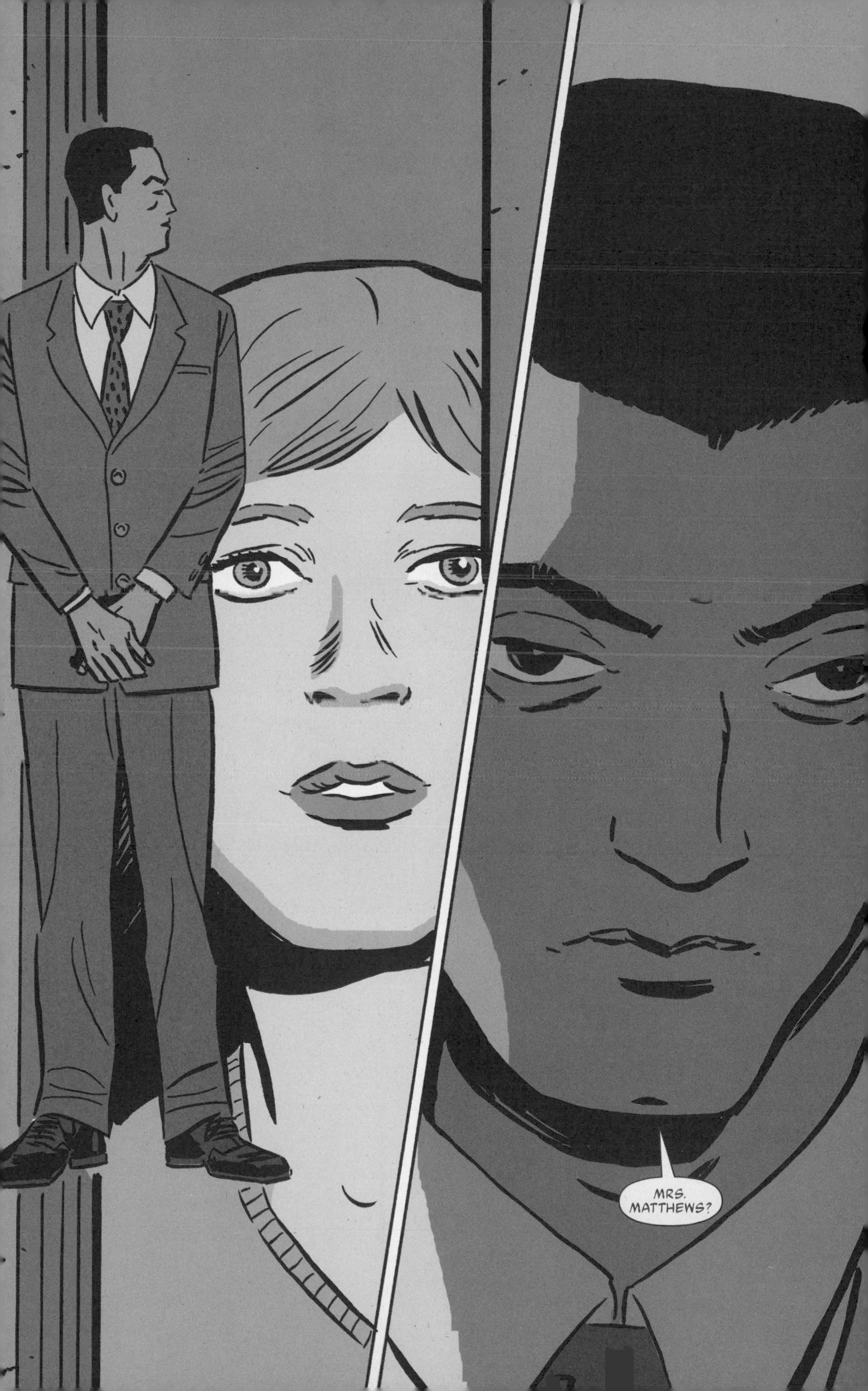
MRS.
MATTHEWS?

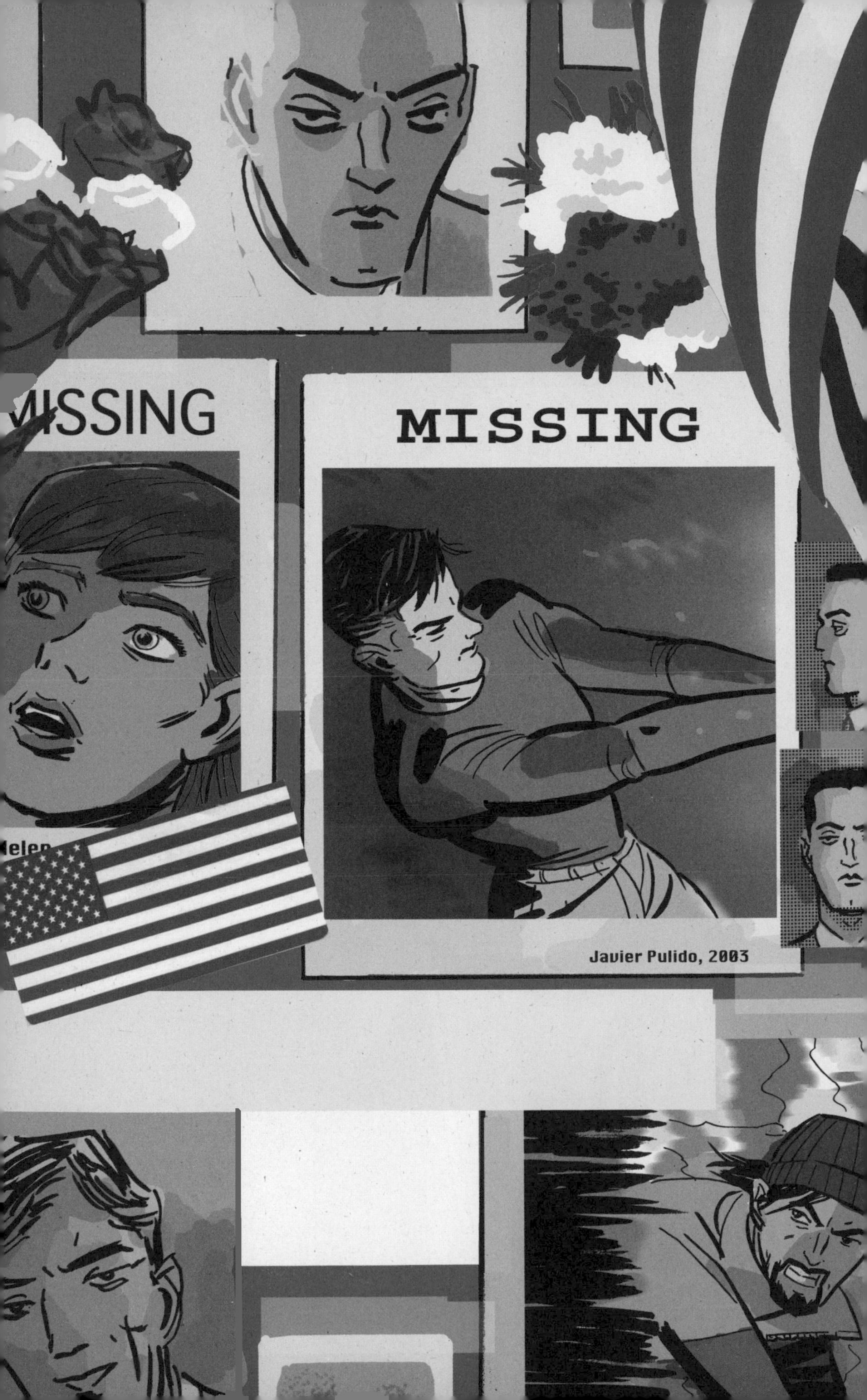
MISSING
MISSING
Javier Pulido, 2003

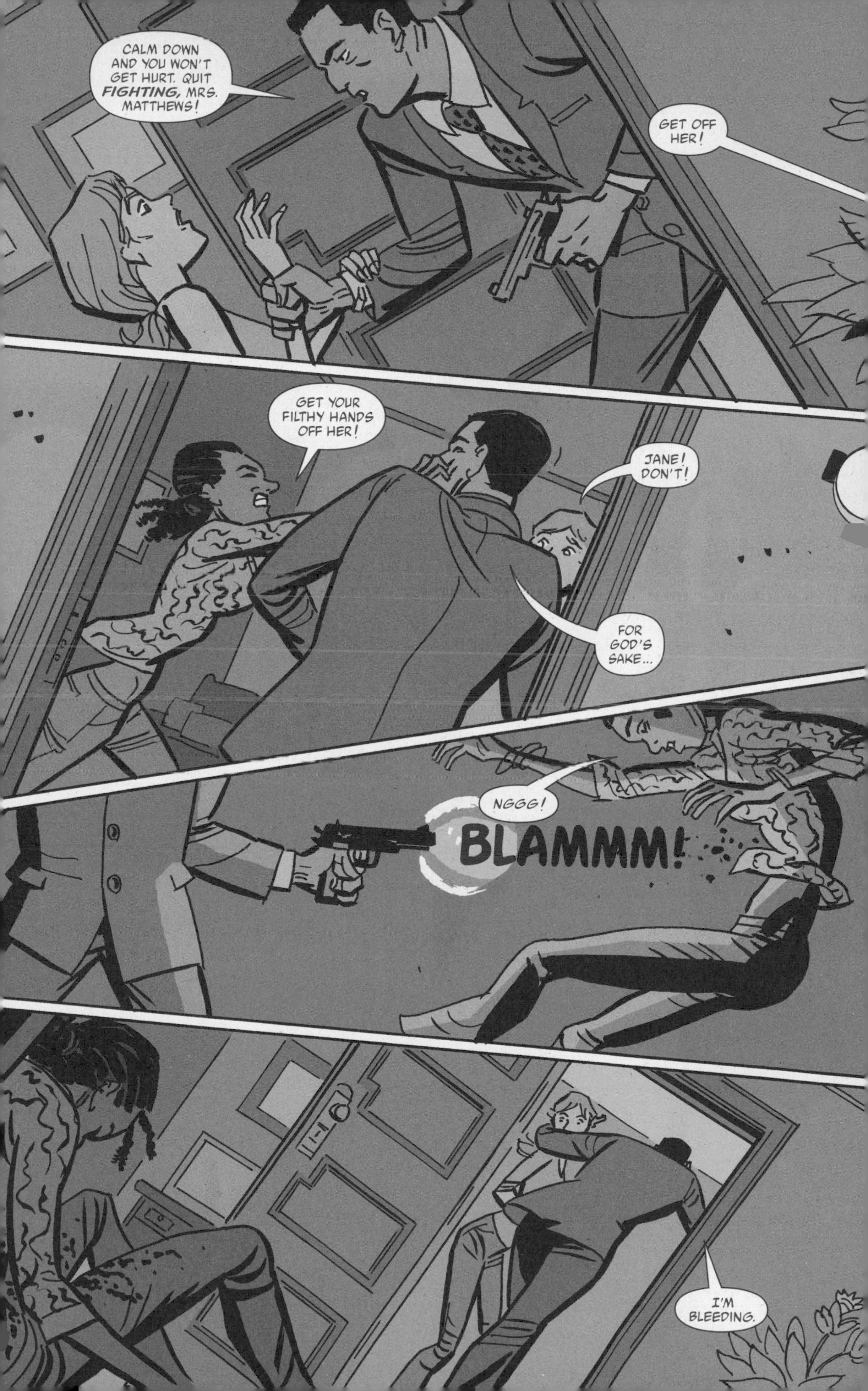
CALM DOWN AND YOU WON'T GET HURT. QUIT *FIGHTING,* MRS. MATTHEWS!
GET OFF HER!
GET YOUR FILTHY HANDS OFF HER!
JANE! DON'T!
FOR GOD'S SAKE...
NGGG!
BLAMMM!
I'M BLEEDING.

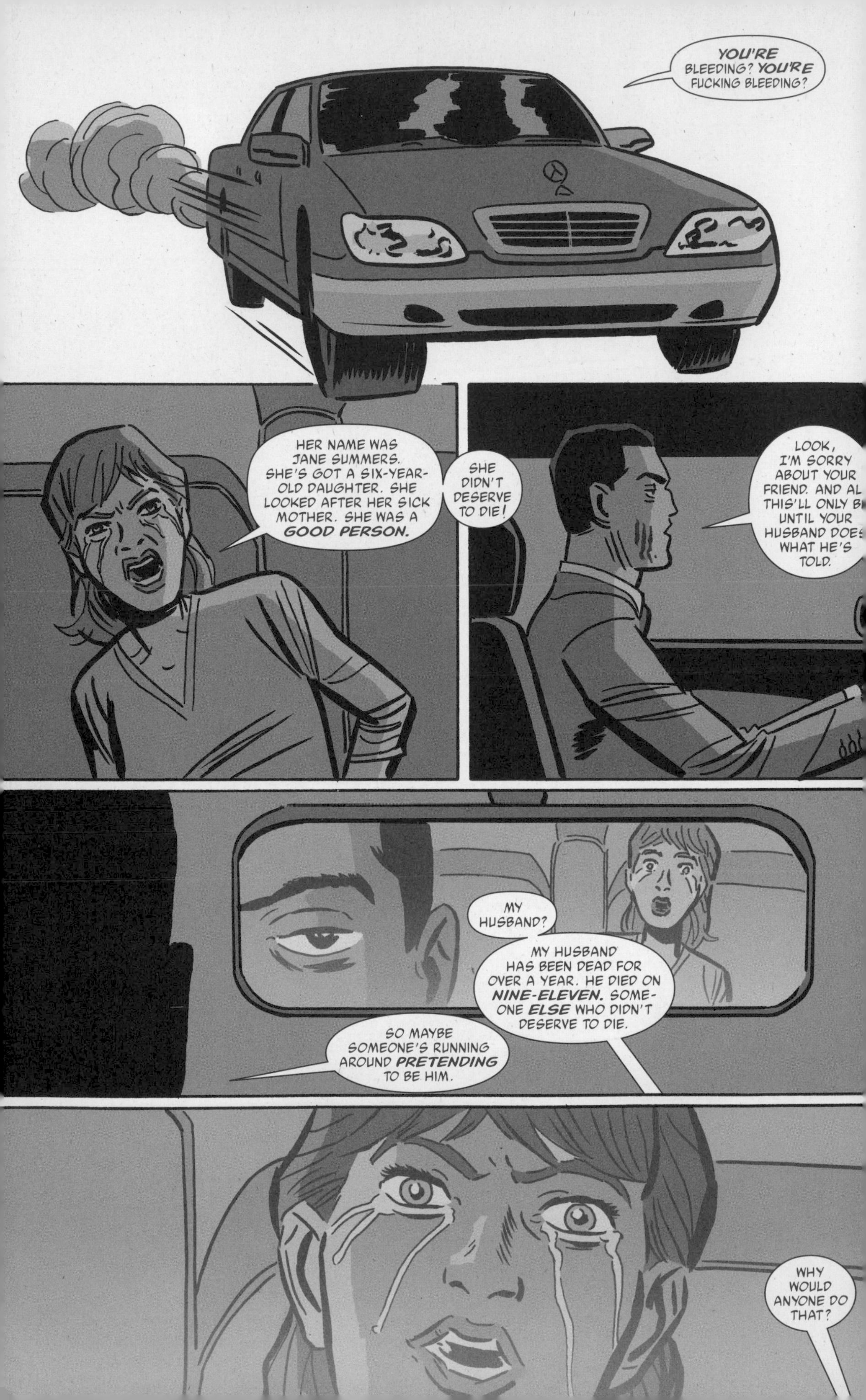
YOU'RE BLEEDING? YOU'RE FUCKING BLEEDING?
HER NAME WAS JANE SUMMERS. SHE'S GOT A SIX-YEAR-OLD DAUGHTER. SHE LOOKED AFTER HER SICK MOTHER. SHE WAS A GOOD PERSON.
SHE DIDN'T DESERVE TO DIE!
LOOK, I'M SORRY ABOUT YOUR FRIEND. AND AL THIS'LL ONLY B UNTIL YOUR HUSBAND DOE WHAT HE'S TOLD.
MY HUSBAND?
MY HUSBAND HAS BEEN DEAD FOR OVER A YEAR. HE DIED ON NINE-ELEVEN. SOME-ONE ELSE WHO DIDN'T DESERVE TO DIE.
SO MAYBE SOMEONE'S RUNNING AROUND PRETENDING TO BE HIM.
WHY WOULD ANYONE DO THAT?

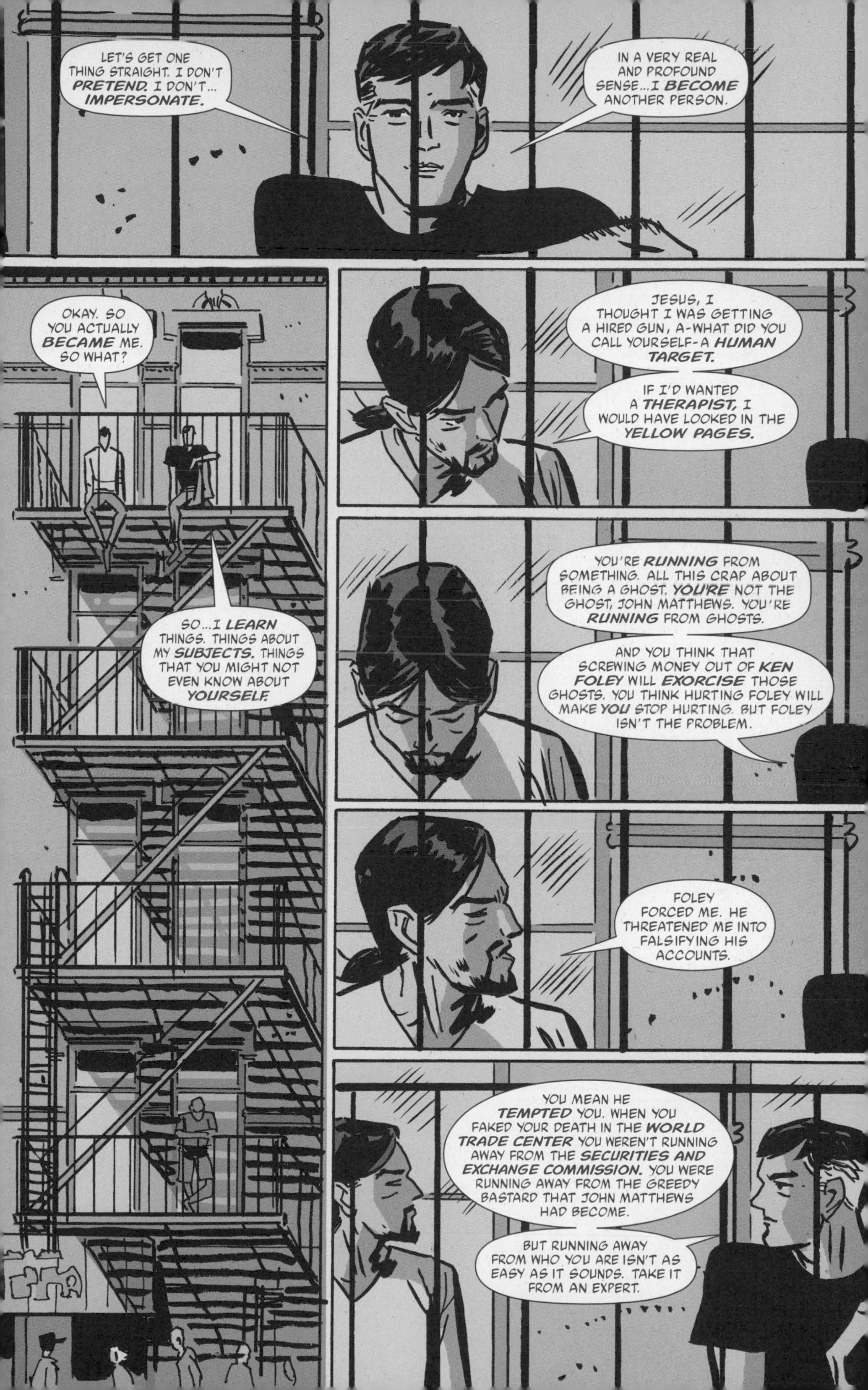

LET'S GET ONE THING STRAIGHT. I DON'T PRETEND. I DON'T... IMPERSONATE.
IN A VERY REAL AND PROFOUND SENSE...I BECOME ANOTHER PERSON.
OKAY. SO YOU ACTUALLY BECAME ME. SO WHAT?
SO...I LEARN THINGS. THINGS ABOUT MY SUBJECTS. THINGS THAT YOU MIGHT NOT EVEN KNOW ABOUT YOURSELF.
JESUS, I THOUGHT I WAS GETTING A HIRED GUN, A-WHAT DID YOU CALL YOURSELF-A HUMAN TARGET.
IF I'D WANTED A THERAPIST, I WOULD HAVE LOOKED IN THE YELLOW PAGES.
YOU'RE RUNNING FROM SOMETHING. ALL THIS CRAP ABOUT BEING A GHOST. YOU'RE NOT THE GHOST, JOHN MATTHEWS. YOU'RE RUNNING FROM GHOSTS.
AND YOU THINK THAT SCREWING MONEY OUT OF KEN FOLEY WILL EXORCISE THOSE GHOSTS. YOU THINK HURTING FOLEY WILL MAKE YOU STOP HURTING. BUT FOLEY ISN'T THE PROBLEM.
FOLEY FORCED ME. HE THREATENED ME INTO FALSIFYING HIS ACCOUNTS.
YOU MEAN HE TEMPTED YOU. WHEN YOU FAKED YOUR DEATH IN THE WORLD TRADE CENTER YOU WEREN'T RUNNING AWAY FROM THE SECURITIES AND EXCHANGE COMMISSION. YOU WERE RUNNING AWAY FROM THE GREEDY BASTARD THAT JOHN MATTHEWS HAD BECOME.
BUT RUNNING AWAY FROM WHO YOU ARE ISN'T AS EASY AS IT SOUNDS. TAKE IT FROM AN EXPERT.

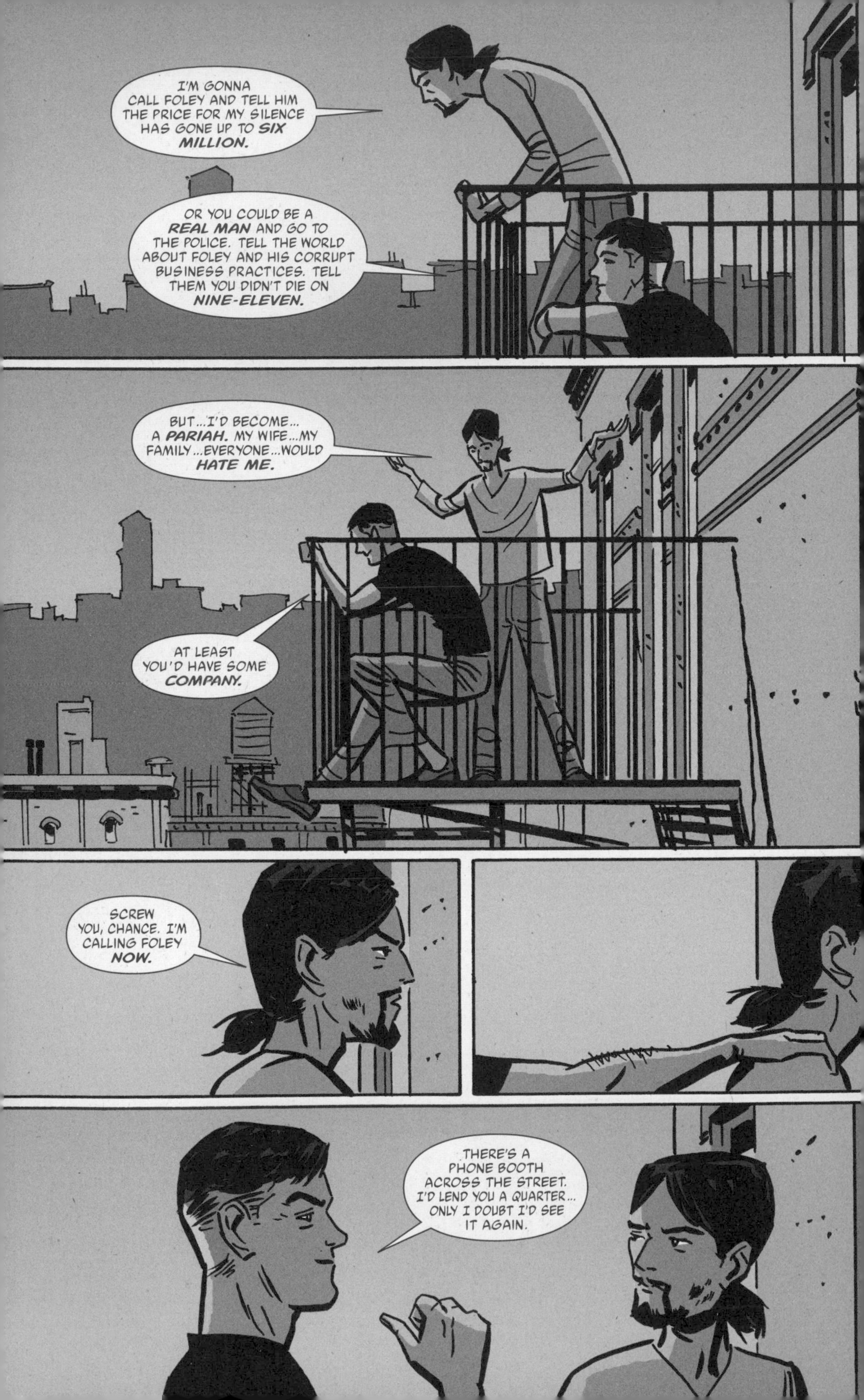
I'M GONNA CALL FOLEY AND TELL HIM THE PRICE FOR MY SILENCE HAS GONE UP TO SIX MILLION.
OR YOU COULD BE A REAL MAN AND GO TO THE POLICE. TELL THE WORLD ABOUT FOLEY AND HIS CORRUPT BUSINESS PRACTICES. TELL THEM YOU DIDN'T DIE ON NINE-ELEVEN.
BUT...I'D BECOME... A PARIAH. MY WIFE...MY FAMILY...EVERYONE...WOULD HATE ME.
AT LEAST YOU'D HAVE SOME COMPANY.
SCREW YOU, CHANCE. I'M CALLING FOLEY NOW.
THERE'S A PHONE BOOTH ACROSS THE STREET. I'D LEND YOU A QUARTER... ONLY I DOUBT I'D SEE IT AGAIN.

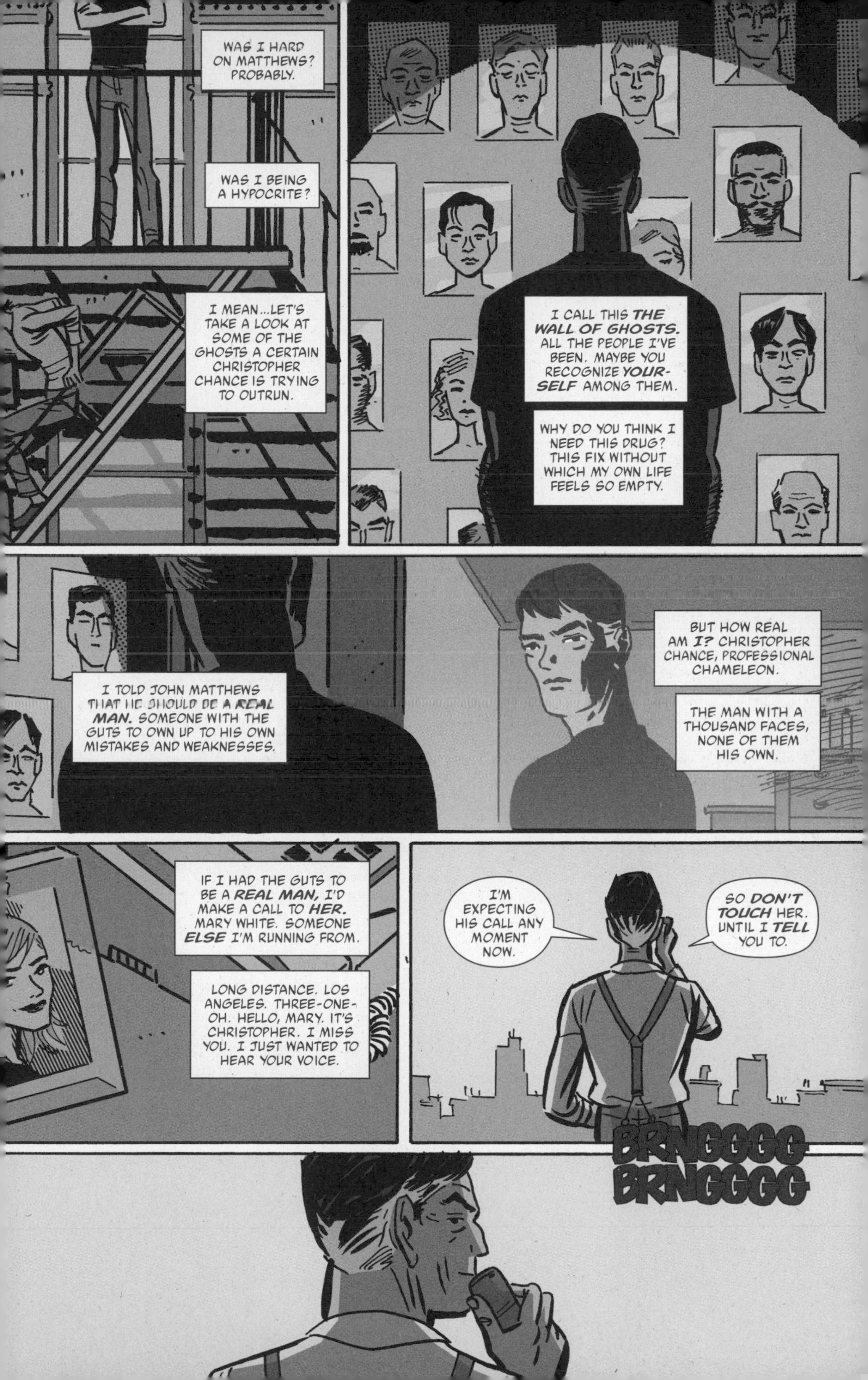
WAS I HARD ON MATTHEWS? PROBABLY.
WAS I BEING A HYPOCRITE?
I MEAN...LET'S TAKE A LOOK AT SOME OF THE GHOSTS A CERTAIN CHRISTOPHER CHANCE IS TRYING TO OUTRUN.
I CALL THIS THE WALL OF GHOSTS. ALL THE PEOPLE I'VE BEEN. MAYBE YOU RECOGNIZE YOURSELF AMONG THEM.
WHY DO YOU THINK I NEED THIS DRUG? THIS FIX WITHOUT WHICH MY OWN LIFE FEELS SO EMPTY.
I TOLD JOHN MATTHEWS THAT HE SHOULD BE A REAL MAN. SOMEONE WITH THE GUTS TO OWN UP TO HIS OWN MISTAKES AND WEAKNESSES.
BUT HOW REAL AM I? CHRISTOPHER CHANCE, PROFESSIONAL CHAMELEON.
THE MAN WITH A THOUSAND FACES, NONE OF THEM HIS OWN.
IF I HAD THE GUTS TO BE A REAL MAN, I'D MAKE A CALL TO HER. MARY WHITE. SOMEONE ELSE I'M RUNNING FROM.
LONG DISTANCE. LOS ANGELES. THREE-ONE-OH. HELLO, MARY. IT'S CHRISTOPHER. I MISS YOU. I JUST WANTED TO HEAR YOUR VOICE.
I'M EXPECTING HIS CALL ANY MOMENT NOW.
SO DON'T TOUCH HER. UNTIL I TELL YOU TO.
BRNGGGG BRNGGGG

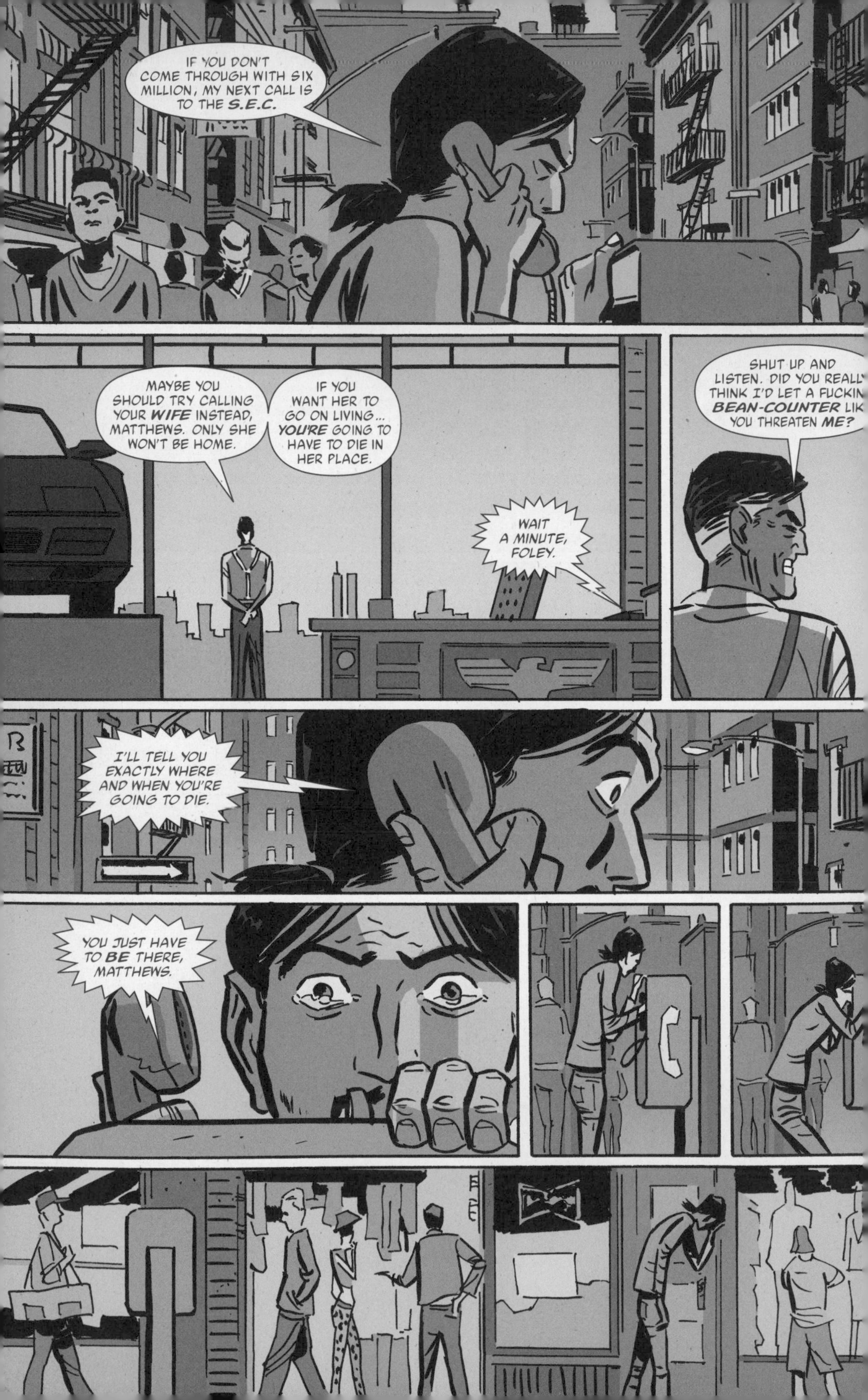
IF YOU DON'T COME THROUGH WITH SIX MILLION, MY NEXT CALL IS TO THE S.E.C.
MAYBE YOU SHOULD TRY CALLING YOUR WIFE INSTEAD, MATTHEWS. ONLY SHE WON'T BE HOME.
IF YOU WANT HER TO GO ON LIVING... YOU'RE GOING TO HAVE TO DIE IN HER PLACE.
WAIT A MINUTE, FOLEY.
SHUT UP AND LISTEN. DID YOU REALL THINK I'D LET A FUCKIN BEAN-COUNTER LIK YOU THREATEN ME?
I'LL TELL YOU EXACTLY WHERE AND WHEN YOU'RE GOING TO DIE.
YOU JUST HAVE TO BE THERE, MATTHEWS.

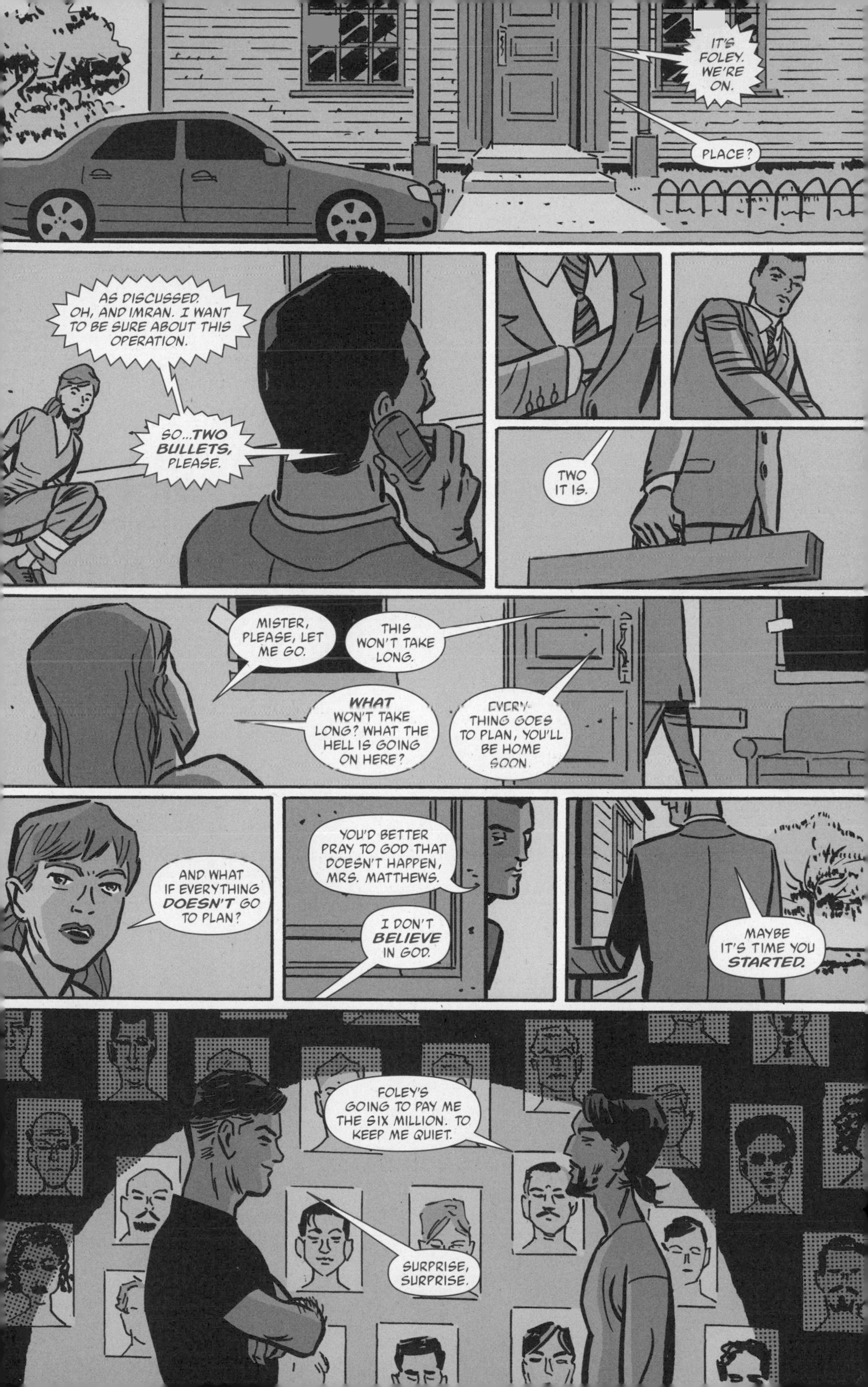
IT'S FOLEY. WE'RE ON.
PLACE?
AS DISCUSSED. OH, AND IMRAN. I WANT TO BE SURE ABOUT THIS OPERATION.
SO...TWO BULLETS, PLEASE.
TWO IT IS.
MISTER, PLEASE, LET ME GO.
THIS WON'T TAKE LONG.
WHAT WON'T TAKE LONG? WHAT THE HELL IS GOING ON HERE?
EVERY-THING GOES TO PLAN, YOU'LL BE HOME SOON.
AND WHAT IF EVERYTHING DOESN'T GO TO PLAN?
YOU'D BETTER PRAY TO GOD THAT DOESN'T HAPPEN, MRS. MATTHEWS.
I DON'T BELIEVE IN GOD.
MAYBE IT'S TIME YOU STARTED.
FOLEY'S GOING TO PAY ME THE SIX MILLION. TO KEEP ME QUIET.
SURPRISE, SURPRISE.

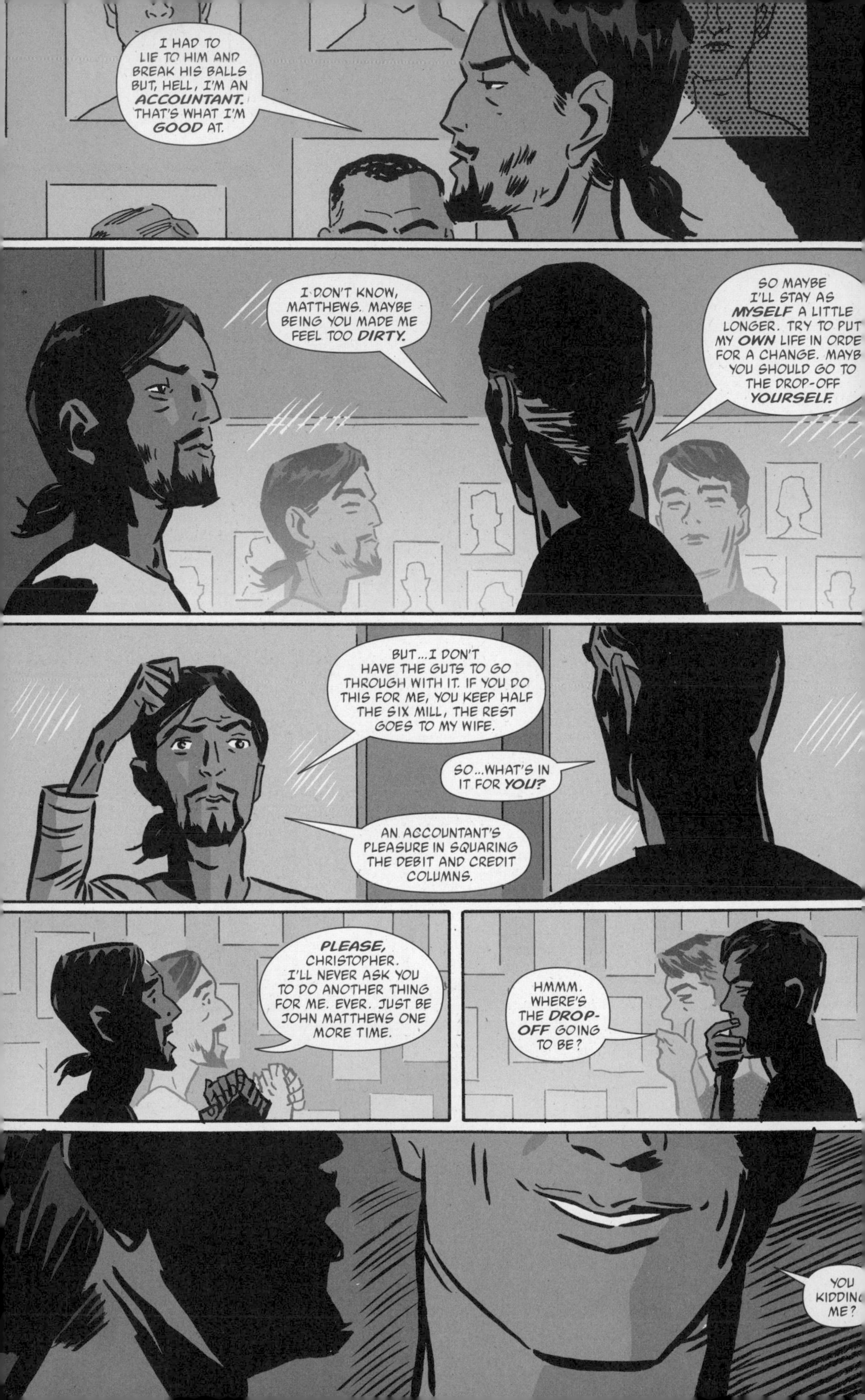
I HAD TO LIE TO HIM AND BREAK HIS BALLS BUT, HELL, I'M AN ACCOUNTANT. THAT'S WHAT I'M GOOD AT.
I DON'T KNOW, MATTHEWS. MAYBE BEING YOU MADE ME FEEL TOO DIRTY.
SO MAYBE I'LL STAY AS MYSELF A LITTLE LONGER. TRY TO PUT MY OWN LIFE IN ORDE FOR A CHANGE. MAYB YOU SHOULD GO TO THE DROP-OFF YOURSELF.
BUT...I DON'T HAVE THE GUTS TO GO THROUGH WITH IT. IF YOU DO THIS FOR ME, YOU KEEP HALF THE SIX MILL, THE REST GOES TO MY WIFE.
SO...WHAT'S IN IT FOR YOU?
AN ACCOUNTANT'S PLEASURE IN SQUARING THE DEBIT AND CREDIT COLUMNS.
PLEASE, CHRISTOPHER. I'LL NEVER ASK YOU TO DO ANOTHER THING FOR ME. EVER. JUST BE JOHN MATTHEWS ONE MORE TIME.
HMMM. WHERE'S THE DROP-OFF GOING TO BE?
YOU KIDDIN ME?

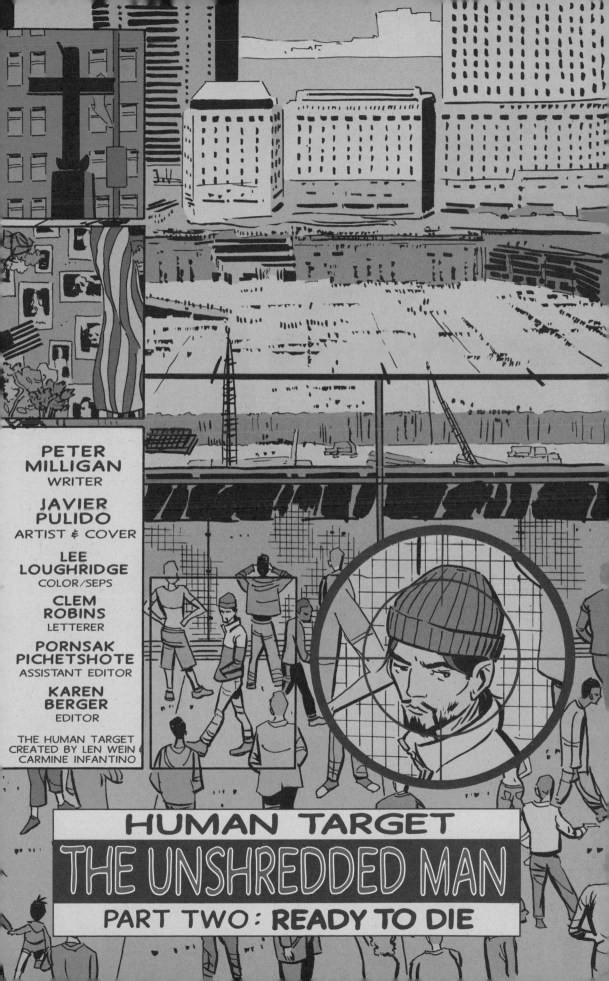

PETER
MILLIGAN
WRITER

JAVIER
PULIDO
ARTIST & COVER

LEE
LOUGHRIDGE
COLOR/SEPS

CLEM
ROBINS
LETTERER

PORNSAK
PICHETSHOTE
ASSISTANT EDITOR

KAREN
BERGER
EDITOR

THE HUMAN TARGET
CREATED BY LEN WEIN &
CARMINE INFANTINO

HUMAN TARGET
THE UNSHREDDED MAN
PART TWO: READY TO DIE

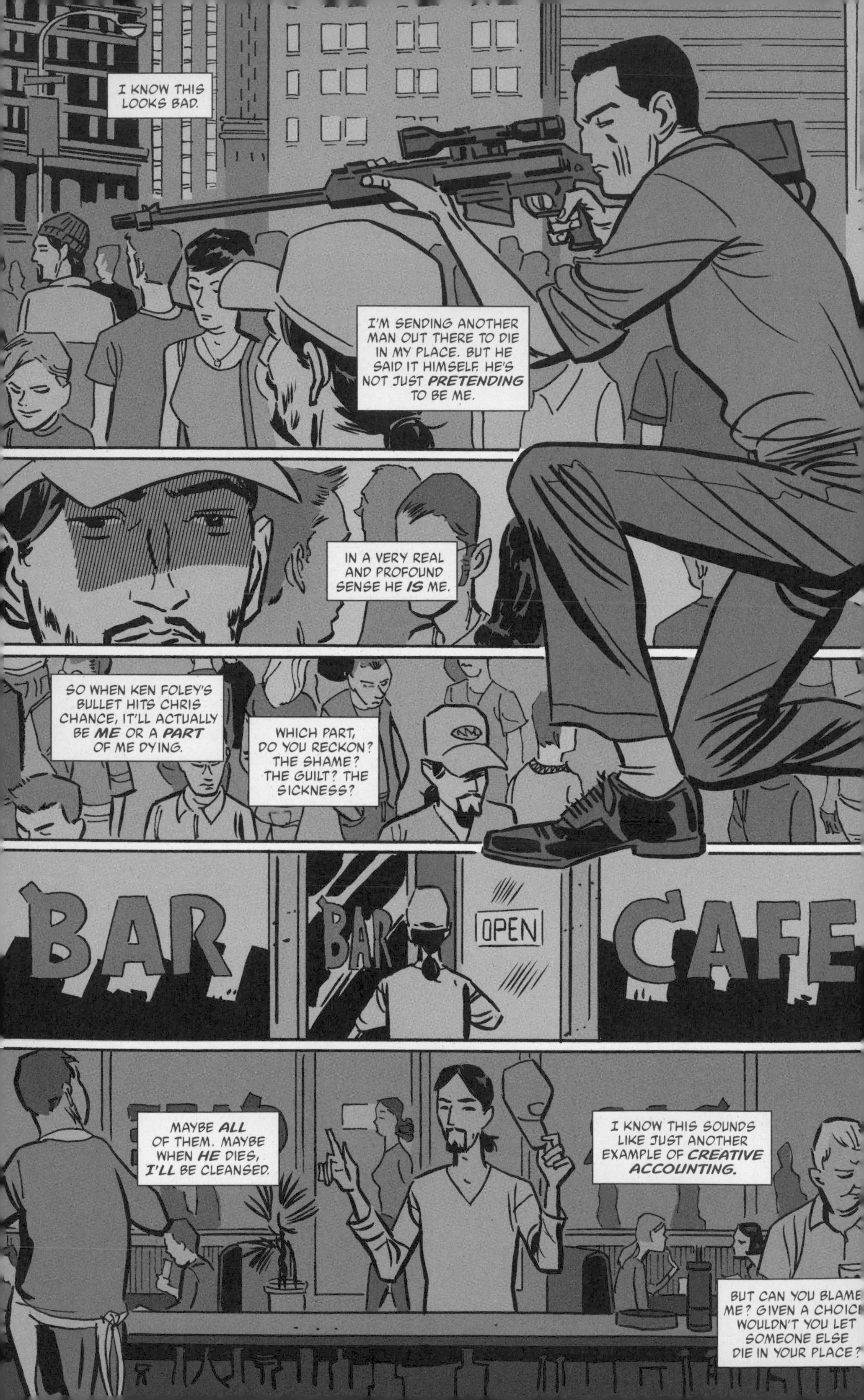
I KNOW THIS LOOKS BAD.
I'M SENDING ANOTHER MAN OUT THERE TO DIE IN MY PLACE. BUT HE SAID IT HIMSELF. HE'S NOT JUST PRETENDING TO BE ME.
IN A VERY REAL AND PROFOUND SENSE HE IS ME.
SO WHEN KEN FOLEY'S BULLET HITS CHRIS CHANCE, IT'LL ACTUALLY BE ME OR A PART OF ME DYING.
WHICH PART, DO YOU RECKON? THE SHAME? THE GUILT? THE SICKNESS?
BAR
BAR
OPEN
CAFE
MAYBE ALL OF THEM. MAYBE WHEN HE DIES, I'LL BE CLEANSED.
I KNOW THIS SOUNDS LIKE JUST ANOTHER EXAMPLE OF CREATIVE ACCOUNTING.
BUT CAN YOU BLAME ME? GIVEN A CHOIC WOULDN'T YOU LET SOMEONE ELSE DIE IN YOUR PLACE?

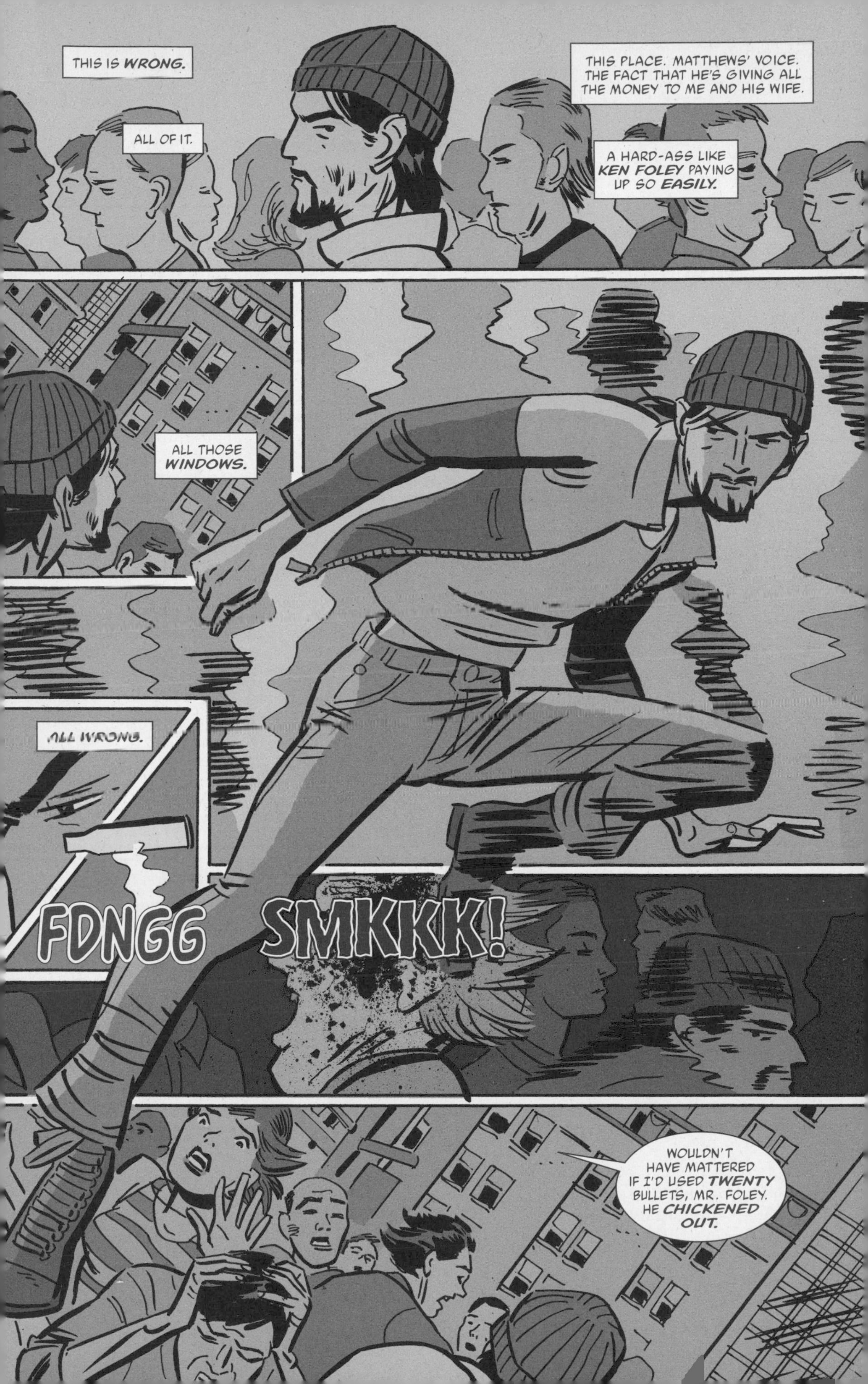
THIS IS WRONG.
ALL OF IT.
THIS PLACE. MATTHEWS' VOICE. THE FACT THAT HE'S GIVING ALL THE MONEY TO ME AND HIS WIFE.
A HARD-ASS LIKE KEN FOLEY PAYING UP SO EASILY.
ALL THOSE WINDOWS.
ALL WRONG.
FDNGG
SMKKK!
WOULDN'T HAVE MATTERED IF I'D USED TWENTY BULLETS, MR. FOLEY. HE CHICKENED OUT.

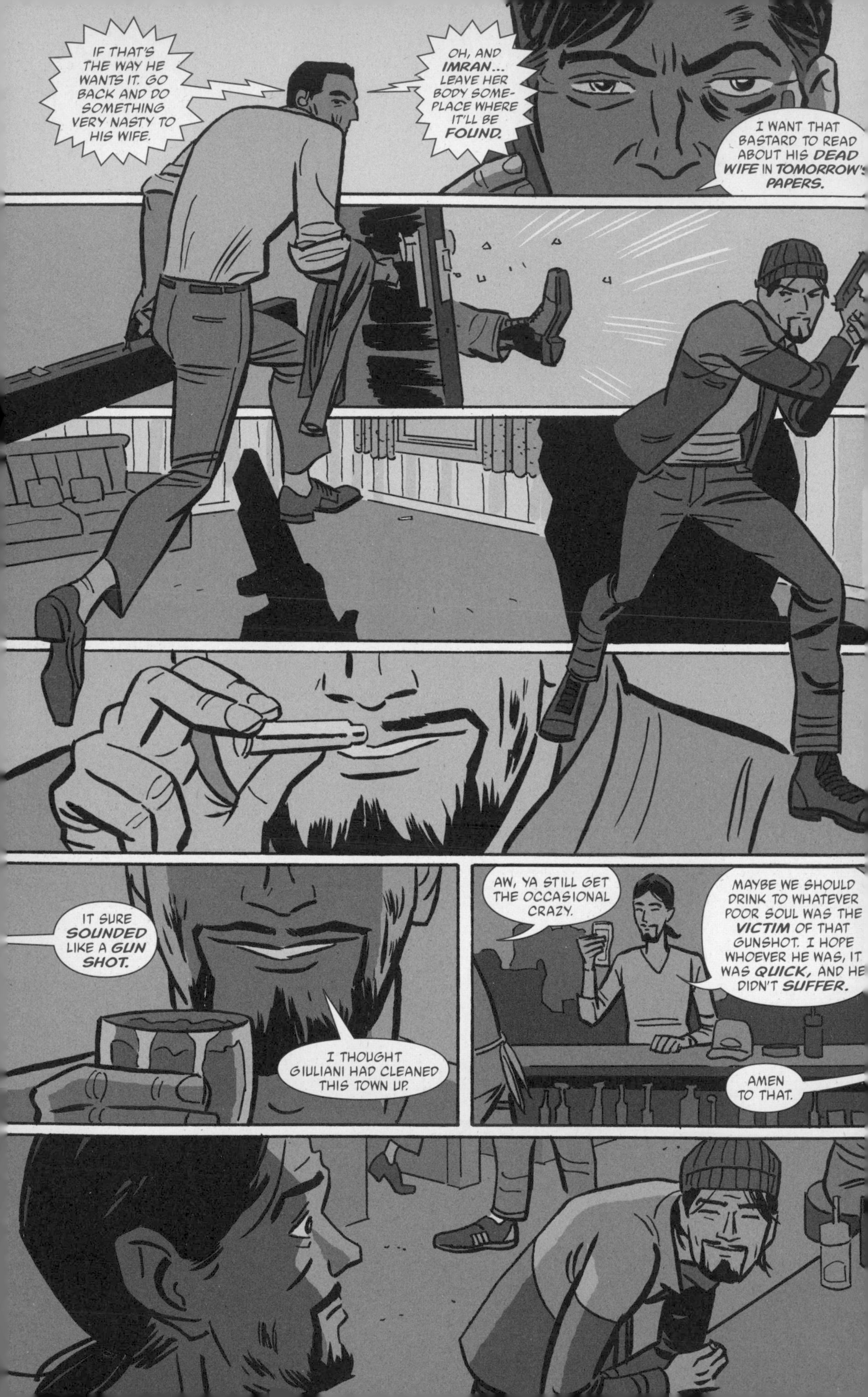
IF THAT'S THE WAY HE WANTS IT. GO BACK AND DO SOMETHING VERY NASTY TO HIS WIFE.
OH, AND IMRAN... LEAVE HER BODY SOMEPLACE WHERE IT'LL BE FOUND.
I WANT THAT BASTARD TO READ ABOUT HIS DEAD WIFE IN TOMORROW'S PAPERS.
IT SURE SOUNDED LIKE A GUN SHOT.
I THOUGHT GIULIANI HAD CLEANED THIS TOWN UP.
AW, YA STILL GET THE OCCASIONAL CRAZY.
MAYBE WE SHOULD DRINK TO WHATEVER POOR SOUL WAS THE VICTIM OF THAT GUNSHOT. I HOPE WHOEVER HE WAS, IT WAS QUICK, AND HE DIDN'T SUFFER.
AMEN TO THAT.

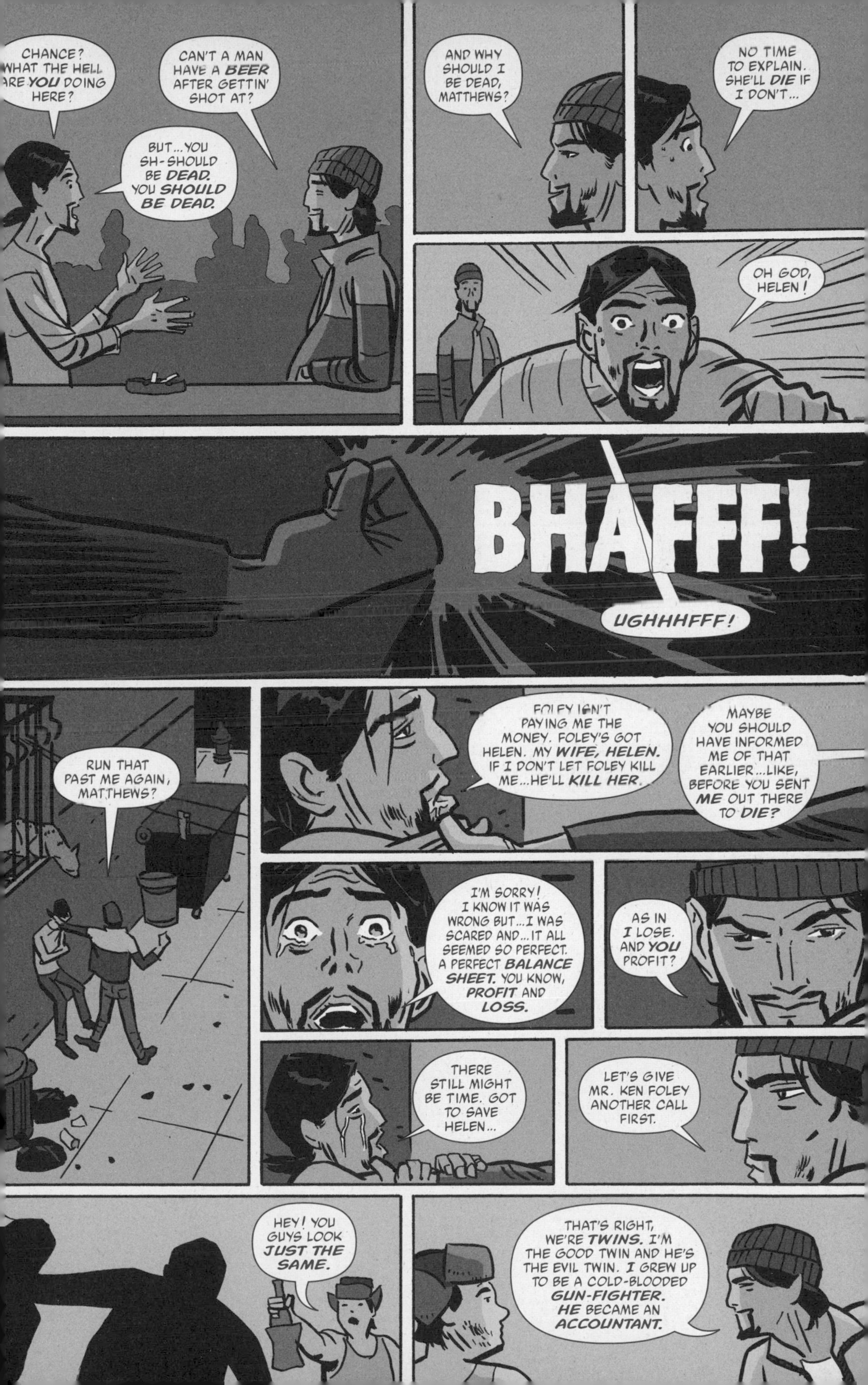
CHANCE? WHAT THE HELL ARE *YOU* DOING HERE?
CAN'T A MAN HAVE A *BEER* AFTER GETTIN' SHOT AT?
BUT...YOU SH-SHOULD BE *DEAD.* YOU *SHOULD BE DEAD.*
AND WHY SHOULD I BE DEAD, MATTHEWS?
NO TIME TO EXPLAIN. SHE'LL *DIE* IF I DON'T...
OH GOD, HELEN!
BHAFFF!
UGHHHFFF!
RUN THAT PAST ME AGAIN, MATTHEWS?
FOLEY ISN'T PAYING ME THE MONEY. FOLEY'S GOT HELEN. MY *WIFE, HELEN.* IF I DON'T LET FOLEY KILL ME...HE'LL *KILL HER.*
MAYBE YOU SHOULD HAVE INFORMED ME OF THAT EARLIER...LIKE, BEFORE YOU SENT *ME* OUT THERE TO *DIE?*
I'M SORRY! I KNOW IT WAS WRONG BUT...I WAS SCARED AND...IT ALL SEEMED SO PERFECT. A PERFECT *BALANCE SHEET.* YOU KNOW, *PROFIT* AND *LOSS.*
AS IN *I* LOSE. AND *YOU* PROFIT?
THERE STILL MIGHT BE TIME. GOT TO SAVE HELEN...
LET'S GIVE MR. KEN FOLEY ANOTHER CALL FIRST.
HEY! YOU GUYS LOOK *JUST THE SAME.*
THAT'S RIGHT, WE'RE *TWINS.* I'M THE GOOD TWIN AND HE'S THE EVIL TWIN. *I* GREW UP TO BE A COLD-BLOODED *GUN-FIGHTER.* *HE* BECAME AN *ACCOUNTANT.*

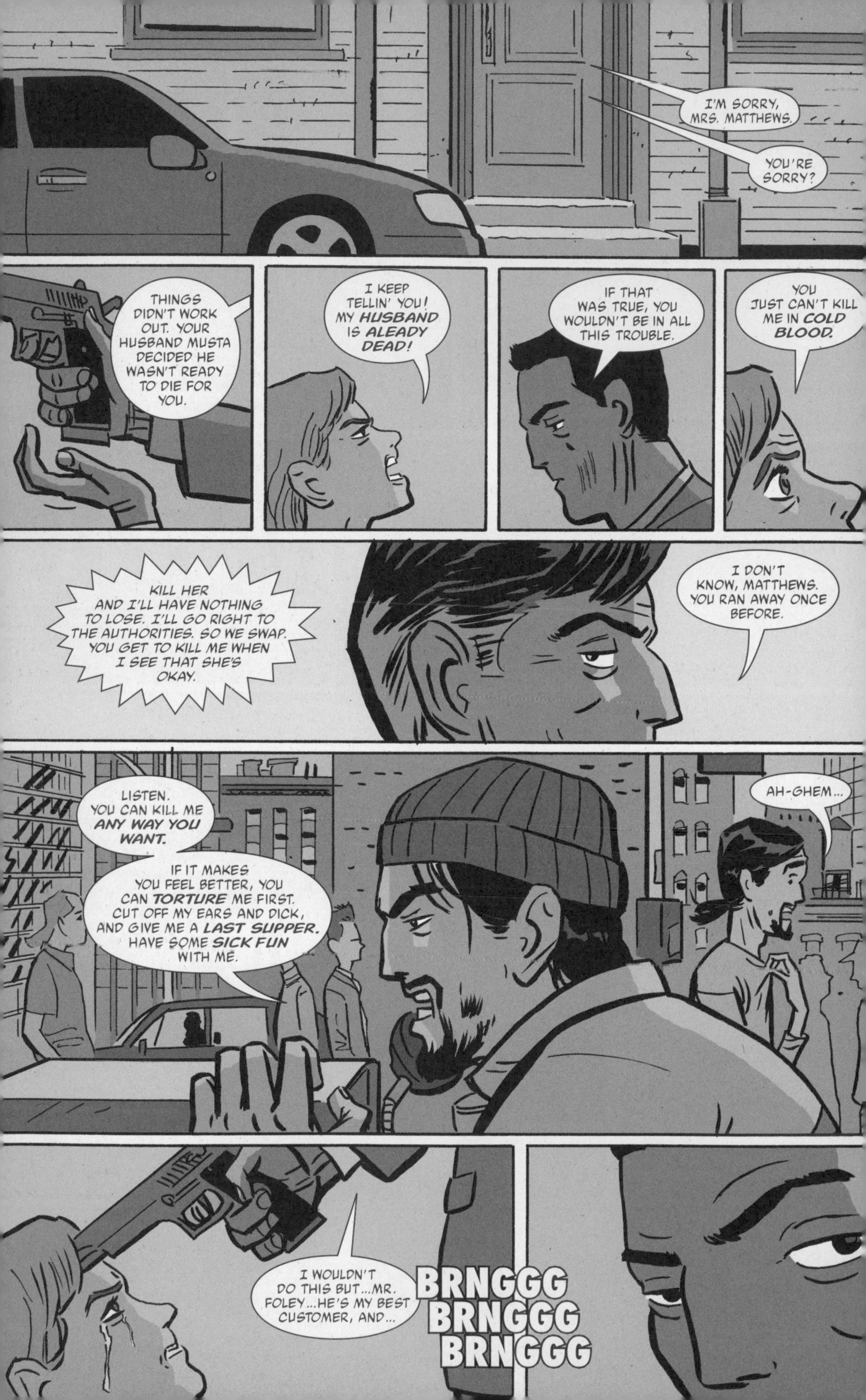
I'M SORRY, MRS. MATTHEWS.
YOU'RE SORRY?
THINGS DIDN'T WORK OUT. YOUR HUSBAND MUSTA DECIDED HE WASN'T READY TO DIE FOR YOU.
I KEEP TELLIN' YOU! MY HUSBAND IS ALEADY DEAD!
IF THAT WAS TRUE, YOU WOULDN'T BE IN ALL THIS TROUBLE.
YOU JUST CAN'T KILL ME IN COLD BLOOD.
KILL HER AND I'LL HAVE NOTHING TO LOSE. I'LL GO RIGHT TO THE AUTHORITIES. SO WE SWAP. YOU GET TO KILL ME WHEN I SEE THAT SHE'S OKAY.
I DON'T KNOW, MATTHEWS. YOU RAN AWAY ONCE BEFORE.
LISTEN. YOU CAN KILL ME ANY WAY YOU WANT.
IF IT MAKES YOU FEEL BETTER, YOU CAN TORTURE ME FIRST. CUT OFF MY EARS AND DICK, AND GIVE ME A LAST SUPPER. HAVE SOME SICK FUN WITH ME.
AH-GHEM...
I WOULDN'T DO THIS BUT...MR. FOLEY...HE'S MY BEST CUSTOMER, AND...
BRNGGG
BRNGGG
BRNGGG

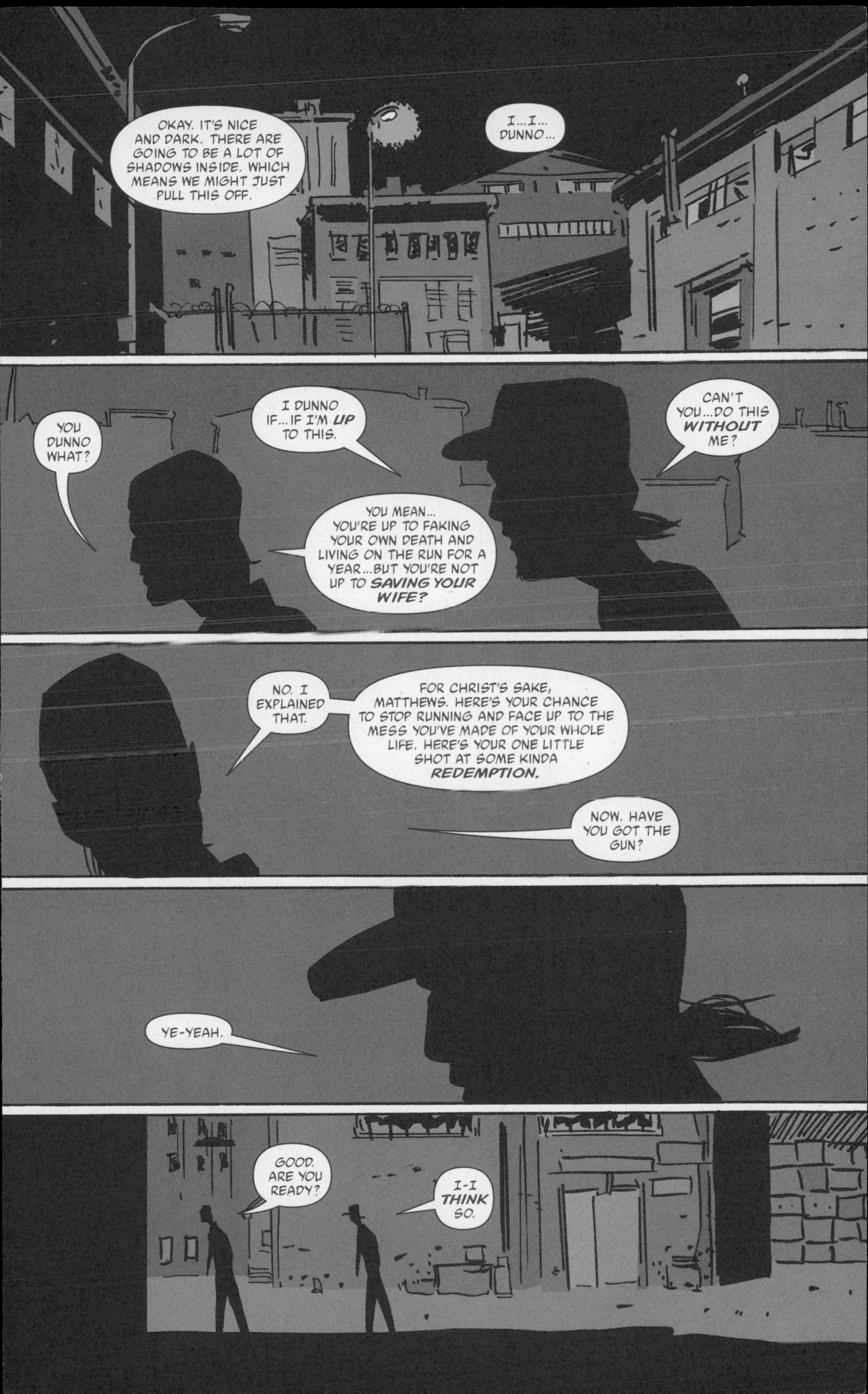
OKAY. IT'S NICE AND DARK. THERE ARE GOING TO BE A LOT OF SHADOWS INSIDE. WHICH MEANS WE MIGHT JUST PULL THIS OFF.
I...I... DUNNO...
YOU DUNNO WHAT?
I DUNNO IF...IF I'M UP TO THIS.
CAN'T YOU...DO THIS WITHOUT ME?
YOU MEAN... YOU'RE UP TO FAKING YOUR OWN DEATH AND LIVING ON THE RUN FOR A YEAR...BUT YOU'RE NOT UP TO SAVING YOUR WIFE?
NO. I EXPLAINED THAT.
FOR CHRIST'S SAKE, MATTHEWS. HERE'S YOUR CHANCE TO STOP RUNNING AND FACE UP TO THE MESS YOU'VE MADE OF YOUR WHOLE LIFE. HERE'S YOUR ONE LITTLE SHOT AT SOME KINDA REDEMPTION.
NOW. HAVE YOU GOT THE GUN?
YE-YEAH.
GOOD. ARE YOU READY?
I-I THINK SO.

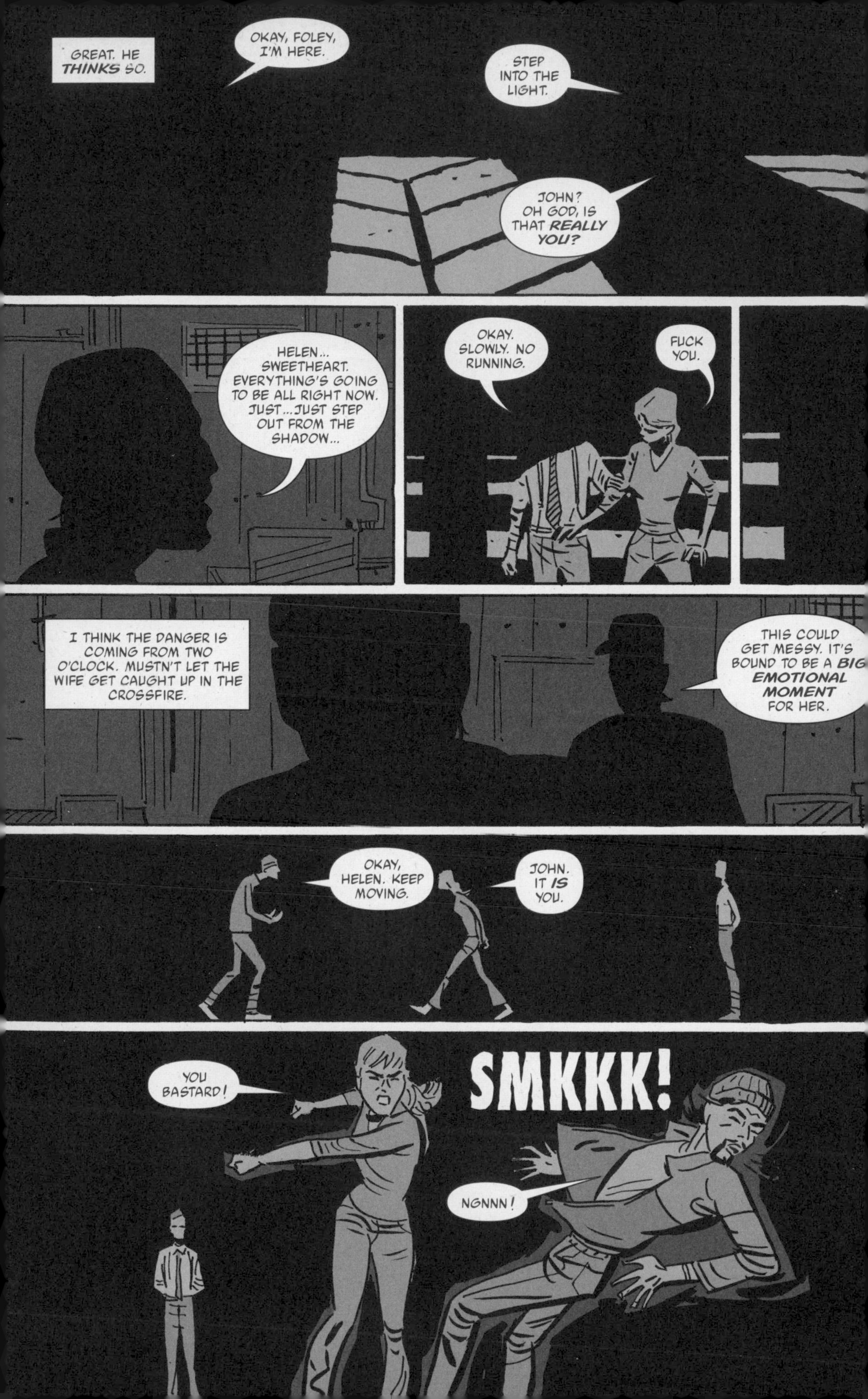
GREAT. HE THINKS SO.
OKAY, FOLEY, I'M HERE.
STEP INTO THE LIGHT.
JOHN? OH GOD, IS THAT REALLY YOU?
HELEN... SWEETHEART. EVERYTHING'S GOING TO BE ALL RIGHT NOW. JUST...JUST STEP OUT FROM THE SHADOW...
OKAY. SLOWLY. NO RUNNING.
FUCK YOU.
I THINK THE DANGER IS COMING FROM TWO O'CLOCK. MUSTN'T LET THE WIFE GET CAUGHT UP IN THE CROSSFIRE.
THIS COULD GET MESSY. IT'S BOUND TO BE A BIG EMOTIONAL MOMENT FOR HER.
OKAY, HELEN. KEEP MOVING.
JOHN. IT IS YOU.
YOU BASTARD!
SMKKK!
NGNNN!

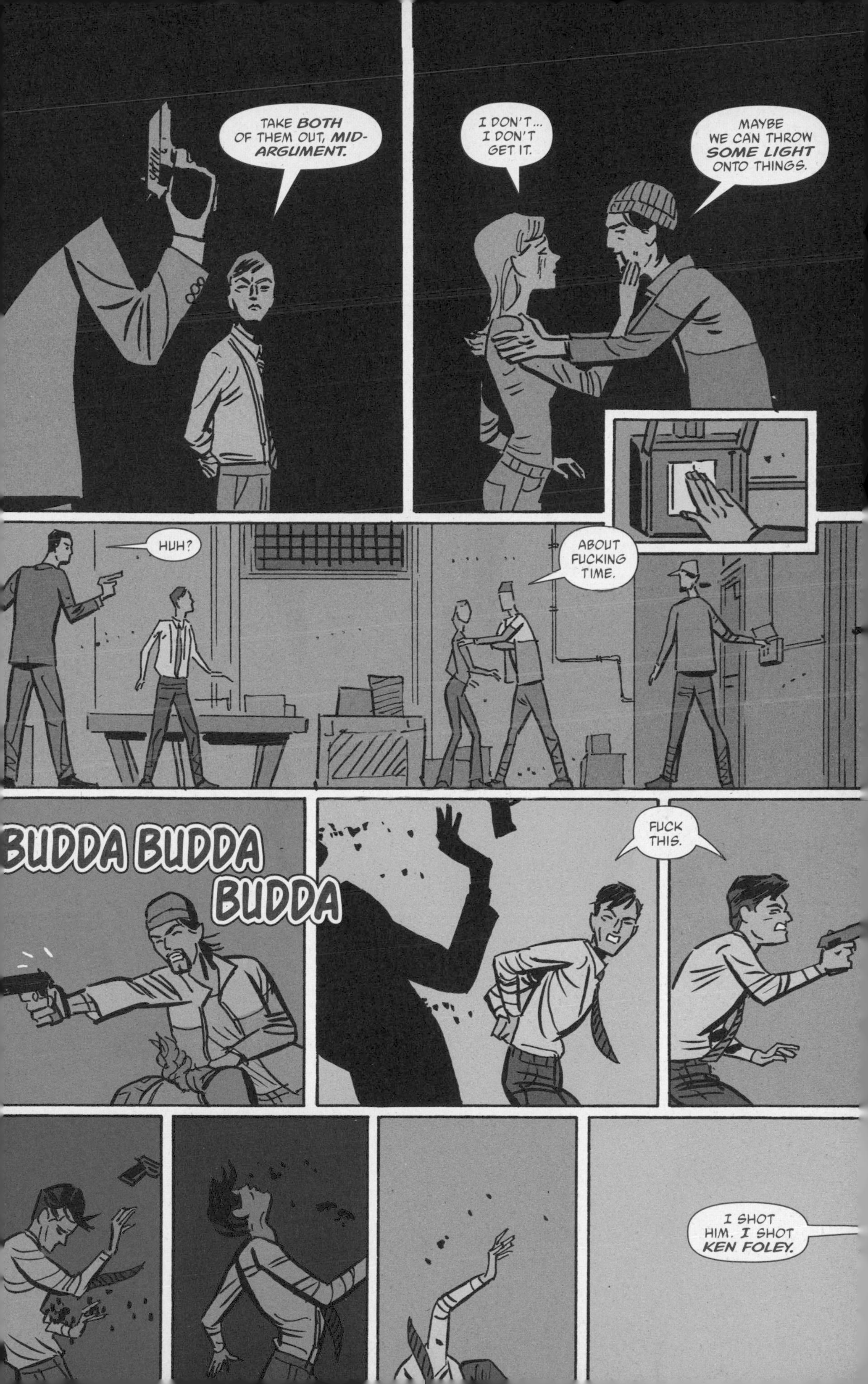

TAKE BOTH OF THEM OUT, MID-ARGUMENT.
I DON'T... I DON'T GET IT.
MAYBE WE CAN THROW SOME LIGHT ONTO THINGS.
HUH?
ABOUT FUCKING TIME.
BUDDA BUDDA BUDDA
FUCK THIS.
I SHOT HIM. I SHOT KEN FOLEY.

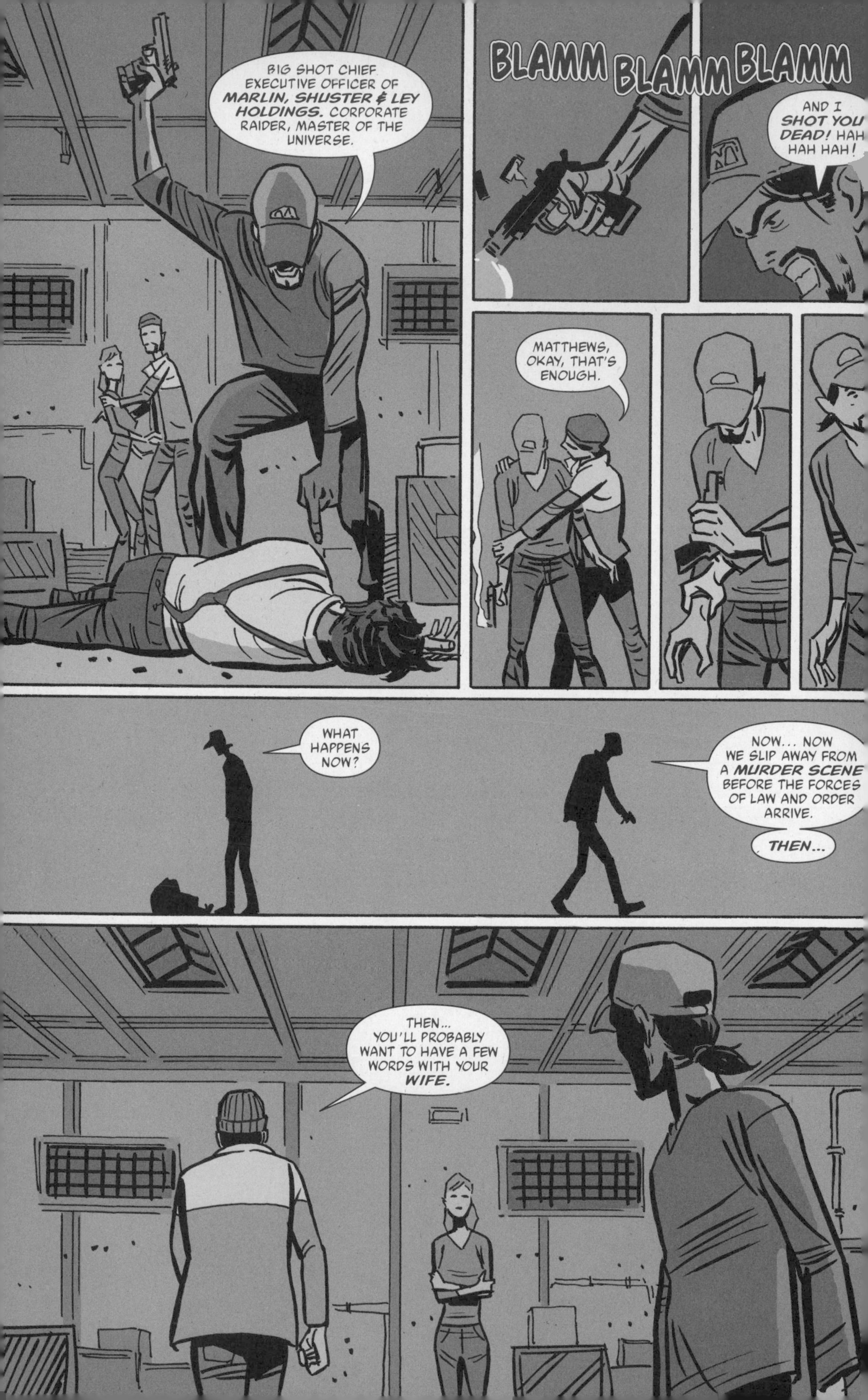

BIG SHOT CHIEF EXECUTIVE OFFICER OF MARLIN, SHUSTER & LEY HOLDINGS. CORPORATE RAIDER, MASTER OF THE UNIVERSE.
BLAMM BLAMM BLAMM
AND I SHOT YOU DEAD! HAH HAH HAH!
MATTHEWS, OKAY, THAT'S ENOUGH.
WHAT HAPPENS NOW?
NOW... NOW WE SLIP AWAY FROM A MURDER SCENE BEFORE THE FORCES OF LAW AND ORDER ARRIVE.
THEN...
THEN... YOU'LL PROBABLY WANT TO HAVE A FEW WORDS WITH YOUR WIFE.

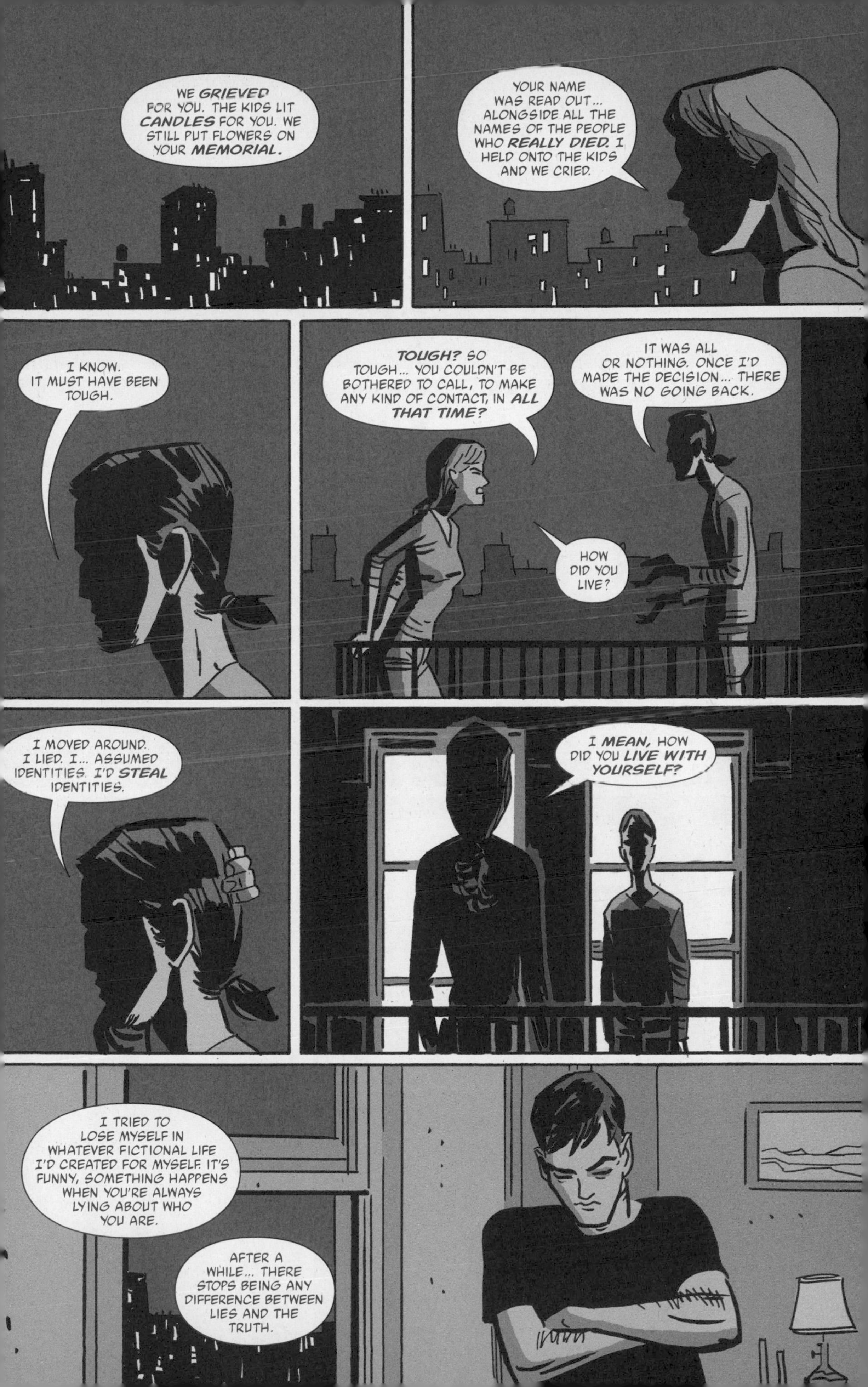
WE GRIEVED FOR YOU. THE KIDS LIT CANDLES FOR YOU. WE STILL PUT FLOWERS ON YOUR MEMORIAL.
YOUR NAME WAS READ OUT... ALONGSIDE ALL THE NAMES OF THE PEOPLE WHO REALLY DIED. I HELD ONTO THE KIDS AND WE CRIED.
I KNOW. IT MUST HAVE BEEN TOUGH.
TOUGH? SO TOUGH... YOU COULDN'T BE BOTHERED TO CALL, TO MAKE ANY KIND OF CONTACT, IN ALL THAT TIME?
IT WAS ALL OR NOTHING. ONCE I'D MADE THE DECISION... THERE WAS NO GOING BACK.
HOW DID YOU LIVE?
I MOVED AROUND. I LIED. I... ASSUMED IDENTITIES. I'D STEAL IDENTITIES.
I MEAN, HOW DID YOU LIVE WITH YOURSELF?
I TRIED TO LOSE MYSELF IN WHATEVER FICTIONAL LIFE I'D CREATED FOR MYSELF. IT'S FUNNY, SOMETHING HAPPENS WHEN YOU'RE ALWAYS LYING ABOUT WHO YOU ARE.
AFTER A WHILE... THERE STOPS BEING ANY DIFFERENCE BETWEEN LIES AND THE TRUTH.

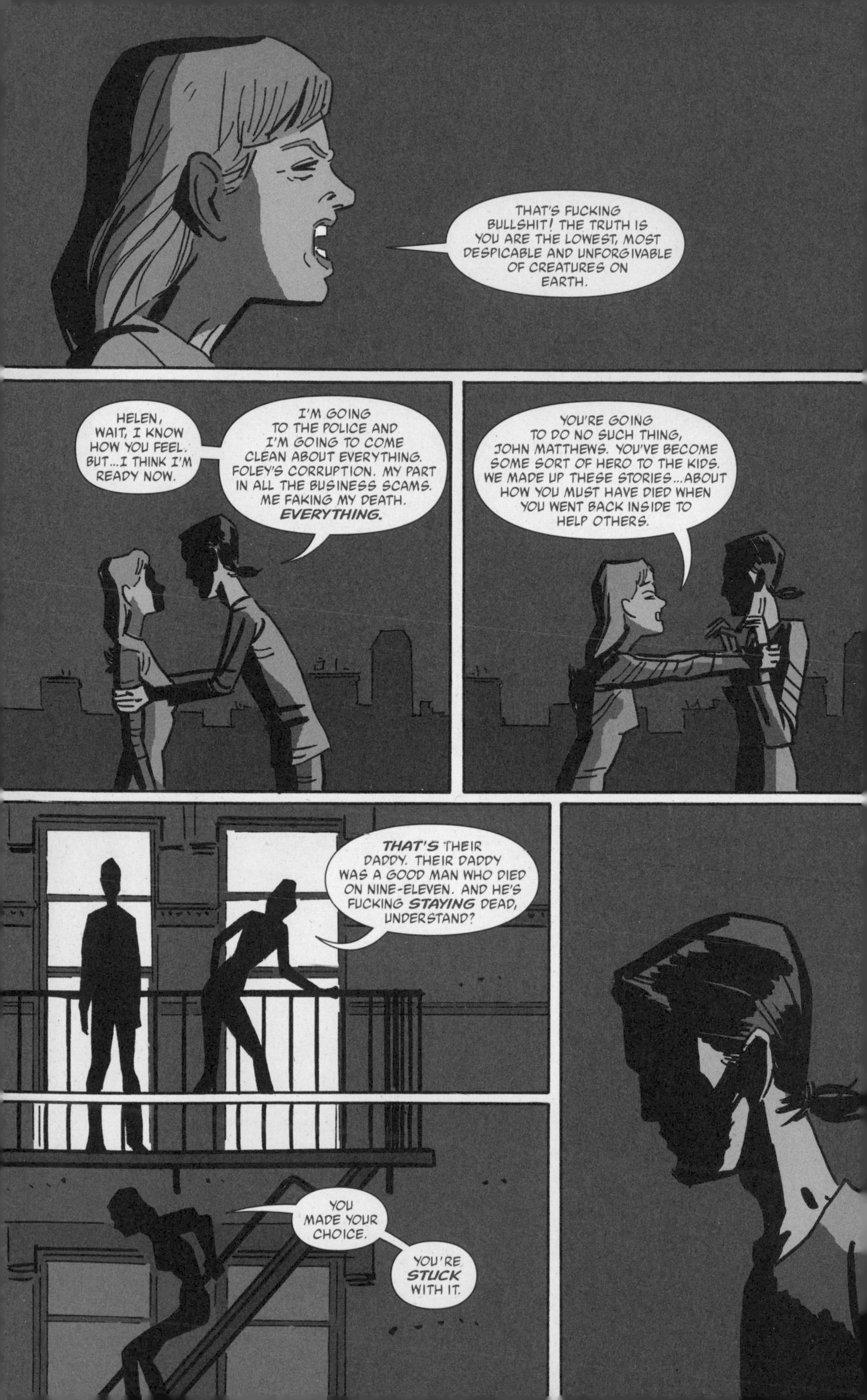
THAT'S FUCKING BULLSHIT! THE TRUTH IS YOU ARE THE LOWEST, MOST DESPICABLE AND UNFORGIVABLE OF CREATURES ON EARTH.
HELEN, WAIT, I KNOW HOW YOU FEEL. BUT...I THINK I'M READY NOW.
I'M GOING TO THE POLICE AND I'M GOING TO COME CLEAN ABOUT EVERYTHING. FOLEY'S CORRUPTION. MY PART IN ALL THE BUSINESS SCAMS. ME FAKING MY DEATH. EVERYTHING.
YOU'RE GOING TO DO NO SUCH THING, JOHN MATTHEWS. YOU'VE BECOME SOME SORT OF HERO TO THE KIDS. WE MADE UP THESE STORIES...ABOUT HOW YOU MUST HAVE DIED WHEN YOU WENT BACK INSIDE TO HELP OTHERS.
THAT'S THEIR DADDY. THEIR DADDY WAS A GOOD MAN WHO DIED ON NINE-ELEVEN. AND HE'S FUCKING STAYING DEAD, UNDERSTAND?
YOU MADE YOUR CHOICE.
YOU'RE STUCK WITH IT.

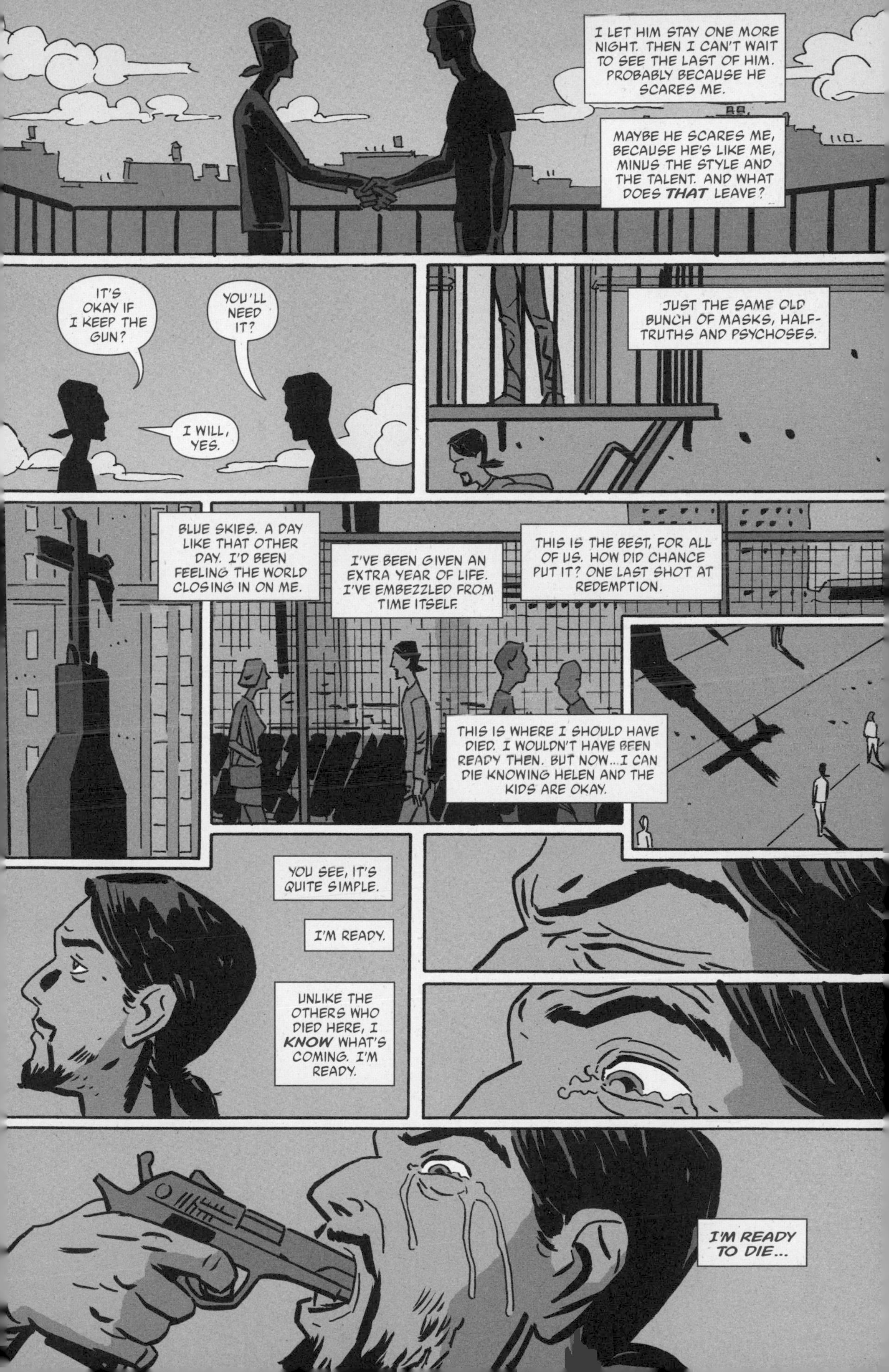
I LET HIM STAY ONE MORE NIGHT. THEN I CAN'T WAIT TO SEE THE LAST OF HIM. PROBABLY BECAUSE HE SCARES ME.
MAYBE HE SCARES ME, BECAUSE HE'S LIKE ME, MINUS THE STYLE AND THE TALENT. AND WHAT DOES **THAT** LEAVE?
IT'S OKAY IF I KEEP THE GUN?
YOU'LL NEED IT?
I WILL, YES.
JUST THE SAME OLD BUNCH OF MASKS, HALF-TRUTHS AND PSYCHOSES.
BLUE SKIES. A DAY LIKE THAT OTHER DAY. I'D BEEN FEELING THE WORLD CLOSING IN ON ME.
I'VE BEEN GIVEN AN EXTRA YEAR OF LIFE. I'VE EMBEZZLED FROM TIME ITSELF.
THIS IS THE BEST, FOR ALL OF US. HOW DID CHANCE PUT IT? ONE LAST SHOT AT REDEMPTION.
THIS IS WHERE I SHOULD HAVE DIED. I WOULDN'T HAVE BEEN READY THEN. BUT NOW...I CAN DIE KNOWING HELEN AND THE KIDS ARE OKAY.
YOU SEE, IT'S QUITE SIMPLE.
I'M READY.
UNLIKE THE OTHERS WHO DIED HERE, I **KNOW** WHAT'S COMING. I'M READY.
I'M READY TO DIE...

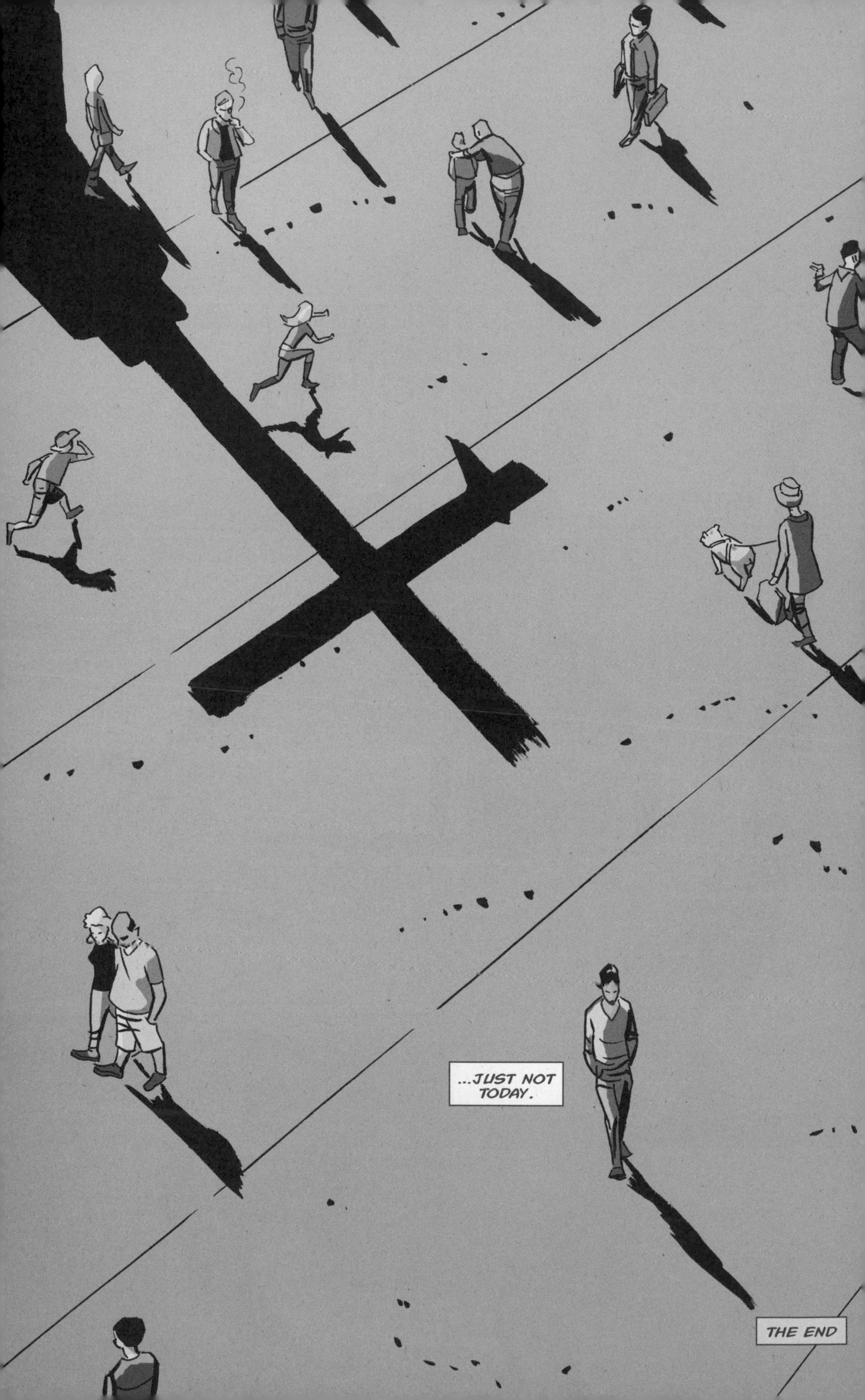
...JUST NOT TODAY.
THE END

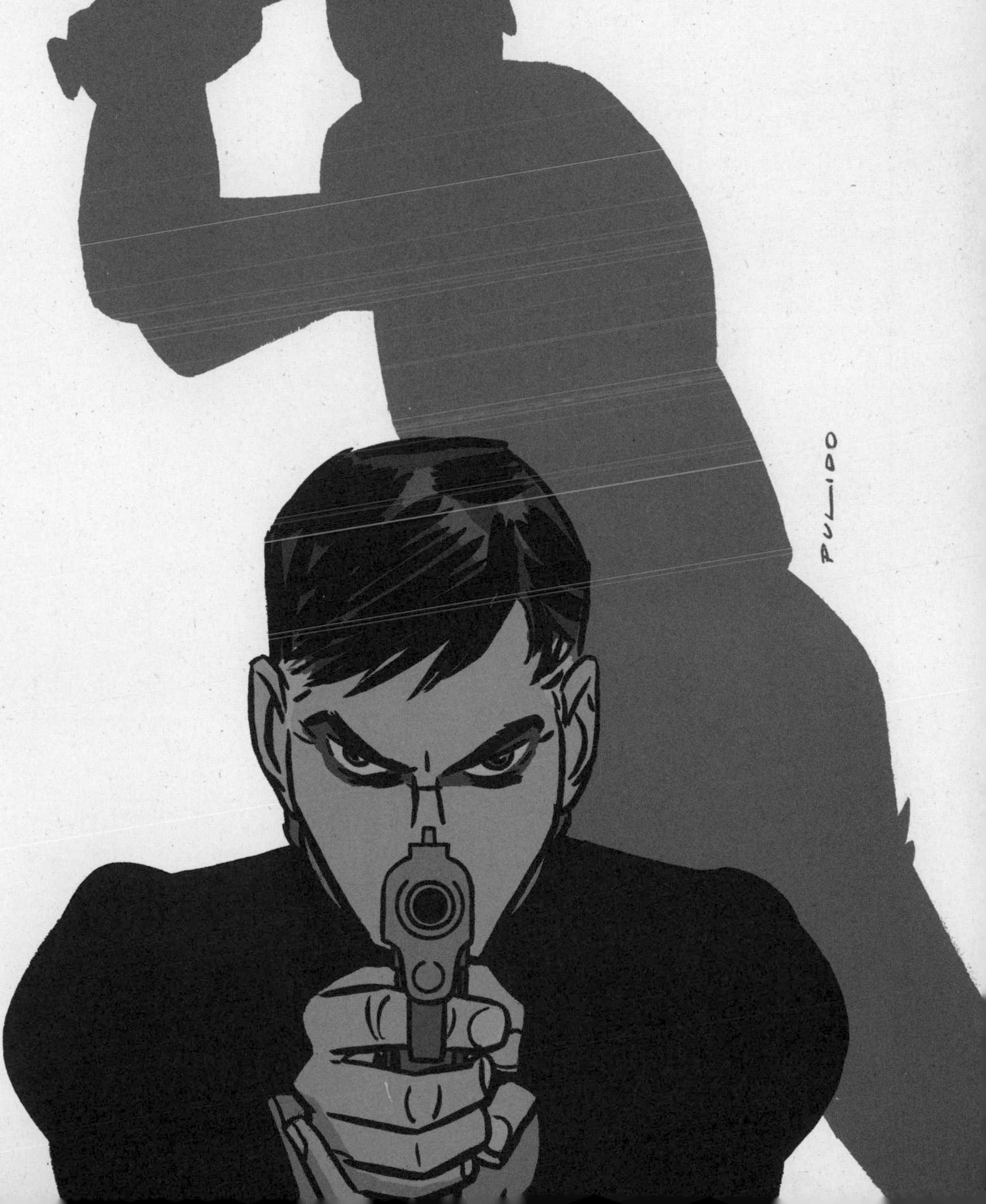
PULIDO

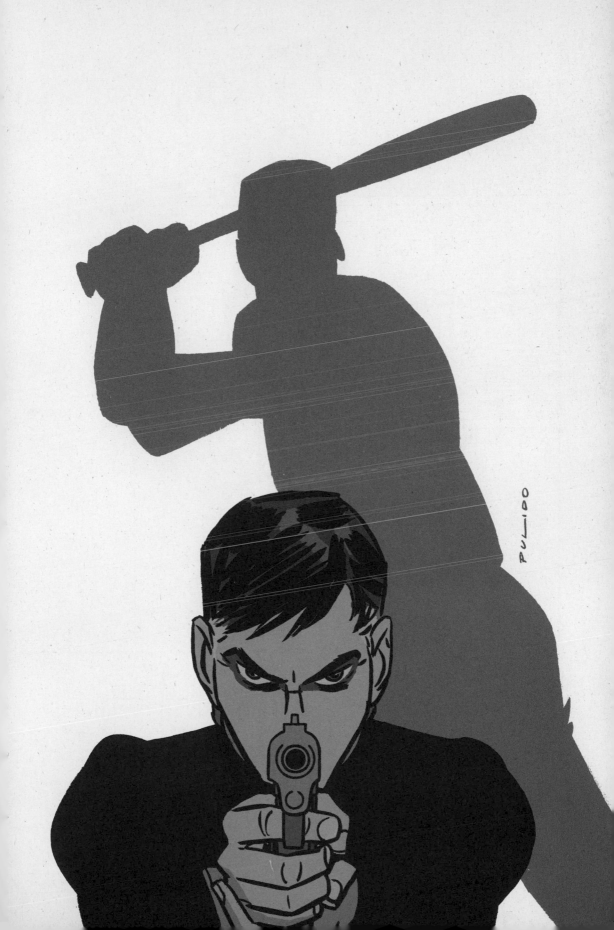

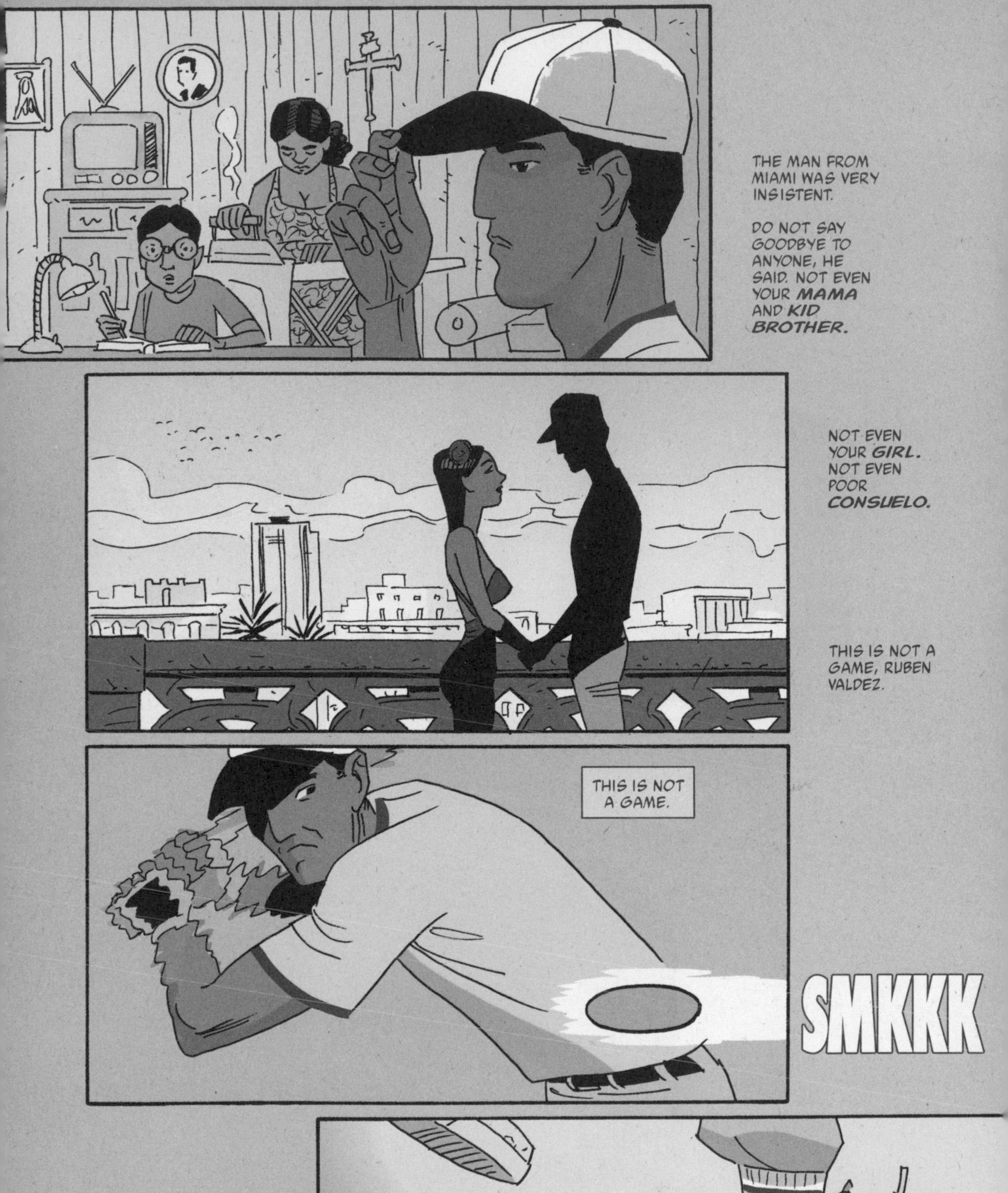
THE MAN FROM MIAMI WAS VERY INSISTENT.
DO NOT SAY GOODBYE TO ANYONE, HE SAID. NOT EVEN YOUR MAMA AND KID BROTHER.
NOT EVEN YOUR GIRL. NOT EVEN POOR CONSUELO.
THIS IS NOT A GAME, RUBEN VALDEZ.
THIS IS NOT A GAME.
SMKKK
TONIGHT YOU BEGIN THE LONG JOURNEY.
TONIGHT YOU RUN.

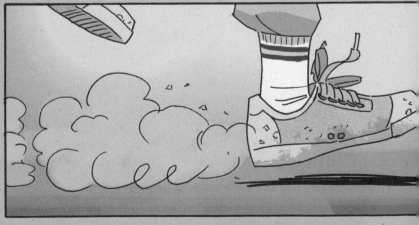

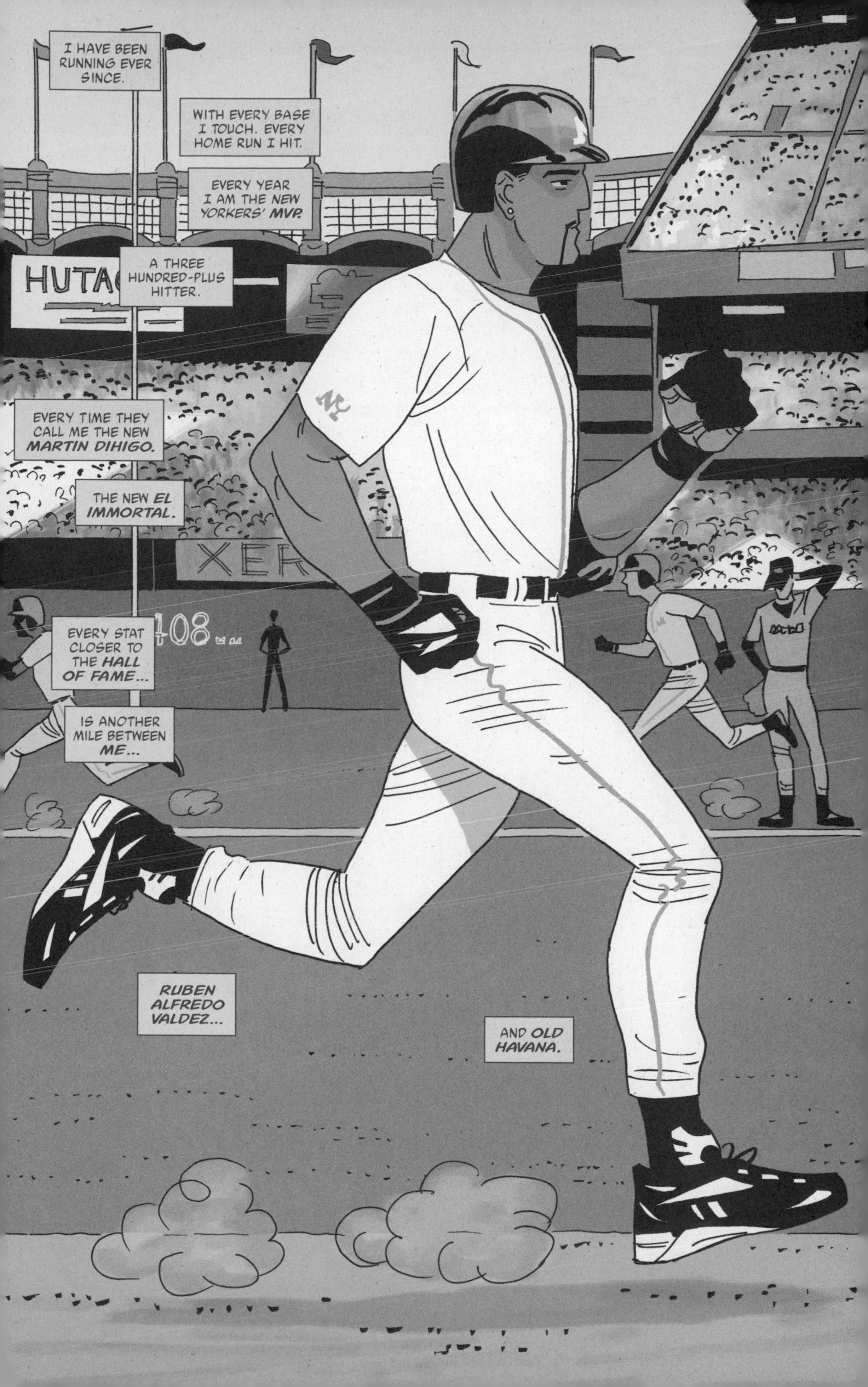
I HAVE BEEN RUNNING EVER SINCE.
WITH EVERY BASE I TOUCH. EVERY HOME RUN I HIT.
EVERY YEAR I AM THE NEW YORKERS' MVP.
A THREE HUNDRED-PLUS HITTER.
EVERY TIME THEY CALL ME THE NEW MARTIN DIHIGO.
THE NEW EL IMMORTAL.
EVERY STAT CLOSER TO THE HALL OF FAME...
IS ANOTHER MILE BETWEEN ME...
RUBEN ALFREDO VALDEZ...
AND OLD HAVANA.

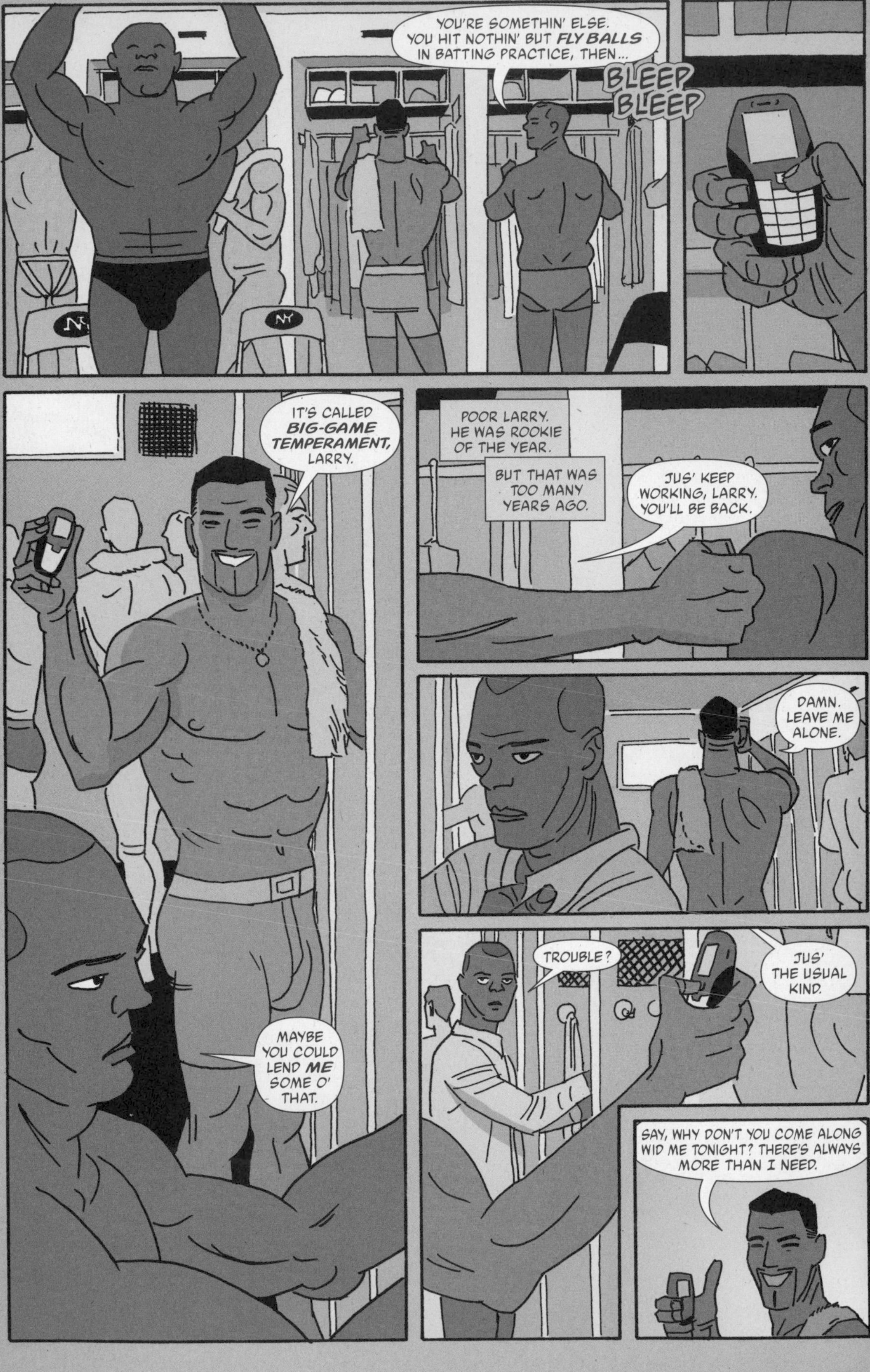

YOU'RE SOMETHIN' ELSE. YOU HIT NOTHIN' BUT FLY BALLS IN BATTING PRACTICE, THEN...
BLEEP BLEEP
IT'S CALLED BIG-GAME TEMPERAMENT, LARRY.
MAYBE YOU COULD LEND ME SOME O' THAT.
POOR LARRY. HE WAS ROOKIE OF THE YEAR.
BUT THAT WAS TOO MANY YEARS AGO.
JUS' KEEP WORKING, LARRY. YOU'LL BE BACK.
DAMN. LEAVE ME ALONE.
TROUBLE?
JUS' THE USUAL KIND.
SAY, WHY DON'T YOU COME ALONG WID ME TONIGHT? THERE'S ALWAYS MORE THAN I NEED.

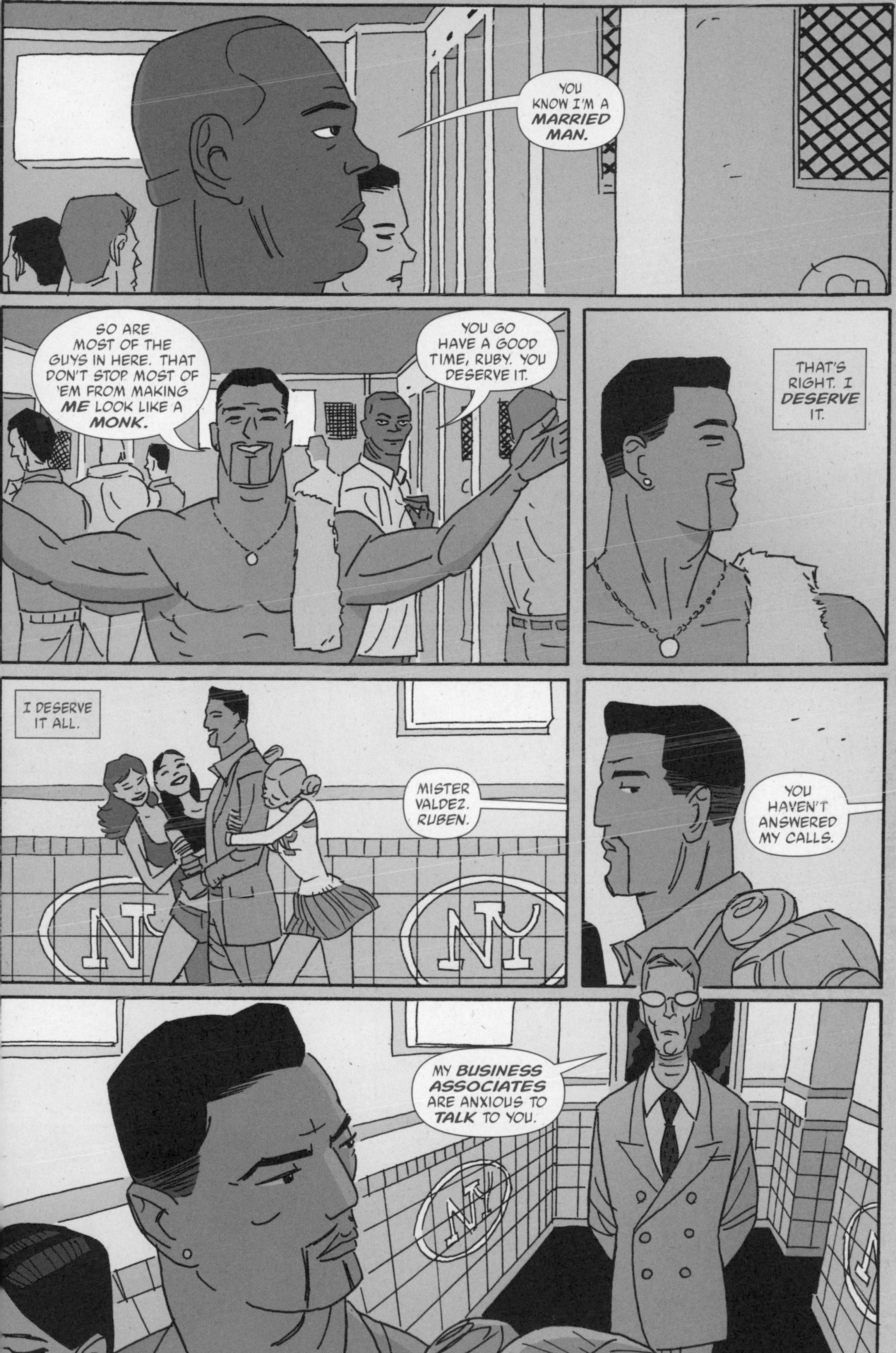
YOU KNOW I'M A MARRIED MAN.
SO ARE MOST OF THE GUYS IN HERE. THAT DON'T STOP MOST OF 'EM FROM MAKING ME LOOK LIKE A MONK.
YOU GO HAVE A GOOD TIME, RUBY. YOU DESERVE IT.
THAT'S RIGHT. I DESERVE IT.
I DESERVE IT ALL.
MISTER VALDEZ. RUBEN.
YOU HAVEN'T ANSWERED MY CALLS.
MY BUSINESS ASSOCIATES ARE ANXIOUS TO TALK TO YOU.

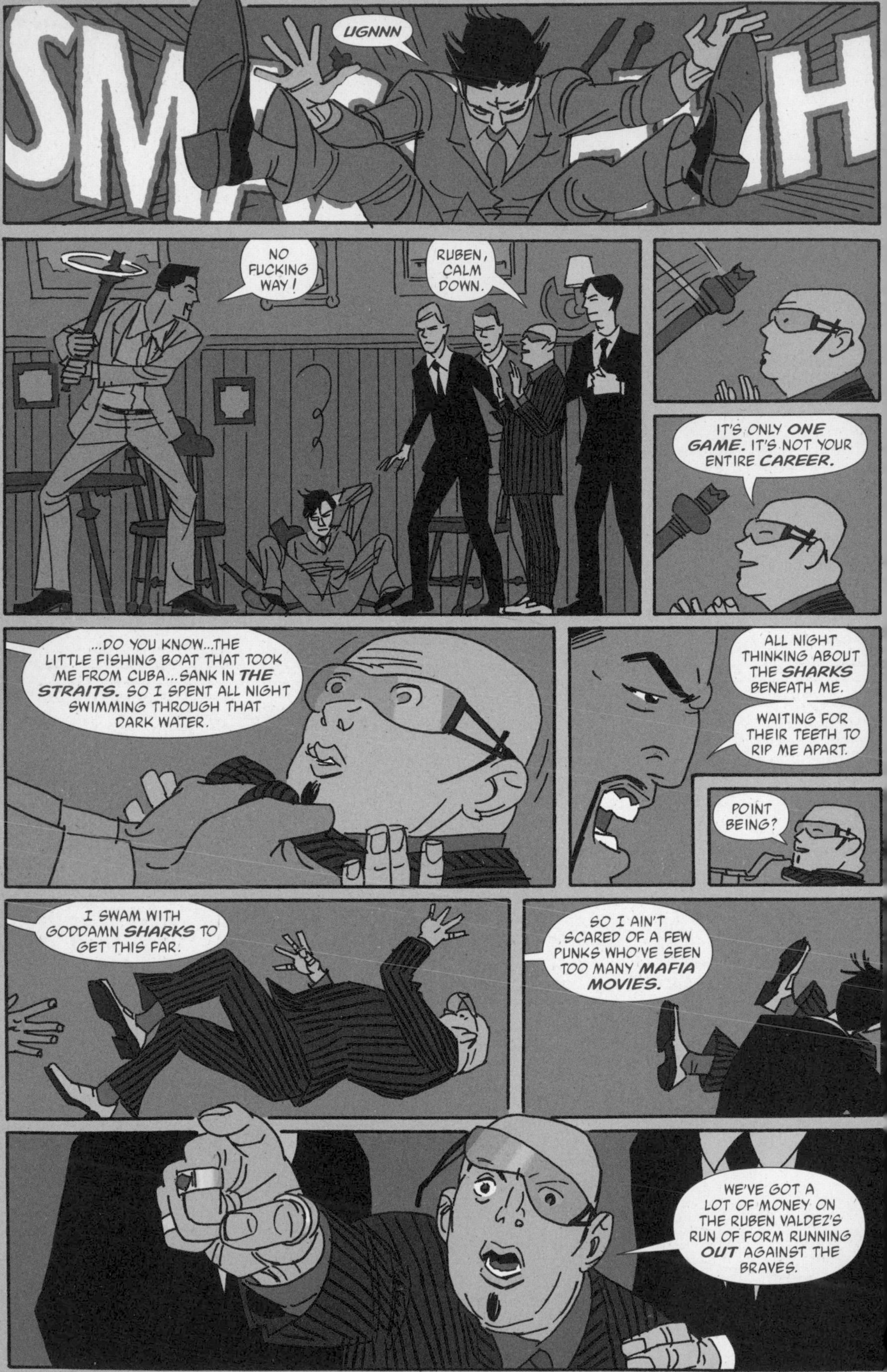
SMASH
UGNNN
NO FUCKING WAY!
RUBEN, CALM DOWN.
IT'S ONLY ONE GAME. IT'S NOT YOUR ENTIRE CAREER.
...DO YOU KNOW...THE LITTLE FISHING BOAT THAT TOOK ME FROM CUBA...SANK IN THE STRAITS. SO I SPENT ALL NIGHT SWIMMING THROUGH THAT DARK WATER.
ALL NIGHT THINKING ABOUT THE SHARKS BENEATH ME.
WAITING FOR THEIR TEETH TO RIP ME APART.
POINT BEING?
I SWAM WITH GODDAMN SHARKS TO GET THIS FAR.
SO I AIN'T SCARED OF A FEW PUNKS WHO'VE SEEN TOO MANY MAFIA MOVIES.
WE'VE GOT A LOT OF MONEY ON THE RUBEN VALDEZ'S RUN OF FORM RUNNING OUT AGAINST THE BRAVES.

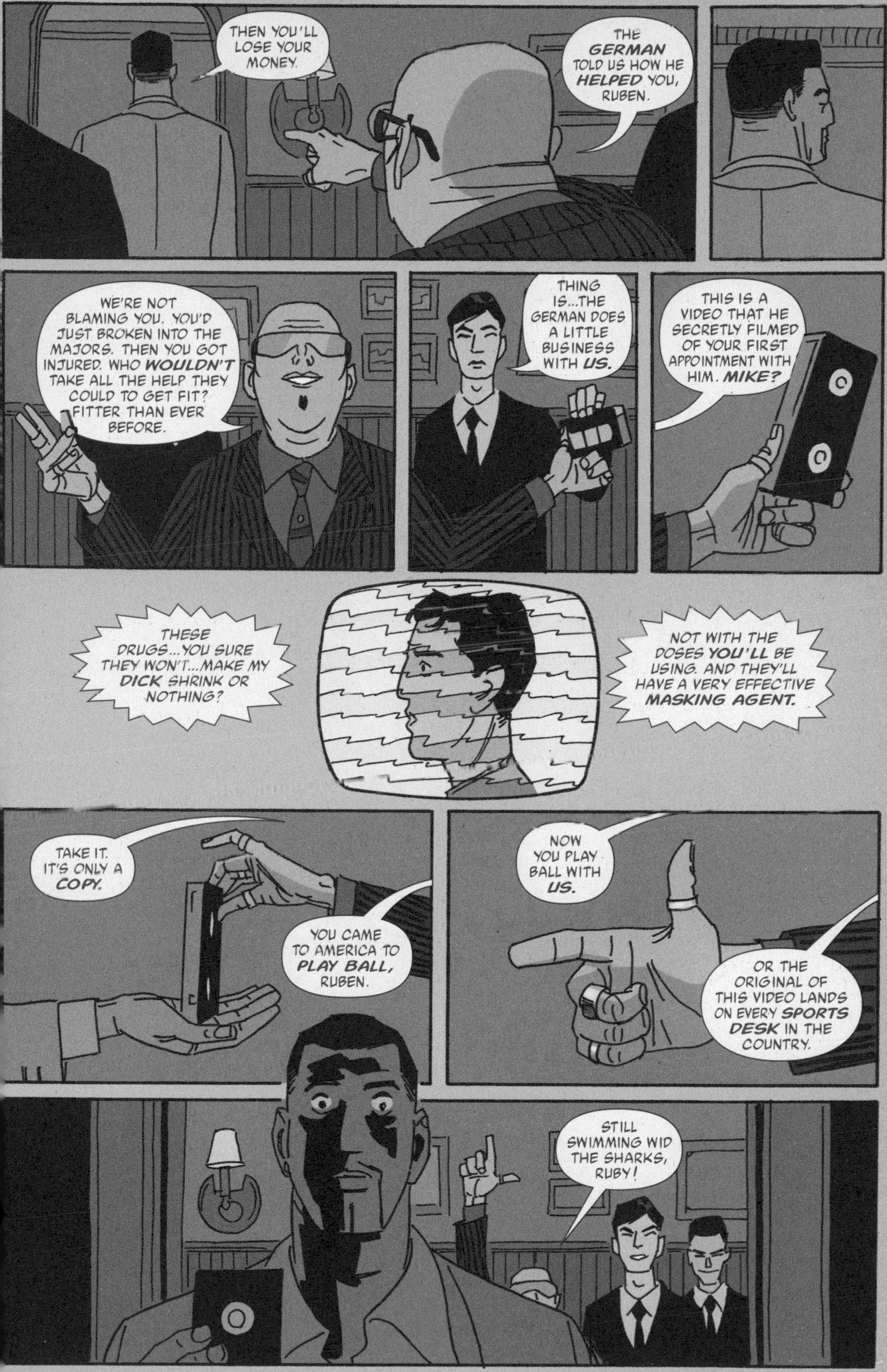
THEN YOU'LL LOSE YOUR MONEY.
THE GERMAN TOLD US HOW HE HELPED YOU, RUBEN.
WE'RE NOT BLAMING YOU. YOU'D JUST BROKEN INTO THE MAJORS. THEN YOU GOT INJURED. WHO WOULDN'T TAKE ALL THE HELP THEY COULD TO GET FIT? FITTER THAN EVER BEFORE.
THING IS...THE GERMAN DOES A LITTLE BUSINESS WITH US.
THIS IS A VIDEO THAT HE SECRETLY FILMED OF YOUR FIRST APPOINTMENT WITH HIM. MIKE?
THESE DRUGS...YOU SURE THEY WON'T...MAKE MY DICK SHRINK OR NOTHING?
NOT WITH THE DOSES YOU'LL BE USING. AND THEY'LL HAVE A VERY EFFECTIVE MASKING AGENT.
TAKE IT. IT'S ONLY A COPY.
YOU CAME TO AMERICA TO PLAY BALL, RUBEN.
NOW YOU PLAY BALL WITH US.
OR THE ORIGINAL OF THIS VIDEO LANDS ON EVERY SPORTS DESK IN THE COUNTRY.
STILL SWIMMING WID THE SHARKS, RUBY!

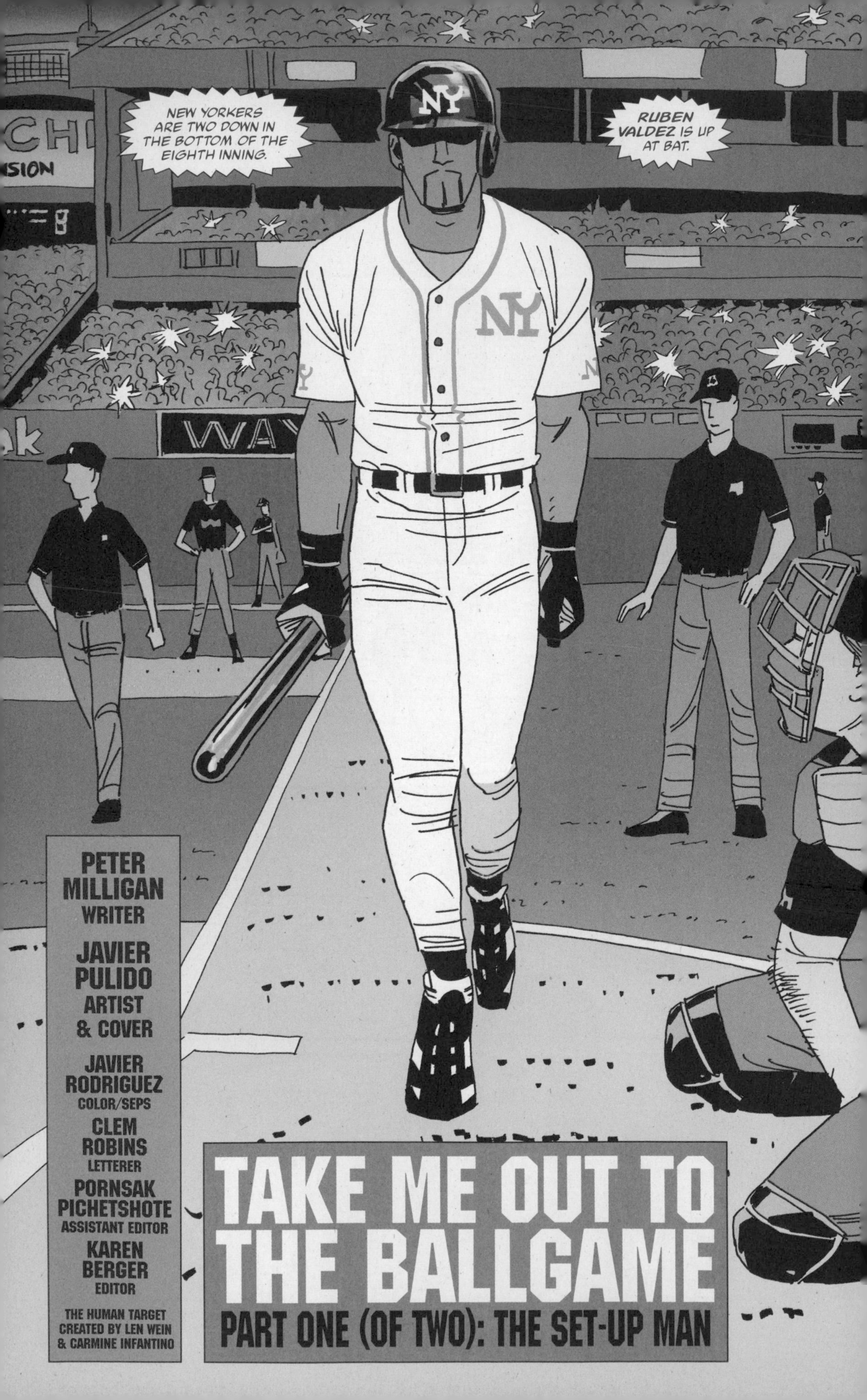
NEW YORKERS ARE TWO DOWN IN THE BOTTOM OF THE EIGHTH INNING.
RUBEN VALDEZ IS UP AT BAT.
PETER MILLIGAN WRITER
JAVIER PULIDO ARTIST & COVER
JAVIER RODRIGUEZ COLOR/SEPS
CLEM ROBINS LETTERER
PORNSAK PICHETSHOTE ASSISTANT EDITOR
KAREN BERGER EDITOR
THE HUMAN TARGET CREATED BY LEN WEIN & CARMINE INFANTINO
TAKE ME OUT TO THE BALLGAME
PART ONE (OF TWO): THE SET-UP MAN

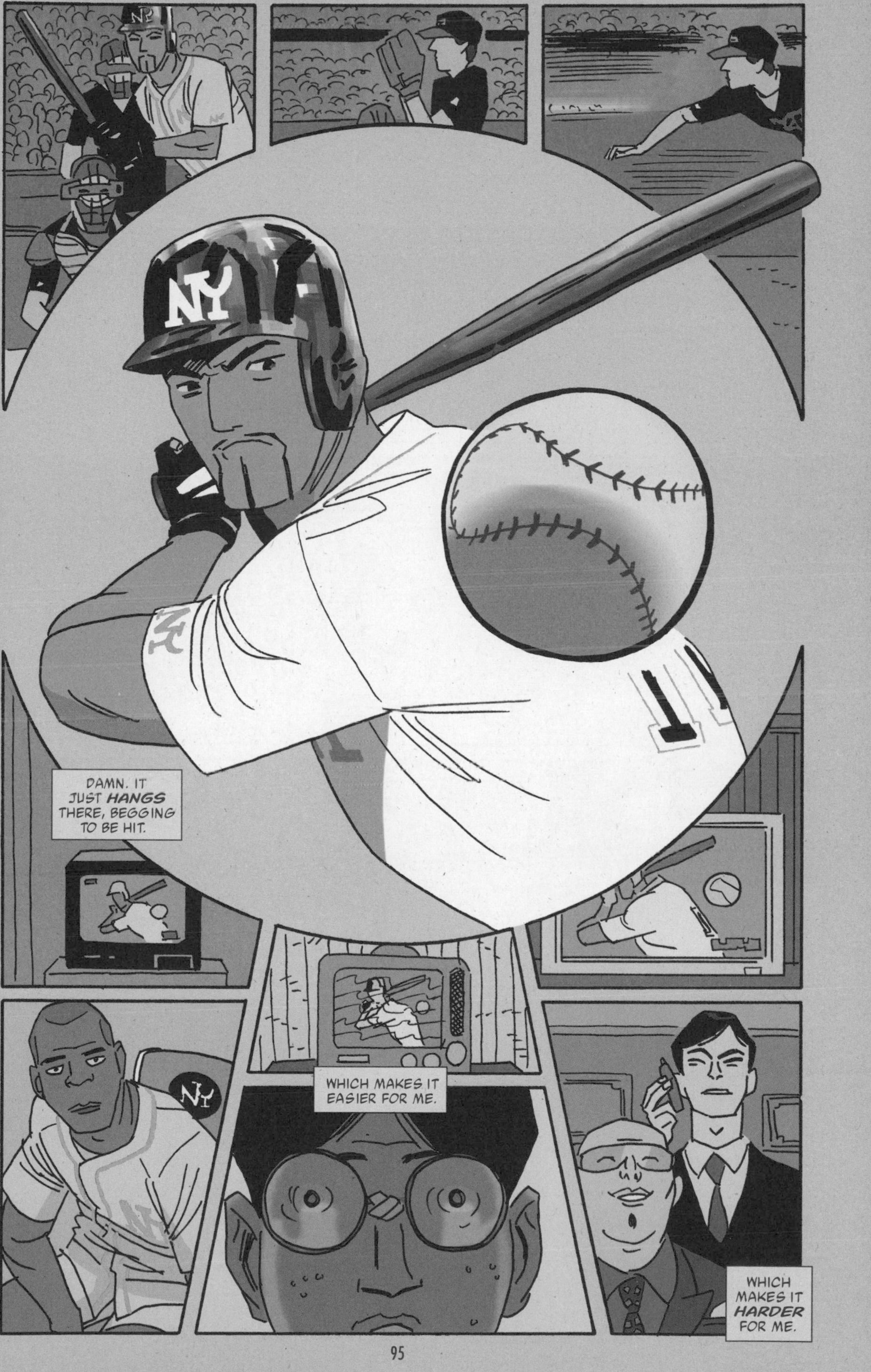
DAMN. IT JUST HANGS THERE, BEGGING TO BE HIT.
WHICH MAKES IT EASIER FOR ME.
WHICH MAKES IT HARDER FOR ME.

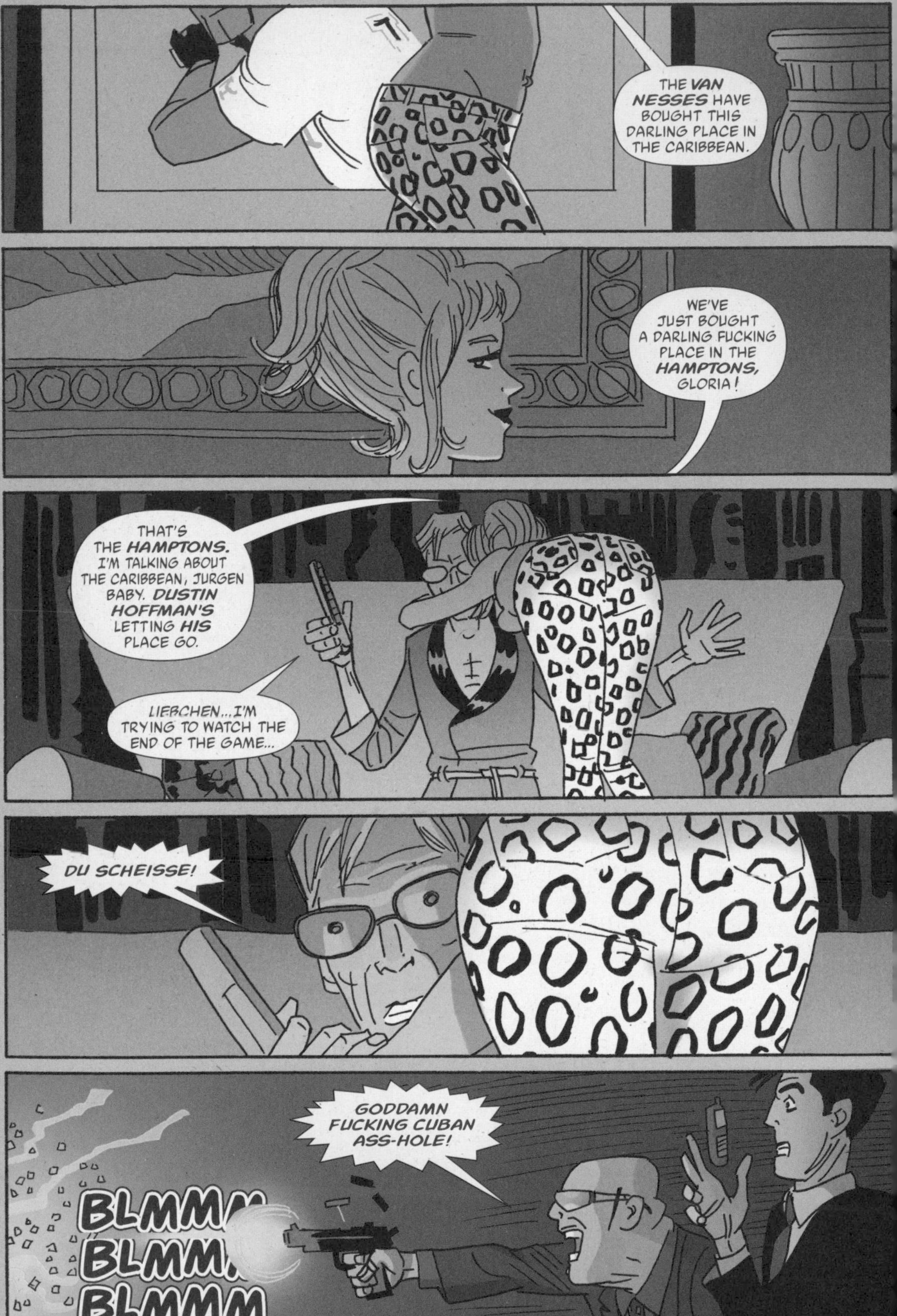
THE VAN NESSES HAVE BOUGHT THIS DARLING PLACE IN THE CARIBBEAN.
WE'VE JUST BOUGHT A DARLING FUCKING PLACE IN THE HAMPTONS, GLORIA!
THAT'S THE HAMPTONS. I'M TALKING ABOUT THE CARIBBEAN, JURGEN BABY. DUSTIN HOFFMAN'S LETTING HIS PLACE GO.
LIEBCHEN... I'M TRYING TO WATCH THE END OF THE GAME...
DU SCHEISSE!
GODDAMN FUCKING CUBAN ASS-HOLE!
BLMMM BLMMM BLMMM

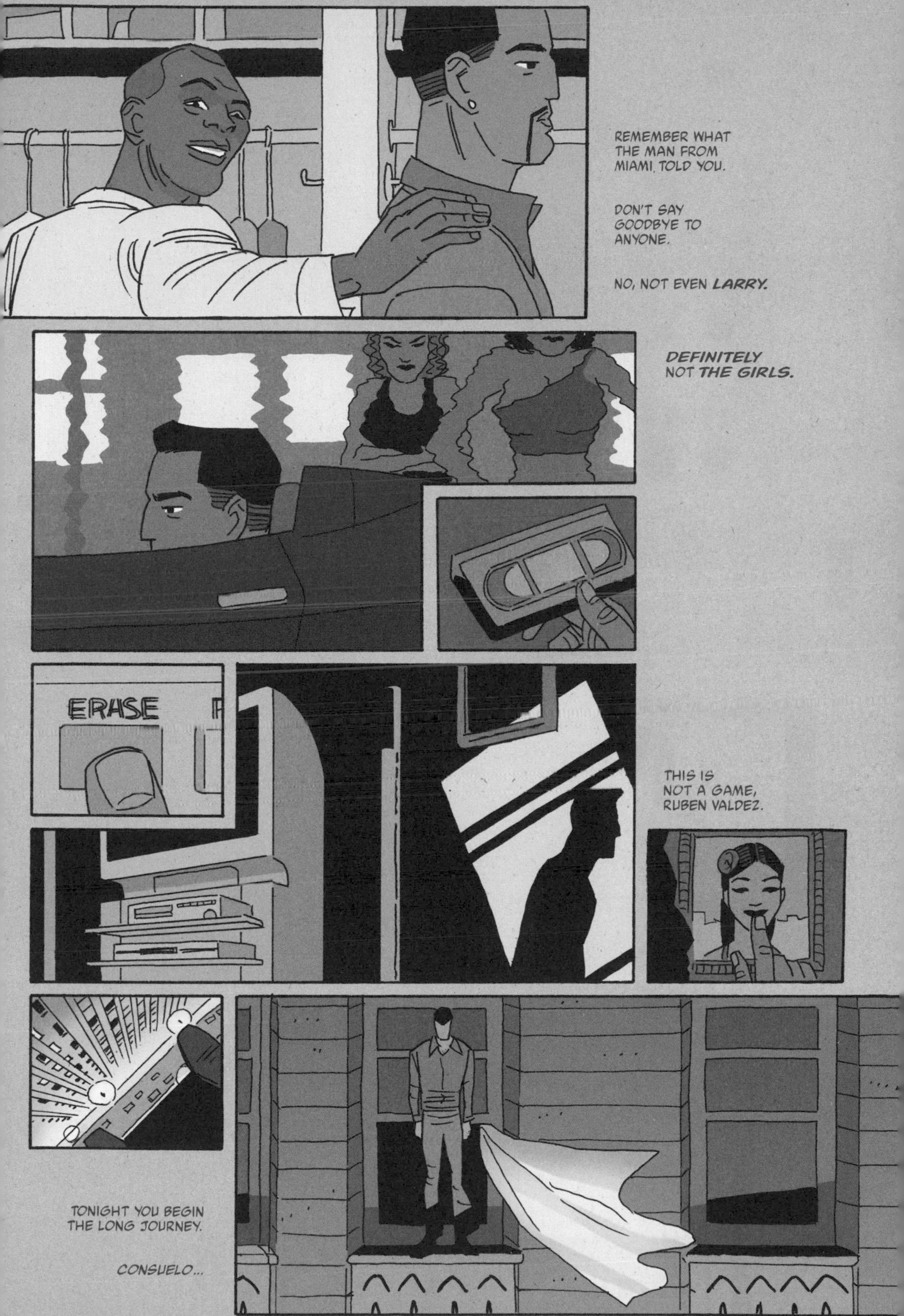
REMEMBER WHAT THE MAN FROM MIAMI TOLD YOU.
DON'T SAY GOODBYE TO ANYONE.
NO, NOT EVEN **LARRY.**
DEFINITELY NOT ***THE GIRLS.***
ERASE
THIS IS NOT A GAME, RUBEN VALDEZ.
TONIGHT YOU BEGIN THE LONG JOURNEY.
CONSUELO...

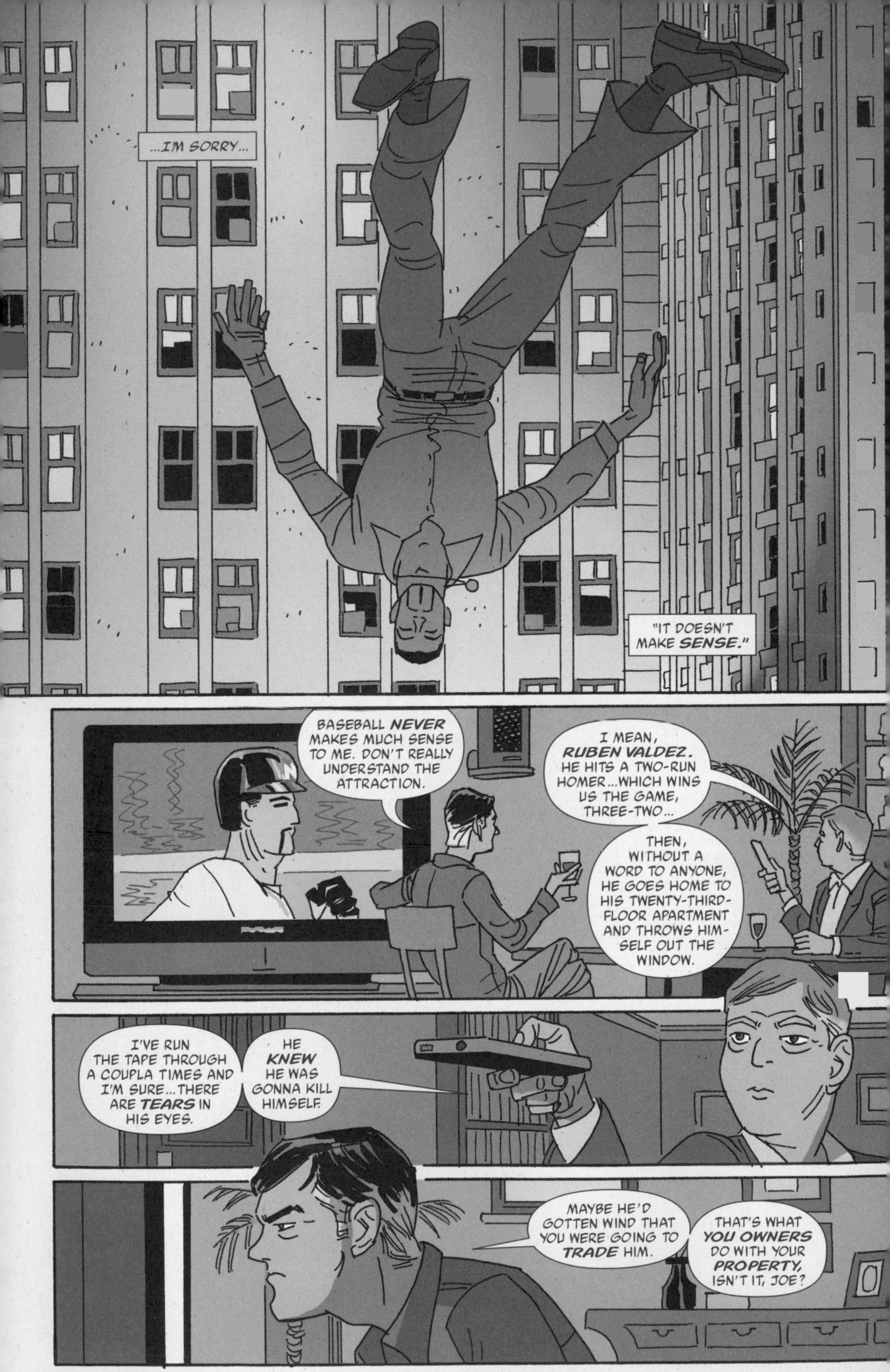
...I'M SORRY...
"IT DOESN'T MAKE SENSE."
BASEBALL NEVER MAKES MUCH SENSE TO ME. DON'T REALLY UNDERSTAND THE ATTRACTION.
I MEAN, RUBEN VALDEZ. HE HITS A TWO-RUN HOMER...WHICH WINS US THE GAME, THREE-TWO...
THEN, WITHOUT A WORD TO ANYONE, HE GOES HOME TO HIS TWENTY-THIRD-FLOOR APARTMENT AND THROWS HIMSELF OUT THE WINDOW.
I'VE RUN THE TAPE THROUGH A COUPLA TIMES AND I'M SURE...THERE ARE TEARS IN HIS EYES.
HE KNEW HE WAS GONNA KILL HIMSELF.
MAYBE HE'D GOTTEN WIND THAT YOU WERE GOING TO TRADE HIM.
THAT'S WHAT YOU OWNERS DO WITH YOUR PROPERTY, ISN'T IT, JOE?

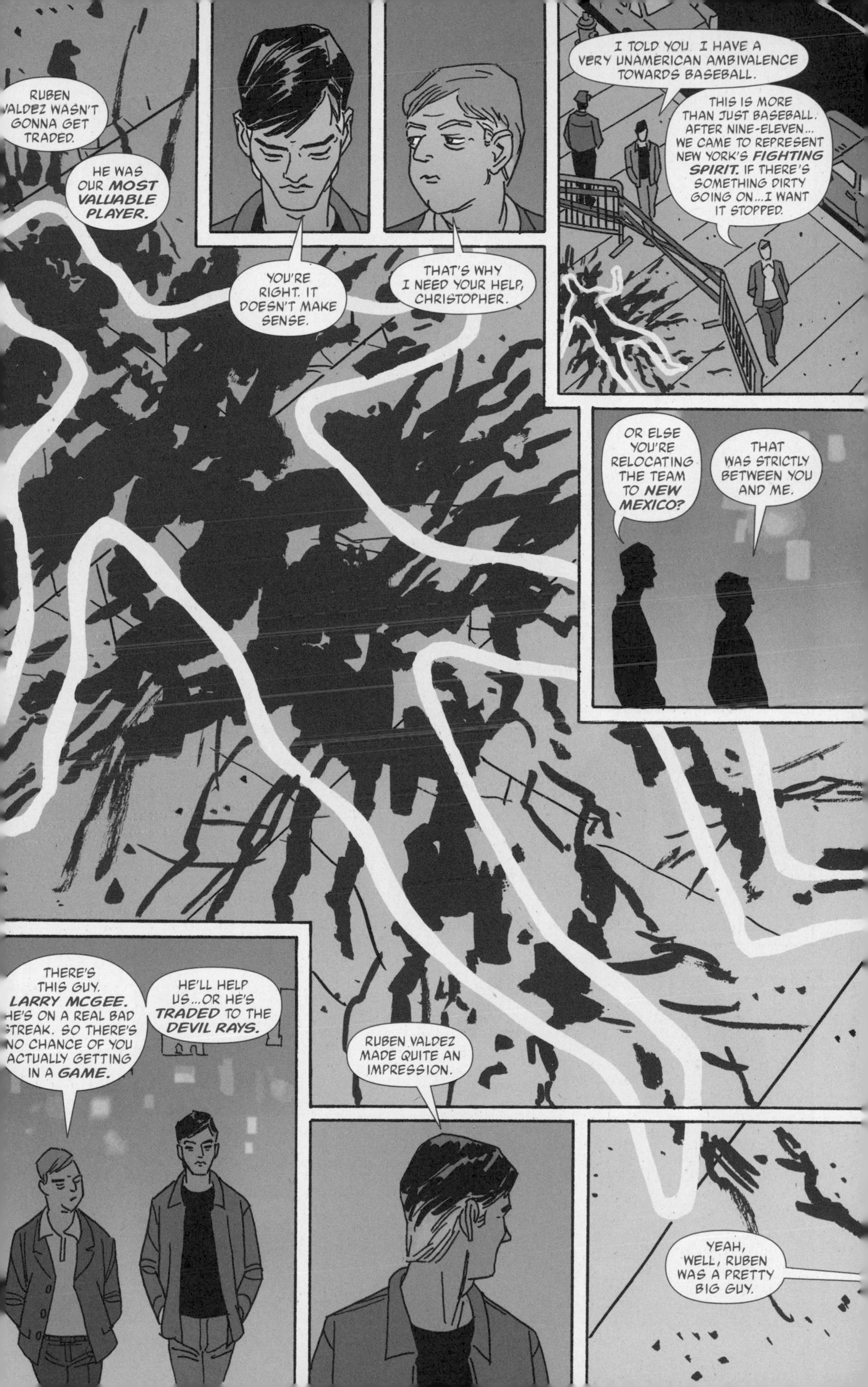
RUBEN VALDEZ WASN'T GONNA GET TRADED.
HE WAS OUR MOST VALUABLE PLAYER.
YOU'RE RIGHT. IT DOESN'T MAKE SENSE.
THAT'S WHY I NEED YOUR HELP, CHRISTOPHER.
I TOLD YOU I HAVE A VERY UNAMERICAN AMBIVALENCE TOWARDS BASEBALL.
THIS IS MORE THAN JUST BASEBALL. AFTER NINE-ELEVEN... WE CAME TO REPRESENT NEW YORK'S FIGHTING SPIRIT. IF THERE'S SOMETHING DIRTY GOING ON...I WANT IT STOPPED.
OR ELSE YOU'RE RELOCATING THE TEAM TO NEW MEXICO?
THAT WAS STRICTLY BETWEEN YOU AND ME.
THERE'S THIS GUY. LARRY MCGEE. HE'S ON A REAL BAD STREAK. SO THERE'S NO CHANCE OF YOU ACTUALLY GETTING IN A GAME.
HE'LL HELP US...OR HE'S TRADED TO THE DEVIL RAYS.
RUBEN VALDEZ MADE QUITE AN IMPRESSION.
YEAH, WELL, RUBEN WAS A PRETTY BIG GUY.

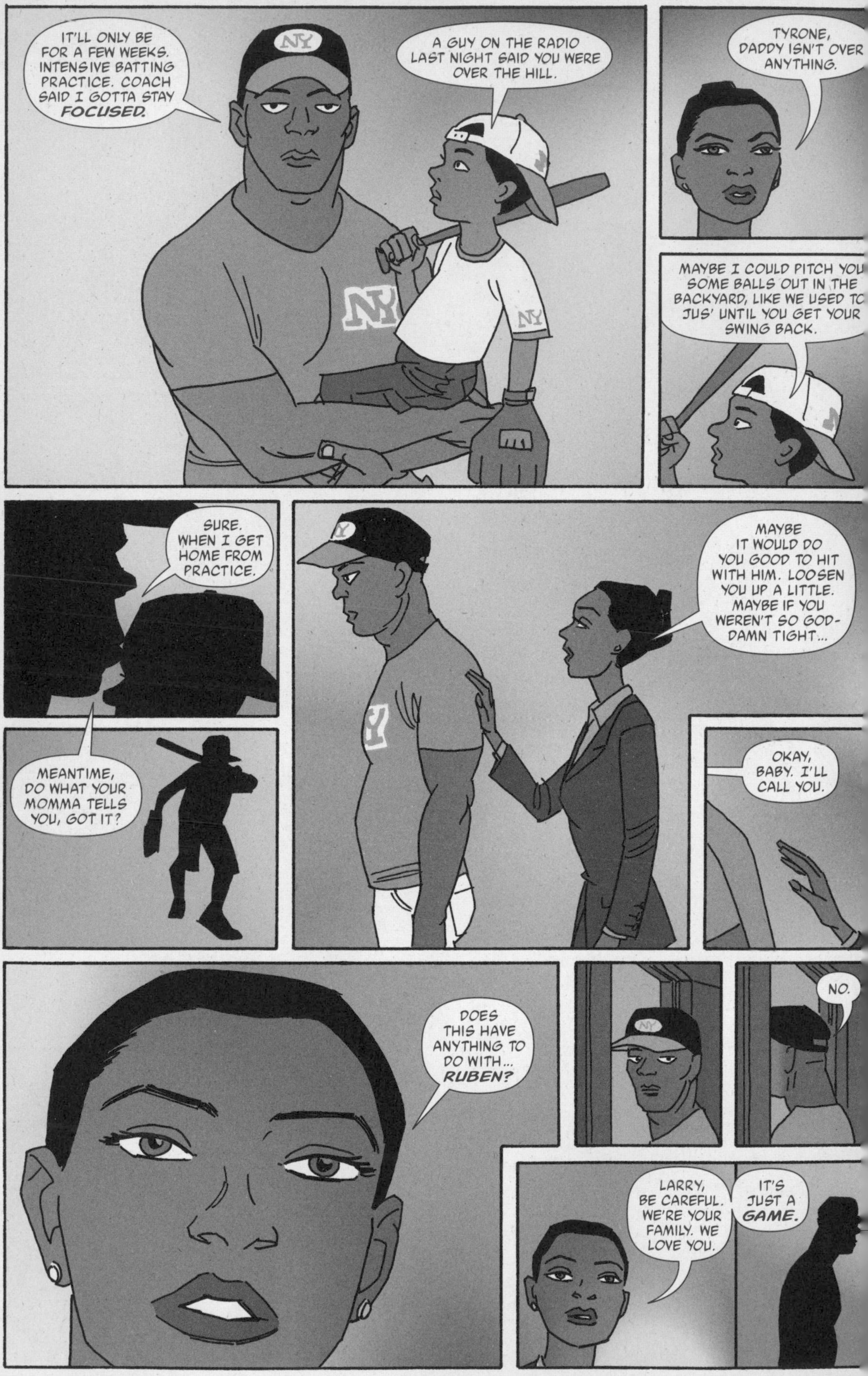
IT'LL ONLY BE FOR A FEW WEEKS. INTENSIVE BATTING PRACTICE. COACH SAID I GOTTA STAY FOCUSED.
A GUY ON THE RADIO LAST NIGHT SAID YOU WERE OVER THE HILL.
TYRONE, DADDY ISN'T OVER ANYTHING.
MAYBE I COULD PITCH YOU SOME BALLS OUT IN THE BACKYARD, LIKE WE USED TO JUS' UNTIL YOU GET YOUR SWING BACK.
SURE. WHEN I GET HOME FROM PRACTICE.
MEANTIME, DO WHAT YOUR MOMMA TELLS YOU, GOT IT?
MAYBE IT WOULD DO YOU GOOD TO HIT WITH HIM. LOOSEN YOU UP A LITTLE. MAYBE IF YOU WEREN'T SO GOD-DAMN TIGHT...
OKAY, BABY. I'LL CALL YOU.
DOES THIS HAVE ANYTHING TO DO WITH... RUBEN?
NO.
LARRY, BE CAREFUL. WE'RE YOUR FAMILY. WE LOVE YOU.
IT'S JUST A GAME.

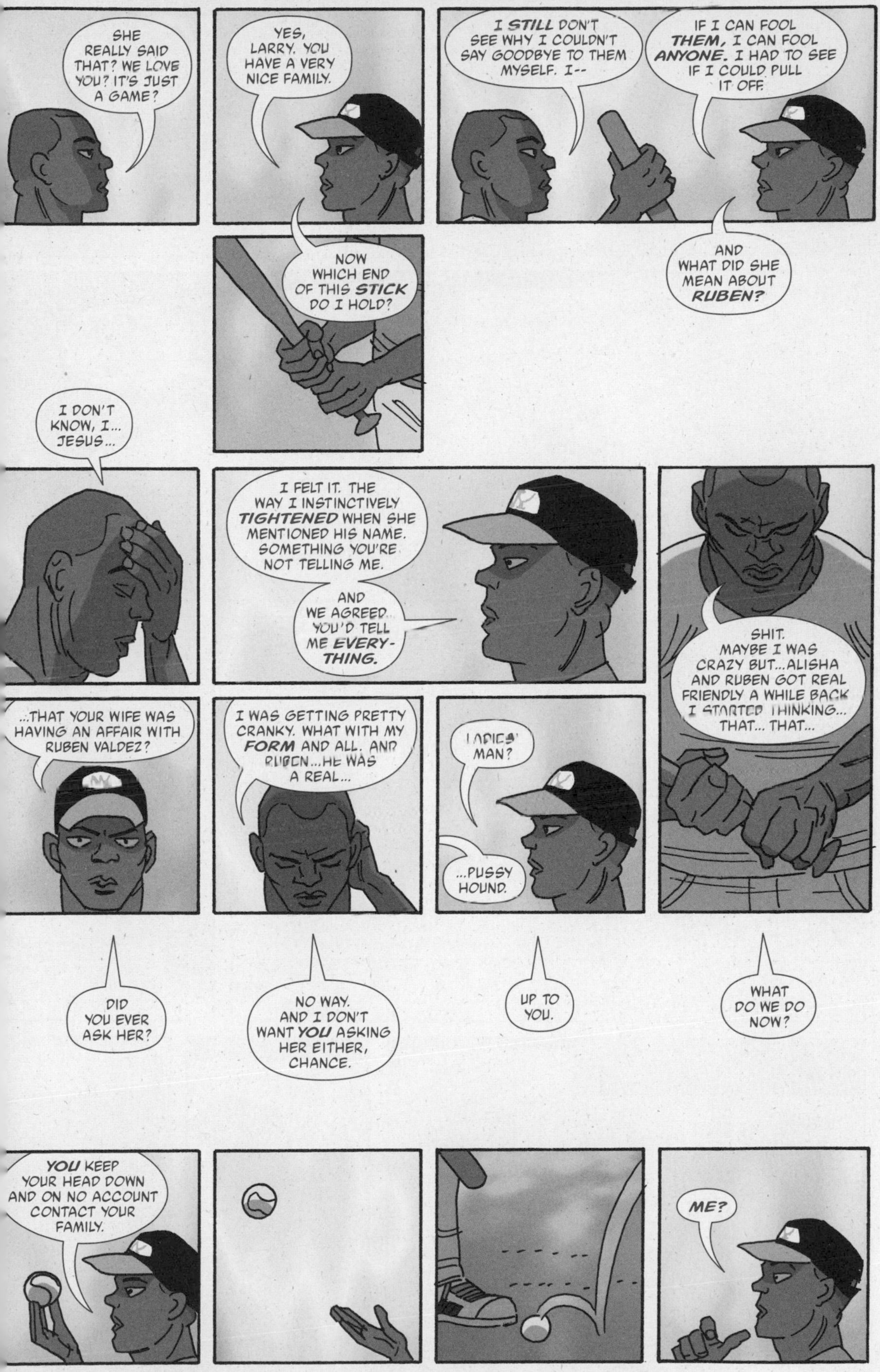
SHE REALLY SAID THAT? WE LOVE YOU? IT'S JUST A GAME?
YES, LARRY. YOU HAVE A VERY NICE FAMILY.
NOW WHICH END OF THIS STICK DO I HOLD?
I STILL DON'T SEE WHY I COULDN'T SAY GOODBYE TO THEM MYSELF. I--
IF I CAN FOOL THEM, I CAN FOOL ANYONE. I HAD TO SEE IF I COULD PULL IT OFF.
AND WHAT DID SHE MEAN ABOUT RUBEN?
I DON'T KNOW, I... JESUS...
I FELT IT. THE WAY I INSTINCTIVELY TIGHTENED WHEN SHE MENTIONED HIS NAME. SOMETHING YOU'RE NOT TELLING ME.
AND WE AGREED YOU'D TELL ME EVERYTHING.
SHIT. MAYBE I WAS CRAZY BUT...ALISHA AND RUBEN GOT REAL FRIENDLY A WHILE BACK I STARTED THINKING... THAT... THAT...
...THAT YOUR WIFE WAS HAVING AN AFFAIR WITH RUBEN VALDEZ?
DID YOU EVER ASK HER?
I WAS GETTING PRETTY CRANKY. WHAT WITH MY FORM AND ALL. AND RUBEN...HE WAS A REAL...
NO WAY. AND I DON'T WANT YOU ASKING HER EITHER, CHANCE.
LADIES' MAN?
...PUSSY HOUND.
UP TO YOU.
WHAT DO WE DO NOW?
YOU KEEP YOUR HEAD DOWN AND ON NO ACCOUNT CONTACT YOUR FAMILY.
ME?

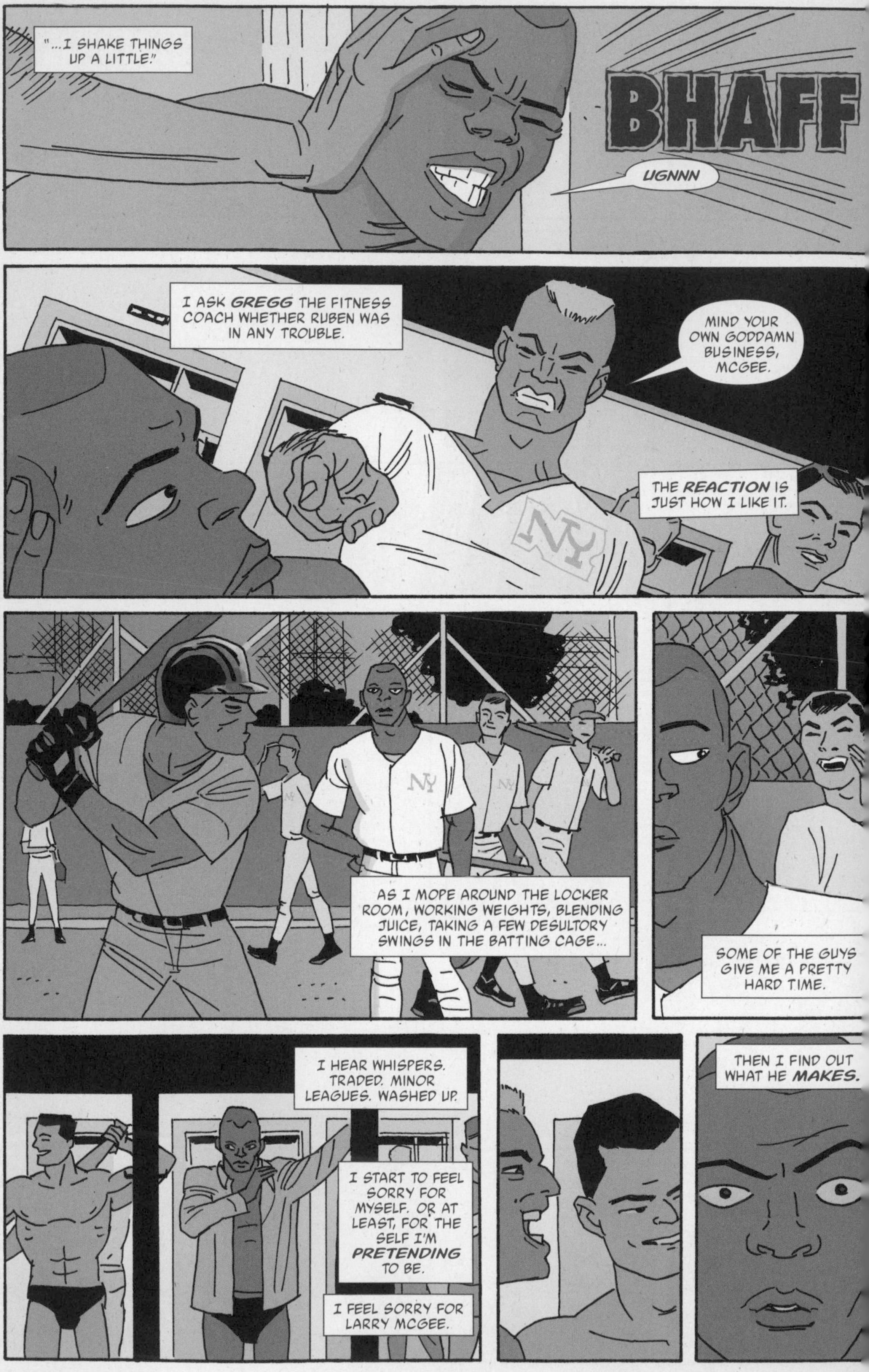

"...I SHAKE THINGS UP A LITTLE."
BHAFF
UGNNN
I ASK GREGG THE FITNESS COACH WHETHER RUBEN WAS IN ANY TROUBLE.
MIND YOUR OWN GODDAMN BUSINESS, MCGEE.
THE REACTION IS JUST HOW I LIKE IT.
AS I MOPE AROUND THE LOCKER ROOM, WORKING WEIGHTS, BLENDING JUICE, TAKING A FEW DESULTORY SWINGS IN THE BATTING CAGE...
SOME OF THE GUYS GIVE ME A PRETTY HARD TIME.
I HEAR WHISPERS. TRADED. MINOR LEAGUES. WASHED UP.
I START TO FEEL SORRY FOR MYSELF. OR AT LEAST, FOR THE SELF I'M PRETENDING TO BE.
I FEEL SORRY FOR LARRY MCGEE.
THEN I FIND OUT WHAT HE MAKES.

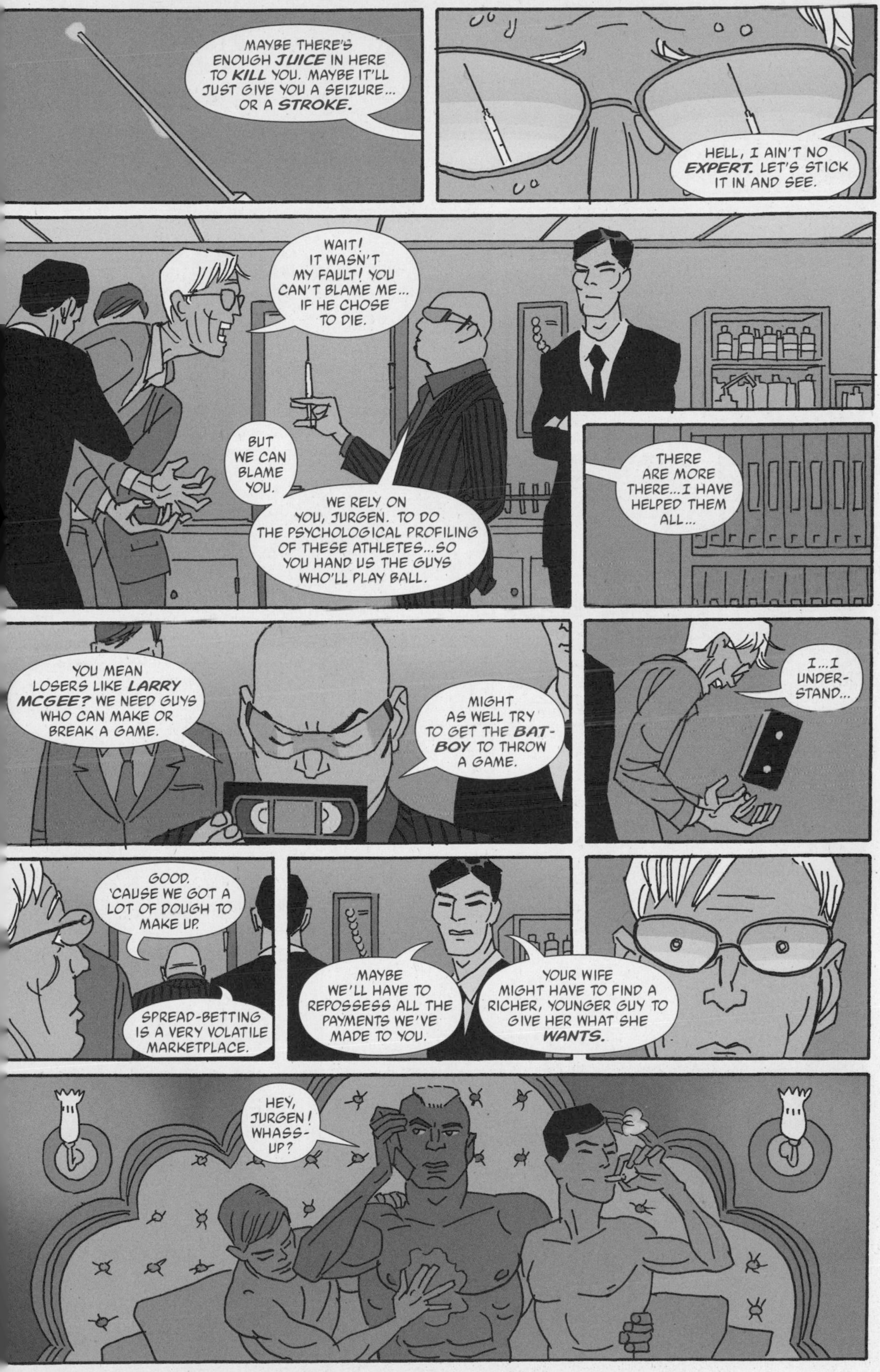
MAYBE THERE'S ENOUGH JUICE IN HERE TO KILL YOU. MAYBE IT'LL JUST GIVE YOU A SEIZURE... OR A STROKE.
HELL, I AIN'T NO EXPERT. LET'S STICK IT IN AND SEE.
WAIT! IT WASN'T MY FAULT! YOU CAN'T BLAME ME... IF HE CHOSE TO DIE.
BUT WE CAN BLAME YOU.
WE RELY ON YOU, JURGEN. TO DO THE PSYCHOLOGICAL PROFILING OF THESE ATHLETES...SO YOU HAND US THE GUYS WHO'LL PLAY BALL.
THERE ARE MORE THERE...I HAVE HELPED THEM ALL...
YOU MEAN LOSERS LIKE LARRY MCGEE? WE NEED GUYS WHO CAN MAKE OR BREAK A GAME.
MIGHT AS WELL TRY TO GET THE BAT-BOY TO THROW A GAME.
I...I UNDER-STAND...
GOOD. 'CAUSE WE GOT A LOT OF DOUGH TO MAKE UP.
SPREAD-BETTING IS A VERY VOLATILE MARKETPLACE.
MAYBE WE'LL HAVE TO REPOSSESS ALL THE PAYMENTS WE'VE MADE TO YOU.
YOUR WIFE MIGHT HAVE TO FIND A RICHER, YOUNGER GUY TO GIVE HER WHAT SHE WANTS.
HEY, JURGEN! WHASS-UP?

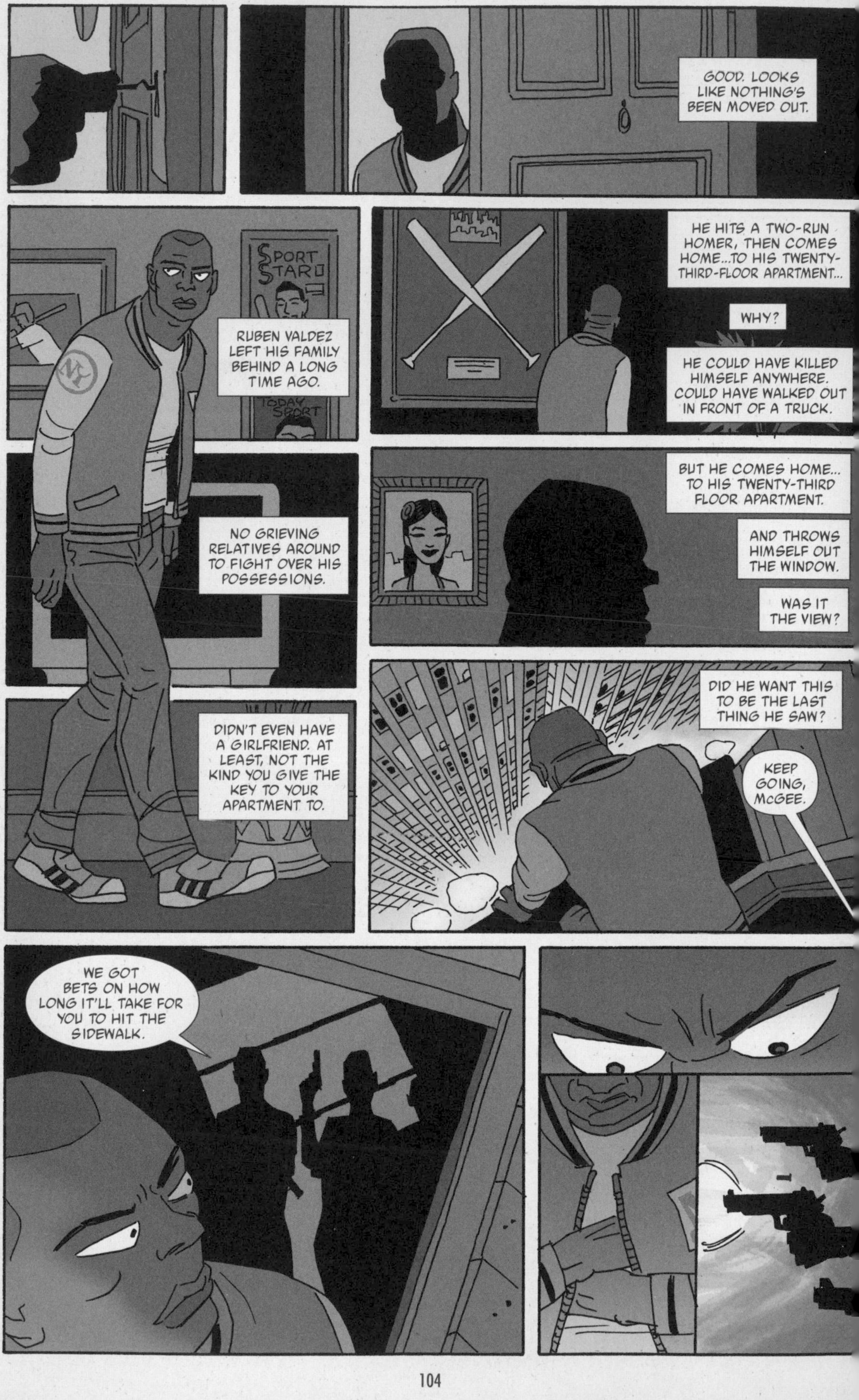

GOOD. LOOKS LIKE NOTHING'S BEEN MOVED OUT.
RUBEN VALDEZ LEFT HIS FAMILY BEHIND A LONG TIME AGO.
SPORT STAR
TODAY SPORT
HE HITS A TWO-RUN HOMER, THEN COMES HOME...TO HIS TWENTY-THIRD-FLOOR APARTMENT...
WHY?
HE COULD HAVE KILLED HIMSELF ANYWHERE. COULD HAVE WALKED OUT IN FRONT OF A TRUCK.
NO GRIEVING RELATIVES AROUND TO FIGHT OVER HIS POSSESSIONS.
BUT HE COMES HOME... TO HIS TWENTY-THIRD FLOOR APARTMENT.
AND THROWS HIMSELF OUT THE WINDOW.
WAS IT THE VIEW?
DIDN'T EVEN HAVE A GIRLFRIEND. AT LEAST, NOT THE KIND YOU GIVE THE KEY TO YOUR APARTMENT TO.
DID HE WANT THIS TO BE THE LAST THING HE SAW?
KEEP GOING, McGEE.
WE GOT BETS ON HOW LONG IT'LL TAKE FOR YOU TO HIT THE SIDEWALK.

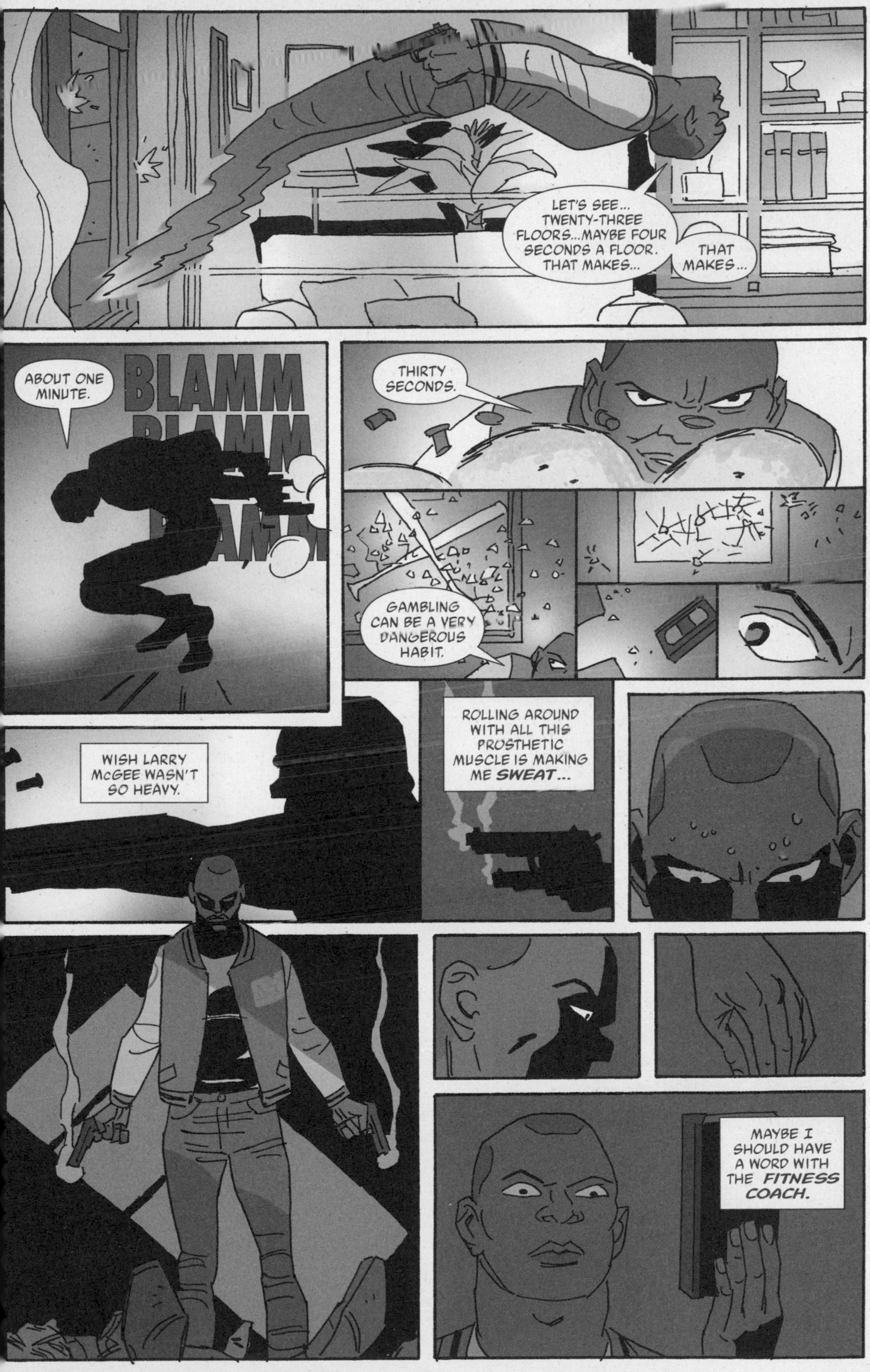
LET'S SEE... TWENTY-THREE FLOORS...MAYBE FOUR SECONDS A FLOOR. THAT MAKES...
THAT MAKES...
ABOUT ONE MINUTE.
BLAMM
BLAMM
THIRTY SECONDS.
GAMBLING CAN BE A VERY DANGEROUS HABIT.
WISH LARRY McGEE WASN'T SO HEAVY.
ROLLING AROUND WITH ALL THIS PROSTHETIC MUSCLE IS MAKING ME **SWEAT**...
MAYBE I SHOULD HAVE A WORD WITH THE **FITNESS COACH.**

JUST ONE WORD, THAT'S ALL. OR TWO WORDS. TWO SHORT WORDS, A SMILE...

I WON'T HAVE TO EXPLAIN WHAT'S HAPPENING. JUST SAY, "I LOVE YOU" ALISHA.

WON'T MENTION RUBEN. WON'T ASK HER OR NOTHING.

JESUS, WHAT HARM IS THERE IN ME SEEING MY OWN GODDAMN WIFE?

WHO THE HELL IS CHRISTOPHER CHANCE ANYWAY? GODDAMN FREAK. DON'T HE HAVE A LIFE OF HIS *OWN*?

JESUS...

WHAT THE FUCK...

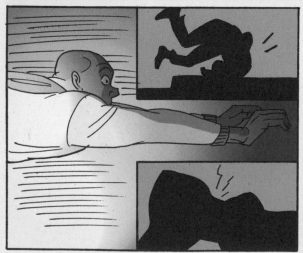

BETTER WATCH YOUR STEP, LARRY.

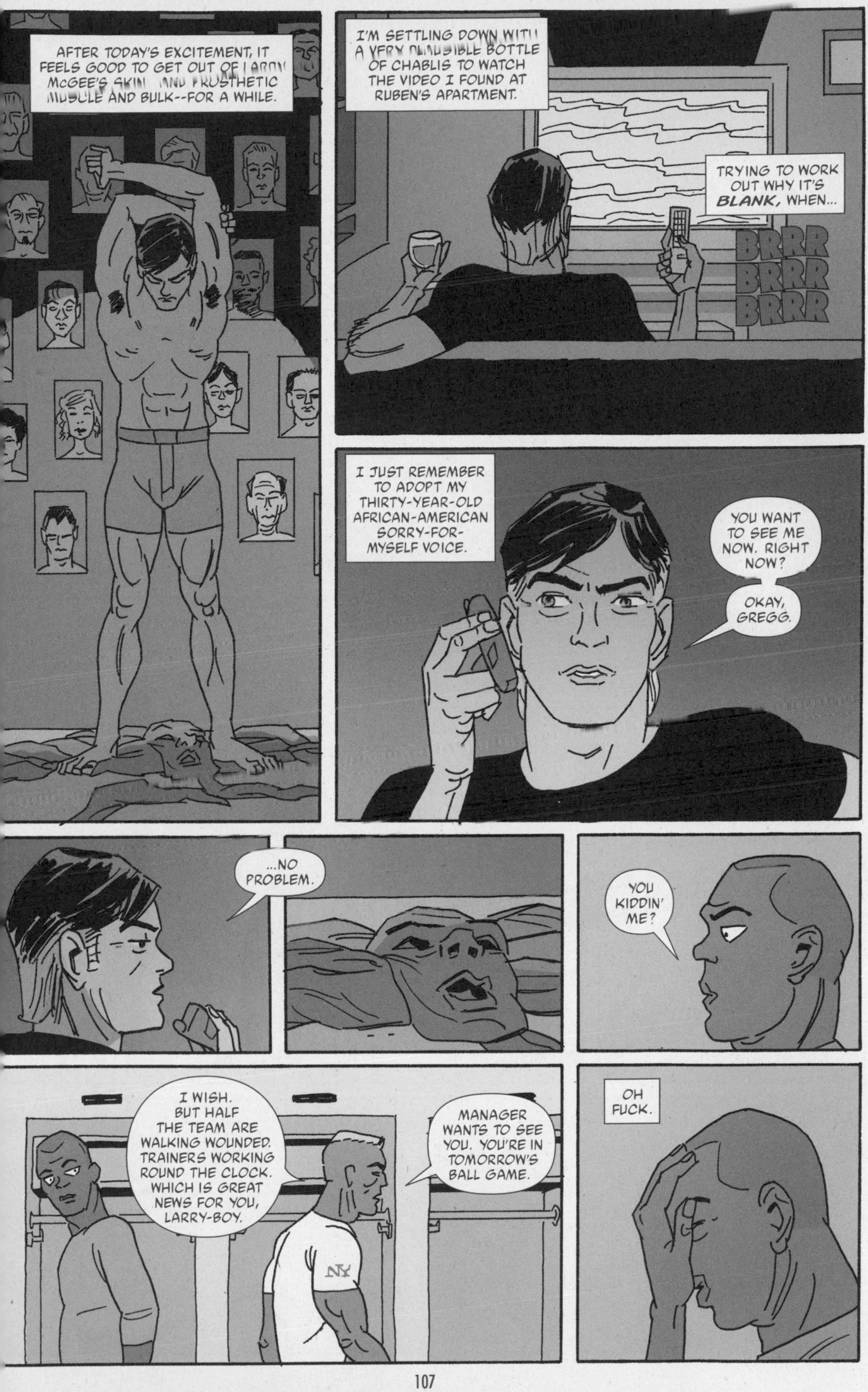
AFTER TODAY'S EXCITEMENT, IT FEELS GOOD TO GET OUT OF LARRY McGEE'S SKIN AND PROSTHETIC MUSCLE AND BULK--FOR A WHILE.
I'M SETTLING DOWN WITH A VERY PLAUSIBLE BOTTLE OF CHABLIS TO WATCH THE VIDEO I FOUND AT RUBEN'S APARTMENT.
TRYING TO WORK OUT WHY IT'S *BLANK,* WHEN...
BRRR BRRR BRRR
I JUST REMEMBER TO ADOPT MY THIRTY-YEAR-OLD AFRICAN-AMERICAN SORRY-FOR-MYSELF VOICE.
YOU WANT TO SEE ME NOW. RIGHT NOW?
OKAY, GREGG.
...NO PROBLEM.
YOU KIDDIN' ME?
I WISH. BUT HALF THE TEAM ARE WALKING WOUNDED. TRAINERS WORKING ROUND THE CLOCK. WHICH IS GREAT NEWS FOR YOU, LARRY-BOY.
MANAGER WANTS TO SEE YOU. YOU'RE IN TOMORROW'S BALL GAME.
NY
OH FUCK.

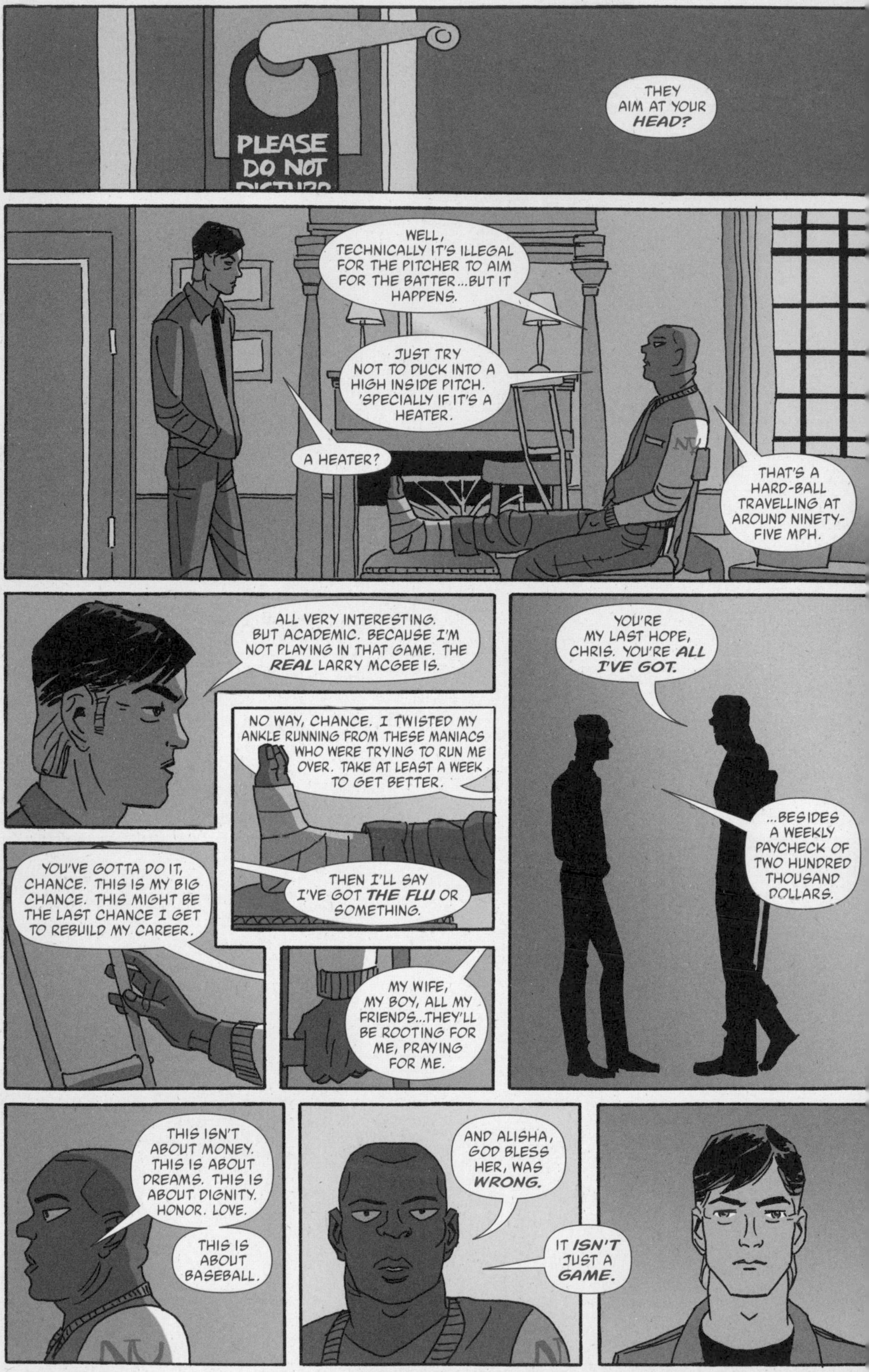
PLEASE DO NOT
THEY AIM AT YOUR HEAD?
WELL, TECHNICALLY IT'S ILLEGAL FOR THE PITCHER TO AIM FOR THE BATTER...BUT IT HAPPENS.
JUST TRY NOT TO DUCK INTO A HIGH INSIDE PITCH. 'SPECIALLY IF IT'S A HEATER.
A HEATER?
THAT'S A HARD-BALL TRAVELLING AT AROUND NINETY-FIVE MPH.
ALL VERY INTERESTING. BUT ACADEMIC. BECAUSE I'M NOT PLAYING IN THAT GAME. THE REAL LARRY MCGEE IS.
NO WAY, CHANCE. I TWISTED MY ANKLE RUNNING FROM THESE MANIACS WHO WERE TRYING TO RUN ME OVER. TAKE AT LEAST A WEEK TO GET BETTER.
THEN I'LL SAY I'VE GOT THE FLU OR SOMETHING.
YOU'VE GOTTA DO IT, CHANCE. THIS IS MY BIG CHANCE. THIS MIGHT BE THE LAST CHANCE I GET TO REBUILD MY CAREER.
MY WIFE, MY BOY, ALL MY FRIENDS...THEY'LL BE ROOTING FOR ME, PRAYING FOR ME.
YOU'RE MY LAST HOPE, CHRIS. YOU'RE ALL I'VE GOT.
...BESIDES A WEEKLY PAYCHECK OF TWO HUNDRED THOUSAND DOLLARS.
THIS ISN'T ABOUT MONEY. THIS IS ABOUT DREAMS. THIS IS ABOUT DIGNITY. HONOR. LOVE.
THIS IS ABOUT BASEBALL.
AND ALISHA, GOD BLESS HER, WAS WRONG.
IT ISN'T JUST A GAME.

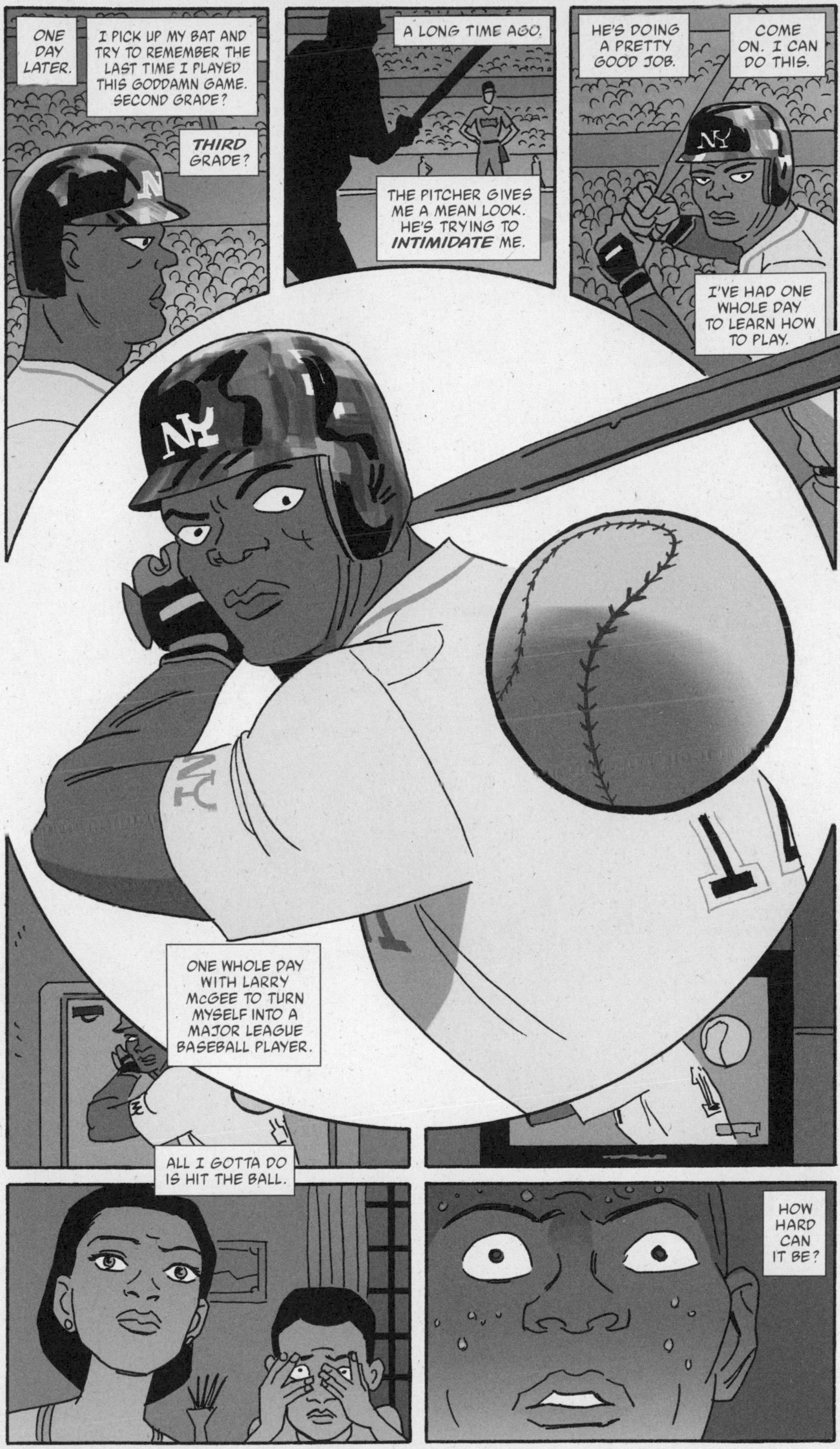
ONE DAY LATER.
I PICK UP MY BAT AND TRY TO REMEMBER THE LAST TIME I PLAYED THIS GODDAMN GAME. SECOND GRADE?
THIRD GRADE?
A LONG TIME AGO.
THE PITCHER GIVES ME A MEAN LOOK. HE'S TRYING TO INTIMIDATE ME.
HE'S DOING A PRETTY GOOD JOB.
COME ON. I CAN DO THIS.
I'VE HAD ONE WHOLE DAY TO LEARN HOW TO PLAY.
ONE WHOLE DAY WITH LARRY McGEE TO TURN MYSELF INTO A MAJOR LEAGUE BASEBALL PLAYER.
ALL I GOTTA DO IS HIT THE BALL.
HOW HARD CAN IT BE?

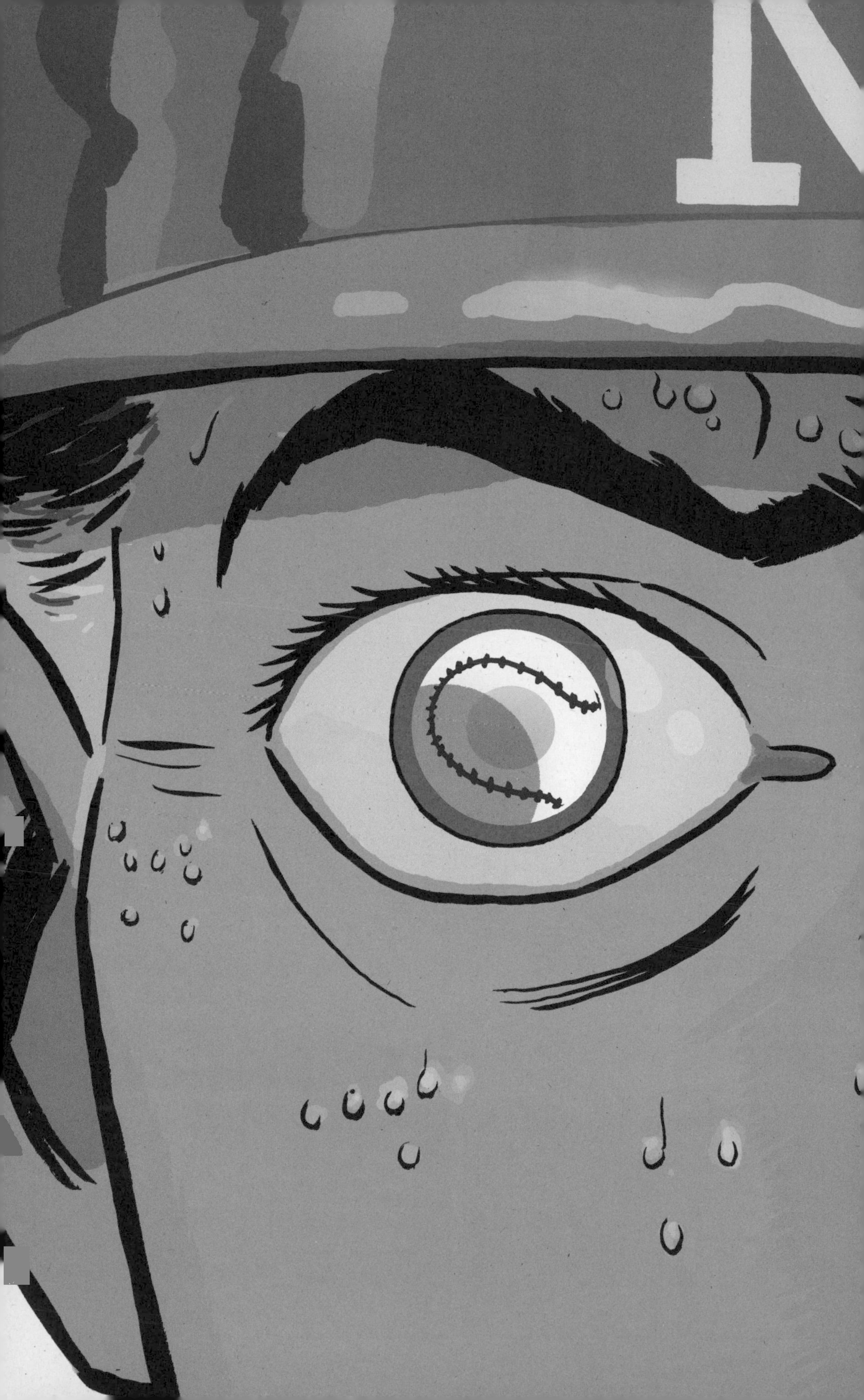

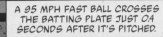

TED WILLIAMS WORKED IT ALL OUT.

A HITTER--THAT'S *ME*--HAS LESS THAN HALF A SECOND TO *REACT*. IN OTHER WORDS...

A 95 MPH FAST BALL CROSSES THE BATTING PLATE JUST 0.4 SECONDS AFTER IT'S PITCHED.

WELL, AT LEAST THAT'S A LOT SLOWER THAN A *BULLET*.

AND I'VE FACED PLENTY OF *THOSE* BEFORE.

PETER MILLIGAN
WRITER

JAVIER PULIDO
ARTIST & COVER

JAVIER RODRIGUEZ
COLOR/SEPS

TAKE ME OUT TO THE BALLGAME
PART TWO (OF TWO): THE STRIKE ZONE

CLEM ROBINS
LETTERER

PORNSAK PICHETSHOTE
ASSISTANT EDITOR

KAREN BERGER
EDITOR

THE HUMAN TARGET CREATED BY LEN WEIN & CARMINE INFANTINO

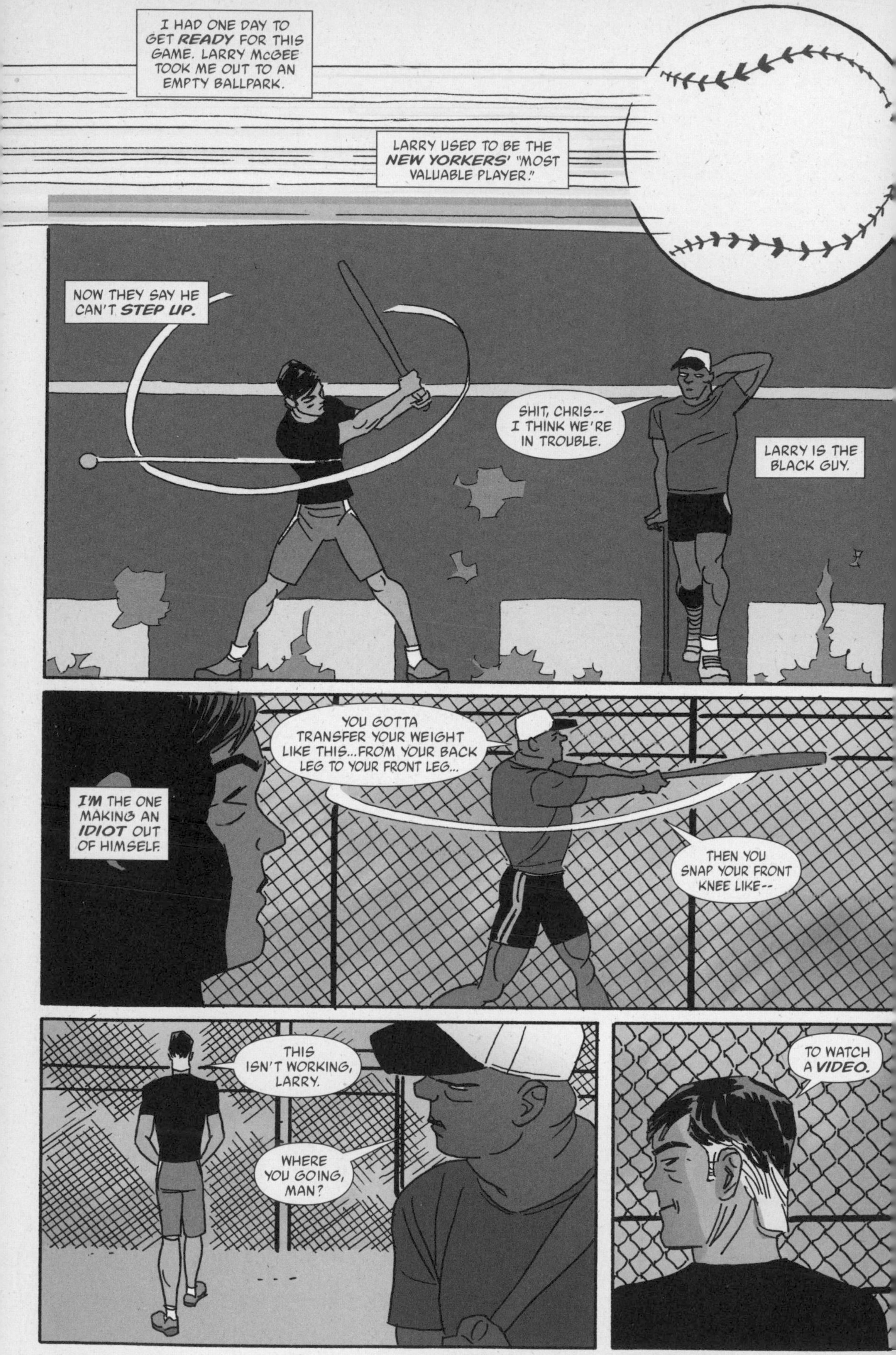
I HAD ONE DAY TO GET READY FOR THIS GAME. LARRY McGEE TOOK ME OUT TO AN EMPTY BALLPARK.
LARRY USED TO BE THE NEW YORKERS' "MOST VALUABLE PLAYER."
NOW THEY SAY HE CAN'T STEP UP.
SHIT, CHRIS-- I THINK WE'RE IN TROUBLE.
LARRY IS THE BLACK GUY.
YOU GOTTA TRANSFER YOUR WEIGHT LIKE THIS...FROM YOUR BACK LEG TO YOUR FRONT LEG...
I'M THE ONE MAKING AN IDIOT OUT OF HIMSELF.
THEN YOU SNAP YOUR FRONT KNEE LIKE--
THIS ISN'T WORKING, LARRY.
WHERE YOU GOING, MAN?
TO WATCH A VIDEO.

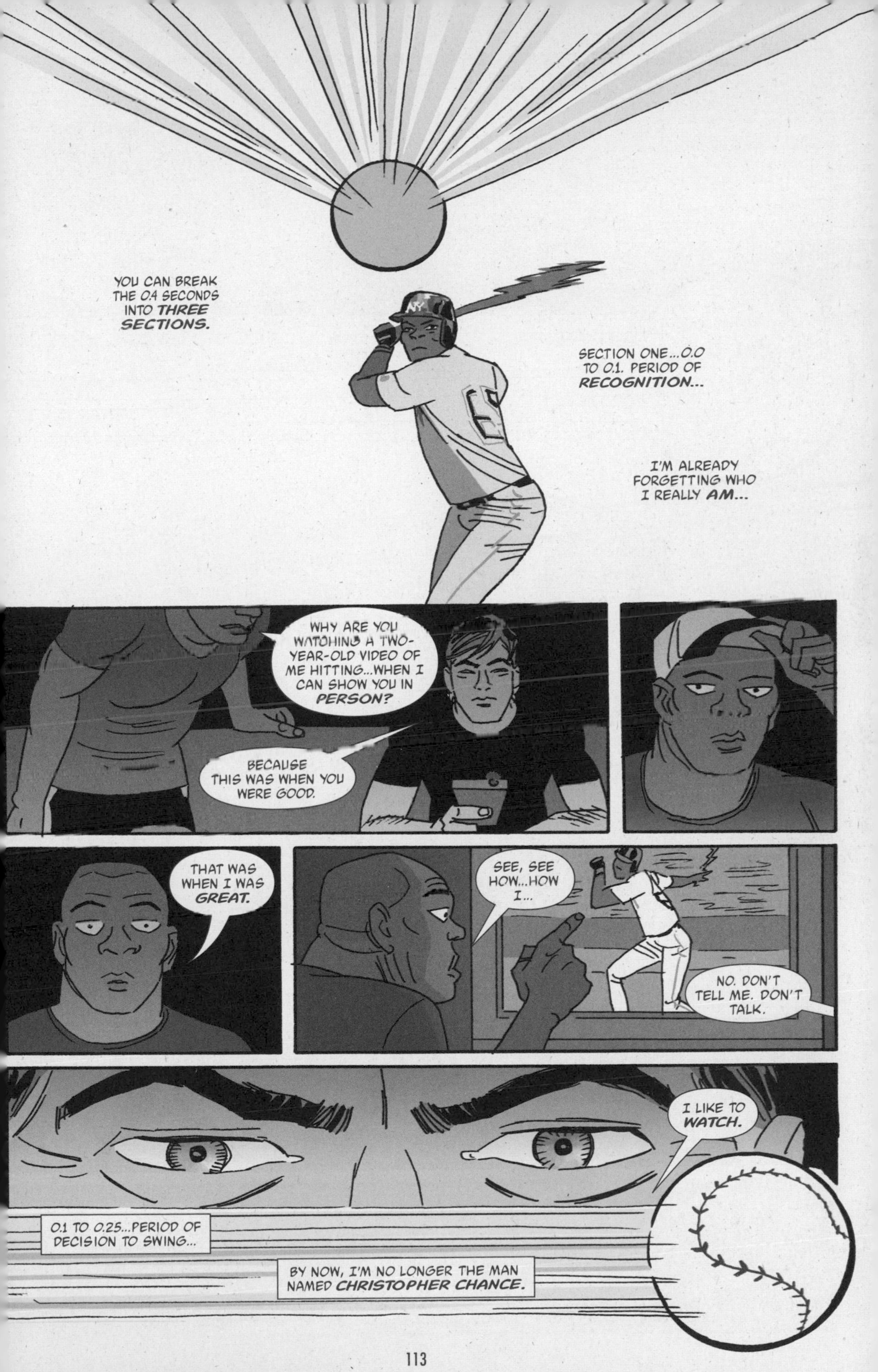
YOU CAN BREAK THE 0.4 SECONDS INTO THREE SECTIONS.
SECTION ONE...0.0 TO 0.1. PERIOD OF RECOGNITION...
I'M ALREADY FORGETTING WHO I REALLY AM...
WHY ARE YOU WATCHING A TWO-YEAR-OLD VIDEO OF ME HITTING...WHEN I CAN SHOW YOU IN PERSON?
BECAUSE THIS WAS WHEN YOU WERE GOOD.
THAT WAS WHEN I WAS GREAT.
SEE, SEE HOW...HOW I...
NO. DON'T TELL ME. DON'T TALK.
I LIKE TO WATCH.
0.1 TO 0.25...PERIOD OF DECISION TO SWING...
BY NOW, I'M NO LONGER THE MAN NAMED CHRISTOPHER CHANCE.

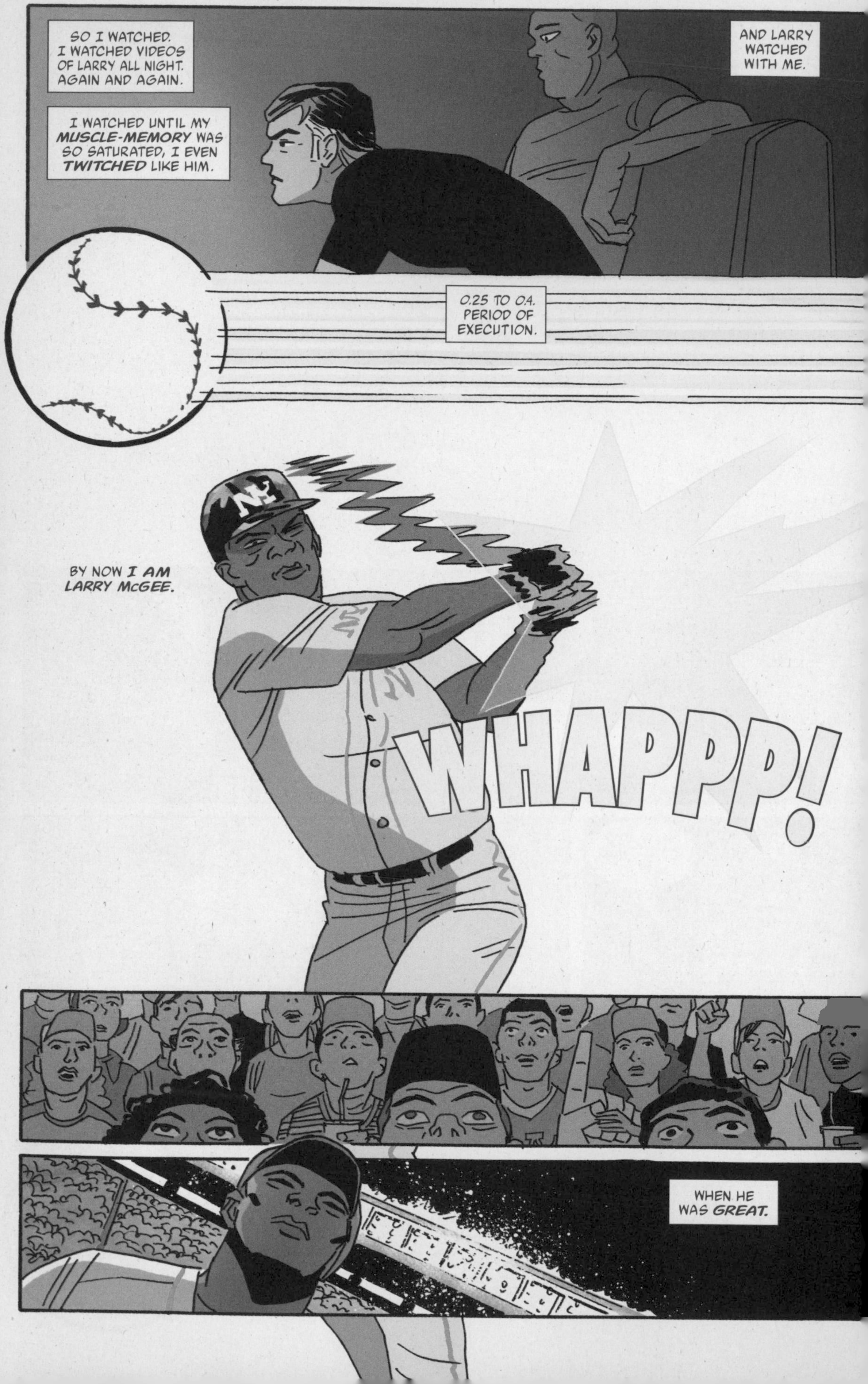
SO I WATCHED. I WATCHED VIDEOS OF LARRY ALL NIGHT. AGAIN AND AGAIN.
I WATCHED UNTIL MY MUSCLE-MEMORY WAS SO SATURATED, I EVEN TWITCHED LIKE HIM.
AND LARRY WATCHED WITH ME.
0.25 TO 0.4. PERIOD OF EXECUTION.
BY NOW I AM LARRY McGEE.
WHAPPP!
WHEN HE WAS GREAT.

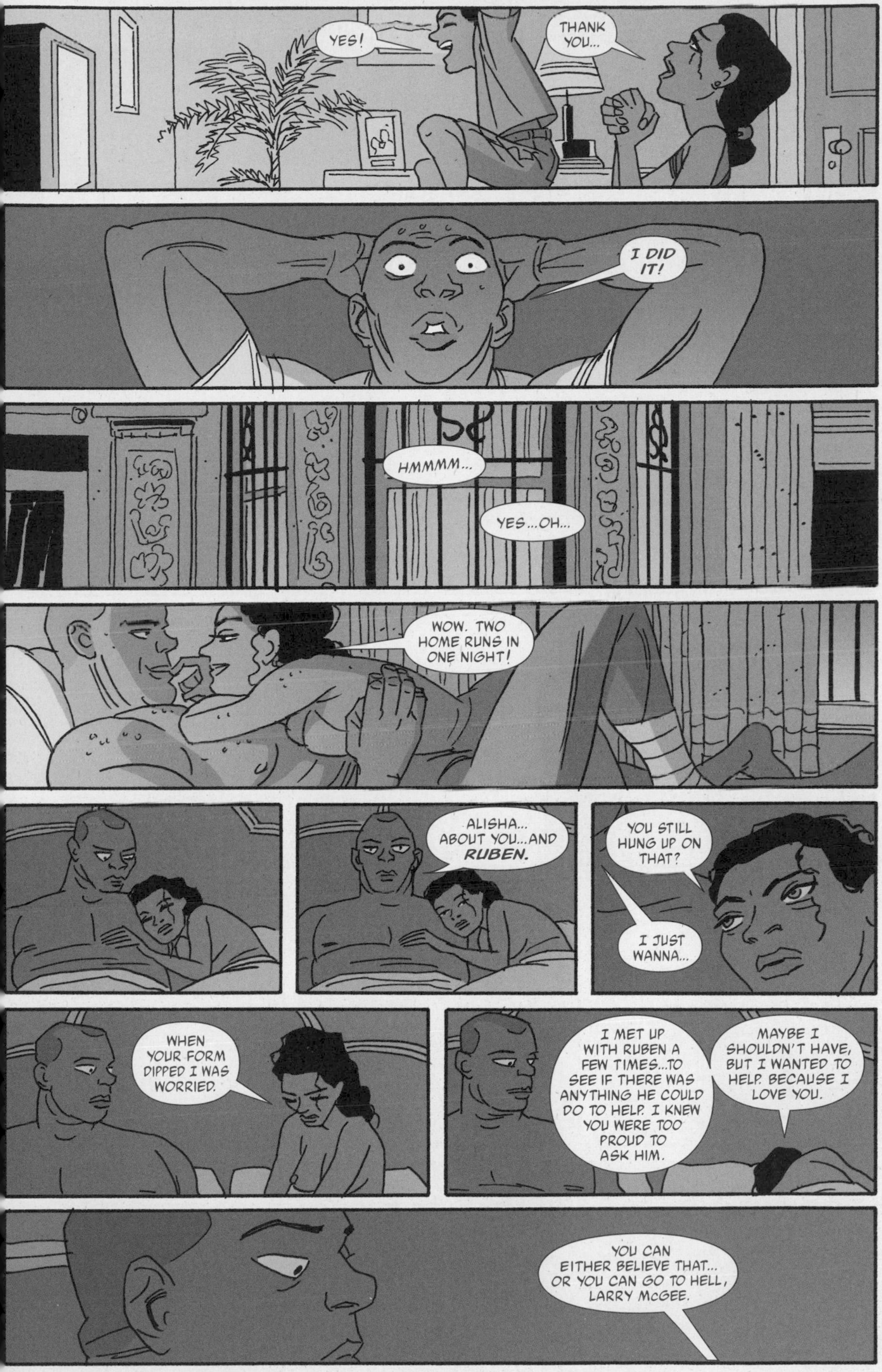
YES!
THANK YOU...
I DID IT!
HMMMM...
YES...OH...
WOW. TWO HOME RUNS IN ONE NIGHT!
ALISHA... ABOUT YOU...AND RUBEN.
YOU STILL HUNG UP ON THAT?
I JUST WANNA...
WHEN YOUR FORM DIPPED I WAS WORRIED.
I MET UP WITH RUBEN A FEW TIMES...TO SEE IF THERE WAS ANYTHING HE COULD DO TO HELP. I KNEW YOU WERE TOO PROUD TO ASK HIM.
MAYBE I SHOULDN'T HAVE, BUT I WANTED TO HELP. BECAUSE I LOVE YOU.
YOU CAN EITHER BELIEVE THAT... OR YOU CAN GO TO HELL, LARRY McGEE.

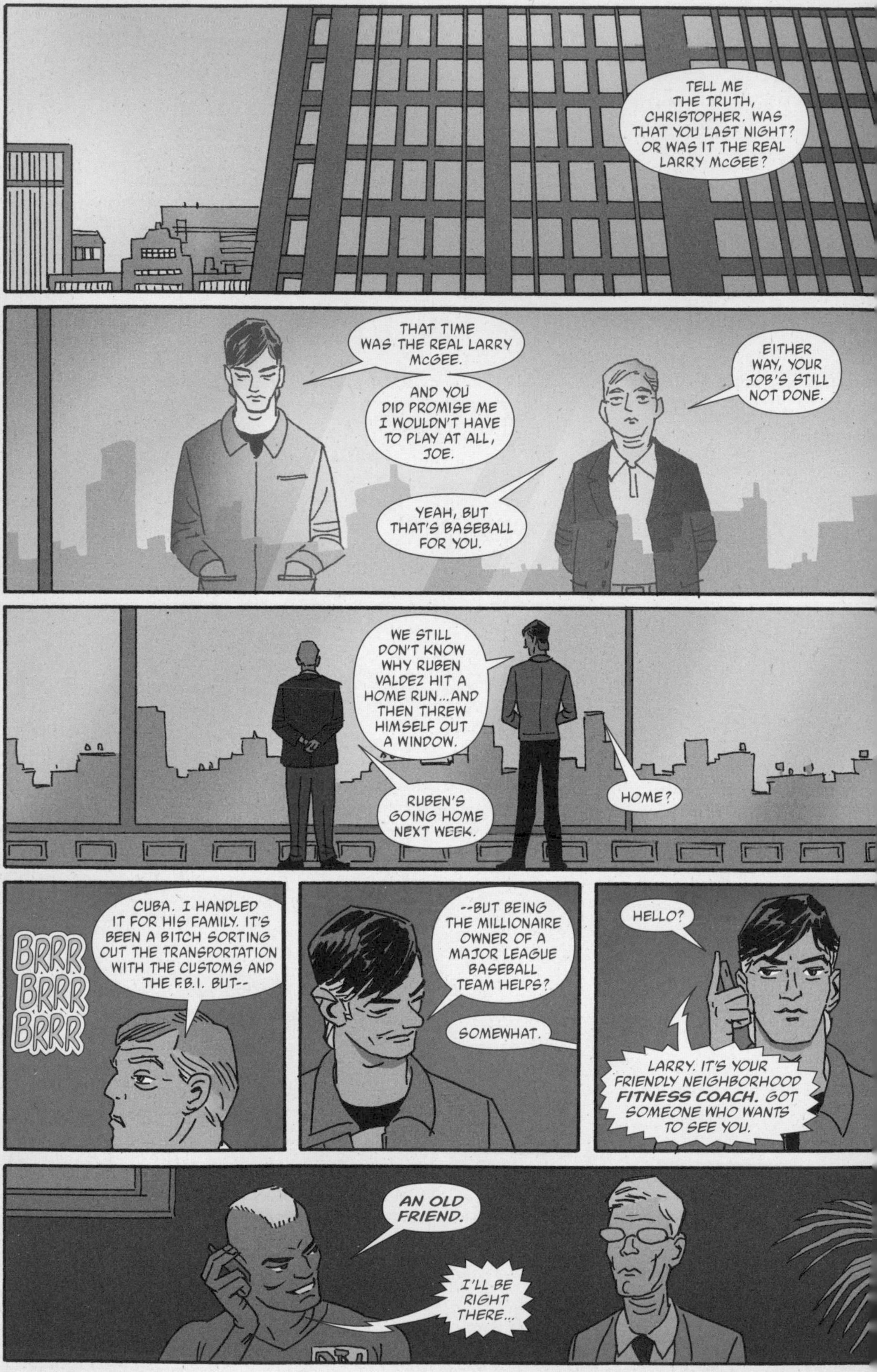
TELL ME THE TRUTH, CHRISTOPHER. WAS THAT YOU LAST NIGHT? OR WAS IT THE REAL LARRY McGEE?
THAT TIME WAS THE REAL LARRY McGEE.
AND YOU DID PROMISE ME I WOULDN'T HAVE TO PLAY AT ALL, JOE.
EITHER WAY, YOUR JOB'S STILL NOT DONE.
YEAH, BUT THAT'S BASEBALL FOR YOU.
WE STILL DON'T KNOW WHY RUBEN VALDEZ HIT A HOME RUN...AND THEN THREW HIMSELF OUT A WINDOW.
RUBEN'S GOING HOME NEXT WEEK.
HOME?
BRRR BRRR BRRR
CUBA. I HANDLED IT FOR HIS FAMILY. IT'S BEEN A BITCH SORTING OUT THE TRANSPORTATION WITH THE CUSTOMS AND THE F.B.I. BUT--
--BUT BEING THE MILLIONAIRE OWNER OF A MAJOR LEAGUE BASEBALL TEAM HELPS?
SOMEWHAT.
HELLO?
LARRY. IT'S YOUR FRIENDLY NEIGHBORHOOD FITNESS COACH. GOT SOMEONE WHO WANTS TO SEE YOU.
AN OLD FRIEND.
I'LL BE RIGHT THERE...

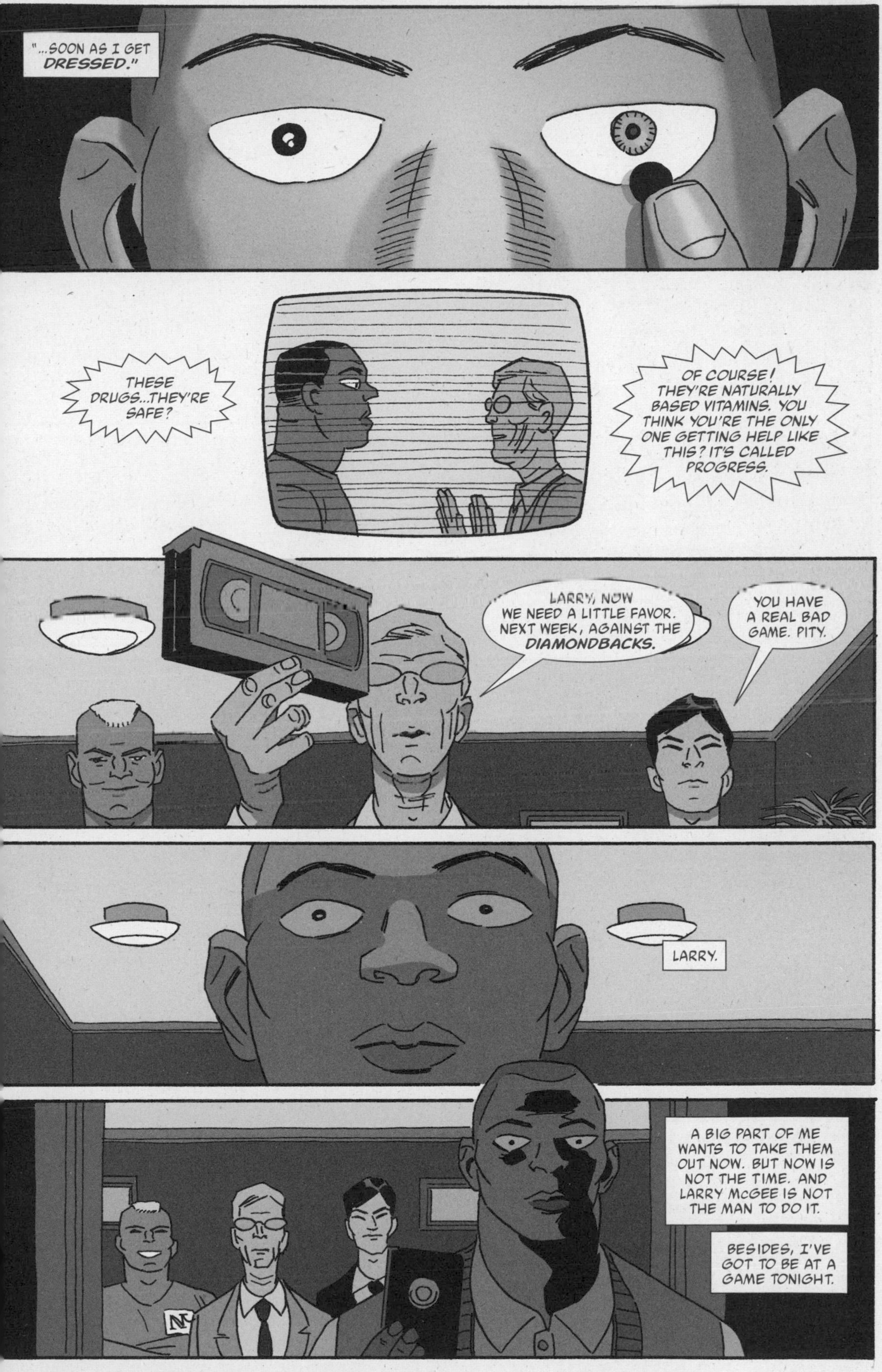
"...SOON AS I GET DRESSED."
THESE DRUGS...THEY'RE SAFE?
OF COURSE! THEY'RE NATURALLY BASED VITAMINS. YOU THINK YOU'RE THE ONLY ONE GETTING HELP LIKE THIS? IT'S CALLED PROGRESS.
LARRY, NOW WE NEED A LITTLE FAVOR. NEXT WEEK, AGAINST THE DIAMONDBACKS.
YOU HAVE A REAL BAD GAME. PITY.
LARRY.
A BIG PART OF ME WANTS TO TAKE THEM OUT NOW. BUT NOW IS NOT THE TIME. AND LARRY McGEE IS NOT THE MAN TO DO IT.
BESIDES, I'VE GOT TO BE AT A GAME TONIGHT.

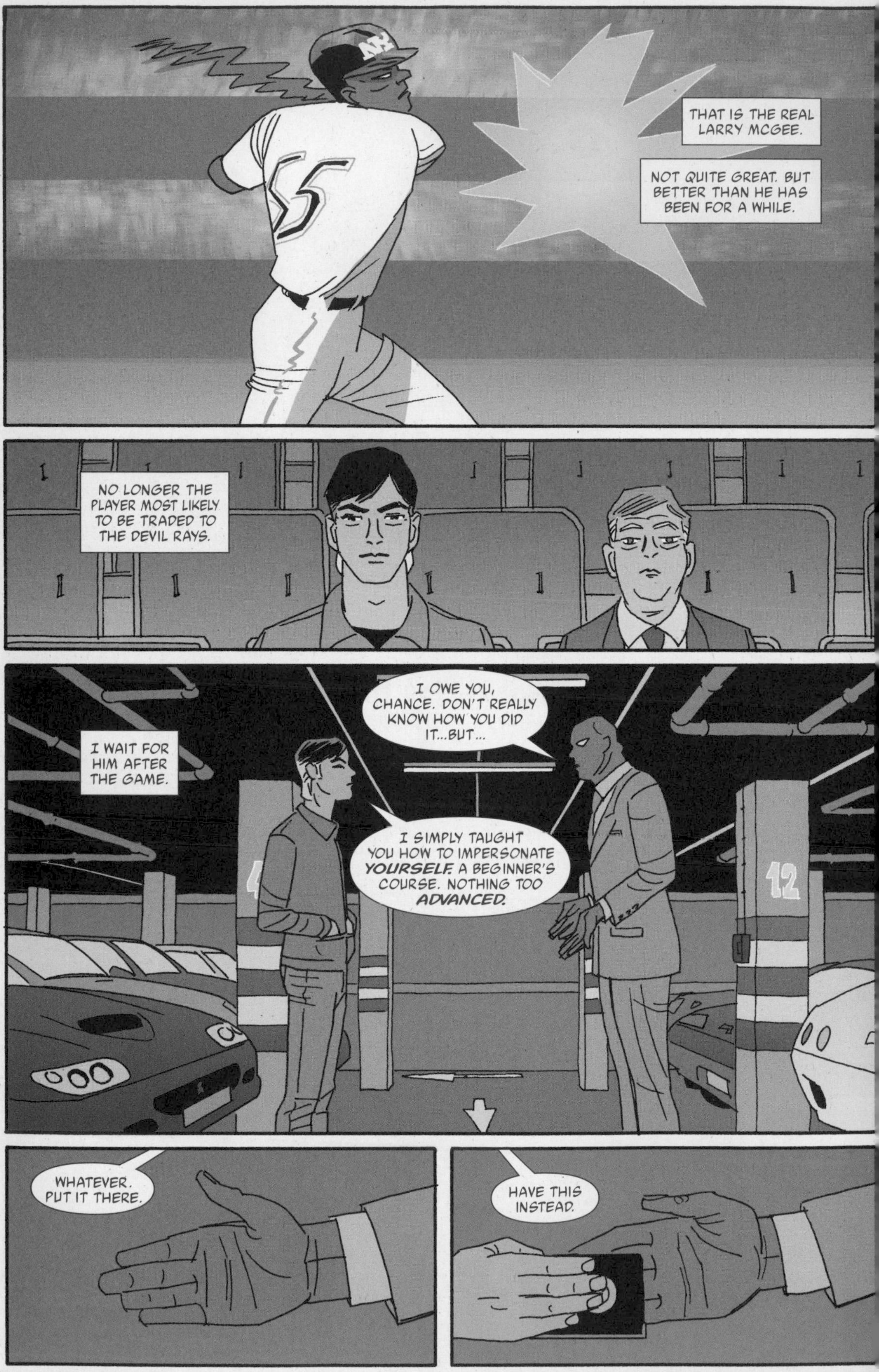
THAT IS THE REAL LARRY MCGEE.
NOT QUITE GREAT. BUT BETTER THAN HE HAS BEEN FOR A WHILE.
NO LONGER THE PLAYER MOST LIKELY TO BE TRADED TO THE DEVIL RAYS.
I WAIT FOR HIM AFTER THE GAME.
I OWE YOU, CHANCE. DON'T REALLY KNOW HOW YOU DID IT...BUT...
I SIMPLY TAUGHT YOU HOW TO IMPERSONATE **YOURSELF.** A BEGINNER'S COURSE. NOTHING TOO **ADVANCED.**
12
WHATEVER. PUT IT THERE.
HAVE THIS INSTEAD.

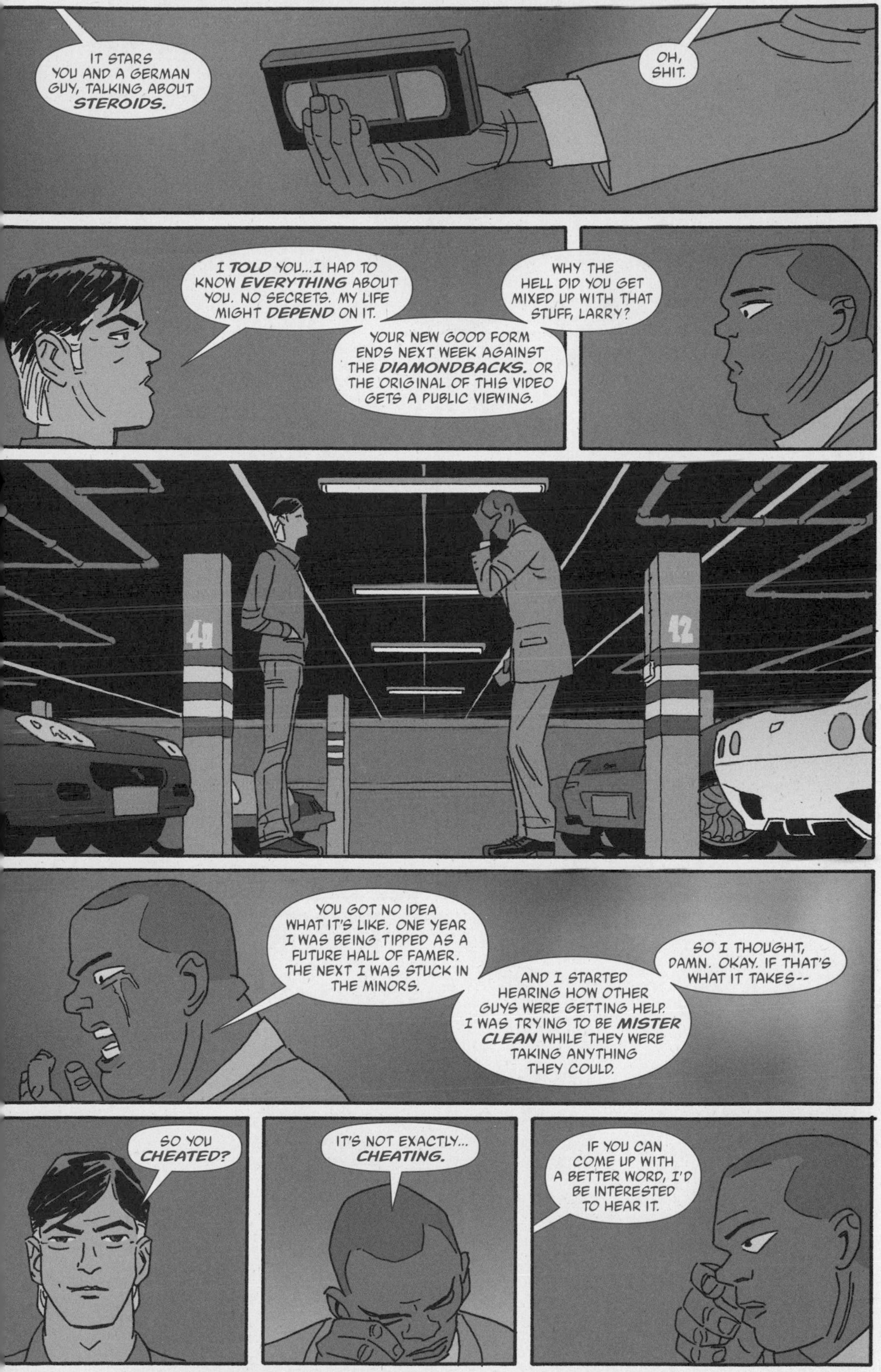
IT STARS YOU AND A GERMAN GUY, TALKING ABOUT STEROIDS.
OH, SHIT.
I TOLD YOU...I HAD TO KNOW EVERYTHING ABOUT YOU. NO SECRETS. MY LIFE MIGHT DEPEND ON IT.
YOUR NEW GOOD FORM ENDS NEXT WEEK AGAINST THE DIAMONDBACKS. OR THE ORIGINAL OF THIS VIDEO GETS A PUBLIC VIEWING.
WHY THE HELL DID YOU GET MIXED UP WITH THAT STUFF, LARRY?
YOU GOT NO IDEA WHAT IT'S LIKE. ONE YEAR I WAS BEING TIPPED AS A FUTURE HALL OF FAMER. THE NEXT I WAS STUCK IN THE MINORS.
AND I STARTED HEARING HOW OTHER GUYS WERE GETTING HELP. I WAS TRYING TO BE MISTER CLEAN WHILE THEY WERE TAKING ANYTHING THEY COULD.
SO I THOUGHT, DAMN. OKAY. IF THAT'S WHAT IT TAKES--
SO YOU CHEATED?
IT'S NOT EXACTLY... CHEATING.
IF YOU CAN COME UP WITH A BETTER WORD, I'D BE INTERESTED TO HEAR IT.

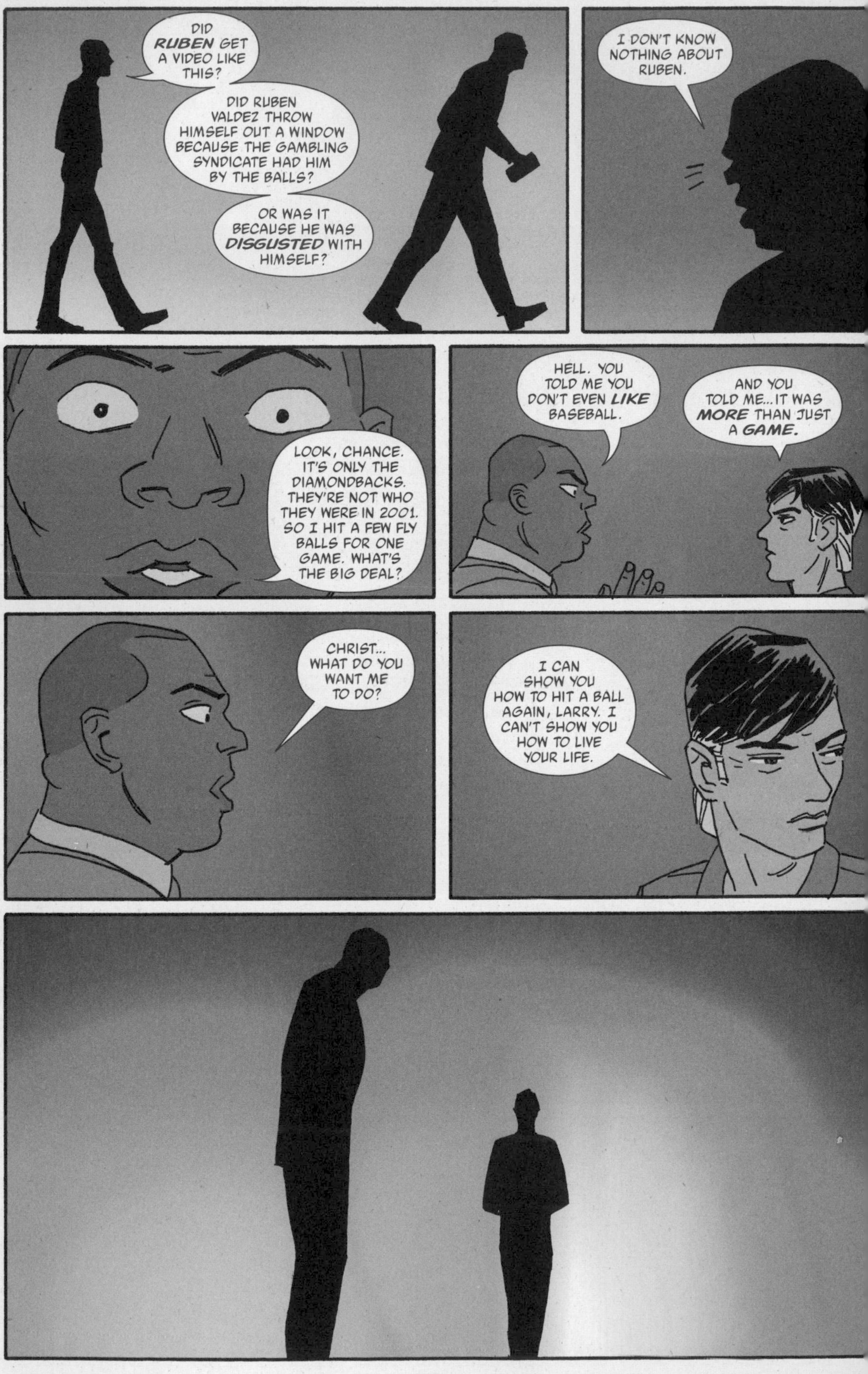
DID RUBEN GET A VIDEO LIKE THIS?
DID RUBEN VALDEZ THROW HIMSELF OUT A WINDOW BECAUSE THE GAMBLING SYNDICATE HAD HIM BY THE BALLS?
OR WAS IT BECAUSE HE WAS DISGUSTED WITH HIMSELF?
I DON'T KNOW NOTHING ABOUT RUBEN.
LOOK, CHANCE. IT'S ONLY THE DIAMONDBACKS. THEY'RE NOT WHO THEY WERE IN 2001. SO I HIT A FEW FLY BALLS FOR ONE GAME. WHAT'S THE BIG DEAL?
HELL. YOU TOLD ME YOU DON'T EVEN LIKE BASEBALL.
AND YOU TOLD ME... IT WAS MORE THAN JUST A GAME.
CHRIST... WHAT DO YOU WANT ME TO DO?
I CAN SHOW YOU HOW TO HIT A BALL AGAIN, LARRY. I CAN'T SHOW YOU HOW TO LIVE YOUR LIFE.

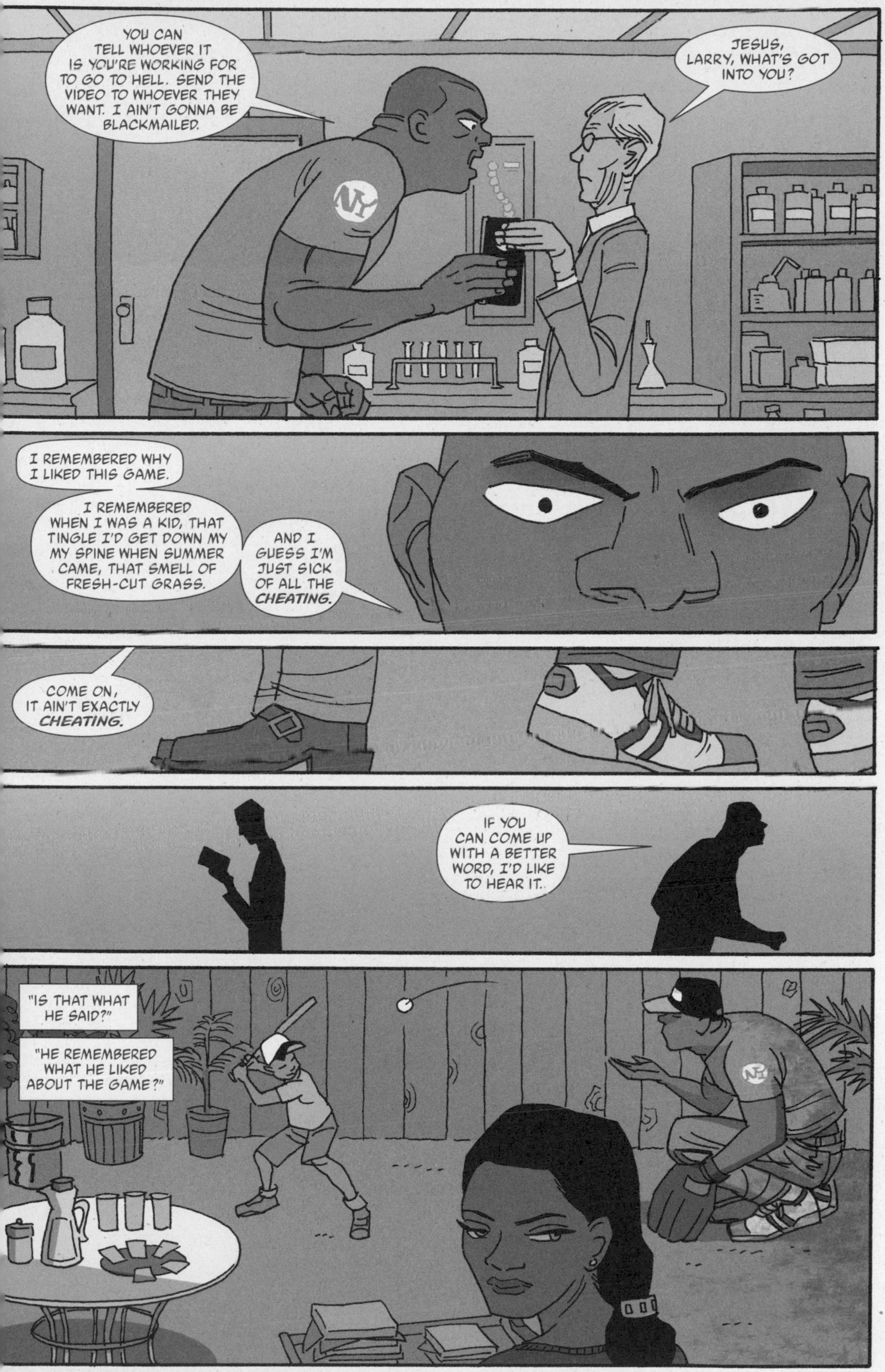

YOU CAN TELL WHOEVER IT IS YOU'RE WORKING FOR TO GO TO HELL. SEND THE VIDEO TO WHOEVER THEY WANT. I AIN'T GONNA BE BLACKMAILED.
JESUS, LARRY, WHAT'S GOT INTO YOU?
I REMEMBERED WHY I LIKED THIS GAME.
I REMEMBERED WHEN I WAS A KID, THAT TINGLE I'D GET DOWN MY MY SPINE WHEN SUMMER CAME, THAT SMELL OF FRESH-CUT GRASS.
AND I GUESS I'M JUST SICK OF ALL THE *CHEATING.*
COME ON, IT AIN'T EXACTLY *CHEATING.*
IF YOU CAN COME UP WITH A BETTER WORD, I'D LIKE TO HEAR IT.
"IS THAT WHAT HE SAID?"
"HE REMEMBERED WHAT HE LIKED ABOUT THE GAME?"

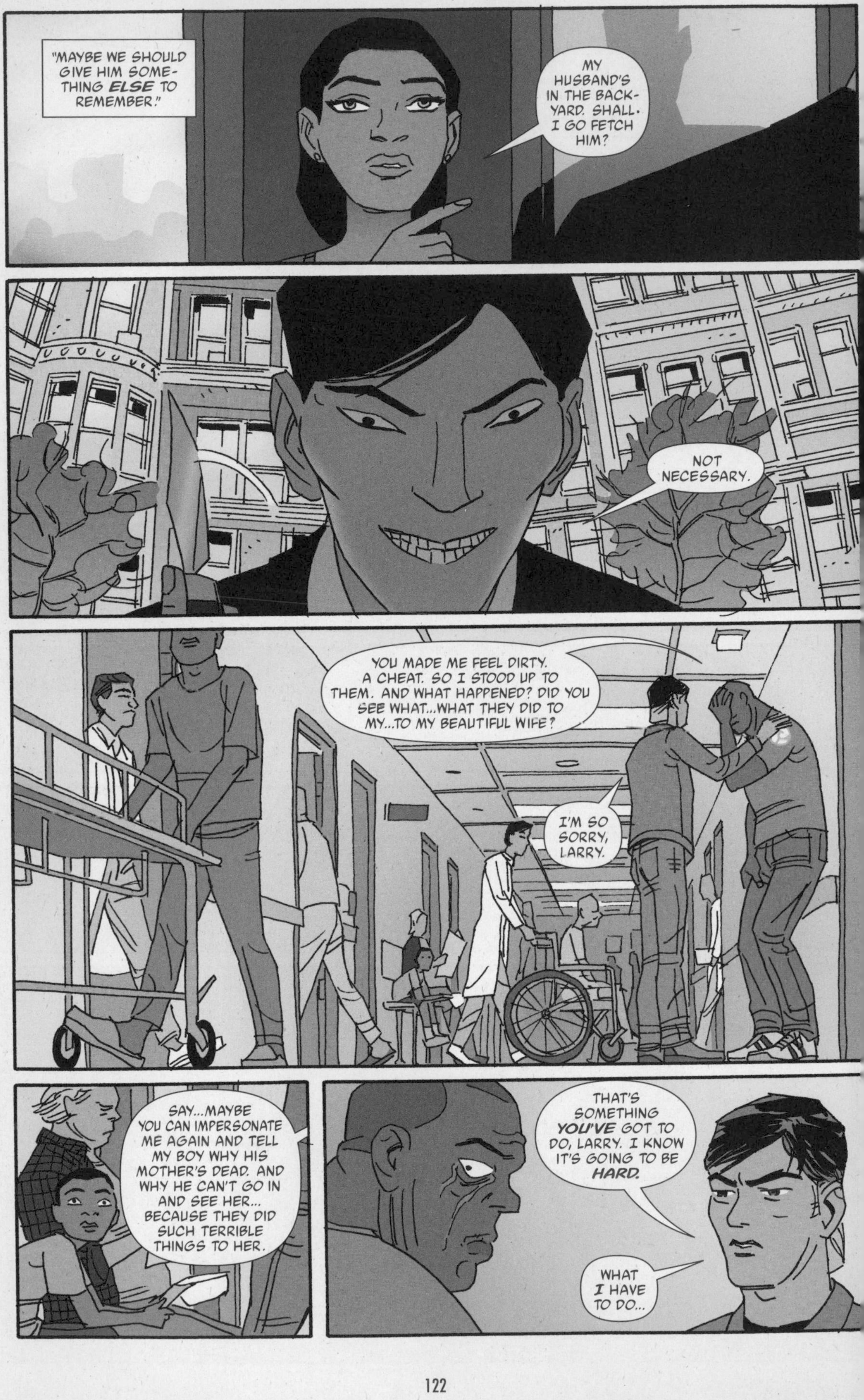
"MAYBE WE SHOULD GIVE HIM SOME-THING ELSE TO REMEMBER."
MY HUSBAND'S IN THE BACK-YARD. SHALL. I GO FETCH HIM?
NOT NECESSARY.
YOU MADE ME FEEL DIRTY. A CHEAT. SO I STOOD UP TO THEM. AND WHAT HAPPENED? DID YOU SEE WHAT...WHAT THEY DID TO MY...TO MY BEAUTIFUL WIFE?
I'M SO SORRY, LARRY.
SAY...MAYBE YOU CAN IMPERSONATE ME AGAIN AND TELL MY BOY WHY HIS MOTHER'S DEAD. AND WHY HE CAN'T GO IN AND SEE HER... BECAUSE THEY DID SUCH TERRIBLE THINGS TO HER.
THAT'S SOMETHING YOU'VE GOT TO DO, LARRY. I KNOW IT'S GOING TO BE HARD.
WHAT I HAVE TO DO...

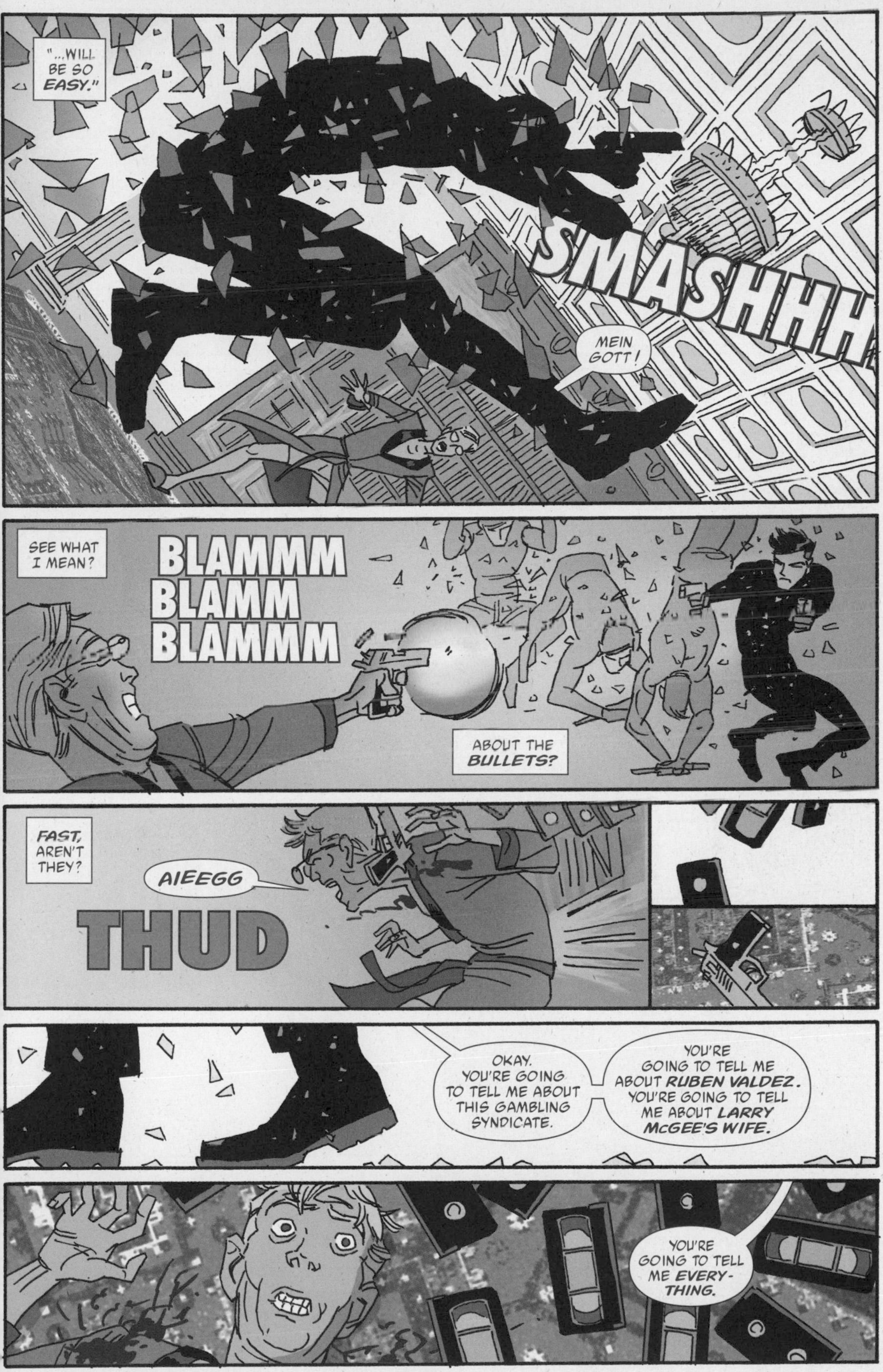
"...WILL BE SO EASY."
SMASHHH
MEIN GOTT!
SEE WHAT I MEAN?
BLAMMM
BLAMM
BLAMMM
ABOUT THE BULLETS?
FAST, AREN'T THEY?
AIEEGG
THUD
OKAY. YOU'RE GOING TO TELL ME ABOUT THIS GAMBLING SYNDICATE.
YOU'RE GOING TO TELL ME ABOUT RUBEN VALDEZ. YOU'RE GOING TO TELL ME ABOUT LARRY McGEE'S WIFE.
YOU'RE GOING TO TELL ME EVERY-THING.

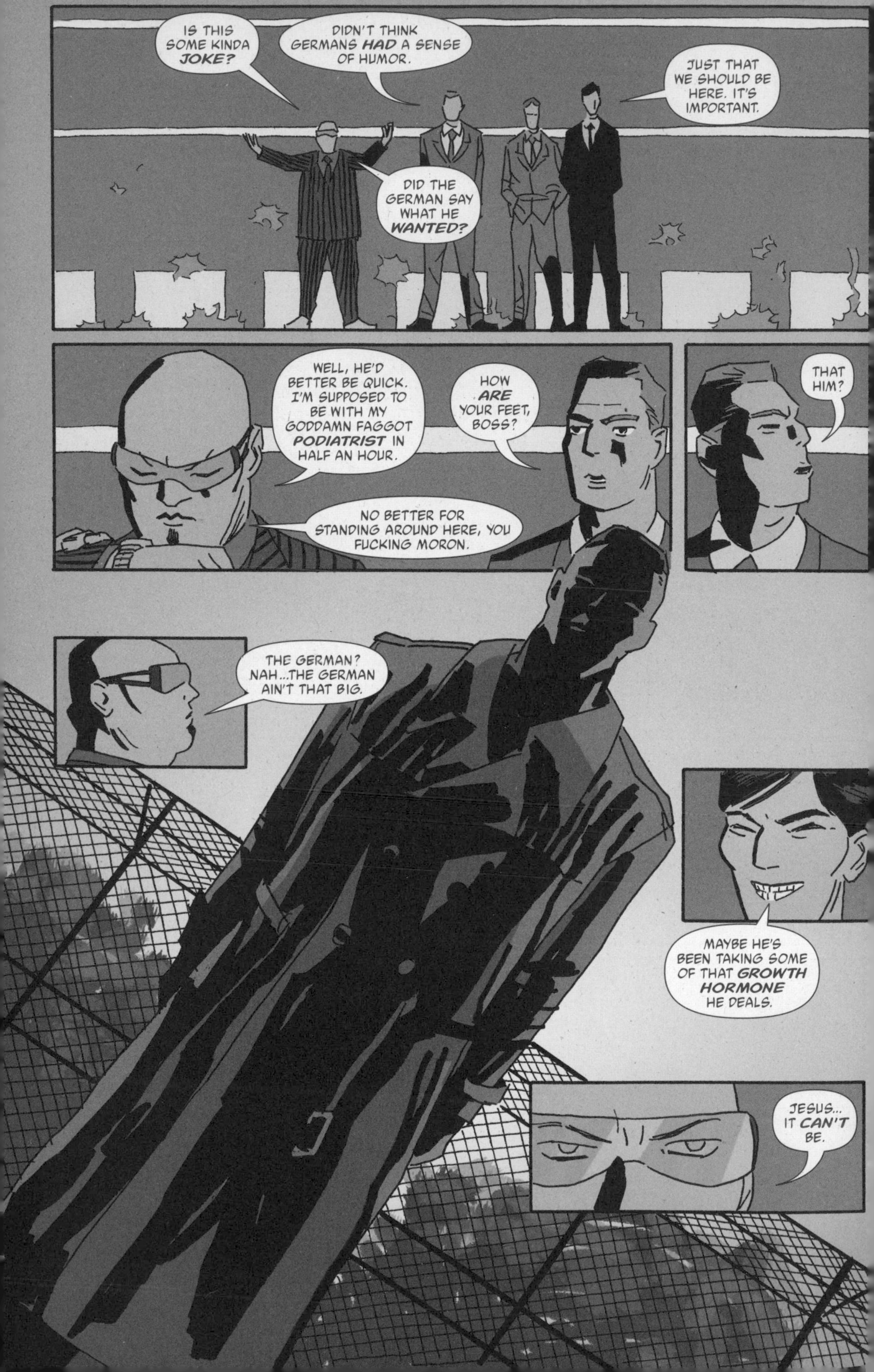
IS THIS SOME KINDA JOKE?
DIDN'T THINK GERMANS HAD A SENSE OF HUMOR.
JUST THAT WE SHOULD BE HERE. IT'S IMPORTANT.
DID THE GERMAN SAY WHAT HE WANTED?
WELL, HE'D BETTER BE QUICK. I'M SUPPOSED TO BE WITH MY GODDAMN FAGGOT PODIATRIST IN HALF AN HOUR.
HOW ARE YOUR FEET, BOSS?
NO BETTER FOR STANDING AROUND HERE, YOU FUCKING MORON.
THAT HIM?
THE GERMAN? NAH...THE GERMAN AIN'T THAT BIG.
MAYBE HE'S BEEN TAKING SOME OF THAT GROWTH HORMONE HE DEALS.
JESUS... IT CAN'T BE.

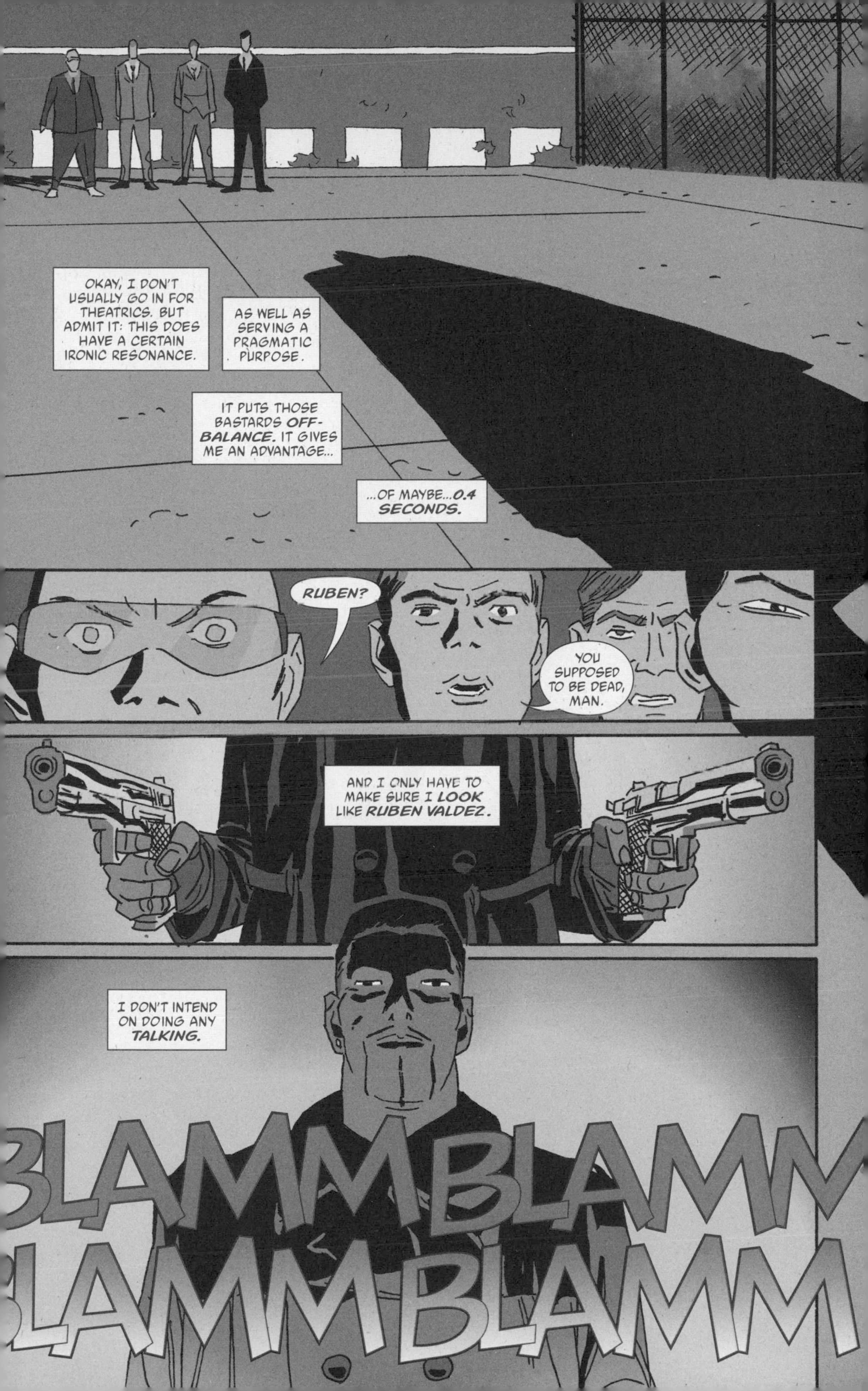
OKAY, I DON'T USUALLY GO IN FOR THEATRICS. BUT ADMIT IT: THIS DOES HAVE A CERTAIN IRONIC RESONANCE.
AS WELL AS SERVING A PRAGMATIC PURPOSE.
IT PUTS THOSE BASTARDS OFF-BALANCE. IT GIVES ME AN ADVANTAGE...
...OF MAYBE...0.4 SECONDS.
RUBEN?
YOU SUPPOSED TO BE DEAD, MAN.
AND I ONLY HAVE TO MAKE SURE I LOOK LIKE RUBEN VALDEZ.
I DON'T INTEND ON DOING ANY TALKING.
BLAMM BLAMM
BLAMM BLAMM

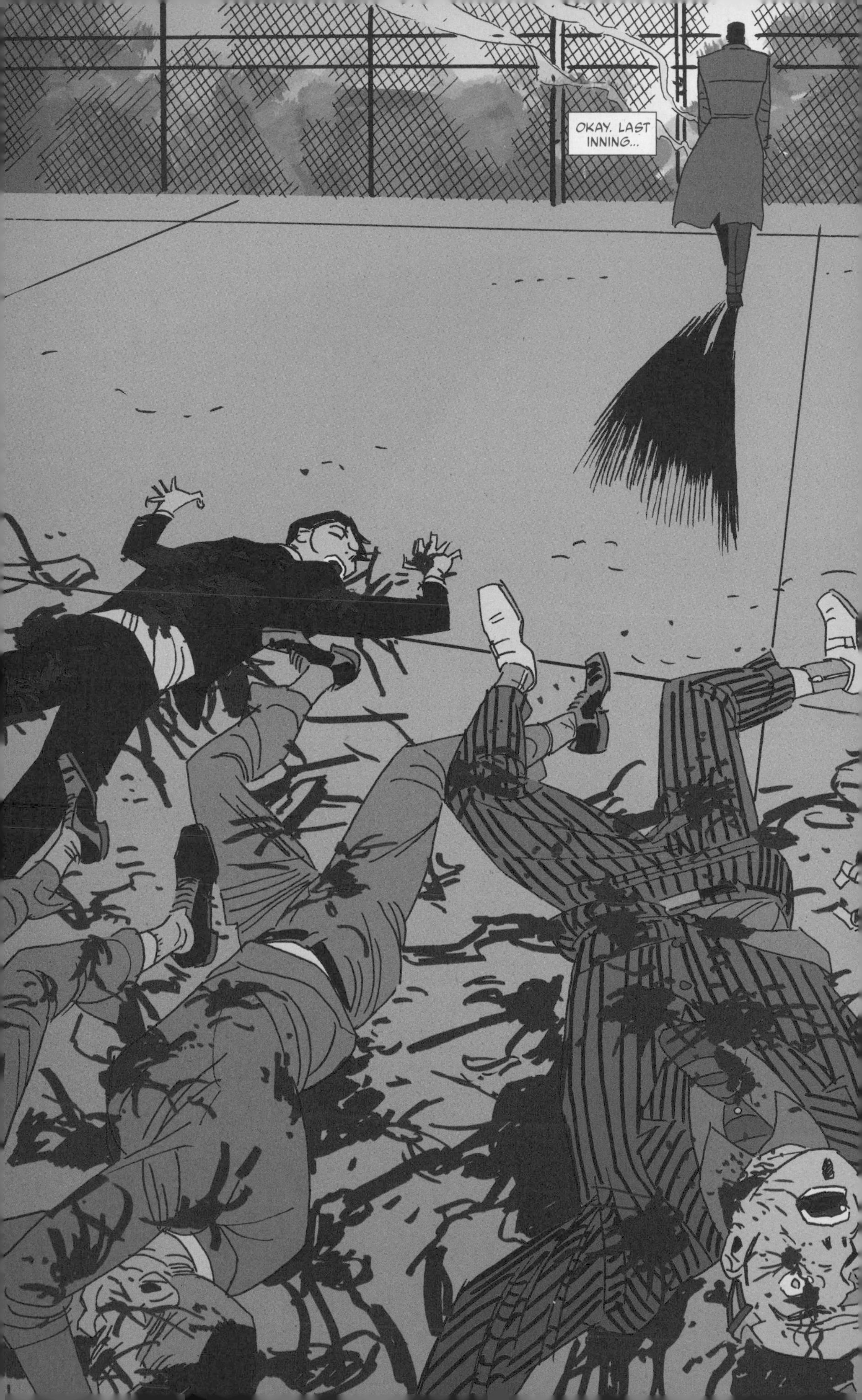
OKAY. LAST INNING...

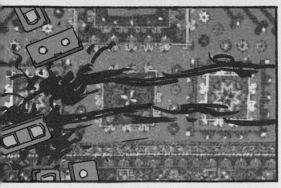

LIEBCHEN... THANK GOD...I GOTTA MAKE A CALL. SOME-ONE'S...SOMEONE'S ATTACKED ME.

I CAN SEE THAT.

WHAT... WHAT ARE YOU DOING?

I REALLY DID WANT THAT PLACE IN THE CARIBBEAN, JURGEN. IT'S A PITY YOU'RE TOO MUCH OF A TIGHTWAD KRAUT TO GET IT FOR ME.

OTHER MEN WOULD HAVE GOT IT FOR ME. OTHER MEN WOULD *APPRECIATE* ME.

LIEBCHEN...IS THIS...A *JOKE*?

NO, BABY. THIS IS AN *OPPORTUNITY*.

TO GET MY HANDS ON YOUR *LIFE INSURANCE*. TO BE ABLE TO LIVE MY LIFE...WITH-OUT RUNNING TO *YOU* EVERY TIME I NEED SOMETHING.

AND PEOPLE WONDER WHY I NEVER GOT *MARRIED*.

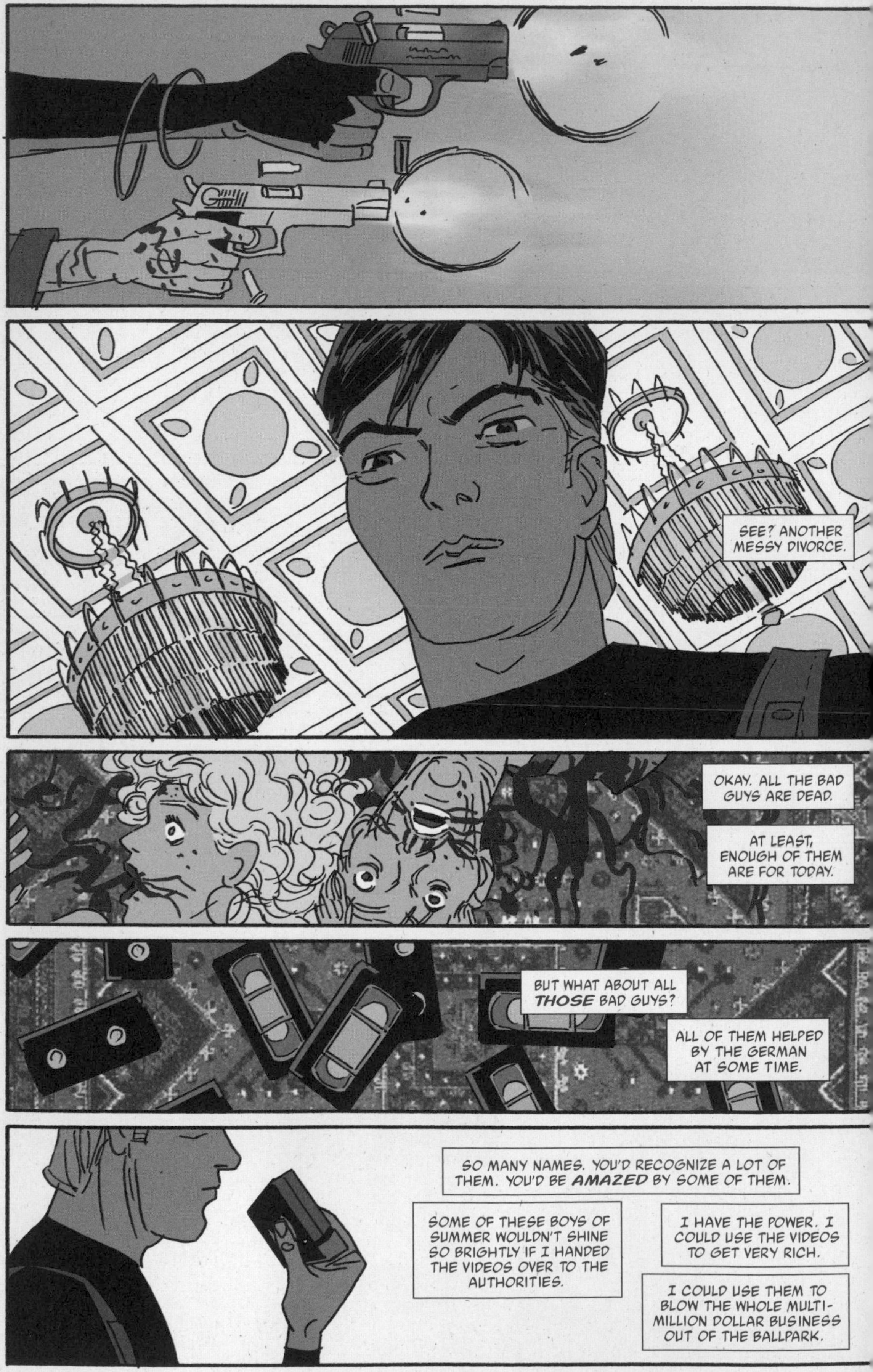

SEE? ANOTHER MESSY DIVORCE.
OKAY. ALL THE BAD GUYS ARE DEAD.
AT LEAST, ENOUGH OF THEM ARE FOR TODAY.
BUT WHAT ABOUT ALL **THOSE** BAD GUYS?
ALL OF THEM HELPED BY THE GERMAN AT SOME TIME.
SO MANY NAMES. YOU'D RECOGNIZE A LOT OF THEM. YOU'D BE **AMAZED** BY SOME OF THEM.
SOME OF THESE BOYS OF SUMMER WOULDN'T SHINE SO BRIGHTLY IF I HANDED THE VIDEOS OVER TO THE AUTHORITIES.
I HAVE THE POWER. I COULD USE THE VIDEOS TO GET VERY RICH.
I COULD USE THEM TO BLOW THE WHOLE MULTI-MILLION DOLLAR BUSINESS OUT OF THE BALLPARK.

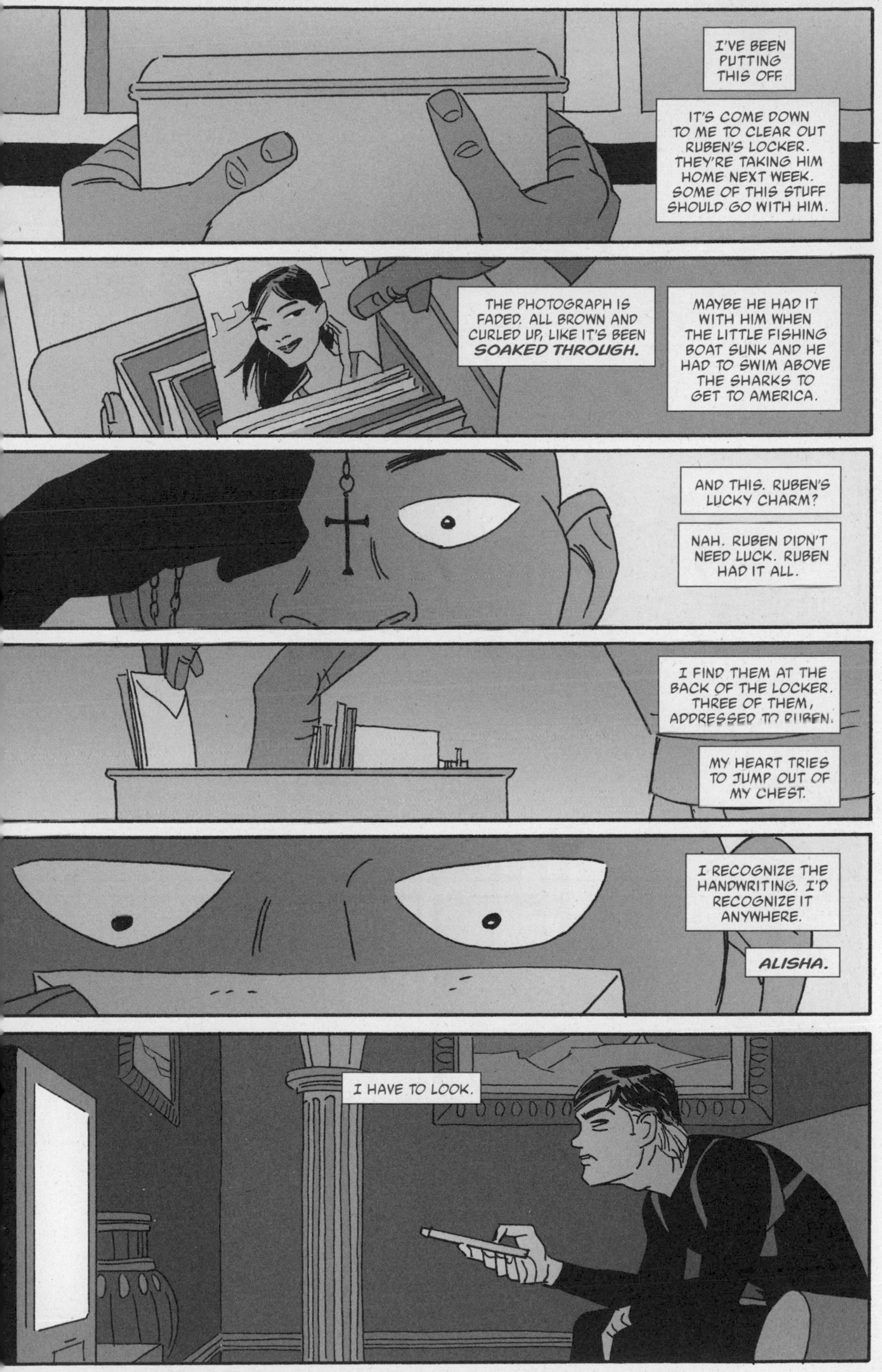
I'VE BEEN PUTTING THIS OFF.
IT'S COME DOWN TO ME TO CLEAR OUT RUBEN'S LOCKER. THEY'RE TAKING HIM HOME NEXT WEEK. SOME OF THIS STUFF SHOULD GO WITH HIM.
THE PHOTOGRAPH IS FADED. ALL BROWN AND CURLED UP, LIKE IT'S BEEN SOAKED THROUGH.
MAYBE HE HAD IT WITH HIM WHEN THE LITTLE FISHING BOAT SUNK AND HE HAD TO SWIM ABOVE THE SHARKS TO GET TO AMERICA.
AND THIS. RUBEN'S LUCKY CHARM?
NAH. RUBEN DIDN'T NEED LUCK. RUBEN HAD IT ALL.
I FIND THEM AT THE BACK OF THE LOCKER. THREE OF THEM, ADDRESSED TO RUBEN.
MY HEART TRIES TO JUMP OUT OF MY CHEST.
I RECOGNIZE THE HANDWRITING. I'D RECOGNIZE IT ANYWHERE.
ALISHA.
I HAVE TO LOOK.

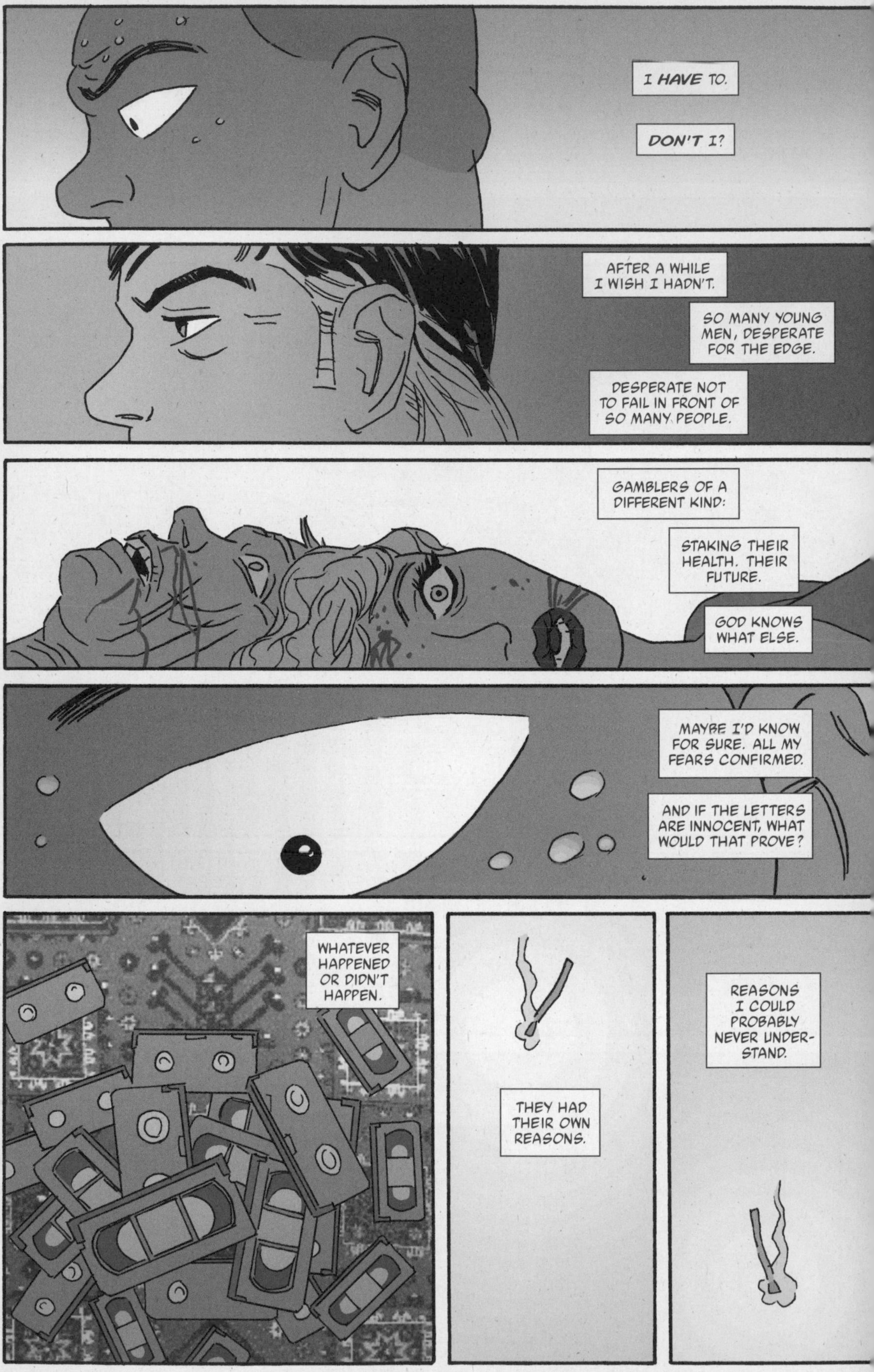
I HAVE TO.
DON'T I?
AFTER A WHILE I WISH I HADN'T.
SO MANY YOUNG MEN, DESPERATE FOR THE EDGE.
DESPERATE NOT TO FAIL IN FRONT OF SO MANY PEOPLE.
GAMBLERS OF A DIFFERENT KIND:
STAKING THEIR HEALTH. THEIR FUTURE.
GOD KNOWS WHAT ELSE.
MAYBE I'D KNOW FOR SURE. ALL MY FEARS CONFIRMED.
AND IF THE LETTERS ARE INNOCENT, WHAT WOULD THAT PROVE?
WHATEVER HAPPENED OR DIDN'T HAPPEN.
THEY HAD THEIR OWN REASONS.
REASONS I COULD PROBABLY NEVER UNDER-STAND.

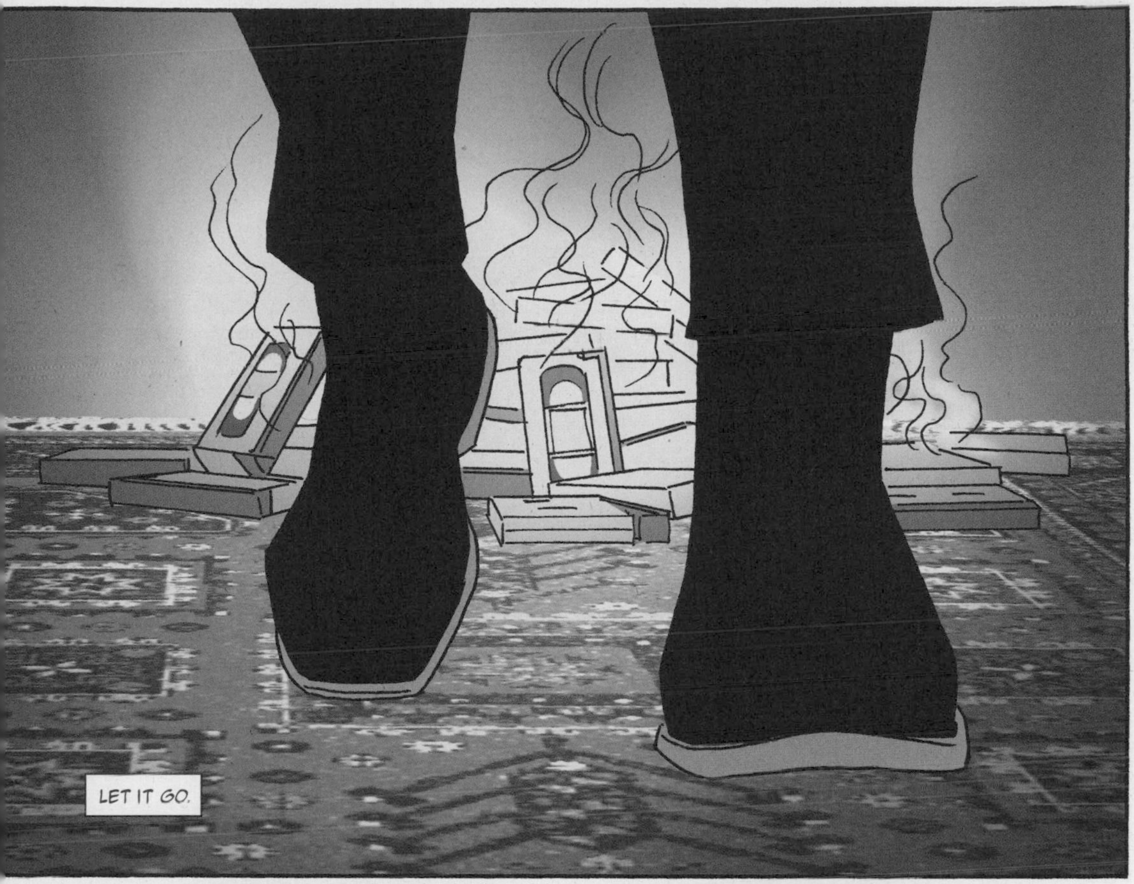
LET IT GO.

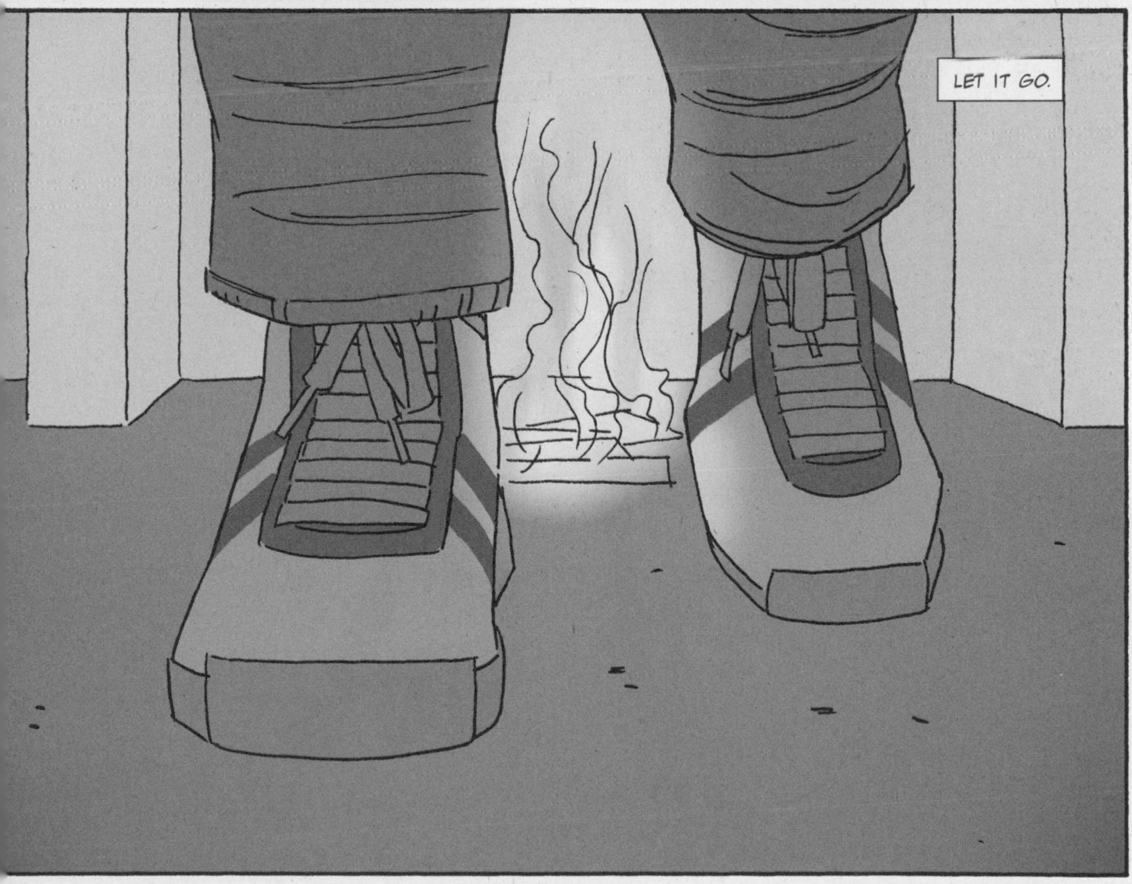
LET IT GO.

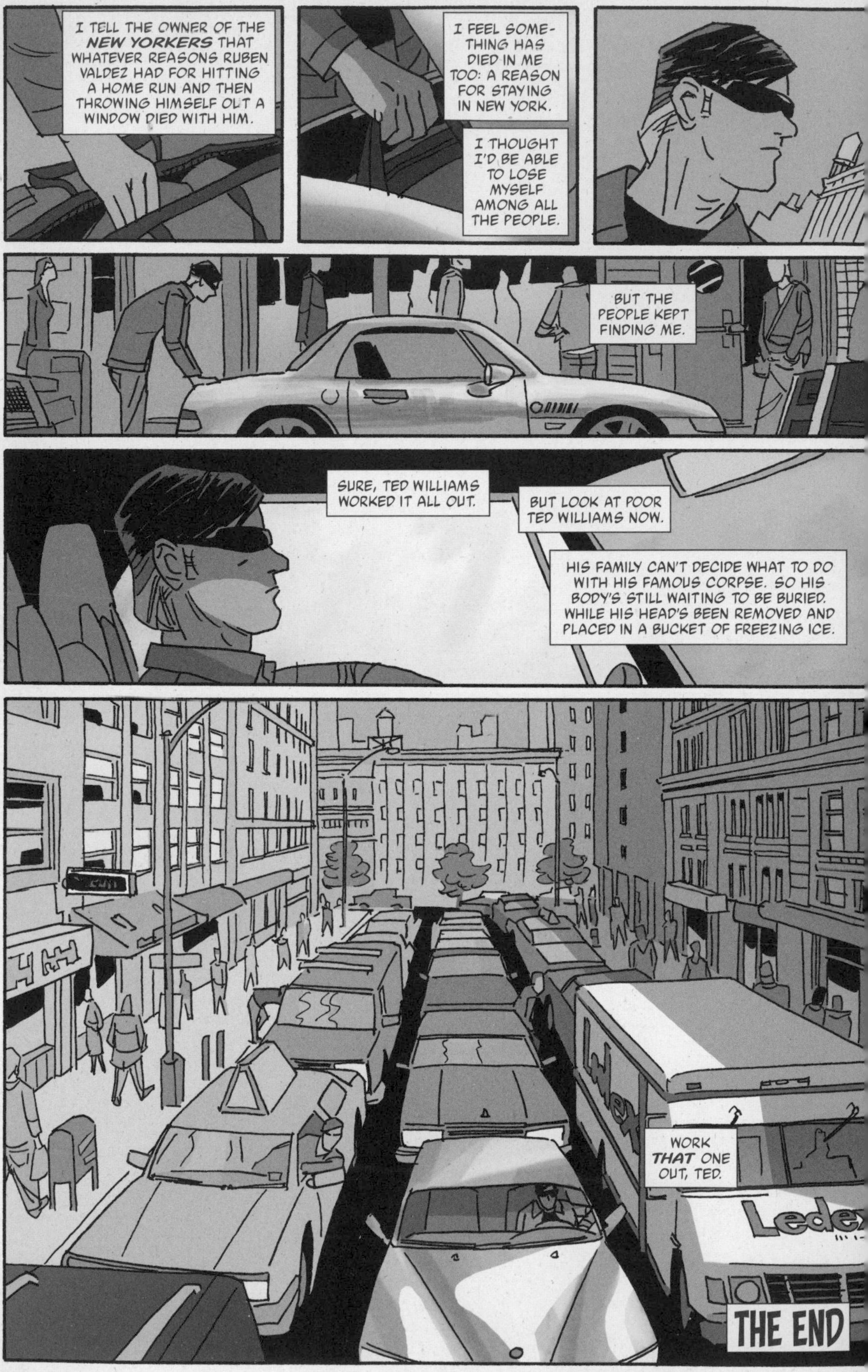
I TELL THE OWNER OF THE **NEW YORKERS** THAT WHATEVER REASONS RUBEN VALDEZ HAD FOR HITTING A HOME RUN AND THEN THROWING HIMSELF OUT A WINDOW DIED WITH HIM.
I FEEL SOMETHING HAS DIED IN ME TOO: A REASON FOR STAYING IN NEW YORK.
I THOUGHT I'D BE ABLE TO LOSE MYSELF AMONG ALL THE PEOPLE.
BUT THE PEOPLE KEPT FINDING ME.
SURE, TED WILLIAMS WORKED IT ALL OUT.
BUT LOOK AT POOR TED WILLIAMS NOW.
HIS FAMILY CAN'T DECIDE WHAT TO DO WITH HIS FAMOUS CORPSE. SO HIS BODY'S STILL WAITING TO BE BURIED. WHILE HIS HEAD'S BEEN REMOVED AND PLACED IN A BUCKET OF FREEZING ICE.
WORK **THAT** ONE OUT, TED.
THE END

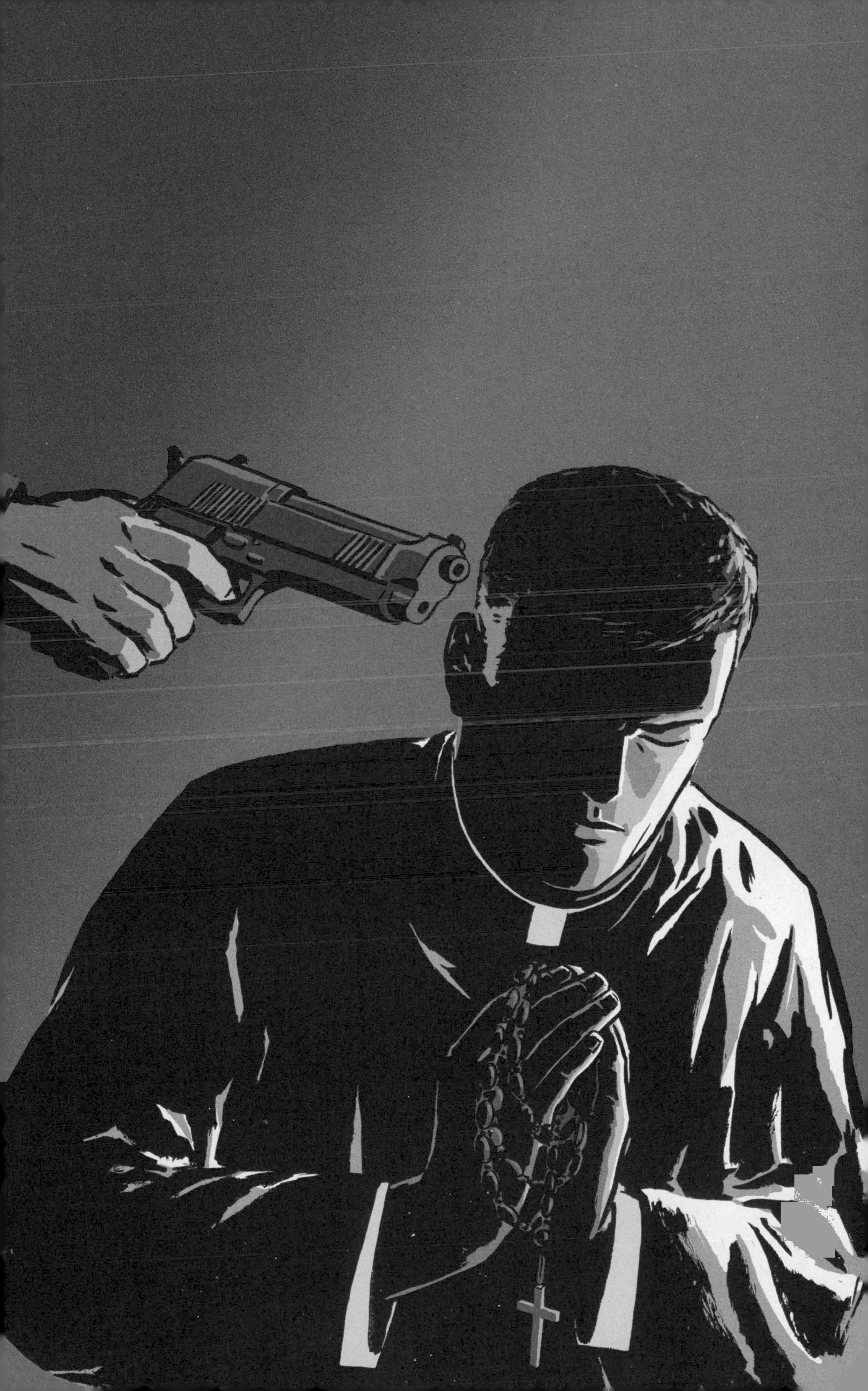

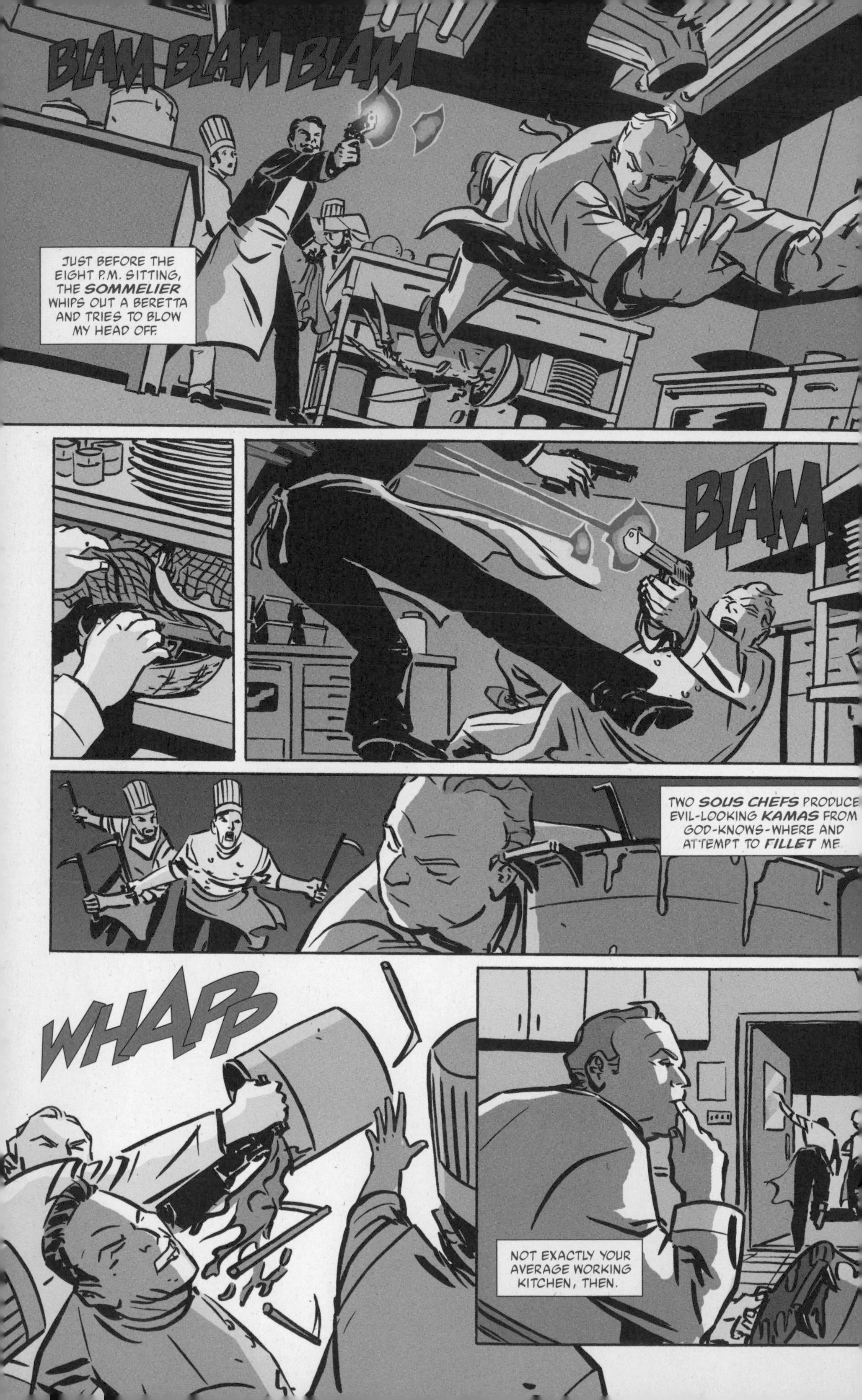
BLAM BLAM BLAM
JUST BEFORE THE EIGHT P.M. SITTING, THE SOMMELIER WHIPS OUT A BERETTA AND TRIES TO BLOW MY HEAD OFF.
BLAM
TWO SOUS CHEFS PRODUCE EVIL-LOOKING KAMAS FROM GOD-KNOWS-WHERE AND ATTEMPT TO FILLET ME.
WHAPP
NOT EXACTLY YOUR AVERAGE WORKING KITCHEN, THEN.

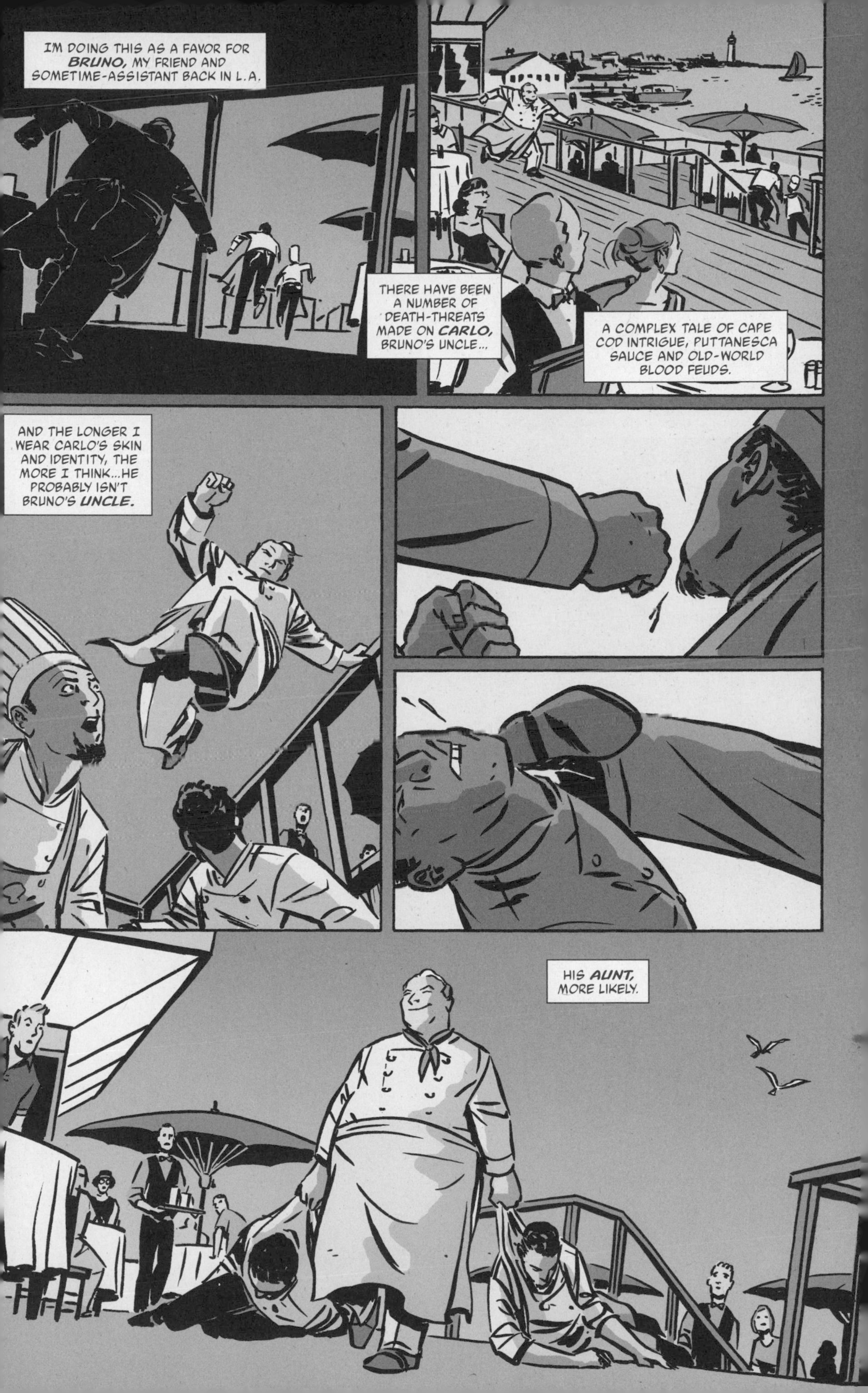
I'M DOING THIS AS A FAVOR FOR BRUNO, MY FRIEND AND SOMETIME-ASSISTANT BACK IN L.A.
THERE HAVE BEEN A NUMBER OF DEATH-THREATS MADE ON CARLO, BRUNO'S UNCLE...
A COMPLEX TALE OF CAPE COD INTRIGUE, PUTTANESCA SAUCE AND OLD-WORLD BLOOD FEUDS.
AND THE LONGER I WEAR CARLO'S SKIN AND IDENTITY, THE MORE I THINK...HE PROBABLY ISN'T BRUNO'S UNCLE.
HIS AUNT, MORE LIKELY.

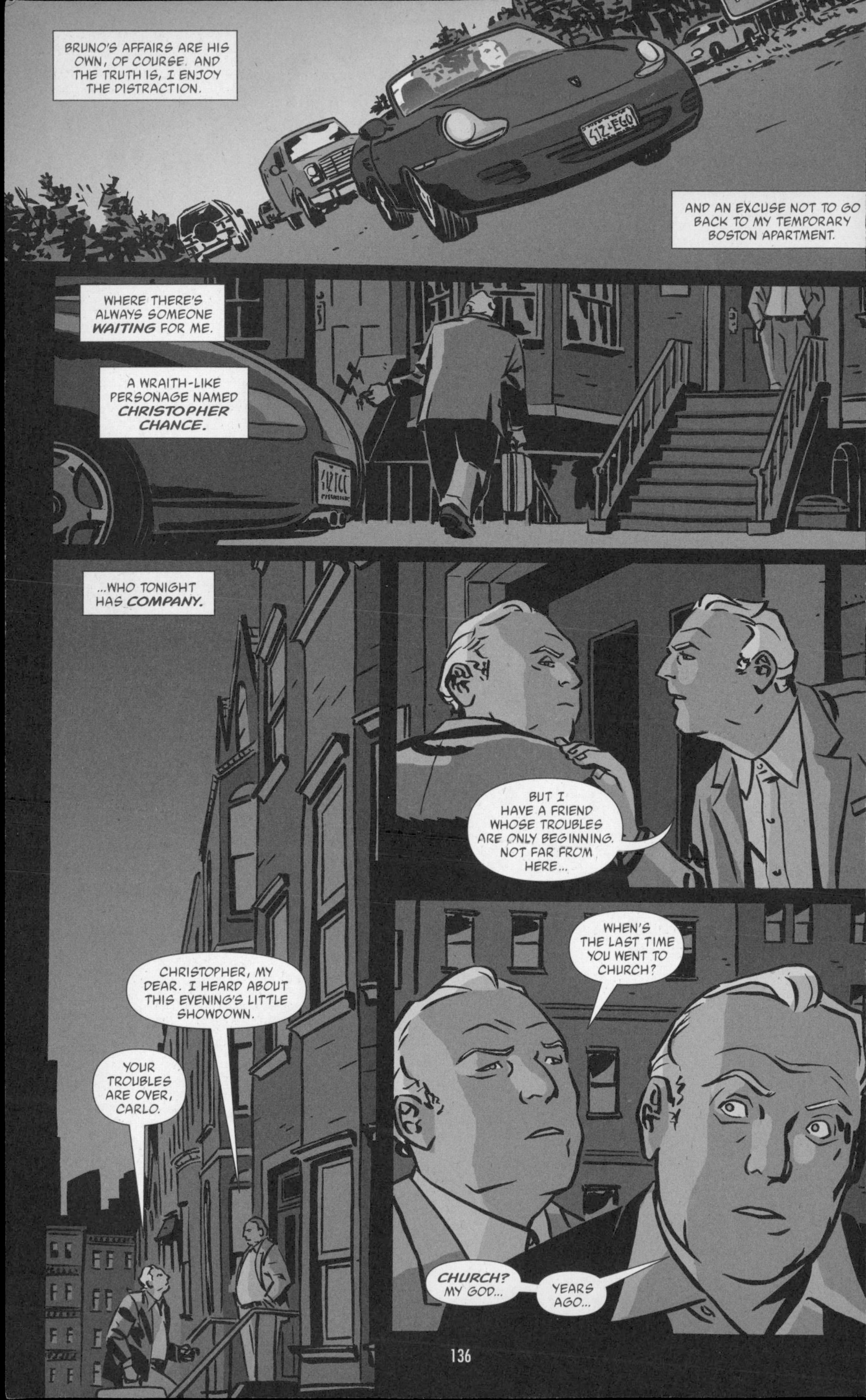
BRUNO'S AFFAIRS ARE HIS OWN, OF COURSE. AND THE TRUTH IS, I ENJOY THE DISTRACTION.
AND AN EXCUSE NOT TO GO BACK TO MY TEMPORARY BOSTON APARTMENT.
WHERE THERE'S ALWAYS SOMEONE WAITING FOR ME.
A WRAITH-LIKE PERSONAGE NAMED CHRISTOPHER CHANCE.
...WHO TONIGHT HAS COMPANY.
CHRISTOPHER, MY DEAR. I HEARD ABOUT THIS EVENING'S LITTLE SHOWDOWN.
YOUR TROUBLES ARE OVER, CARLO.
BUT I HAVE A FRIEND WHOSE TROUBLES ARE ONLY BEGINNING. NOT FAR FROM HERE...
WHEN'S THE LAST TIME YOU WENT TO CHURCH?
CHURCH? MY GOD...
YEARS AGO...

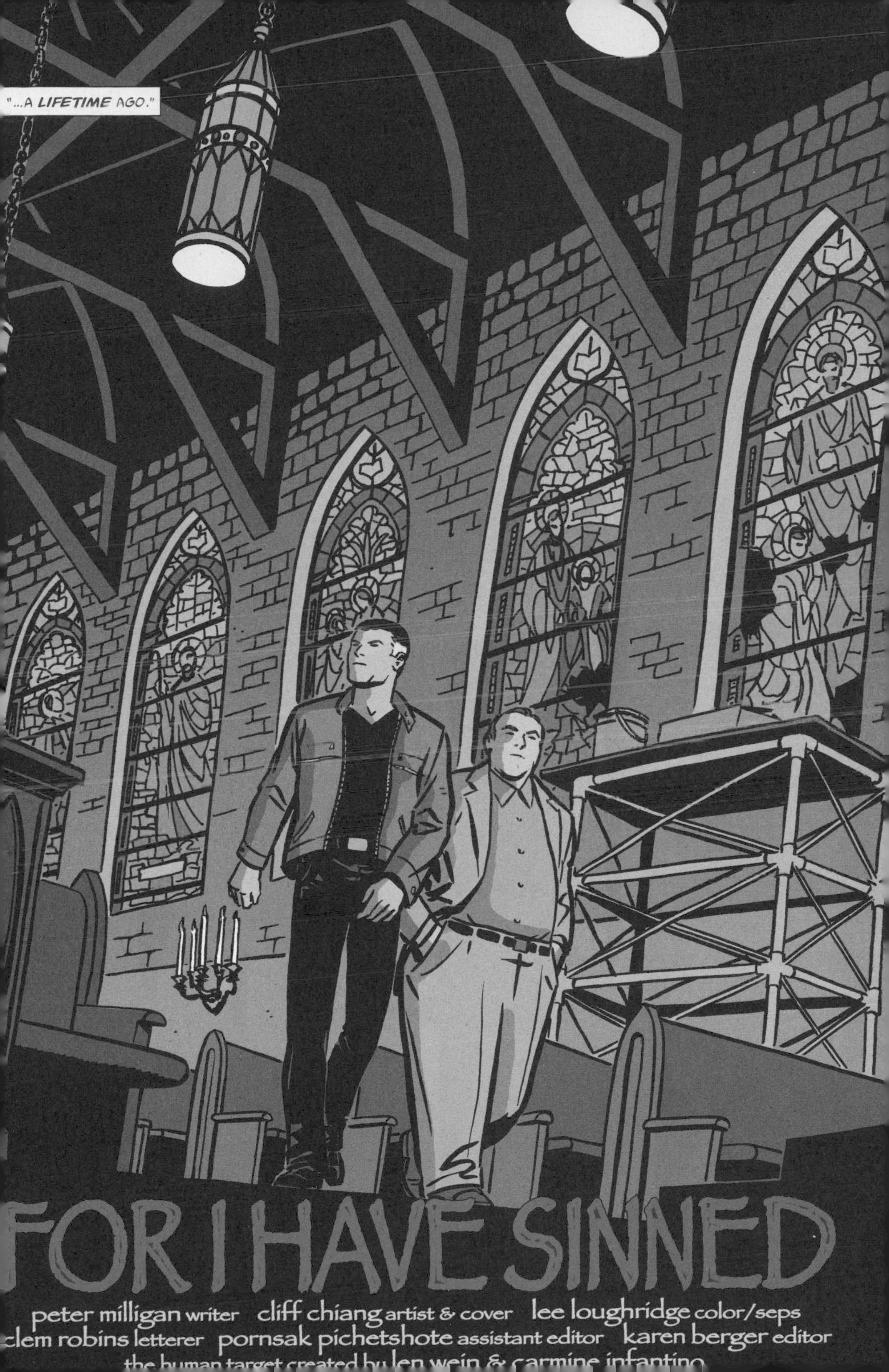
"...A LIFETIME AGO."
FOR I HAVE SINNED
peter milligan writer cliff chiang artist & cover lee loughridge color/seps
clem robins letterer pornsak pichetshote assistant editor karen berger editor
the human target created by len wein & carmine infantino

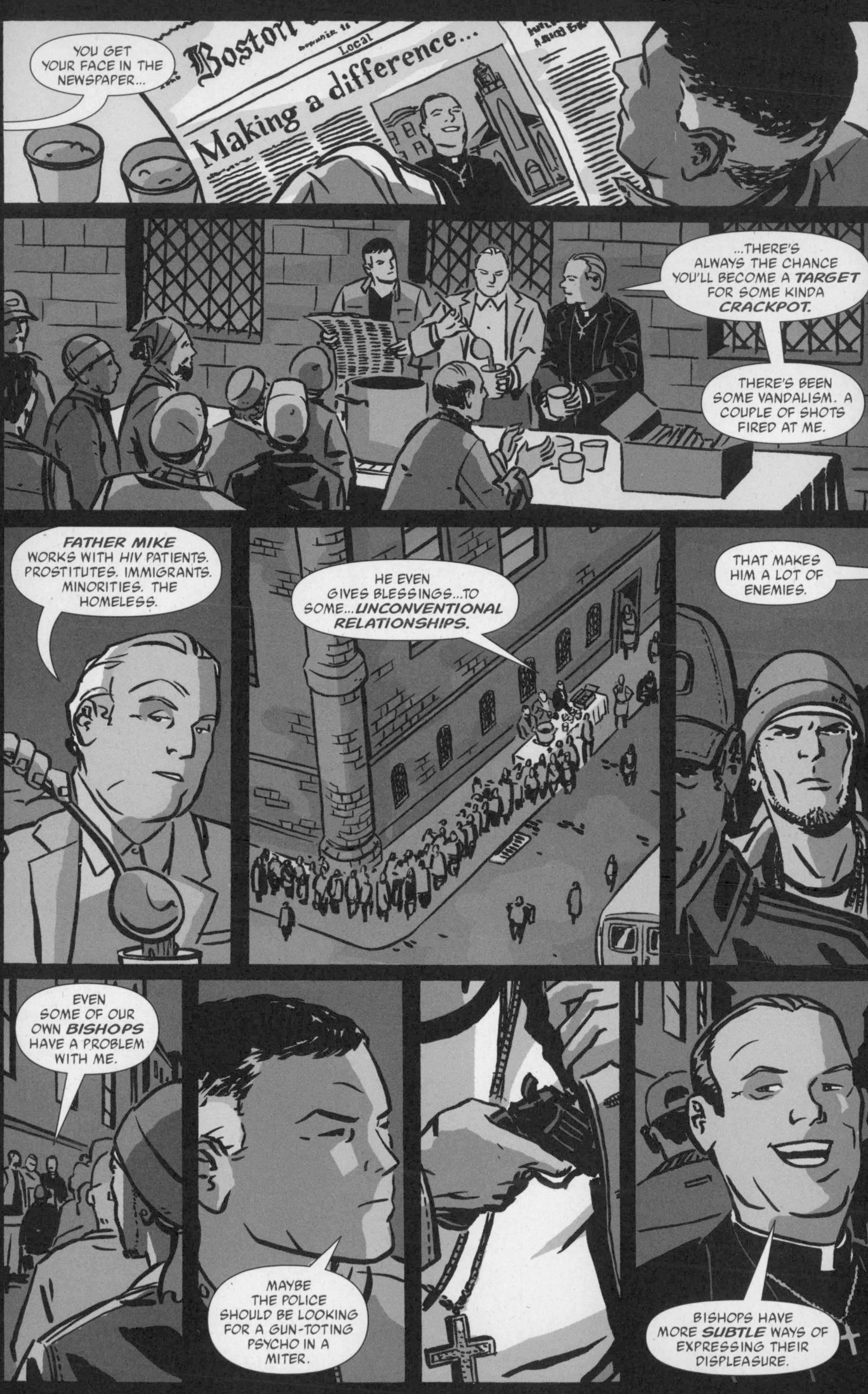
YOU GET YOUR FACE IN THE NEWSPAPER...
Boston
Local
Making a difference...
...THERE'S ALWAYS THE CHANCE YOU'LL BECOME A TARGET FOR SOME KINDA CRACKPOT.
THERE'S BEEN SOME VANDALISM. A COUPLE OF SHOTS FIRED AT ME.
FATHER MIKE WORKS WITH HIV PATIENTS. PROSTITUTES. IMMIGRANTS. MINORITIES. THE HOMELESS.
HE EVEN GIVES BLESSINGS...TO SOME...UNCONVENTIONAL RELATIONSHIPS.
THAT MAKES HIM A LOT OF ENEMIES.
EVEN SOME OF OUR OWN BISHOPS HAVE A PROBLEM WITH ME.
MAYBE THE POLICE SHOULD BE LOOKING FOR A GUN-TOTING PSYCHO IN A MITER.
BISHOPS HAVE MORE SUBTLE WAYS OF EXPRESSING THEIR DISPLEASURE.

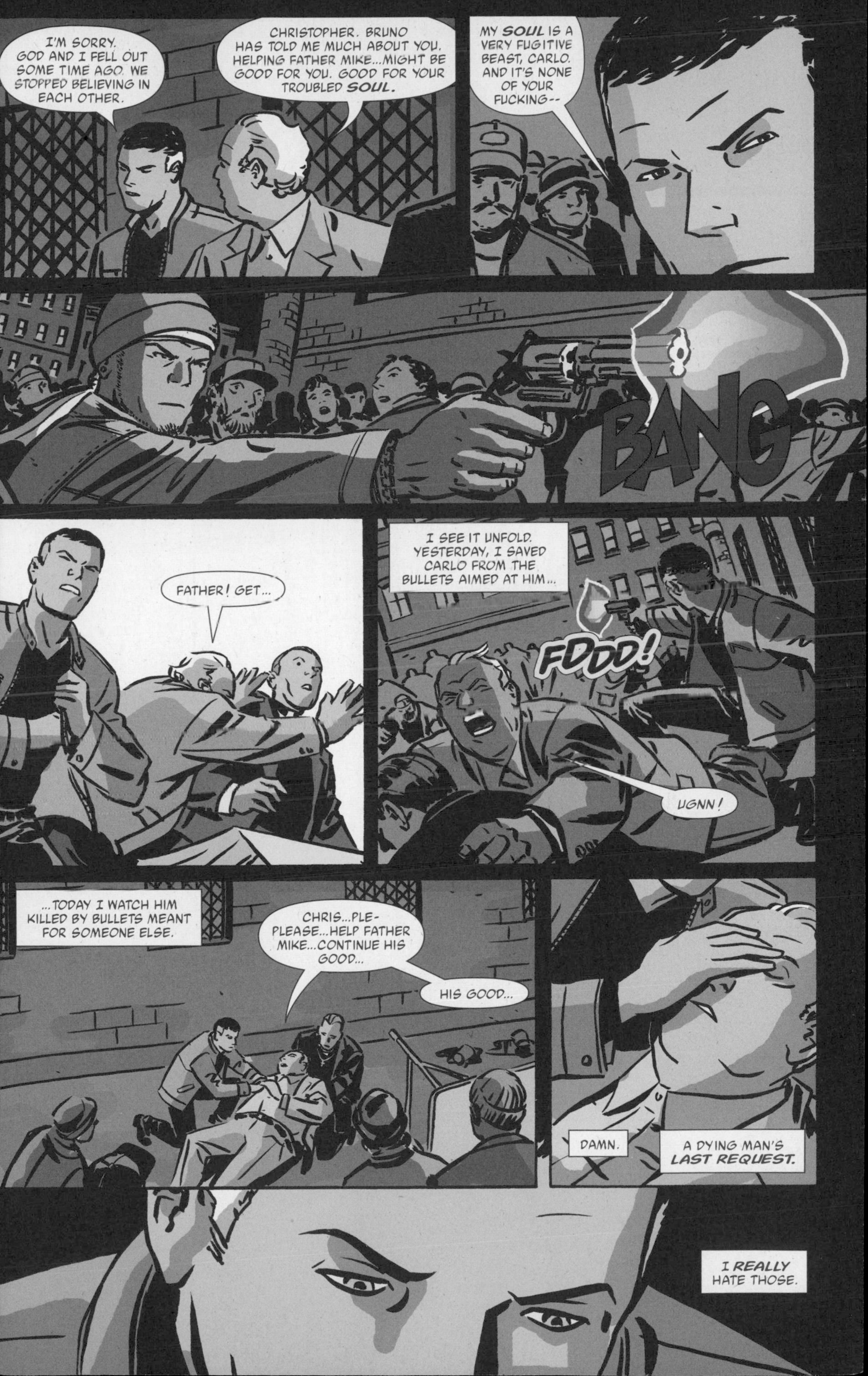

I'M SORRY. GOD AND I FELL OUT SOME TIME AGO. WE STOPPED BELIEVING IN EACH OTHER.
CHRISTOPHER. BRUNO HAS TOLD ME MUCH ABOUT YOU. HELPING FATHER MIKE...MIGHT BE GOOD FOR YOU. GOOD FOR YOUR TROUBLED SOUL.
MY SOUL IS A VERY FUGITIVE BEAST, CARLO. AND IT'S NONE OF YOUR FUCKING--
BANG
FATHER! GET...
I SEE IT UNFOLD. YESTERDAY, I SAVED CARLO FROM THE BULLETS AIMED AT HIM...
FDDD!
UGNN!
...TODAY I WATCH HIM KILLED BY BULLETS MEANT FOR SOMEONE ELSE.
CHRIS...PLE-PLEASE...HELP FATHER MIKE...CONTINUE HIS GOOD...
HIS GOOD...
DAMN.
A DYING MAN'S LAST REQUEST.
I REALLY HATE THOSE.

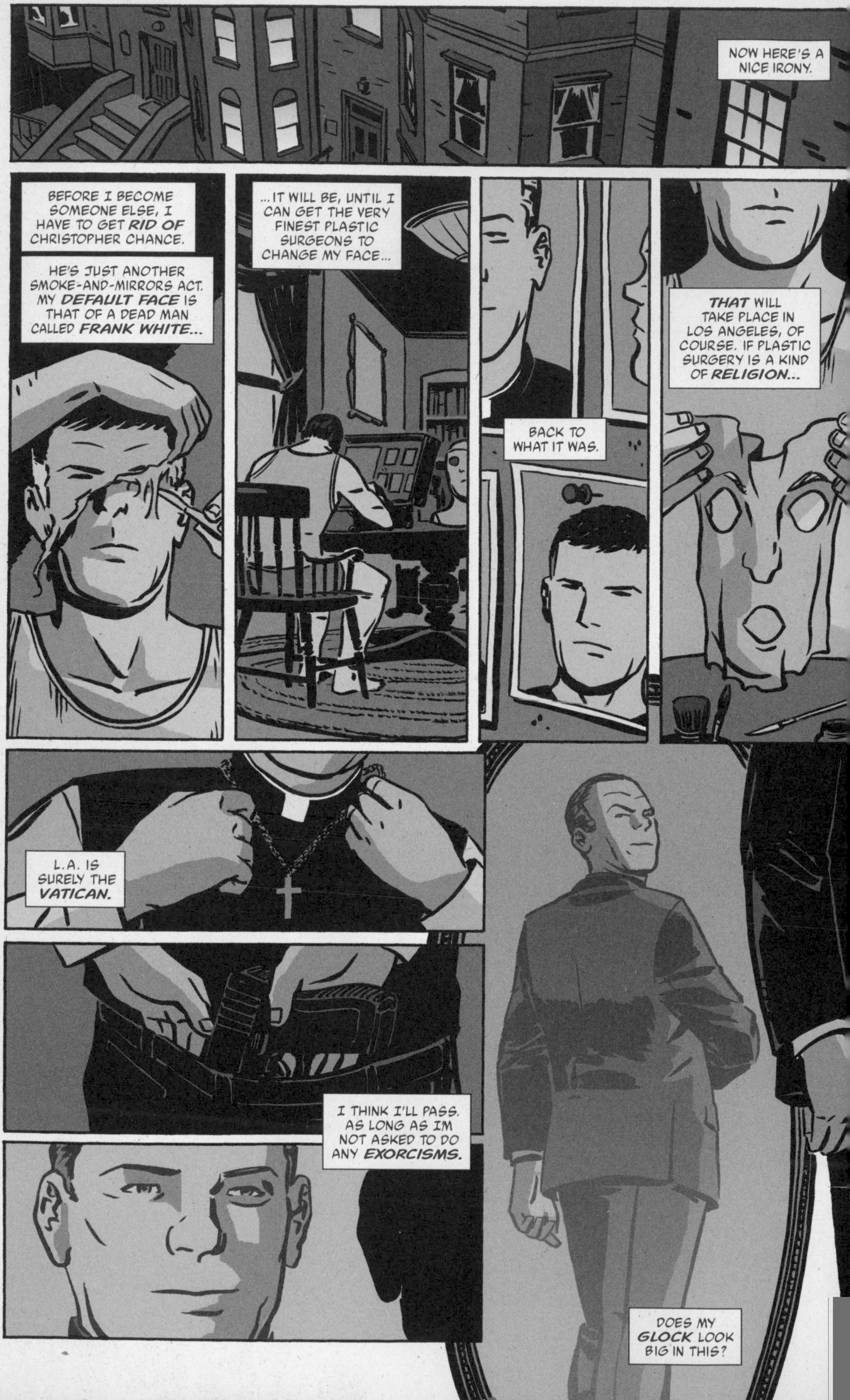
NOW HERE'S A NICE IRONY.
BEFORE I BECOME SOMEONE ELSE, I HAVE TO GET RID OF CHRISTOPHER CHANCE.
HE'S JUST ANOTHER SMOKE-AND-MIRRORS ACT. MY DEFAULT FACE IS THAT OF A DEAD MAN CALLED FRANK WHITE...
...IT WILL BE, UNTIL I CAN GET THE VERY FINEST PLASTIC SURGEONS TO CHANGE MY FACE...
BACK TO WHAT IT WAS.
THAT WILL TAKE PLACE IN LOS ANGELES, OF COURSE. IF PLASTIC SURGERY IS A KIND OF RELIGION...
L.A. IS SURELY THE VATICAN.
I THINK I'LL PASS. AS LONG AS I'M NOT ASKED TO DO ANY EXORCISMS.
DOES MY GLOCK LOOK BIG IN THIS?

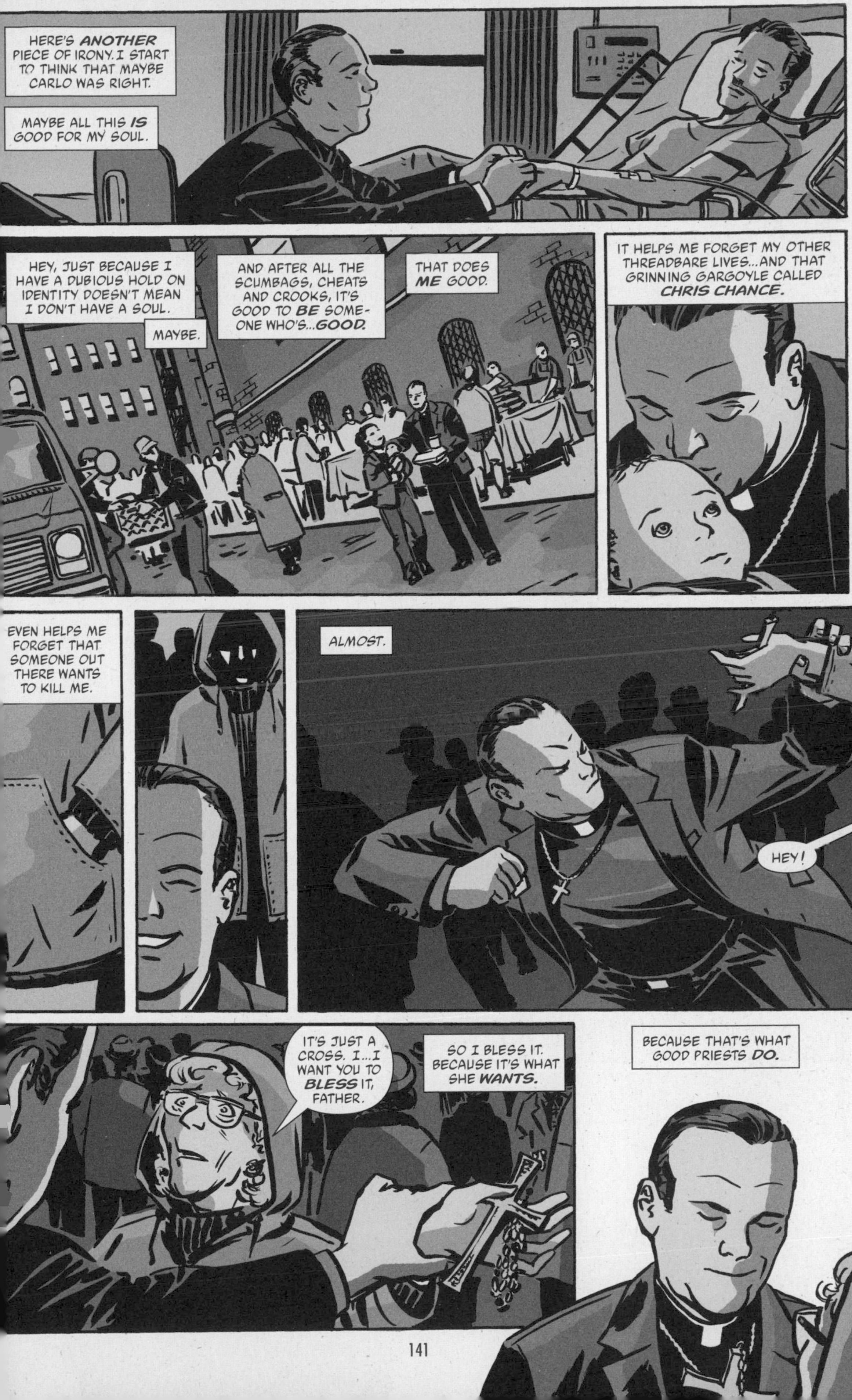
HERE'S ANOTHER PIECE OF IRONY. I START TO THINK THAT MAYBE CARLO WAS RIGHT.
MAYBE ALL THIS IS GOOD FOR MY SOUL.
HEY, JUST BECAUSE I HAVE A DUBIOUS HOLD ON IDENTITY DOESN'T MEAN I DON'T HAVE A SOUL.
MAYBE.
AND AFTER ALL THE SCUMBAGS, CHEATS AND CROOKS, IT'S GOOD TO BE SOME-ONE WHO'S...GOOD.
THAT DOES ME GOOD.
IT HELPS ME FORGET MY OTHER THREADBARE LIVES...AND THAT GRINNING GARGOYLE CALLED CHRIS CHANCE.
EVEN HELPS ME FORGET THAT SOMEONE OUT THERE WANTS TO KILL ME.
ALMOST.
HEY!
IT'S JUST A CROSS. I...I WANT YOU TO BLESS IT, FATHER.
SO I BLESS IT. BECAUSE IT'S WHAT SHE WANTS.
BECAUSE THAT'S WHAT GOOD PRIESTS DO.

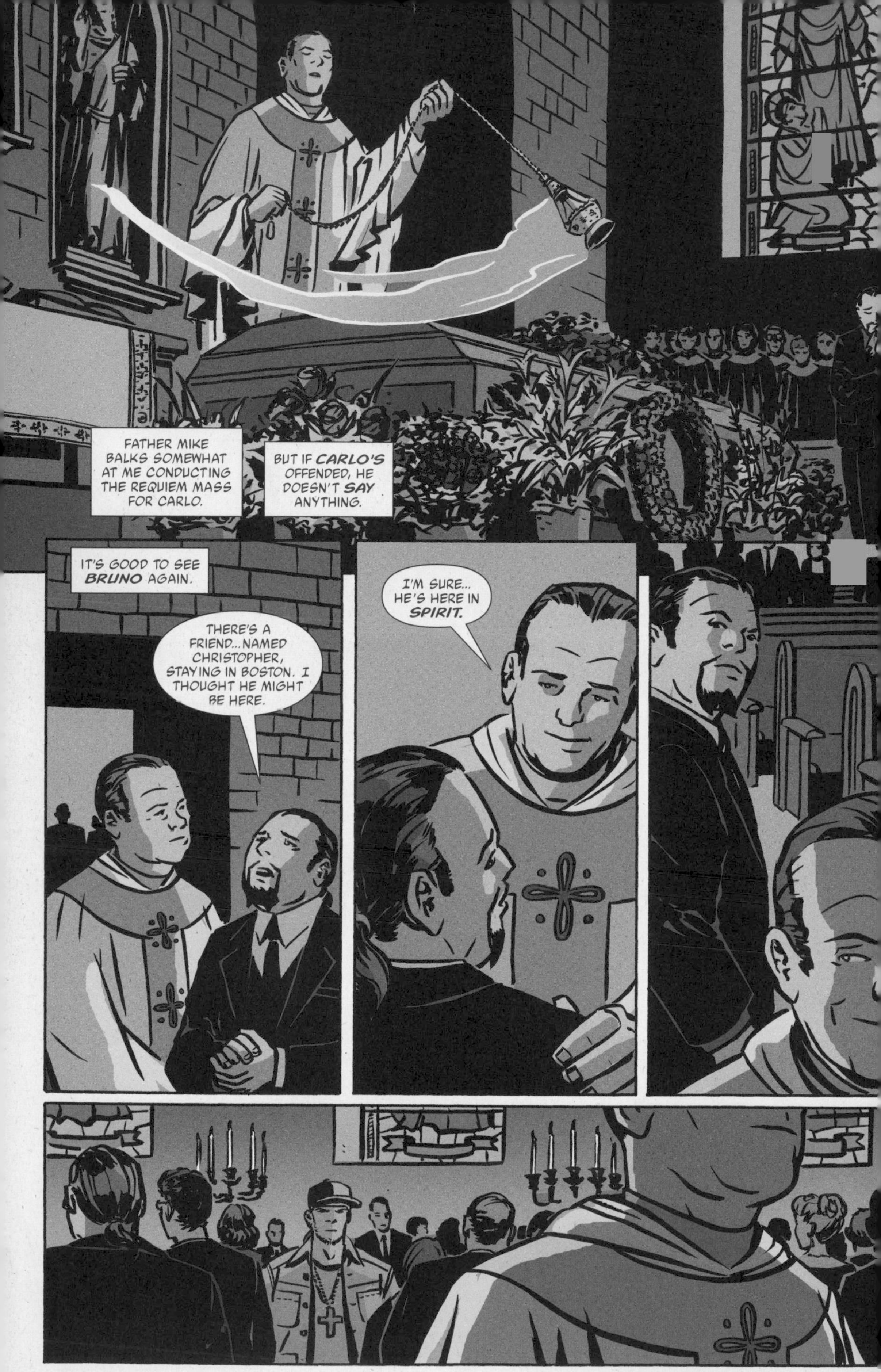
FATHER MIKE BALKS SOMEWHAT AT ME CONDUCTING THE REQUIEM MASS FOR CARLO.
BUT IF CARLO'S OFFENDED, HE DOESN'T SAY ANYTHING.
IT'S GOOD TO SEE BRUNO AGAIN.
THERE'S A FRIEND...NAMED CHRISTOPHER, STAYING IN BOSTON. I THOUGHT HE MIGHT BE HERE.
I'M SURE... HE'S HERE IN SPIRIT.

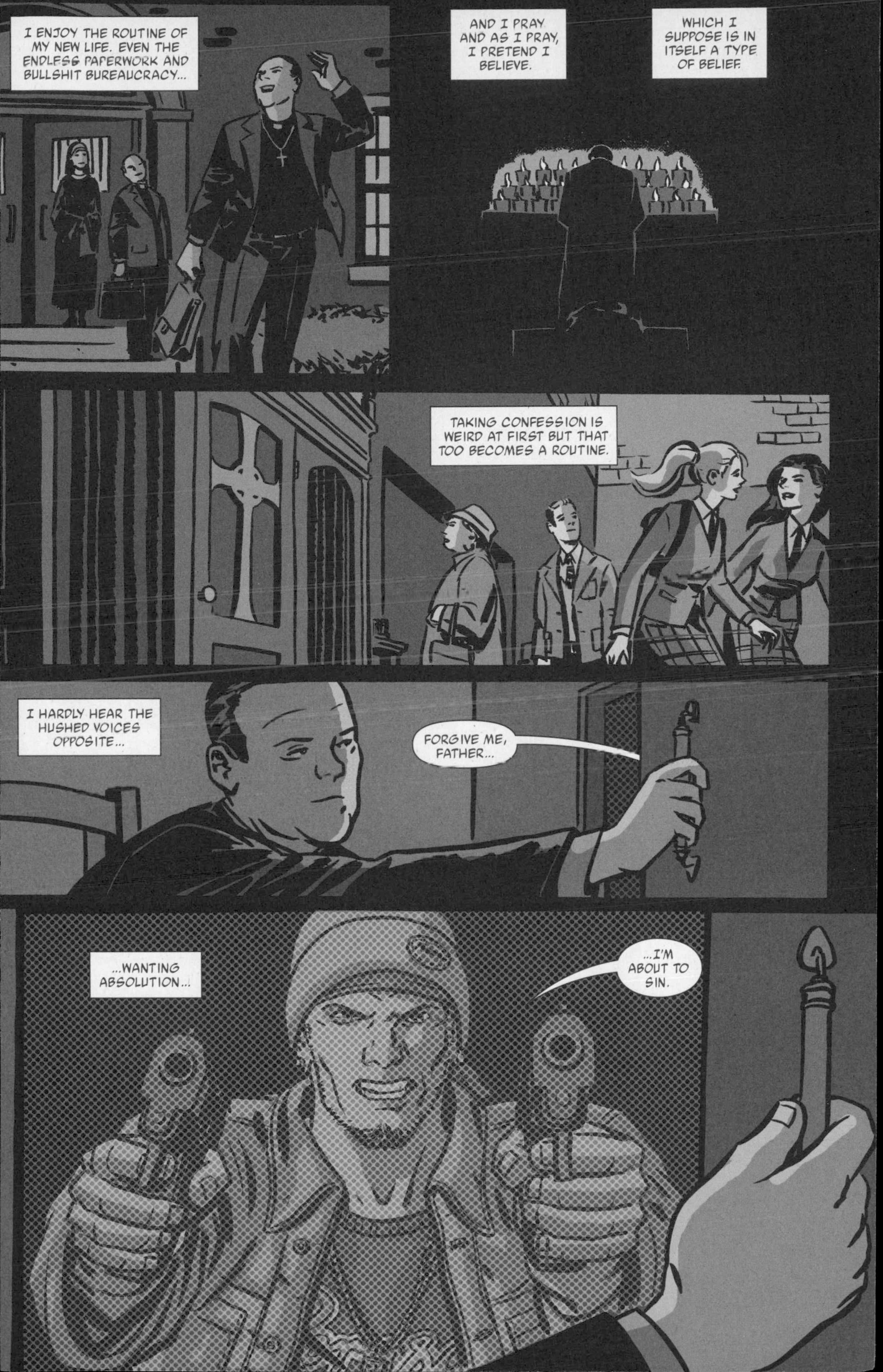
I ENJOY THE ROUTINE OF MY NEW LIFE. EVEN THE ENDLESS PAPERWORK AND BULLSHIT BUREAUCRACY...
AND I PRAY AND AS I PRAY, I PRETEND I BELIEVE.
WHICH I SUPPOSE IS IN ITSELF A TYPE OF BELIEF.
TAKING CONFESSION IS WEIRD AT FIRST BUT THAT TOO BECOMES A ROUTINE.
I HARDLY HEAR THE HUSHED VOICES OPPOSITE...
FORGIVE ME, FATHER...
...WANTING ABSOLUTION...
...I'M ABOUT TO SIN.

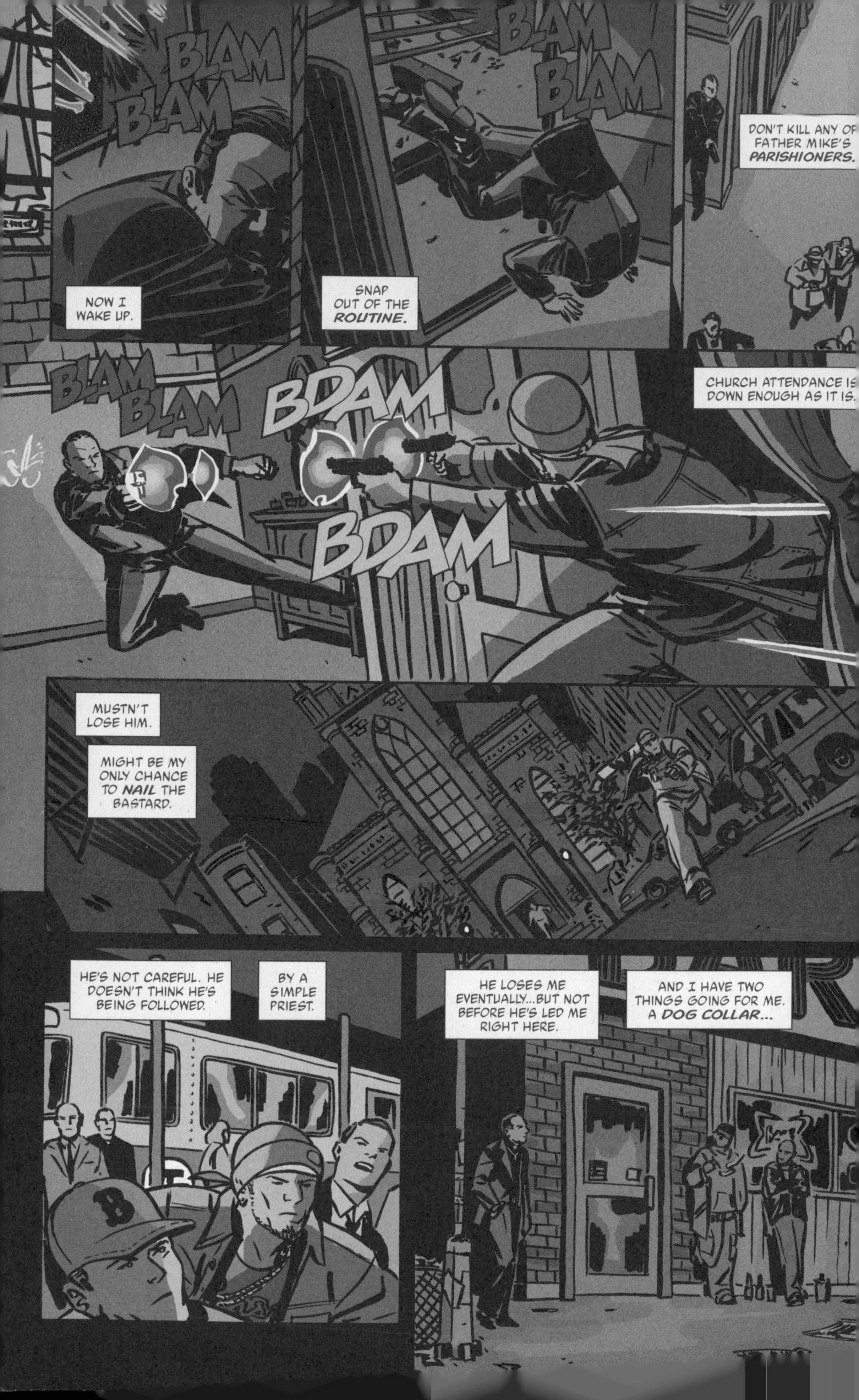
BLAM
BLAM
NOW I WAKE UP.
BLAM
BLAM
SNAP OUT OF THE ROUTINE.
DON'T KILL ANY OF FATHER MIKE'S PARISHIONERS.
BLAM
BLAM
BDAM
BDAM
CHURCH ATTENDANCE IS DOWN ENOUGH AS IT IS.
MUSTN'T LOSE HIM.
MIGHT BE MY ONLY CHANCE TO NAIL THE BASTARD.
HE'S NOT CAREFUL. HE DOESN'T THINK HE'S BEING FOLLOWED.
BY A SIMPLE PRIEST.
HE LOSES ME EVENTUALLY...BUT NOT BEFORE HE'S LED ME RIGHT HERE.
AND I HAVE TWO THINGS GOING FOR ME. A DOG COLLAR...

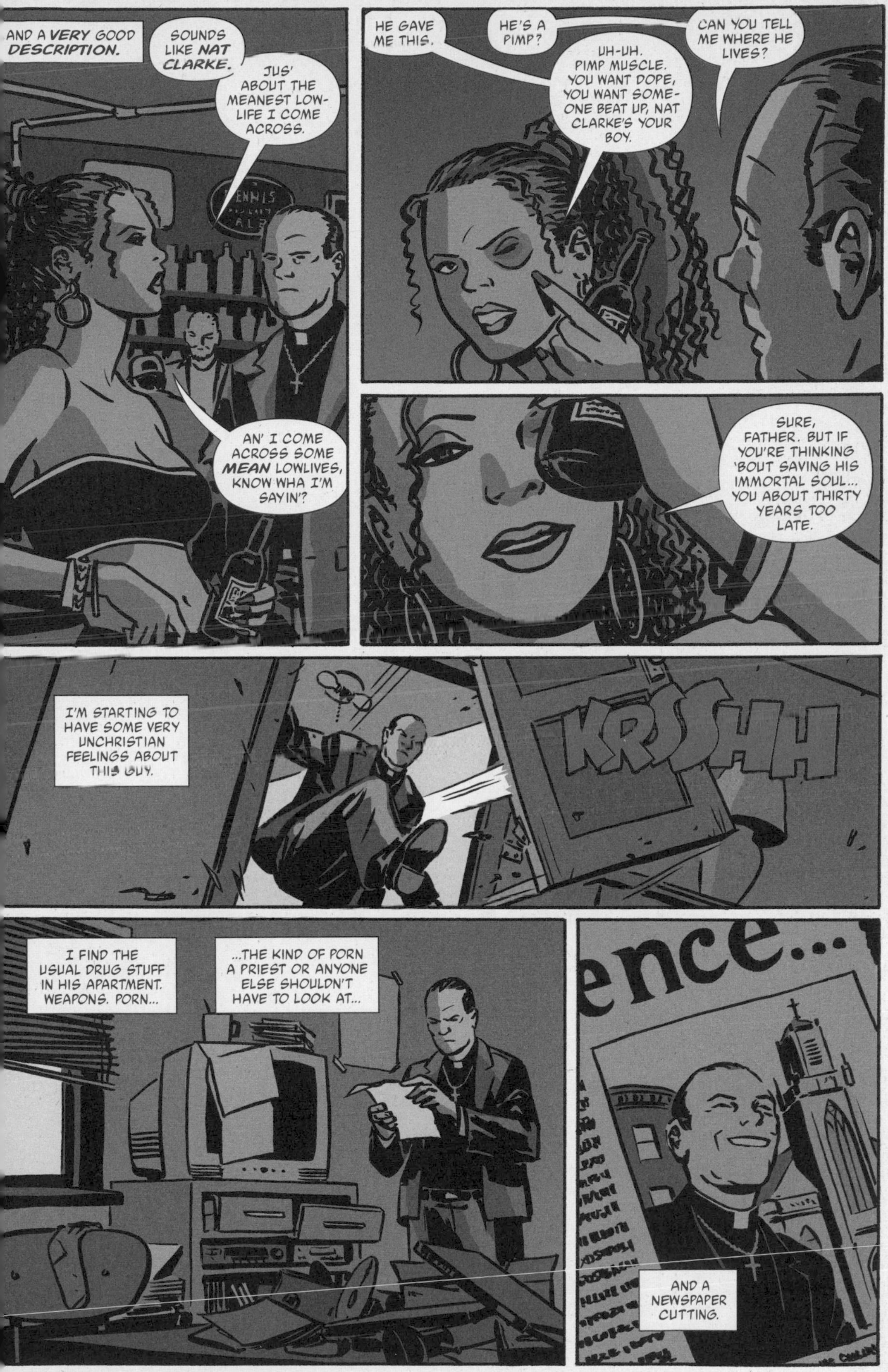
AND A VERY GOOD DESCRIPTION.
SOUNDS LIKE NAT CLARKE.
JUS' ABOUT THE MEANEST LOW-LIFE I COME ACROSS.
AN' I COME ACROSS SOME MEAN LOWLIVES, KNOW WHA I'M SAYIN'?
HE GAVE ME THIS.
HE'S A PIMP?
UH-UH. PIMP MUSCLE. YOU WANT DOPE, YOU WANT SOME-ONE BEAT UP, NAT CLARKE'S YOUR BOY.
CAN YOU TELL ME WHERE HE LIVES?
SURE, FATHER. BUT IF YOU'RE THINKING 'BOUT SAVING HIS IMMORTAL SOUL... YOU ABOUT THIRTY YEARS TOO LATE.
I'M STARTING TO HAVE SOME VERY UNCHRISTIAN FEELINGS ABOUT THIS GUY.
KRSSHH
I FIND THE USUAL DRUG STUFF IN HIS APARTMENT. WEAPONS. PORN...
...THE KIND OF PORN A PRIEST OR ANYONE ELSE SHOULDN'T HAVE TO LOOK AT...
ence...
AND A NEWSPAPER CUTTING.

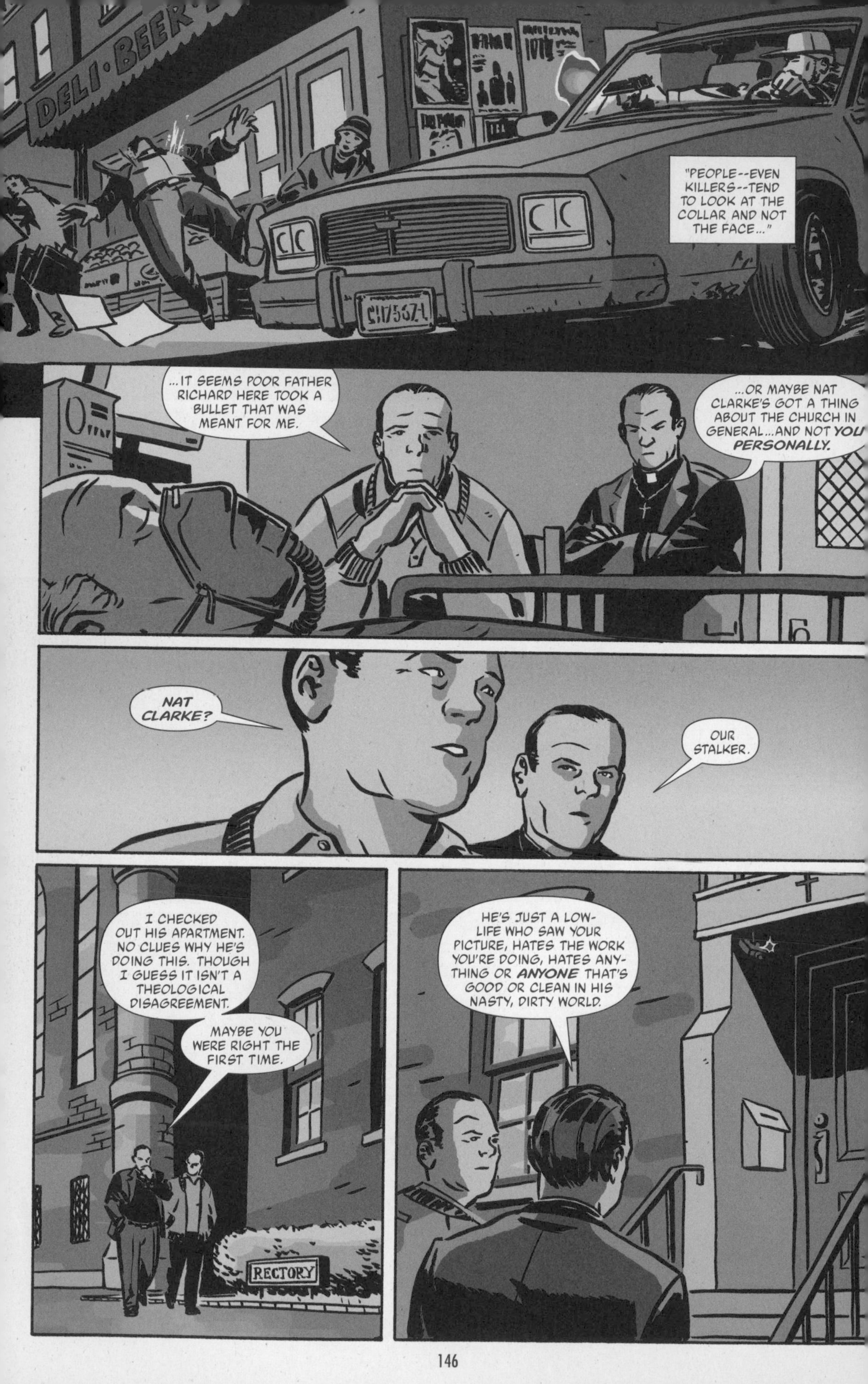
DELI · BEER
"PEOPLE--EVEN KILLERS--TEND TO LOOK AT THE COLLAR AND NOT THE FACE..."
...IT SEEMS POOR FATHER RICHARD HERE TOOK A BULLET THAT WAS MEANT FOR ME.
...OR MAYBE NAT CLARKE'S GOT A THING ABOUT THE CHURCH IN GENERAL...AND NOT YOU PERSONALLY.
NAT CLARKE?
OUR STALKER.
I CHECKED OUT HIS APARTMENT. NO CLUES WHY HE'S DOING THIS. THOUGH I GUESS IT ISN'T A THEOLOGICAL DISAGREEMENT.
MAYBE YOU WERE RIGHT THE FIRST TIME.
RECTORY
HE'S JUST A LOW-LIFE WHO SAW YOUR PICTURE, HATES THE WORK YOU'RE DOING, HATES ANYTHING OR ANYONE THAT'S GOOD OR CLEAN IN HIS NASTY, DIRTY WORLD.

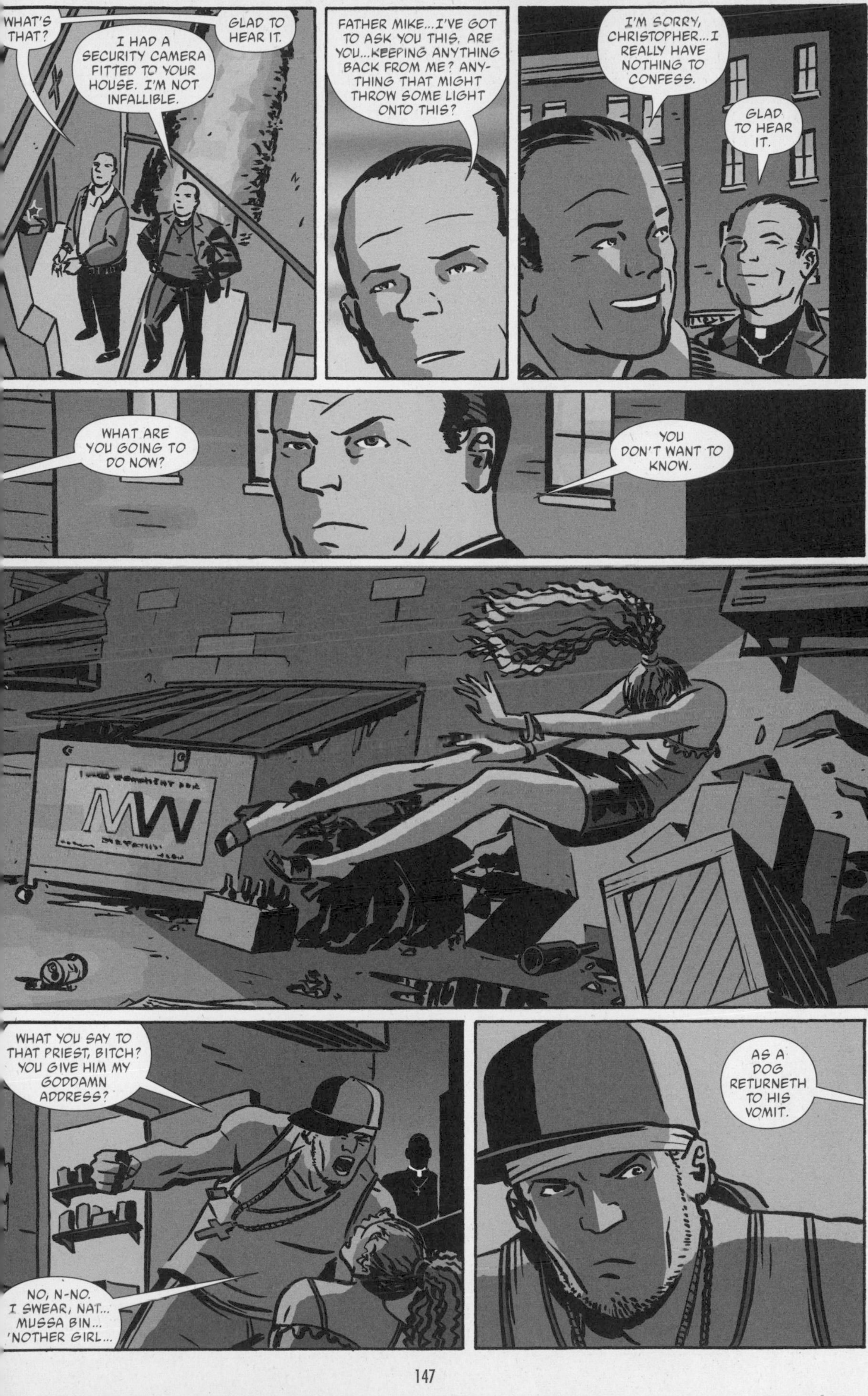
WHAT'S THAT?
I HAD A SECURITY CAMERA FITTED TO YOUR HOUSE. I'M NOT INFALLIBLE.
GLAD TO HEAR IT.
FATHER MIKE...I'VE GOT TO ASK YOU THIS. ARE YOU...KEEPING ANYTHING BACK FROM ME? ANYTHING THAT MIGHT THROW SOME LIGHT ONTO THIS?
I'M SORRY, CHRISTOPHER...I REALLY HAVE NOTHING TO CONFESS.
GLAD TO HEAR IT.
WHAT ARE YOU GOING TO DO NOW?
YOU DON'T WANT TO KNOW.
MW
WHAT YOU SAY TO THAT PRIEST, BITCH? YOU GIVE HIM MY GODDAMN ADDRESS?
NO, N-NO. I SWEAR, NAT... MUSSA BIN... 'NOTHER GIRL...
AS A DOG RETURNETH TO HIS VOMIT.

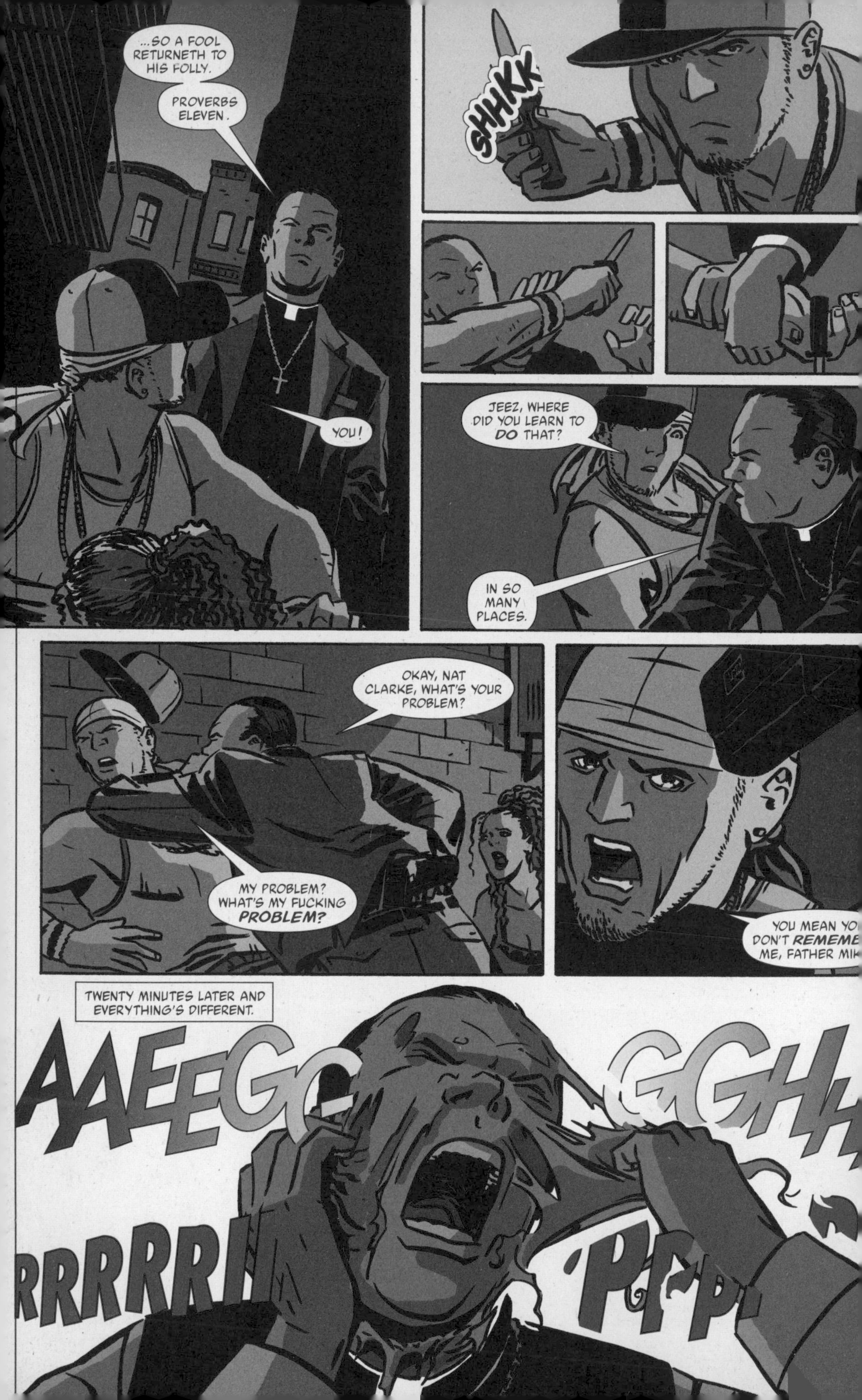
...SO A FOOL RETURNETH TO HIS FOLLY.
PROVERBS ELEVEN.
YOU!
SHHKK
JEEZ, WHERE DID YOU LEARN TO DO THAT?
IN SO MANY PLACES.
OKAY, NAT CLARKE, WHAT'S YOUR PROBLEM?
MY PROBLEM? WHAT'S MY FUCKING PROBLEM?
YOU MEAN YO DON'T REMEME ME, FATHER MIK
TWENTY MINUTES LATER AND EVERYTHING'S DIFFERENT.
AAEEGG GGH
RRRRRI PPP

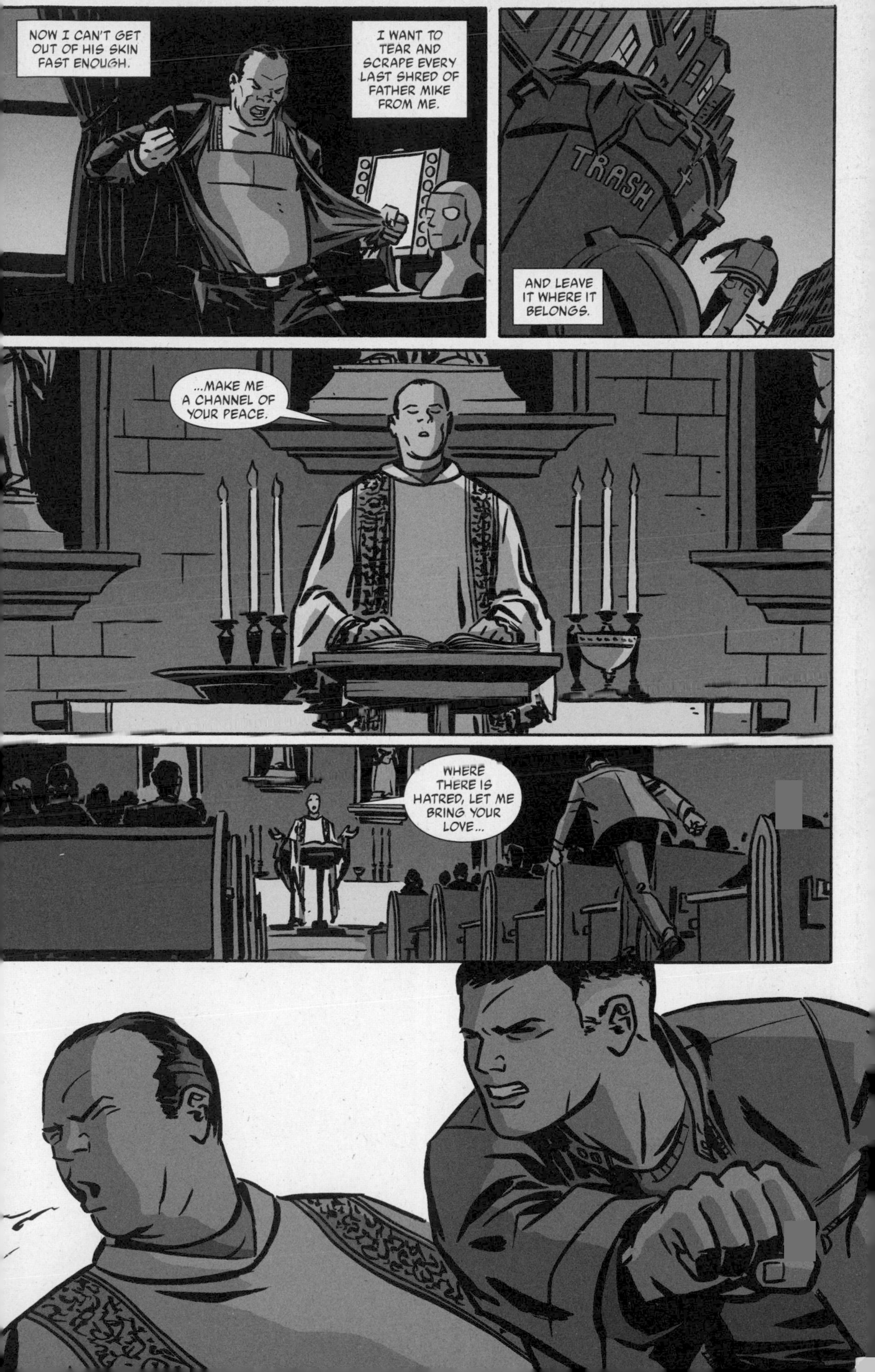
NOW I CAN'T GET OUT OF HIS SKIN FAST ENOUGH.
I WANT TO TEAR AND SCRAPE EVERY LAST SHRED OF FATHER MIKE FROM ME.
TRASH
AND LEAVE IT WHERE IT BELONGS.
...MAKE ME A CHANNEL OF YOUR PEACE.
WHERE THERE IS HATRED, LET ME BRING YOUR LOVE...

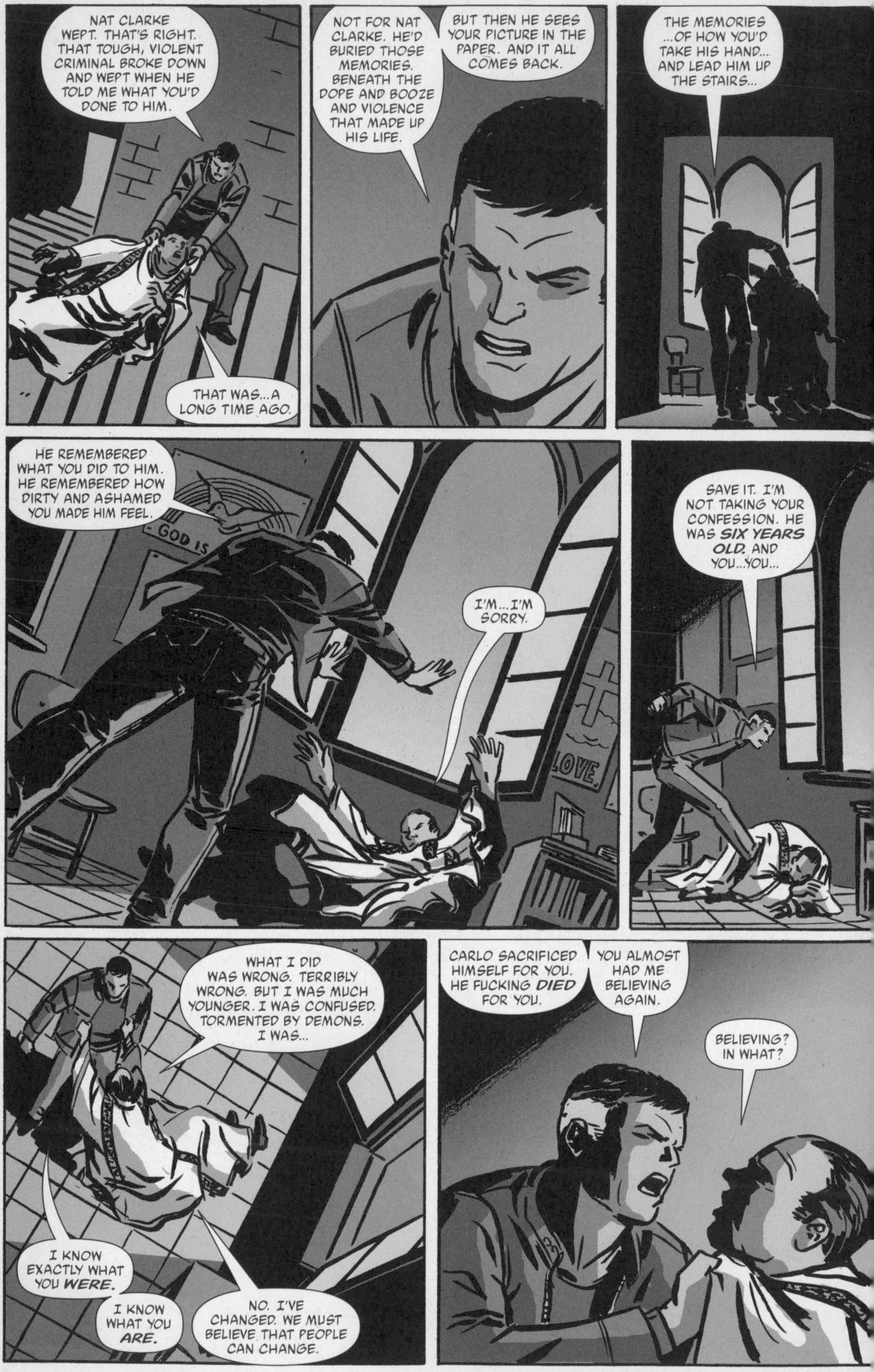

NAT CLARKE WEPT. THAT'S RIGHT. THAT TOUGH, VIOLENT CRIMINAL BROKE DOWN AND WEPT WHEN HE TOLD ME WHAT YOU'D DONE TO HIM.
THAT WAS...A LONG TIME AGO.
NOT FOR NAT CLARKE. HE'D BURIED THOSE MEMORIES. BENEATH THE DOPE AND BOOZE AND VIOLENCE THAT MADE UP HIS LIFE.
BUT THEN HE SEES YOUR PICTURE IN THE PAPER. AND IT ALL COMES BACK.
THE MEMORIES ...OF HOW YOU'D TAKE HIS HAND... AND LEAD HIM UP THE STAIRS...
HE REMEMBERED WHAT YOU DID TO HIM. HE REMEMBERED HOW DIRTY AND ASHAMED YOU MADE HIM FEEL.
GOD IS
LOVE.
I'M...I'M SORRY.
SAVE IT. I'M NOT TAKING YOUR CONFESSION. HE WAS **SIX YEARS OLD**. AND YOU...YOU...
WHAT I DID WAS WRONG. TERRIBLY WRONG. BUT I WAS MUCH YOUNGER. I WAS CONFUSED. TORMENTED BY DEMONS. I WAS...
I KNOW EXACTLY WHAT YOU **WERE.**
I KNOW WHAT YOU **ARE.**
NO. I'VE CHANGED. WE MUST BELIEVE THAT PEOPLE CAN CHANGE.
CARLO SACRIFICED HIMSELF FOR YOU. HE FUCKING **DIED** FOR YOU.
YOU ALMOST HAD ME BELIEVING AGAIN.
BELIEVING? IN WHAT?

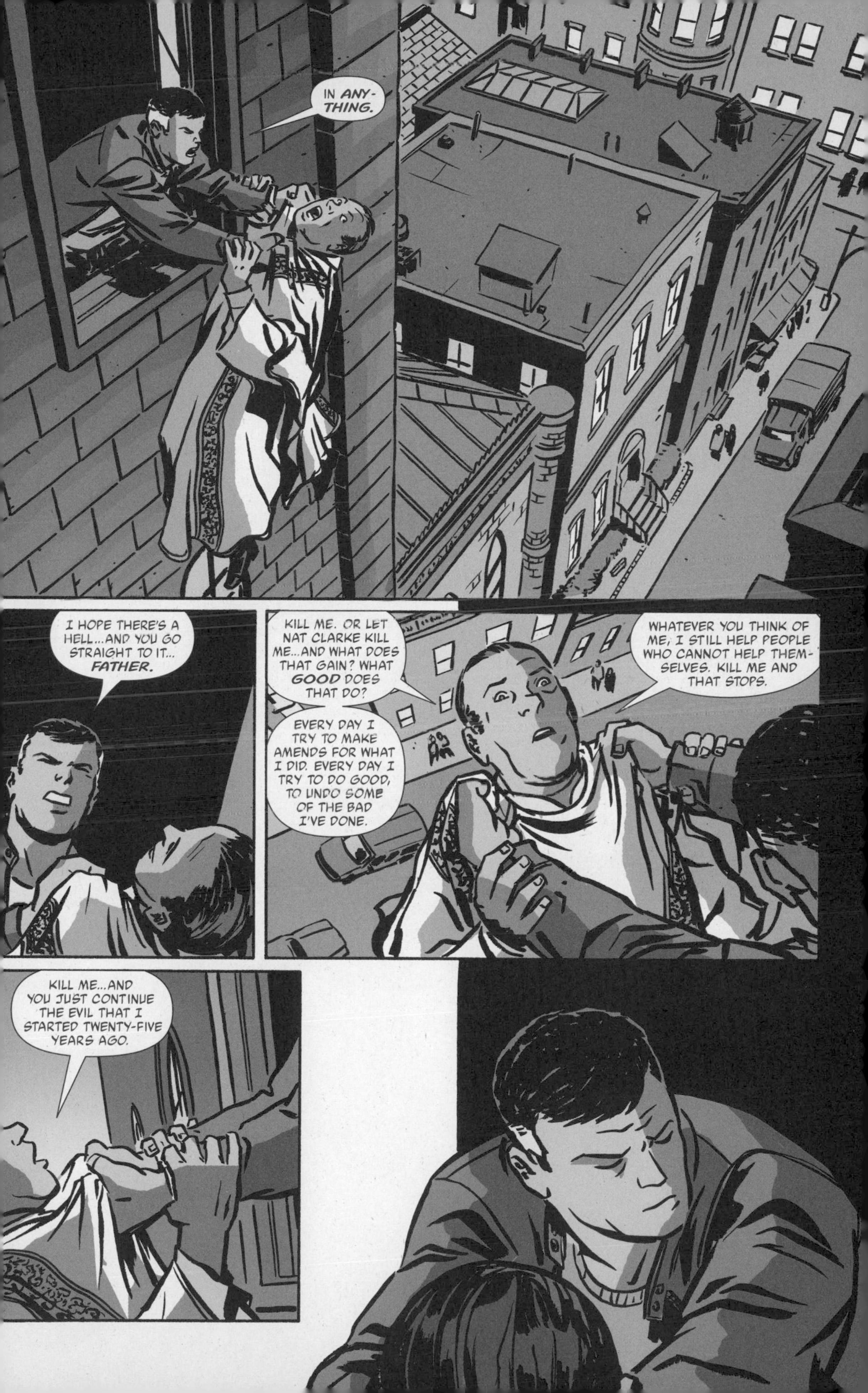
IN ANY-THING.
I HOPE THERE'S A HELL...AND YOU GO STRAIGHT TO IT... FATHER.
KILL ME. OR LET NAT CLARKE KILL ME...AND WHAT DOES THAT GAIN? WHAT GOOD DOES THAT DO?
EVERY DAY I TRY TO MAKE AMENDS FOR WHAT I DID. EVERY DAY I TRY TO DO GOOD, TO UNDO SOME OF THE BAD I'VE DONE.
WHATEVER YOU THINK OF ME, I STILL HELP PEOPLE WHO CANNOT HELP THEM-SELVES. KILL ME AND THAT STOPS.
KILL ME...AND YOU JUST CONTINUE THE EVIL THAT I STARTED TWENTY-FIVE YEARS AGO.

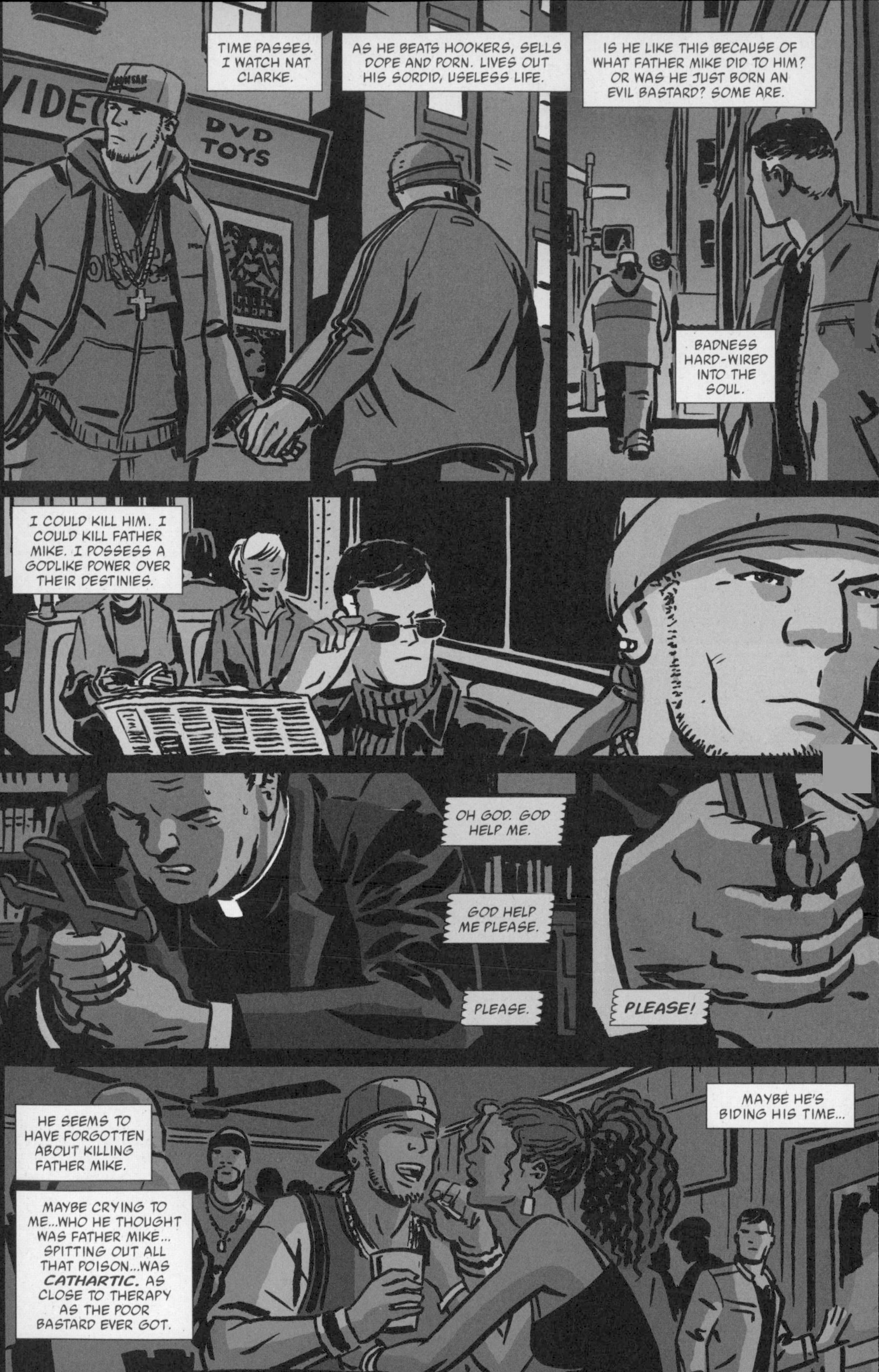
TIME PASSES. I WATCH NAT CLARKE.
AS HE BEATS HOOKERS, SELLS DOPE AND PORN. LIVES OUT HIS SORDID, USELESS LIFE.
DVD TOYS
IS HE LIKE THIS BECAUSE OF WHAT FATHER MIKE DID TO HIM? OR WAS HE JUST BORN AN EVIL BASTARD? SOME ARE.
BADNESS HARD-WIRED INTO THE SOUL.
I COULD KILL HIM. I COULD KILL FATHER MIKE. I POSSESS A GODLIKE POWER OVER THEIR DESTINIES.
OH GOD. GOD HELP ME.
GOD HELP ME PLEASE.
PLEASE.
PLEASE!
HE SEEMS TO HAVE FORGOTTEN ABOUT KILLING FATHER MIKE.
MAYBE CRYING TO ME...WHO HE THOUGHT WAS FATHER MIKE... SPITTING OUT ALL THAT POISON...WAS CATHARTIC. AS CLOSE TO THERAPY AS THE POOR BASTARD EVER GOT.
MAYBE HE'S BIDING HIS TIME...

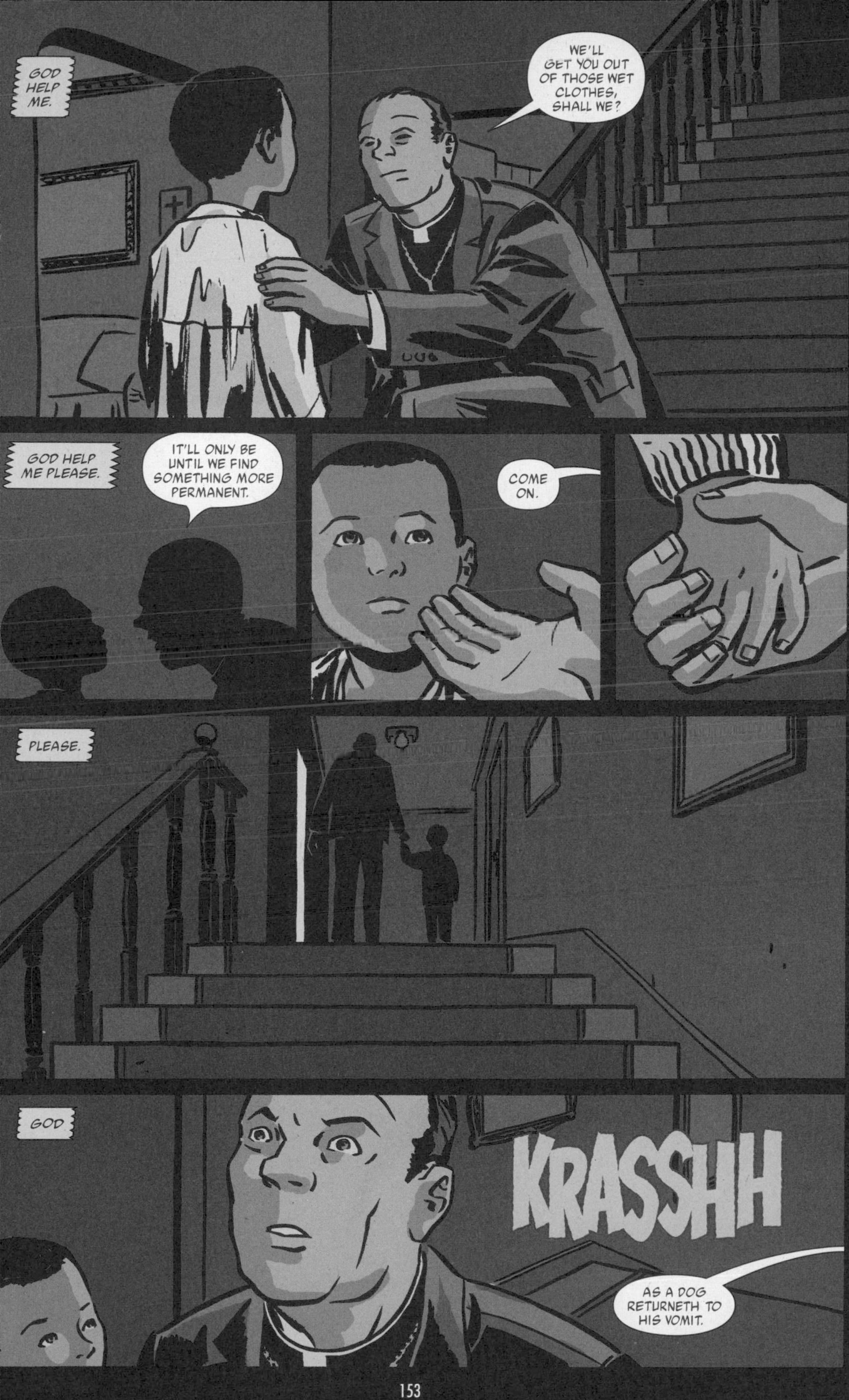
GOD HELP ME.
WE'LL GET YOU OUT OF THOSE WET CLOTHES, SHALL WE?
GOD HELP ME PLEASE.
IT'LL ONLY BE UNTIL WE FIND SOMETHING MORE PERMANENT.
COME ON.
PLEASE.
GOD
KRASSHH
AS A DOG RETURNETH TO HIS VOMIT.

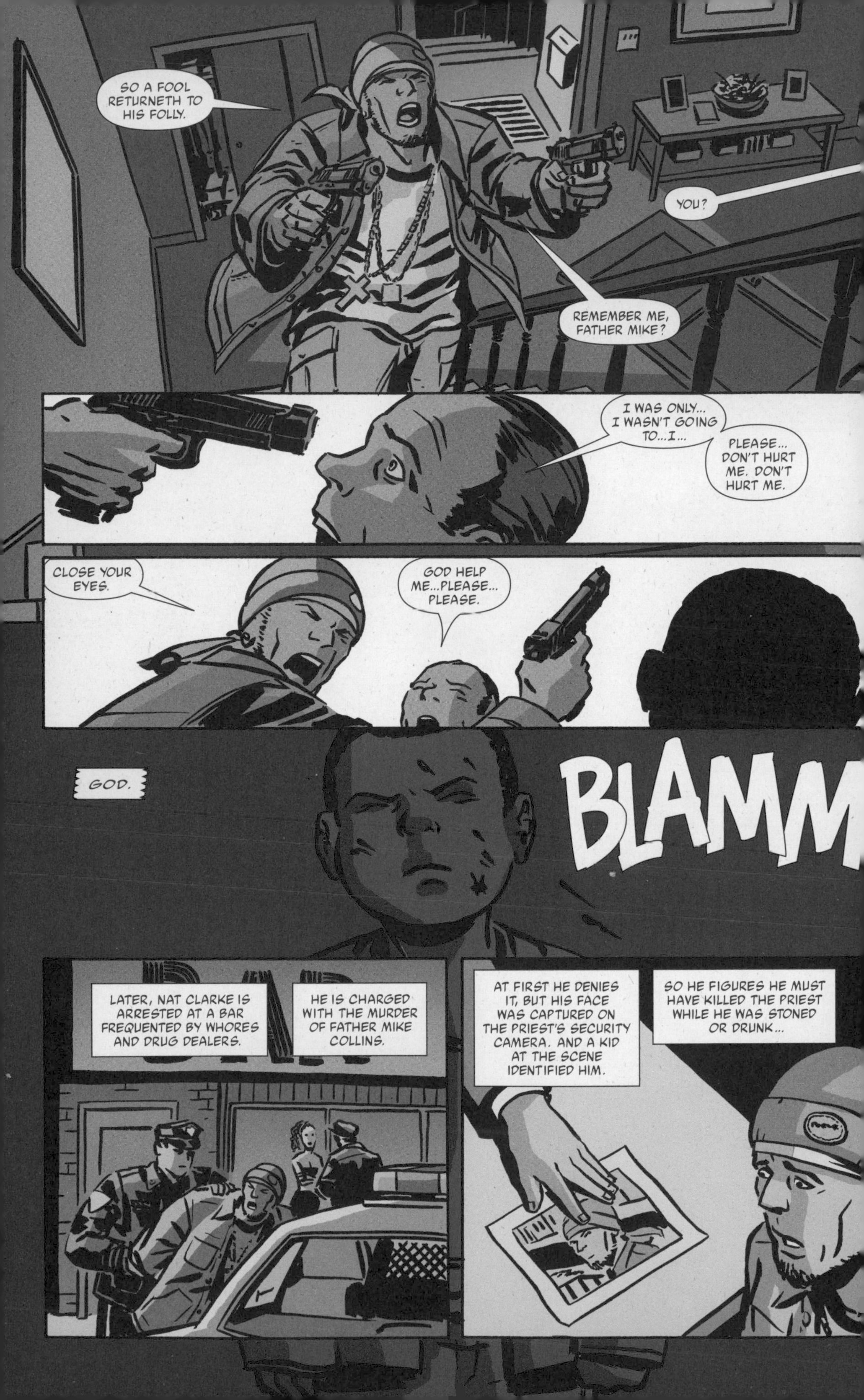

SO A FOOL RETURNETH TO HIS FOLLY.
YOU?
REMEMBER ME, FATHER MIKE?
I WAS ONLY... I WASN'T GOING TO...I...
PLEASE... DON'T HURT ME. DON'T HURT ME.
CLOSE YOUR EYES.
GOD HELP ME...PLEASE... PLEASE.
GOD.
BLAMM
LATER, NAT CLARKE IS ARRESTED AT A BAR FREQUENTED BY WHORES AND DRUG DEALERS.
HE IS CHARGED WITH THE MURDER OF FATHER MIKE COLLINS.
AT FIRST HE DENIES IT, BUT HIS FACE WAS CAPTURED ON THE PRIEST'S SECURITY CAMERA. AND A KID AT THE SCENE IDENTIFIED HIM.
SO HE FIGURES HE MUST HAVE KILLED THE PRIEST WHILE HE WAS STONED OR DRUNK...

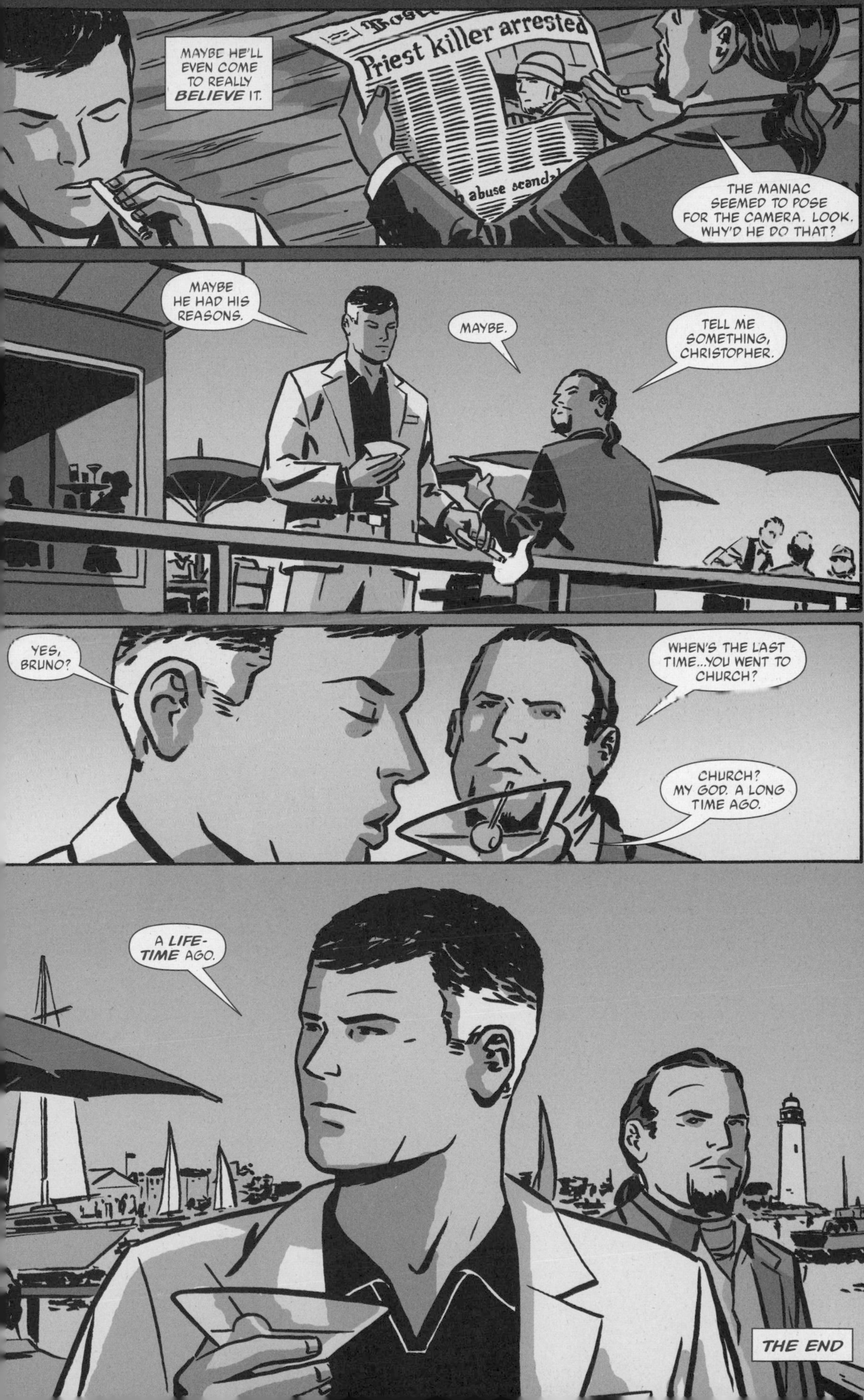
MAYBE HE'LL EVEN COME TO REALLY BELIEVE IT.
Priest killer arrested
abuse scandal
THE MANIAC SEEMED TO POSE FOR THE CAMERA. LOOK. WHY'D HE DO THAT?
MAYBE HE HAD HIS REASONS.
MAYBE.
TELL ME SOMETHING, CHRISTOPHER.
YES, BRUNO?
WHEN'S THE LAST TIME...YOU WENT TO CHURCH?
CHURCH? MY GOD. A LONG TIME AGO.
A LIFE-TIME AGO.
THE END

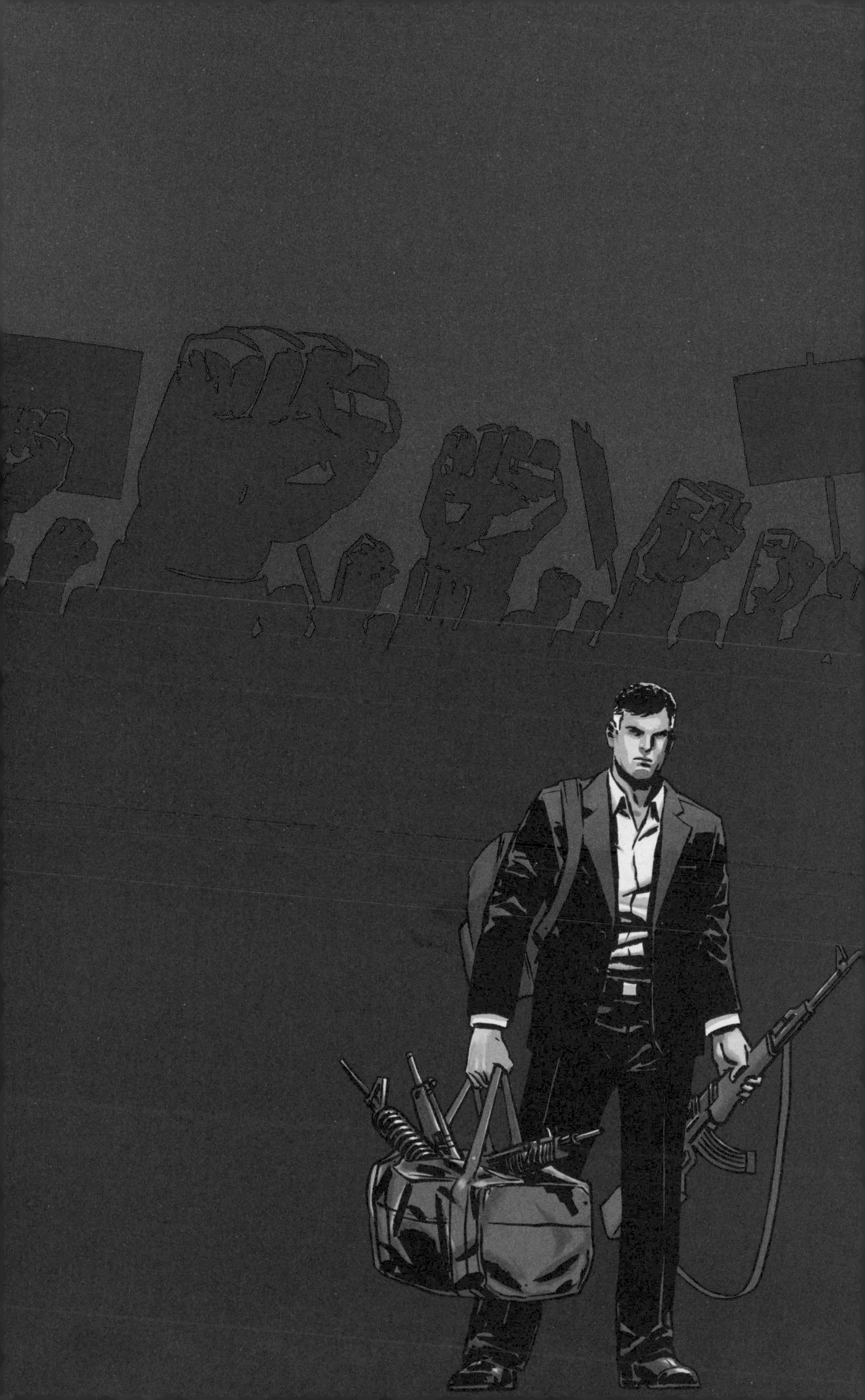

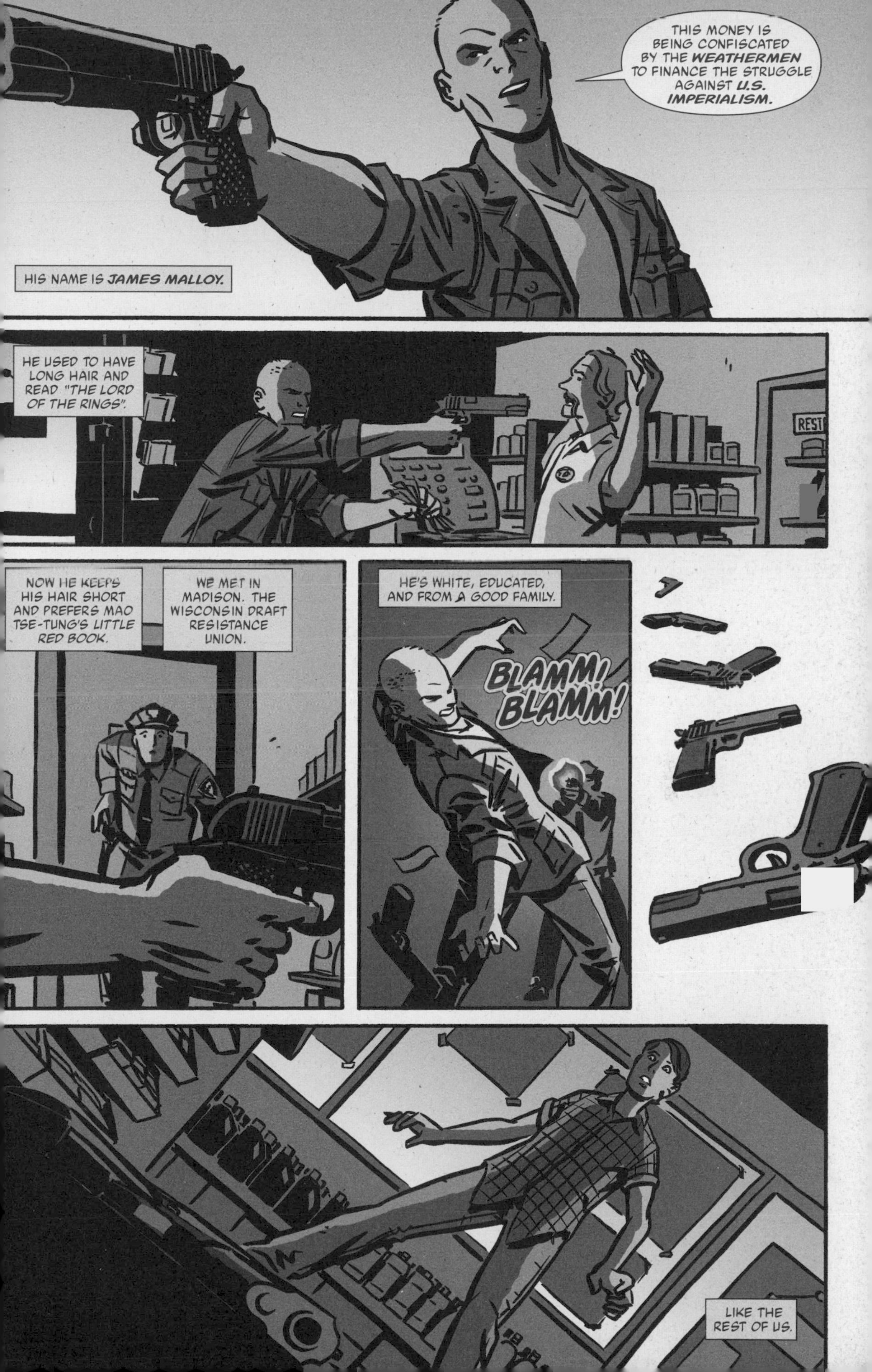
THIS MONEY IS BEING CONFISCATED BY THE WEATHERMEN TO FINANCE THE STRUGGLE AGAINST U.S. IMPERIALISM.
HIS NAME IS JAMES MALLOY.
HE USED TO HAVE LONG HAIR AND READ "THE LORD OF THE RINGS".
REST
NOW HE KEEPS HIS HAIR SHORT AND PREFERS MAO TSE-TUNG'S LITTLE RED BOOK.
WE MET IN MADISON. THE WISCONSIN DRAFT RESISTANCE UNION.
HE'S WHITE, EDUCATED, AND FROM A GOOD FAMILY.
BLAMM! BLAMM!
LIKE THE REST OF US.

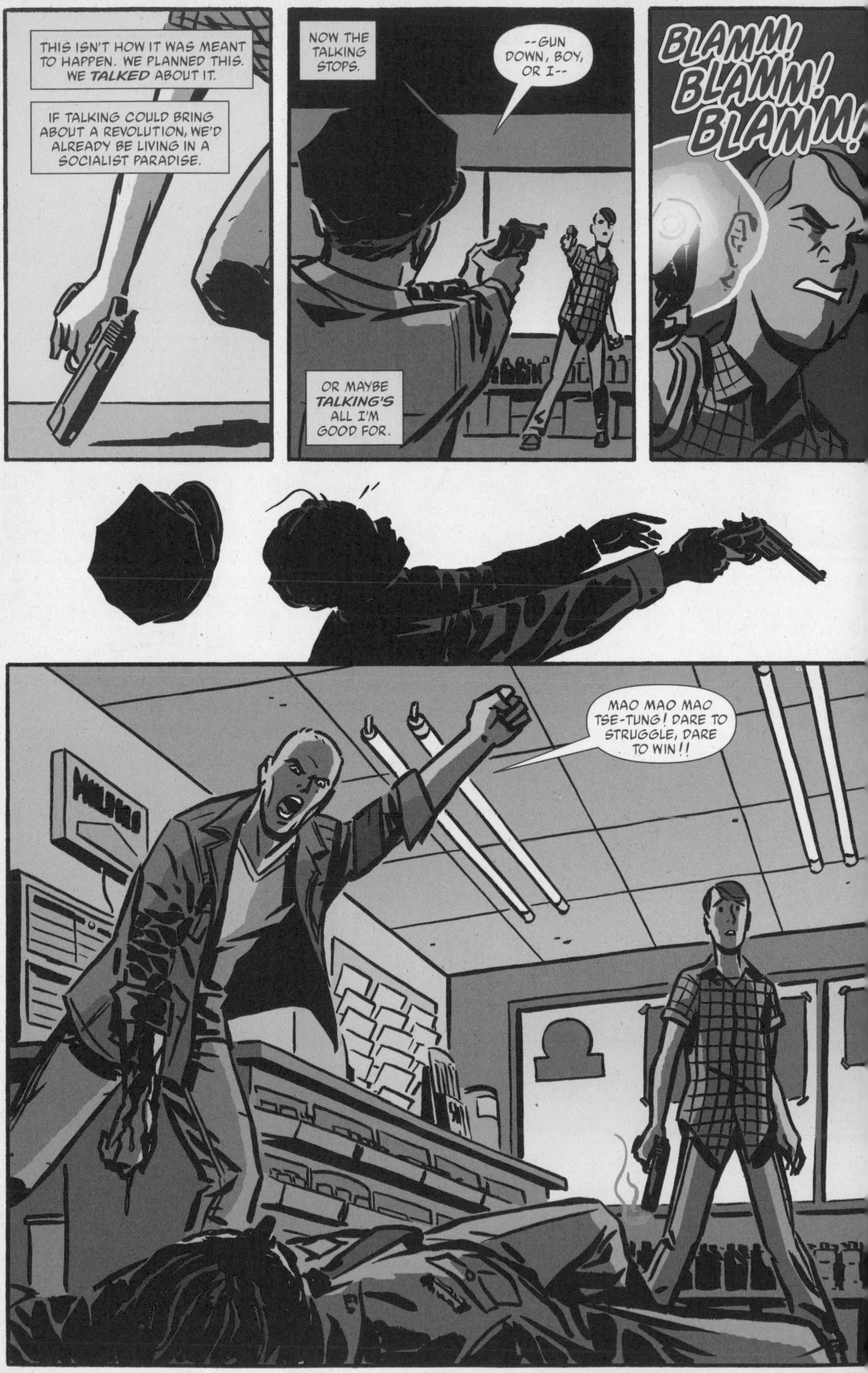

THIS ISN'T HOW IT WAS MEANT TO HAPPEN. WE PLANNED THIS. WE *TALKED* ABOUT IT.
IF TALKING COULD BRING ABOUT A REVOLUTION, WE'D ALREADY BE LIVING IN A SOCIALIST PARADISE.
NOW THE TALKING STOPS.
--GUN DOWN, BOY, OR I--
OR MAYBE *TALKING'S* ALL I'M GOOD FOR.
BLAMM! BLAMM! BLAMM!
MAO MAO MAO TSE-TUNG! DARE TO STRUGGLE, DARE TO WIN!!

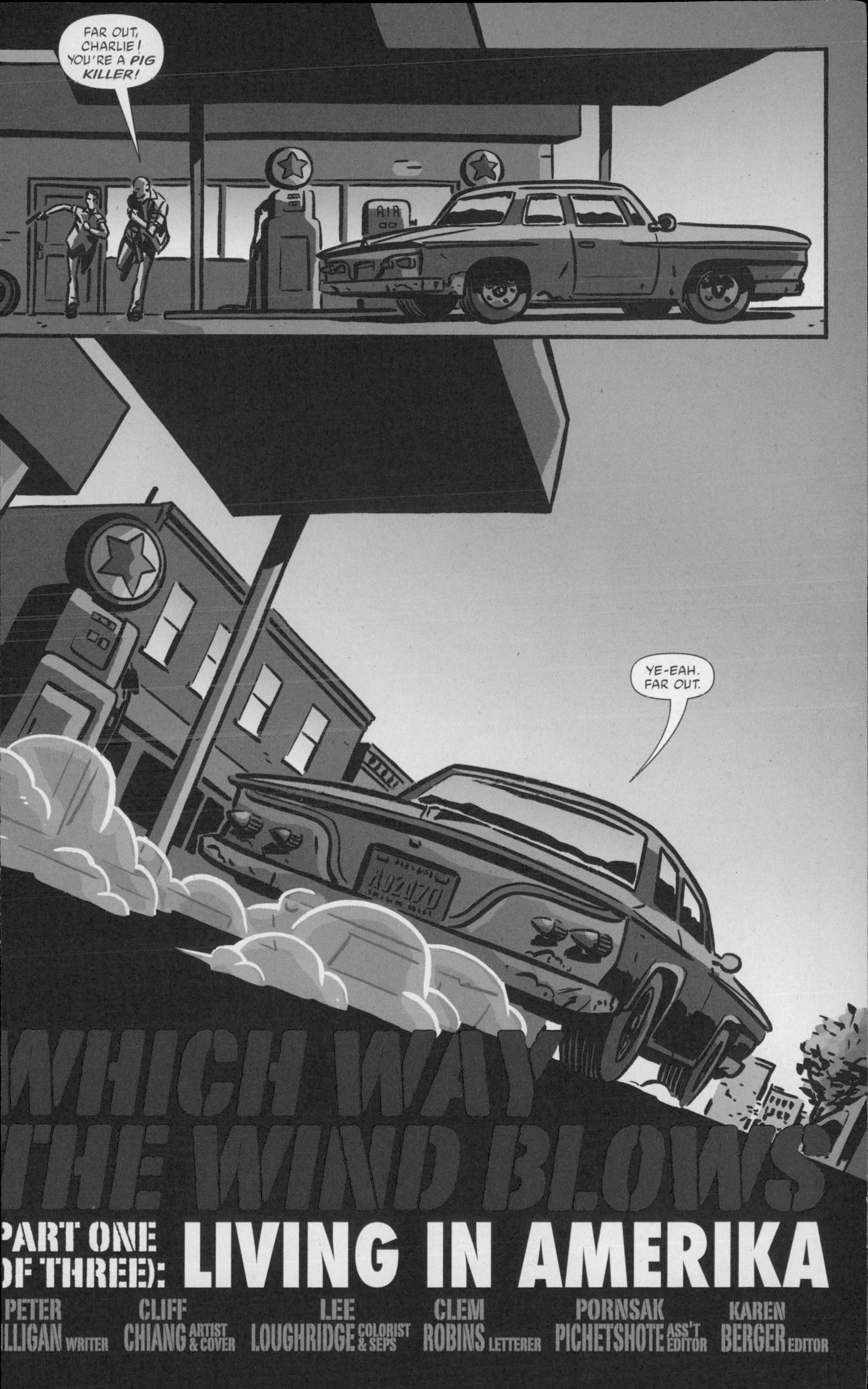

FAR OUT, CHARLIE! YOU'RE A PIG KILLER!
AIR
YE-EAH. FAR OUT.
WHICH WAY THE WIND BLOWS
PART ONE (OF THREE): LIVING IN AMERIKA
PETER ILLIGAN WRITER
CLIFF CHIANG ARTIST & COVER
LEE LOUGHRIDGE COLORIST & SEPS
CLEM ROBINS LETTERER
PORNSAK PICHETSHOTE ASS'T EDITOR
KAREN BERGER EDITOR

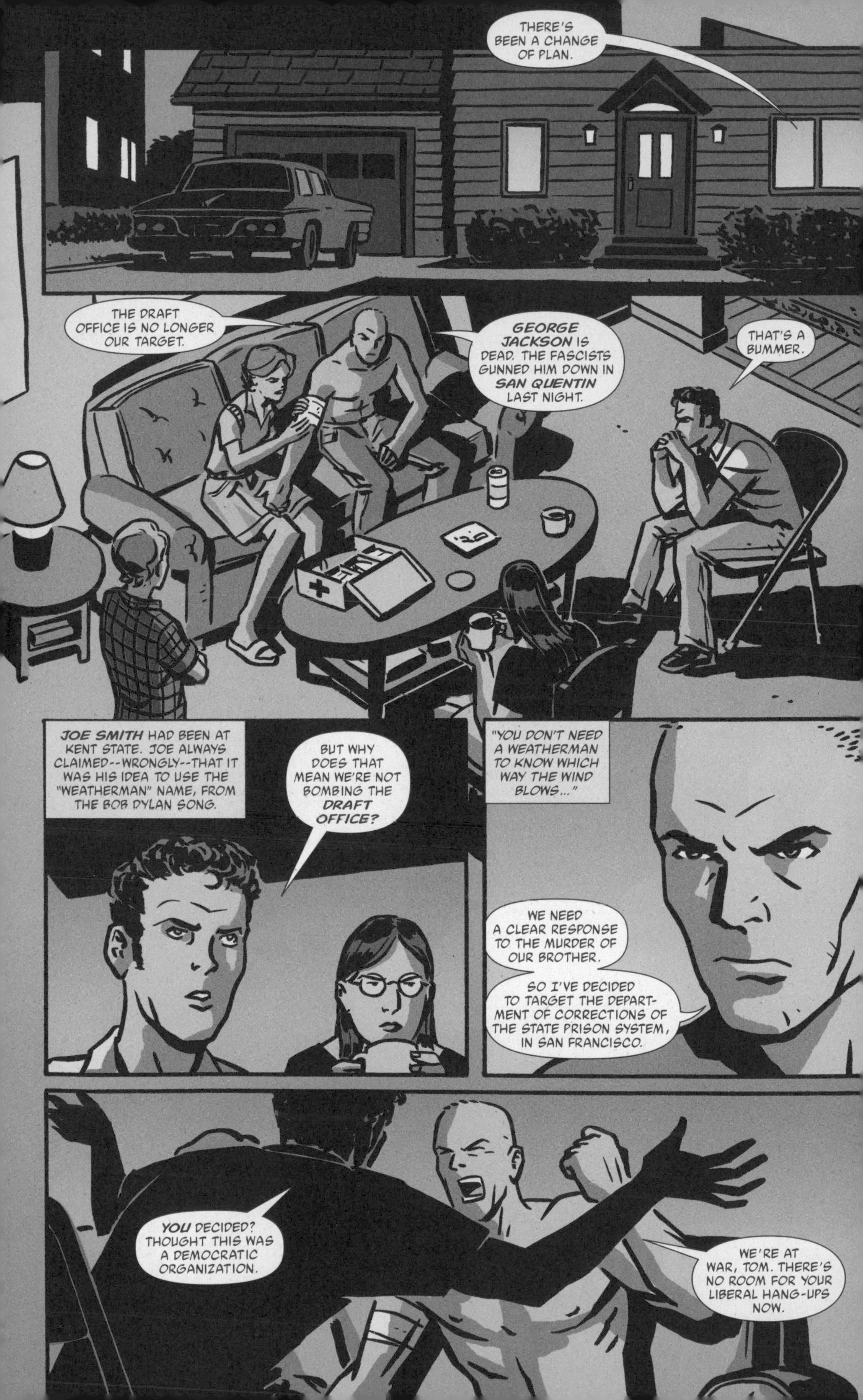
THERE'S BEEN A CHANGE OF PLAN.
THE DRAFT OFFICE IS NO LONGER OUR TARGET.
GEORGE JACKSON IS DEAD. THE FASCISTS GUNNED HIM DOWN IN SAN QUENTIN LAST NIGHT.
THAT'S A BUMMER.
JOE SMITH HAD BEEN AT KENT STATE. JOE ALWAYS CLAIMED--WRONGLY--THAT IT WAS HIS IDEA TO USE THE "WEATHERMAN" NAME, FROM THE BOB DYLAN SONG.
BUT WHY DOES THAT MEAN WE'RE NOT BOMBING THE DRAFT OFFICE?
"YOU DON'T NEED A WEATHERMAN TO KNOW WHICH WAY THE WIND BLOWS..."
WE NEED A CLEAR RESPONSE TO THE MURDER OF OUR BROTHER.
SO I'VE DECIDED TO TARGET THE DEPARTMENT OF CORRECTIONS OF THE STATE PRISON SYSTEM, IN SAN FRANCISCO.
YOU DECIDED? THOUGHT THIS WAS A DEMOCRATIC ORGANIZATION.
WE'RE AT WAR, TOM. THERE'S NO ROOM FOR YOUR LIBERAL HANG-UPS NOW.

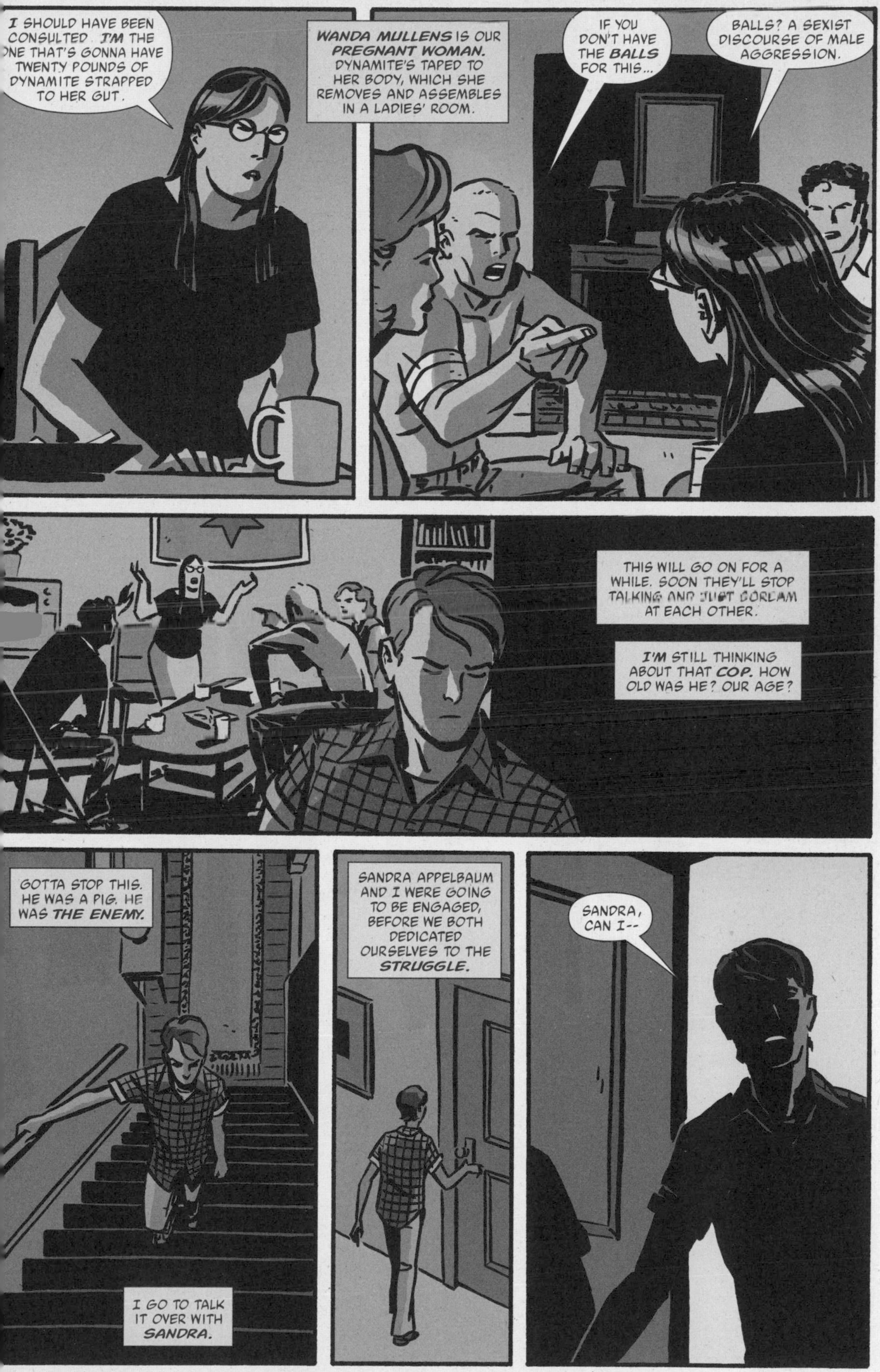
I SHOULD HAVE BEEN CONSULTED. I'M THE ONE THAT'S GONNA HAVE TWENTY POUNDS OF DYNAMITE STRAPPED TO HER GUT.
WANDA MULLENS IS OUR PREGNANT WOMAN. DYNAMITE'S TAPED TO HER BODY, WHICH SHE REMOVES AND ASSEMBLES IN A LADIES' ROOM.
IF YOU DON'T HAVE THE BALLS FOR THIS...
BALLS? A SEXIST DISCOURSE OF MALE AGGRESSION.
THIS WILL GO ON FOR A WHILE. SOON THEY'LL STOP TALKING AND JUST SCREAM AT EACH OTHER.
I'M STILL THINKING ABOUT THAT COP. HOW OLD WAS HE? OUR AGE?
GOTTA STOP THIS. HE WAS A PIG. HE WAS THE ENEMY.
I GO TO TALK IT OVER WITH SANDRA.
SANDRA APPELBAUM AND I WERE GOING TO BE ENGAGED, BEFORE WE BOTH DEDICATED OURSELVES TO THE STRUGGLE.
SANDRA, CAN I--

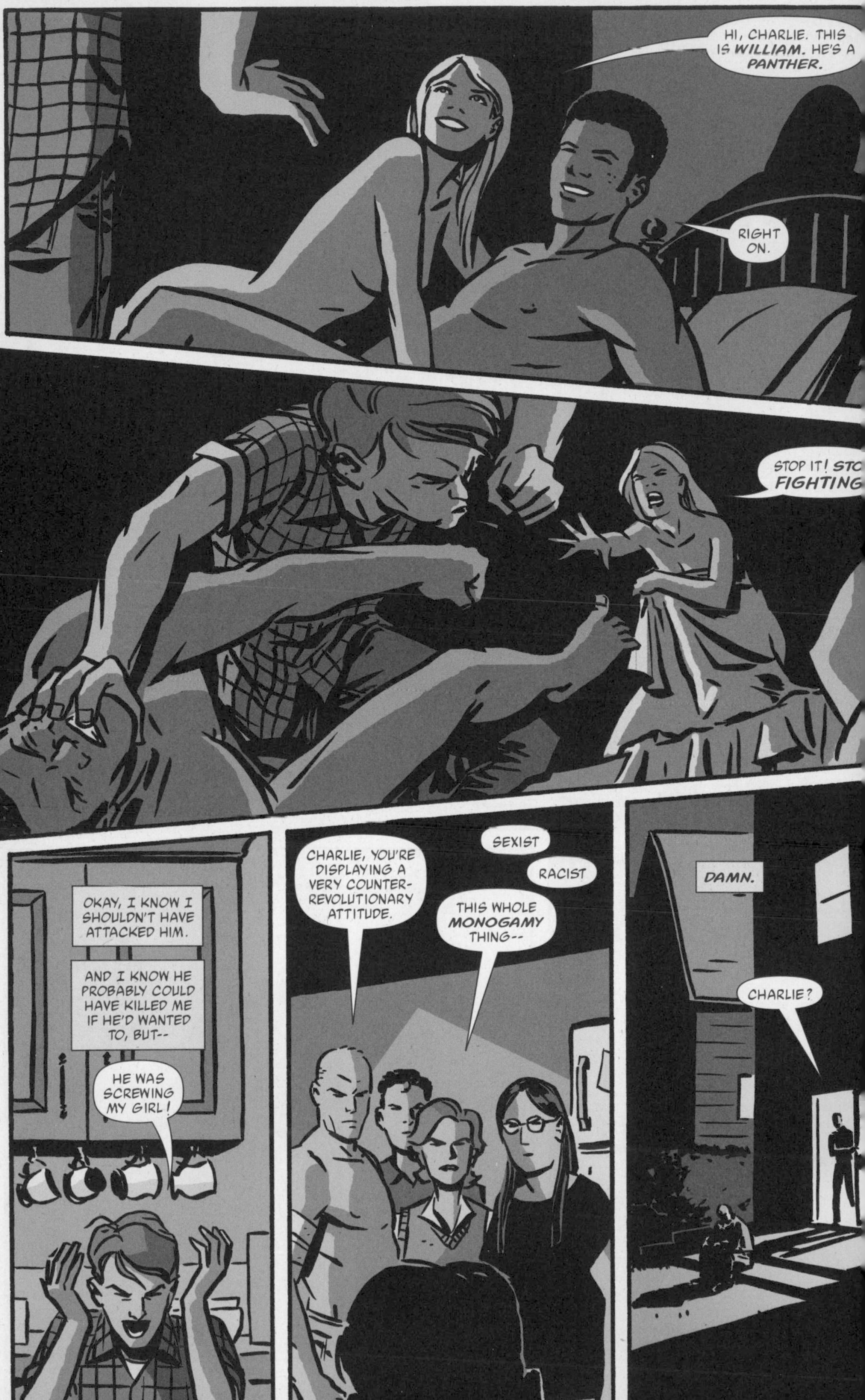
HI, CHARLIE. THIS IS *WILLIAM.* HE'S A *PANTHER.*
RIGHT ON.
STOP IT! *STO*
FIGHTING
OKAY, I KNOW I SHOULDN'T HAVE ATTACKED HIM.
AND I KNOW HE PROBABLY COULD HAVE KILLED ME IF HE'D WANTED TO, BUT--
HE WAS SCREWING MY GIRL!
CHARLIE, YOU'RE DISPLAYING A VERY COUNTER-REVOLUTIONARY ATTITUDE.
SEXIST
RACIST
THIS WHOLE *MONOGAMY* THING--
DAMN.
CHARLIE?

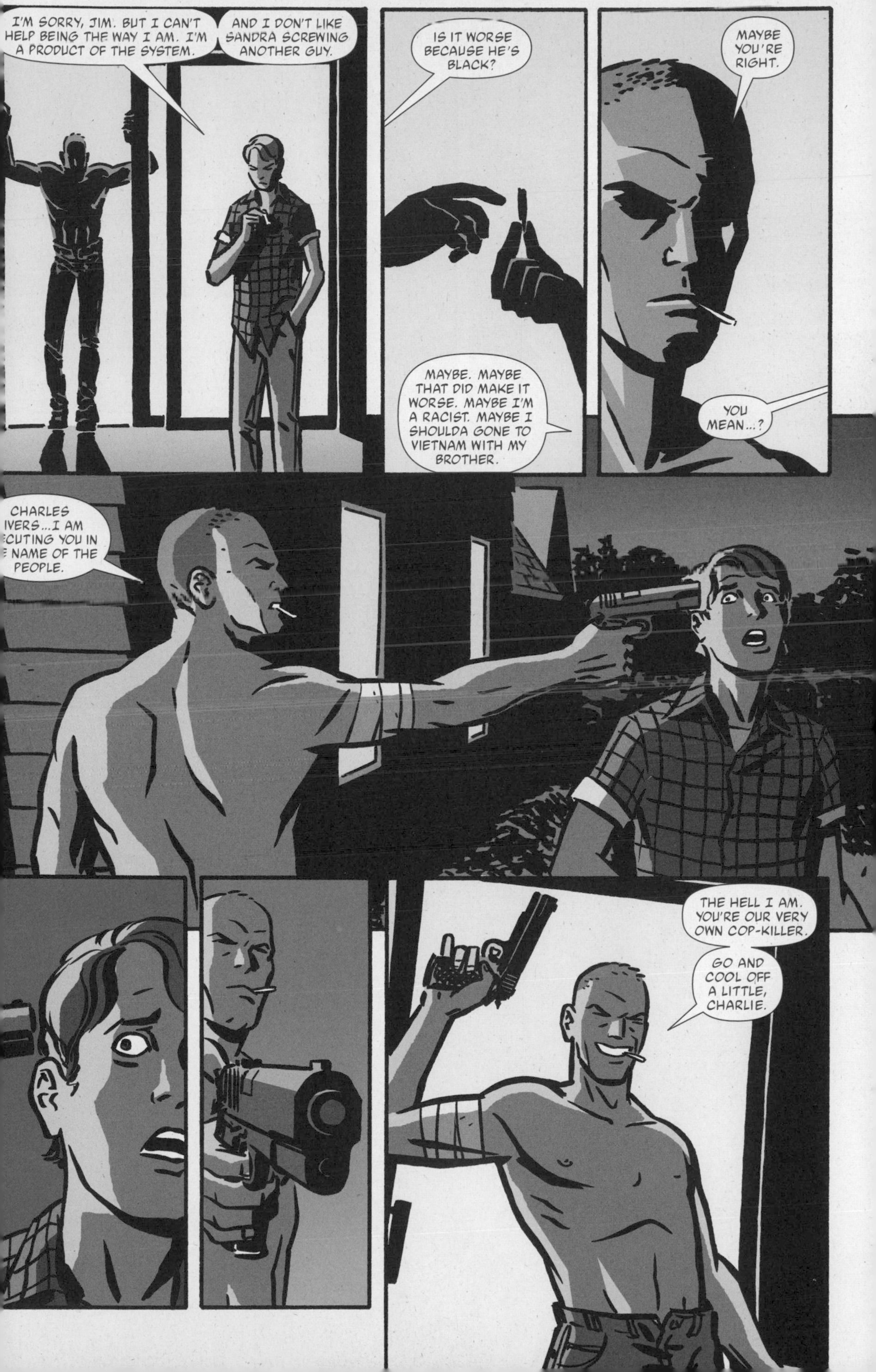
I'M SORRY, JIM. BUT I CAN'T HELP BEING THE WAY I AM. I'M A PRODUCT OF THE SYSTEM.
AND I DON'T LIKE SANDRA SCREWING ANOTHER GUY.
IS IT WORSE BECAUSE HE'S BLACK?
MAYBE. MAYBE THAT DID MAKE IT WORSE. MAYBE I'M A RACIST. MAYBE I SHOULDA GONE TO VIETNAM WITH MY BROTHER.
MAYBE YOU'RE RIGHT.
YOU MEAN...?
CHARLES IVERS...I AM ECUTING YOU IN E NAME OF THE PEOPLE.
THE HELL I AM. YOU'RE OUR VERY OWN COP-KILLER.
GO AND COOL OFF A LITTLE, CHARLIE.

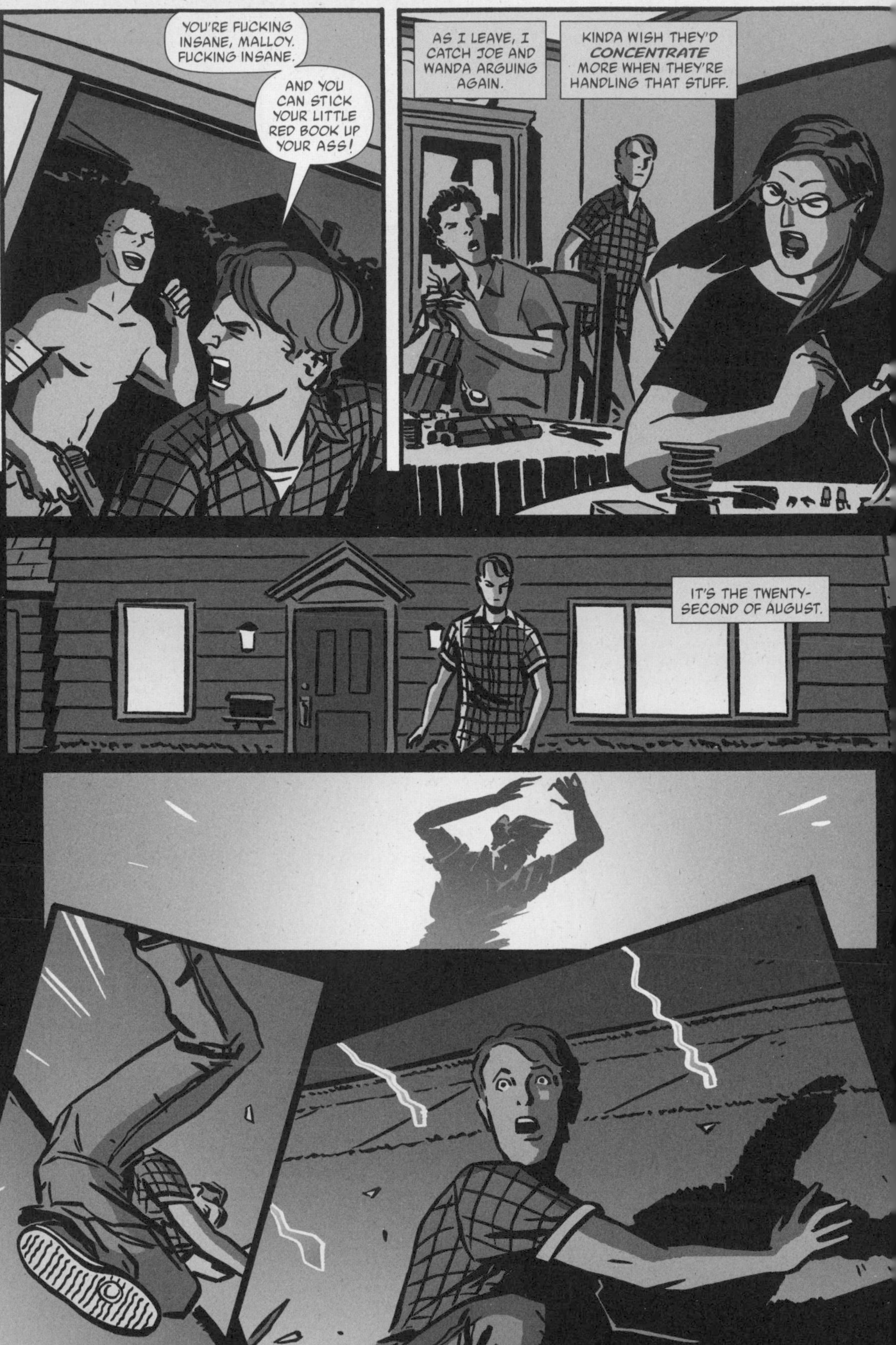
YOU'RE FUCKING INSANE, MALLOY. FUCKING INSANE.
AND YOU CAN STICK YOUR LITTLE RED BOOK UP YOUR ASS!
AS I LEAVE, I CATCH JOE AND WANDA ARGUING AGAIN.
KINDA WISH THEY'D CONCENTRATE MORE WHEN THEY'RE HANDLING THAT STUFF.
IT'S THE TWENTY-SECOND OF AUGUST.

"IT HAS BEEN OVER THIRTY YEARS SINCE THE 'BOMB FACTORY EXPLOSION' PUT AN END TO THE TERRORIST ACTIVITIES OF THE WEATHERMEN CELL KNOWN AS THE **MALLOY GANG.**

"AS SHOWN ELSEWHERE, THE WEATHERMEN--KNOWN ALSO AS THE WEATHER UNDERGROUND--WERE A SMALL THOUGH AGGRESSIVE GROUP OF REVOLUTIONARIES THAT GREW OUT OF THE NEW LEFT IN GENERAL, AND THE 'STUDENTS FOR A DEMOCRATIC SOCIETY' IN PARTICULAR...

DUE TO RECENT UNEXPECTED EVENTS, I SHALL ATTEMPT TO INCLUDE ALL KNOWN FACTS IN THIS EXTRAORDINARY REPORT.

"**JOE SMITH** TOOK THE FULL BLAST OF THE EXPLOSION AND WAS ONLY IDENTIFIED THROUGH DENTAL RECORDS.

"HE BECAME A SMALL FOOTNOTE IN THE MODERN AMERICAN HISTORY COURSE OF A MINOR UNIVERSITY.

JOSEPH SMITH
1949 – 1971

"**WANDA MULLENS** WAS PARTIALLY BLINDED, AND CONFINED TO A WHEELCHAIR FOR LIFE.

"SHE SERVED FIVE YEARS FOR HER ACTIONS BEFORE BECOMING A LEGAL ASSISTANT IN A LAW FIRM THAT SUPPORTS AND CREATES FEMINIST SOCIAL CHANGE."

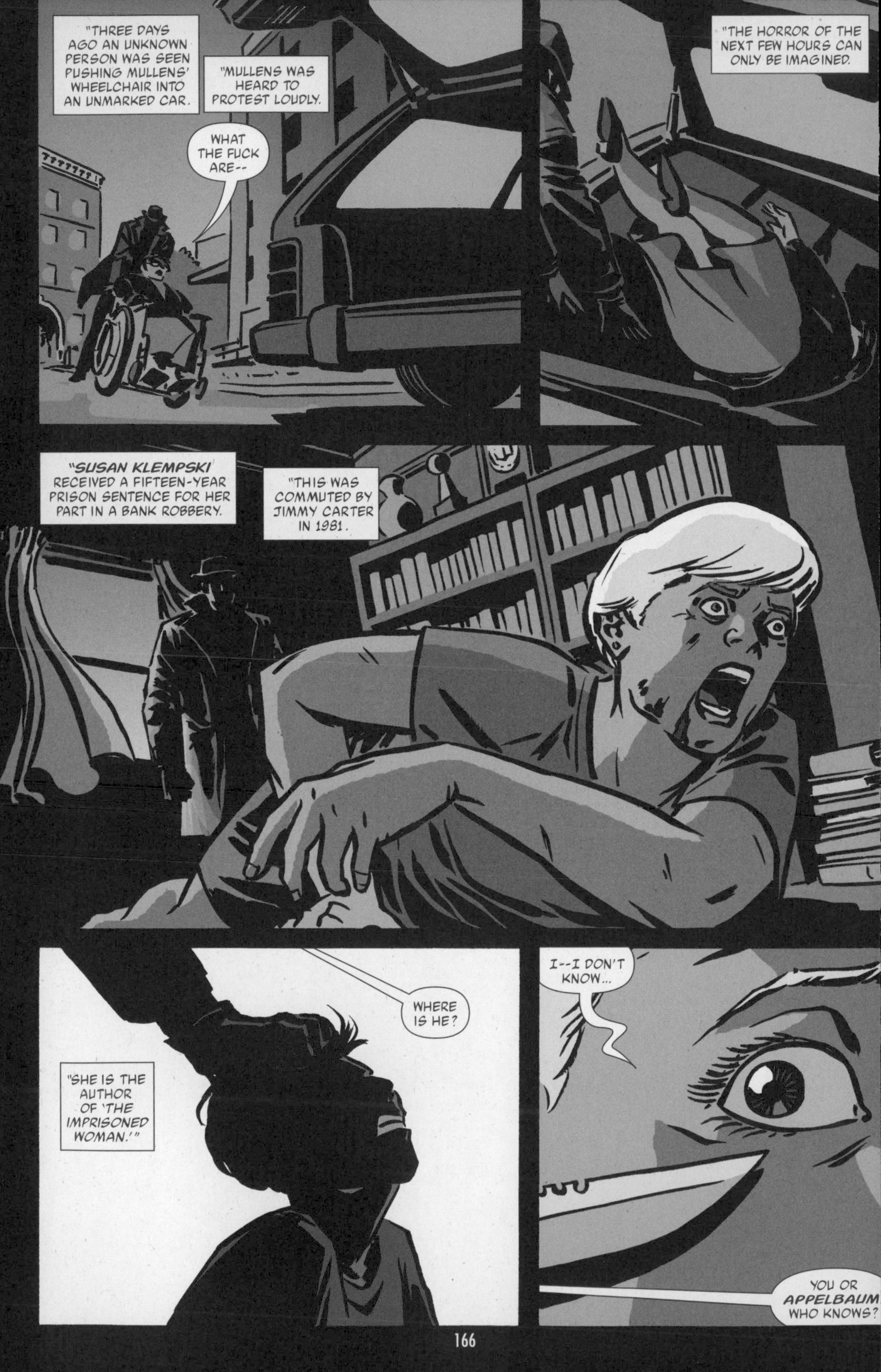
"THREE DAYS AGO AN UNKNOWN PERSON WAS SEEN PUSHING MULLENS' WHEELCHAIR INTO AN UNMARKED CAR.
"MULLENS WAS HEARD TO PROTEST LOUDLY.
WHAT THE FUCK ARE--
"THE HORROR OF THE NEXT FEW HOURS CAN ONLY BE IMAGINED.
"SUSAN KLEMPSKI RECEIVED A FIFTEEN-YEAR PRISON SENTENCE FOR HER PART IN A BANK ROBBERY.
"THIS WAS COMMUTED BY JIMMY CARTER IN 1981.
WHERE IS HE?
"SHE IS THE AUTHOR OF 'THE IMPRISONED WOMAN.'"
I--I DON'T KNOW...
YOU OR APPELBAUM WHO KNOWS?

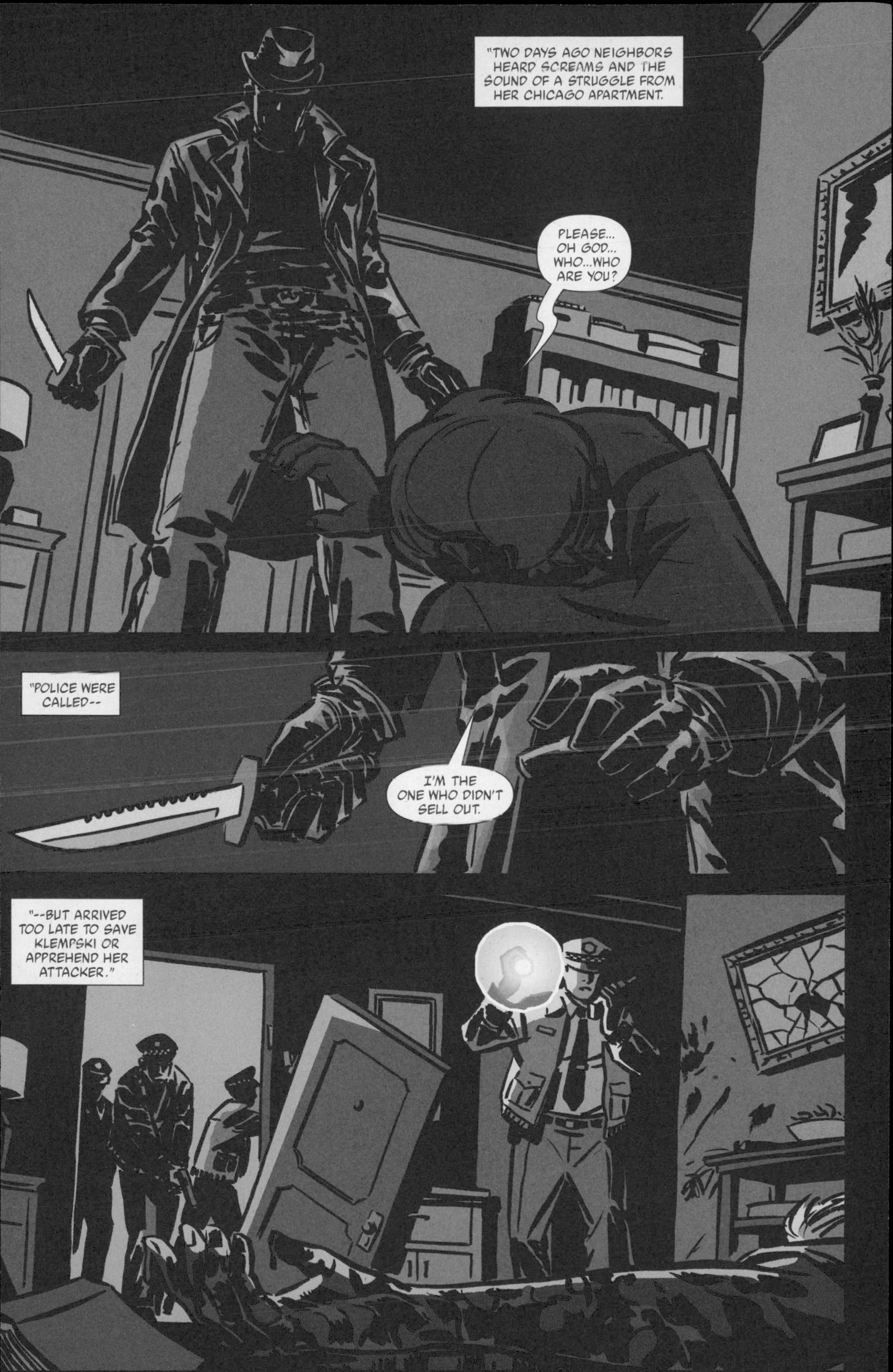
"TWO DAYS AGO NEIGHBORS HEARD SCREAMS AND THE SOUND OF A STRUGGLE FROM HER CHICAGO APARTMENT.
PLEASE... OH GOD... WHO...WHO ARE YOU?
"POLICE WERE CALLED--
I'M THE ONE WHO DIDN'T SELL OUT.
"--BUT ARRIVED TOO LATE TO SAVE KLEMPSKI OR APPREHEND HER ATTACKER."

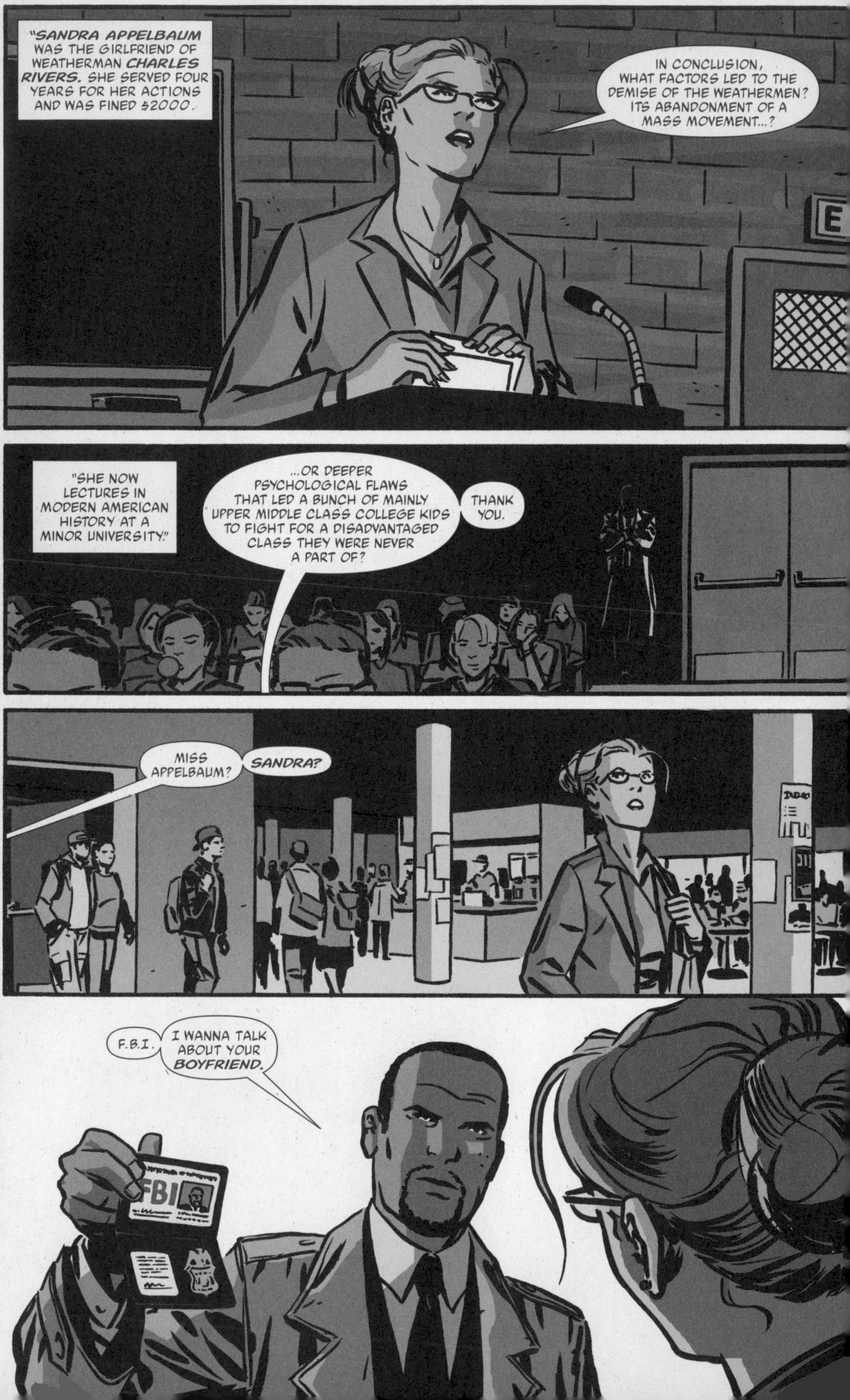
"SANDRA APPELBAUM WAS THE GIRLFRIEND OF WEATHERMAN CHARLES RIVERS. SHE SERVED FOUR YEARS FOR HER ACTIONS AND WAS FINED $2000.
IN CONCLUSION, WHAT FACTORS LED TO THE DEMISE OF THE WEATHERMEN? ITS ABANDONMENT OF A MASS MOVEMENT...?
"SHE NOW LECTURES IN MODERN AMERICAN HISTORY AT A MINOR UNIVERSITY."
...OR DEEPER PSYCHOLOGICAL FLAWS THAT LED A BUNCH OF MAINLY UPPER MIDDLE CLASS COLLEGE KIDS TO FIGHT FOR A DISADVANTAGED CLASS THEY WERE NEVER A PART OF?
THANK YOU.
MISS APPELBAUM?
SANDRA?
F.B.I.
I WANNA TALK ABOUT YOUR BOYFRIEND.
FBI

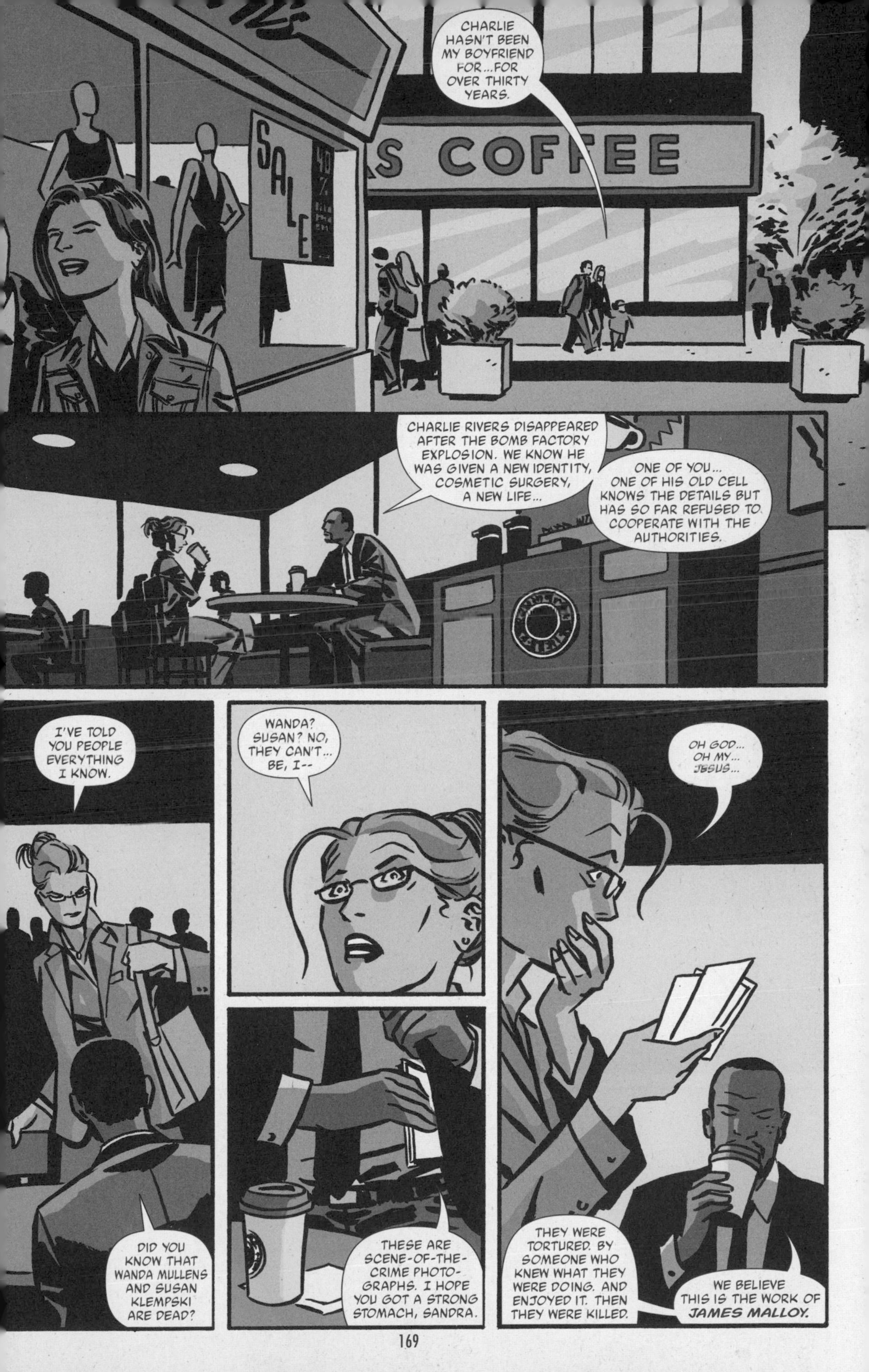
CHARLIE HASN'T BEEN MY BOYFRIEND FOR...FOR OVER THIRTY YEARS.
SALE
S COFFEE
CHARLIE RIVERS DISAPPEARED AFTER THE BOMB FACTORY EXPLOSION. WE KNOW HE WAS GIVEN A NEW IDENTITY, COSMETIC SURGERY, A NEW LIFE...
ONE OF YOU... ONE OF HIS OLD CELL KNOWS THE DETAILS BUT HAS SO FAR REFUSED TO COOPERATE WITH THE AUTHORITIES.
I'VE TOLD YOU PEOPLE EVERYTHING I KNOW.
DID YOU KNOW THAT WANDA MULLENS AND SUSAN KLEMPSKI ARE DEAD?
WANDA? SUSAN? NO, THEY CAN'T... BE, I--
THESE ARE SCENE-OF-THE-CRIME PHOTO-GRAPHS. I HOPE YOU GOT A STRONG STOMACH, SANDRA.
OH GOD... OH MY... JESUS...
THEY WERE TORTURED. BY SOMEONE WHO KNEW WHAT THEY WERE DOING. AND ENJOYED IT. THEN THEY WERE KILLED.
WE BELIEVE THIS IS THE WORK OF JAMES MALLOY.

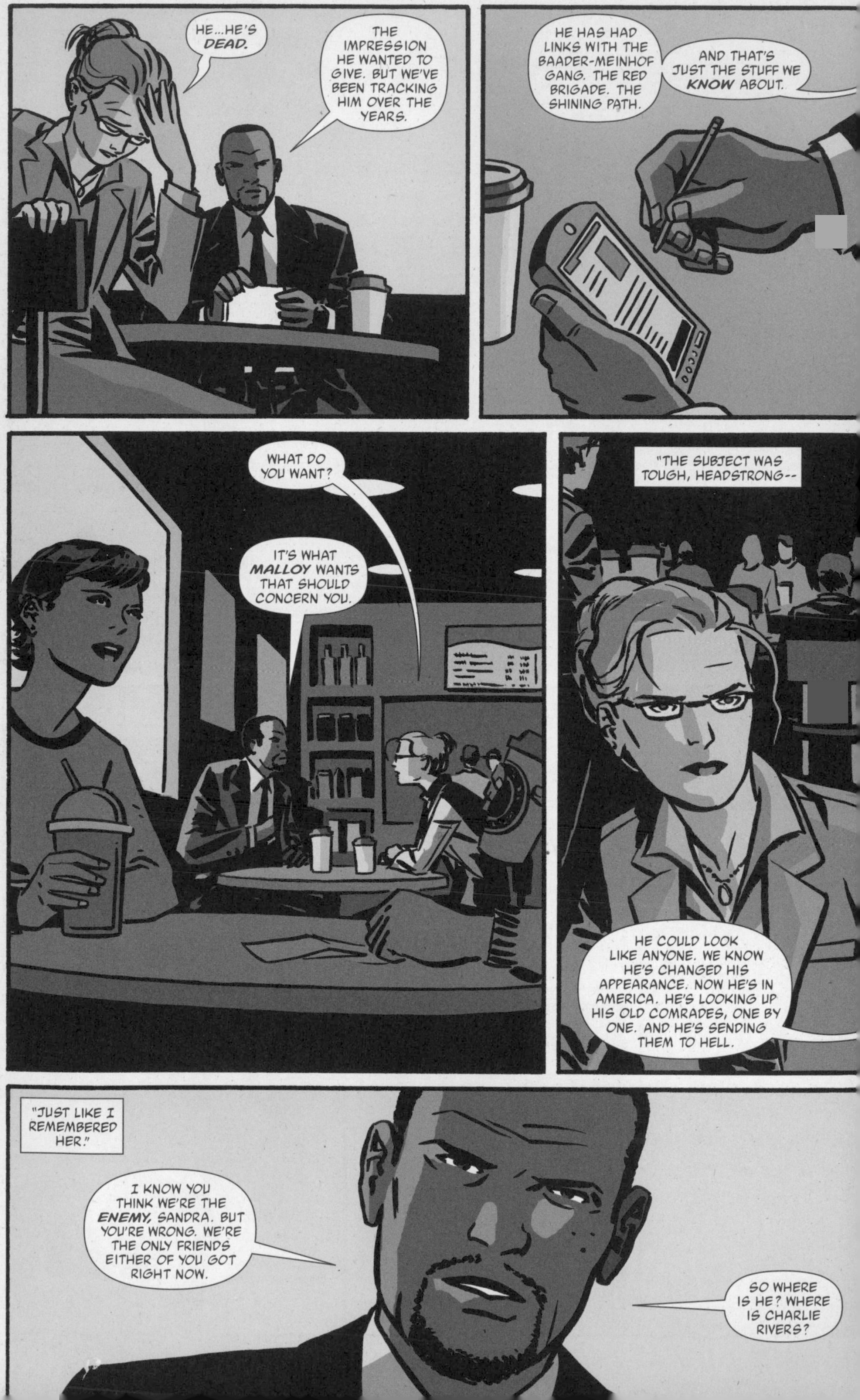
HE...HE'S DEAD.
THE IMPRESSION HE WANTED TO GIVE. BUT WE'VE BEEN TRACKING HIM OVER THE YEARS.
HE HAS HAD LINKS WITH THE BAADER-MEINHOF GANG. THE RED BRIGADE. THE SHINING PATH.
AND THAT'S JUST THE STUFF WE KNOW ABOUT.
WHAT DO YOU WANT?
IT'S WHAT MALLOY WANTS THAT SHOULD CONCERN YOU.
"THE SUBJECT WAS TOUGH, HEADSTRONG--
HE COULD LOOK LIKE ANYONE. WE KNOW HE'S CHANGED HIS APPEARANCE. NOW HE'S IN AMERICA. HE'S LOOKING UP HIS OLD COMRADES, ONE BY ONE. AND HE'S SENDING THEM TO HELL.
"JUST LIKE I REMEMBERED HER."
I KNOW YOU THINK WE'RE THE ENEMY, SANDRA. BUT YOU'RE WRONG. WE'RE THE ONLY FRIENDS EITHER OF YOU GOT RIGHT NOW.
SO WHERE IS HE? WHERE IS CHARLIE RIVERS?

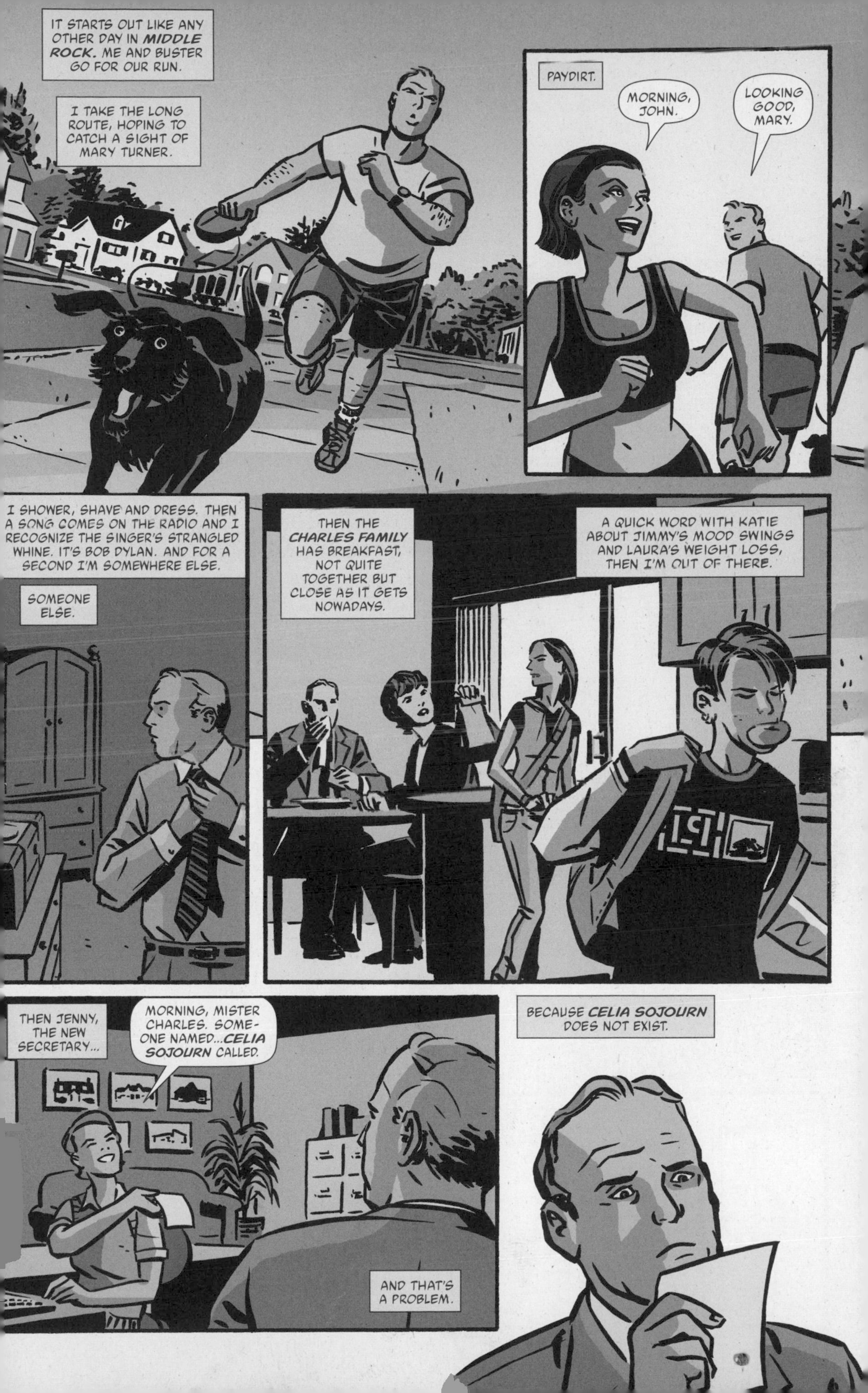
IT STARTS OUT LIKE ANY OTHER DAY IN **MIDDLE ROCK.** ME AND BUSTER GO FOR OUR RUN.
I TAKE THE LONG ROUTE, HOPING TO CATCH A SIGHT OF MARY TURNER.
PAYDIRT.
MORNING, JOHN.
LOOKING GOOD, MARY.
I SHOWER, SHAVE AND DRESS. THEN A SONG COMES ON THE RADIO AND I RECOGNIZE THE SINGER'S STRANGLED WHINE. IT'S BOB DYLAN. AND FOR A SECOND I'M SOMEWHERE ELSE.
SOMEONE ELSE.
THEN THE **CHARLES FAMILY** HAS BREAKFAST, NOT QUITE TOGETHER BUT CLOSE AS IT GETS NOWADAYS.
A QUICK WORD WITH KATIE ABOUT JIMMY'S MOOD SWINGS AND LAURA'S WEIGHT LOSS, THEN I'M OUT OF THERE.
THEN JENNY, THE NEW SECRETARY...
MORNING, MISTER CHARLES. SOME-ONE NAMED...**CELIA SOJOURN** CALLED.
AND THAT'S A PROBLEM.
BECAUSE **CELIA SOJOURN** DOES NOT EXIST.

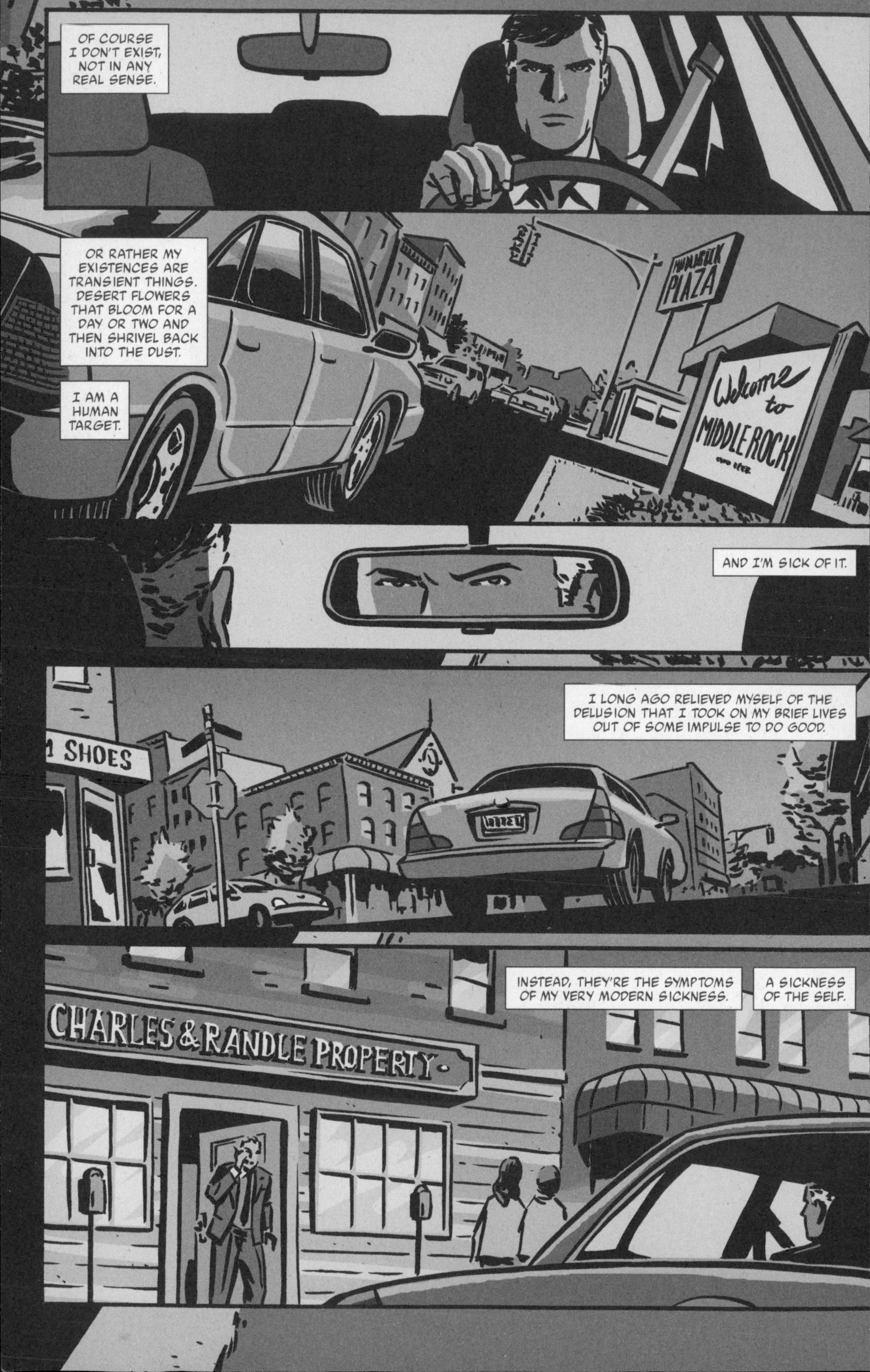
OF COURSE I DON'T EXIST, NOT IN ANY REAL SENSE.
OR RATHER MY EXISTENCES ARE TRANSIENT THINGS. DESERT FLOWERS THAT BLOOM FOR A DAY OR TWO AND THEN SHRIVEL BACK INTO THE DUST.
I AM A HUMAN TARGET.
PLAZA
Welcome to MIDDLE ROCK
AND I'M SICK OF IT.
I LONG AGO RELIEVED MYSELF OF THE DELUSION THAT I TOOK ON MY BRIEF LIVES OUT OF SOME IMPULSE TO DO GOOD.
SHOES
INSTEAD, THEY'RE THE SYMPTOMS OF MY VERY MODERN SICKNESS.
A SICKNESS OF THE SELF.
CHARLES & RANDLE PROPERTY

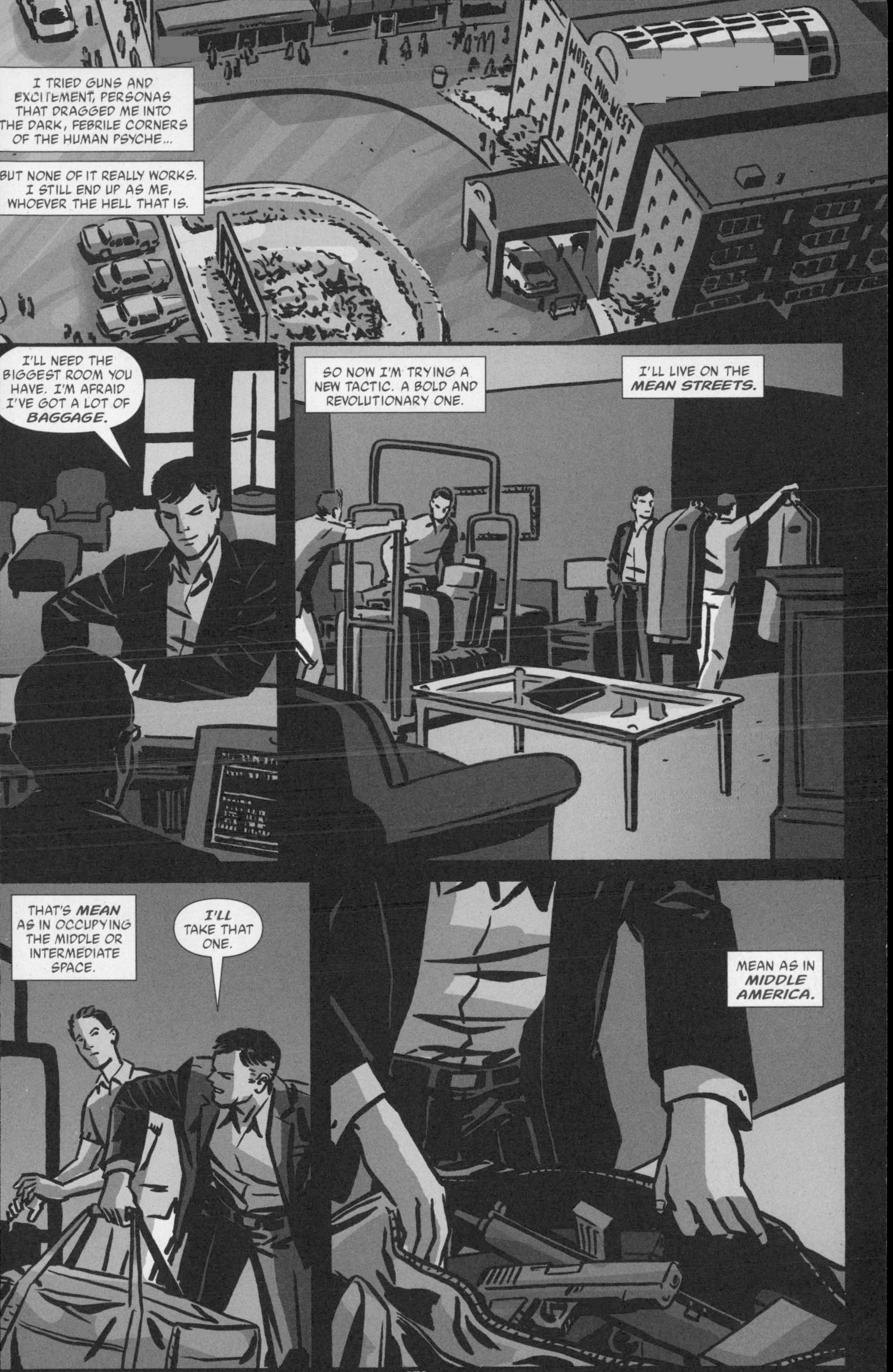

I TRIED GUNS AND EXCITEMENT, PERSONAS THAT DRAGGED ME INTO THE DARK, FEBRILE CORNERS OF THE HUMAN PSYCHE...
BUT NONE OF IT REALLY WORKS. I STILL END UP AS ME, WHOEVER THE HELL THAT IS.
HOTEL MID-WEST
I'LL NEED THE BIGGEST ROOM YOU HAVE. I'M AFRAID I'VE GOT A LOT OF BAGGAGE.
SO NOW I'M TRYING A NEW TACTIC. A BOLD AND REVOLUTIONARY ONE.
I'LL LIVE ON THE MEAN STREETS.
THAT'S MEAN AS IN OCCUPYING THE MIDDLE OR INTERMEDIATE SPACE.
I'LL TAKE THAT ONE.
MEAN AS IN MIDDLE AMERICA.

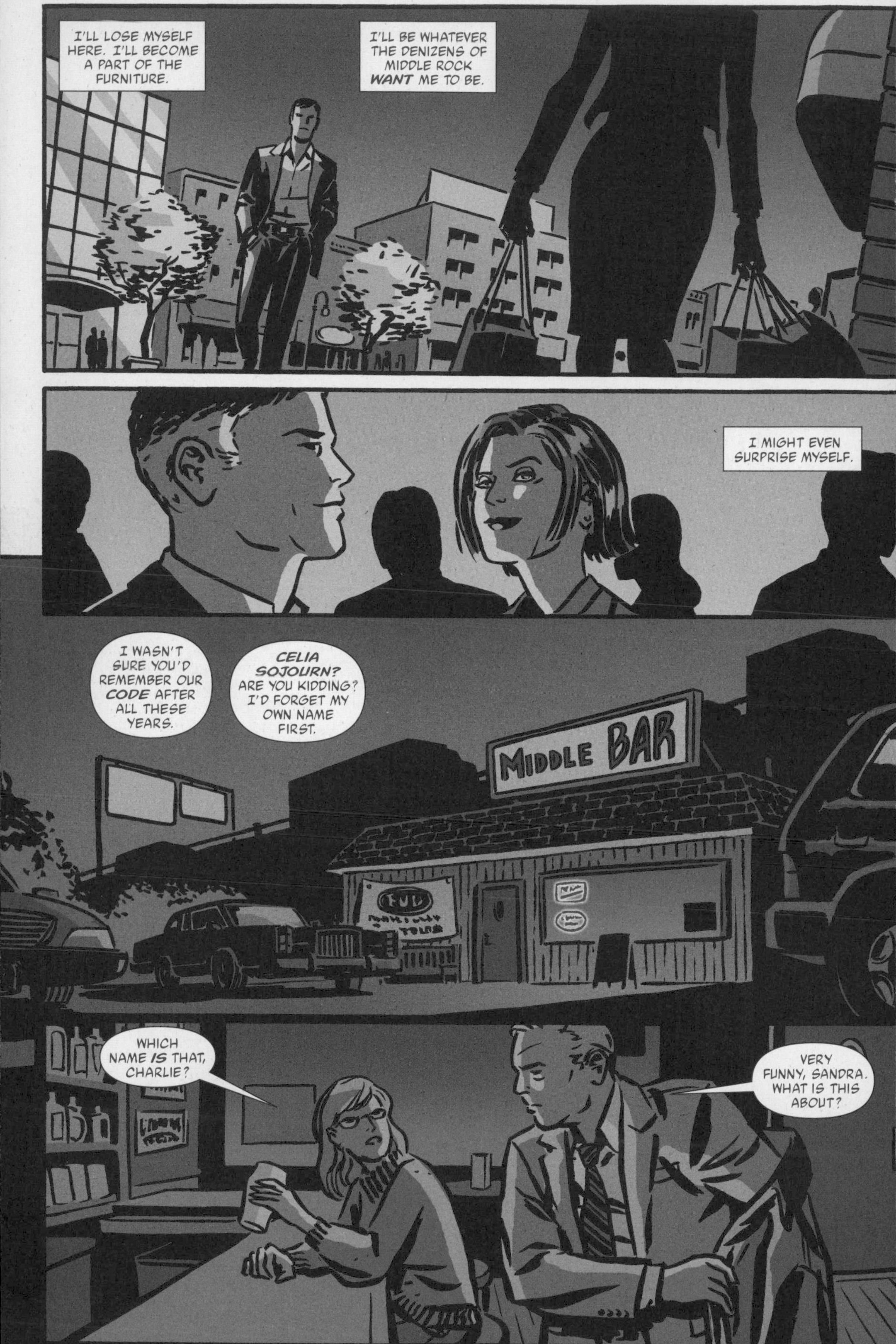

I'LL LOSE MYSELF HERE. I'LL BECOME A PART OF THE FURNITURE.
I'LL BE WHATEVER THE DENIZENS OF MIDDLE ROCK WANT ME TO BE.
I MIGHT EVEN SURPRISE MYSELF.
I WASN'T SURE YOU'D REMEMBER OUR CODE AFTER ALL THESE YEARS.
CELIA SOJOURN? ARE YOU KIDDING? I'D FORGET MY OWN NAME FIRST.
MIDDLE BAR
WHICH NAME IS THAT, CHARLIE?
VERY FUNNY, SANDRA. WHAT IS THIS ABOUT?

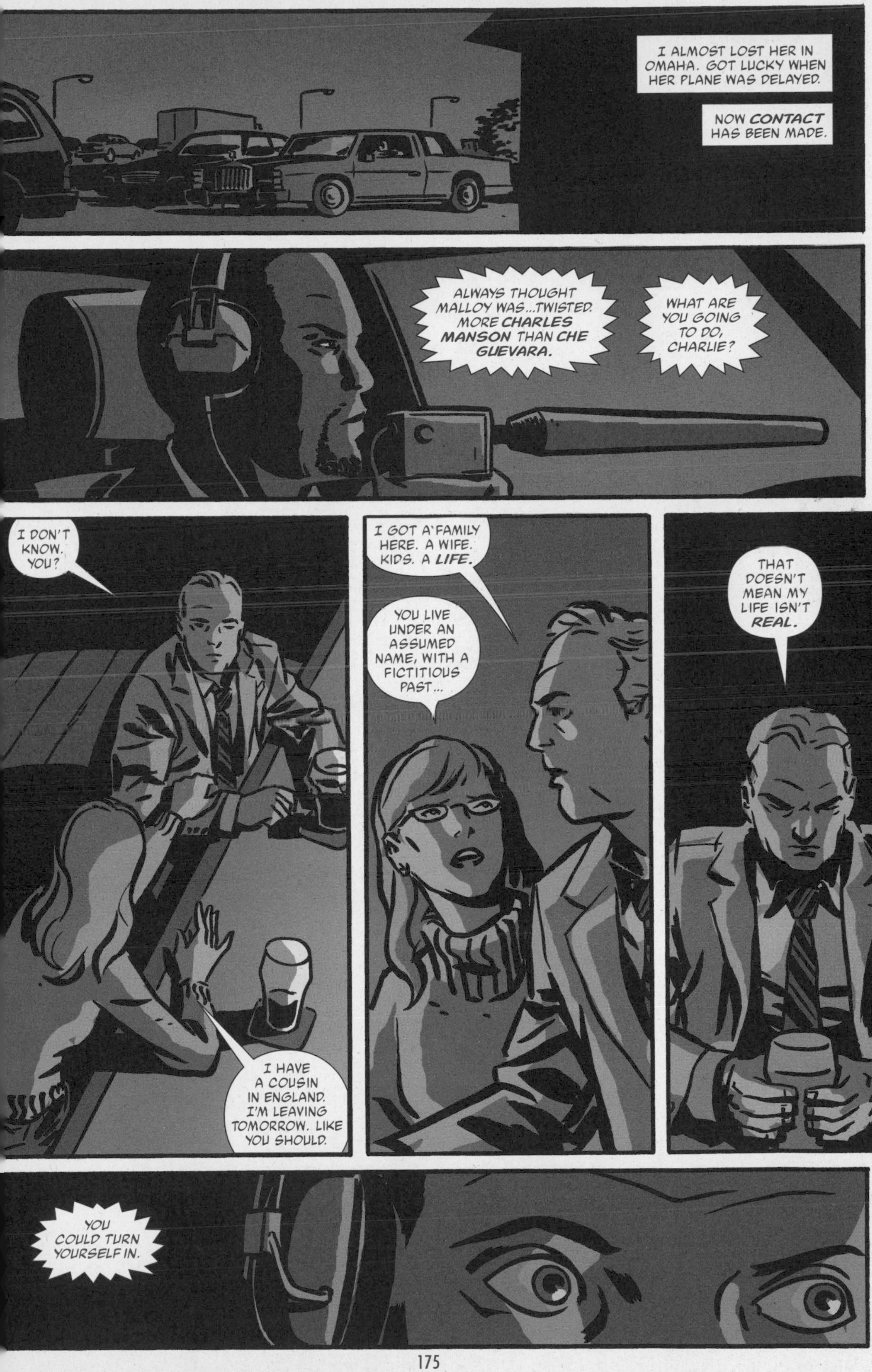
I ALMOST LOST HER IN OMAHA. GOT LUCKY WHEN HER PLANE WAS DELAYED.
NOW CONTACT HAS BEEN MADE.
ALWAYS THOUGHT MALLOY WAS...TWISTED. MORE CHARLES MANSON THAN CHE GUEVARA.
WHAT ARE YOU GOING TO DO, CHARLIE?
I DON'T KNOW. YOU?
I HAVE A COUSIN IN ENGLAND. I'M LEAVING TOMORROW. LIKE YOU SHOULD.
I GOT A FAMILY HERE. A WIFE. KIDS. A LIFE.
YOU LIVE UNDER AN ASSUMED NAME, WITH A FICTITIOUS PAST...
THAT DOESN'T MEAN MY LIFE ISN'T REAL.
YOU COULD TURN YOURSELF IN.

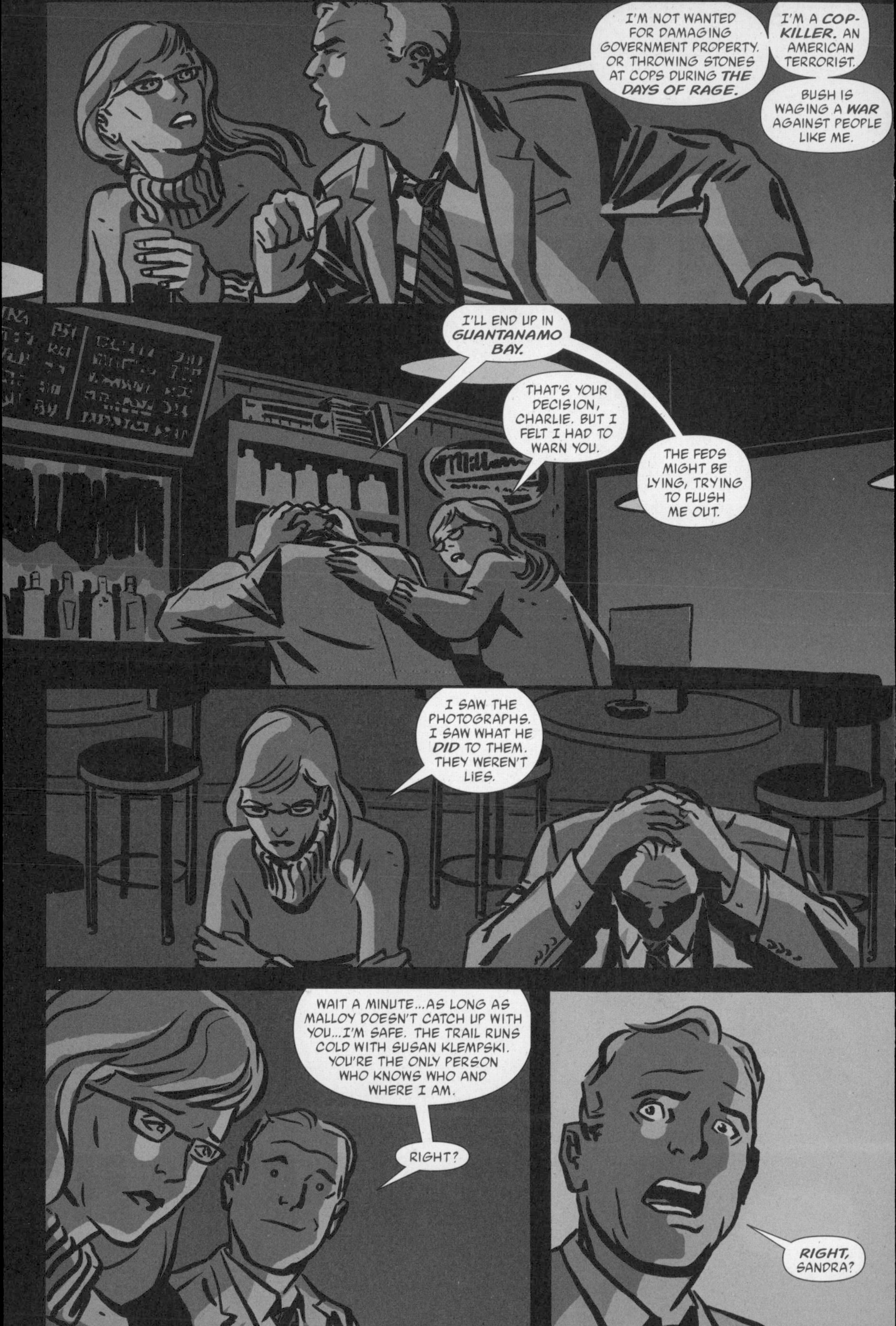
I'M NOT WANTED FOR DAMAGING GOVERNMENT PROPERTY. OR THROWING STONES AT COPS DURING THE DAYS OF RAGE.
I'M A COP-KILLER. AN AMERICAN TERRORIST.
BUSH IS WAGING A WAR AGAINST PEOPLE LIKE ME.
I'LL END UP IN GUANTANAMO BAY.
THAT'S YOUR DECISION, CHARLIE. BUT I FELT I HAD TO WARN YOU.
THE FEDS MIGHT BE LYING, TRYING TO FLUSH ME OUT.
I SAW THE PHOTOGRAPHS. I SAW WHAT HE DID TO THEM. THEY WEREN'T LIES.
WAIT A MINUTE...AS LONG AS MALLOY DOESN'T CATCH UP WITH YOU...I'M SAFE. THE TRAIL RUNS COLD WITH SUSAN KLEMPSKI. YOU'RE THE ONLY PERSON WHO KNOWS WHO AND WHERE I AM.
RIGHT?
RIGHT, SANDRA?

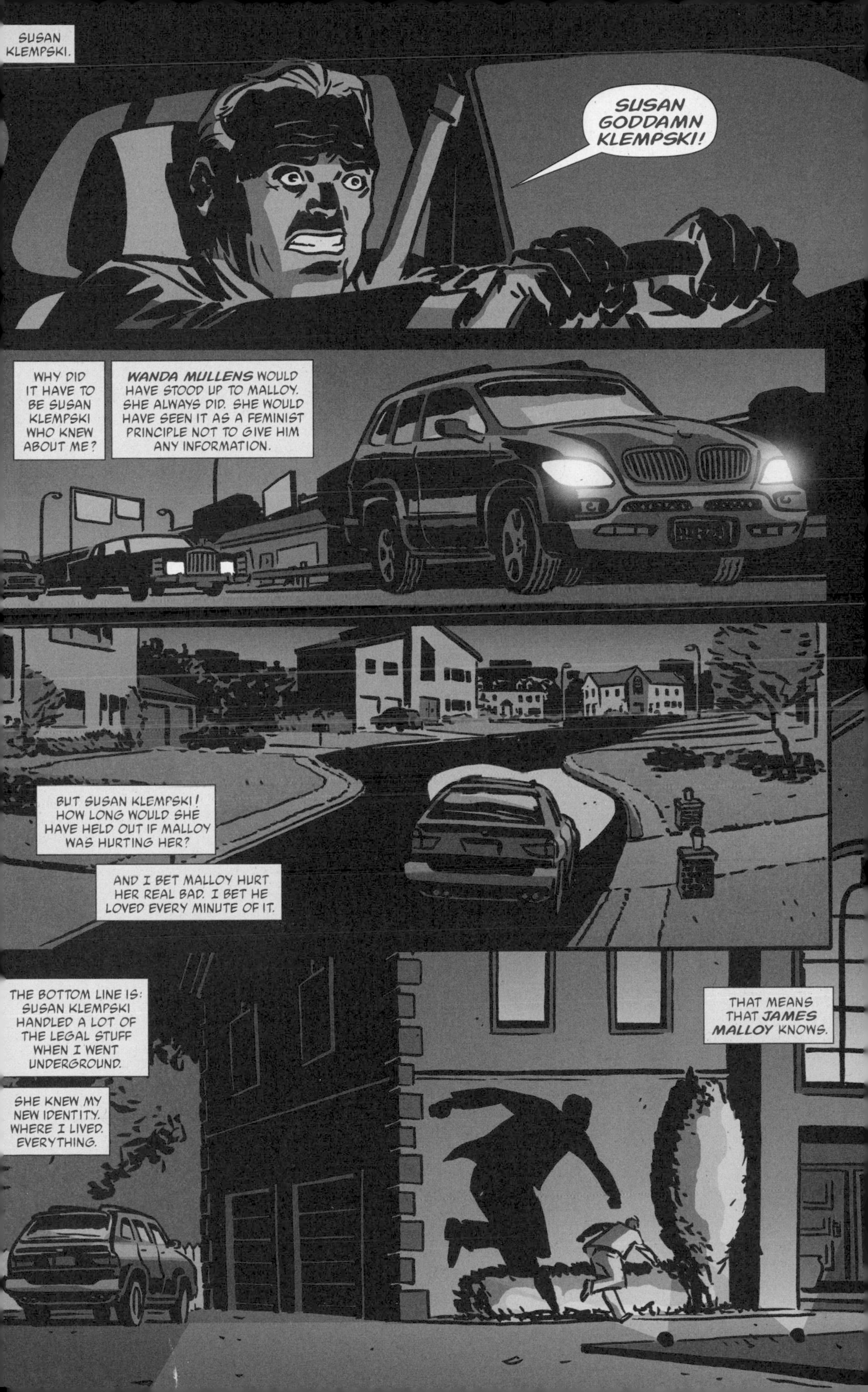
SUSAN KLEMPSKI.
SUSAN GODDAMN KLEMPSKI!
WHY DID IT HAVE TO BE SUSAN KLEMPSKI WHO KNEW ABOUT ME?
WANDA MULLENS WOULD HAVE STOOD UP TO MALLOY. SHE ALWAYS DID. SHE WOULD HAVE SEEN IT AS A FEMINIST PRINCIPLE NOT TO GIVE HIM ANY INFORMATION.
BUT SUSAN KLEMPSKI! HOW LONG WOULD SHE HAVE HELD OUT IF MALLOY WAS HURTING HER?
AND I BET MALLOY HURT HER REAL BAD. I BET HE LOVED EVERY MINUTE OF IT.
THE BOTTOM LINE IS: SUSAN KLEMPSKI HANDLED A LOT OF THE LEGAL STUFF WHEN I WENT UNDERGROUND.
SHE KNEW MY NEW IDENTITY. WHERE I LIVED. EVERYTHING.
THAT MEANS THAT JAMES MALLOY KNOWS.

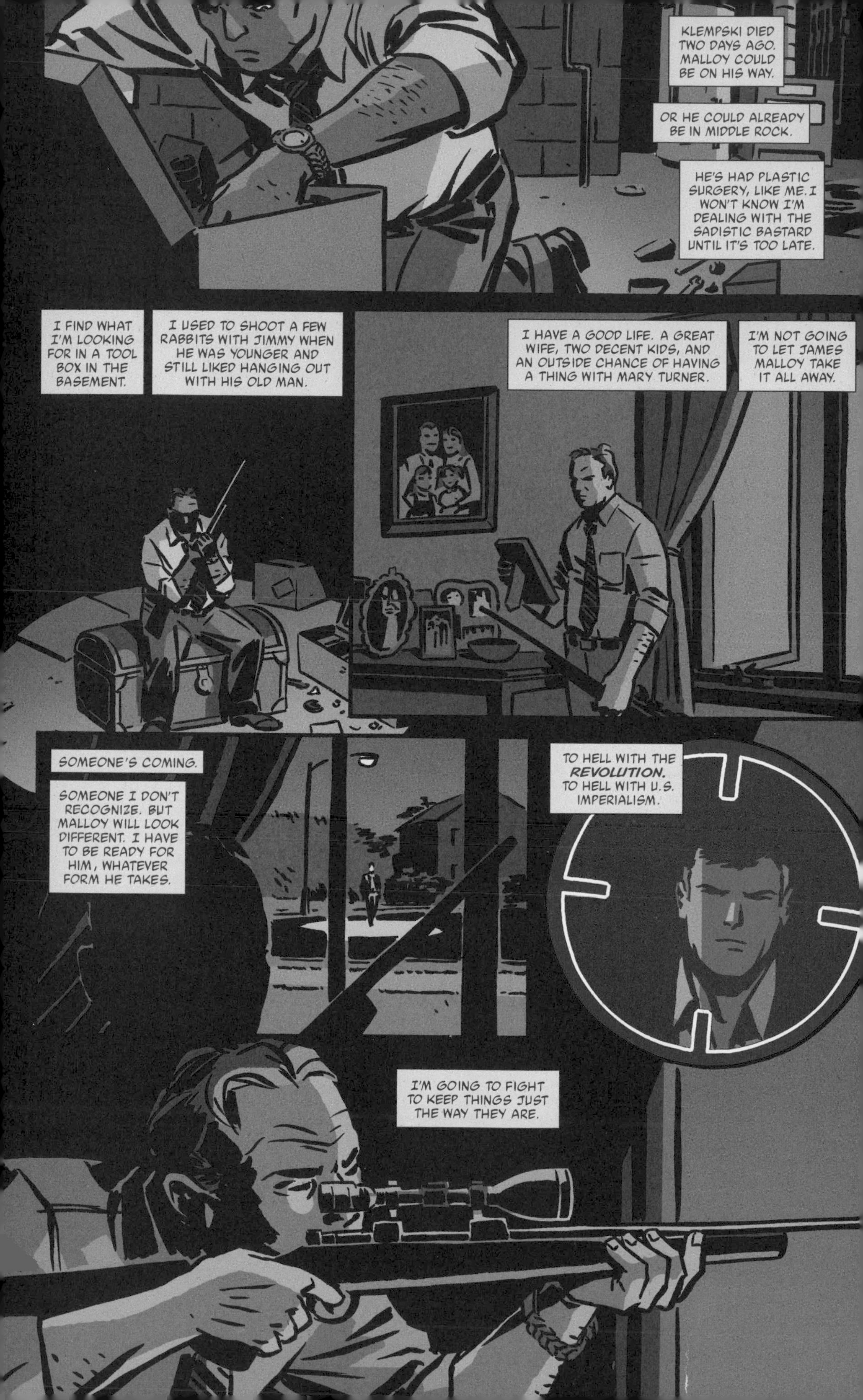
KLEMPSKI DIED TWO DAYS AGO. MALLOY COULD BE ON HIS WAY.
OR HE COULD ALREADY BE IN MIDDLE ROCK.
HE'S HAD PLASTIC SURGERY, LIKE ME. I WON'T KNOW I'M DEALING WITH THE SADISTIC BASTARD UNTIL IT'S TOO LATE.
I FIND WHAT I'M LOOKING FOR IN A TOOL BOX IN THE BASEMENT.
I USED TO SHOOT A FEW RABBITS WITH JIMMY WHEN HE WAS YOUNGER AND STILL LIKED HANGING OUT WITH HIS OLD MAN.
I HAVE A GOOD LIFE. A GREAT WIFE, TWO DECENT KIDS, AND AN OUTSIDE CHANCE OF HAVING A THING WITH MARY TURNER.
I'M NOT GOING TO LET JAMES MALLOY TAKE IT ALL AWAY.
SOMEONE'S COMING.
SOMEONE I DON'T RECOGNIZE. BUT MALLOY WILL LOOK DIFFERENT. I HAVE TO BE READY FOR HIM, WHATEVER FORM HE TAKES.
TO HELL WITH THE ***REVOLUTION.*** TO HELL WITH U.S. IMPERIALISM.
I'M GOING TO FIGHT TO KEEP THINGS JUST THE WAY THEY ARE.

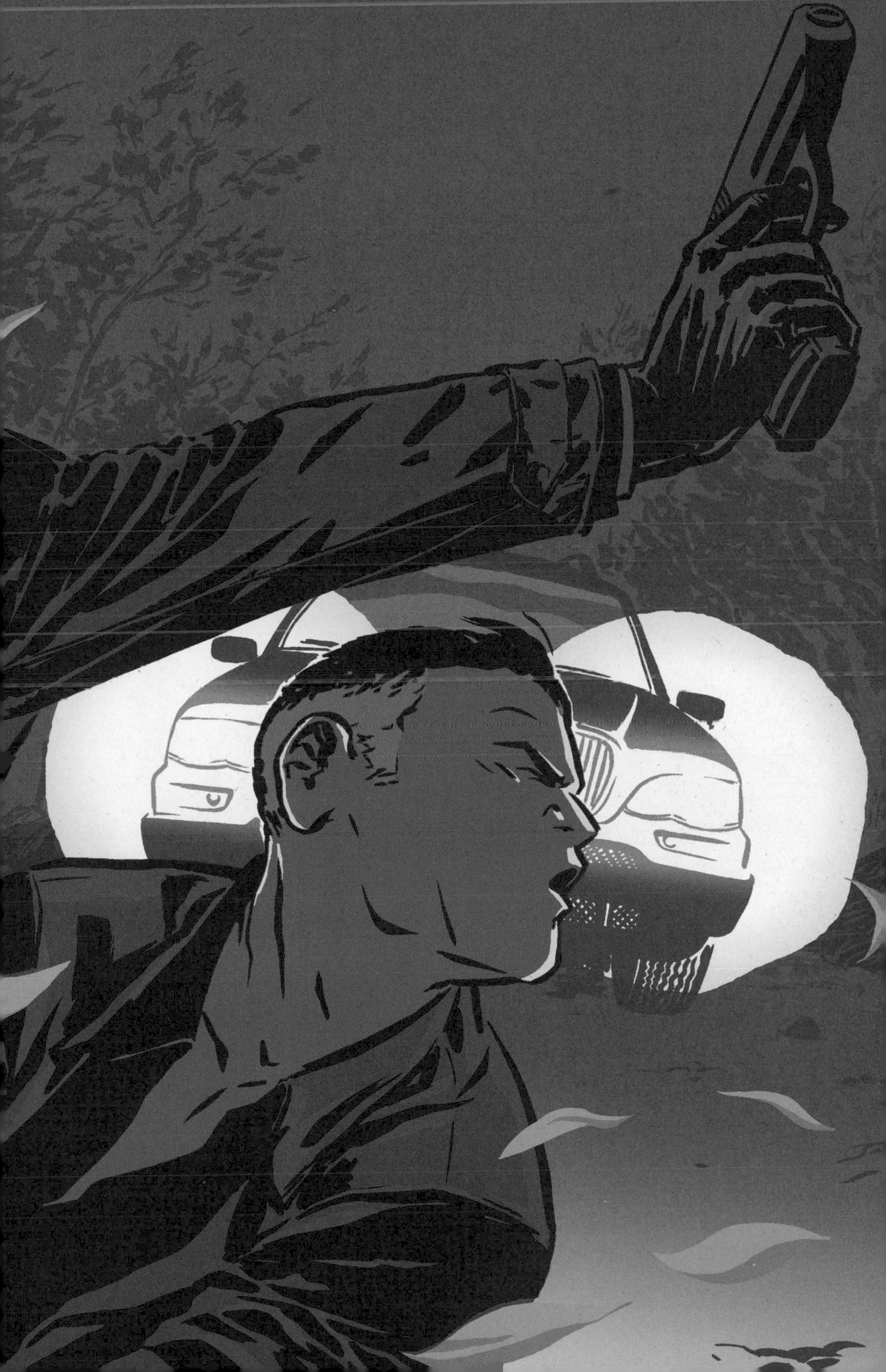

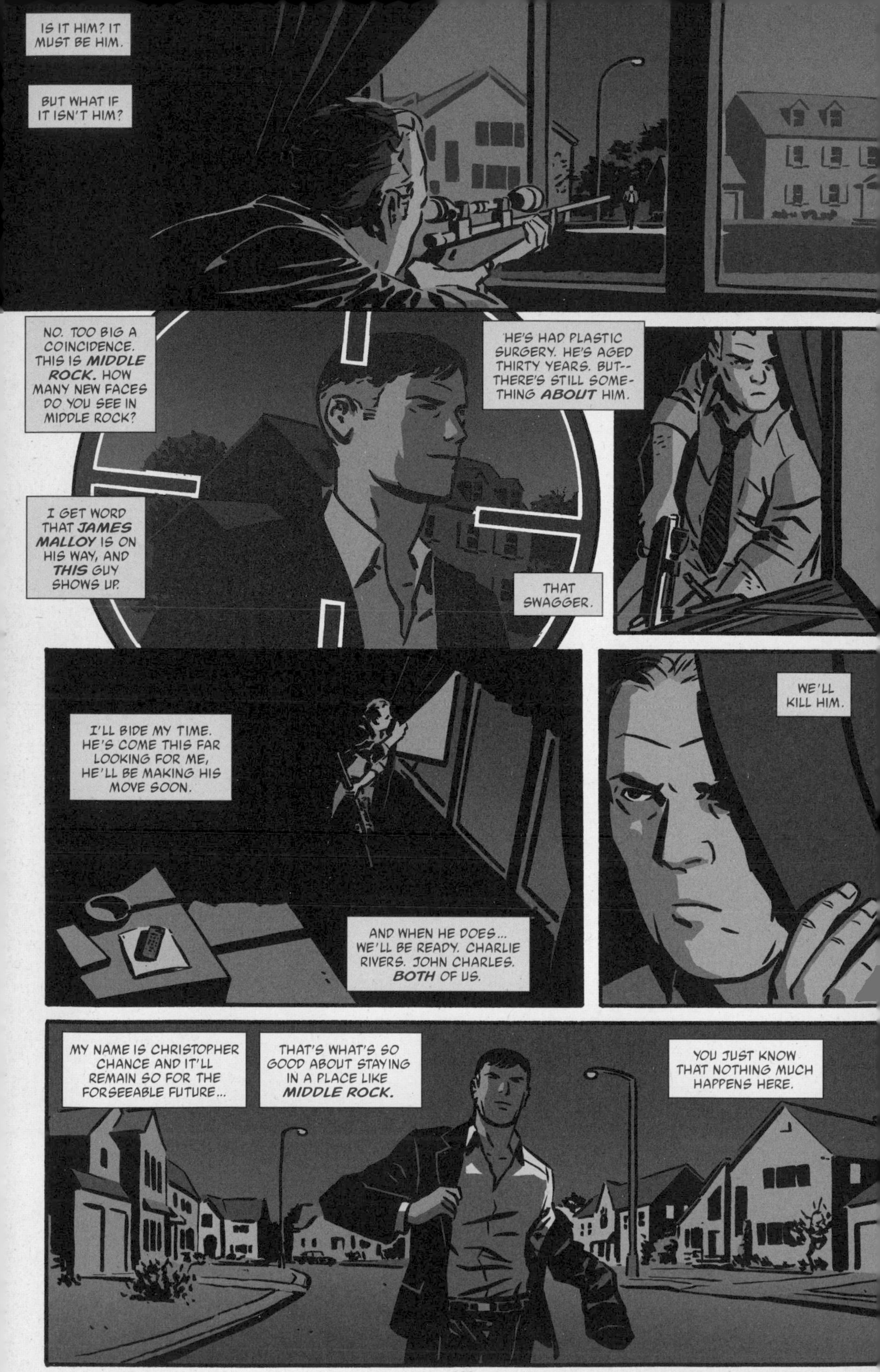

IS IT HIM? IT MUST BE HIM.
BUT WHAT IF IT ISN'T HIM?
NO. TOO BIG A COINCIDENCE. THIS IS MIDDLE ROCK. HOW MANY NEW FACES DO YOU SEE IN MIDDLE ROCK?
I GET WORD THAT JAMES MALLOY IS ON HIS WAY, AND THIS GUY SHOWS UP.
HE'S HAD PLASTIC SURGERY. HE'S AGED THIRTY YEARS. BUT-- THERE'S STILL SOMETHING ABOUT HIM.
THAT SWAGGER.
I'LL BIDE MY TIME. HE'S COME THIS FAR LOOKING FOR ME, HE'LL BE MAKING HIS MOVE SOON.
AND WHEN HE DOES... WE'LL BE READY. CHARLIE RIVERS. JOHN CHARLES. BOTH OF US.
WE'LL KILL HIM.
MY NAME IS CHRISTOPHER CHANCE AND IT'LL REMAIN SO FOR THE FORSEEABLE FUTURE...
THAT'S WHAT'S SO GOOD ABOUT STAYING IN A PLACE LIKE MIDDLE ROCK.
YOU JUST KNOW THAT NOTHING MUCH HAPPENS HERE.

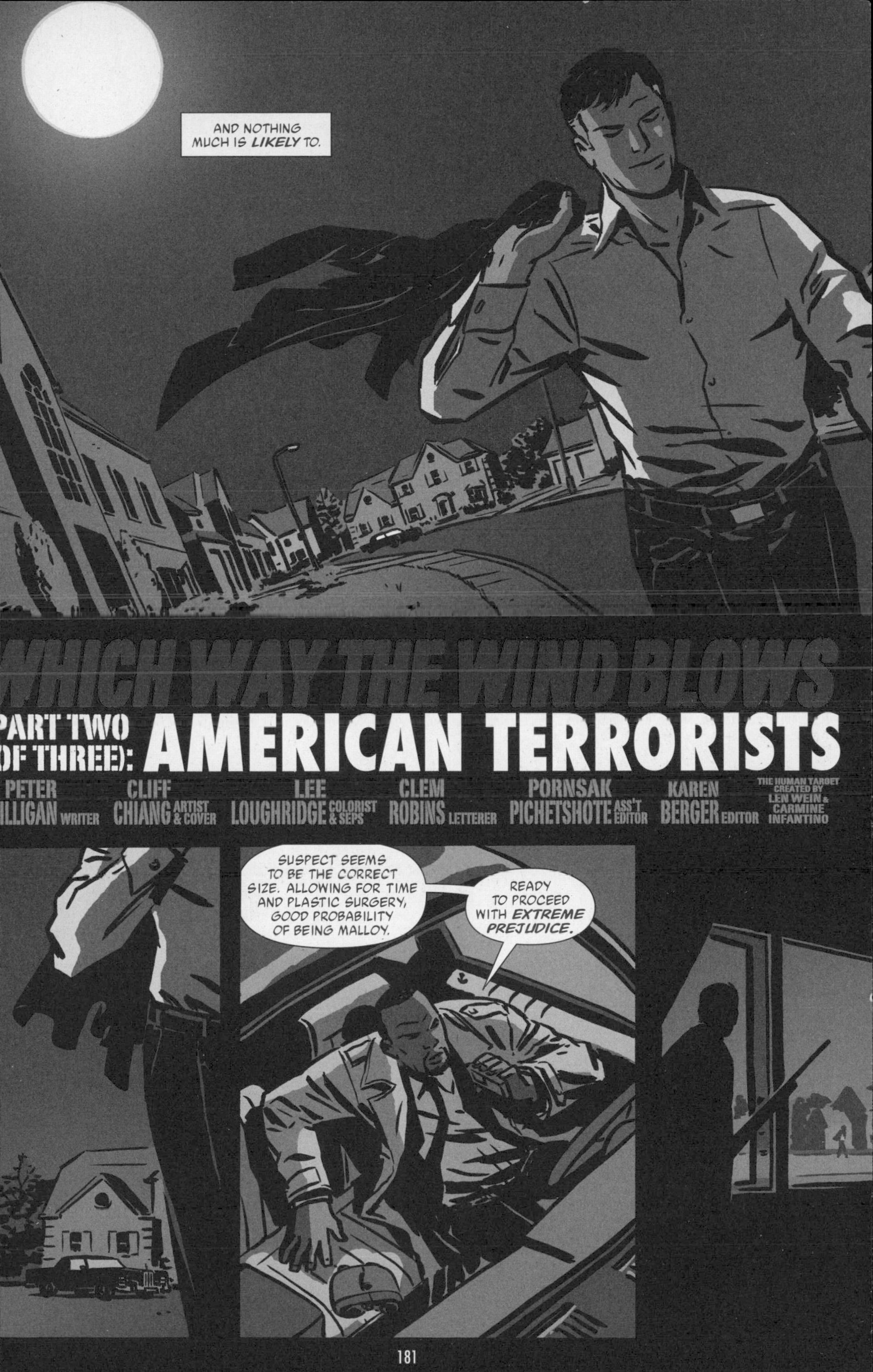
AND NOTHING MUCH IS *LIKELY* TO.
WHICH WAY THE WIND BLOWS
PART TWO (OF THREE): AMERICAN TERRORISTS
PETER ILLIGAN WRITER
CLIFF CHIANG ARTIST & COVER
LEE LOUGHRIDGE COLORIST & SEPS
CLEM ROBINS LETTERER
PORNSAK PICHETSHOTE ASS'T EDITOR
KAREN BERGER EDITOR
THE HUMAN TARGET CREATED BY LEN WEIN & CARMINE INFANTINO
SUSPECT SEEMS TO BE THE CORRECT SIZE. ALLOWING FOR TIME AND PLASTIC SURGERY, GOOD PROBABILITY OF BEING MALLOY.
READY TO PROCEED WITH *EXTREME PREJUDICE.*

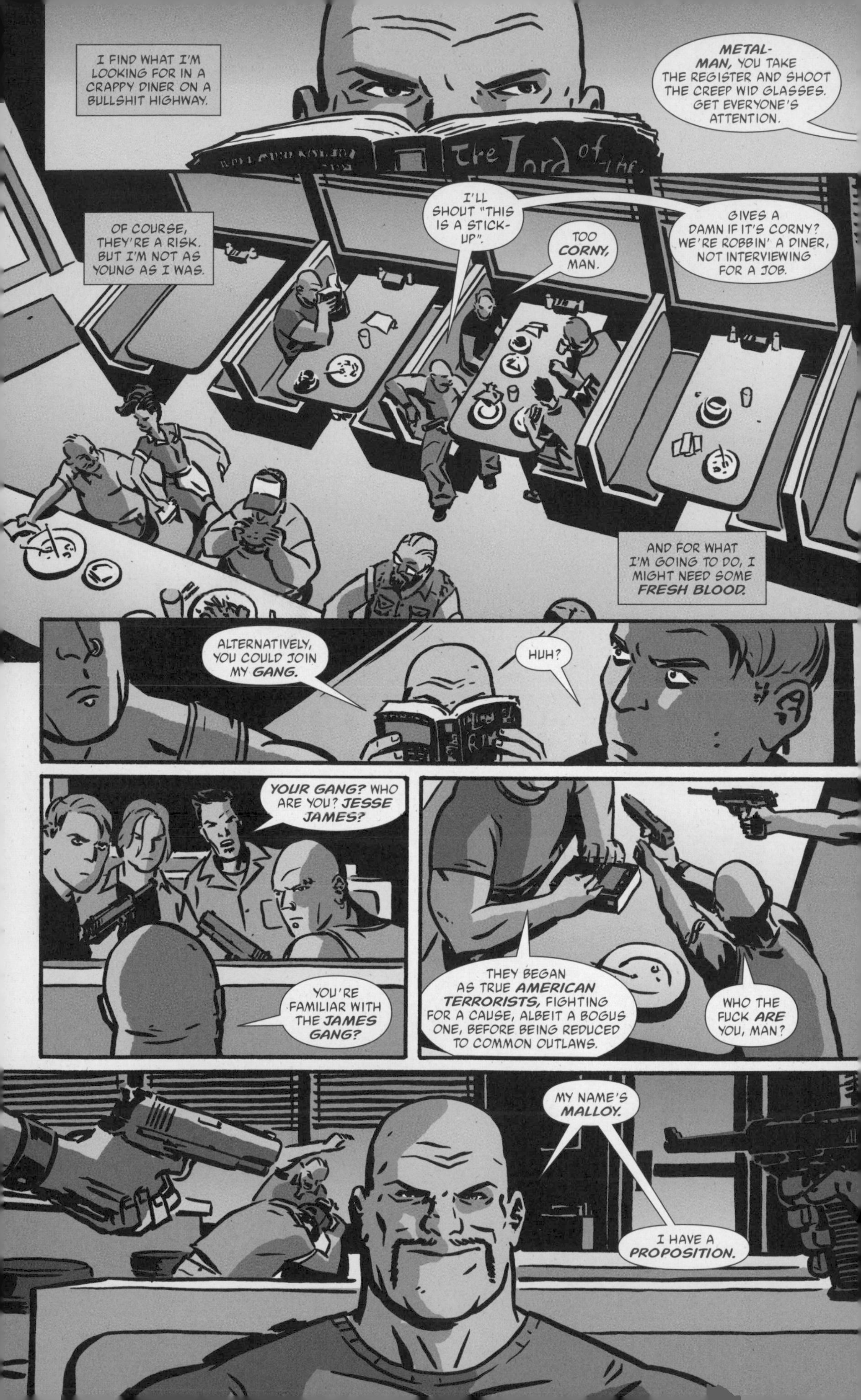
I FIND WHAT I'M LOOKING FOR IN A CRAPPY DINER ON A BULLSHIT HIGHWAY.
METAL-MAN, YOU TAKE THE REGISTER AND SHOOT THE CREEP WID GLASSES. GET EVERYONE'S ATTENTION.
OF COURSE, THEY'RE A RISK. BUT I'M NOT AS YOUNG AS I WAS.
I'LL SHOUT "THIS IS A STICK-UP".
TOO CORNY, MAN.
GIVES A DAMN IF IT'S CORNY? WE'RE ROBBIN' A DINER, NOT INTERVIEWING FOR A JOB.
AND FOR WHAT I'M GOING TO DO, I MIGHT NEED SOME FRESH BLOOD.
ALTERNATIVELY, YOU COULD JOIN MY GANG.
HUH?
YOUR GANG? WHO ARE YOU? JESSE JAMES?
YOU'RE FAMILIAR WITH THE JAMES GANG?
THEY BEGAN AS TRUE AMERICAN TERRORISTS, FIGHTING FOR A CAUSE, ALBEIT A BOGUS ONE, BEFORE BEING REDUCED TO COMMON OUTLAWS.
WHO THE FUCK ARE YOU, MAN?
MY NAME'S MALLOY.
I HAVE A PROPOSITION.

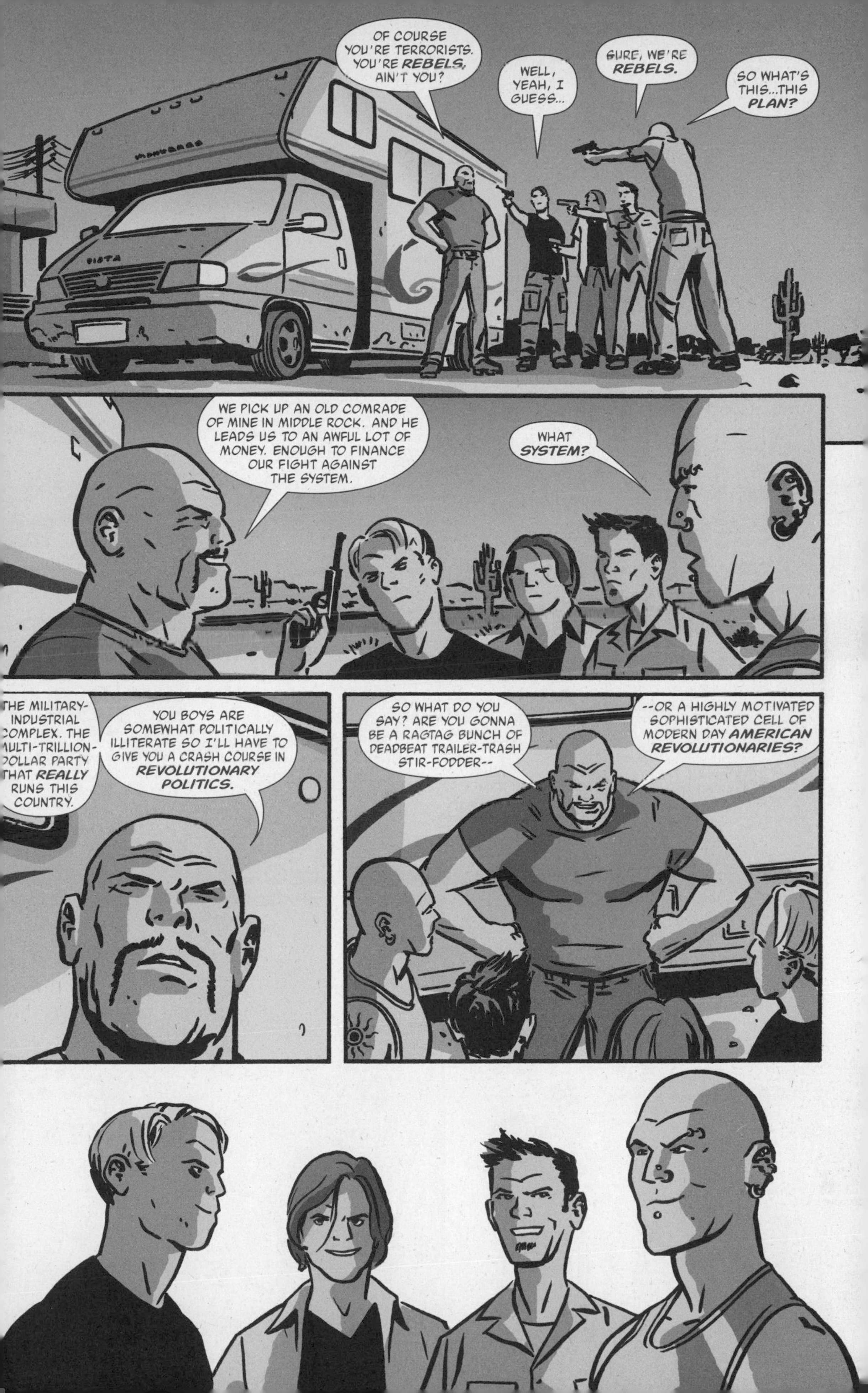
OF COURSE YOU'RE TERRORISTS. YOU'RE REBELS, AIN'T YOU?
WELL, YEAH, I GUESS...
SURE, WE'RE REBELS.
SO WHAT'S THIS...THIS PLAN?
WE PICK UP AN OLD COMRADE OF MINE IN MIDDLE ROCK. AND HE LEADS US TO AN AWFUL LOT OF MONEY. ENOUGH TO FINANCE OUR FIGHT AGAINST THE SYSTEM.
WHAT SYSTEM?
THE MILITARY-INDUSTRIAL COMPLEX. THE MULTI-TRILLION-DOLLAR PARTY THAT REALLY RUNS THIS COUNTRY.
YOU BOYS ARE SOMEWHAT POLITICALLY ILLITERATE SO I'LL HAVE TO GIVE YOU A CRASH COURSE IN REVOLUTIONARY POLITICS.
SO WHAT DO YOU SAY? ARE YOU GONNA BE A RAGTAG BUNCH OF DEADBEAT TRAILER-TRASH STIR-FODDER--
--OR A HIGHLY MOTIVATED SOPHISTICATED CELL OF MODERN DAY AMERICAN REVOLUTIONARIES?

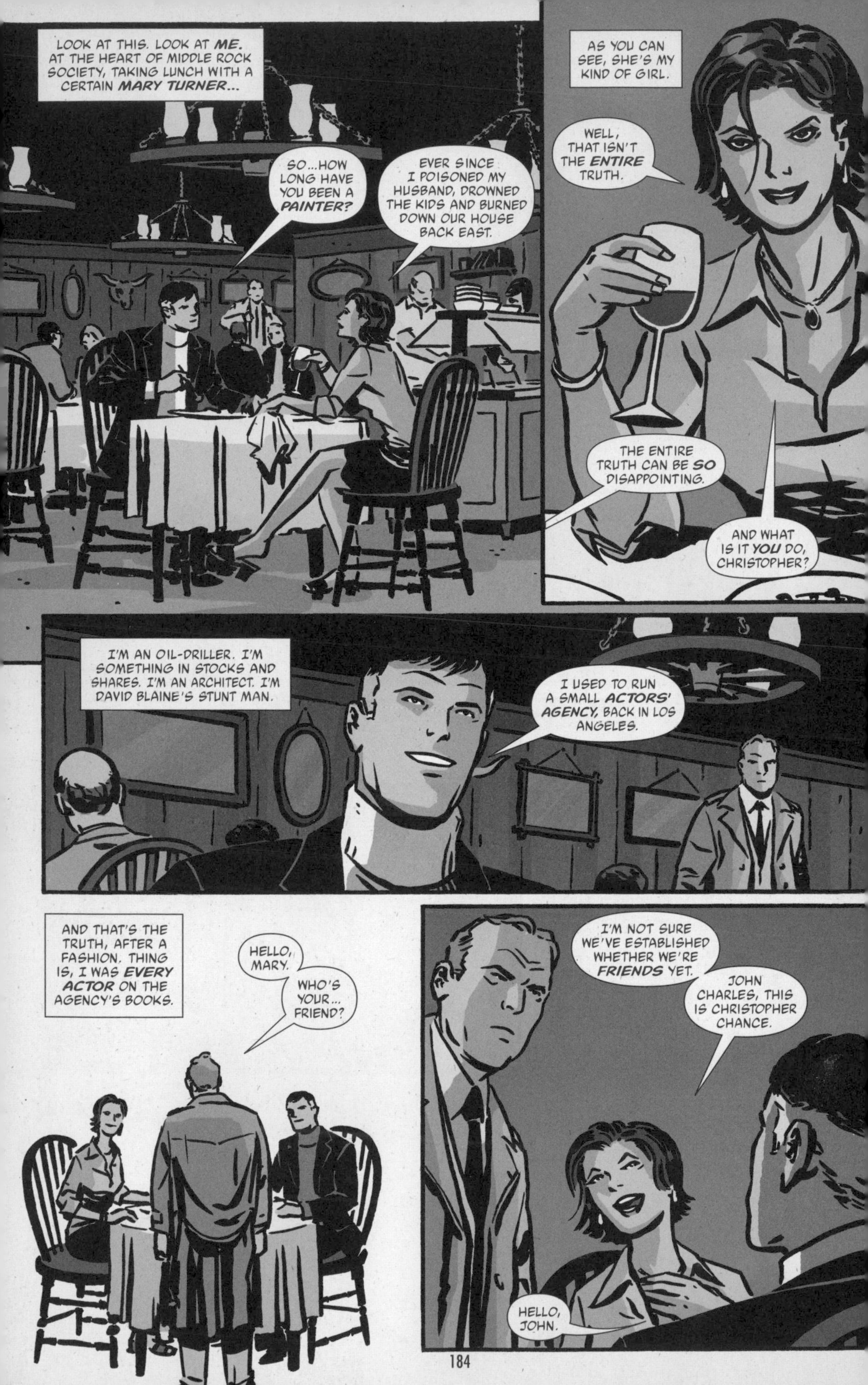
LOOK AT THIS. LOOK AT **ME.** AT THE HEART OF MIDDLE ROCK SOCIETY, TAKING LUNCH WITH A CERTAIN **MARY TURNER...**
SO...HOW LONG HAVE YOU BEEN A **PAINTER?**
EVER SINCE I POISONED MY HUSBAND, DROWNED THE KIDS AND BURNED DOWN OUR HOUSE BACK EAST.
AS YOU CAN SEE, SHE'S MY KIND OF GIRL.
WELL, THAT ISN'T THE **ENTIRE** TRUTH.
THE ENTIRE TRUTH CAN BE **SO** DISAPPOINTING.
AND WHAT IS IT **YOU** DO, CHRISTOPHER?
I'M AN OIL-DRILLER. I'M SOMETHING IN STOCKS AND SHARES. I'M AN ARCHITECT. I'M DAVID BLAINE'S STUNT MAN.
I USED TO RUN A SMALL **ACTORS' AGENCY,** BACK IN LOS ANGELES.
AND THAT'S THE TRUTH, AFTER A FASHION. THING IS, I WAS **EVERY ACTOR** ON THE AGENCY'S BOOKS.
HELLO, MARY.
WHO'S YOUR... FRIEND?
I'M NOT SURE WE'VE ESTABLISHED WHETHER WE'RE **FRIENDS** YET.
JOHN CHARLES, THIS IS CHRISTOPHER CHANCE.
HELLO, JOHN.

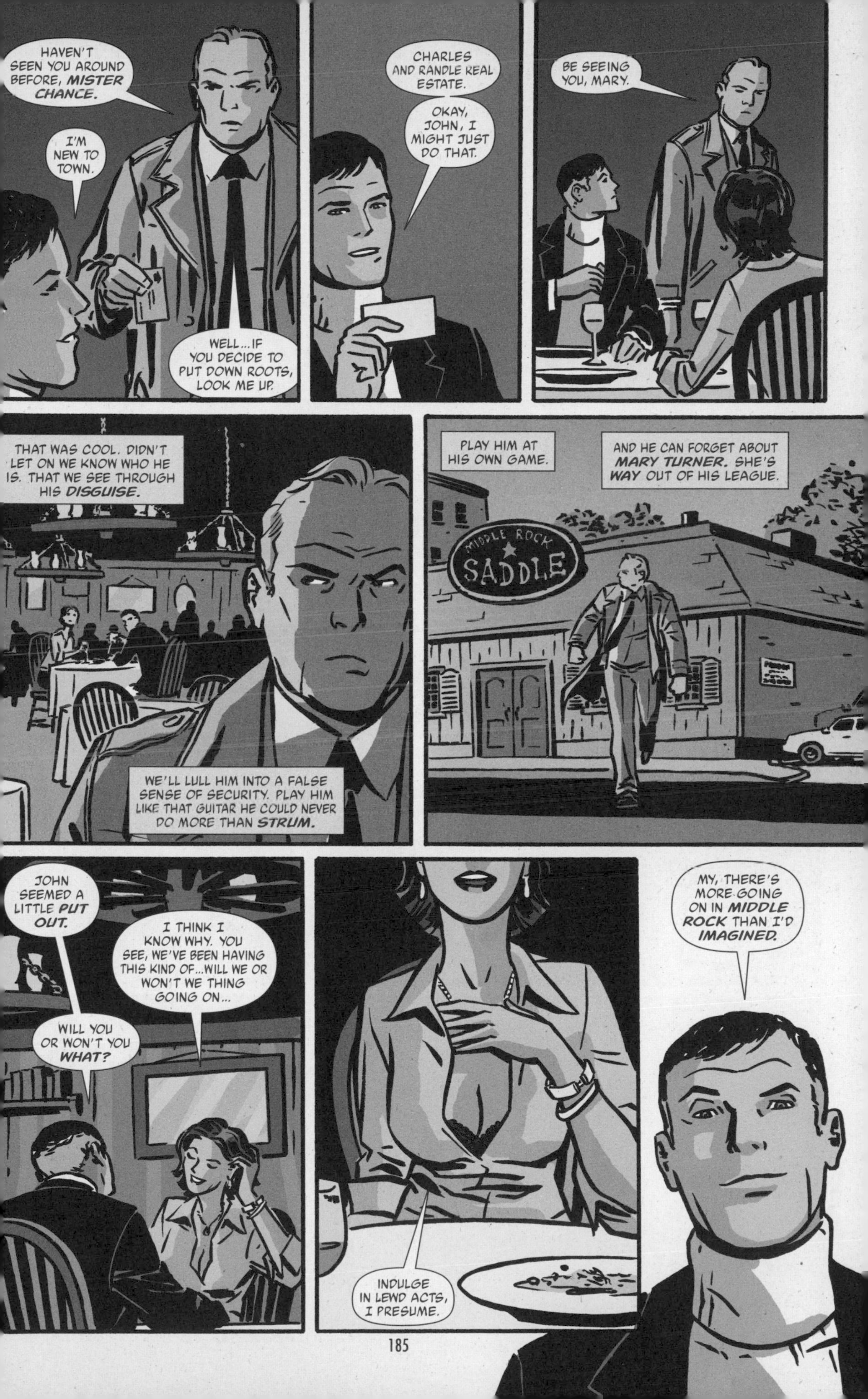
HAVEN'T SEEN YOU AROUND BEFORE, MISTER CHANCE.
I'M NEW TO TOWN.
WELL...IF YOU DECIDE TO PUT DOWN ROOTS, LOOK ME UP.
CHARLES AND RANDLE REAL ESTATE.
OKAY, JOHN, I MIGHT JUST DO THAT.
BE SEEING YOU, MARY.
THAT WAS COOL. DIDN'T LET ON WE KNOW WHO HE IS. THAT WE SEE THROUGH HIS DISGUISE.
WE'LL LULL HIM INTO A FALSE SENSE OF SECURITY. PLAY HIM LIKE THAT GUITAR HE COULD NEVER DO MORE THAN STRUM.
PLAY HIM AT HIS OWN GAME.
AND HE CAN FORGET ABOUT MARY TURNER. SHE'S WAY OUT OF HIS LEAGUE.
MIDDLE ROCK SADDLE
JOHN SEEMED A LITTLE PUT OUT.
I THINK I KNOW WHY. YOU SEE, WE'VE BEEN HAVING THIS KIND OF...WILL WE OR WON'T WE THING GOING ON...
WILL YOU OR WON'T YOU WHAT?
INDULGE IN LEWD ACTS, I PRESUME.
MY, THERE'S MORE GOING ON IN MIDDLE ROCK THAN I'D IMAGINED.

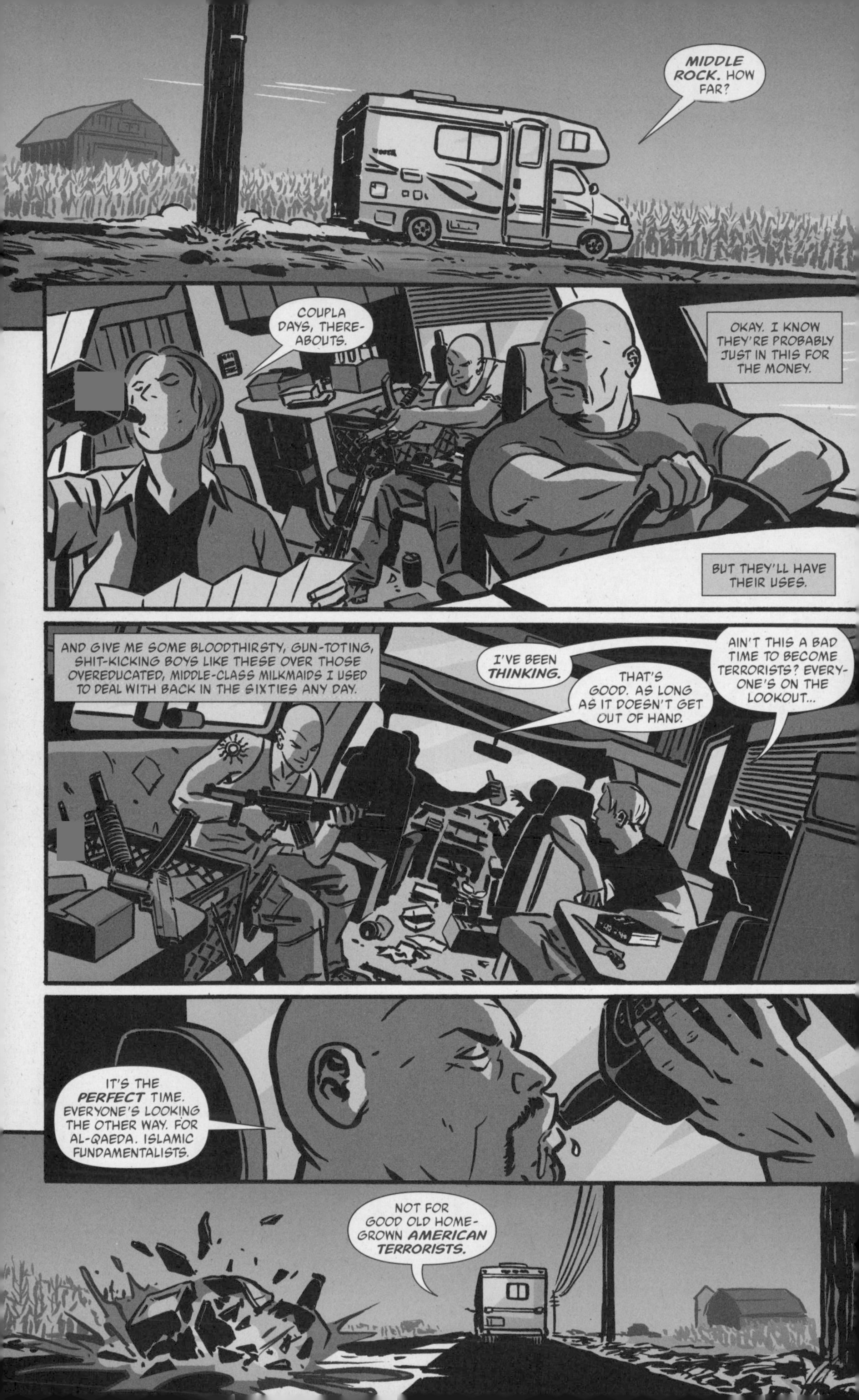
MIDDLE ROCK. HOW FAR?
COUPLA DAYS, THERE-ABOUTS.
OKAY. I KNOW THEY'RE PROBABLY JUST IN THIS FOR THE MONEY.
BUT THEY'LL HAVE THEIR USES.
AND GIVE ME SOME BLOODTHIRSTY, GUN-TOTING, SHIT-KICKING BOYS LIKE THESE OVER THOSE OVEREDUCATED, MIDDLE-CLASS MILKMAIDS I USED TO DEAL WITH BACK IN THE SIXTIES ANY DAY.
I'VE BEEN THINKING.
THAT'S GOOD. AS LONG AS IT DOESN'T GET OUT OF HAND.
AIN'T THIS A BAD TIME TO BECOME TERRORISTS? EVERY-ONE'S ON THE LOOKOUT...
IT'S THE PERFECT TIME. EVERYONE'S LOOKING THE OTHER WAY. FOR AL-QAEDA. ISLAMIC FUNDAMENTALISTS.
NOT FOR GOOD OLD HOME-GROWN AMERICAN TERRORISTS.

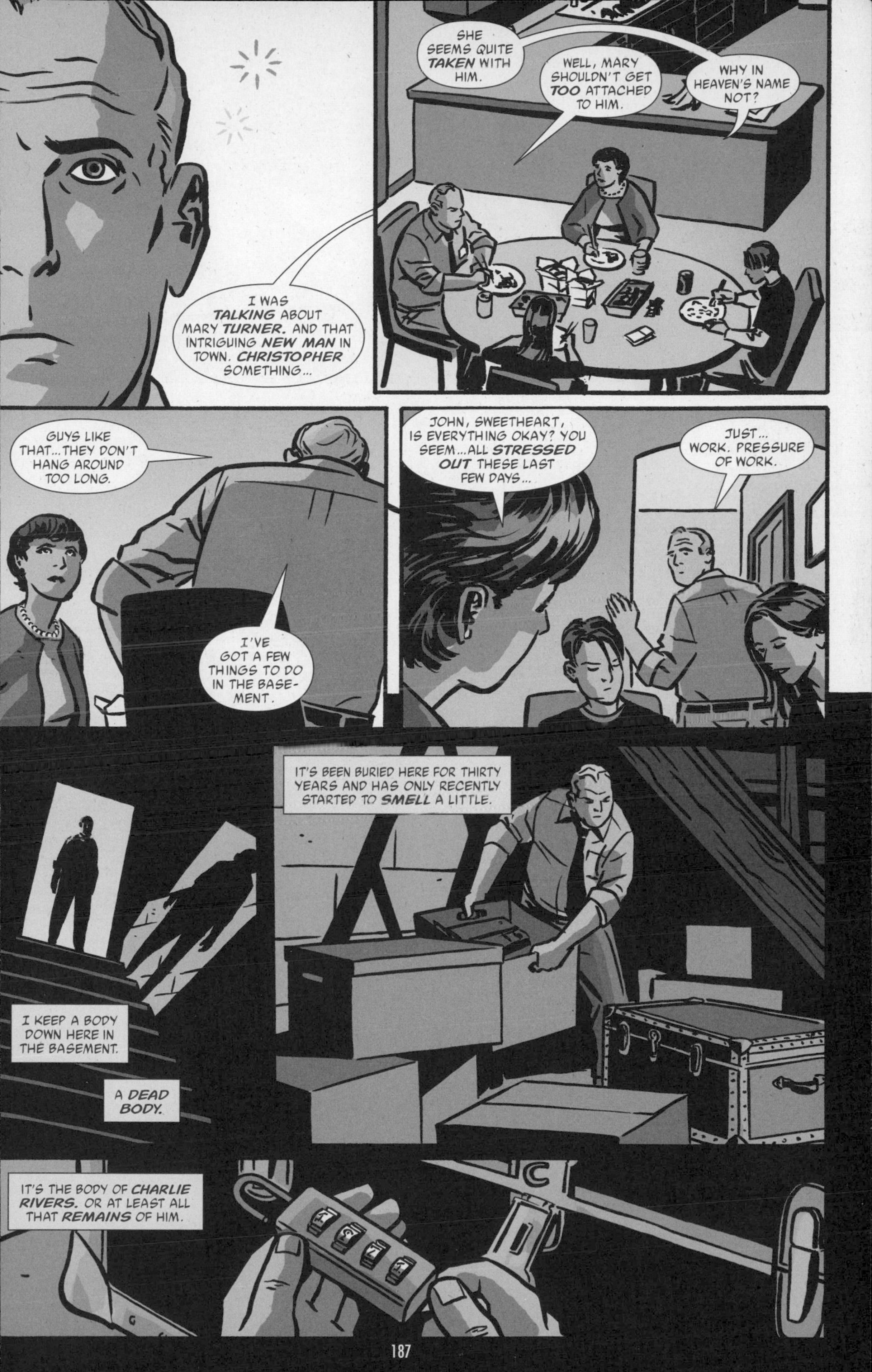
SHE SEEMS QUITE TAKEN WITH HIM.
WELL, MARY SHOULDN'T GET TOO ATTACHED TO HIM.
WHY IN HEAVEN'S NAME NOT?
I WAS TALKING ABOUT MARY TURNER. AND THAT INTRIGUING NEW MAN IN TOWN. CHRISTOPHER SOMETHING...
GUYS LIKE THAT...THEY DON'T HANG AROUND TOO LONG.
I'VE GOT A FEW THINGS TO DO IN THE BASE-MENT.
JOHN, SWEETHEART, IS EVERYTHING OKAY? YOU SEEM...ALL STRESSED OUT THESE LAST FEW DAYS...
JUST... WORK. PRESSURE OF WORK.
I KEEP A BODY DOWN HERE IN THE BASEMENT.
A DEAD BODY.
IT'S BEEN BURIED HERE FOR THIRTY YEARS AND HAS ONLY RECENTLY STARTED TO SMELL A LITTLE.
IT'S THE BODY OF CHARLIE RIVERS. OR AT LEAST ALL THAT REMAINS OF HIM.

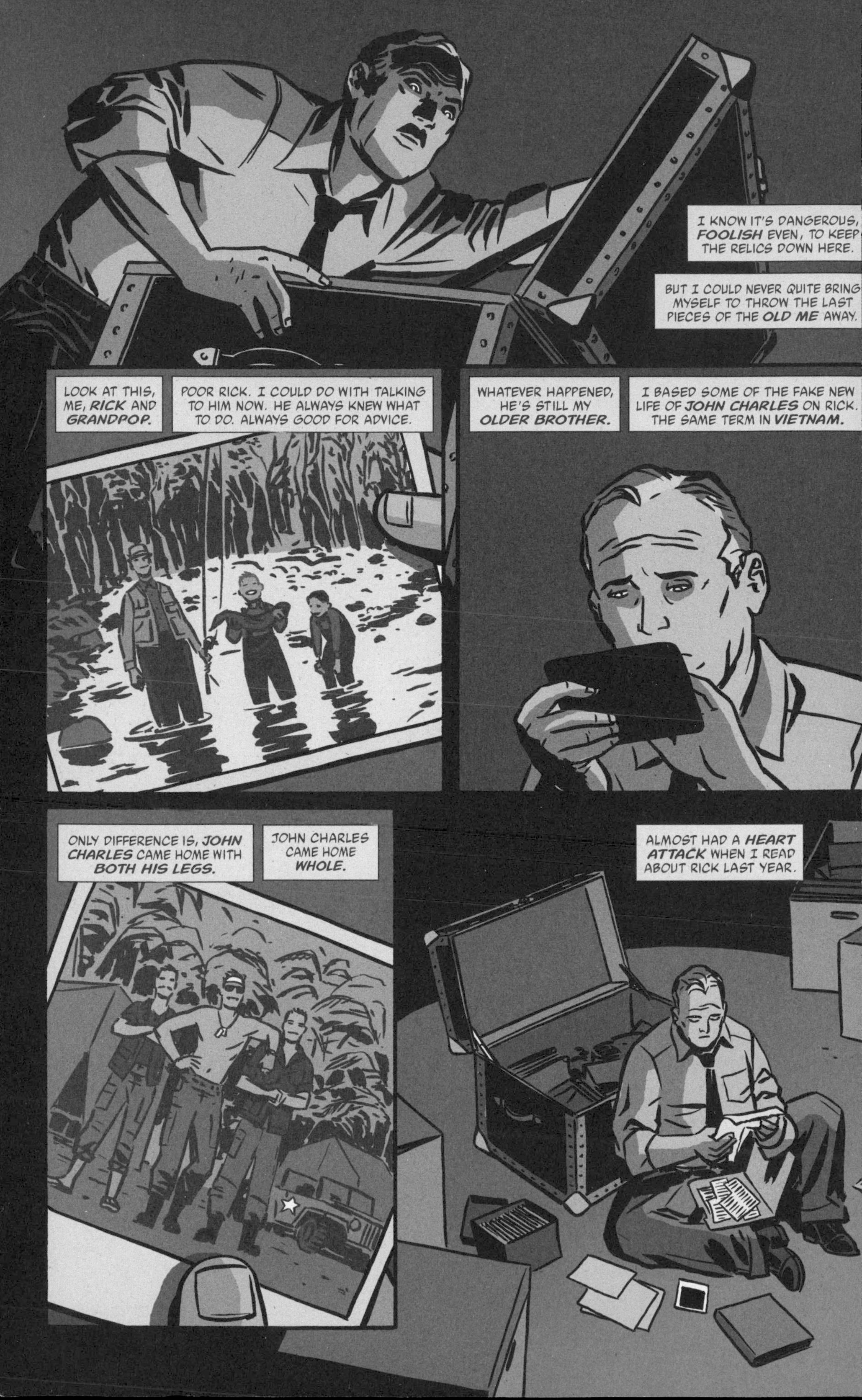
I KNOW IT'S DANGEROUS, FOOLISH EVEN, TO KEEP THE RELICS DOWN HERE.
BUT I COULD NEVER QUITE BRING MYSELF TO THROW THE LAST PIECES OF THE OLD ME AWAY.
LOOK AT THIS, ME, RICK AND GRANDPOP.
POOR RICK. I COULD DO WITH TALKING TO HIM NOW. HE ALWAYS KNEW WHAT TO DO. ALWAYS GOOD FOR ADVICE.
WHATEVER HAPPENED, HE'S STILL MY OLDER BROTHER.
I BASED SOME OF THE FAKE NEW LIFE OF JOHN CHARLES ON RICK. THE SAME TERM IN VIETNAM.
ONLY DIFFERENCE IS, JOHN CHARLES CAME HOME WITH BOTH HIS LEGS.
JOHN CHARLES CAME HOME WHOLE.
ALMOST HAD A HEART ATTACK WHEN I READ ABOUT RICK LAST YEAR.

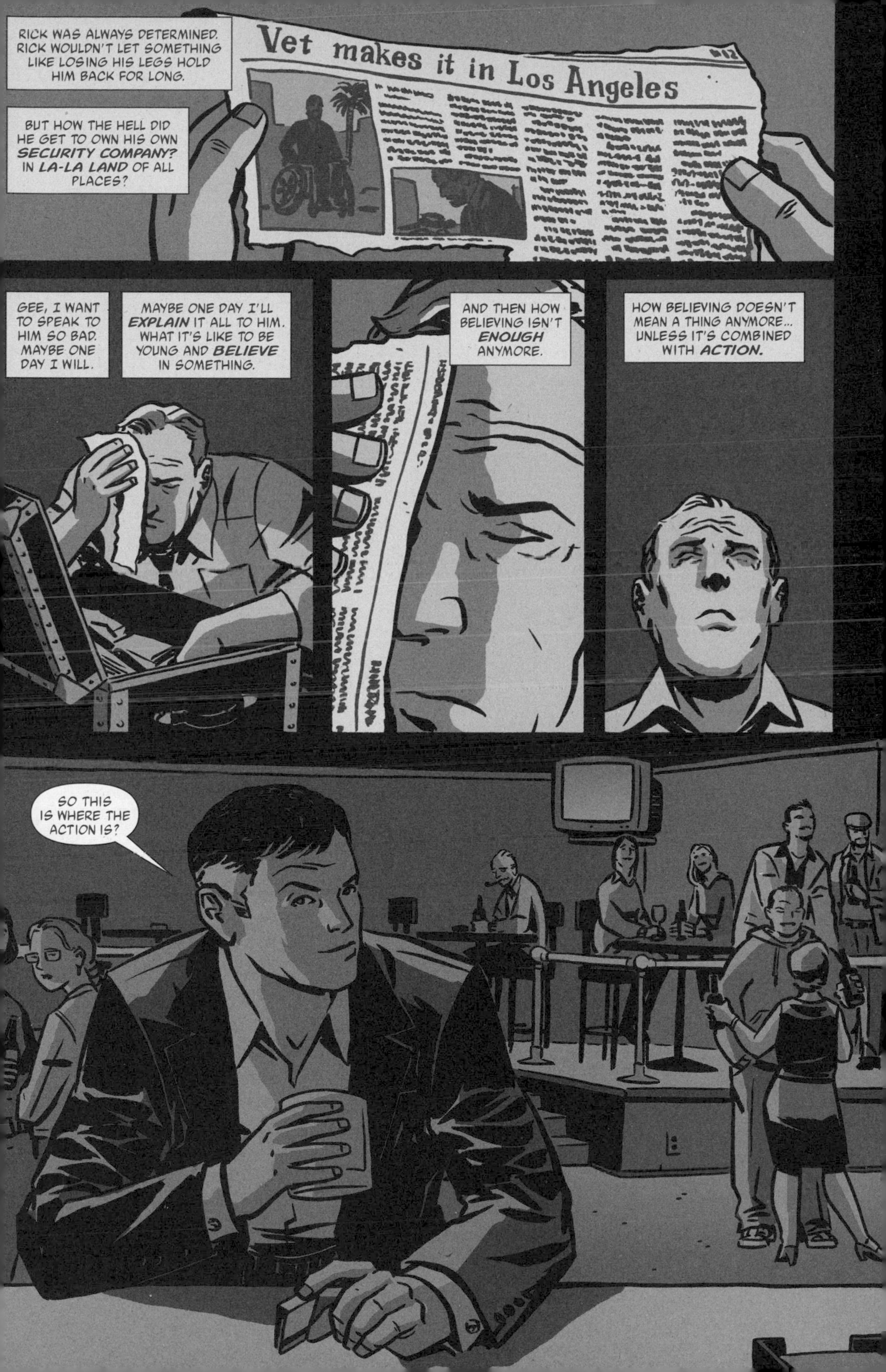
RICK WAS ALWAYS DETERMINED. RICK WOULDN'T LET SOMETHING LIKE LOSING HIS LEGS HOLD HIM BACK FOR LONG.
Vet makes it in Los Angeles
BUT HOW THE HELL DID HE GET TO OWN HIS OWN SECURITY COMPANY? IN LA-LA LAND OF ALL PLACES?
GEE, I WANT TO SPEAK TO HIM SO BAD. MAYBE ONE DAY I WILL.
MAYBE ONE DAY I'LL EXPLAIN IT ALL TO HIM. WHAT IT'S LIKE TO BE YOUNG AND BELIEVE IN SOMETHING.
AND THEN HOW BELIEVING ISN'T ENOUGH ANYMORE.
HOW BELIEVING DOESN'T MEAN A THING ANYMORE... UNLESS IT'S COMBINED WITH ACTION.
SO THIS IS WHERE THE ACTION IS?

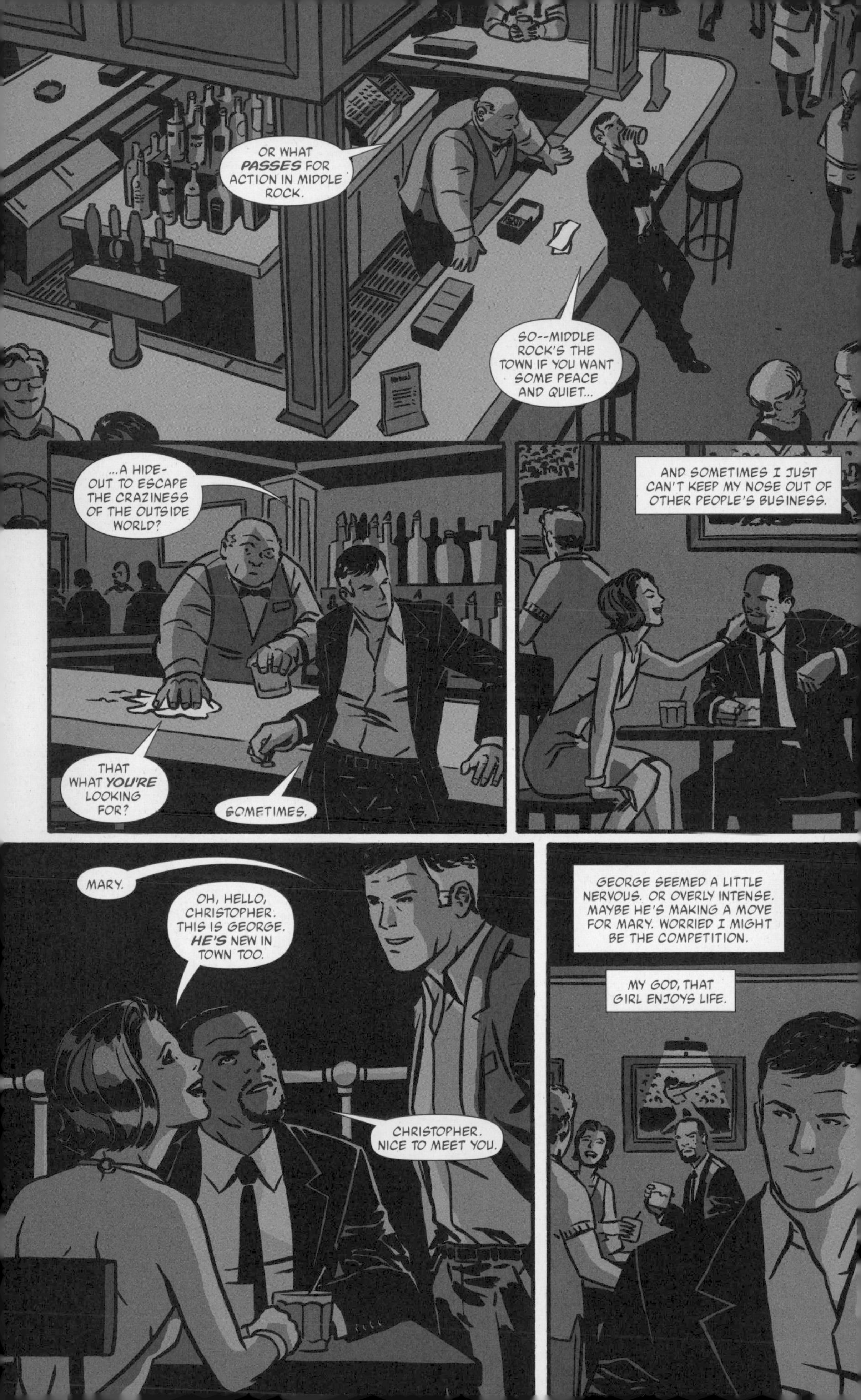
OR WHAT PASSES FOR ACTION IN MIDDLE ROCK.
SO--MIDDLE ROCK'S THE TOWN IF YOU WANT SOME PEACE AND QUIET...
...A HIDE-OUT TO ESCAPE THE CRAZINESS OF THE OUTSIDE WORLD?
THAT WHAT YOU'RE LOOKING FOR?
SOMETIMES.
AND SOMETIMES I JUST CAN'T KEEP MY NOSE OUT OF OTHER PEOPLE'S BUSINESS.
MARY.
OH, HELLO, CHRISTOPHER. THIS IS GEORGE. HE'S NEW IN TOWN TOO.
CHRISTOPHER. NICE TO MEET YOU.
GEORGE SEEMED A LITTLE NERVOUS. OR OVERLY INTENSE. MAYBE HE'S MAKING A MOVE FOR MARY. WORRIED I MIGHT BE THE COMPETITION.
MY GOD, THAT GIRL ENJOYS LIFE.

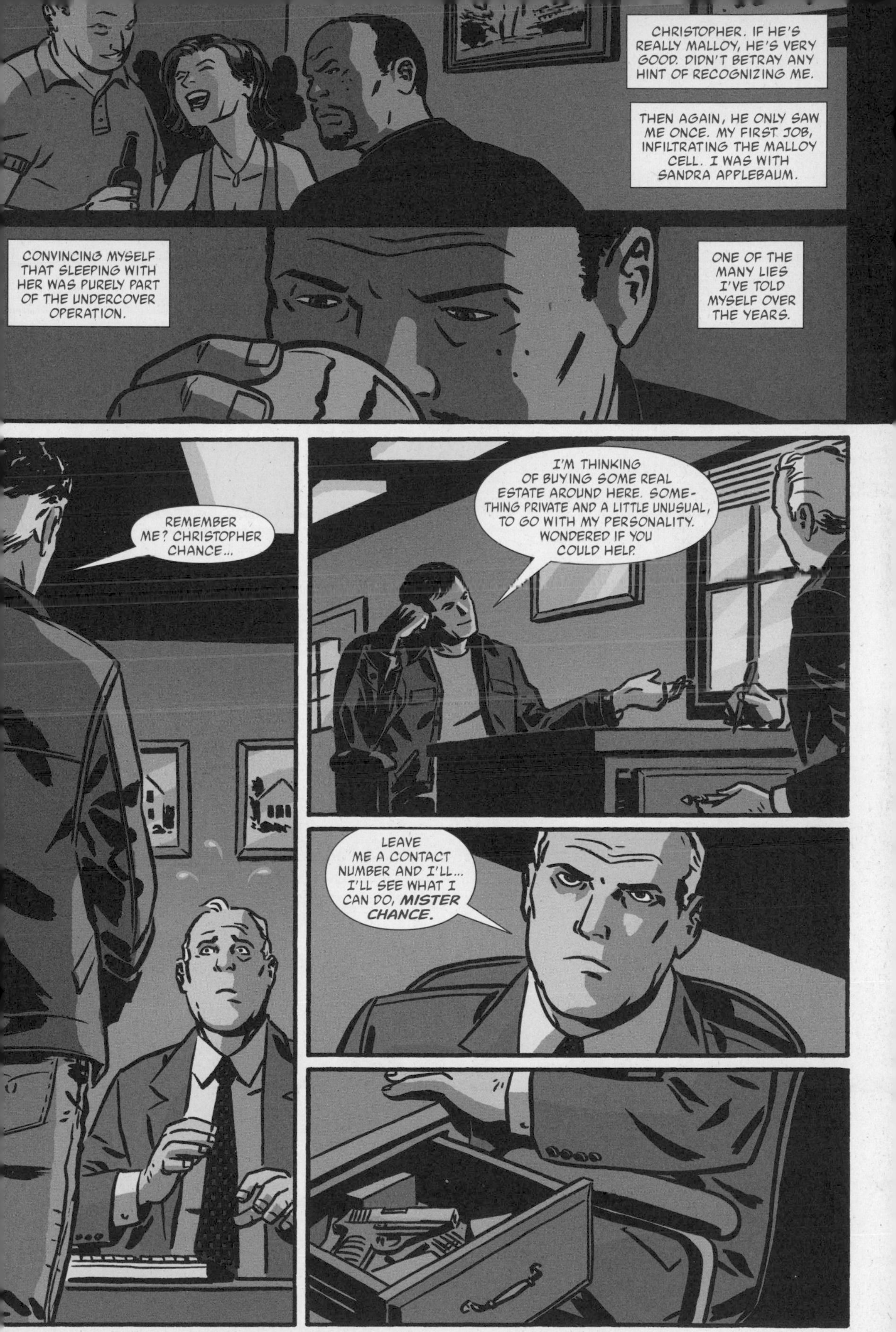

CHRISTOPHER. IF HE'S REALLY MALLOY, HE'S VERY GOOD. DIDN'T BETRAY ANY HINT OF RECOGNIZING ME.
THEN AGAIN, HE ONLY SAW ME ONCE. MY FIRST JOB, INFILTRATING THE MALLOY CELL. I WAS WITH SANDRA APPLEBAUM.
CONVINCING MYSELF THAT SLEEPING WITH HER WAS PURELY PART OF THE UNDERCOVER OPERATION.
ONE OF THE MANY LIES I'VE TOLD MYSELF OVER THE YEARS.
REMEMBER ME? CHRISTOPHER CHANCE...
I'M THINKING OF BUYING SOME REAL ESTATE AROUND HERE. SOMETHING PRIVATE AND A LITTLE UNUSUAL, TO GO WITH MY PERSONALITY. WONDERED IF YOU COULD HELP.
LEAVE ME A CONTACT NUMBER AND I'LL... I'LL SEE WHAT I CAN DO, MISTER CHANCE.

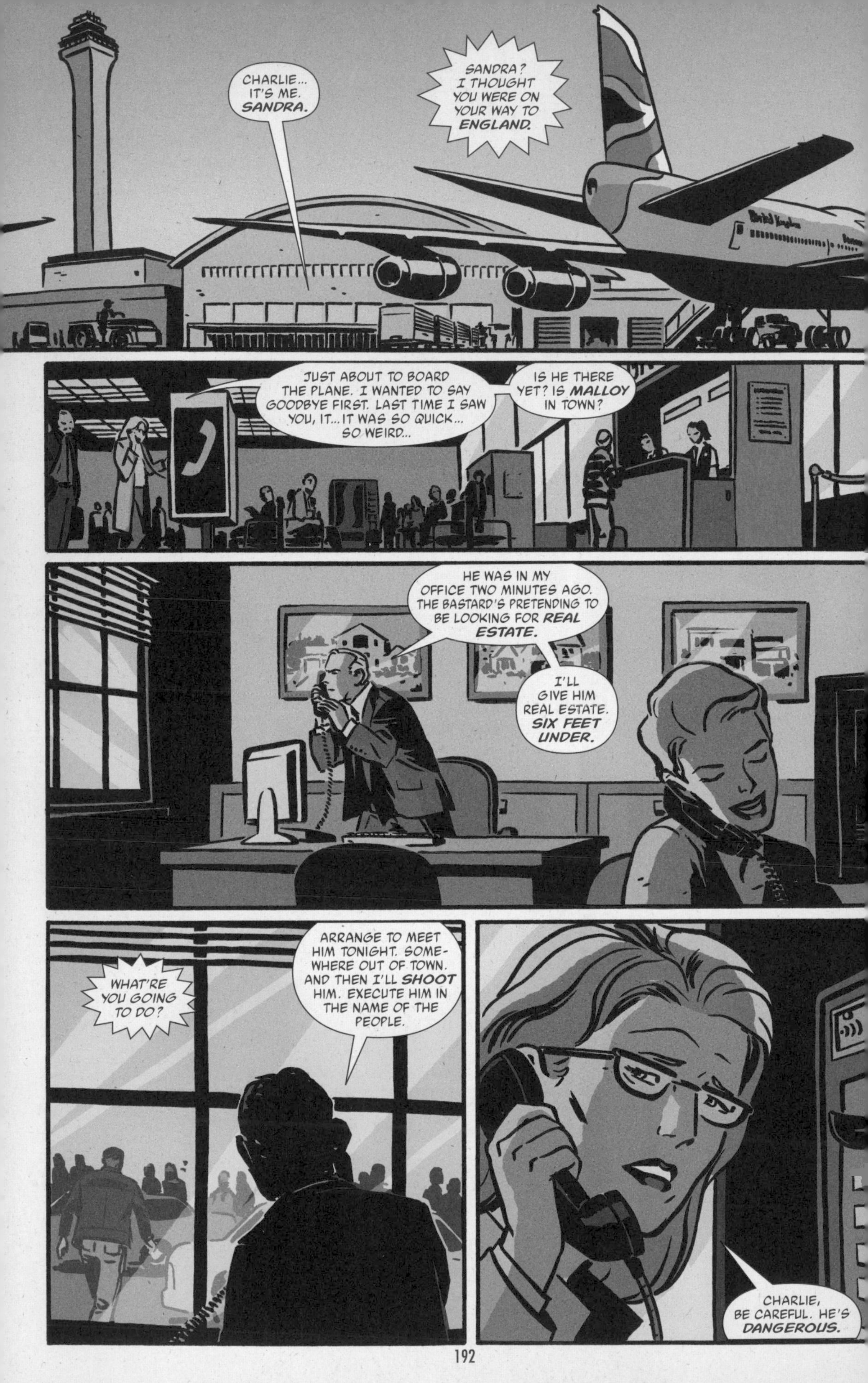
CHARLIE... IT'S ME. SANDRA.
SANDRA? I THOUGHT YOU WERE ON YOUR WAY TO ENGLAND.
JUST ABOUT TO BOARD THE PLANE. I WANTED TO SAY GOODBYE FIRST. LAST TIME I SAW YOU, IT... IT WAS SO QUICK... SO WEIRD...
IS HE THERE YET? IS MALLOY IN TOWN?
HE WAS IN MY OFFICE TWO MINUTES AGO. THE BASTARD'S PRETENDING TO BE LOOKING FOR REAL ESTATE.
I'LL GIVE HIM REAL ESTATE. SIX FEET UNDER.
WHAT'RE YOU GOING TO DO?
ARRANGE TO MEET HIM TONIGHT. SOMEWHERE OUT OF TOWN. AND THEN I'LL SHOOT HIM. EXECUTE HIM IN THE NAME OF THE PEOPLE.
CHARLIE, BE CAREFUL. HE'S DANGEROUS.

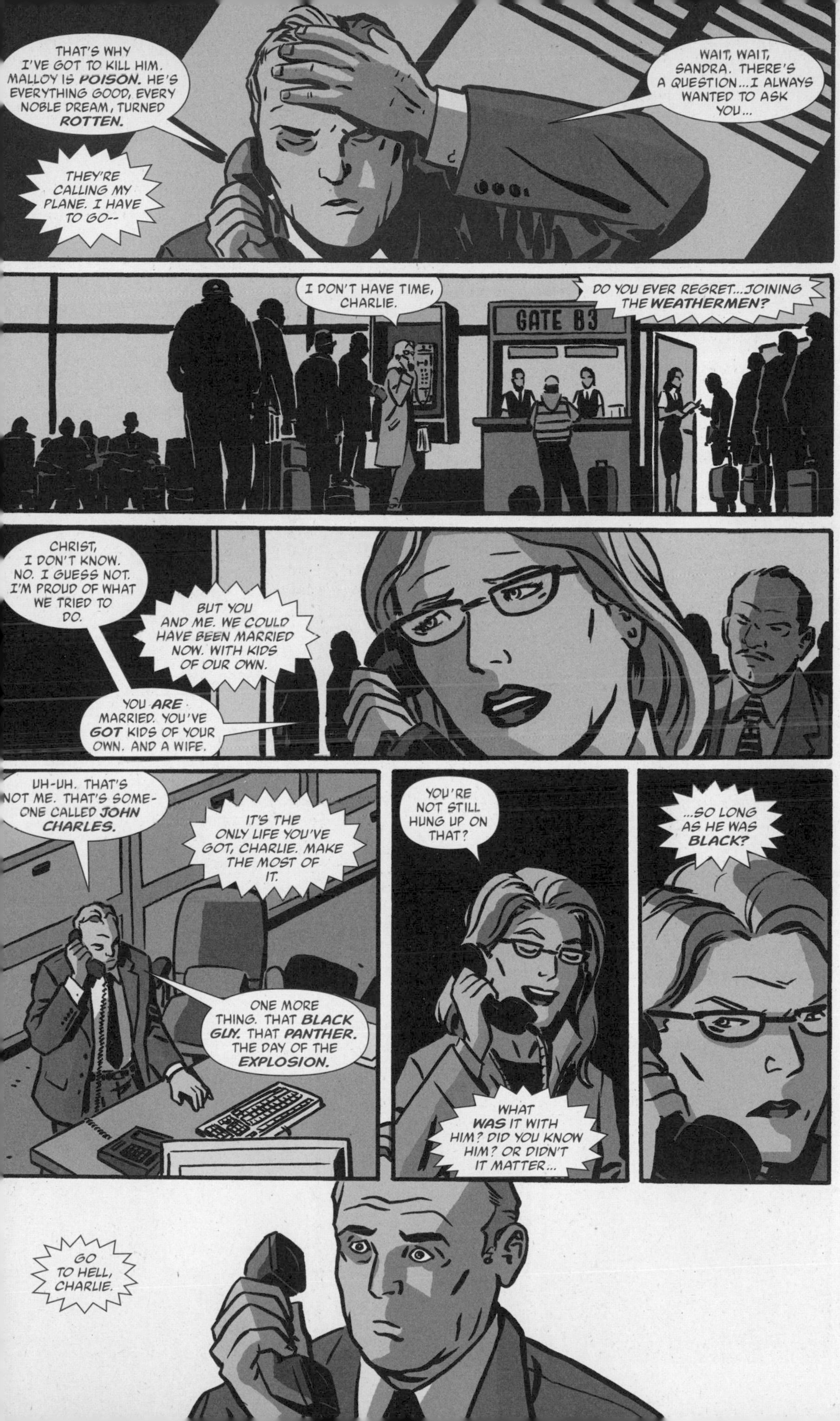
THAT'S WHY I'VE GOT TO KILL HIM. MALLOY IS POISON. HE'S EVERYTHING GOOD, EVERY NOBLE DREAM, TURNED ROTTEN.
WAIT, WAIT, SANDRA. THERE'S A QUESTION... I ALWAYS WANTED TO ASK YOU...
THEY'RE CALLING MY PLANE. I HAVE TO GO--
I DON'T HAVE TIME, CHARLIE.
DO YOU EVER REGRET... JOINING THE WEATHERMEN?
GATE B3
CHRIST, I DON'T KNOW. NO. I GUESS NOT. I'M PROUD OF WHAT WE TRIED TO DO.
BUT YOU AND ME. WE COULD HAVE BEEN MARRIED NOW. WITH KIDS OF OUR OWN.
YOU ARE MARRIED. YOU'VE GOT KIDS OF YOUR OWN. AND A WIFE.
UH-UH. THAT'S NOT ME. THAT'S SOMEONE CALLED JOHN CHARLES.
IT'S THE ONLY LIFE YOU'VE GOT, CHARLIE. MAKE THE MOST OF IT.
ONE MORE THING. THAT BLACK GUY. THAT PANTHER. THE DAY OF THE EXPLOSION.
YOU'RE NOT STILL HUNG UP ON THAT?
WHAT WAS IT WITH HIM? DID YOU KNOW HIM? OR DIDN'T IT MATTER...
...SO LONG AS HE WAS BLACK?
GO TO HELL, CHARLIE.

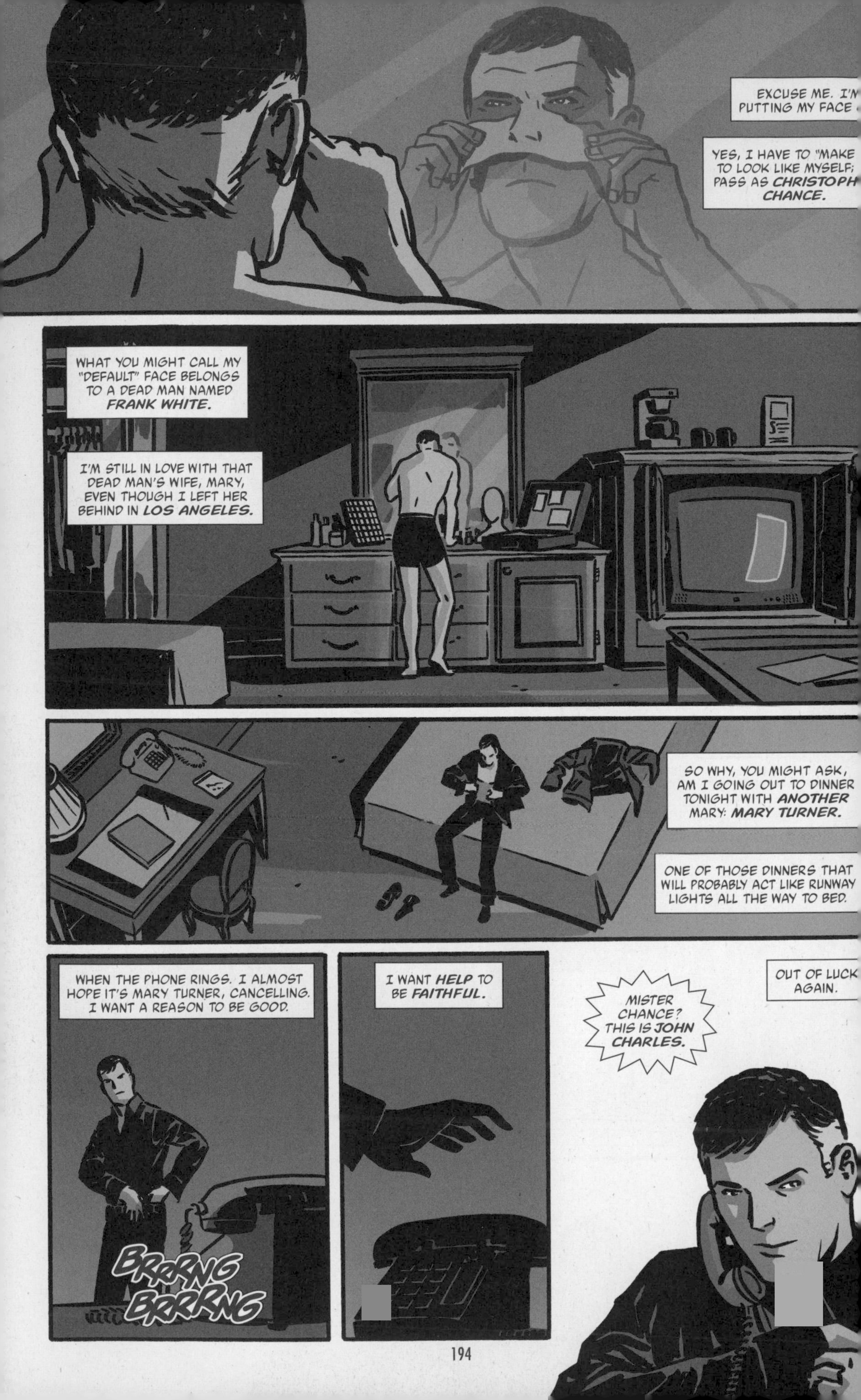

EXCUSE ME. I'M PUTTING MY FACE
YES, I HAVE TO "MAKE TO LOOK LIKE MYSELF; PASS AS CHRISTOPH CHANCE.
WHAT YOU MIGHT CALL MY "DEFAULT" FACE BELONGS TO A DEAD MAN NAMED FRANK WHITE.
I'M STILL IN LOVE WITH THAT DEAD MAN'S WIFE, MARY, EVEN THOUGH I LEFT HER BEHIND IN LOS ANGELES.
SO WHY, YOU MIGHT ASK, AM I GOING OUT TO DINNER TONIGHT WITH ANOTHER MARY: MARY TURNER.
ONE OF THOSE DINNERS THAT WILL PROBABLY ACT LIKE RUNWAY LIGHTS ALL THE WAY TO BED.
WHEN THE PHONE RINGS. I ALMOST HOPE IT'S MARY TURNER, CANCELLING. I WANT A REASON TO BE GOOD.
BRRRNG BRRRNG
I WANT HELP TO BE FAITHFUL.
MISTER CHANCE? THIS IS JOHN CHARLES.
OUT OF LUCK AGAIN.

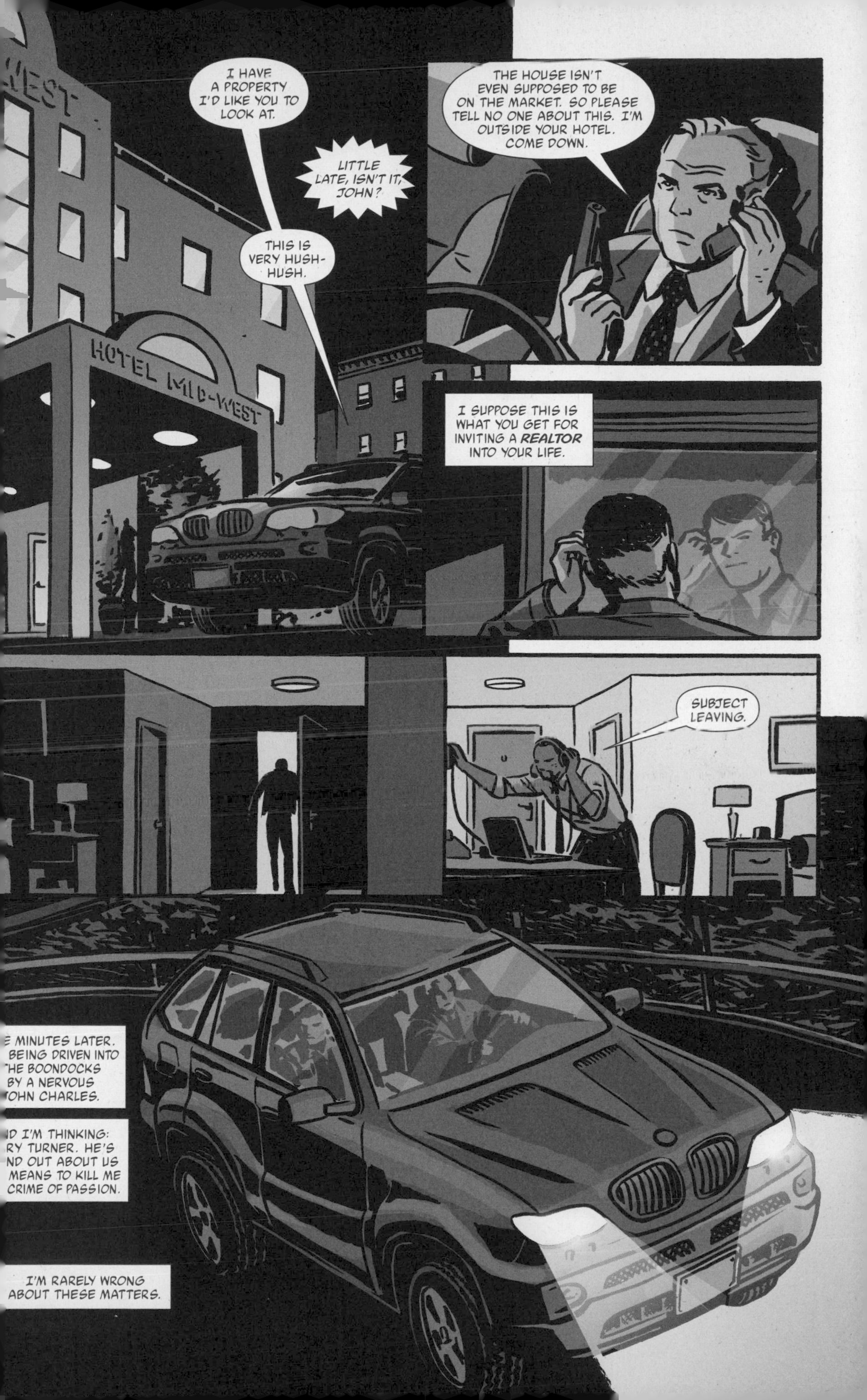
I HAVE A PROPERTY I'D LIKE YOU TO LOOK AT.
LITTLE LATE, ISN'T IT, JOHN?
THIS IS VERY HUSH-HUSH.
HOTEL MID-WEST
THE HOUSE ISN'T EVEN SUPPOSED TO BE ON THE MARKET. SO PLEASE TELL NO ONE ABOUT THIS. I'M OUTSIDE YOUR HOTEL. COME DOWN.
I SUPPOSE THIS IS WHAT YOU GET FOR INVITING A **REALTOR** INTO YOUR LIFE.
SUBJECT LEAVING.
E MINUTES LATER. BEING DRIVEN INTO THE BOONDOCKS BY A NERVOUS JOHN CHARLES.
D I'M THINKING: RY TURNER. HE'S ND OUT ABOUT US MEANS TO KILL ME CRIME OF PASSION.
I'M RARELY WRONG ABOUT THESE MATTERS.

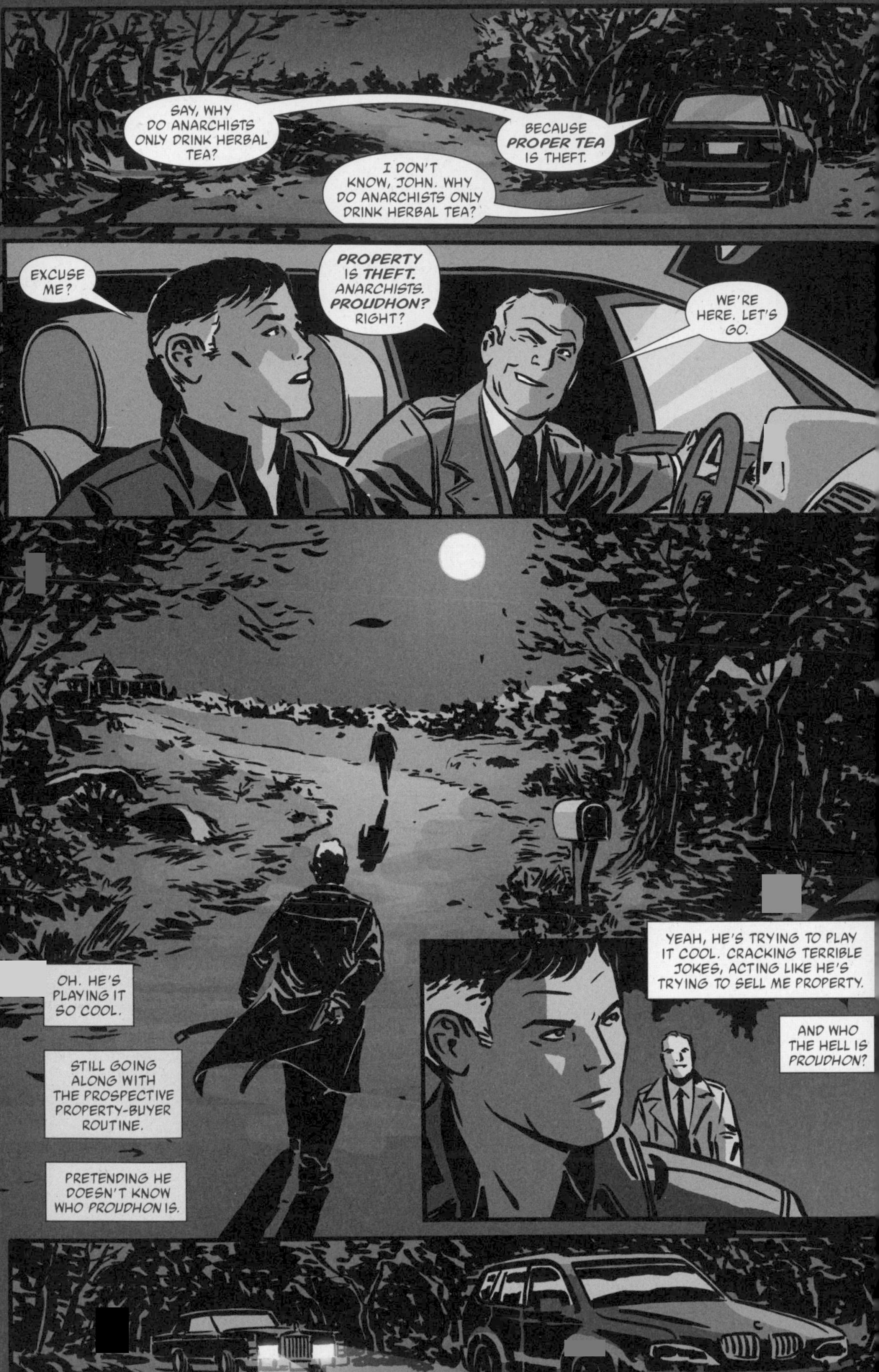
SAY, WHY DO ANARCHISTS ONLY DRINK HERBAL TEA?
I DON'T KNOW, JOHN. WHY DO ANARCHISTS ONLY DRINK HERBAL TEA?
BECAUSE PROPER TEA IS THEFT.
EXCUSE ME?
PROPERTY IS THEFT. ANARCHISTS. PROUDHON? RIGHT?
WE'RE HERE. LET'S GO.
OH. HE'S PLAYING IT SO COOL.
STILL GOING ALONG WITH THE PROSPECTIVE PROPERTY-BUYER ROUTINE.
PRETENDING HE DOESN'T KNOW WHO PROUDHON IS.
YEAH, HE'S TRYING TO PLAY IT COOL. CRACKING TERRIBLE JOKES, ACTING LIKE HE'S TRYING TO SELL ME PROPERTY.
AND WHO THE HELL IS PROUDHON?

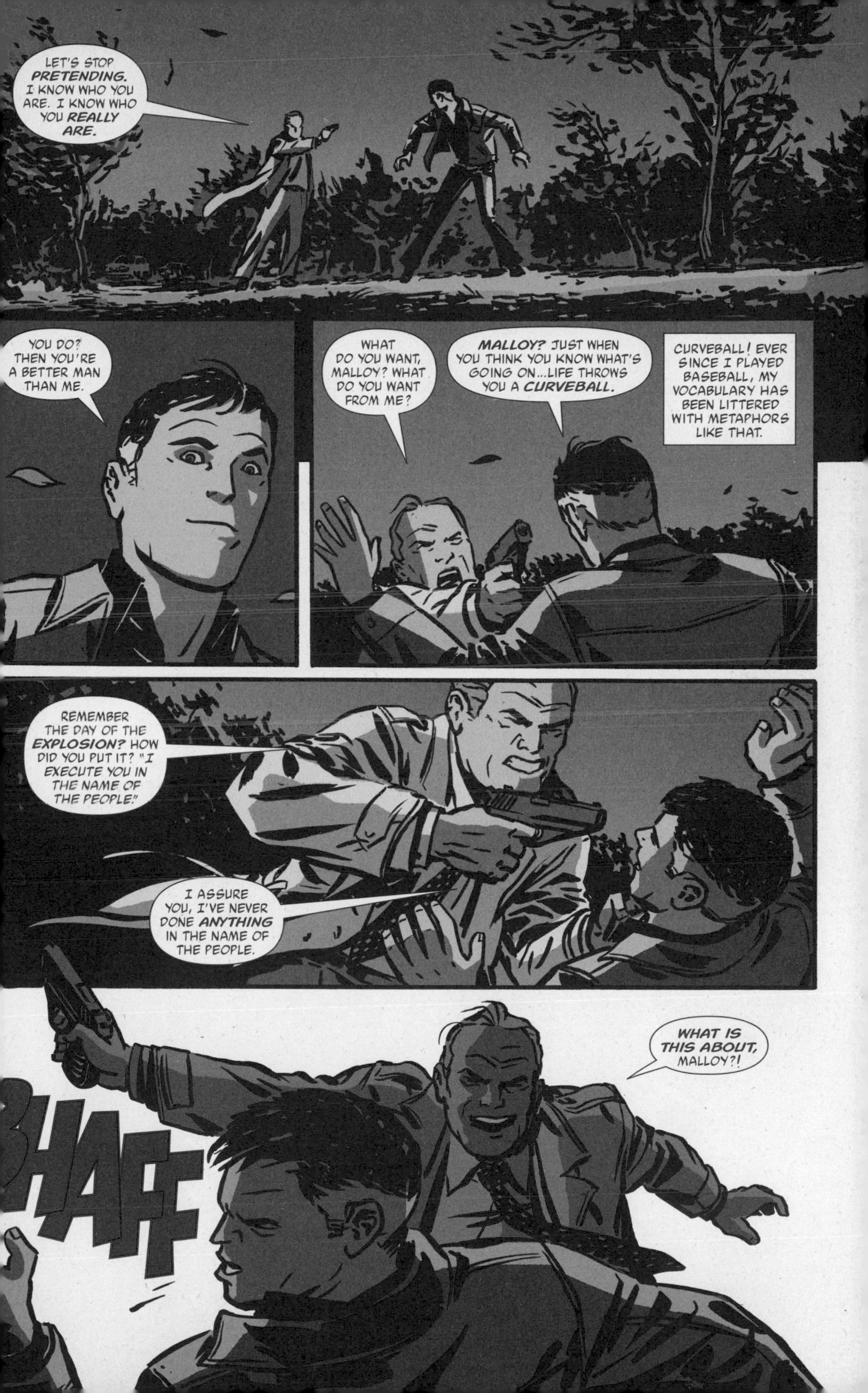
LET'S STOP PRETENDING. I KNOW WHO YOU ARE. I KNOW WHO YOU REALLY ARE.
YOU DO? THEN YOU'RE A BETTER MAN THAN ME.
WHAT DO YOU WANT, MALLOY? WHAT DO YOU WANT FROM ME?
MALLOY? JUST WHEN YOU THINK YOU KNOW WHAT'S GOING ON...LIFE THROWS YOU A CURVEBALL.
CURVEBALL! EVER SINCE I PLAYED BASEBALL, MY VOCABULARY HAS BEEN LITTERED WITH METAPHORS LIKE THAT.
REMEMBER THE DAY OF THE EXPLOSION? HOW DID YOU PUT IT? "I EXECUTE YOU IN THE NAME OF THE PEOPLE."
I ASSURE YOU, I'VE NEVER DONE ANYTHING IN THE NAME OF THE PEOPLE.
WHAT IS THIS ABOUT, MALLOY?!
BHAFF

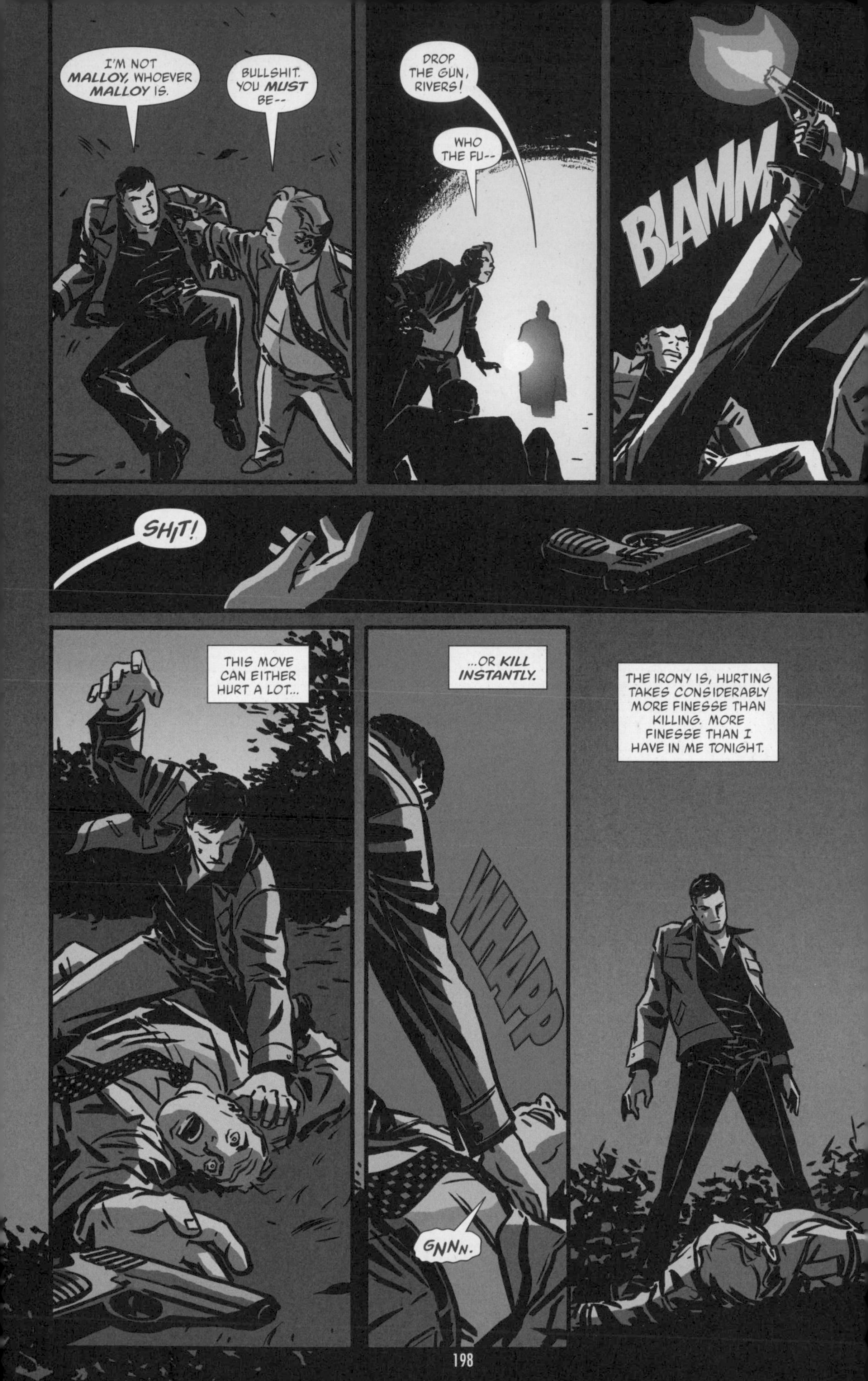
I'M NOT MALLOY, WHOEVER MALLOY IS.
BULLSHIT. YOU MUST BE--
DROP THE GUN, RIVERS!
WHO THE FU--
BLAMM
SHIT!
THIS MOVE CAN EITHER HURT A LOT...
...OR KILL INSTANTLY.
WHAPP
GNNN.
THE IRONY IS, HURTING TAKES CONSIDERABLY MORE FINESSE THAN KILLING. MORE FINESSE THAN I HAVE IN ME TONIGHT.

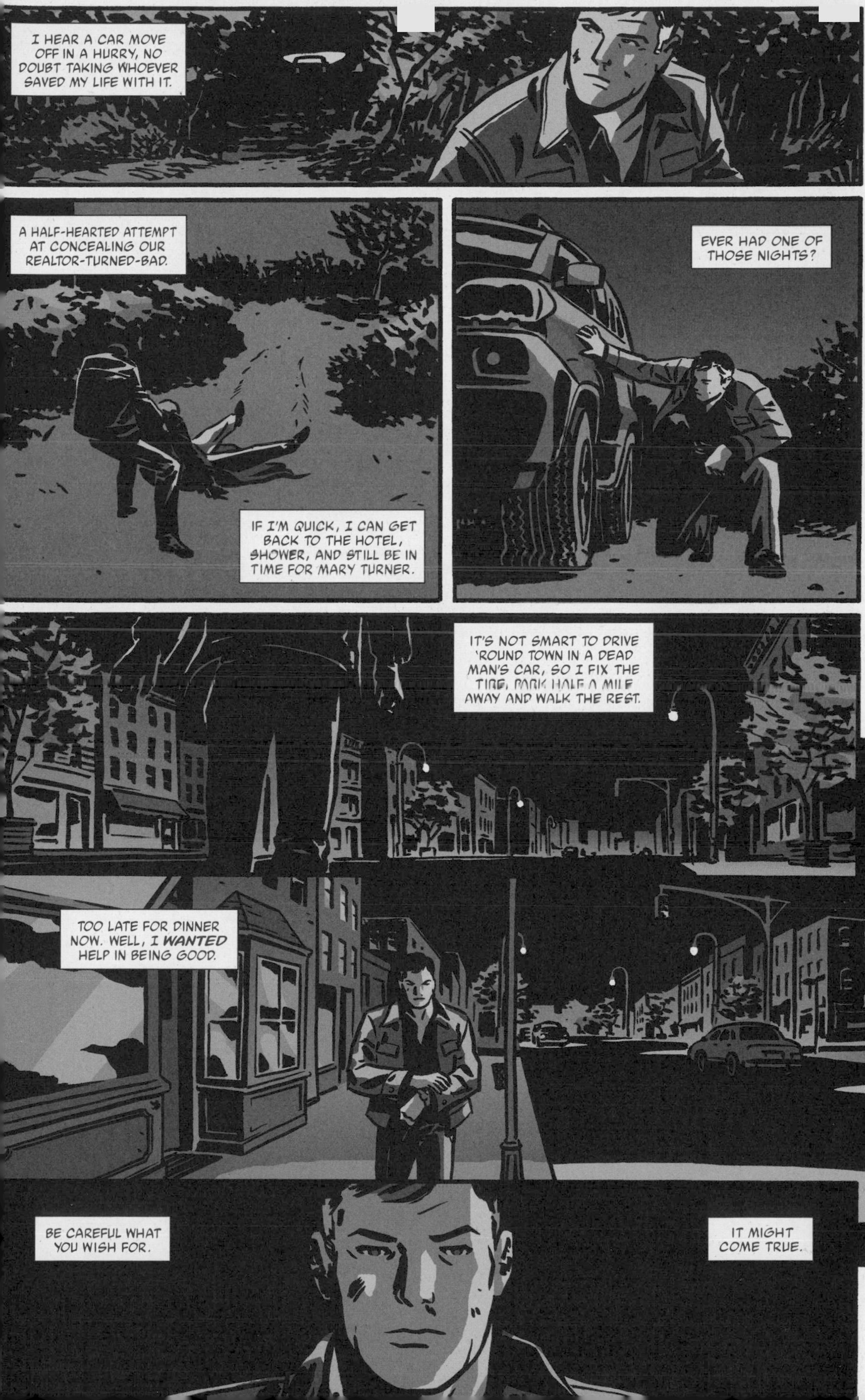
I HEAR A CAR MOVE OFF IN A HURRY, NO DOUBT TAKING WHOEVER SAVED MY LIFE WITH IT.
A HALF-HEARTED ATTEMPT AT CONCEALING OUR REALTOR-TURNED-BAD.
IF I'M QUICK, I CAN GET BACK TO THE HOTEL, SHOWER, AND STILL BE IN TIME FOR MARY TURNER.
EVER HAD ONE OF THOSE NIGHTS?
IT'S NOT SMART TO DRIVE 'ROUND TOWN IN A DEAD MAN'S CAR, SO I FIX THE TIRE, PARK HALF A MILE AWAY AND WALK THE REST.
TOO LATE FOR DINNER NOW. WELL, I WANTED HELP IN BEING GOOD.
BE CAREFUL WHAT YOU WISH FOR.
IT MIGHT COME TRUE.

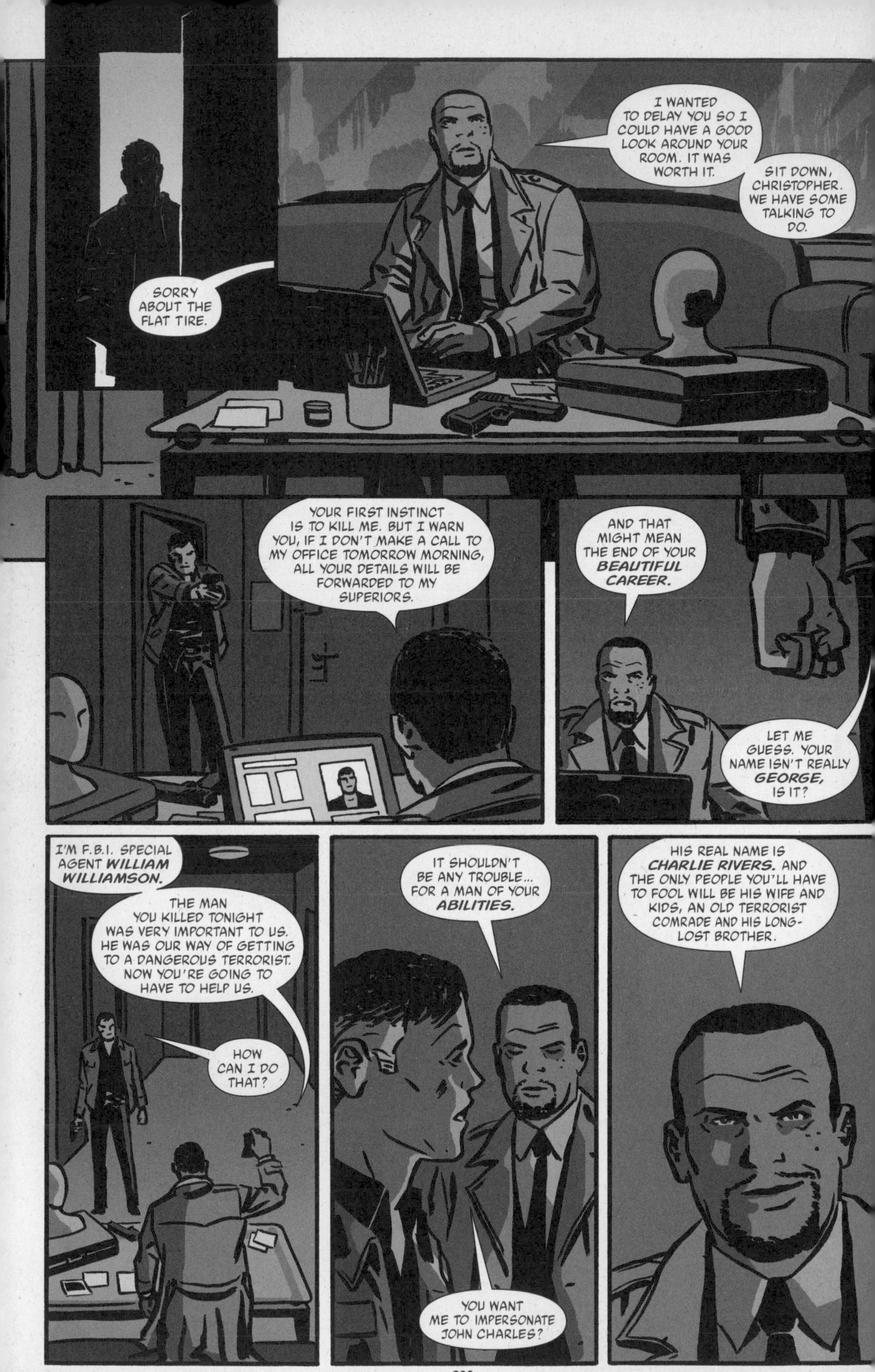
I WANTED TO DELAY YOU SO I COULD HAVE A GOOD LOOK AROUND YOUR ROOM. IT WAS WORTH IT.
SIT DOWN, CHRISTOPHER. WE HAVE SOME TALKING TO DO.
SORRY ABOUT THE FLAT TIRE.
YOUR FIRST INSTINCT IS TO KILL ME. BUT I WARN YOU, IF I DON'T MAKE A CALL TO MY OFFICE TOMORROW MORNING, ALL YOUR DETAILS WILL BE FORWARDED TO MY SUPERIORS.
AND THAT MIGHT MEAN THE END OF YOUR **BEAUTIFUL CAREER.**
LET ME GUESS. YOUR NAME ISN'T REALLY **GEORGE,** IS IT?
I'M F.B.I. SPECIAL AGENT **WILLIAM WILLIAMSON.**
THE MAN YOU KILLED TONIGHT WAS VERY IMPORTANT TO US. HE WAS OUR WAY OF GETTING TO A DANGEROUS TERRORIST. NOW YOU'RE GOING TO HAVE TO HELP US.
HOW CAN I DO THAT?
IT SHOULDN'T BE ANY TROUBLE... FOR A MAN OF YOUR **ABILITIES.**
YOU WANT ME TO IMPERSONATE JOHN CHARLES?
HIS REAL NAME IS **CHARLIE RIVERS.** AND THE ONLY PEOPLE YOU'LL HAVE TO FOOL WILL BE HIS WIFE AND KIDS, AN OLD TERRORIST COMRADE AND HIS LONG-LOST BROTHER.

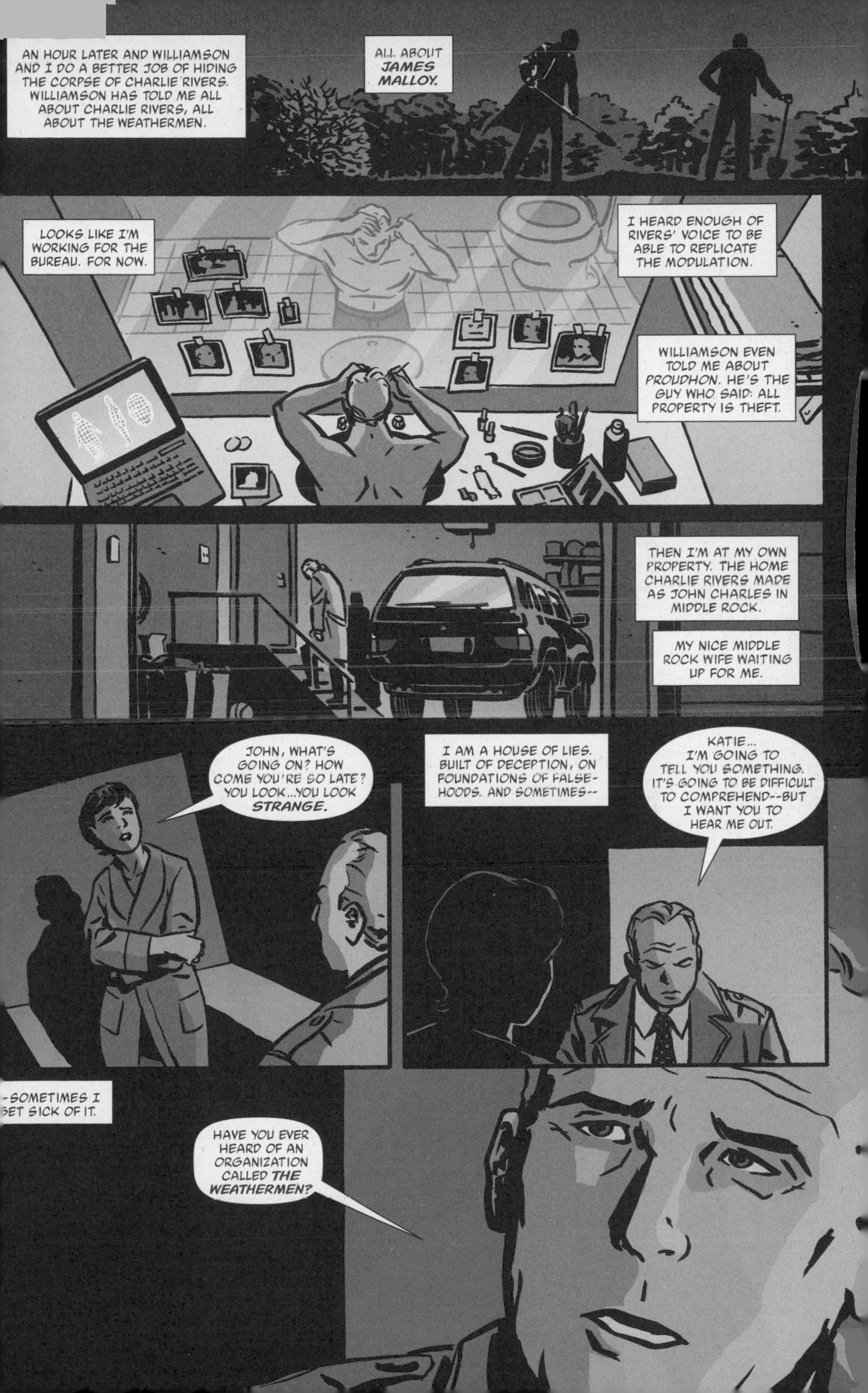
AN HOUR LATER AND WILLIAMSON AND I DO A BETTER JOB OF HIDING THE CORPSE OF CHARLIE RIVERS. WILLIAMSON HAS TOLD ME ALL ABOUT CHARLIE RIVERS, ALL ABOUT THE WEATHERMEN.
ALL ABOUT JAMES MALLOY.
LOOKS LIKE I'M WORKING FOR THE BUREAU. FOR NOW.
I HEARD ENOUGH OF RIVERS' VOICE TO BE ABLE TO REPLICATE THE MODULATION.
WILLIAMSON EVEN TOLD ME ABOUT PROUDHON. HE'S THE GUY WHO SAID: ALL PROPERTY IS THEFT.
THEN I'M AT MY OWN PROPERTY. THE HOME CHARLIE RIVERS MADE AS JOHN CHARLES IN MIDDLE ROCK.
MY NICE MIDDLE ROCK WIFE WAITING UP FOR ME.
JOHN, WHAT'S GOING ON? HOW COME YOU'RE SO LATE? YOU LOOK...YOU LOOK STRANGE.
I AM A HOUSE OF LIES. BUILT OF DECEPTION, ON FOUNDATIONS OF FALSE-HOODS. AND SOMETIMES--
KATIE... I'M GOING TO TELL YOU SOMETHING. IT'S GOING TO BE DIFFICULT TO COMPREHEND--BUT I WANT YOU TO HEAR ME OUT.
-SOMETIMES I GET SICK OF IT.
HAVE YOU EVER HEARD OF AN ORGANIZATION CALLED THE WEATHERMEN?

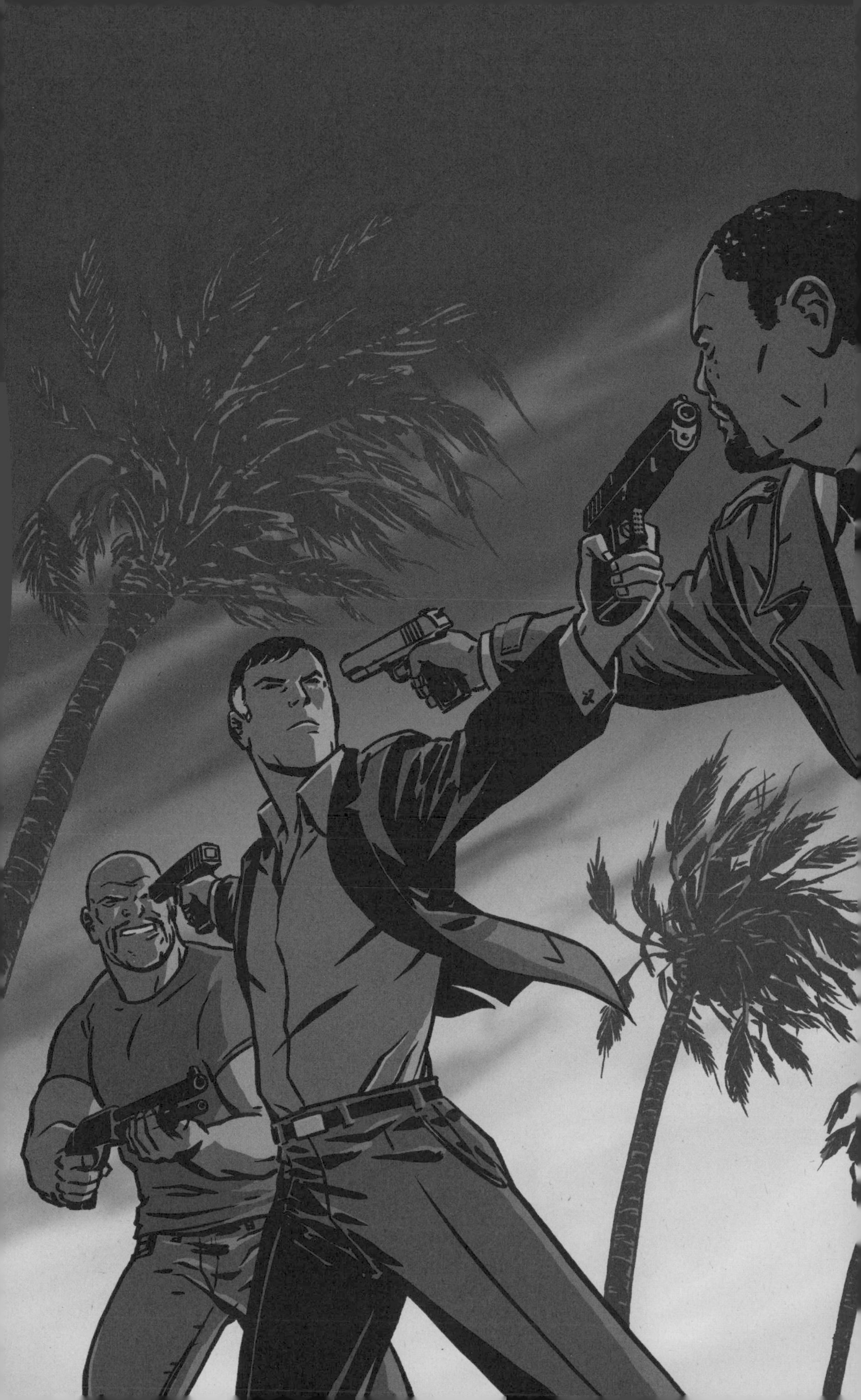

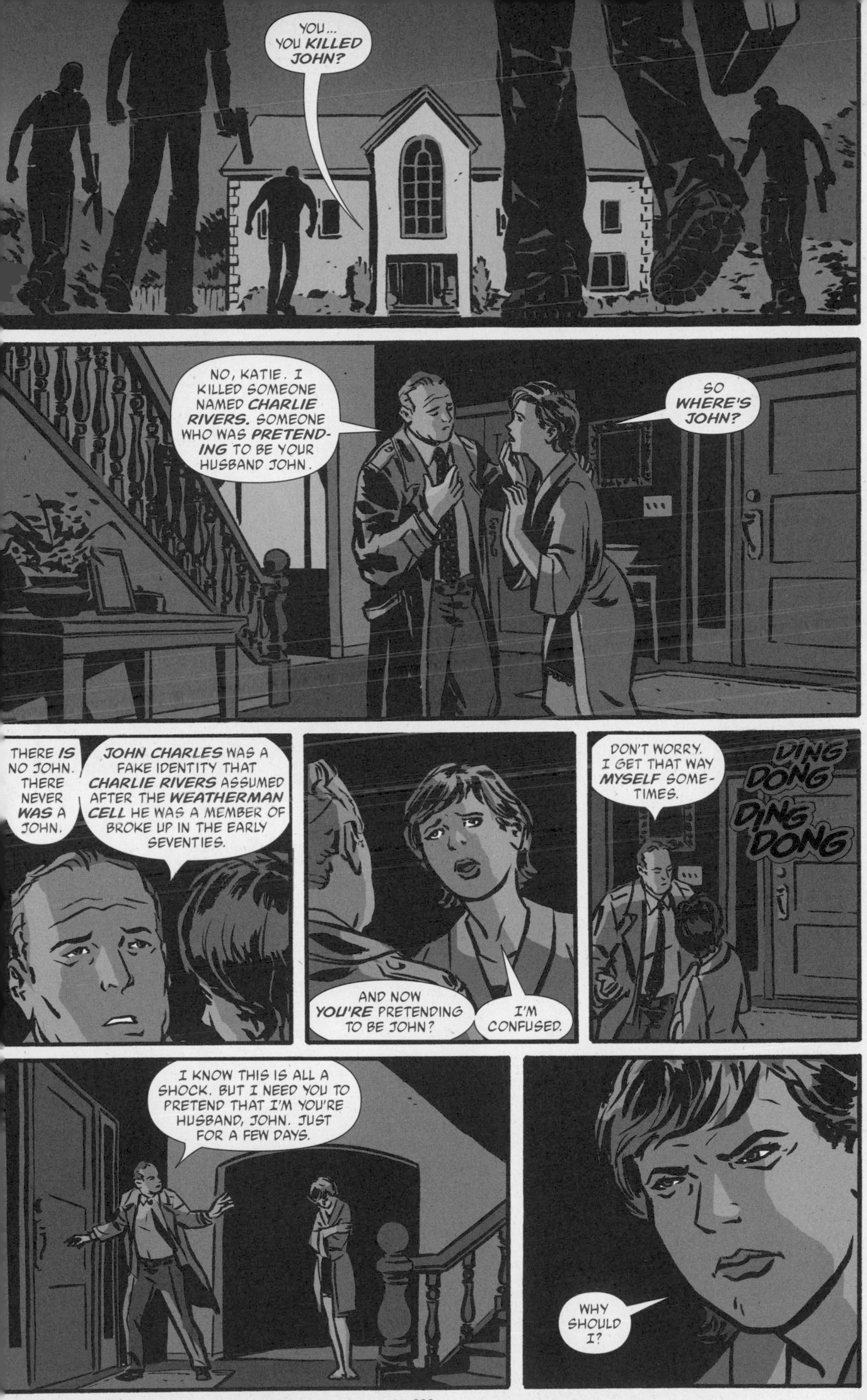
YOU... YOU KILLED JOHN?
NO, KATIE. I KILLED SOMEONE NAMED CHARLIE RIVERS. SOMEONE WHO WAS PRETENDING TO BE YOUR HUSBAND JOHN.
SO WHERE'S JOHN?
THERE IS NO JOHN. THERE NEVER WAS A JOHN.
JOHN CHARLES WAS A FAKE IDENTITY THAT CHARLIE RIVERS ASSUMED AFTER THE WEATHERMAN CELL HE WAS A MEMBER OF BROKE UP IN THE EARLY SEVENTIES.
AND NOW YOU'RE PRETENDING TO BE JOHN?
I'M CONFUSED.
DON'T WORRY. I GET THAT WAY MYSELF SOMETIMES.
DING DONG
DING DONG
I KNOW THIS IS ALL A SHOCK. BUT I NEED YOU TO PRETEND THAT I'M YOU'RE HUSBAND, JOHN. JUST FOR A FEW DAYS.
WHY SHOULD I?

VERY GOOD QUESTION.

NO, IT WON'T BE NECESSARY TO *TORTURE* HIM.

WHICH WAY THE WIND BLOWS

PART THREE: BRINGING IT ALL BACK HOME

PETER MILLIGAN WRITER · CLIFF CHIANG ARTIST & COVER · LEE LOUGHRIDGE COLORIST & SEPS · CLEM ROBINS LETTERER · PORNSAK PICHETSHOTE ASS'T EDITOR · KAREN BERGER EDITOR · THE HUMAN TA... CREATED BY LEN WEIN... CARMINE INFANTIN...

HELLO? CAN I HELP YOU?

HELLO, *CHARLIE*. LIVING THE LIFE OF A *FAT CAPITALIST*, I SEE.

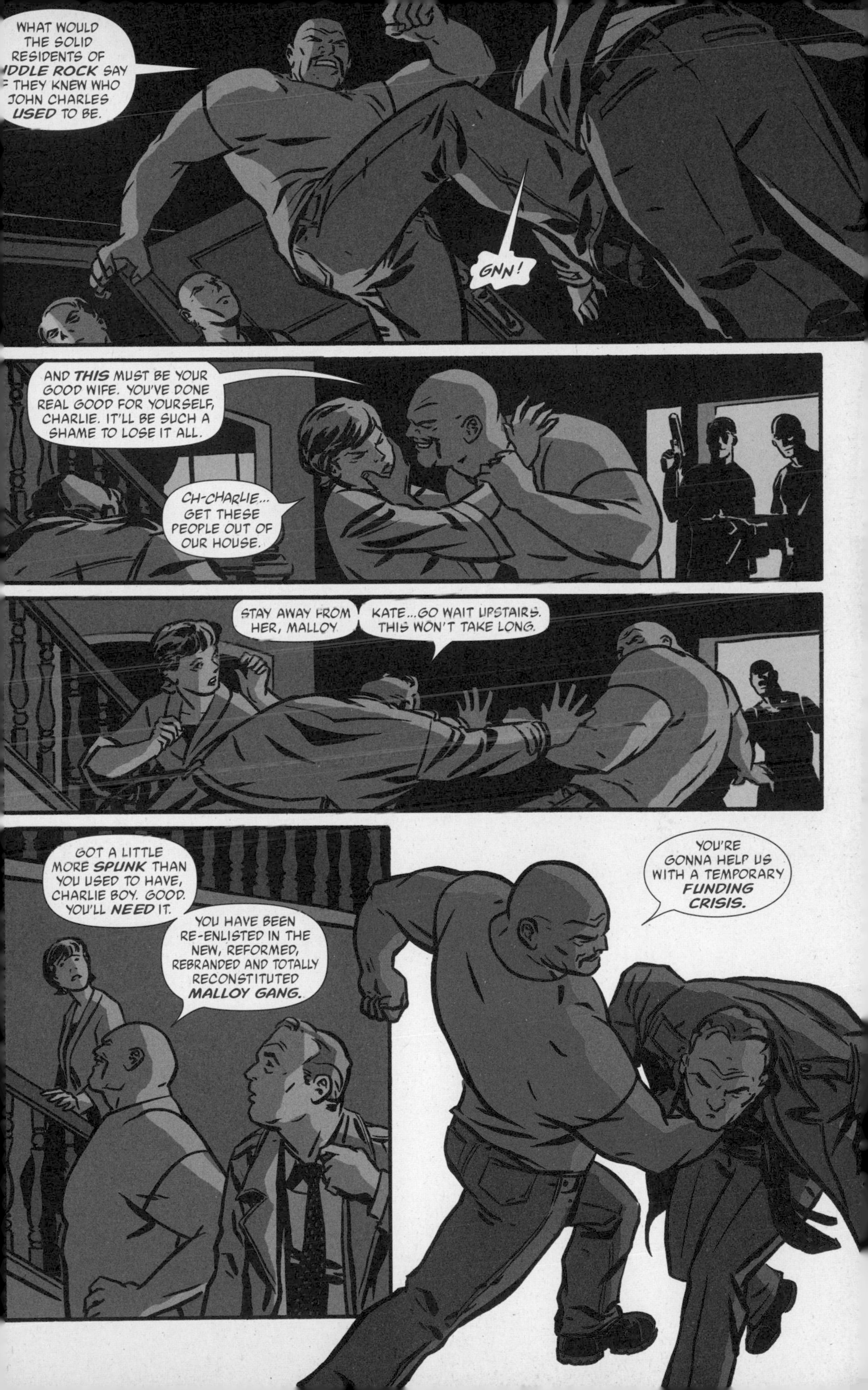
WHAT WOULD THE SOLID RESIDENTS OF IDDLE ROCK SAY F THEY KNEW WHO JOHN CHARLES USED TO BE.
GNN!
AND THIS MUST BE YOUR GOOD WIFE. YOU'VE DONE REAL GOOD FOR YOURSELF, CHARLIE. IT'LL BE SUCH A SHAME TO LOSE IT ALL.
CH-CHARLIE... GET THESE PEOPLE OUT OF OUR HOUSE.
STAY AWAY FROM HER, MALLOY
KATE...GO WAIT UPSTAIRS. THIS WON'T TAKE LONG.
GOT A LITTLE MORE SPUNK THAN YOU USED TO HAVE, CHARLIE BOY. GOOD. YOU'LL NEED IT.
YOU HAVE BEEN RE-ENLISTED IN THE NEW, REFORMED, REBRANDED AND TOTALLY RECONSTITUTED MALLOY GANG.
YOU'RE GONNA HELP US WITH A TEMPORARY FUNDING CRISIS.

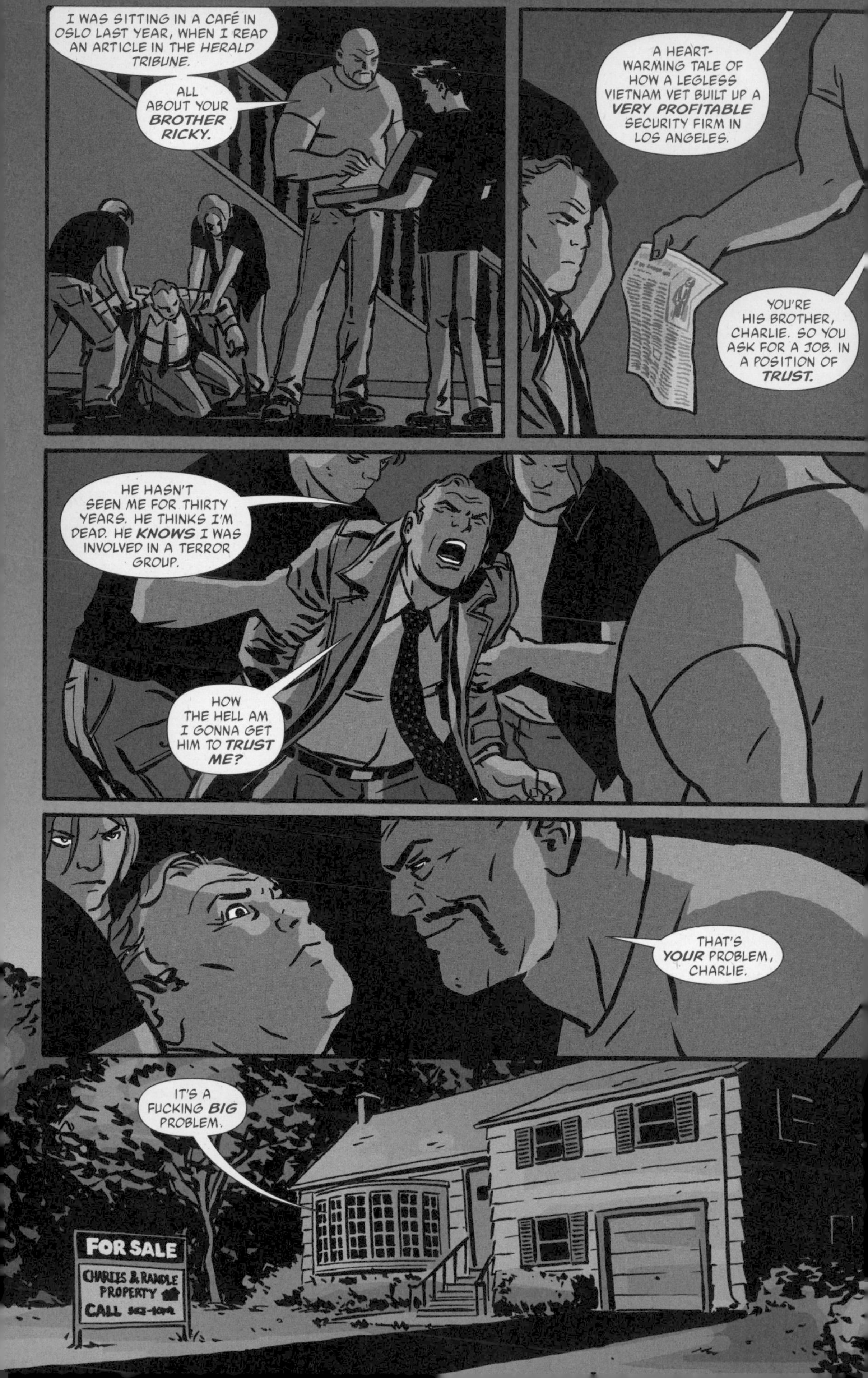
I WAS SITTING IN A CAFÉ IN OSLO LAST YEAR, WHEN I READ AN ARTICLE IN THE HERALD TRIBUNE.
ALL ABOUT YOUR **BROTHER RICKY.**
A HEART-WARMING TALE OF HOW A LEGLESS VIETNAM VET BUILT UP A **VERY PROFITABLE** SECURITY FIRM IN LOS ANGELES.
YOU'RE HIS BROTHER, CHARLIE. SO YOU ASK FOR A JOB. IN A POSITION OF **TRUST.**
HE HASN'T SEEN ME FOR THIRTY YEARS. HE THINKS I'M DEAD. HE **KNOWS** I WAS INVOLVED IN A TERROR GROUP.
HOW THE HELL AM I GONNA GET HIM TO **TRUST ME?**
THAT'S **YOUR** PROBLEM, CHARLIE.
IT'S A FUCKING **BIG** PROBLEM.
FOR SALE
CHARLES & RANDLE PROPERTY
CALL

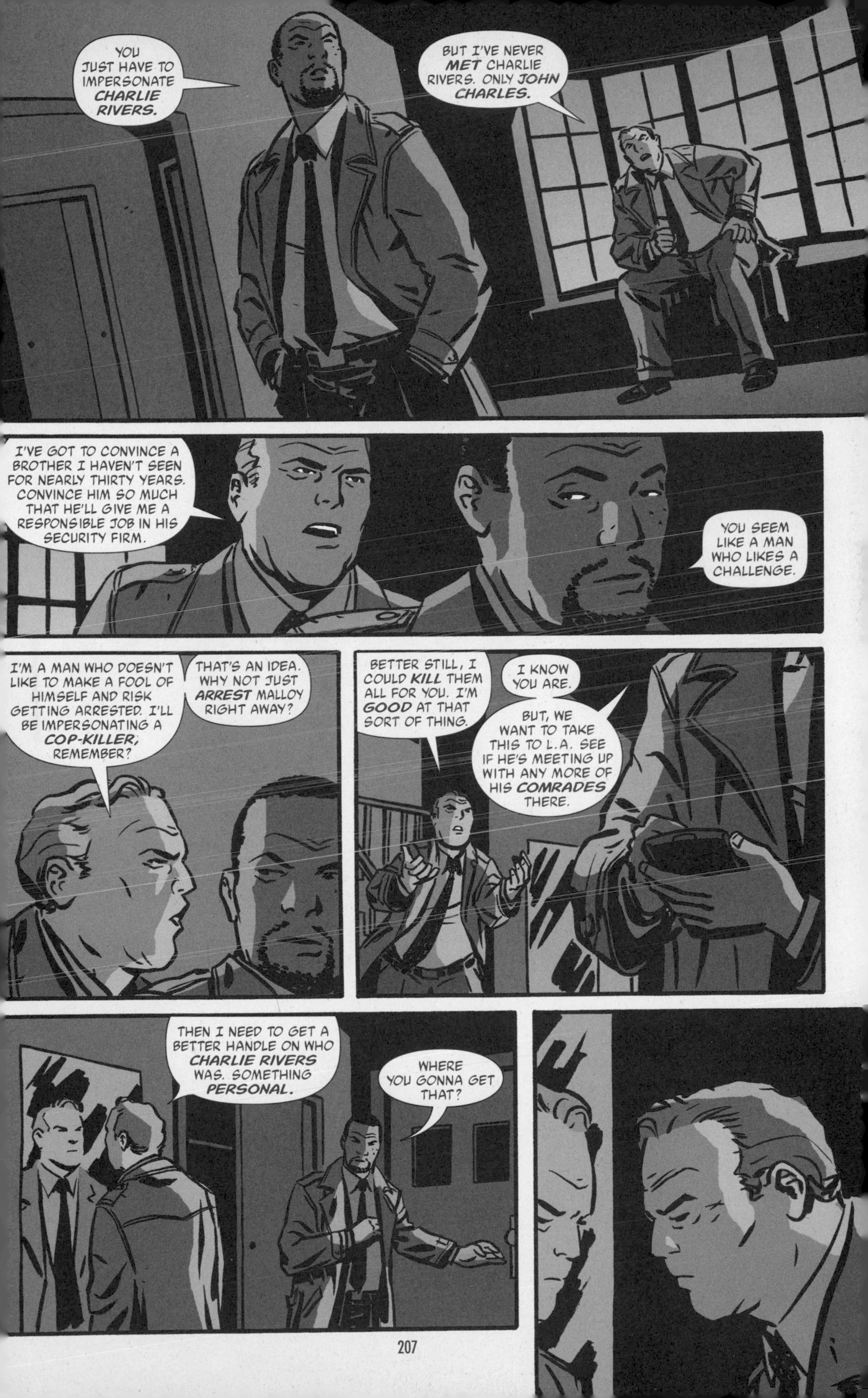
YOU JUST HAVE TO IMPERSONATE CHARLIE RIVERS.
BUT I'VE NEVER MET CHARLIE RIVERS. ONLY JOHN CHARLES.
I'VE GOT TO CONVINCE A BROTHER I HAVEN'T SEEN FOR NEARLY THIRTY YEARS. CONVINCE HIM SO MUCH THAT HE'LL GIVE ME A RESPONSIBLE JOB IN HIS SECURITY FIRM.
YOU SEEM LIKE A MAN WHO LIKES A CHALLENGE.
I'M A MAN WHO DOESN'T LIKE TO MAKE A FOOL OF HIMSELF AND RISK GETTING ARRESTED. I'LL BE IMPERSONATING A COP-KILLER, REMEMBER?
THAT'S AN IDEA. WHY NOT JUST ARREST MALLOY RIGHT AWAY?
BETTER STILL, I COULD KILL THEM ALL FOR YOU. I'M GOOD AT THAT SORT OF THING.
I KNOW YOU ARE.
BUT, WE WANT TO TAKE THIS TO L.A. SEE IF HE'S MEETING UP WITH ANY MORE OF HIS COMRADES THERE.
THEN I NEED TO GET A BETTER HANDLE ON WHO CHARLIE RIVERS WAS. SOMETHING PERSONAL.
WHERE YOU GONNA GET THAT?

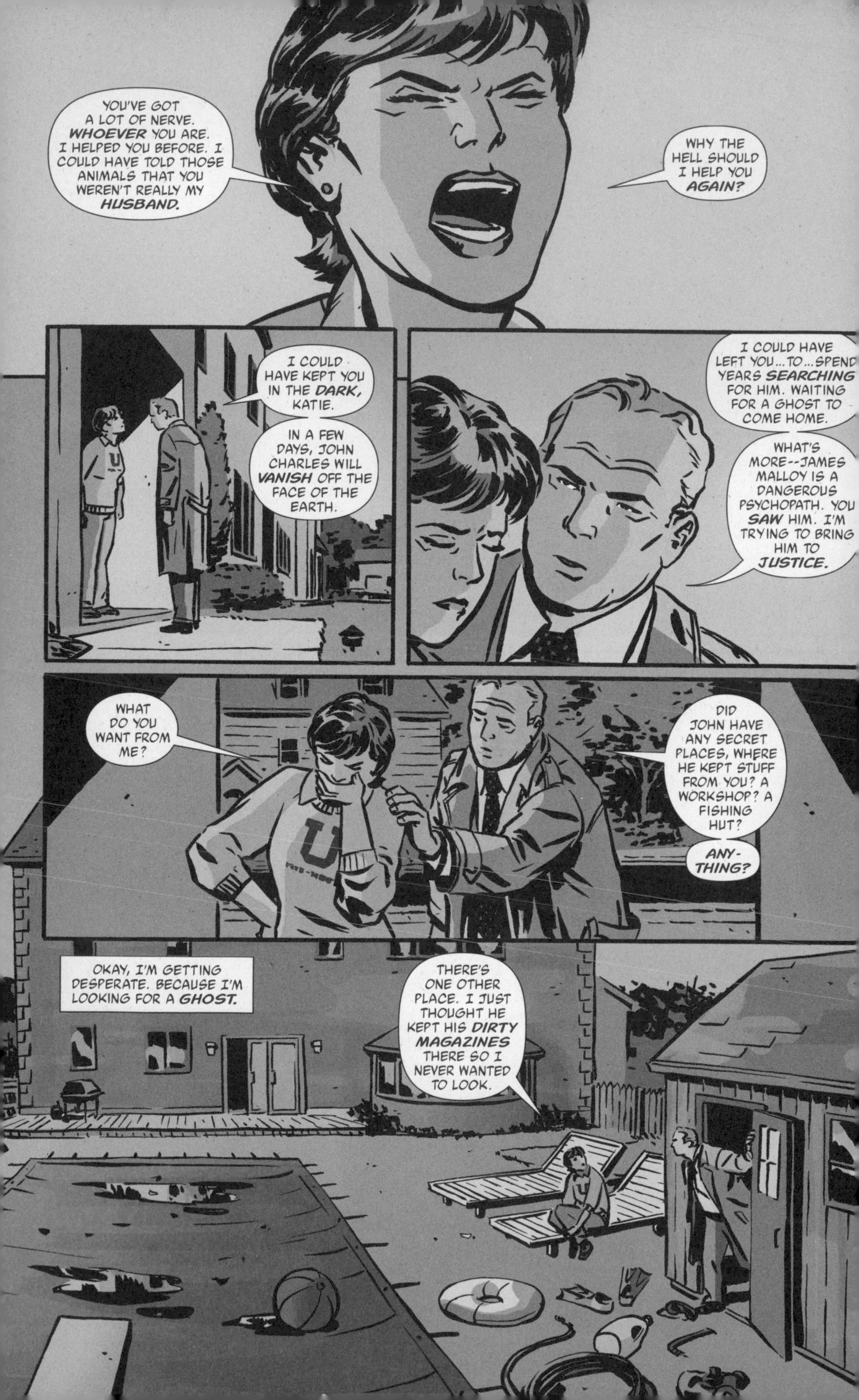
YOU'VE GOT A LOT OF NERVE. WHOEVER YOU ARE. I HELPED YOU BEFORE. I COULD HAVE TOLD THOSE ANIMALS THAT YOU WEREN'T REALLY MY HUSBAND.
WHY THE HELL SHOULD I HELP YOU AGAIN?
I COULD HAVE KEPT YOU IN THE DARK, KATIE.
IN A FEW DAYS, JOHN CHARLES WILL VANISH OFF THE FACE OF THE EARTH.
I COULD HAVE LEFT YOU...TO...SPEND YEARS SEARCHING FOR HIM. WAITING FOR A GHOST TO COME HOME.
WHAT'S MORE--JAMES MALLOY IS A DANGEROUS PSYCHOPATH. YOU SAW HIM. I'M TRYING TO BRING HIM TO JUSTICE.
WHAT DO YOU WANT FROM ME?
DID JOHN HAVE ANY SECRET PLACES, WHERE HE KEPT STUFF FROM YOU? A WORKSHOP? A FISHING HUT?
ANY-THING?
OKAY, I'M GETTING DESPERATE. BECAUSE I'M LOOKING FOR A GHOST.
THERE'S ONE OTHER PLACE. I JUST THOUGHT HE KEPT HIS DIRTY MAGAZINES THERE SO I NEVER WANTED TO LOOK.

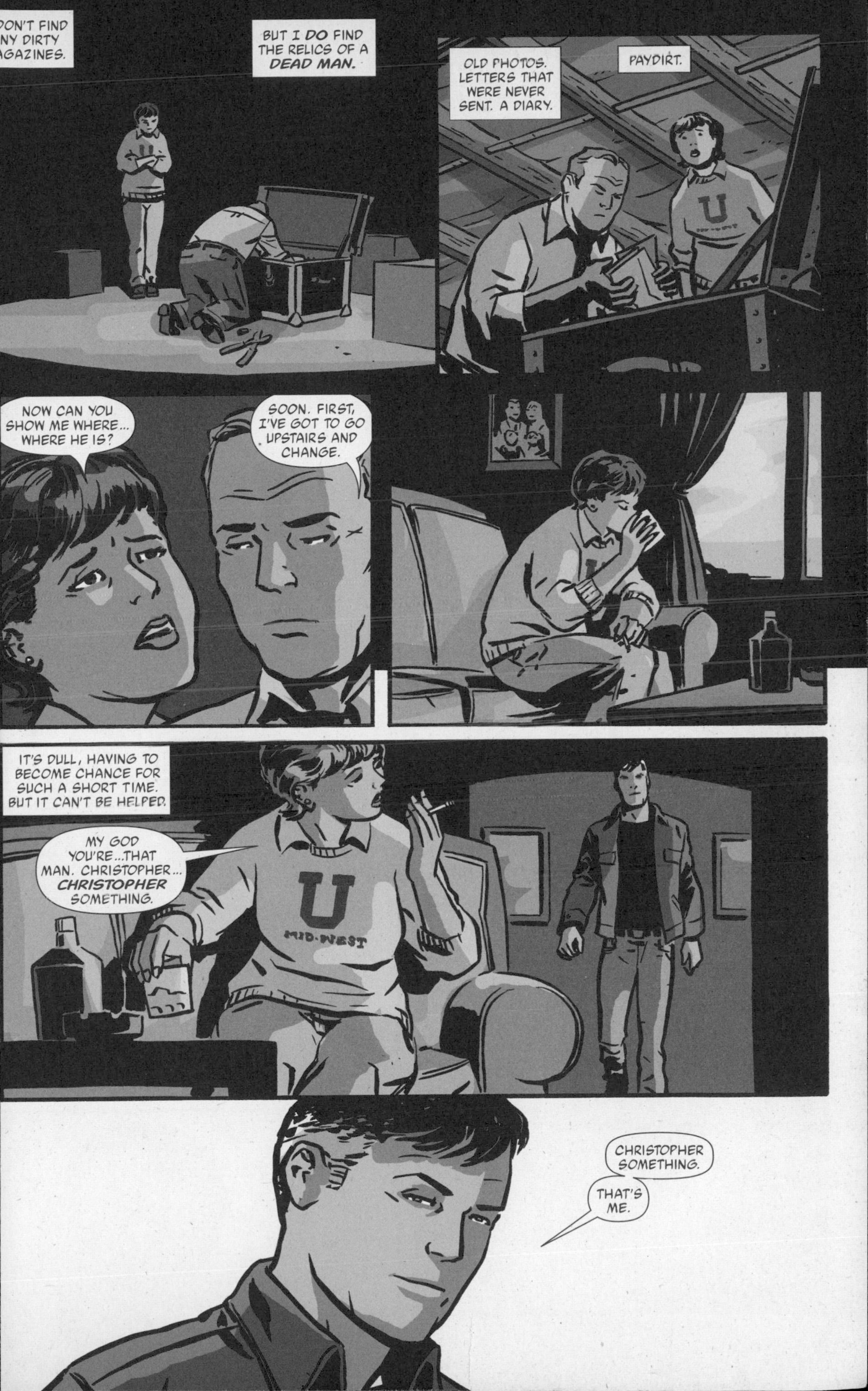
...DON'T FIND
...NY DIRTY
...AGAZINES.
BUT I DO FIND THE RELICS OF A DEAD MAN.
OLD PHOTOS. LETTERS THAT WERE NEVER SENT. A DIARY.
PAYDIRT.
NOW CAN YOU SHOW ME WHERE... WHERE HE IS?
SOON. FIRST, I'VE GOT TO GO UPSTAIRS AND CHANGE.
IT'S DULL, HAVING TO BECOME CHANCE FOR SUCH A SHORT TIME. BUT IT CAN'T BE HELPED.
MY GOD YOU'RE...THAT MAN. CHRISTOPHER... CHRISTOPHER SOMETHING.
U
MID-WEST
CHRISTOPHER SOMETHING.
THAT'S ME.

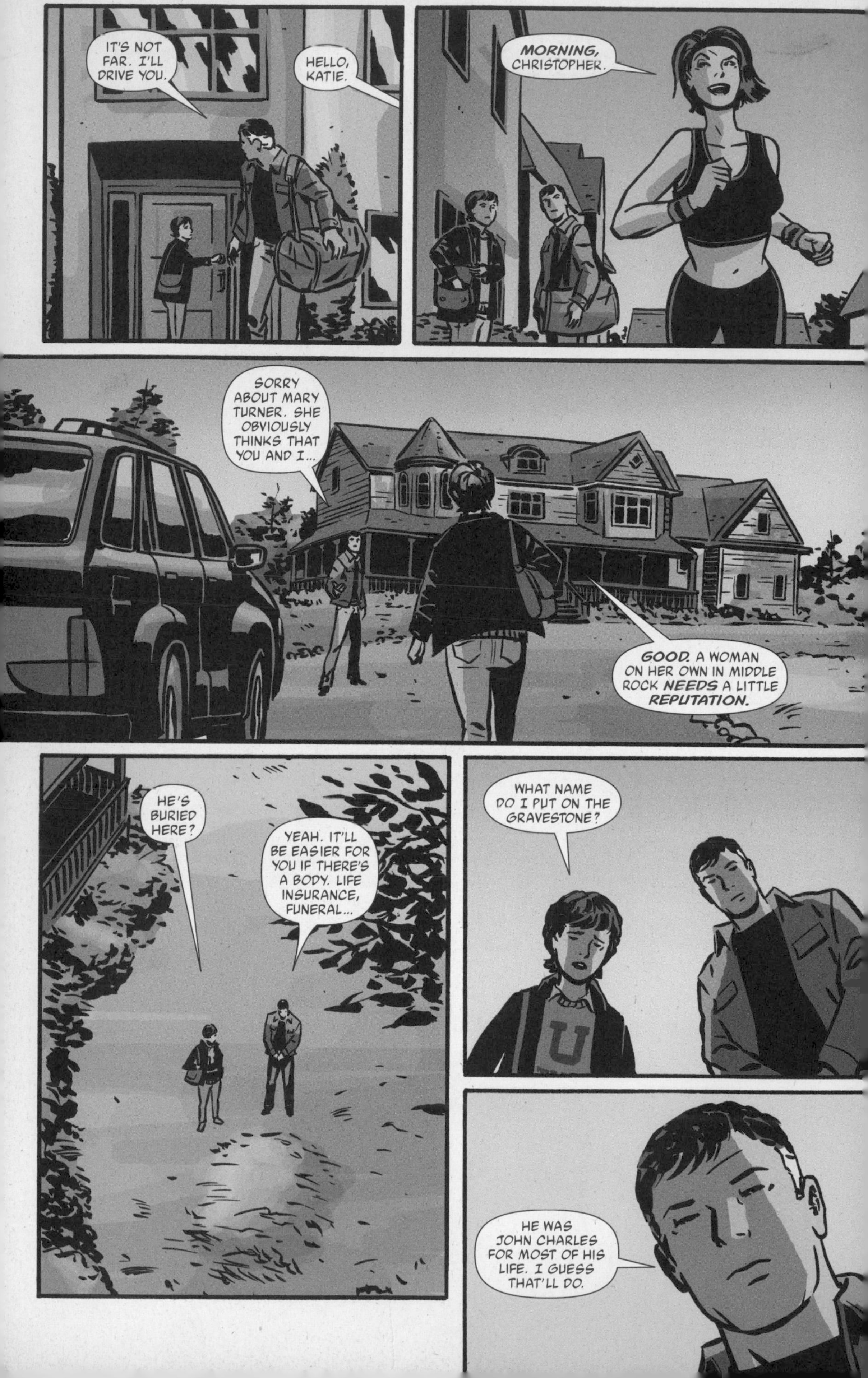
IT'S NOT FAR. I'LL DRIVE YOU.
HELLO, KATIE.
MORNING, CHRISTOPHER.
SORRY ABOUT MARY TURNER. SHE OBVIOUSLY THINKS THAT YOU AND I...
GOOD. A WOMAN ON HER OWN IN MIDDLE ROCK NEEDS A LITTLE REPUTATION.
HE'S BURIED HERE?
YEAH. IT'LL BE EASIER FOR YOU IF THERE'S A BODY. LIFE INSURANCE, FUNERAL...
WHAT NAME DO I PUT ON THE GRAVESTONE?
HE WAS JOHN CHARLES FOR MOST OF HIS LIFE. I GUESS THAT'LL DO.

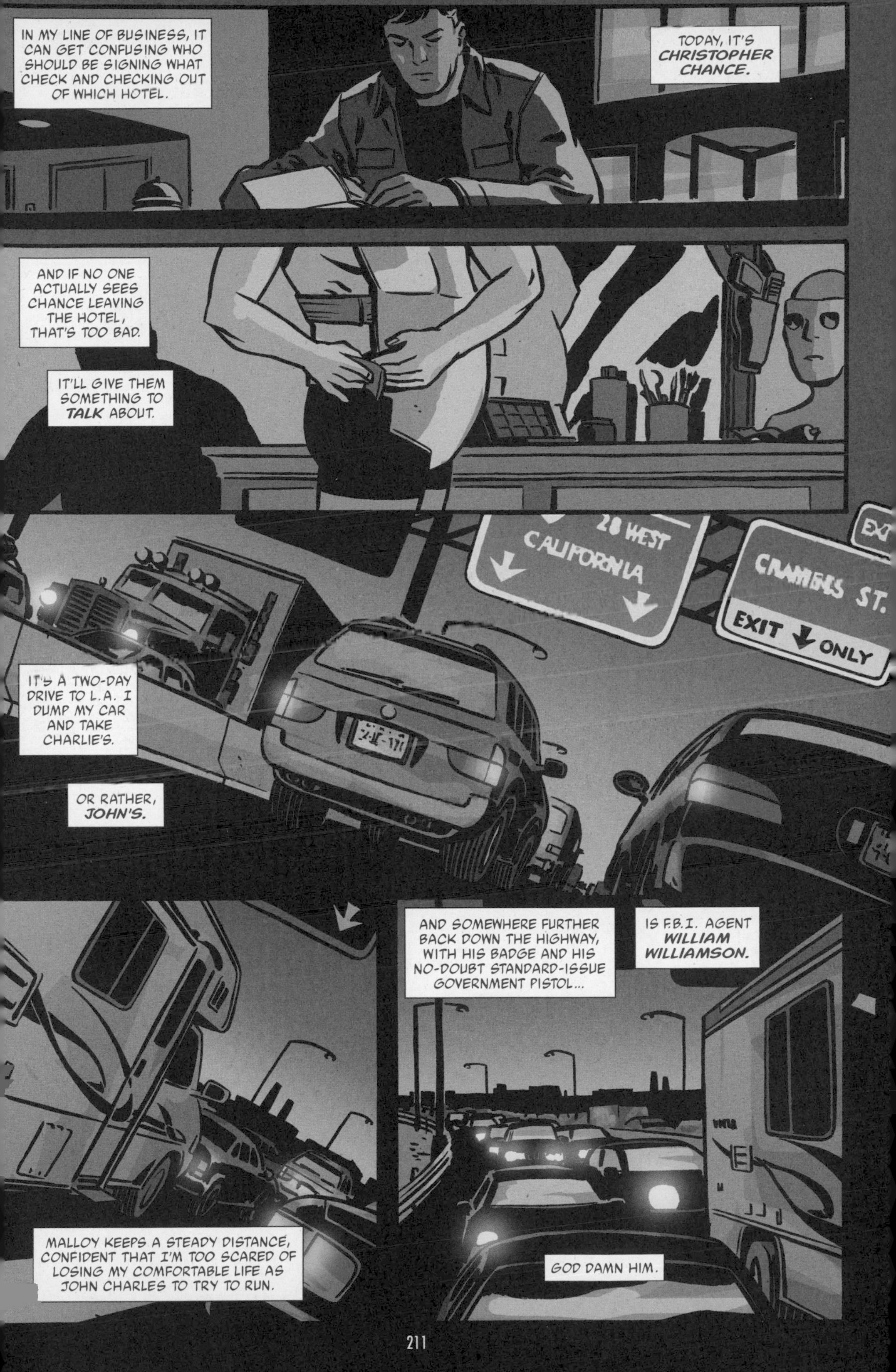
IN MY LINE OF BUSINESS, IT CAN GET CONFUSING WHO SHOULD BE SIGNING WHAT CHECK AND CHECKING OUT OF WHICH HOTEL.
TODAY, IT'S CHRISTOPHER CHANCE.
AND IF NO ONE ACTUALLY SEES CHANCE LEAVING THE HOTEL, THAT'S TOO BAD.
IT'LL GIVE THEM SOMETHING TO TALK ABOUT.
28 WEST
CALIFORNIA
CRAMBES ST.
EXIT ONLY
IT'S A TWO-DAY DRIVE TO L.A. I DUMP MY CAR AND TAKE CHARLIE'S.
OR RATHER, JOHN'S.
MALLOY KEEPS A STEADY DISTANCE, CONFIDENT THAT I'M TOO SCARED OF LOSING MY COMFORTABLE LIFE AS JOHN CHARLES TO TRY TO RUN.
AND SOMEWHERE FURTHER BACK DOWN THE HIGHWAY, WITH HIS BADGE AND HIS NO-DOUBT STANDARD-ISSUE GOVERNMENT PISTOL...
IS F.B.I. AGENT WILLIAM WILLIAMSON.
GOD DAMN HIM.

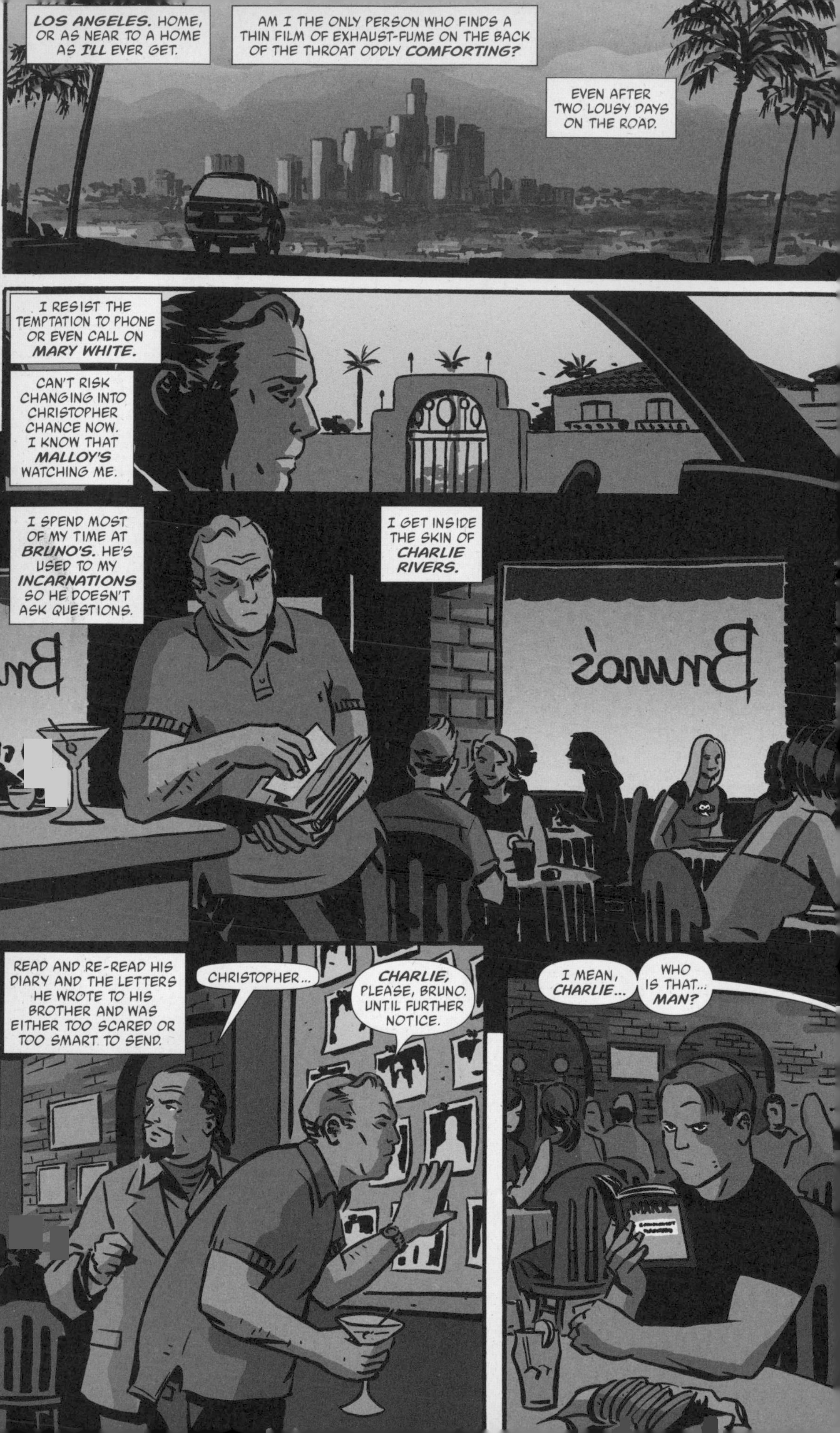

LOS ANGELES. HOME, OR AS NEAR TO A HOME AS I'LL EVER GET.
AM I THE ONLY PERSON WHO FINDS A THIN FILM OF EXHAUST-FUME ON THE BACK OF THE THROAT ODDLY COMFORTING?
EVEN AFTER TWO LOUSY DAYS ON THE ROAD.
I RESIST THE TEMPTATION TO PHONE OR EVEN CALL ON MARY WHITE.
CAN'T RISK CHANGING INTO CHRISTOPHER CHANCE NOW. I KNOW THAT MALLOY'S WATCHING ME.
I SPEND MOST OF MY TIME AT BRUNO'S. HE'S USED TO MY INCARNATIONS SO HE DOESN'T ASK QUESTIONS.
I GET INSIDE THE SKIN OF CHARLIE RIVERS.
READ AND RE-READ HIS DIARY AND THE LETTERS HE WROTE TO HIS BROTHER AND WAS EITHER TOO SCARED OR TOO SMART TO SEND.
CHRISTOPHER...
CHARLIE, PLEASE, BRUNO. UNTIL FURTHER NOTICE.
I MEAN, CHARLIE...
WHO IS THAT... MAN?

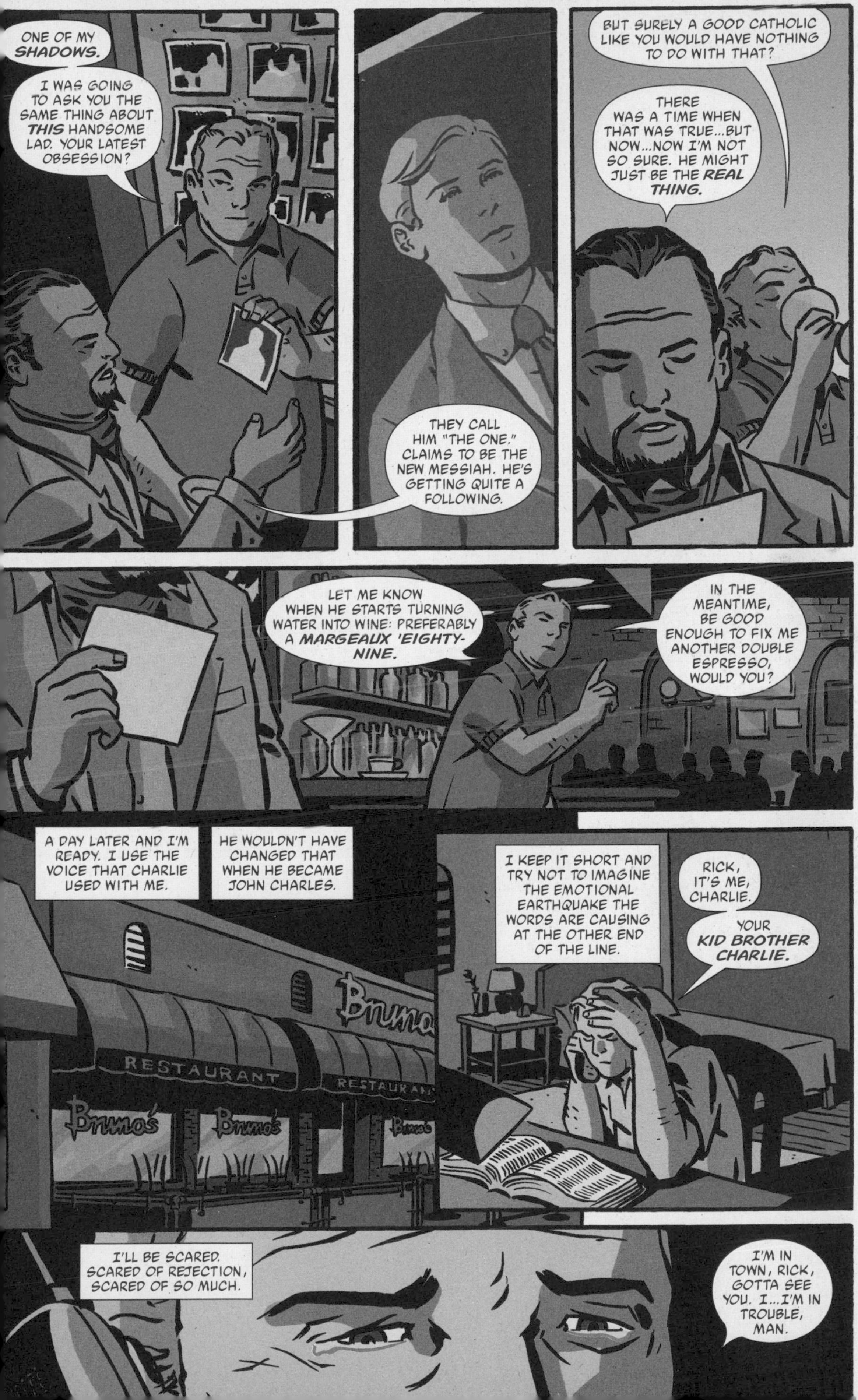
ONE OF MY SHADOWS.
I WAS GOING TO ASK YOU THE SAME THING ABOUT THIS HANDSOME LAD. YOUR LATEST OBSESSION?
THEY CALL HIM "THE ONE." CLAIMS TO BE THE NEW MESSIAH. HE'S GETTING QUITE A FOLLOWING.
BUT SURELY A GOOD CATHOLIC LIKE YOU WOULD HAVE NOTHING TO DO WITH THAT?
THERE WAS A TIME WHEN THAT WAS TRUE...BUT NOW...NOW I'M NOT SO SURE. HE MIGHT JUST BE THE REAL THING.
LET ME KNOW WHEN HE STARTS TURNING WATER INTO WINE: PREFERABLY A MARGEAUX 'EIGHTY-NINE.
IN THE MEANTIME, BE GOOD ENOUGH TO FIX ME ANOTHER DOUBLE ESPRESSO, WOULD YOU?
A DAY LATER AND I'M READY. I USE THE VOICE THAT CHARLIE USED WITH ME.
HE WOULDN'T HAVE CHANGED THAT WHEN HE BECAME JOHN CHARLES.
Bruno's
RESTAURANT
RESTAURANT
Bruno's
Bruno's
Bruno's
I KEEP IT SHORT AND TRY NOT TO IMAGINE THE EMOTIONAL EARTHQUAKE THE WORDS ARE CAUSING AT THE OTHER END OF THE LINE.
RICK, IT'S ME, CHARLIE.
YOUR KID BROTHER CHARLIE.
I'LL BE SCARED. SCARED OF REJECTION, SCARED OF SO MUCH.
I'M IN TOWN, RICK, GOTTA SEE YOU. I...I'M IN TROUBLE, MAN.

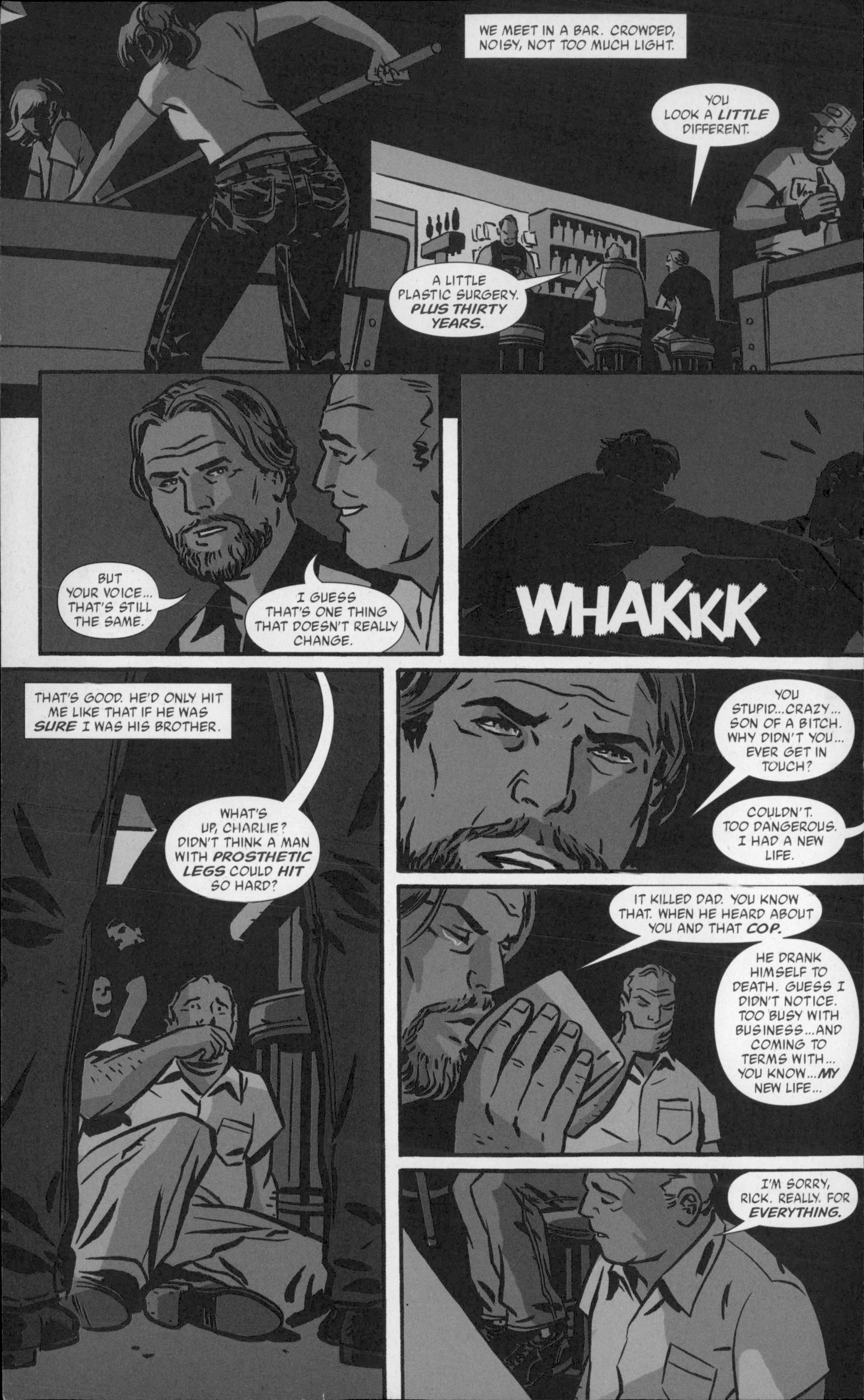
WE MEET IN A BAR. CROWDED, NOISY, NOT TOO MUCH LIGHT.
YOU LOOK A LITTLE DIFFERENT.
A LITTLE PLASTIC SURGERY. PLUS THIRTY YEARS.
BUT YOUR VOICE... THAT'S STILL THE SAME.
I GUESS THAT'S ONE THING THAT DOESN'T REALLY CHANGE.
WHAKKK
THAT'S GOOD. HE'D ONLY HIT ME LIKE THAT IF HE WAS SURE I WAS HIS BROTHER.
WHAT'S UP, CHARLIE? DIDN'T THINK A MAN WITH PROSTHETIC LEGS COULD HIT SO HARD?
YOU STUPID...CRAZY... SON OF A BITCH. WHY DIDN'T YOU... EVER GET IN TOUCH?
COULDN'T. TOO DANGEROUS. I HAD A NEW LIFE.
IT KILLED DAD. YOU KNOW THAT. WHEN HE HEARD ABOUT YOU AND THAT COP.
HE DRANK HIMSELF TO DEATH. GUESS I DIDN'T NOTICE. TOO BUSY WITH BUSINESS...AND COMING TO TERMS WITH... YOU KNOW...MY NEW LIFE...
I'M SORRY, RICK. REALLY. FOR EVERYTHING.

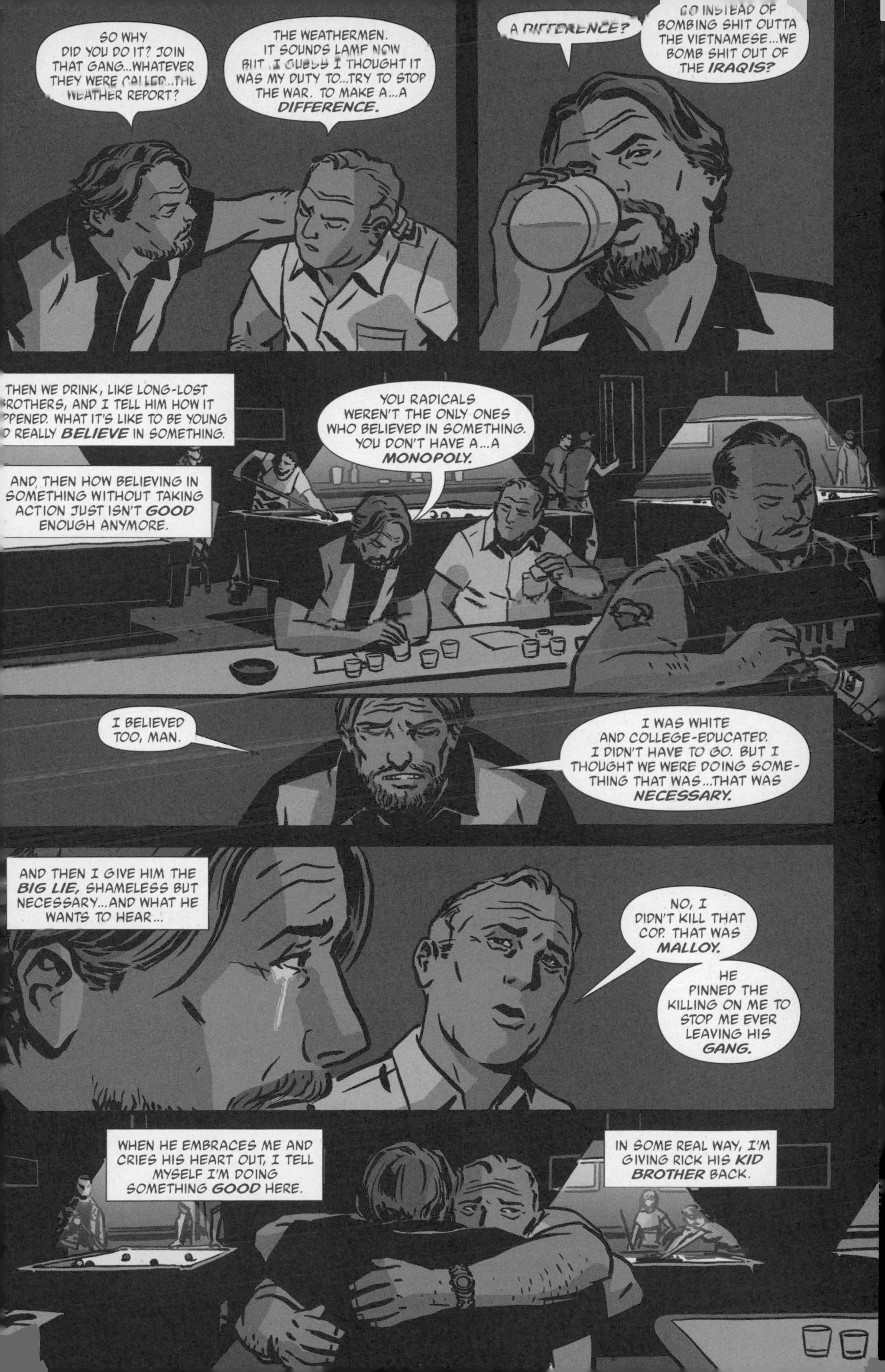
SO WHY DID YOU DO IT? JOIN THAT GANG...WHATEVER THEY WERE CALLED...THE WEATHER REPORT?
THE WEATHERMEN. IT SOUNDS LAME NOW BUT I GUESS I THOUGHT IT WAS MY DUTY TO...TRY TO STOP THE WAR. TO MAKE A...A *DIFFERENCE.*
A *DIFFERENCE?*
SO INSTEAD OF BOMBING SHIT OUTTA THE VIETNAMESE...WE BOMB SHIT OUT OF THE *IRAQIS?*
THEN WE DRINK, LIKE LONG-LOST ROTHERS, AND I TELL HIM HOW IT PPENED. WHAT IT'S LIKE TO BE YOUNG D REALLY *BELIEVE* IN SOMETHING.
AND, THEN HOW BELIEVING IN SOMETHING WITHOUT TAKING ACTION JUST ISN'T *GOOD* ENOUGH ANYMORE.
YOU RADICALS WEREN'T THE ONLY ONES WHO BELIEVED IN SOMETHING. YOU DON'T HAVE A...A *MONOPOLY.*
I BELIEVED TOO, MAN.
I WAS WHITE AND COLLEGE-EDUCATED. I DIDN'T HAVE TO GO. BUT I THOUGHT WE WERE DOING SOMETHING THAT WAS...THAT WAS *NECESSARY.*
AND THEN I GIVE HIM THE *BIG LIE,* SHAMELESS BUT NECESSARY...AND WHAT HE WANTS TO HEAR...
NO, I DIDN'T KILL THAT COP. THAT WAS *MALLOY.*
HE PINNED THE KILLING ON ME TO STOP ME EVER LEAVING HIS *GANG.*
WHEN HE EMBRACES ME AND CRIES HIS HEART OUT, I TELL MYSELF I'M DOING SOMETHING *GOOD* HERE.
IN SOME REAL WAY, I'M GIVING RICK HIS *KID BROTHER* BACK.

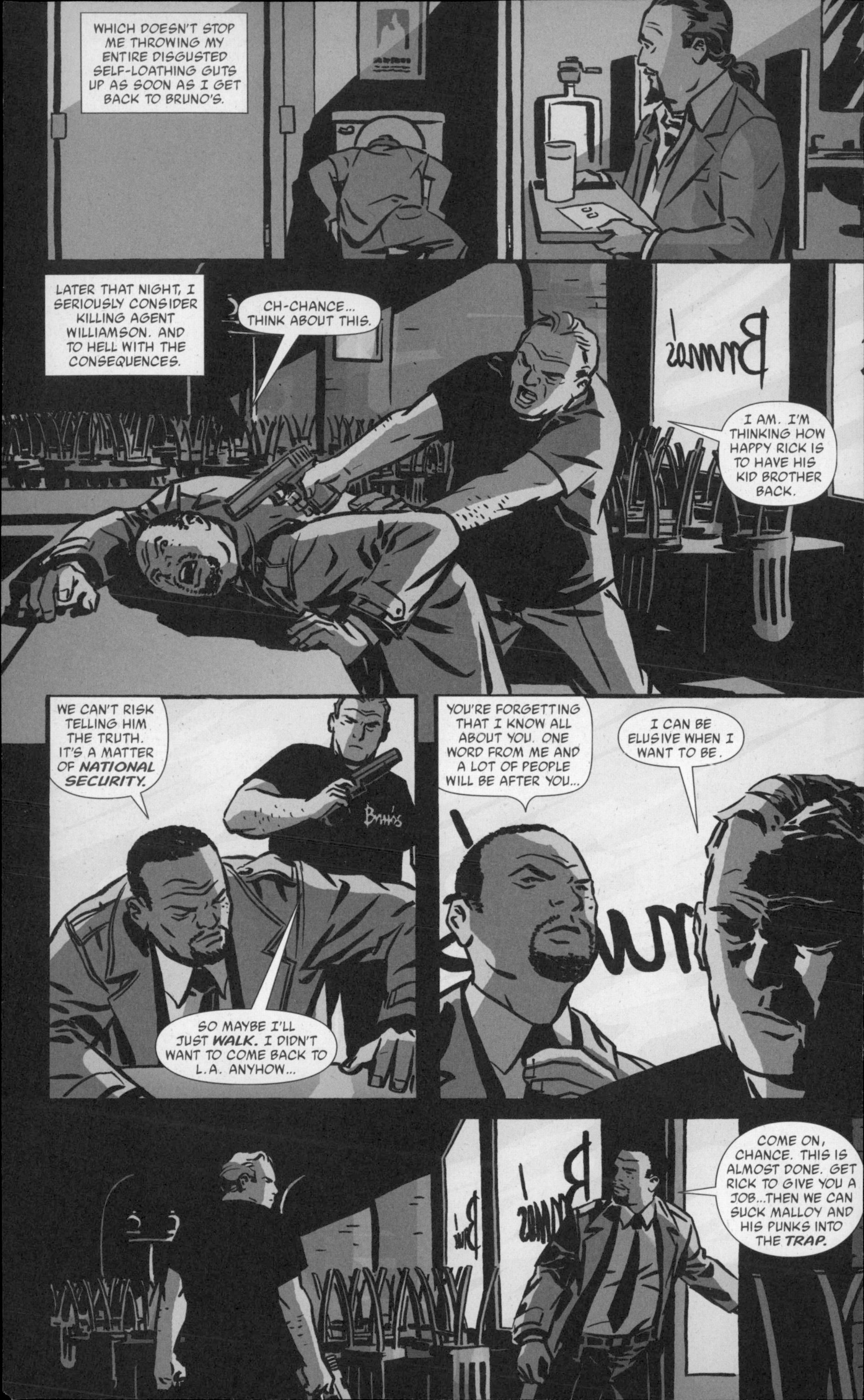
WHICH DOESN'T STOP ME THROWING MY ENTIRE DISGUSTED SELF-LOATHING GUTS UP AS SOON AS I GET BACK TO BRUNO'S.
LATER THAT NIGHT, I SERIOUSLY CONSIDER KILLING AGENT WILLIAMSON. AND TO HELL WITH THE CONSEQUENCES.
CH-CHANCE... THINK ABOUT THIS.
I AM. I'M THINKING HOW HAPPY RICK IS TO HAVE HIS KID BROTHER BACK.
WE CAN'T RISK TELLING HIM THE TRUTH. IT'S A MATTER OF NATIONAL SECURITY.
SO MAYBE I'LL JUST WALK. I DIDN'T WANT TO COME BACK TO L.A. ANYHOW...
YOU'RE FORGETTING THAT I KNOW ALL ABOUT YOU. ONE WORD FROM ME AND A LOT OF PEOPLE WILL BE AFTER YOU...
I CAN BE ELUSIVE WHEN I WANT TO BE.
COME ON, CHANCE. THIS IS ALMOST DONE. GET RICK TO GIVE YOU A JOB...THEN WE CAN SUCK MALLOY AND HIS PUNKS INTO THE TRAP.

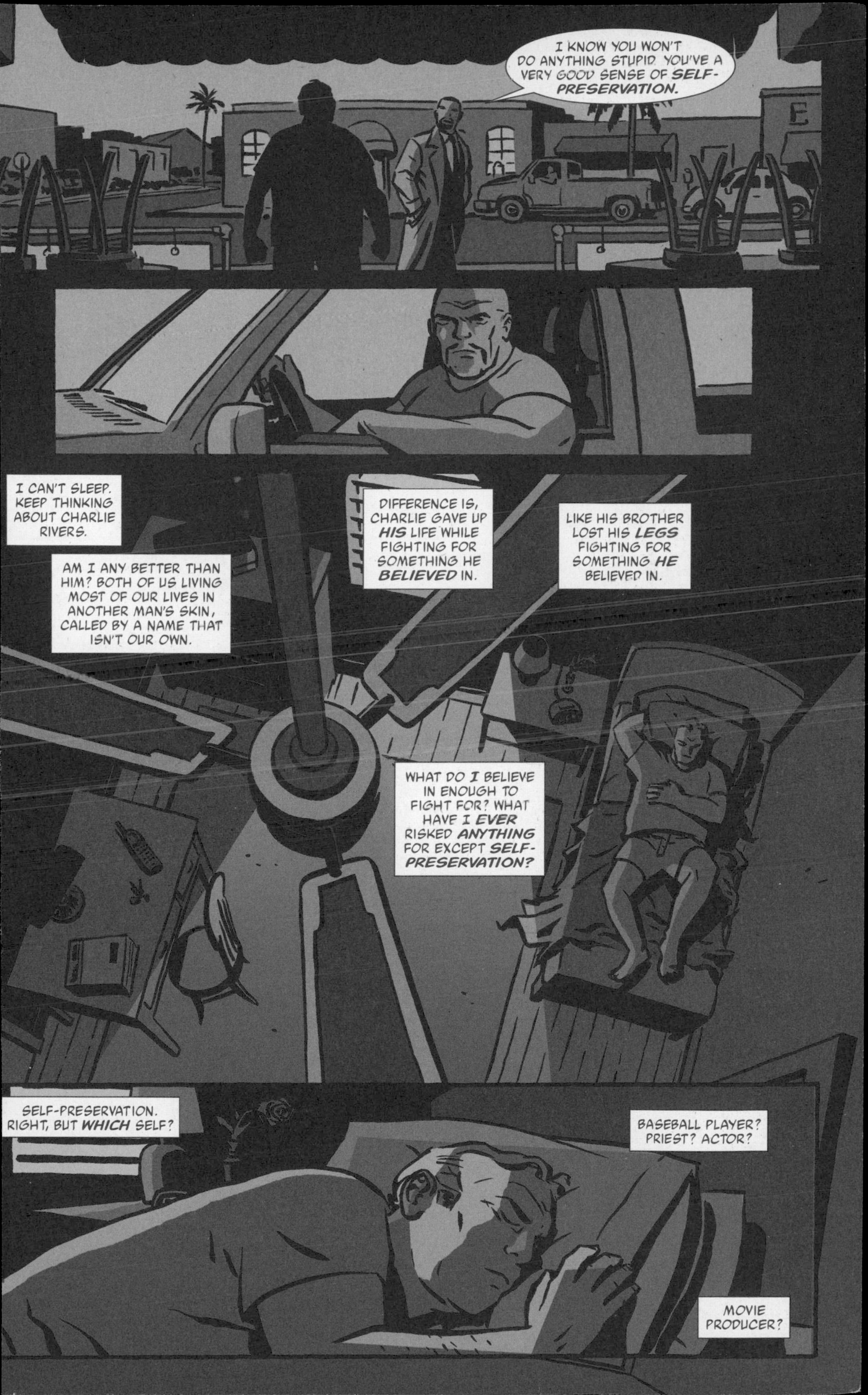
I KNOW YOU WON'T DO ANYTHING STUPID. YOU'VE A VERY GOOD SENSE OF SELF-PRESERVATION.
I CAN'T SLEEP. KEEP THINKING ABOUT CHARLIE RIVERS.
AM I ANY BETTER THAN HIM? BOTH OF US LIVING MOST OF OUR LIVES IN ANOTHER MAN'S SKIN, CALLED BY A NAME THAT ISN'T OUR OWN.
DIFFERENCE IS, CHARLIE GAVE UP HIS LIFE WHILE FIGHTING FOR SOMETHING HE BELIEVED IN.
LIKE HIS BROTHER LOST HIS LEGS FIGHTING FOR SOMETHING HE BELIEVED IN.
WHAT DO I BELIEVE IN ENOUGH TO FIGHT FOR? WHAT HAVE I EVER RISKED ANYTHING FOR EXCEPT SELF-PRESERVATION?
SELF-PRESERVATION. RIGHT, BUT WHICH SELF?
BASEBALL PLAYER? PRIEST? ACTOR?
MOVIE PRODUCER?

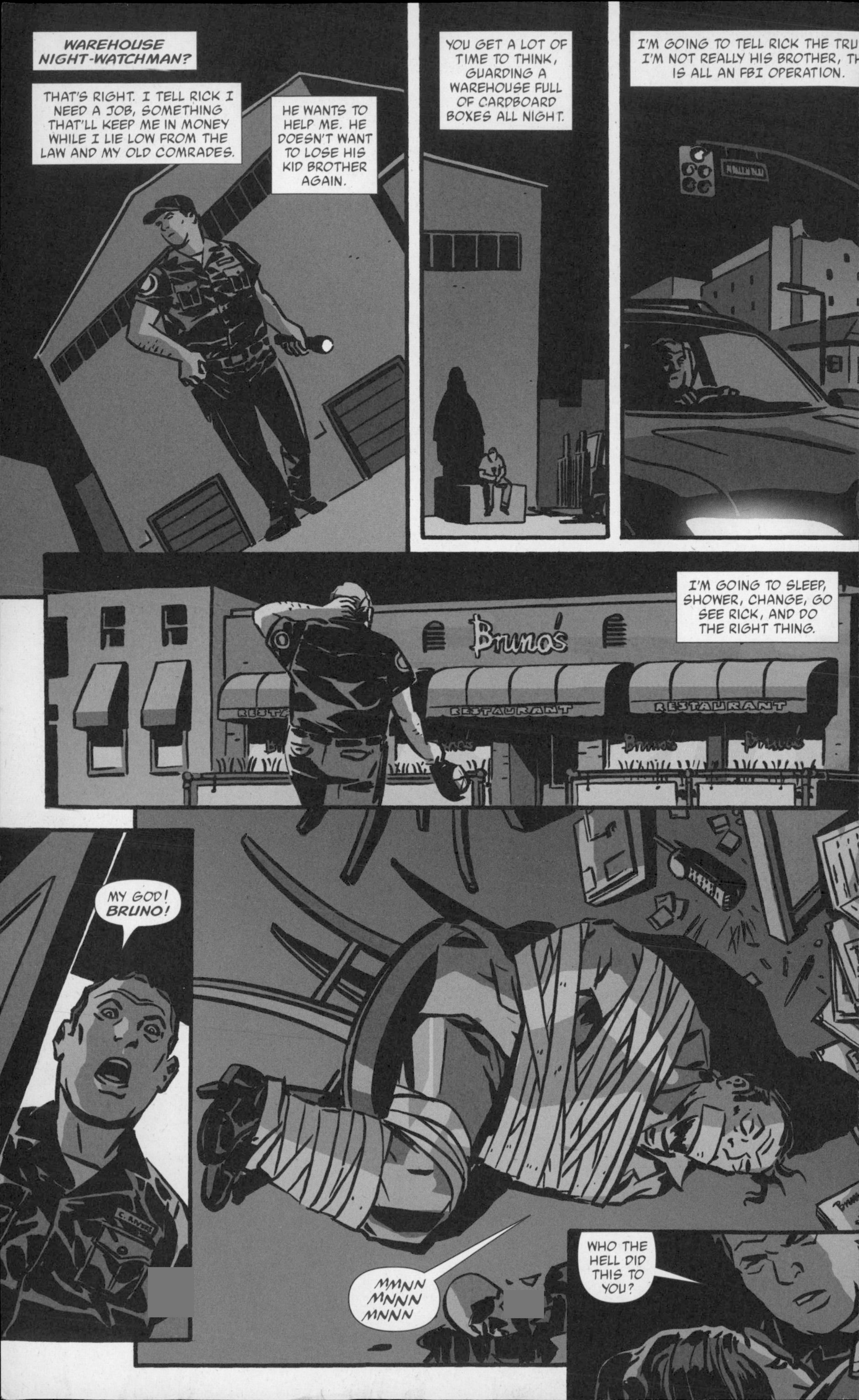
WAREHOUSE NIGHT-WATCHMAN?
THAT'S RIGHT. I TELL RICK I NEED A JOB, SOMETHING THAT'LL KEEP ME IN MONEY WHILE I LIE LOW FROM THE LAW AND MY OLD COMRADES.
HE WANTS TO HELP ME. HE DOESN'T WANT TO LOSE HIS KID BROTHER AGAIN.
YOU GET A LOT OF TIME TO THINK, GUARDING A WAREHOUSE FULL OF CARDBOARD BOXES ALL NIGHT.
I'M GOING TO TELL RICK THE TRU
I'M NOT REALLY HIS BROTHER, TH
IS ALL AN FBI OPERATION.
I'M GOING TO SLEEP, SHOWER, CHANGE, GO SEE RICK, AND DO THE RIGHT THING.
Bruno's
RESTAURANT
RESTAURANT
MY GOD! BRUNO!
MMNN MNNN MNNN
WHO THE HELL DID THIS TO YOU?

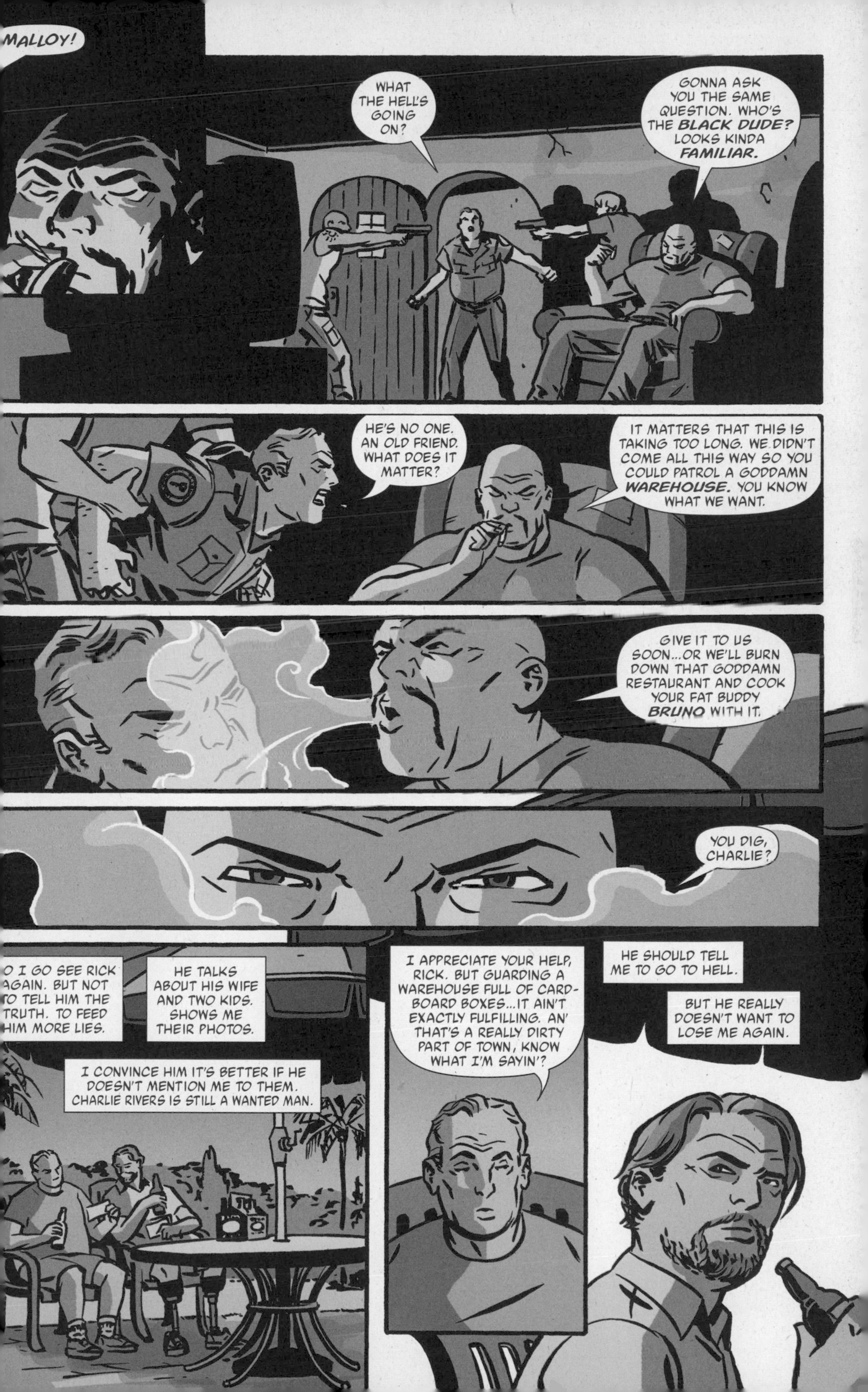
MALLOY!
WHAT THE HELL'S GOING ON?
GONNA ASK YOU THE SAME QUESTION. WHO'S THE BLACK DUDE? LOOKS KINDA FAMILIAR.
HE'S NO ONE. AN OLD FRIEND. WHAT DOES IT MATTER?
IT MATTERS THAT THIS IS TAKING TOO LONG. WE DIDN'T COME ALL THIS WAY SO YOU COULD PATROL A GODDAMN WAREHOUSE. YOU KNOW WHAT WE WANT.
GIVE IT TO US SOON...OR WE'LL BURN DOWN THAT GODDAMN RESTAURANT AND COOK YOUR FAT BUDDY BRUNO WITH IT.
YOU DIG, CHARLIE?
O I GO SEE RICK AGAIN. BUT NOT TO TELL HIM THE TRUTH. TO FEED HIM MORE LIES.
HE TALKS ABOUT HIS WIFE AND TWO KIDS. SHOWS ME THEIR PHOTOS.
I CONVINCE HIM IT'S BETTER IF HE DOESN'T MENTION ME TO THEM. CHARLIE RIVERS IS STILL A WANTED MAN.
I APPRECIATE YOUR HELP, RICK. BUT GUARDING A WAREHOUSE FULL OF CARDBOARD BOXES...IT AIN'T EXACTLY FULFILLING. AN' THAT'S A REALLY DIRTY PART OF TOWN, KNOW WHAT I'M SAYIN'?
HE SHOULD TELL ME TO GO TO HELL.
BUT HE REALLY DOESN'T WANT TO LOSE ME AGAIN.

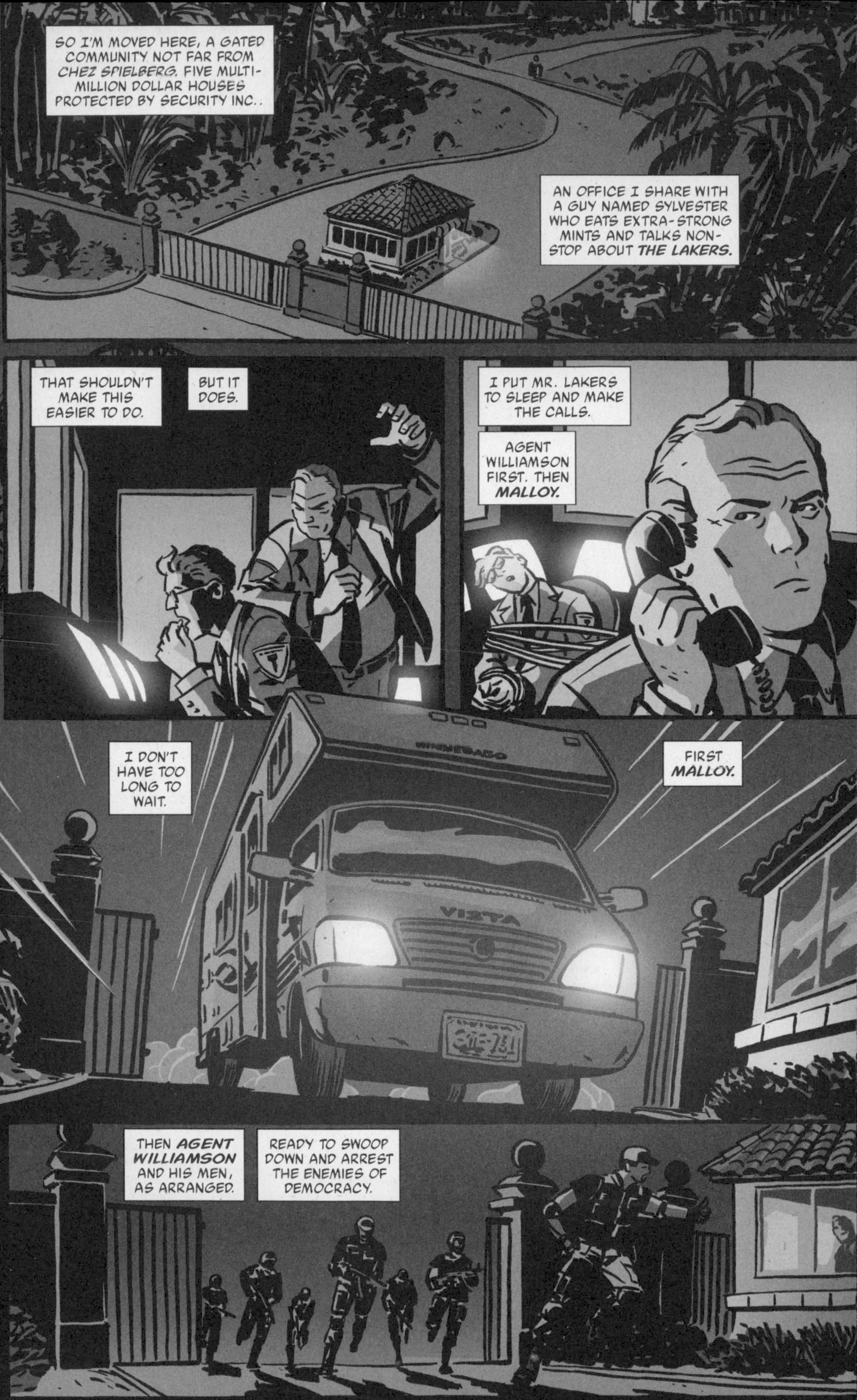
SO I'M MOVED HERE, A GATED COMMUNITY NOT FAR FROM CHEZ SPIELBERG, FIVE MULTI-MILLION DOLLAR HOUSES PROTECTED BY SECURITY INC..
AN OFFICE I SHARE WITH A GUY NAMED SYLVESTER WHO EATS EXTRA-STRONG MINTS AND TALKS NON-STOP ABOUT *THE LAKERS.*
THAT SHOULDN'T MAKE THIS EASIER TO DO.
BUT IT DOES.
I PUT MR. LAKERS TO SLEEP AND MAKE THE CALLS.
AGENT WILLIAMSON FIRST. THEN *MALLOY.*
I DON'T HAVE TOO LONG TO WAIT.
FIRST *MALLOY.*
VISTA
THEN *AGENT WILLIAMSON* AND HIS MEN, AS ARRANGED.
READY TO SWOOP DOWN AND ARREST THE ENEMIES OF DEMOCRACY.

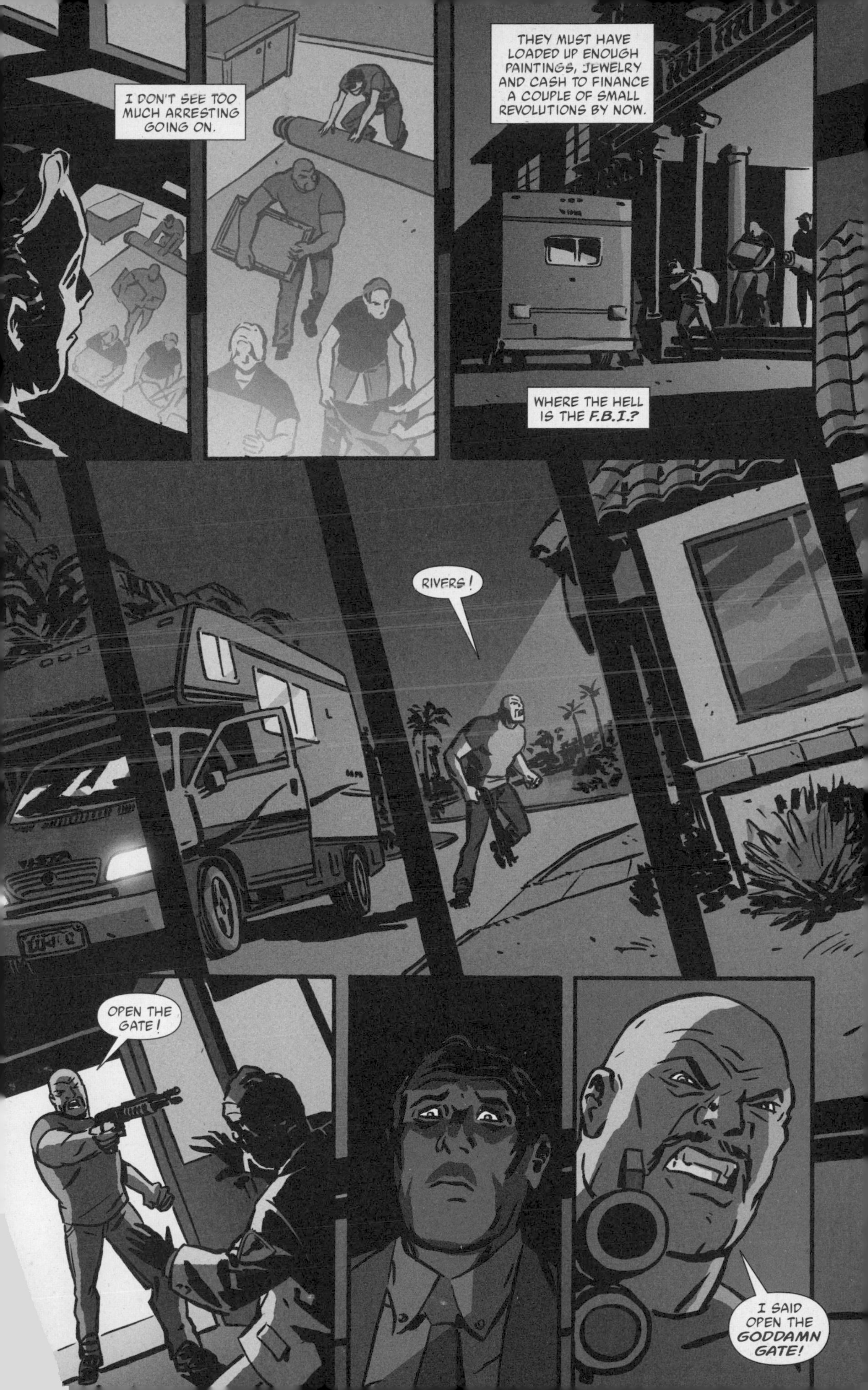
I DON'T SEE TOO MUCH ARRESTING GOING ON.
THEY MUST HAVE LOADED UP ENOUGH PAINTINGS, JEWELRY AND CASH TO FINANCE A COUPLE OF SMALL REVOLUTIONS BY NOW.
WHERE THE HELL IS THE *F.B.I.?*
RIVERS!
OPEN THE GATE!
I SAID OPEN THE ***GODDAMN GATE!***

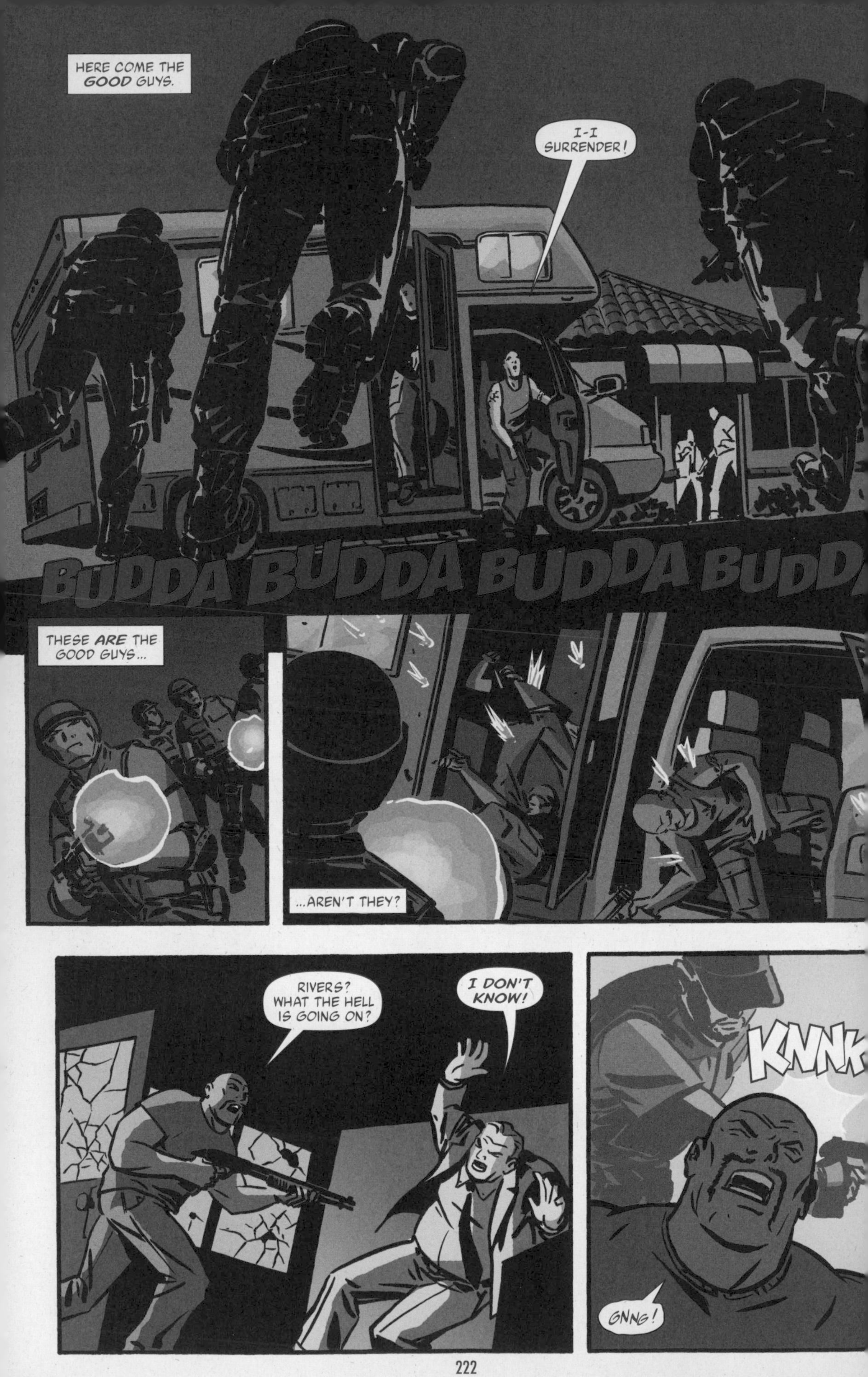
HERE COME THE GOOD GUYS.
I-I SURRENDER!
BUDDA BUDDA BUDDA BUDD
THESE ARE THE GOOD GUYS...
...AREN'T THEY?
RIVERS? WHAT THE HELL IS GOING ON?
I DON'T KNOW!
KNNK
GNNG!

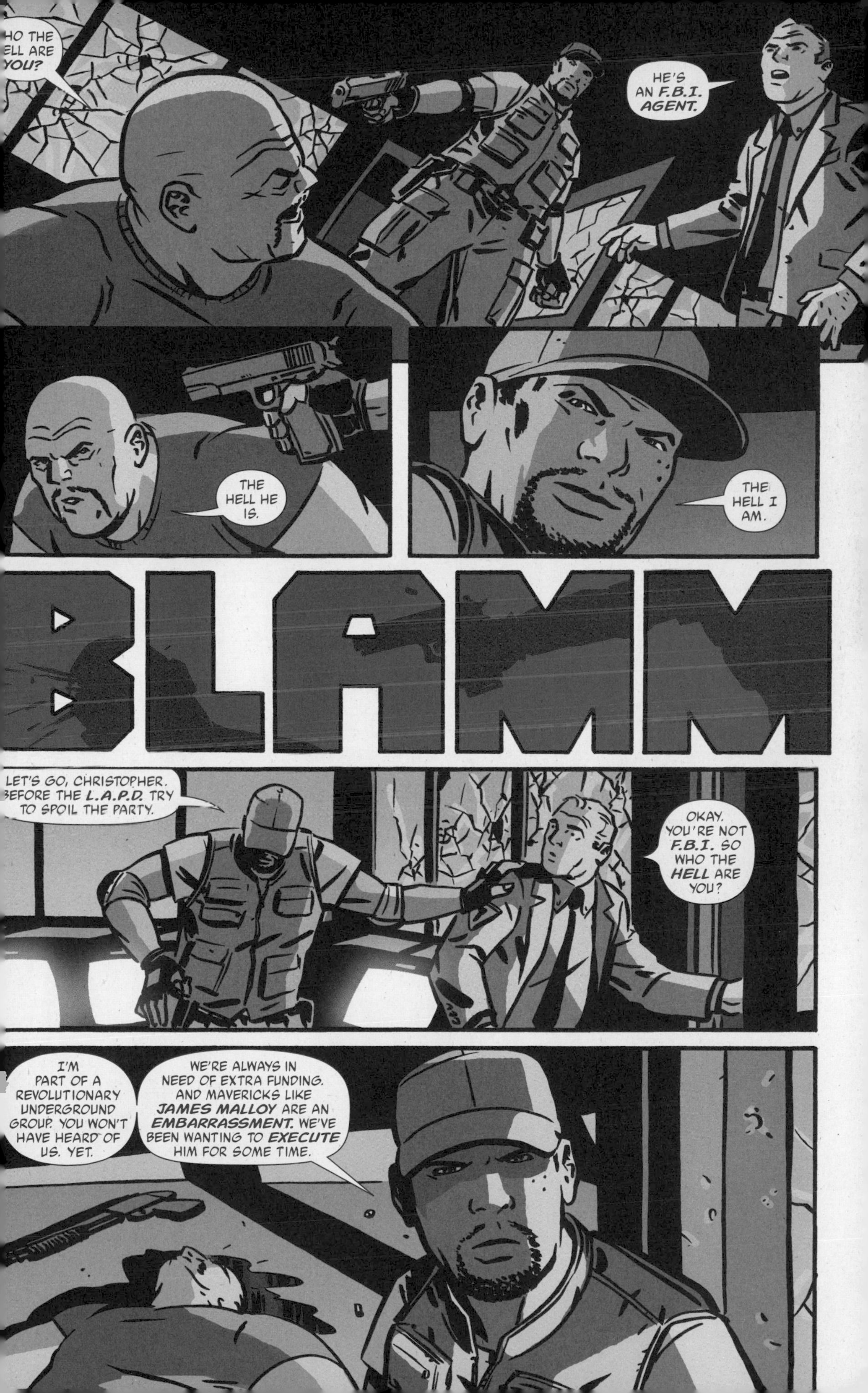
HO THE
ELL ARE
YOU?
HE'S AN F.B.I. AGENT.
THE HELL HE IS.
THE HELL I AM.
BLAMM
LET'S GO, CHRISTOPHER. BEFORE THE L.A.P.D. TRY TO SPOIL THE PARTY.
OKAY. YOU'RE NOT F.B.I. SO WHO THE HELL ARE YOU?
I'M PART OF A REVOLUTIONARY UNDERGROUND GROUP. YOU WON'T HAVE HEARD OF US. YET.
WE'RE ALWAYS IN NEED OF EXTRA FUNDING. AND MAVERICKS LIKE JAMES MALLOY ARE AN EMBARRASSMENT. WE'VE BEEN WANTING TO EXECUTE HIM FOR SOME TIME.

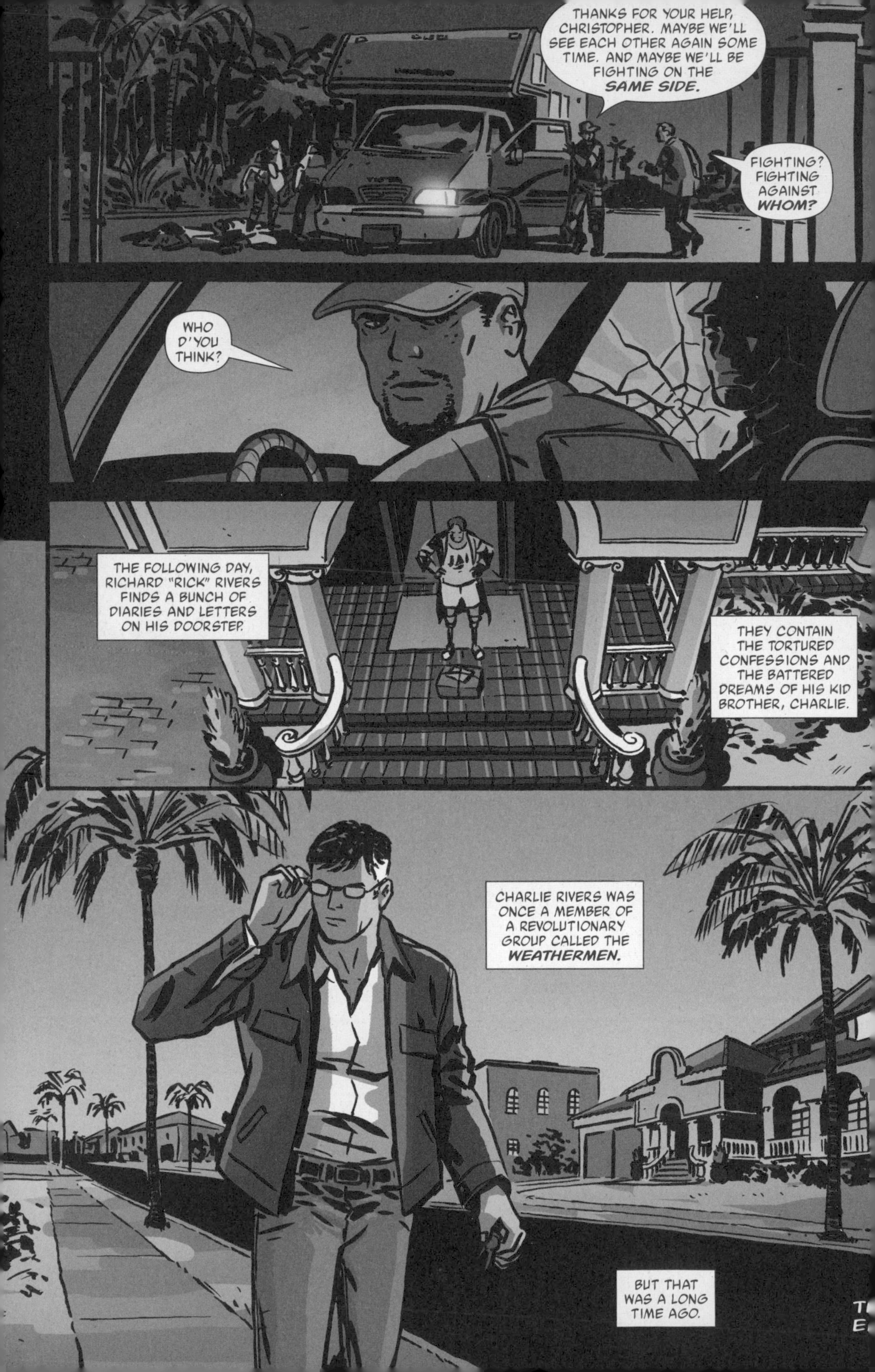
THANKS FOR YOUR HELP, CHRISTOPHER. MAYBE WE'LL SEE EACH OTHER AGAIN SOME TIME. AND MAYBE WE'LL BE FIGHTING ON THE SAME SIDE.
FIGHTING? FIGHTING AGAINST WHOM?
WHO D'YOU THINK?
THE FOLLOWING DAY, RICHARD "RICK" RIVERS FINDS A BUNCH OF DIARIES AND LETTERS ON HIS DOORSTEP.
THEY CONTAIN THE TORTURED CONFESSIONS AND THE BATTERED DREAMS OF HIS KID BROTHER, CHARLIE.
CHARLIE RIVERS WAS ONCE A MEMBER OF A REVOLUTIONARY GROUP CALLED THE WEATHERMEN.
BUT THAT WAS A LONG TIME AGO.

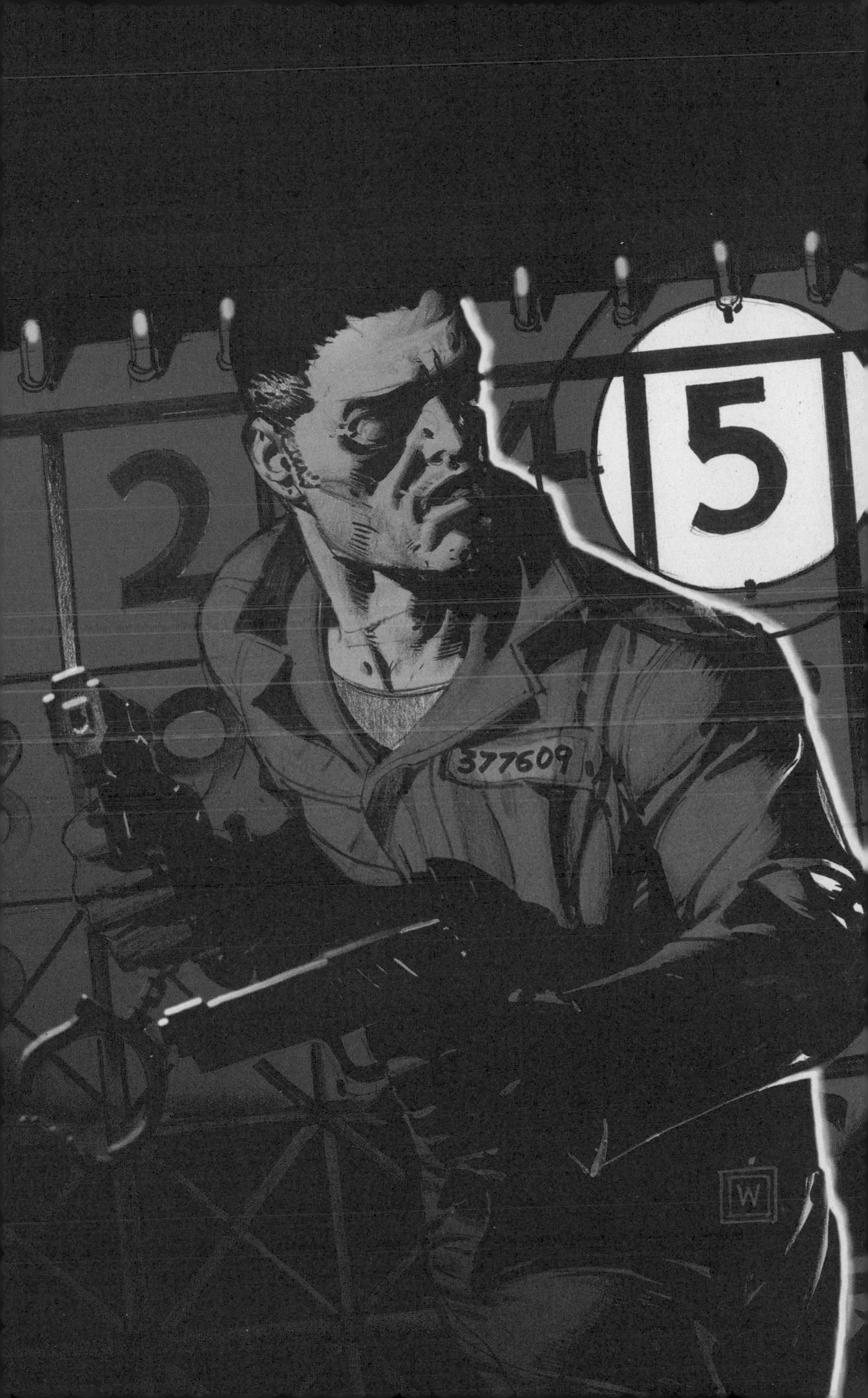
2
5
377609

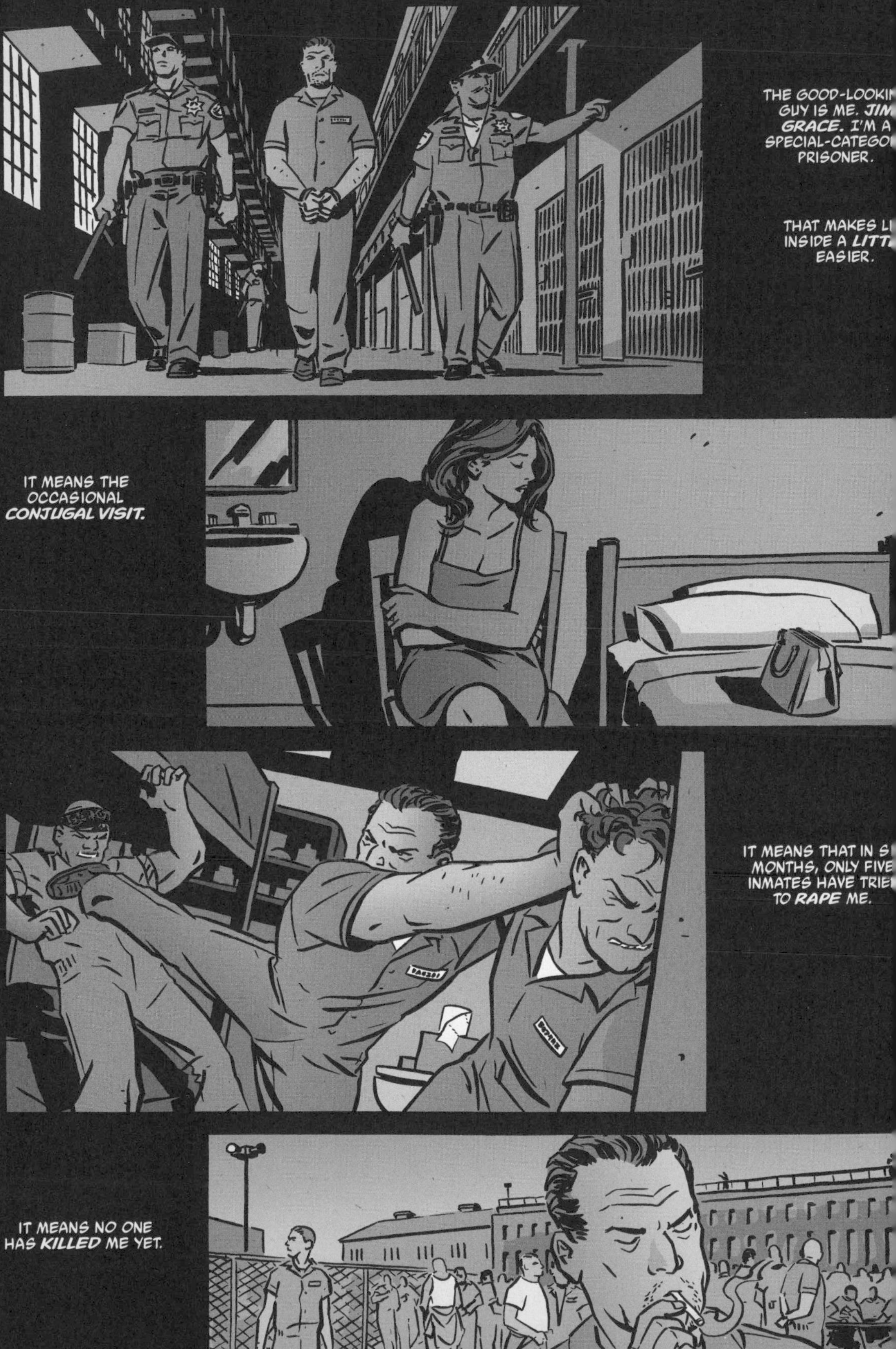
THE GOOD-LOOKI GUY IS ME. JIM GRACE. I'M A SPECIAL-CATEGO PRISONER.
THAT MAKES LI INSIDE A LITT EASIER.
IT MEANS THE OCCASIONAL CONJUGAL VISIT.
IT MEANS THAT IN S MONTHS, ONLY FIVE INMATES HAVE TRIE TO RAPE ME.
IT MEANS NO ONE HAS KILLED ME YET.

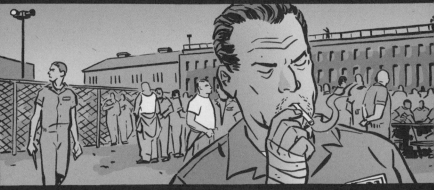

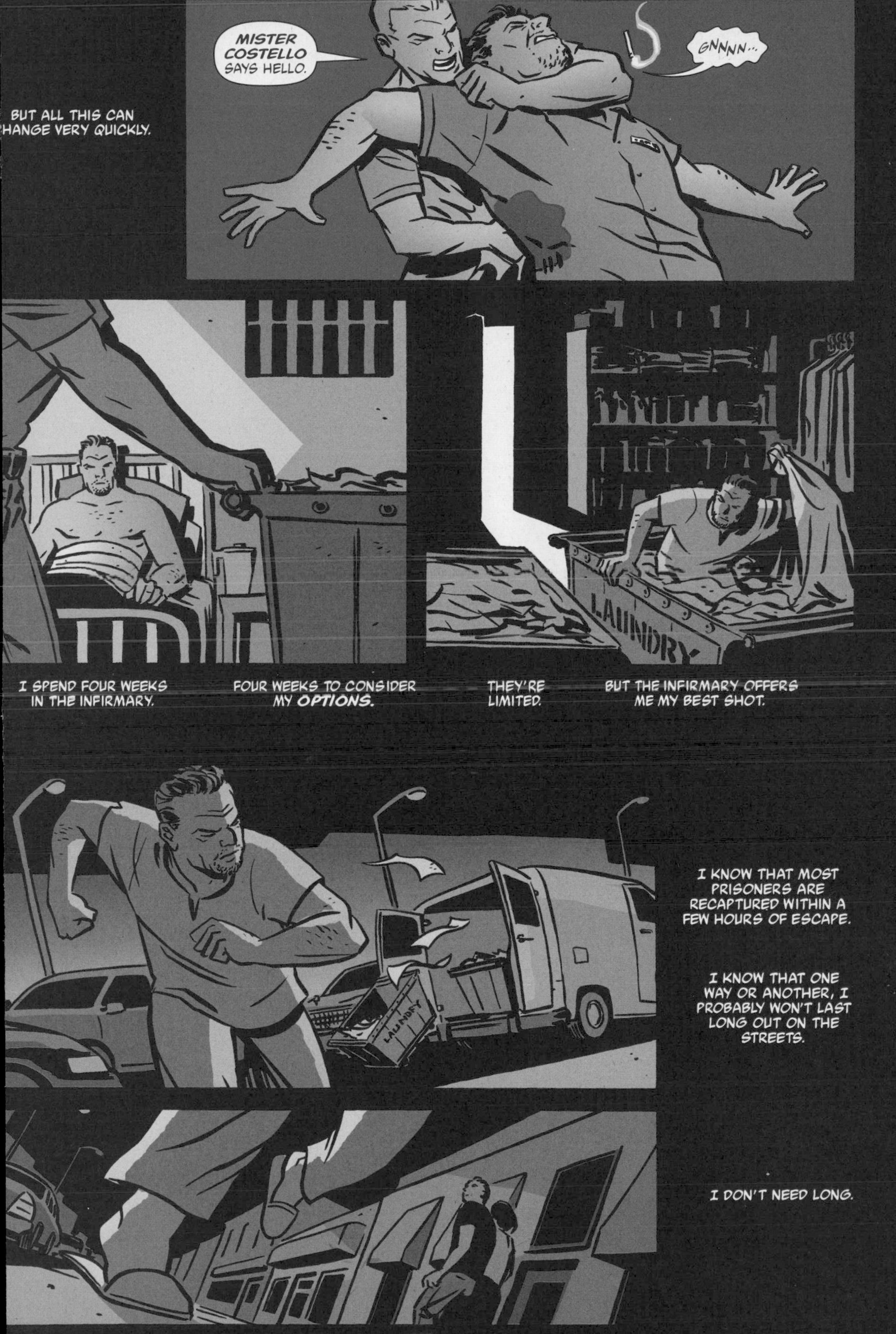
BUT ALL THIS CAN
HANGE VERY QUICKLY.
MISTER COSTELLO SAYS HELLO.
GNNNN...
I SPEND FOUR WEEKS IN THE INFIRMARY.
FOUR WEEKS TO CONSIDER MY OPTIONS.
THEY'RE LIMITED.
BUT THE INFIRMARY OFFERS ME MY BEST SHOT.
LAUNDRY
I KNOW THAT MOST PRISONERS ARE RECAPTURED WITHIN A FEW HOURS OF ESCAPE.
I KNOW THAT ONE WAY OR ANOTHER, I PROBABLY WON'T LAST LONG OUT ON THE STREETS.
I DON'T NEED LONG.

ONE WEEK.

THAT'S ALL I NEED, CHRIS.

THEN I'LL WALK BACK THROUGH THOSE PENITENTIARY GATES WITH A SMILE ON MY FACE.

I DON'T USUALLY DO **PRO BONO** WORK, JIMMY.

IF YOU DON'T WANNA DO THIS FOR **ME**...DO IT FOR **MARIA**.

TWO DAYS WAS ALL WE HAD TOGETHER AS MAN AND WIFE, BEFORE THE COPS DRAGGED ME OFF TO JAIL.

COME ON, CHRIS. **SEVEN DAYS.** DON'T TELL ME YOU CAN'T SPARE AN OLD BUDDY SEVEN LOUSY DAYS.

I'LL GIVE YOU FIVE. TAKE IT OR LEAVE IT.

THE HUMAN TARGET
FIVE DAYS GRACE

PETER MILLIGAN WRITER — CLIFF CHIANG ARTIST — LEE LOUGHRIDGE COLORIST — CLEM ROBINS LETTERER — PORNSAK PICHETSHOTE ASST. EDITOR — KARE BERGI EDITO

THE HUMAN TARGET CREATED BY **LEN WEIN** & **CARMINE INFANTING**

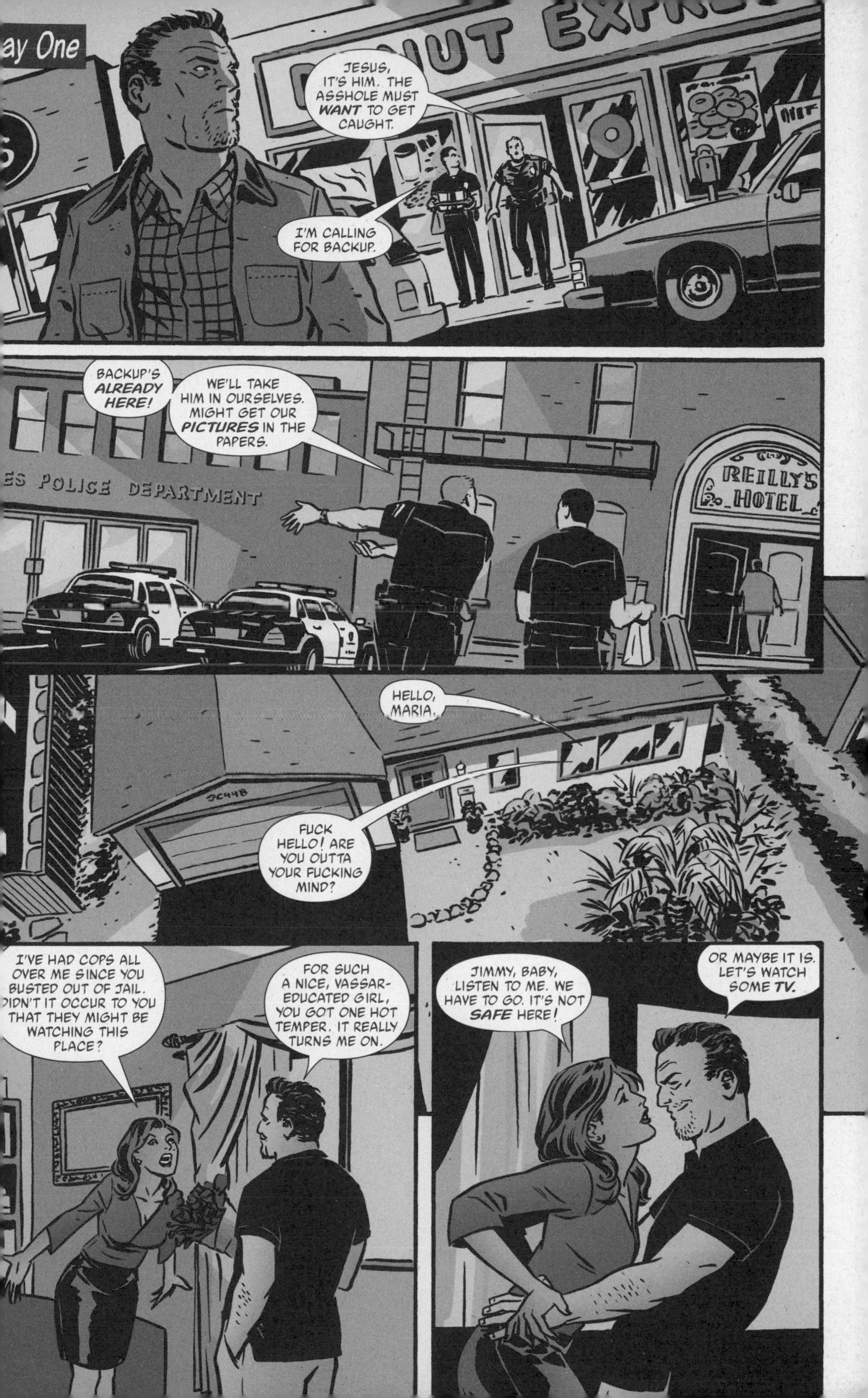
ay One
DONUT EXPR
JESUS, IT'S HIM. THE ASSHOLE MUST WANT TO GET CAUGHT.
I'M CALLING FOR BACKUP.
BACKUP'S ALREADY HERE!
WE'LL TAKE HIM IN OURSELVES. MIGHT GET OUR PICTURES IN THE PAPERS.
ES POLICE DEPARTMENT
REILLY'S HOTEL
HELLO, MARIA.
FUCK HELLO! ARE YOU OUTTA YOUR FUCKING MIND?
I'VE HAD COPS ALL OVER ME SINCE YOU BUSTED OUT OF JAIL. DIDN'T IT OCCUR TO YOU THAT THEY MIGHT BE WATCHING THIS PLACE?
FOR SUCH A NICE, VASSAR-EDUCATED GIRL, YOU GOT ONE HOT TEMPER. IT REALLY TURNS ME ON.
JIMMY, BABY, LISTEN TO ME. WE HAVE TO GO. IT'S NOT SAFE HERE!
OR MAYBE IT IS. LET'S WATCH SOME TV.

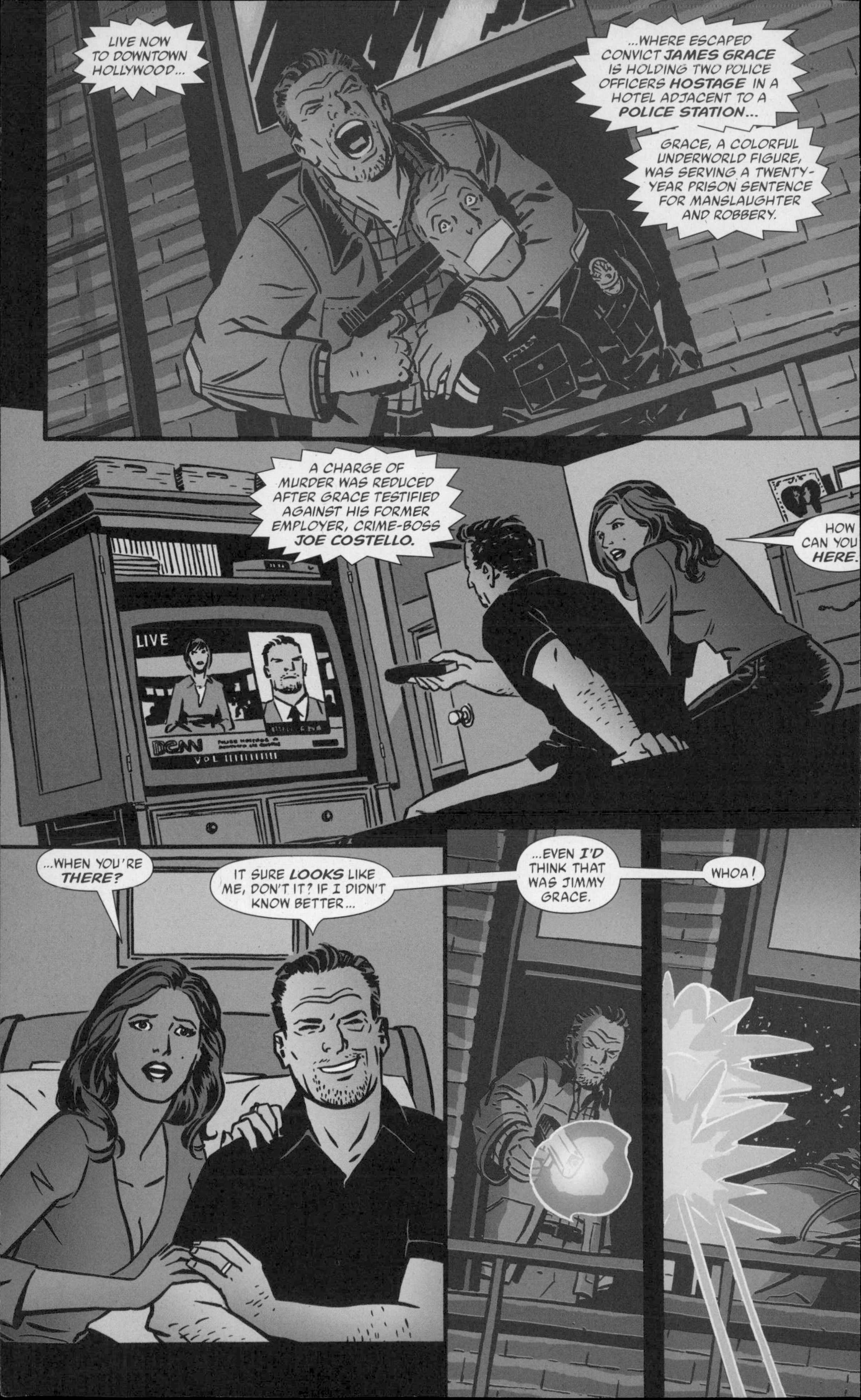
LIVE NOW TO DOWNTOWN HOLLYWOOD...
...WHERE ESCAPED CONVICT JAMES GRACE IS HOLDING TWO POLICE OFFICERS HOSTAGE IN A HOTEL ADJACENT TO A POLICE STATION...
GRACE, A COLORFUL UNDERWORLD FIGURE, WAS SERVING A TWENTY-YEAR PRISON SENTENCE FOR MANSLAUGHTER AND ROBBERY.
A CHARGE OF MURDER WAS REDUCED AFTER GRACE TESTIFIED AGAINST HIS FORMER EMPLOYER, CRIME-BOSS JOE COSTELLO.
LIVE
VOL
HOW CAN YOU HERE.
...WHEN YOU'RE THERE?
IT SURE LOOKS LIKE ME, DON'T IT? IF I DIDN'T KNOW BETTER...
...EVEN I'D THINK THAT WAS JIMMY GRACE.
WHOA!

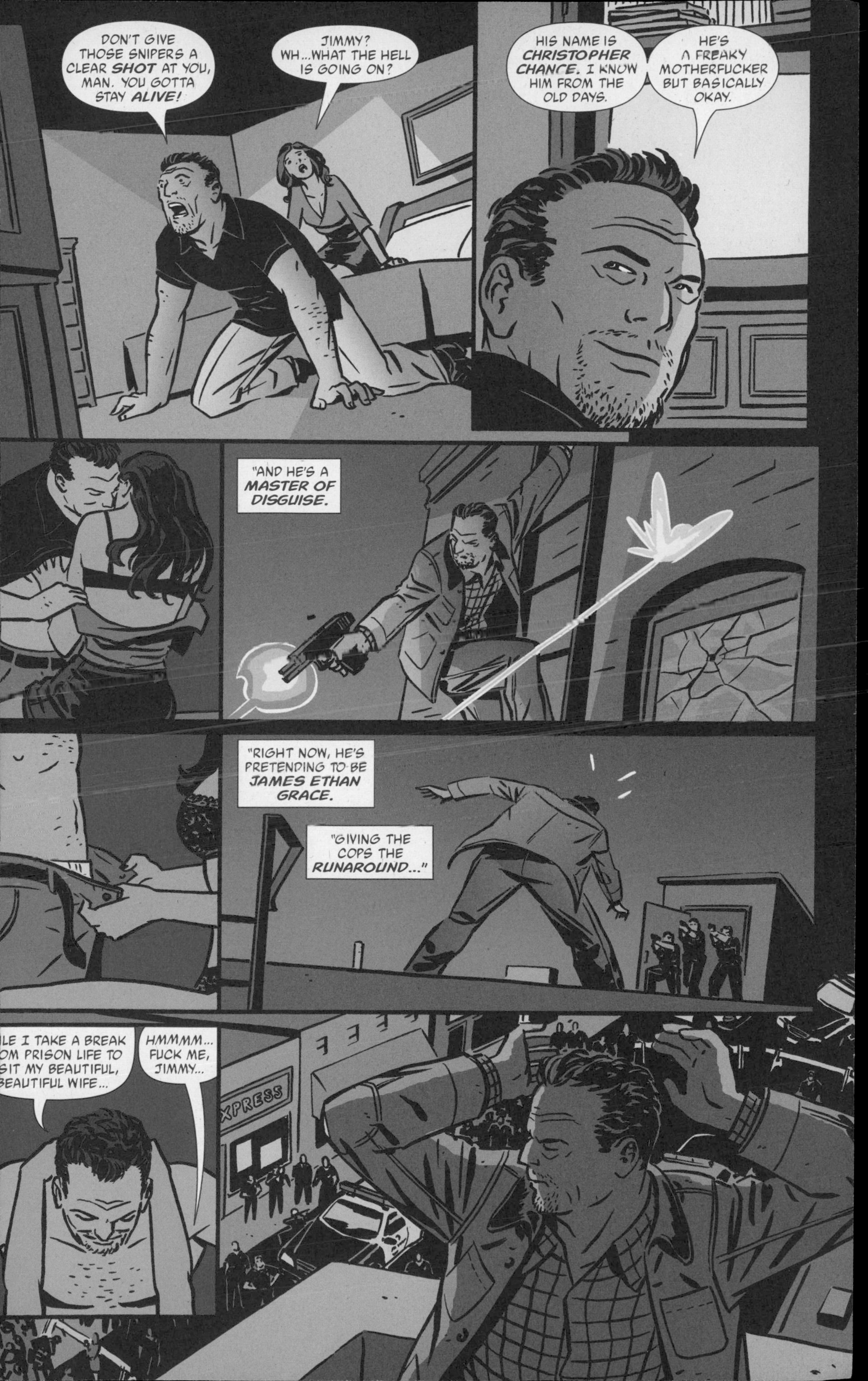
DON'T GIVE THOSE SNIPERS A CLEAR SHOT AT YOU, MAN. YOU GOTTA STAY ALIVE!
JIMMY? WH...WHAT THE HELL IS GOING ON?
HIS NAME IS CHRISTOPHER CHANCE. I KNOW HIM FROM THE OLD DAYS.
HE'S A FREAKY MOTHERFUCKER BUT BASICALLY OKAY.
"AND HE'S A MASTER OF DISGUISE.
"RIGHT NOW, HE'S PRETENDING TO BE JAMES ETHAN GRACE.
"GIVING THE COPS THE RUNAROUND..."
ILE I TAKE A BREAK OM PRISON LIFE TO SIT MY BEAUTIFUL, BEAUTIFUL WIFE...
HMMMM... FUCK ME, JIMMY...
XPRESS

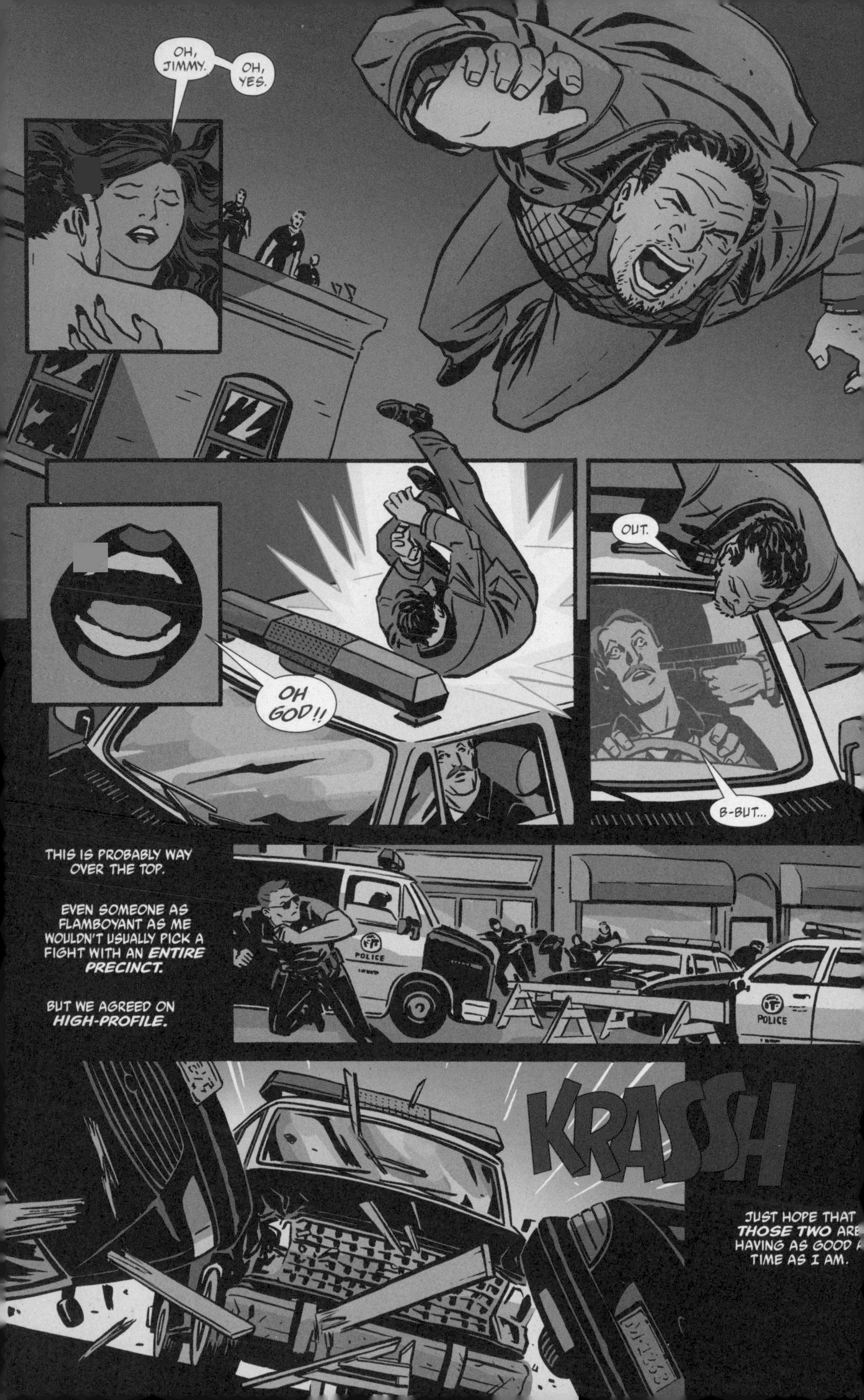

OH, JIMMY.
OH, YES.
OH GOD!!
OUT.
B-BUT...
THIS IS PROBABLY WAY OVER THE TOP.
EVEN SOMEONE AS FLAMBOYANT AS ME WOULDN'T USUALLY PICK A FIGHT WITH AN *ENTIRE PRECINCT.*
BUT WE AGREED ON ***HIGH-PROFILE.***
POLICE
POLICE
KRASSH
JUST HOPE THAT ***THOSE TWO*** ARE HAVING AS GOOD A TIME AS I AM.

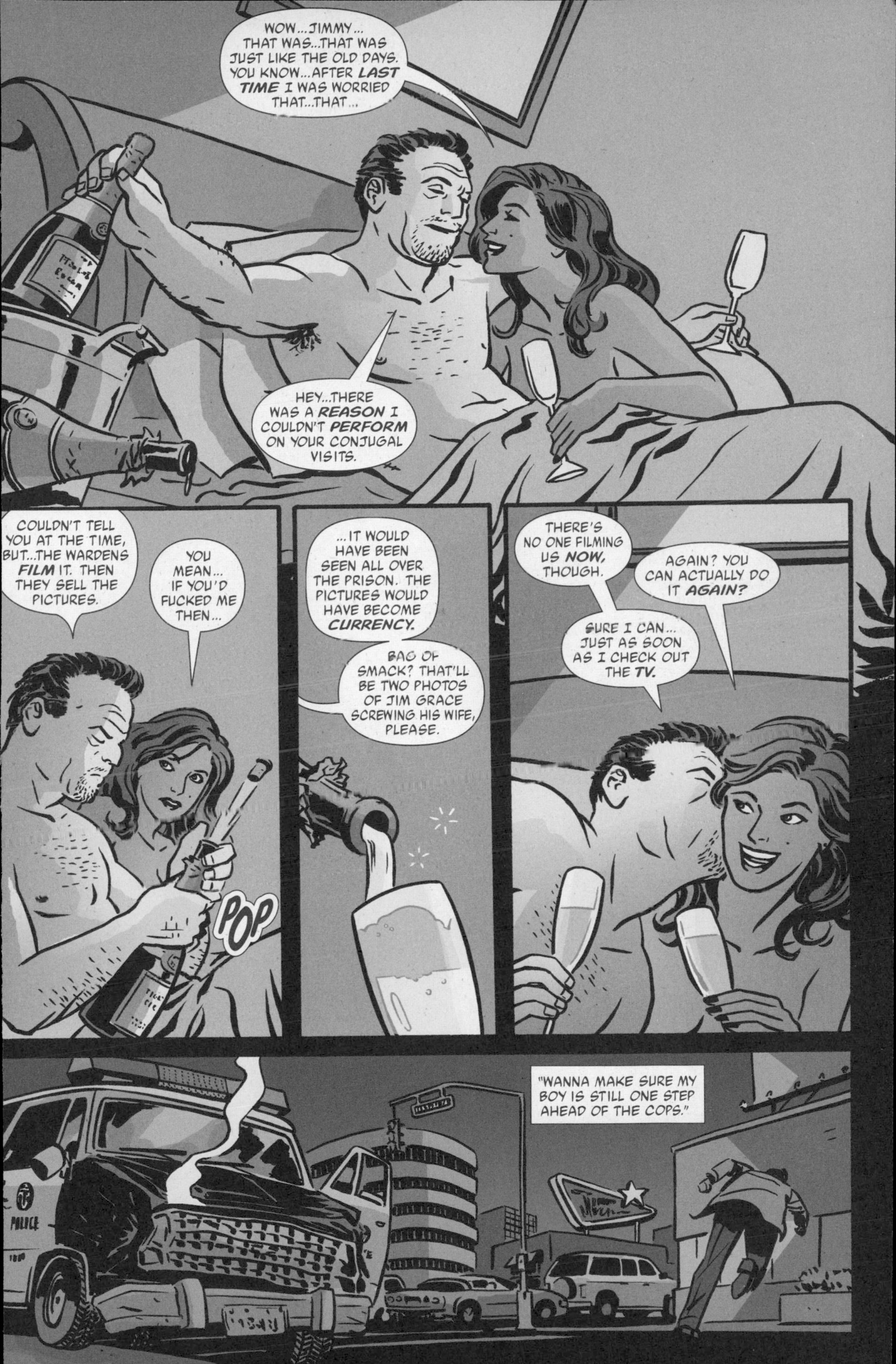
WOW... JIMMY... THAT WAS... THAT WAS JUST LIKE THE OLD DAYS. YOU KNOW... AFTER LAST TIME I WAS WORRIED THAT... THAT...
HEY... THERE WAS A REASON I COULDN'T PERFORM ON YOUR CONJUGAL VISITS.
COULDN'T TELL YOU AT THE TIME, BUT... THE WARDENS FILM IT. THEN THEY SELL THE PICTURES.
YOU MEAN... IF YOU'D FUCKED ME THEN...
POP
...IT WOULD HAVE BEEN SEEN ALL OVER THE PRISON. THE PICTURES WOULD HAVE BECOME CURRENCY.
BAG OF SMACK? THAT'LL BE TWO PHOTOS OF JIM GRACE SCREWING HIS WIFE, PLEASE.
THERE'S NO ONE FILMING US NOW, THOUGH.
AGAIN? YOU CAN ACTUALLY DO IT AGAIN?
SURE I CAN... JUST AS SOON AS I CHECK OUT THE TV.
"WANNA MAKE SURE MY BOY IS STILL ONE STEP AHEAD OF THE COPS."
POLICE

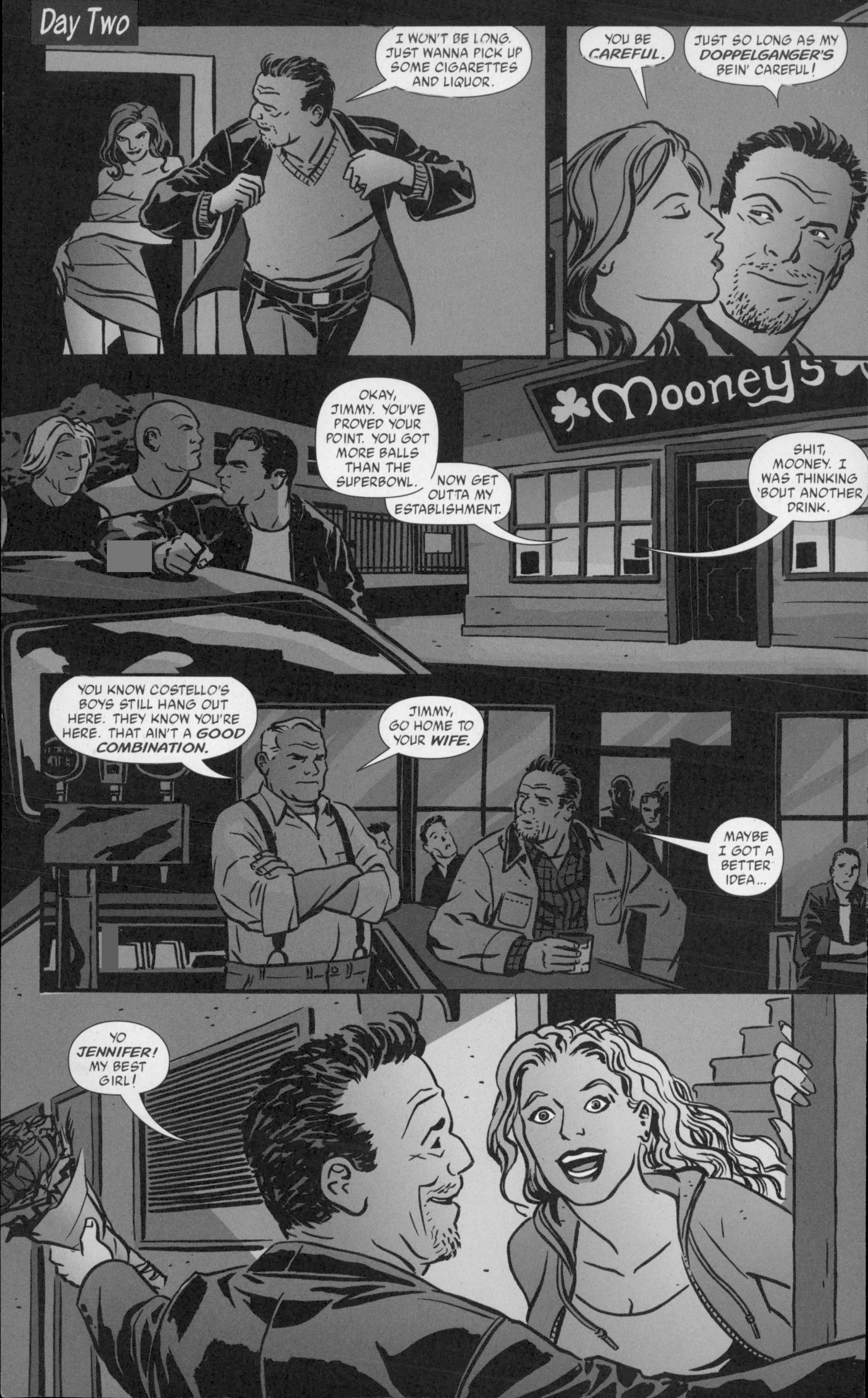
Day Two
I WON'T BE LONG. JUST WANNA PICK UP SOME CIGARETTES AND LIQUOR.
YOU BE CAREFUL.
JUST SO LONG AS MY DOPPELGANGER'S BEIN' CAREFUL!
Mooney's
OKAY, JIMMY. YOU'VE PROVED YOUR POINT. YOU GOT MORE BALLS THAN THE SUPERBOWL.
NOW GET OUTTA MY ESTABLISHMENT.
SHIT, MOONEY. I WAS THINKING 'BOUT ANOTHER DRINK.
YOU KNOW COSTELLO'S BOYS STILL HANG OUT HERE. THEY KNOW YOU'RE HERE. THAT AIN'T A GOOD COMBINATION.
JIMMY, GO HOME TO YOUR WIFE.
MAYBE I GOT A BETTER IDEA...
YO JENNIFER! MY BEST GIRL!

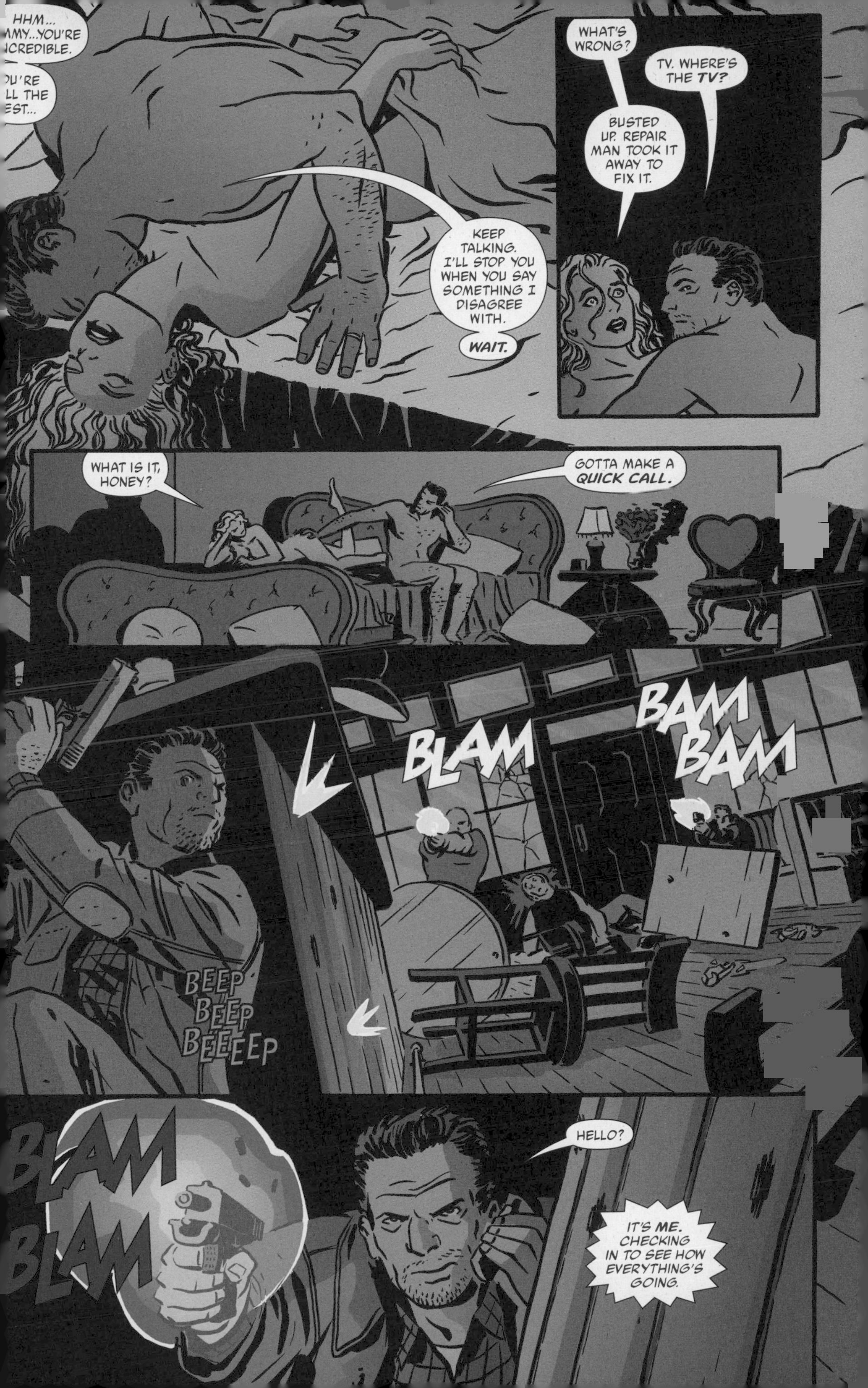
HHM... MMY...YOU'RE INCREDIBLE.
OU'RE LL THE EST...
KEEP TALKING. I'LL STOP YOU WHEN YOU SAY SOMETHING I DISAGREE WITH.
WAIT.
WHAT'S WRONG?
TV. WHERE'S THE TV?
BUSTED UP. REPAIR MAN TOOK IT AWAY TO FIX IT.
WHAT IS IT, HONEY?
GOTTA MAKE A QUICK CALL.
BLAM
BAM BAM
BEEP BEEP BEEEEP
BLAM BLAM
HELLO?
IT'S ME. CHECKING IN TO SEE HOW EVERYTHING'S GOING.

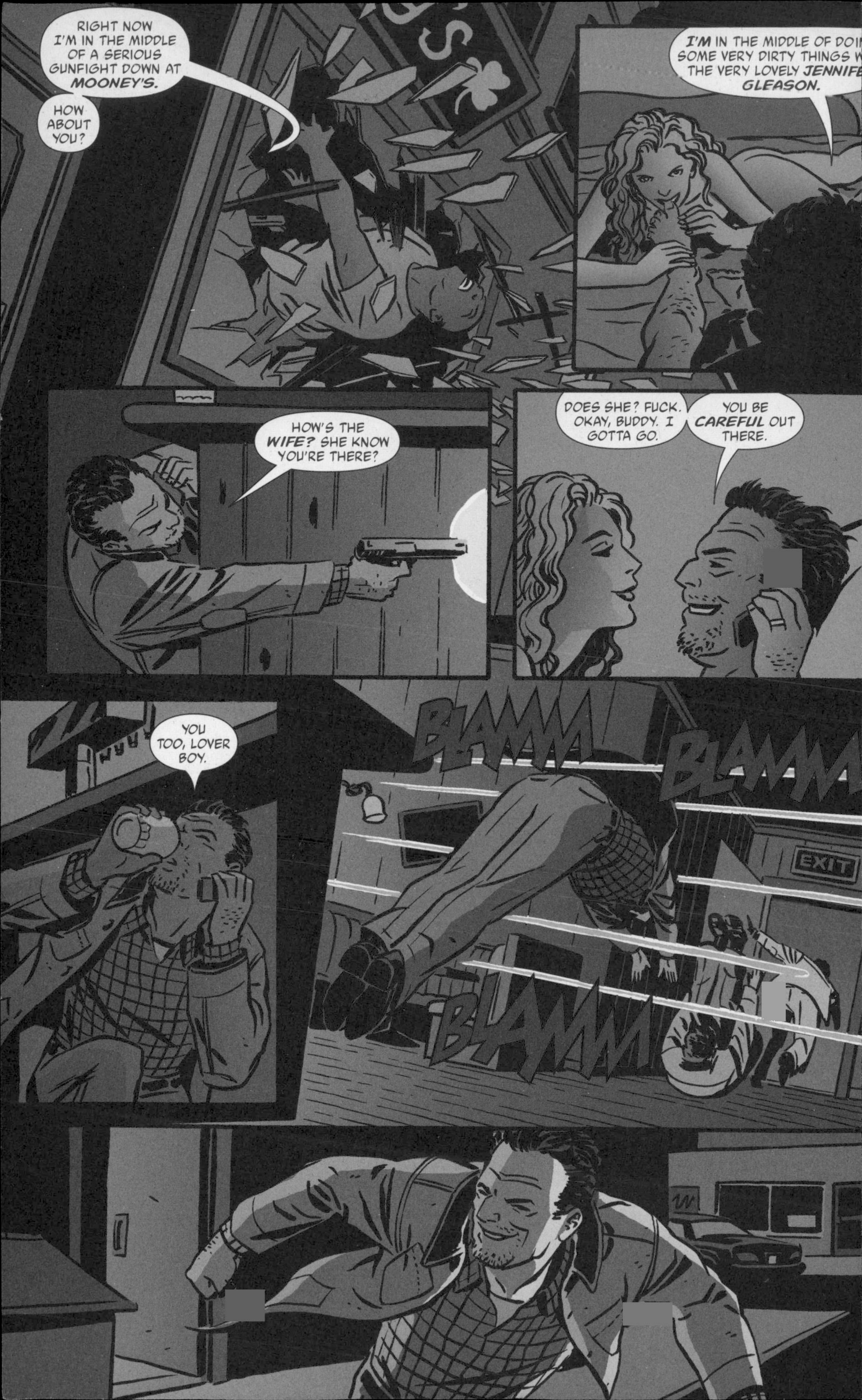

RIGHT NOW I'M IN THE MIDDLE OF A SERIOUS GUNFIGHT DOWN AT MOONEY'S.
HOW ABOUT YOU?
I'M IN THE MIDDLE OF DOIN
SOME VERY DIRTY THINGS W
THE VERY LOVELY JENNIFE
GLEASON.
HOW'S THE WIFE? SHE KNOW YOU'RE THERE?
DOES SHE? FUCK. OKAY, BUDDY. I GOTTA GO.
YOU BE CAREFUL OUT THERE.
YOU TOO, LOVER BOY.
BLAMM
BLAMM
BLAMM
EXIT

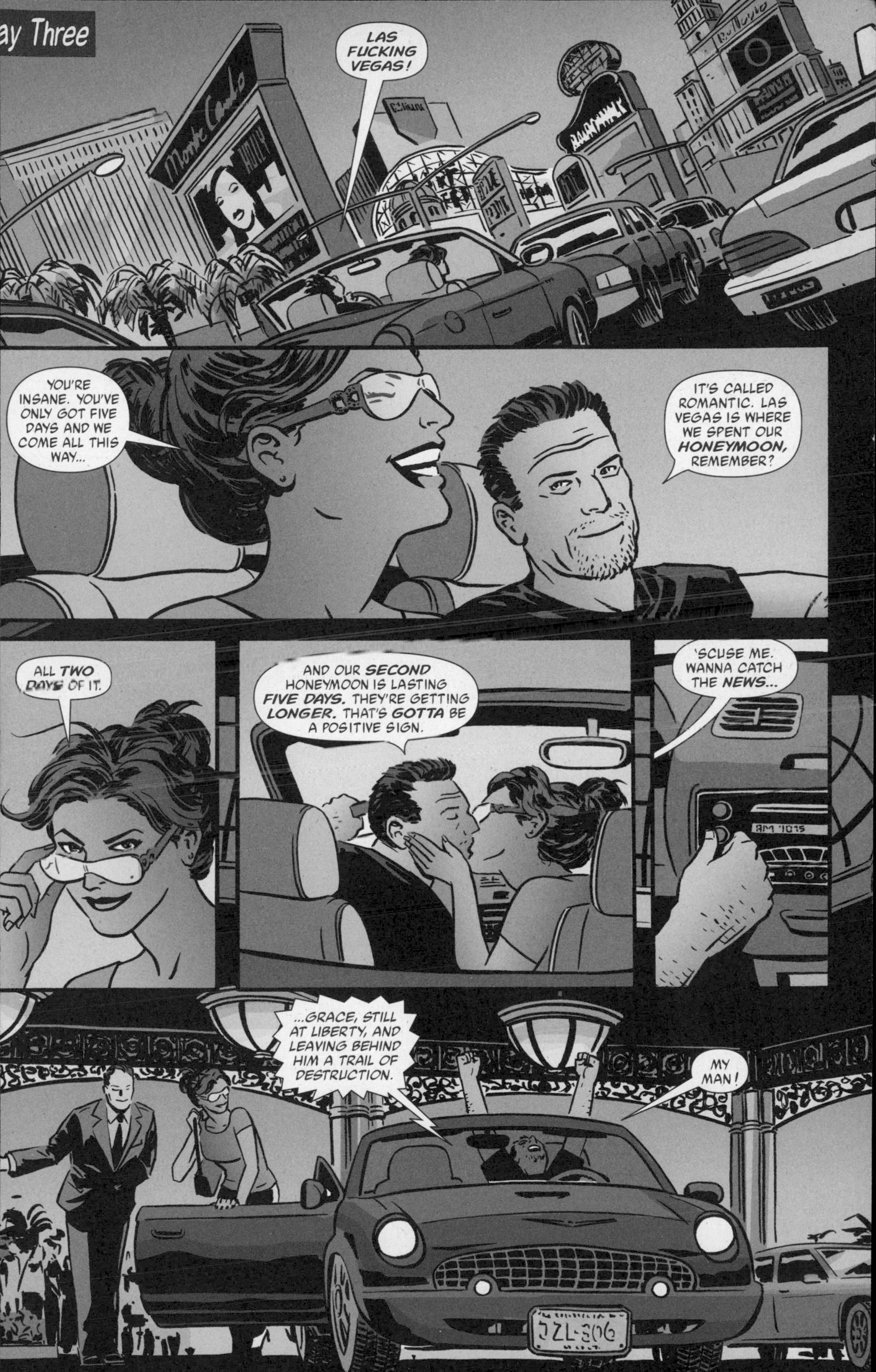
ay Three
LAS FUCKING VEGAS!
YOU'RE INSANE. YOU'VE ONLY GOT FIVE DAYS AND WE COME ALL THIS WAY...
IT'S CALLED ROMANTIC. LAS VEGAS IS WHERE WE SPENT OUR HONEYMOON, REMEMBER?
ALL TWO DAYS OF IT.
AND OUR SECOND HONEYMOON IS LASTING FIVE DAYS. THEY'RE GETTING LONGER. THAT'S GOTTA BE A POSITIVE SIGN.
'SCUSE ME. WANNA CATCH THE NEWS...
...GRACE, STILL AT LIBERTY, AND LEAVING BEHIND HIM A TRAIL OF DESTRUCTION.
MY MAN!
JZL-306

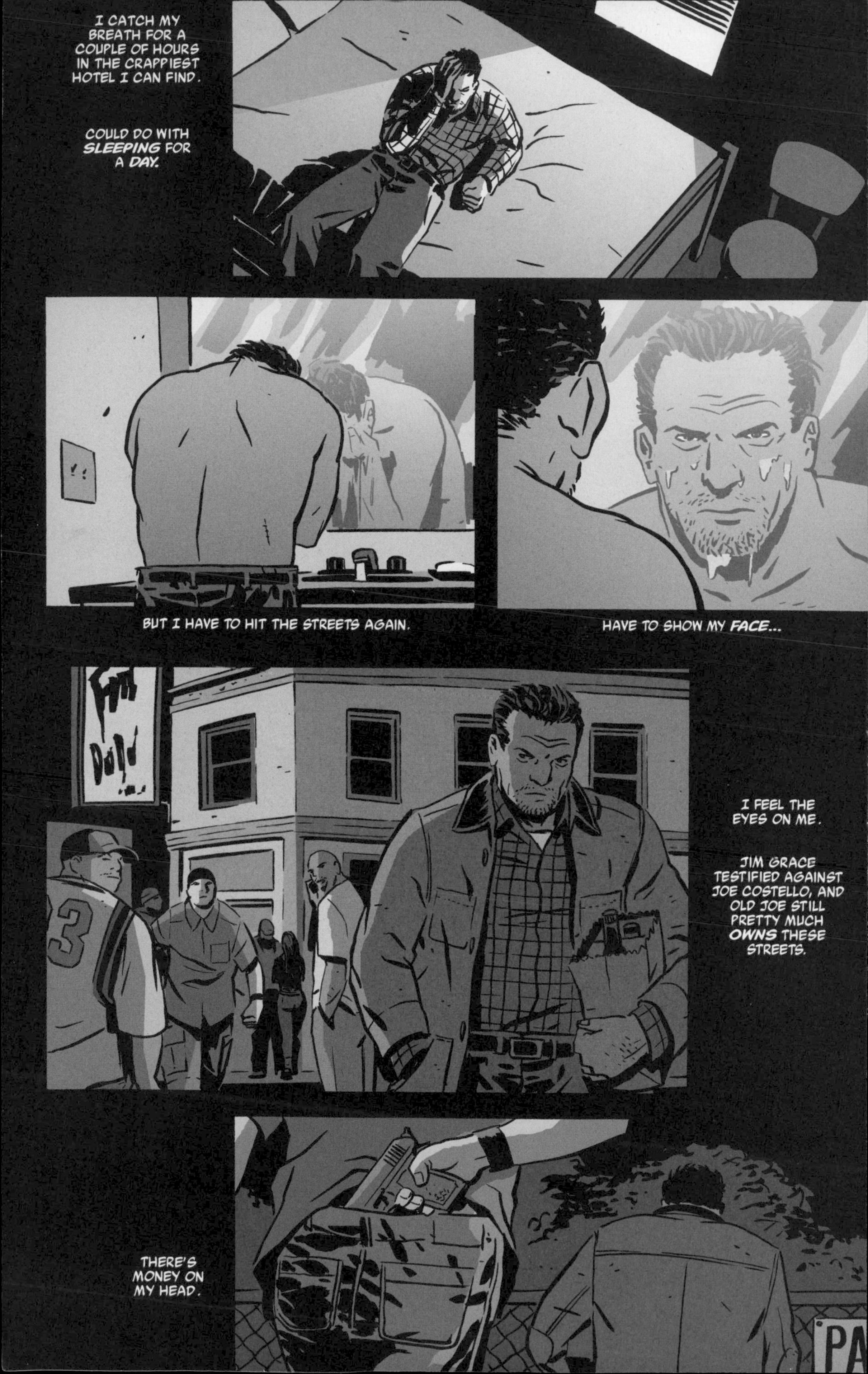
I CATCH MY BREATH FOR A COUPLE OF HOURS IN THE CRAPPIEST HOTEL I CAN FIND.
COULD DO WITH SLEEPING FOR A DAY.
BUT I HAVE TO HIT THE STREETS AGAIN.
HAVE TO SHOW MY FACE...
I FEEL THE EYES ON ME.
JIM GRACE TESTIFIED AGAINST JOE COSTELLO, AND OLD JOE STILL PRETTY MUCH OWNS THESE STREETS.
THERE'S MONEY ON MY HEAD.

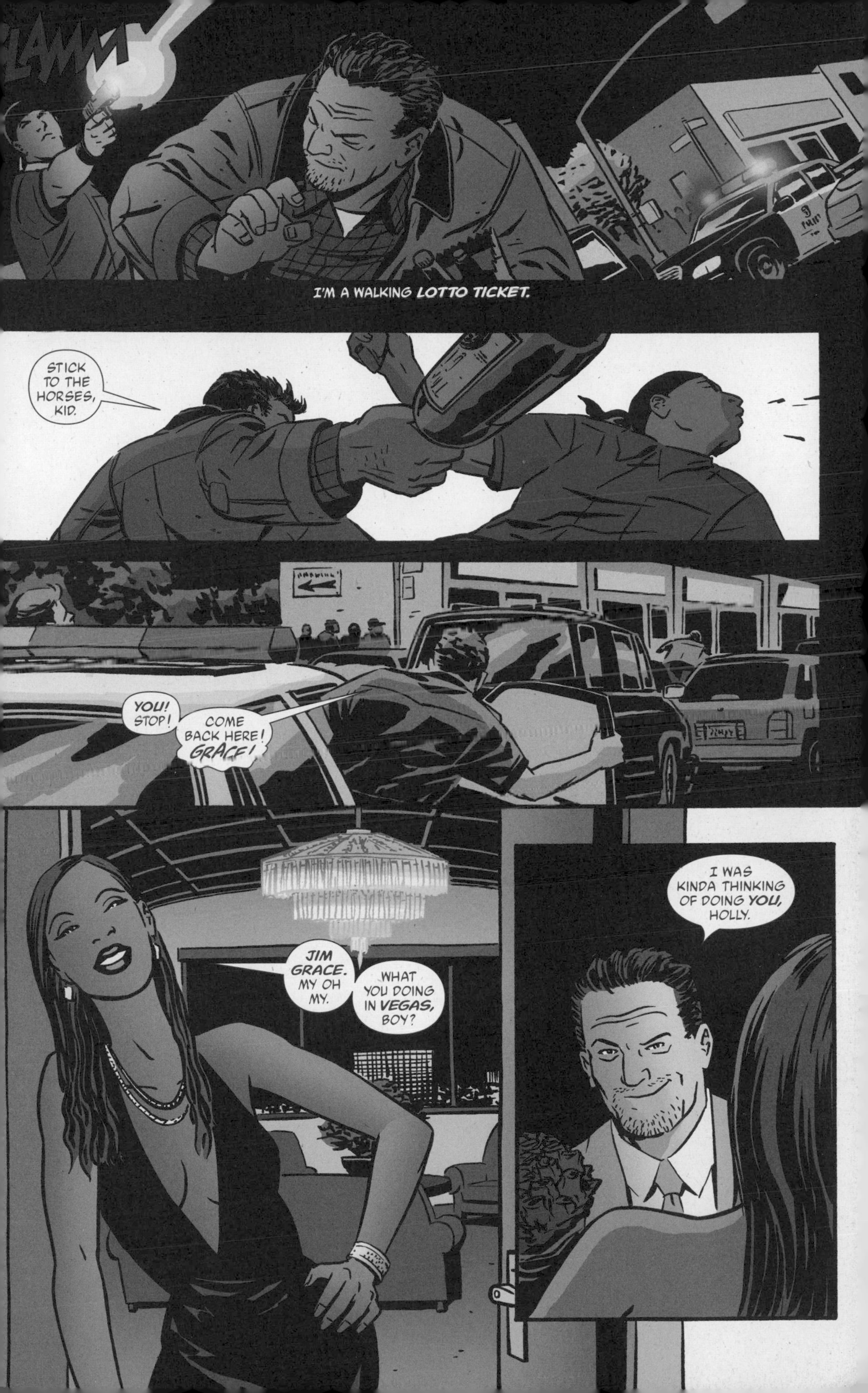
I'M A WALKING LOTTO TICKET.
STICK TO THE HORSES, KID.
YOU! STOP!
COME BACK HERE! GRACE!
JIM GRACE. MY OH MY.
WHAT YOU DOING IN VEGAS, BOY?
I WAS KINDA THINKING OF DOING YOU, HOLLY.

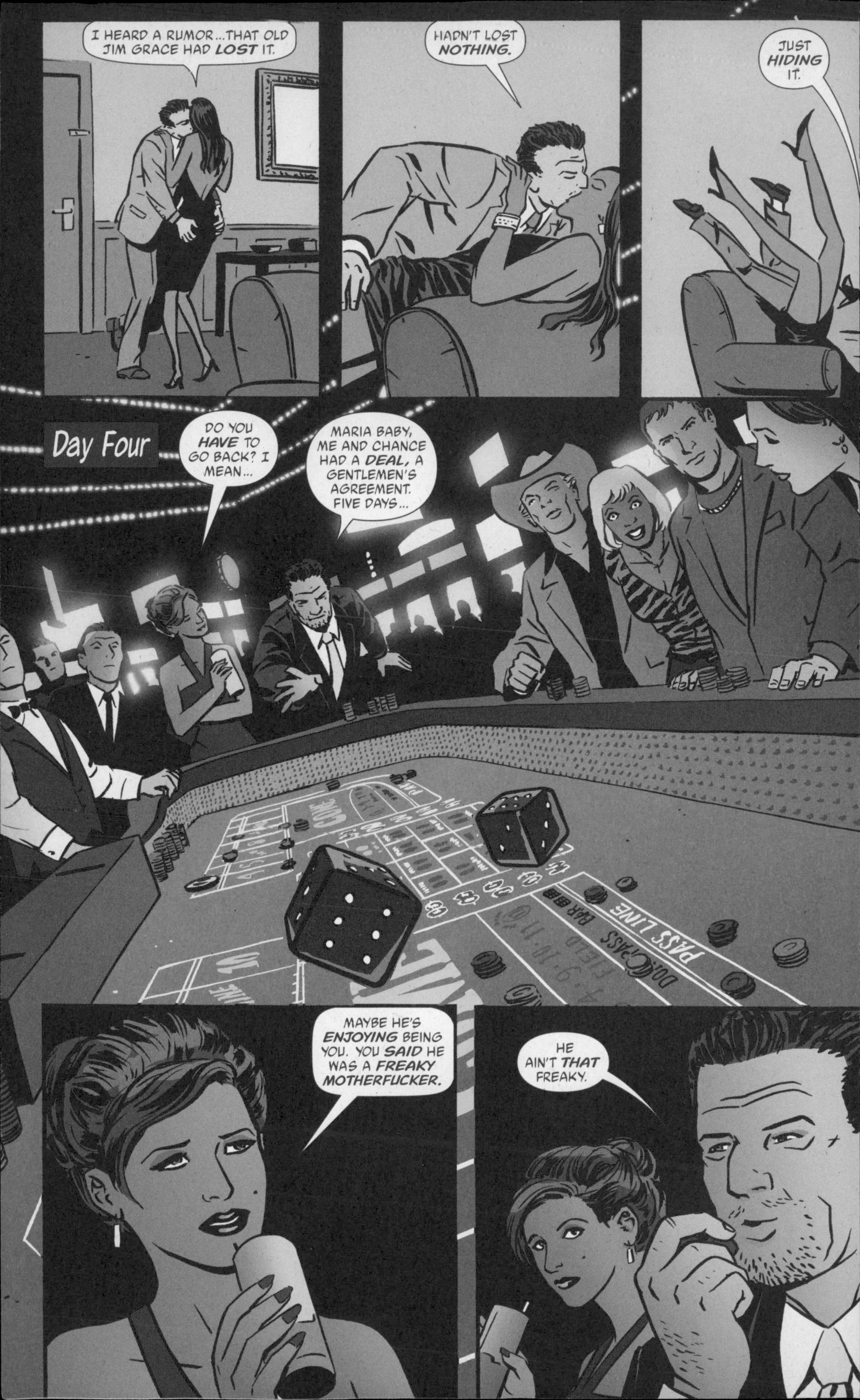

I HEARD A RUMOR...THAT OLD JIM GRACE HAD LOST IT.
HADN'T LOST NOTHING.
JUST HIDING IT.
Day Four
DO YOU HAVE TO GO BACK? I MEAN...
MARIA BABY, ME AND CHANCE HAD A DEAL, A GENTLEMEN'S AGREEMENT. FIVE DAYS...
PASS LINE
DON'T PASS
FIELD
MAYBE HE'S ENJOYING BEING YOU. YOU SAID HE WAS A FREAKY MOTHERFUCKER.
HE AIN'T THAT FREAKY.

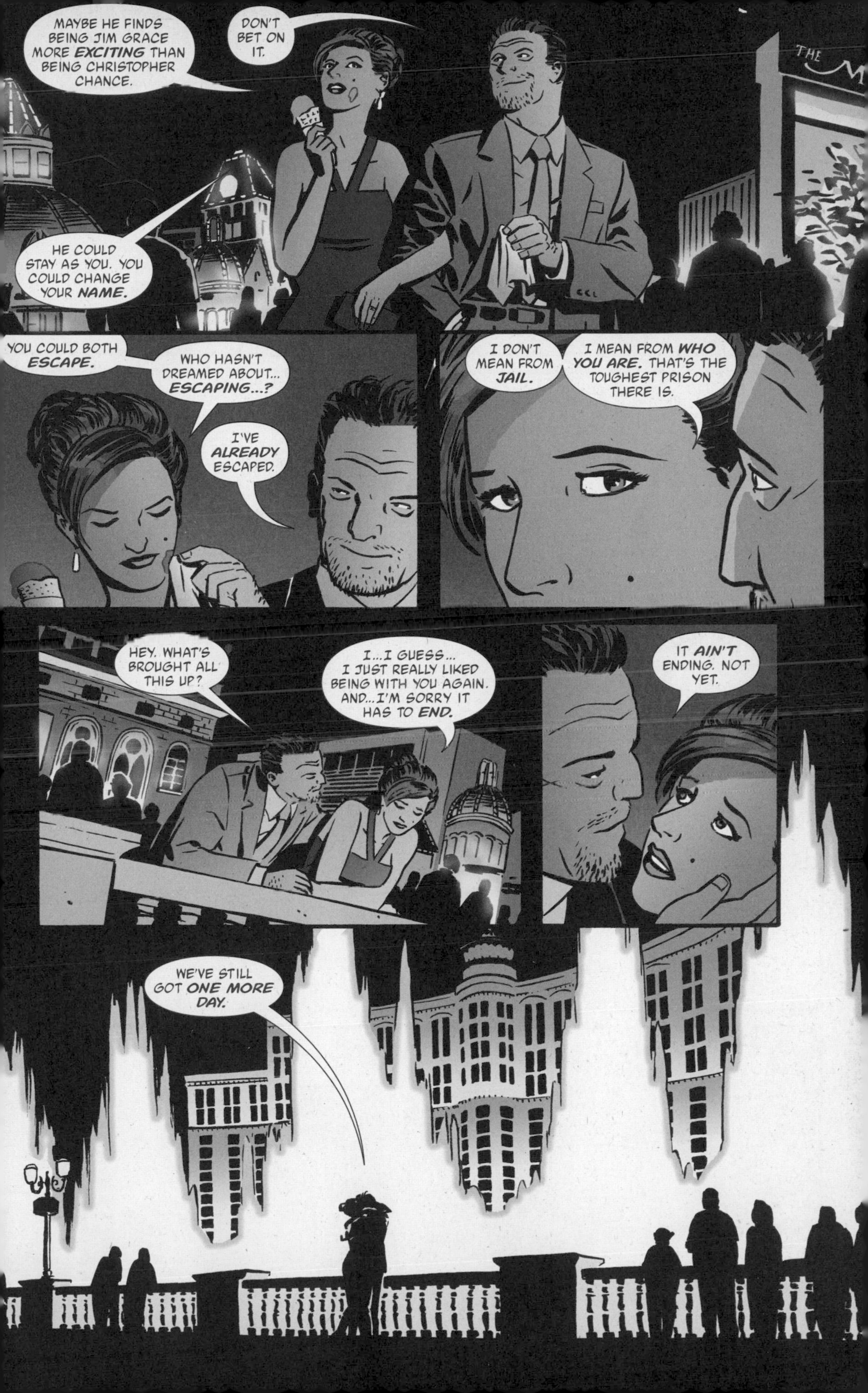
MAYBE HE FINDS BEING JIM GRACE MORE EXCITING THAN BEING CHRISTOPHER CHANCE.
DON'T BET ON IT.
HE COULD STAY AS YOU. YOU COULD CHANGE YOUR NAME.
YOU COULD BOTH ESCAPE.
WHO HASN'T DREAMED ABOUT... ESCAPING...?
I'VE ALREADY ESCAPED.
I DON'T MEAN FROM JAIL.
I MEAN FROM WHO YOU ARE. THAT'S THE TOUGHEST PRISON THERE IS.
HEY. WHAT'S BROUGHT ALL THIS UP?
I...I GUESS... I JUST REALLY LIKED BEING WITH YOU AGAIN. AND...I'M SORRY IT HAS TO END.
IT AIN'T ENDING. NOT YET.
WE'VE STILL GOT ONE MORE DAY.

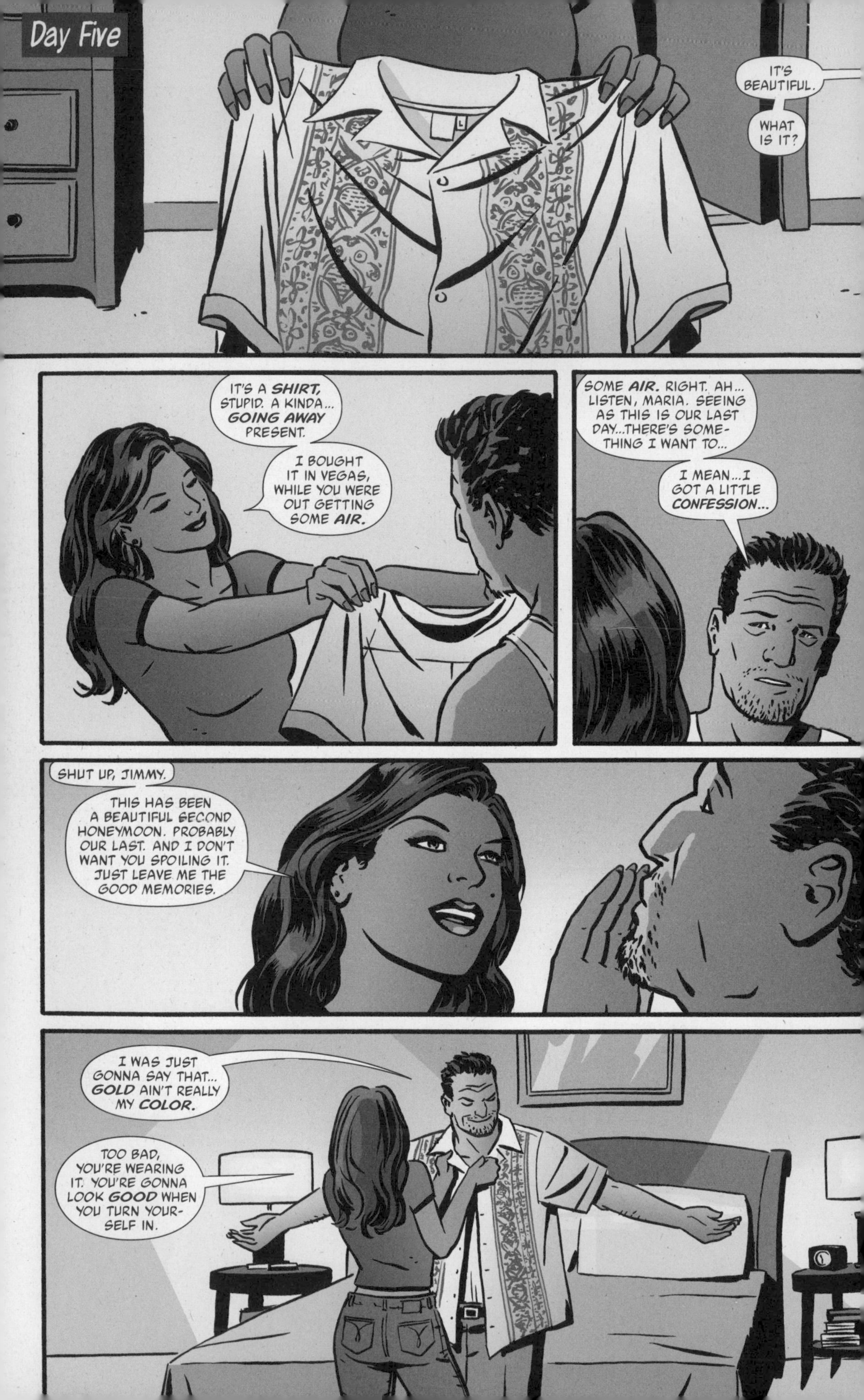
Day Five
IT'S BEAUTIFUL.
WHAT IS IT?
IT'S A SHIRT, STUPID. A KINDA... GOING AWAY PRESENT.
I BOUGHT IT IN VEGAS, WHILE YOU WERE OUT GETTING SOME AIR.
SOME AIR. RIGHT. AH... LISTEN, MARIA. SEEING AS THIS IS OUR LAST DAY...THERE'S SOMETHING I WANT TO...
I MEAN...I GOT A LITTLE CONFESSION...
SHUT UP, JIMMY.
THIS HAS BEEN A BEAUTIFUL SECOND HONEYMOON. PROBABLY OUR LAST. AND I DON'T WANT YOU SPOILING IT. JUST LEAVE ME THE GOOD MEMORIES.
I WAS JUST GONNA SAY THAT... GOLD AIN'T REALLY MY COLOR.
TOO BAD, YOU'RE WEARING IT. YOU'RE GONNA LOOK GOOD WHEN YOU TURN YOURSELF IN.

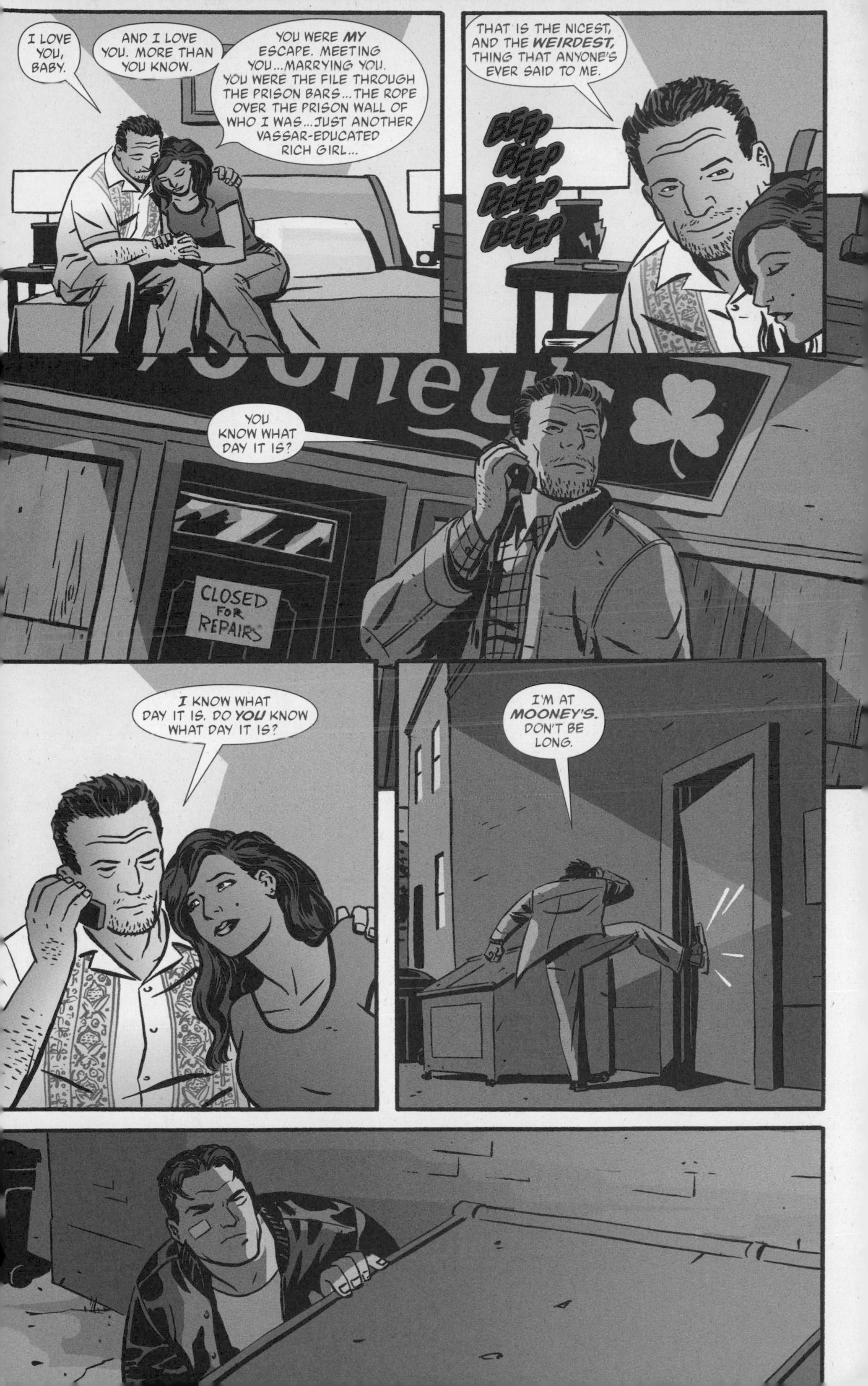
I LOVE YOU, BABY.
AND I LOVE YOU. MORE THAN YOU KNOW.
YOU WERE MY ESCAPE. MEETING YOU...MARRYING YOU. YOU WERE THE FILE THROUGH THE PRISON BARS...THE ROPE OVER THE PRISON WALL OF WHO I WAS...JUST ANOTHER VASSAR-EDUCATED RICH GIRL...
THAT IS THE NICEST, AND THE WEIRDEST, THING THAT ANYONE'S EVER SAID TO ME.
BEEP BEEP BEEEP BEEEP
YOU KNOW WHAT DAY IT IS?
CLOSED FOR REPAIRS
I KNOW WHAT DAY IT IS. DO YOU KNOW WHAT DAY IT IS?
I'M AT MOONEY'S. DON'T BE LONG.

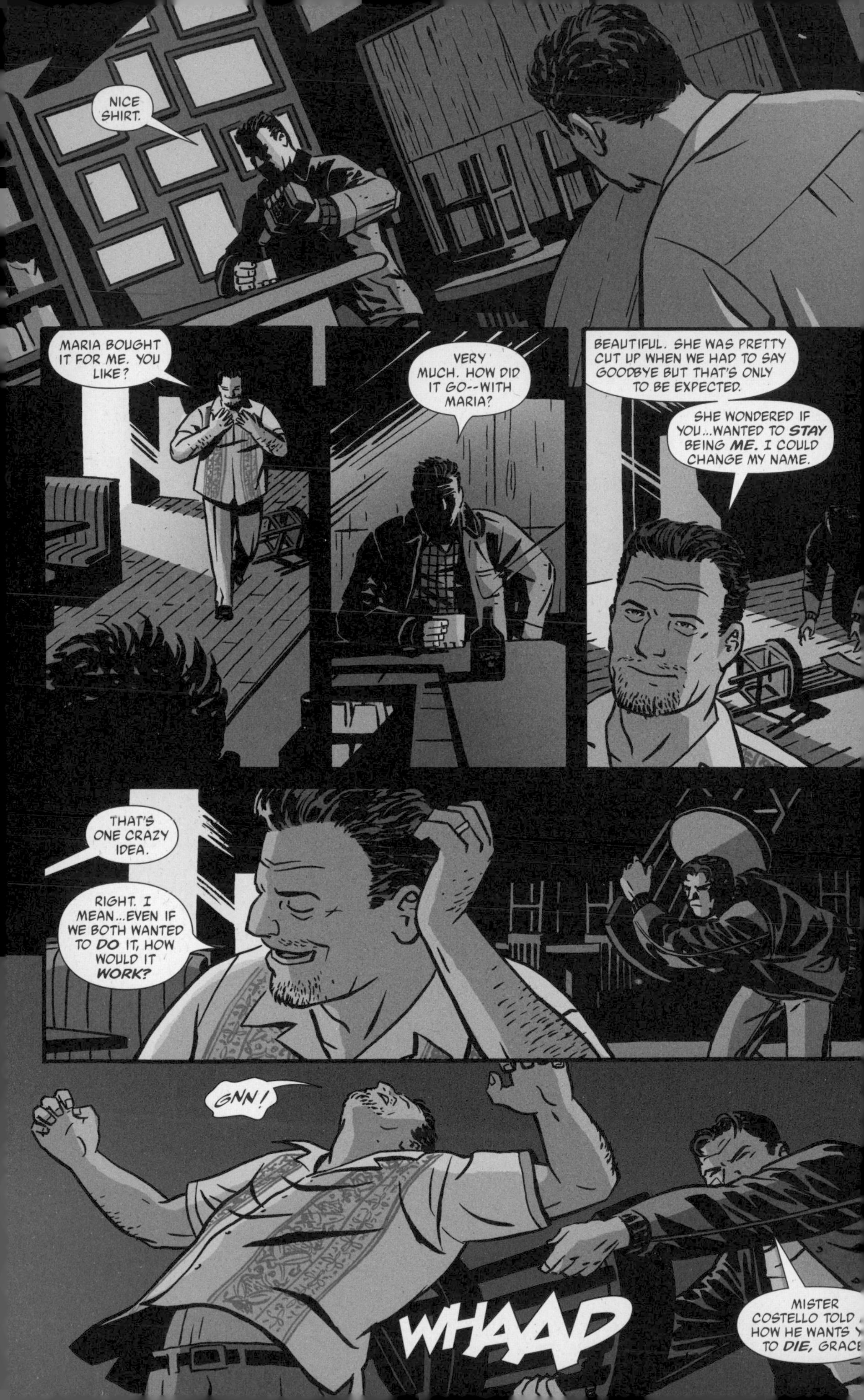
NICE SHIRT.
MARIA BOUGHT IT FOR ME. YOU LIKE?
VERY MUCH. HOW DID IT GO--WITH MARIA?
BEAUTIFUL. SHE WAS PRETTY CUT UP WHEN WE HAD TO SAY GOODBYE BUT THAT'S ONLY TO BE EXPECTED.
SHE WONDERED IF YOU...WANTED TO STAY BEING ME. I COULD CHANGE MY NAME.
THAT'S ONE CRAZY IDEA.
RIGHT. I MEAN...EVEN IF WE BOTH WANTED TO DO IT, HOW WOULD IT WORK?
GNN!
WHAAD
MISTER COSTELLO TOLD HOW HE WANTS TO DIE, GRACE

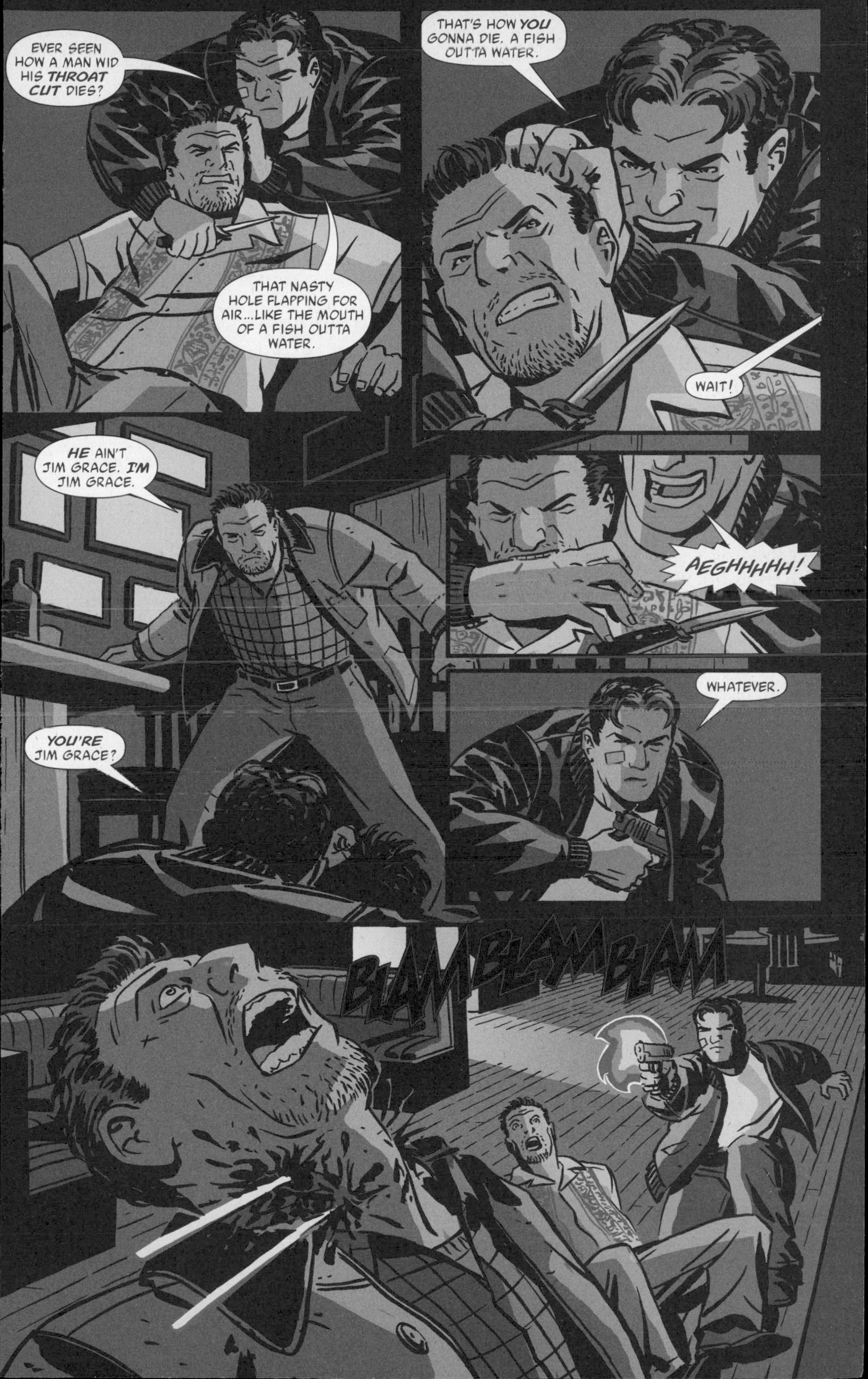
EVER SEEN HOW A MAN WID HIS THROAT CUT DIES?
THAT NASTY HOLE FLAPPING FOR AIR...LIKE THE MOUTH OF A FISH OUTTA WATER.
THAT'S HOW YOU GONNA DIE. A FISH OUTTA WATER.
WAIT!
HE AIN'T JIM GRACE. I'M JIM GRACE.
AEGHHHHH!
YOU'RE JIM GRACE?
WHATEVER.
BLAM BLAM BLAM

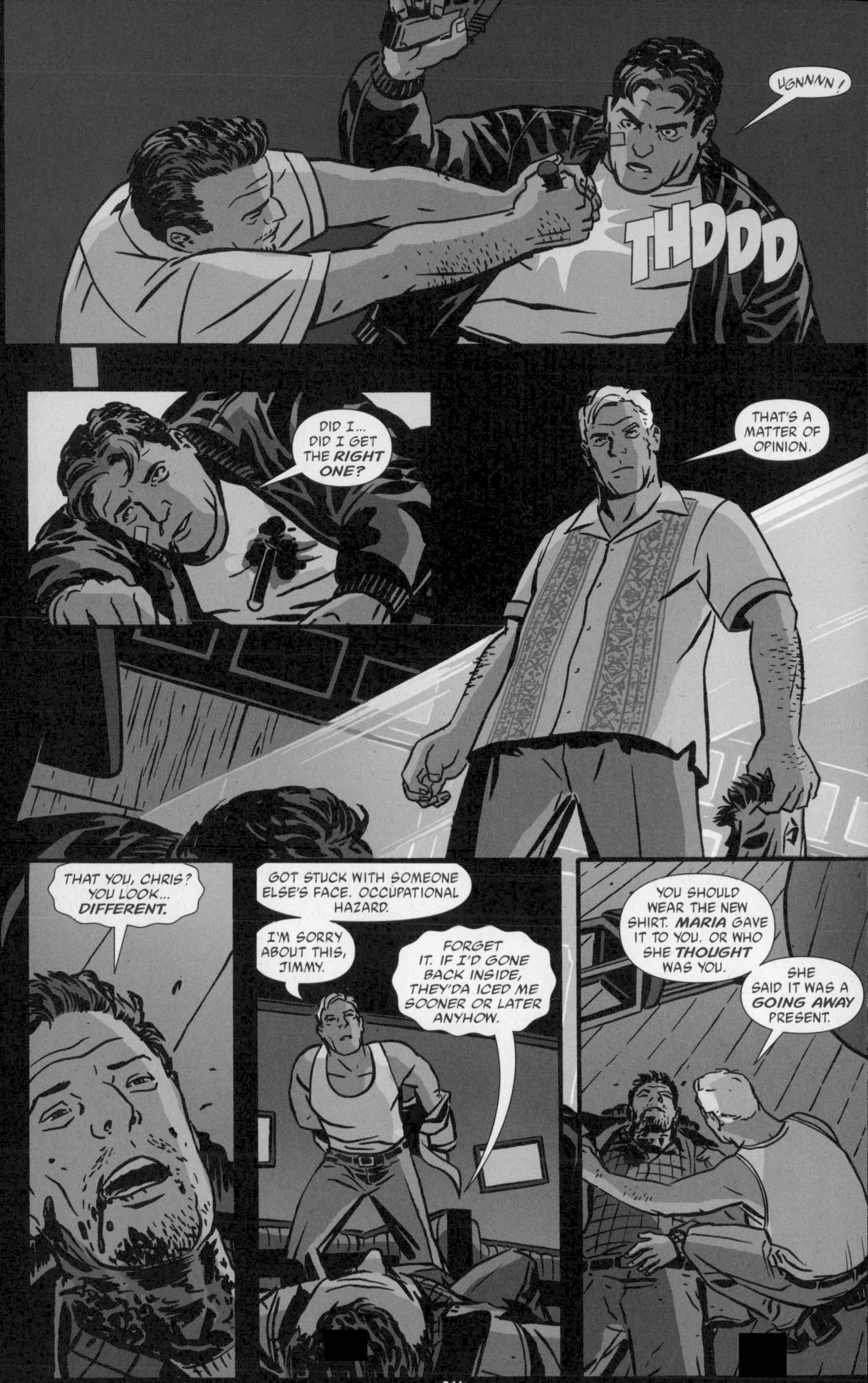
UGNNNN!
THDDD
DID I... DID I GET THE RIGHT ONE?
THAT'S A MATTER OF OPINION.
THAT YOU, CHRIS? YOU LOOK... DIFFERENT.
GOT STUCK WITH SOMEONE ELSE'S FACE. OCCUPATIONAL HAZARD.
I'M SORRY ABOUT THIS, JIMMY.
FORGET IT. IF I'D GONE BACK INSIDE, THEY'DA ICED ME SOONER OR LATER ANYHOW.
YOU SHOULD WEAR THE NEW SHIRT. MARIA GAVE IT TO YOU. OR WHO SHE THOUGHT WAS YOU.
SHE SAID IT WAS A GOING AWAY PRESENT.

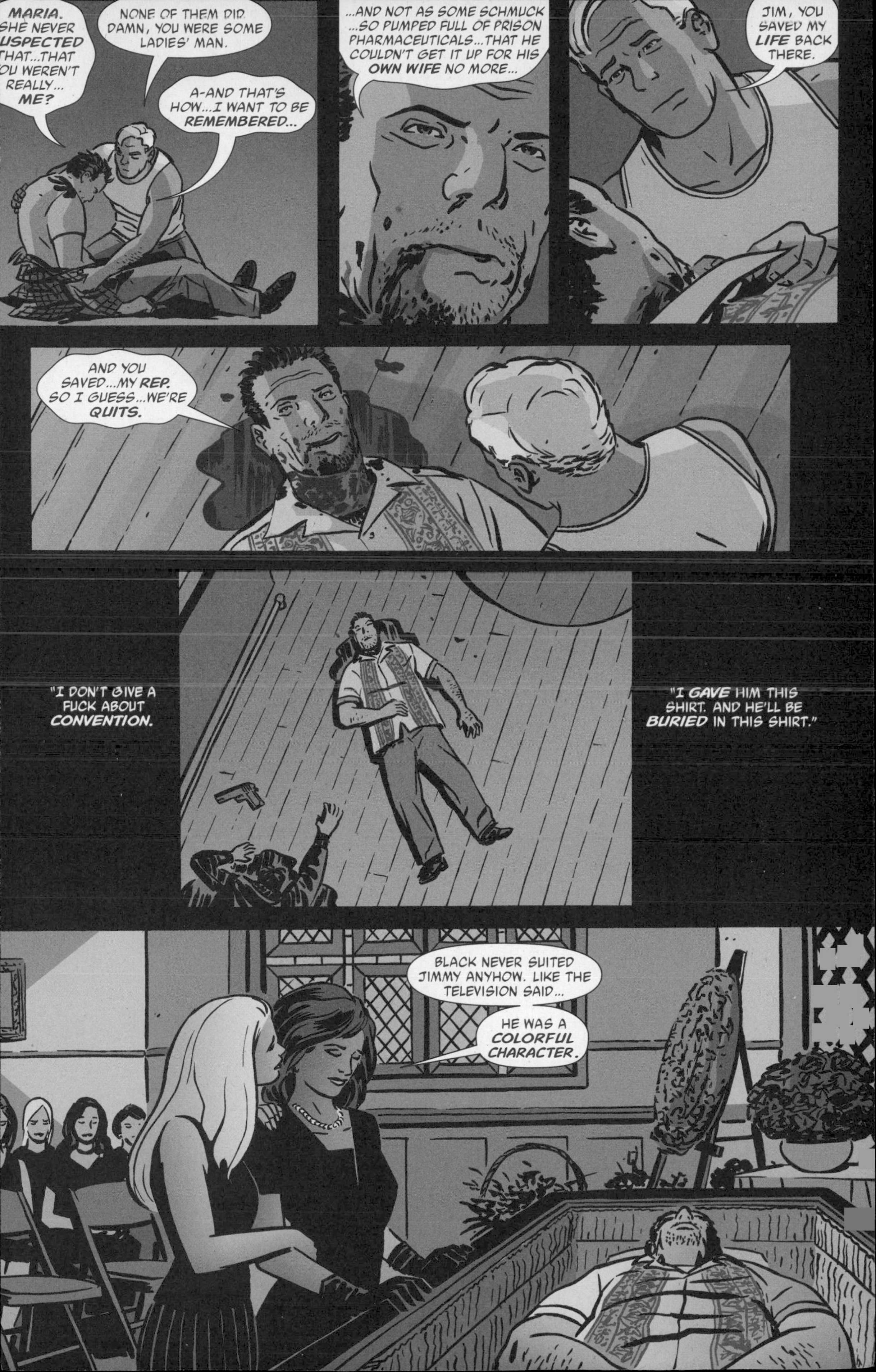
MARIA. SHE NEVER SUSPECTED THAT...THAT YOU WEREN'T REALLY... ME?
NONE OF THEM DID. DAMN, YOU WERE SOME LADIES' MAN.
A-AND THAT'S HOW...I WANT TO BE REMEMBERED...
...AND NOT AS SOME SCHMUCK ...SO PUMPED FULL OF PRISON PHARMACEUTICALS...THAT HE COULDN'T GET IT UP FOR HIS OWN WIFE NO MORE...
JIM, YOU SAVED MY LIFE BACK THERE.
AND YOU SAVED...MY REP. SO I GUESS...WE'RE QUITS.
"I DON'T GIVE A FUCK ABOUT CONVENTION.
"I GAVE HIM THIS SHIRT. AND HE'LL BE BURIED IN THIS SHIRT."
BLACK NEVER SUITED JIMMY ANYHOW. LIKE THE TELEVISION SAID...
HE WAS A COLORFUL CHARACTER.

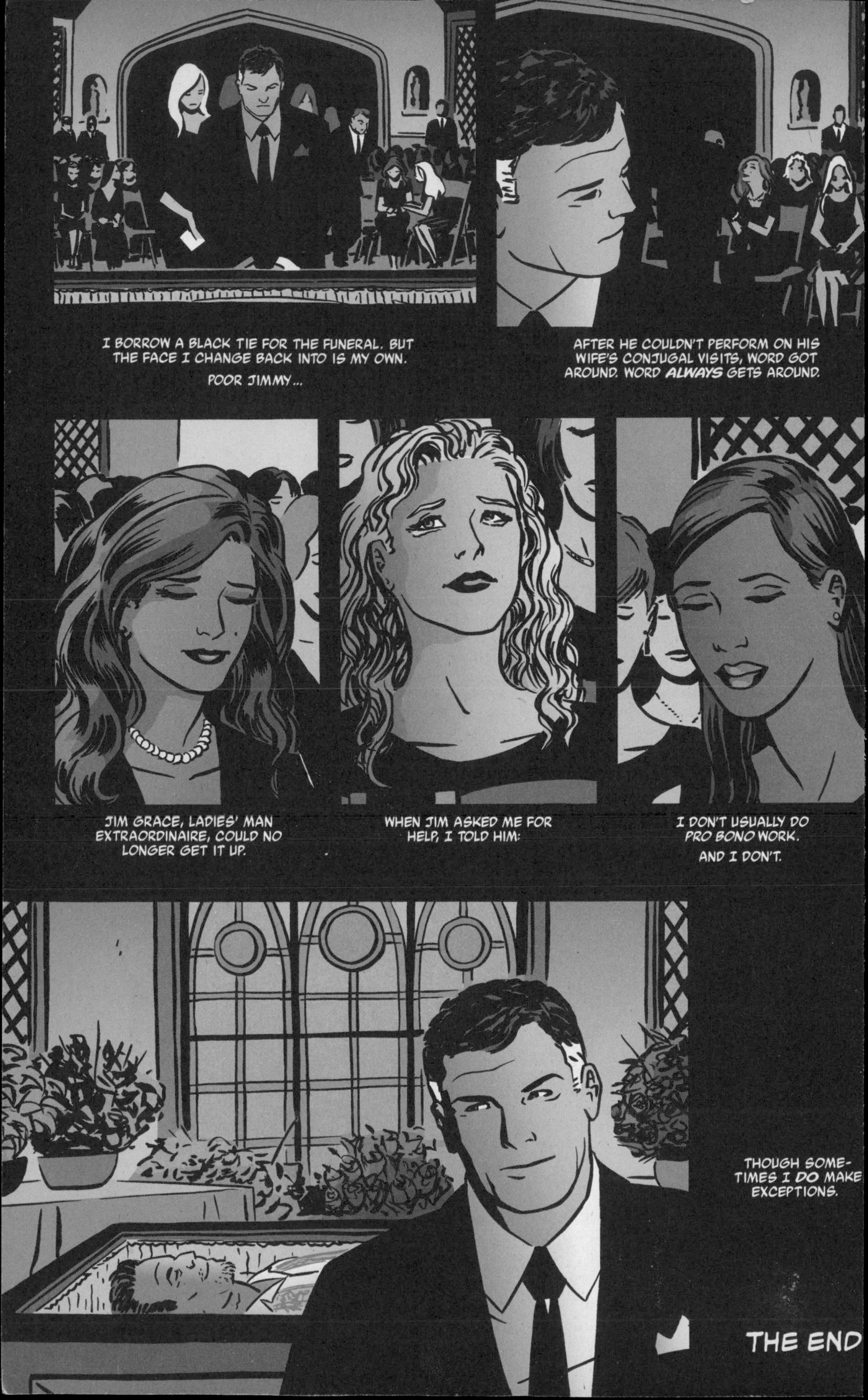

I BORROW A BLACK TIE FOR THE FUNERAL. BUT THE FACE I CHANGE BACK INTO IS MY OWN.
POOR JIMMY...
AFTER HE COULDN'T PERFORM ON HIS WIFE'S CONJUGAL VISITS, WORD GOT AROUND. WORD *ALWAYS* GETS AROUND.
JIM GRACE, LADIES' MAN EXTRAORDINAIRE, COULD NO LONGER GET IT UP.
WHEN JIM ASKED ME FOR HELP, I TOLD HIM:
I DON'T USUALLY DO *PRO BONO* WORK.
AND I DON'T.
THOUGH SOMETIMES I *DO* MAKE EXCEPTIONS.
THE END

MAKING IT LOOK EASY

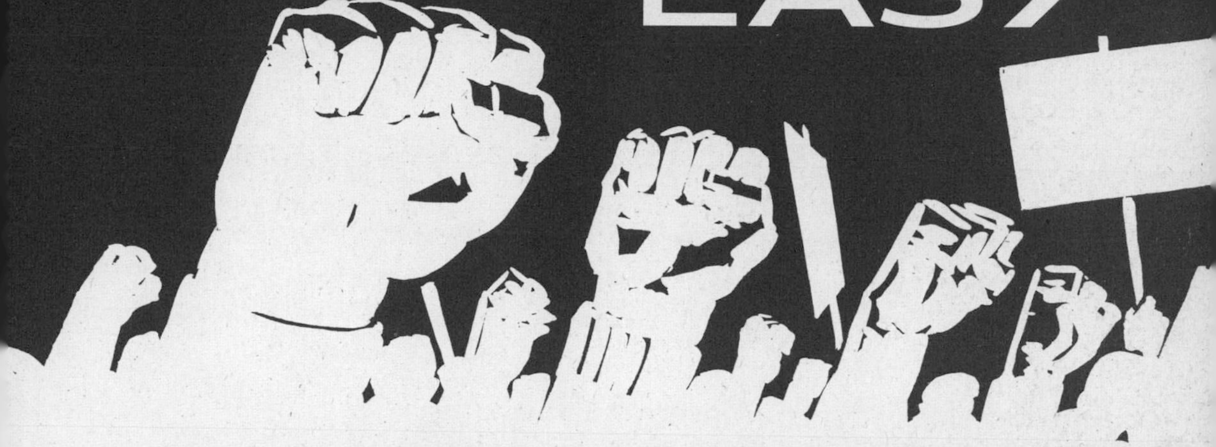

A SPECIAL BEHIND-THE-SCENES LOOK AT DRAWING THE HUMAN TARGET BY ARTIST CLIFF CHIANG.

I've been thinking for a long time about the bonus material for this collection. Given the hectic pace of a monthly title's schedule, I don't normally have the time to do a lot of background design work, and only occasionally do I work up full character sketches. Imagine my surprise, then, when I found myself with pages and pages of charming character model sheets for the last story in this volume ("Five Days Grace"). I'd had very specific Hollywood actors in mind for that story, and it was an enormously fun exercise to take that inspiration and push the drawing a bit more towards caricature. (In the end, the main character turned out a little *too* recognizable, so I consciously pulled away from it. But there you go.)

Now imagine my horror when, after a fit of frenzied and ultimately futile studio cleaning, I discovered that I'd trashed all of those pages. I've since vowed never to throw anything away, so my life is now spent trying not to topple large piles of paper, punctuated by intervals of sleeping on a mattress made of FedEx boxes.

Fortunately, I've got some other development material to show, and hopefully this peek behind the curtain will turn out to be more satisfying than a bunch of possibly dodgy drawings that I remember fondly only because they went missing.

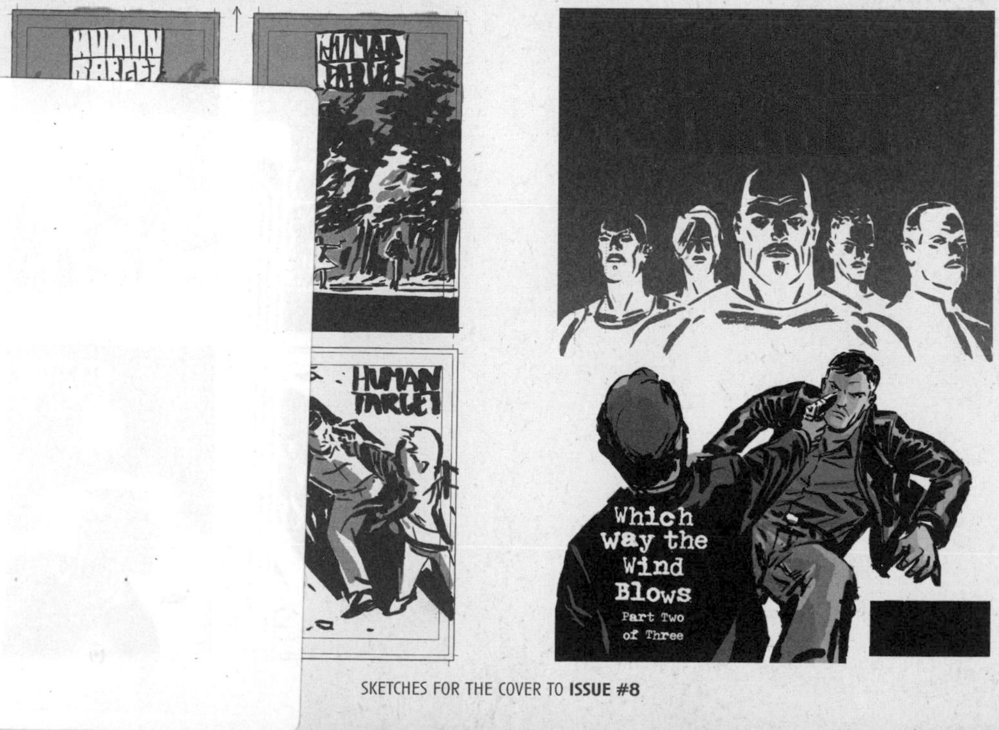
HUMAN TARGET
Which way the Wind Blows
Part Two of Three

SKETCHES FOR THE COVER TO **ISSUE #8**

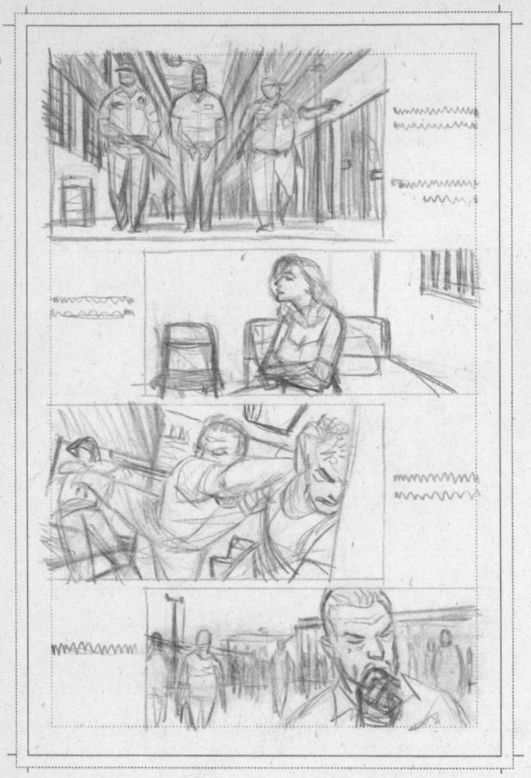

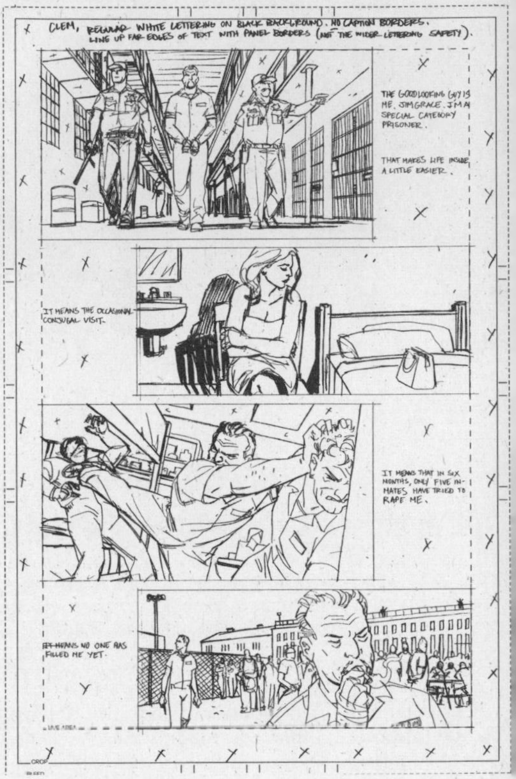

CLEM, REGULAR WHITE LETTERING ON BLACK BACKGROUND. NO CAPTION BORDERS.
LINE UP FAR EDGES OF TEXT WITH PANEL BORDERS (NOT THE WIDER LETTERING SAFETY).
THE GOOD LOOKING GUY IS ME. JIM GRACE. I'M A SPECIAL CATEGORY PRISONER.
THAT MAKES LIFE INSIDE A LITTLE EASIER.
IT MEANS THE OCCASIONAL CONJUGAL VISIT.
IT MEANS THAT IN SIX MONTHS, ONLY FIVE INMATES HAVE TRIED TO RAPE ME.
IT MEANS NO ONE HAS FILLED ME YET.
CROP

Some of the more eagle-eyed readers may have noticed that Christopher Chance's narrative captions always appear in white. While it's an apt metaphor for Chance's lack of a firm identity, it did present some story problems in "Five Days Grace." The color coding would have given away the elaborate joke we were playing on the reader, so Assistant Editor Pornsak Pichetshote and I worked out the solution shown here. By putting all the internal monologue captions outside of the panels, we were able to sidestep any color coding. Also, weeks before, I'd been struck by Dave Gibbons's use of image and text in the preview to his upcoming graphic novel THE ORIGINALS, so yeah, I had to steal it. Thanks, Dave!

Of course, I wasn't sure it would actually work until I hit the inks, so it was a bit of a crap shoot. One unexpected benefit of the black borders

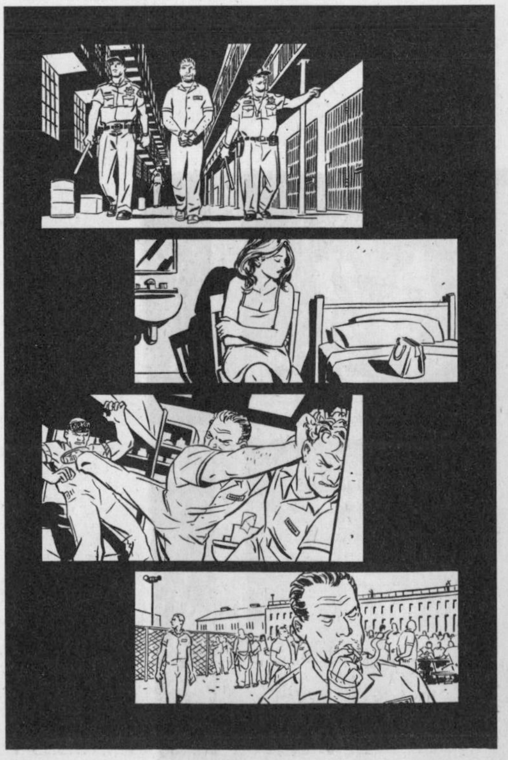

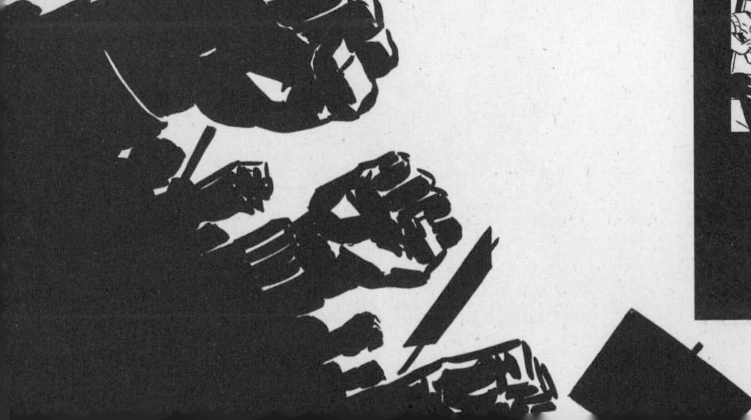

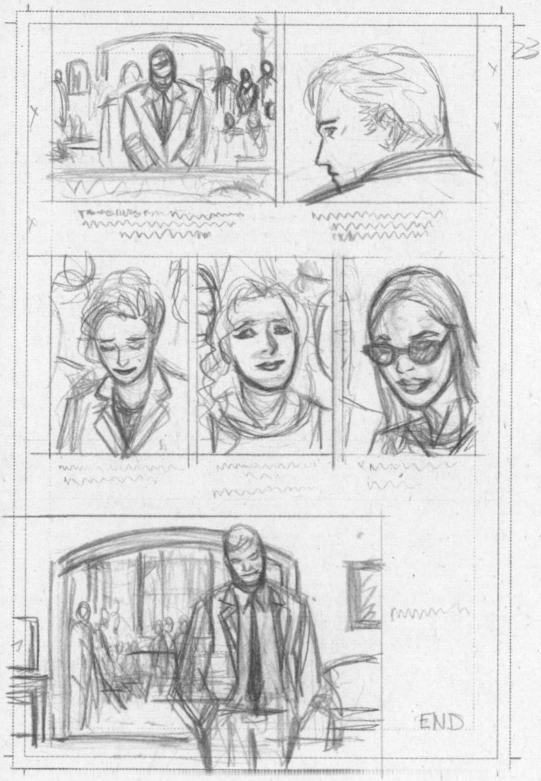
END

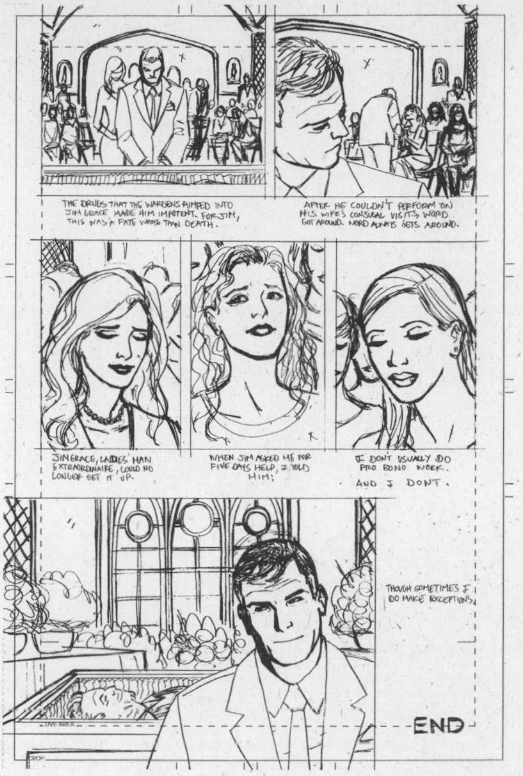
THE DRUGS THAT THE WARDENS PUMPED INTO JIM GRACE MADE HIM IMPOTENT. FOR JIM, THIS WAS A FATE WORSE THAN DEATH.
AFTER HE COULDN'T PERFORM ON HIS WIFE'S CONJUGAL VISITS, WORD GOT AROUND. WORD ALWAYS GETS AROUND.
JIM GRACE, LADIES' MAN EXTRAORDINAIRE, COULD NO LONGER GET IT UP.
WHEN JIM ASKED ME FOR FIVE DAYS HELP, I TOLD HIM:
I DON'T USUALLY DO PRO BONO WORK.
AND I DONT.
THOUGH SOMETIMES I DO MAKE EXCEPTIONS.
END

is the rather cinematic look of the pages. I wanted this story to feel like a crazy action flick (put a mole on Jim Grace's cheekbone and you'll have a good idea who the lead actor would be), so I was quite relieved when it all worked out.

Meanwhile, I do my layouts at print size (about 7" x 10") so I can get a real feel for how the actual comic will read. The blue pencil somehow feels less "final" to me, and it allows me to rework drawings easier than if they were in regular graphite.

More often than not, I do have to revisit my thinking on the layouts. Here, on the last page for "Five Days Grace," it was important to maintain the dry comedic tone of the story. My initial layout had a much more distant (and admittedly bland) shot of Chance walking away from Jim Grace's funeral.

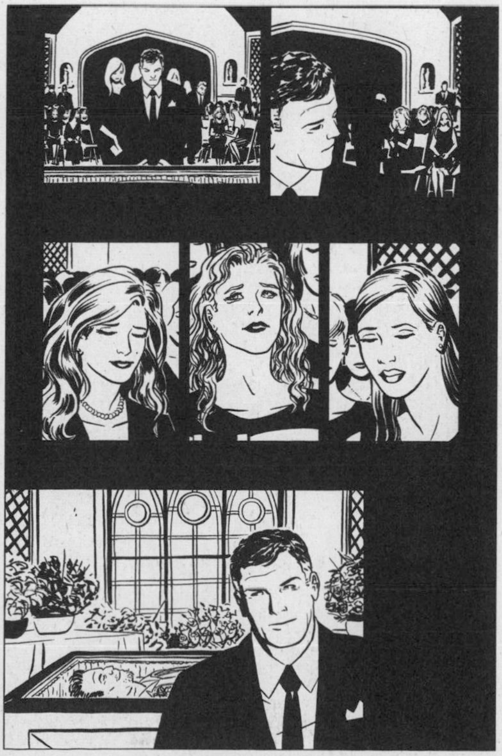

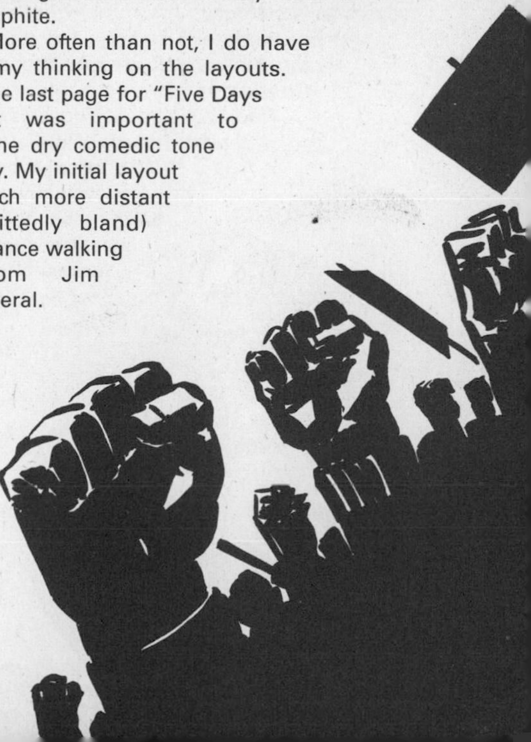

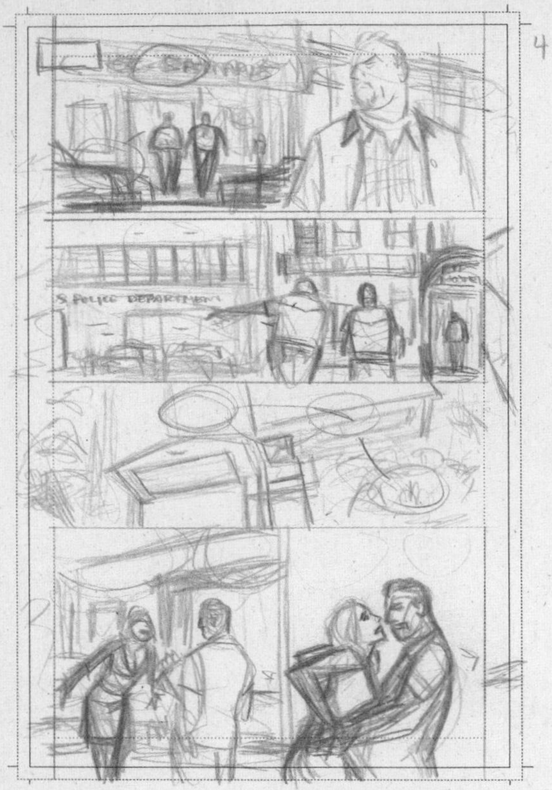

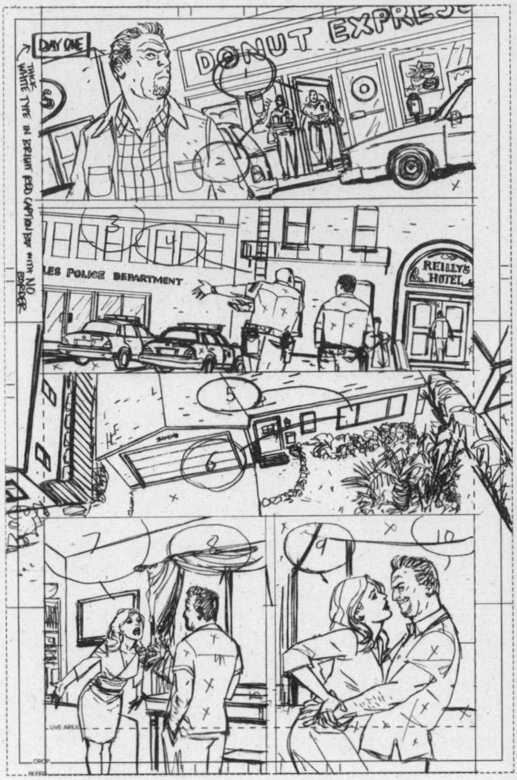

DAY ONE
DONUT EXPRES
LES POLICE DEPARTMENT
REILLY'S HOTEL

It lacked the humor we'd seen throughout the issue, so I opted for a close-up of Chance and a smiling Jim in his coffin. Talk about taking a secret to the grave!

I like to tweak my panel compositions a little to get some more energy out of them. Often it's as simple as tilting the "camera," but not always!

I enlarge my layouts to the full 11" x 17" dimensions of the comic boards, and then proceed to tighten up the drawings. Perspective gets figured out, proportions are fixed, and the women get a lot cuter at this stage.

For example, on the following page, a scene involving Christopher Chance as John Charles: In my layout, I was going for a cinematic approach to this page, but it lacked the atmosphere Peter called for in the script — one of those hot, stuffy nights where you just can't sleep. One valuable lesson I've learned is that you

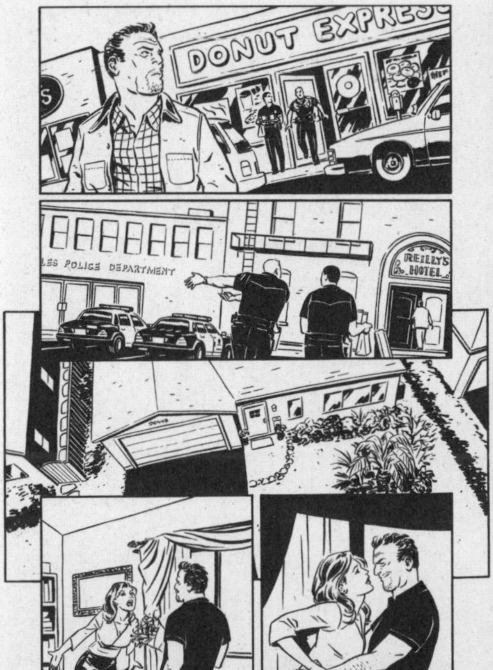

DONUT EXPRES
LES POLICE DEPARTMENT
REILLY'S HOTEL

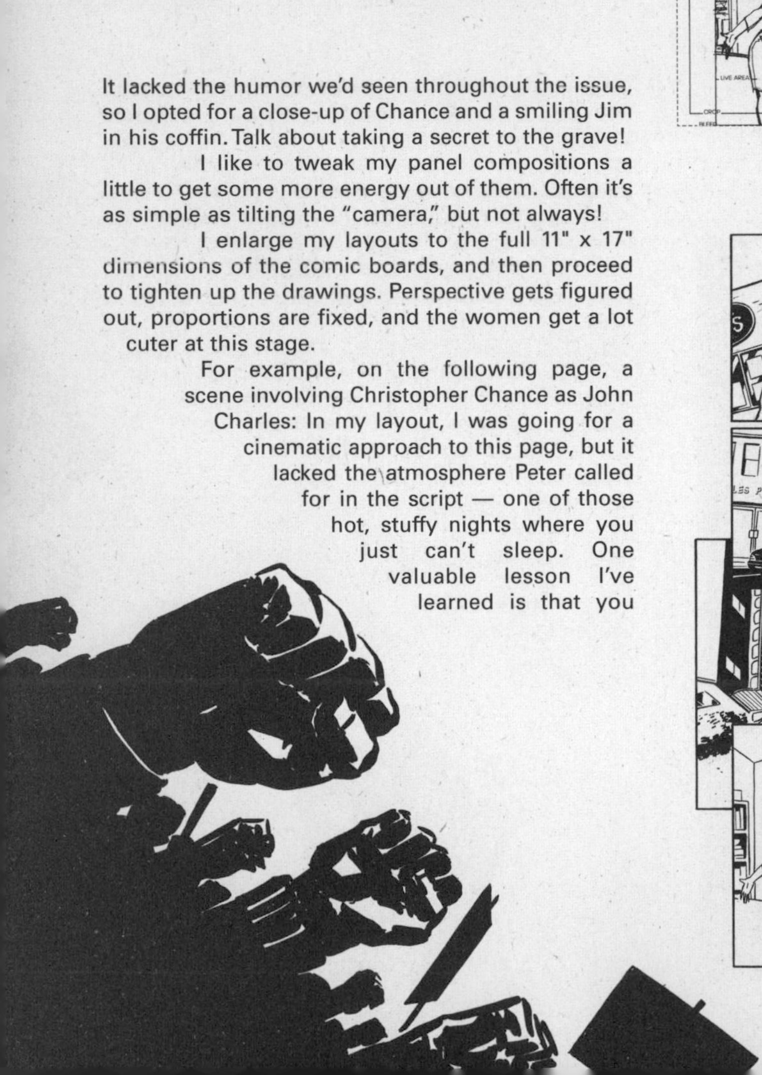

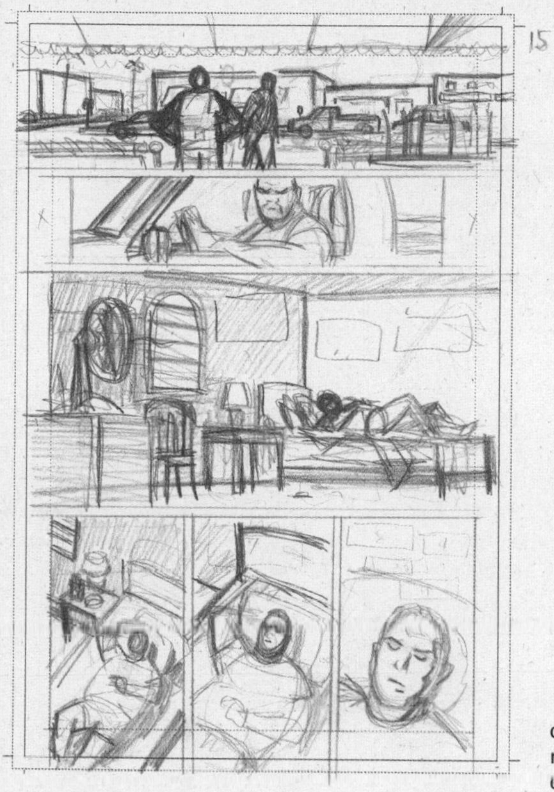
15

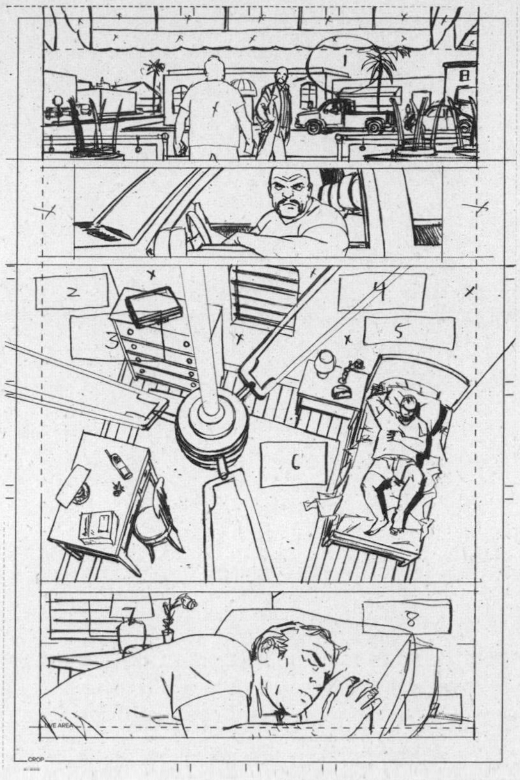

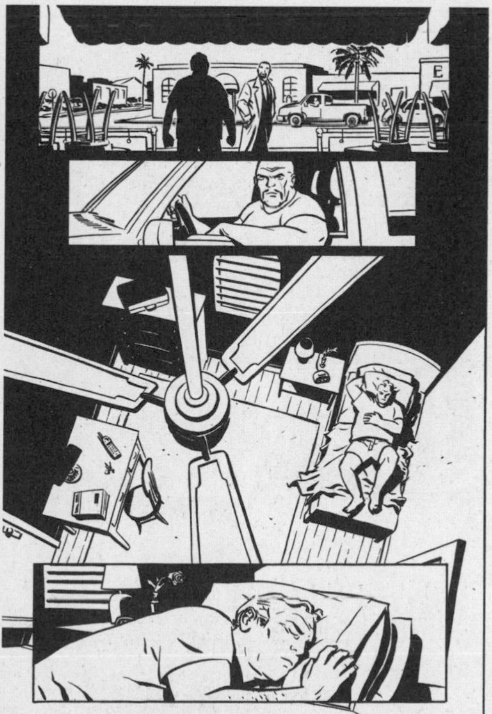

can't become too attached to anything. Even small revisions can make a world of difference. In this case especially it was worth the extra time and thought. Lee really drove it home with the colors, too.

The pencils are pretty basic — just outlines, really. In my head I know where all the ink goes and where the shadows fall, so I just jump into it.

Inking is by far my favorite part of the process. With all the planning that I do, this is the stage where I'm able to loosen up and get into the meat of the drawing. I'll fix some of it as I go, but mostly I just like slapping down ink. I never know exactly how a page will turn out, but that's part of the thrill. It feels a little bit like performance, and you just have to trust your instincts.

— Cliff Chiang
August 2004

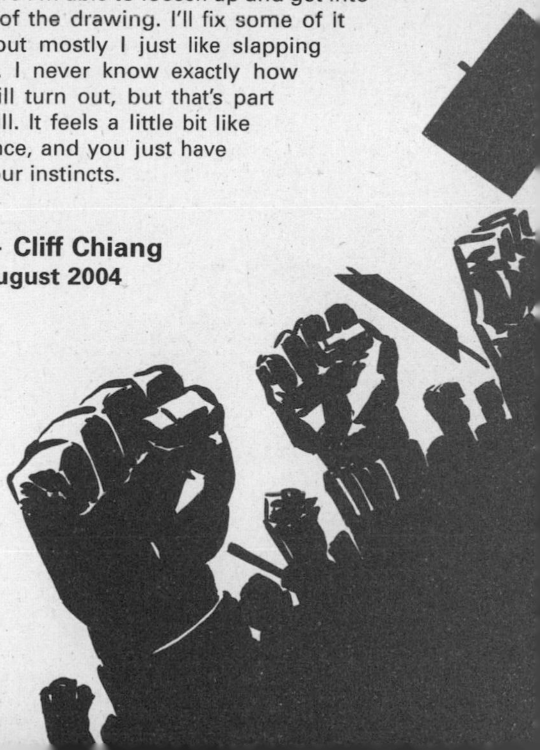

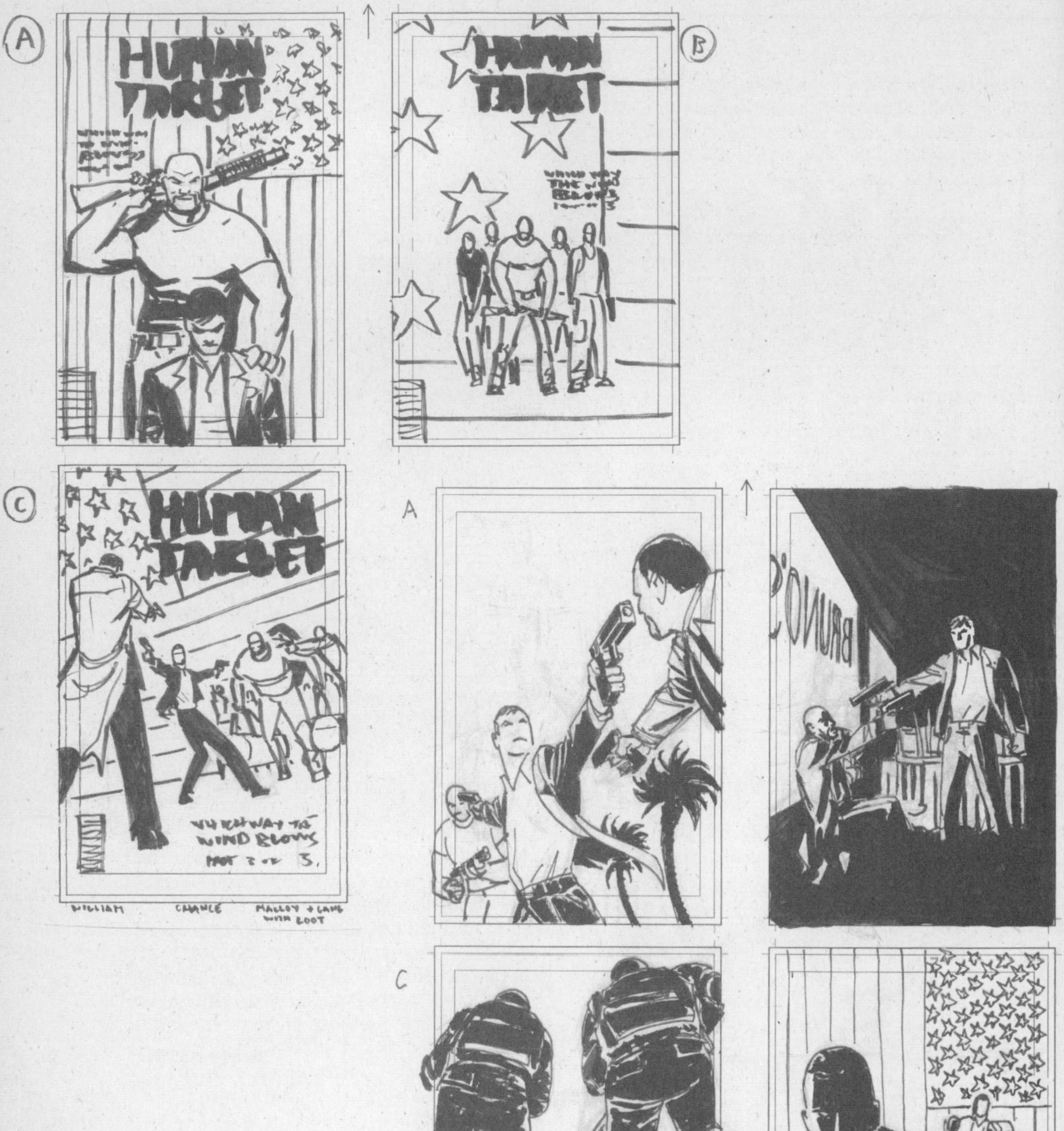
A
B
C
HUMAN TARGET
WILLIAM
CHANCE
MALLOY + GANG WITH LOOT
A
BRUNO'S
C
FBI
WILLIAMSON'S MEN
CHANCE IN SECURITY CLOTHES
MALLOY
RICK
BRUNO TIED UP

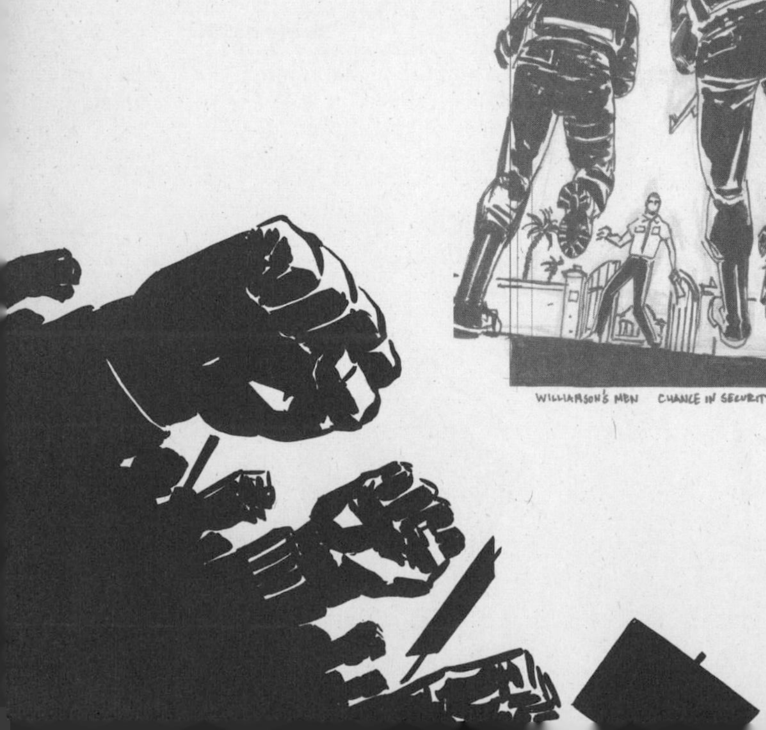

Various cover sketches for **issue #9**. It's interesting how some of these images ended up as the basis for interior art. Another reminder never to throw anything away!

Quick color sketches for the cover art to the original LIVING IN AMERIKA trade paperback collection. Riffing off the title, they were partly inspired by Soviet propaganda posters and partly by pulp novels from the '60s.

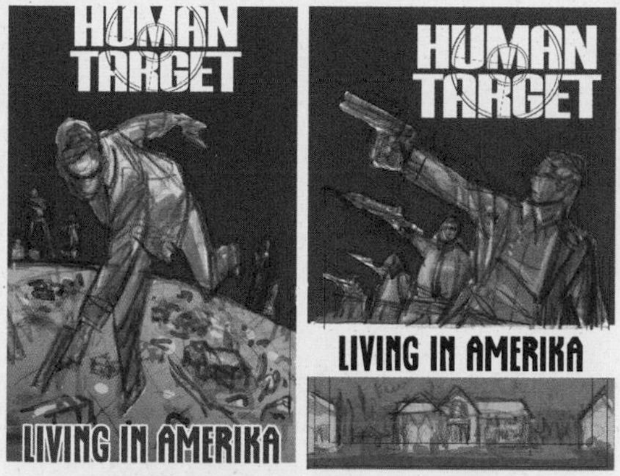
HUMAN TARGET
LIVING IN AMERIKA
HUMAN TARGET
LIVING IN AMERIKA

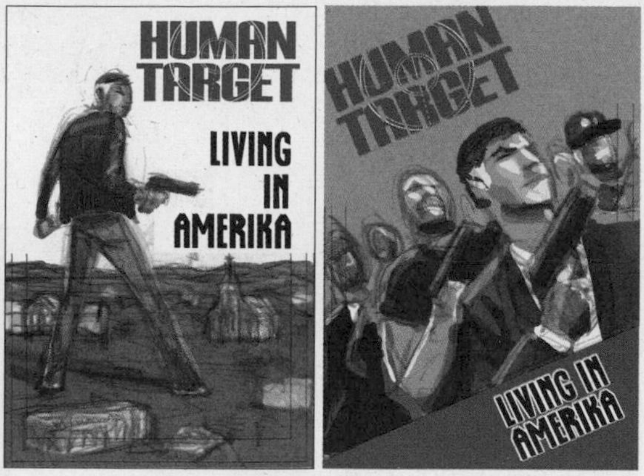
HUMAN TARGET
LIVING IN AMERIKA
HUMAN TARGET
LIVING IN AMERIKA

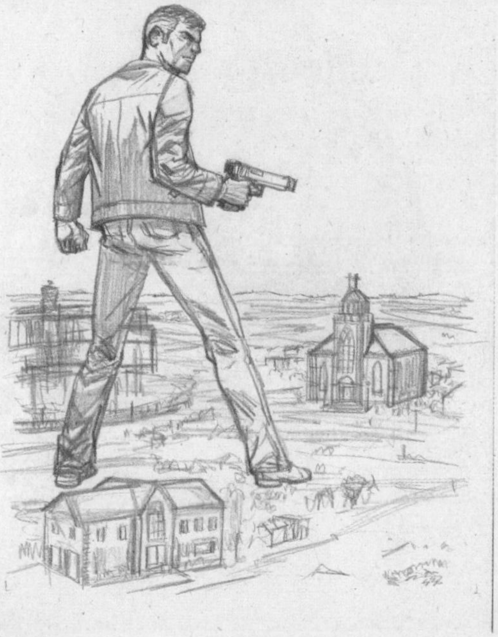

Rough pencils.

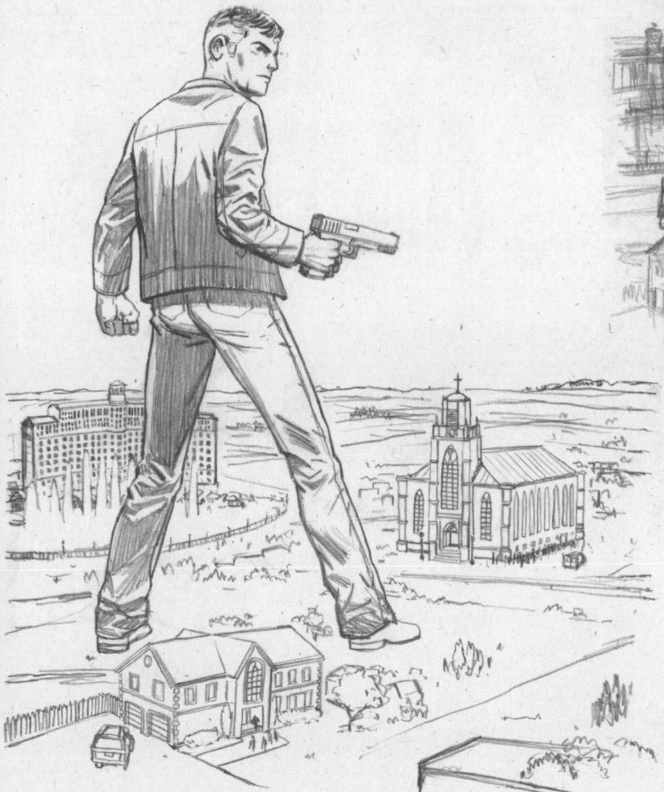

Hoping for a more painted look, I skipped the inks and scanned the final pencil drawing in grayscale and finished the coloring in PhotoShop. Hope you like the way it turned out — if not, I blame the computer.

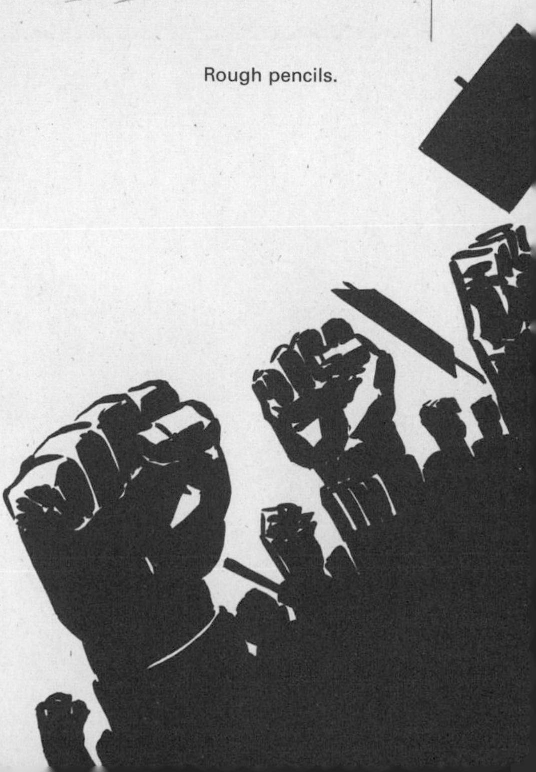

Final art.

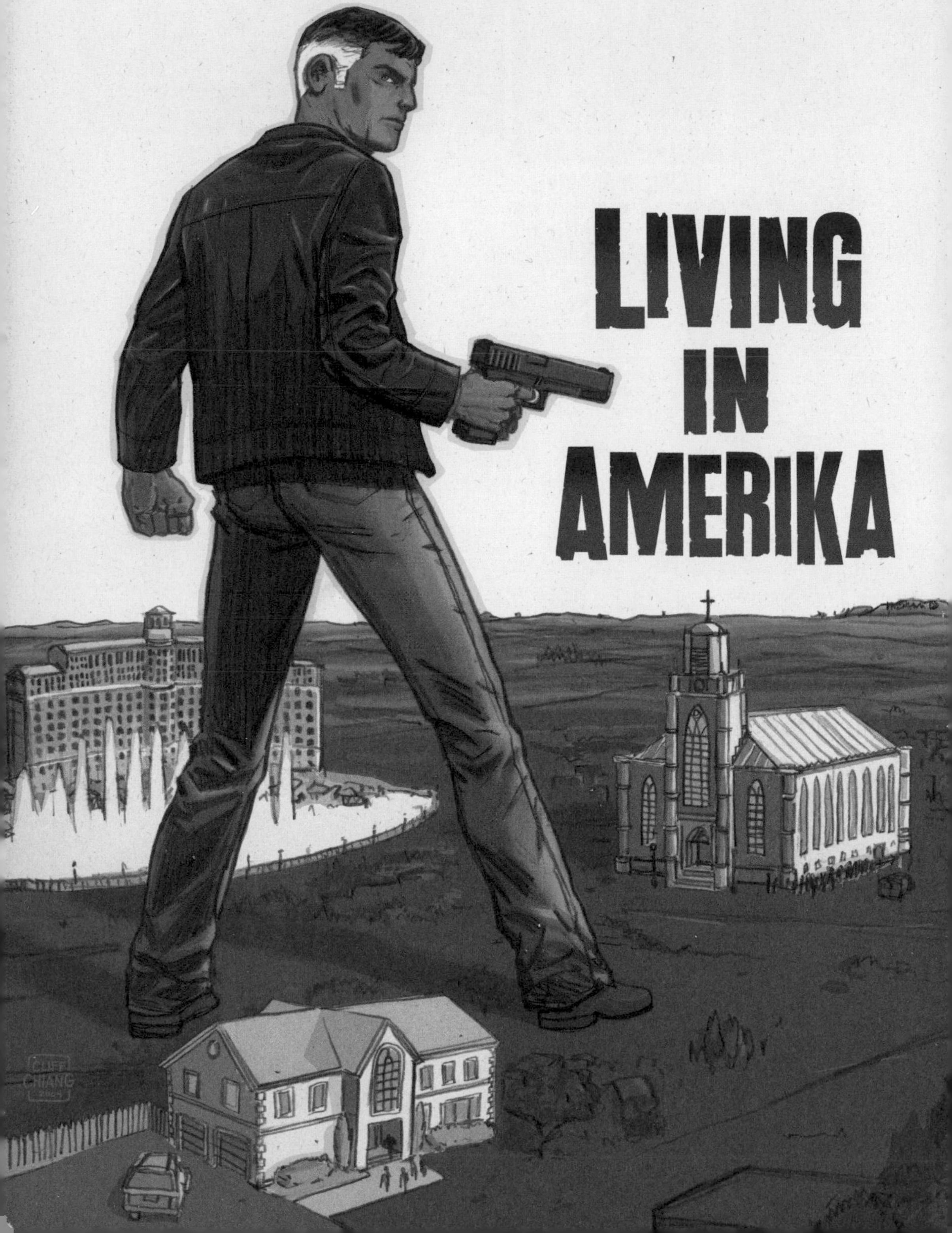
LIVING
IN
AMERIKA
CLIFF CHIANG